What's New in *Sams Teach Yourself Microsoft SQL Server 2000 in 21 Days*

With Microsoft's newest version of its enterprise-level relational database management system, SQL Server 2000, come many new features and improvements, including new administrative tools and a desktop installation. Throughout the step-by-step guides in this book and by using the evaluation version of SQL Server 2000 included with this book, you'll leverage new wizards and graphical dialogs to create database objects, set permissions, and manage your database. You'll also learn traditional coding methods. The following are some of the features and new tools you'll learn to use:

- On Day 1, "Introducing Relational Databases and Microsoft SQL Server 2000," you'll learn the history of SQL Server, up to and including this release.
- On Day 2, "Installing Microsoft SQL Server 2000," you'll learn important information and the steps to install SQL Server with both Windows NT/2000 and the Windows 98/ME platforms.
- Day 3, "Working with SQL Server 2000 Management Tools and Utilities," outlines the features of such tools as the Enterprise Manager, as well as the dramatic enhancements to Query Analyzer.
- Day 13, "Indexing for Performance," shows you how easily you can create indexed views to dramatically enhance the performance of multiple-join queries.
- Day 14, "Ensuring Data Integrity," shows you how to use the exciting new cascading delete and update functionality.
- Day 15, "Creating Views, Triggers, Stored Procedures, and Functions," covers the new features of `INSTEAD OF` triggers and user-defined functions, both long-awaited additions to SQL Server.
- Just like SQL Server 7.0, SQL Server 2000 offers significant replication enhancements. Day 16, "Understanding Replication Design Methodologies," and Day 17, "Implementing Replication Methodologies," offer expanded coverage to help make the planning phase and process easier to follow.
- On Day 21, "Using XML with SQL Server 2000," you'll look at SQL Server 2000's exciting new XML capabilities, and how to access SQL Server from Internet Information Server via XML.

Also new to this edition are two bonus days:

- Day 22, "An Overview of Analysis Services," will give you a very brief overview of SQL Server 2000's OLAP and data-mining capabilities.
- Day 23, "An Overview of English Query," will give you a brief overview of the English Query application.

You can find the electronic files for all the databases and code written for this book at `www.samspublishing.com`.

Richard Waymire
MCDBA, MCSE, MCSD, MCT
Rick Sawtell
MCT, MCSD

SAMS Teach Yourself

Microsoft® SQL Server™ 2000 in 21 Days

SECOND EDITION

SAMS
800 East 96th Street, Indianapolis, Indiana, 46240 USA

Sams Teach Yourself Microsoft SQL Server 2000 in 21 Days Second Edition

International Standard Book Number: 0-672-32469-5

Library of Congress Catalog Number: 200211054

Printed in the United States of America

First Printing: November 2002

06 05 04 03 6 5 3

Trademarks

Warning and Disclaimer

Bulk Sales

Sams Publishing offers excellent discounts on this book when ordered in quantity for bulk purchases or special sales. For more information, please contact

U.S. Corporate and Government Sales
1-800-382-3419
corpsales@pearsontechgroup.com

For sales outside of the U.S., please contact

International Sales
1-317-428-3341
international@pearsontechgroup.com

Associate Publisher
Michael Stephens

Acquisitions Editor
Michelle Newcomb
Kim Spiker

Development Editor
Kevin Howard

Managing Editor
Charlotte Clapp

Project Editor
George E. Nedeff

Copy Editor
Charles A. Hutchinson

Indexer
Mandie Frank

Proofreader
Kevin Ober

Technical Editors
Rob Hawthorne
Euan Garden

Team Coordinator
Lynne Williams

Software Specialist
Dan Scherf

Interior Designer
Gary Adair

Cover Designer
Aren Howell

Contents at a Glance

Contents

Dedication

This book is dedicated to SQL Server professionals—both the experienced and the newly ordained. SQL Server 2000 is better than Microsoft has ever done before, and you're going to love it!

Acknowledgments

I want to thank Rick for all his hard work. Writing a book is truly a labor of love—and a few late-night phone calls to your coauthor. I also think all the people at Sams Publishing did a great job. Thanks for all your support and understanding as we again wrote this book during the beta, with everything changing while we wrote.

I also want to thank all the wonderful folks on the SQL Server team at Microsoft, who have patiently put up with my questions, bug reports, and queries (pardon the pun) while writing this book.

This project, like any extracurricular project, has been the hardest on my family. My wife, Tracy, and two girls have been extremely patient and understanding. I couldn't have done it without their love and understanding. I dedicate my contribution to this book to my daughters, Kathryn and Elizabeth. I'm done now—let's go play at the park! Thanks for understanding, even though you were too young for me to expect that of you!

Mom, thanks for everything! You *know* I couldn't have done it without you.

—Richard

I want to thank Richard for doing such a wonderful job with this book. I also want to thank the staff at Sams Publishing for keeping everything together. When you have 25 or so elements of a book running around, as well as hundreds of screen shots, it can get crazy. A special thanks to Matthew Bridges for his hard work and expertise in putting together a phenomenal chapter on XML.

Thank you, Mom and Dad, for all the love and support over the years. It has made a huge difference in my life.

—Rick

About the Authors

Richard Waymire, a group program manager with the SQL Server development team at Microsoft, is also a Microsoft Certified Database Administrator and Systems Engineer. He's been working on various versions of SQL Server since 1994, and joined the Microsoft development team in 1998. Richard has been a programmer, DBA, and trainer on SQL Server before joining Microsoft. Richard still considers himself a database administrator at heart. You can reach Richard at `rwaymi@hotmail.com`.

Rick Sawtell is a Microsoft Certified Solutions Developer and Certified Trainer. He owns his own consulting firm based in the Hawaiian Islands and currently consults, trains, and writes computer books on several Microsoft products. He has more than 17 years of experience in the consulting and programming arena, with emphasis on database front-end and back-end development. You can reach Rick at `r_sawtell@hotmail.com`.

Tell Us What You Think!

As the reader of this book, *you* are our most important critic and commentator. We value your opinion and want to know what we're doing right, what we could do better, what areas you'd like to see us publish in, and any other words of wisdom you're willing to pass our way.

As an Associate Publisher for Sams, I welcome your comments. You can email or write me directly to let me know what you did or didn't like about this book—as well as what we can do to make our books stronger.

Please note that I cannot help you with technical problems related to the topic of this book, and that due to the high volume of mail I receive, I might not be able to reply to every message.

When you write, please be sure to include this book's title and author as well as your name and phone or fax number. I will carefully review your comments and share them with the author and editors who worked on the book.

Email: `feedback@samspublishing.com`
Mail: Michael Stephens, Associate Publisher
Sams Publishing
800 East 96th Street
Indianapolis, IN 46240 USA

For more information about this book or another Sams Publishing title, visit our Web site at `www.samspublishing.com`. Type the ISBN (excluding hyphens) or the title of a book in the Search field to find the page you're looking for.

Introduction

Welcome to *Sams Teach Yourself Microsoft SQL Server 2000 in 21 Days, Second Edition*. We hope this book will not only help teach you about SQL Server but also prove valuable for everyday work involving SQL Server. We have worked hard to see that the skills you learn from this book will easily translate into real-world methods and solutions.

You need certain skills to successfully install, administer, troubleshoot, and configure SQL Server. The kinds of skills you must know can be divided into two general categories:

- SQL Server programmer
- SQL Server administrator

> In a small company, the developer, programmer, and system administrator/database administrator might be the same person. In large companies, these functions are usually separate, with one or more people in each role.

A SQL Server developer is generally responsible for designing, programming, and populating the database. *Sams Teach Yourself Transact-SQL in 21 Days, Second Edition,* is a great place to start for beginning SQL programmers. After the database design is created, responsibility for the database is often turned over to an administrator, who takes care of the ongoing maintenance.

A SQL Server administrator is usually responsible for the day-to-day administration of the database. This book is designed more for administrators, although many lessons apply to programmers as well. Although some administrators might never have to do any SQL programming, we have created these lessons in enough detail so that they can begin to pick up on SQL programming if they want to. Programming tasks covered here relate to skills administrators might be called on to perform, such as creating tables, creating indexes, and writing complex queries.

About This Book

This book is designed to teach you to become a SQL Server administrator. It has been divided into 21 lessons, which you can complete in 21 days. Although some lessons are longer than others, no lesson should take more than four hours—the average is about two hours.

This book starts with the basics of SQL Server and progresses through various skills and techniques a SQL Server administrator needs to perform his or her job. We wrote this book with the beginner in mind; we have tried very hard to explain not only what to do, but also why it should be done.

This book's 21 lessons are designed to teach you the skills necessary to become proficient in SQL Server. The lessons are composed of roughly 21 equal days' worth of instruction. Because the lessons build on each other, it's important that you go through them in order, or at least understand what is in a given day's lesson if you skip over it.

Week 1's Lessons

Week 1's lessons describe how to use SQL Server and build databases. It is a week of fundamentals, when you will lay the groundwork for the more detailed discussions found in Weeks 2 and 3.

During Week 1, the actual days' lessons, and the skills you will learn, are as follows:

- On Day 1, "Introducing Relational Databases and Microsoft SQL Server 2000," you learn about SQL Server and what makes up a relational database. You also learn about the history of SQL Server.
- On Day 2, "Installing Microsoft SQL Server 2000," you learn the requirements for SQL Server, how to install it, and some simple configuration settings for both Windows 9*x* and a Windows NT/2000 installation.
- On Day 3, "Working with SQL Server 2000 Management Tools and Utilities," you learn about the tools and utilities that ship with SQL Server and when to best use them.
- On Day 4, "Creating and Administering Databases and Data Files," you learn how SQL Server stores databases and how to create, edit, and delete databases and database files.
- On Day 5, "Setting Up Login and User Security," you learn how to add login accounts to SQL Server and how to create users and roles for each database.
- On Day 6, "Establishing Database Permissions," you learn how to assign permissions to users and roles inside SQL Server. You also learn what permissions the default system and database roles contain.
- On Day 7, "Backing Up Your Databases," you learn how to handle one of the most important tasks in SQL Server—creating and saving backups of your databases and transaction logs.

Week 2's Lessons

The next seven days expand on the foundation of skills and understanding you built in the first week of this book. Week 2 is geared toward retrieving and manipulating your data:

- On Day 8, "Restoring Your Databases," you learn how to recover and restore your databases in SQL Server. You also learn some strategies to keep in mind when you are developing your emergency procedures.
- On Day 9, "Data Types and Creating Tables," you learn about the different data types that make up the columns in a table. You then learn how to combine those columns and their associated data types to create new tables in your databases.
- On Day 10, "Retrieving Data with the `SELECT` Statement," you learn the ins and outs of using `SELECT` statements to gather data and manipulate your data. You also learn some more advanced queries using data aggregation as well as correlated subqueries.
- On Day 11, "Modifying Data," you learn how to modify data by using the `INSERT`, `UPDATE`, and `DELETE` statements.
- On Day 12, "Using Transact-SQL Extensions," you learn how to use the programming features of SQL Server, as well as details about transactions and locking. This lesson is an excellent introduction to the programming concepts related to SQL Server 2000.
- On Day 13, "Indexing for Performance," you learn how to plan and build indexes so that queries run more efficiently. You also learn about Indexed Views, one of the most exciting new features of SQL Server 2000.
- On Day 14, "Ensuring Data Integrity," you learn techniques to ensure that your data stays reliable, accurate, and consistent. The concepts presented in this lesson are often referred to as *DRI* (declarative referential integrity).

Week 3's Lessons

The third week contains various advanced topics dealing with SQL Server:

- On Day 15, "Creating Views, Triggers, Stored Procedures, and Functions," you learn the uses of and how to create views, stored procedures, triggers, and user-defined functions. This day will almost certainly be your longest while you're working through the book.
- On Day 16, "Understanding Replication Design Methodologies," you learn the concepts of replication, the terminology, and the various styles and methods you can use to set up replication.

- On Day 17, "Implementing Replication Methodologies," you learn how to implement replication from a publisher and a subscriber.
- On Day 18, "Scheduling Jobs with SQL Server Agent," you see how to use the SQL Server Agent to automate many SQL Server tasks.
- On Day 19, "Migrating Data Between Database Servers," you learn how to move data into and out of SQL Server and other OLE DB data sources.
- On Day 20, "Performance Monitoring Basics and Tools," you learn that, although SQL Server is mostly self-tuning, it's still good to understand what the different configuration options actually accomplish in your SQL Server database. You also learn how to monitor the performance of your SQL Server databases and applications.
- On Day 21, "Using XML with SQL Server 2000," you learn various methods to integrate SQL Server with the exciting world of XML and the Internet. You see how to access SQL Server from XML as well as get XML-formatted data back from SQL Server 2000.

Bonus Days

After you complete the three-week course, you can continue to learn with these bonus lessons:

- On Day 22, "An Overview of Analysis Services," you get a brief introduction to the capabilities of SQL Server 2000 Analysis Services and Microsoft Meta Data Services. These products are part of SQL Server 2000 but in many ways constitute a separate product worthy of an entire 21 days to themselves.
- On Day 23, "An Overview of English Query," you get a brief overview of the other major part of SQL Server, Microsoft English Query. English Query allows users to enter English sentences and have them automatically translated to SQL and return results from SQL Server.

Who Should Read This Book?

This book assumes that you have no prior SQL Server knowledge. If you've already had some exposure to SQL Server, you will only be the better for it.

Windows NT or Windows 2000 experience, although not required, is useful when you're dealing with SQL Server because many of the optional features of SQL Server require interaction with Windows NT/2000. If you find your Windows NT/2000 experience lacking, try reading *Sams Teach Yourself Windows 2000 Server in 24 Hours*.

Conventions Used in This Book

SQL Server can be installed in a case-sensitive format (although we don't do so in this book), so we have put commands in the following format. Also, note that most Transact-SQL (the language of SQL Server) is shown in all capital letters, even though the proper case is all lowercase:

```
CREATE DATABASE
```

We used this convention to show you which words are Transact-SQL reserved words and which words are parameters.

Occasionally, we show you output or code generated by SQL Server. This code might not follow the same capitalization that our code does, but you should be able to recognize the same keywords.

NEW TERM You'll find new terms marked with this icon for quick reference—especially if you're looking for the definition as a reference from the page number in the index. Each new term is also *italicized* in the text when it's being defined. You'll also find a glossary of terms at the end of the book.

INPUT/ OUTPUT Look for the Input and Output icons so you can practice using examples of code. All code examples also follow these conventions:

- Code lines, commands, statements, variables, and any text you see onscreen appear in a `monospaced` typeface. **`Bold monospace`** typeface represents user input.
- Placeholders in syntax descriptions appear in an *`italic monospace`* typeface. Replace the placeholder with the actual filename, parameter, or whatever element it represents.

Also, notice that we use a code continuation character, ➥, to denote that a line had to be broken to fit the width of the printed page. Just treat such instances as you would one long line as you type.

The Analysis icon denotes the explanation of code.

You'll find helpful information set off in boxes like this one. Watch for helpful pointers (tips), and pay particular attention to the cautions.

WEEK 1

At a Glance

In this first week, you will learn enough information about Microsoft SQL Server 2000 that you can do some light database administration and initial database design.

Day 1 introduces you to SQL Server and gives you some background information on relational databases and database design. On Day 2, you actually install SQL Server and examine several setup options.

Day 3 covers the tools and utilities that come packaged with SQL Server. You'll use these tools extensively for the rest of your career with SQL Server.

Day 4 covers storage. You'll learn about databases, files, and filegroups. On Day 5, you examine the process of securing your SQL Server system, including creating logins and database users.

Day 6 discusses the creation and management of database roles and the permissions that can be granted to these database users and roles.

Day 7 begins one of the most important aspects of working with any database—backups. We authors have often been called paranoid because of the amount of importance we place on database backups (and restorations). Then again, we've never been released from a company because our databases were unrecoverable. This lesson outlines the database backup process and some tips for keeping your job.

This information might seem a little overwhelming at first, but relax. This book was intended for you. You will take each new concept from a solid fundamental principle and then add new concepts to it each day. For this reason, it's important that you do all the exercises at the end of each day. They reinforce the fundamentals and give you a good foundation on which to build the other two weeks.

WEEK 1

DAY 1

Introducing Relational Databases and Microsoft SQL Server 2000

SQL Server developers are responsible for designing and implementing the database, whereas SQL Server administrators are responsible for the day-to-day management tasks. However, these tasks are becoming less distinct as SQL Server becomes more widely deployed.

Today's lesson starts with background material on SQL Server and Windows (both Windows 9*x* and Windows NT/2000/XP). You then look at databases and what makes up a client/server environment. Databases and their contents are the next subject. Finally, you end the lesson with a look at designing databases. Your exercise for this day is to go through a simulated interview with a client and look at a design for a simple database.

SQL Server Is *Hot*!

SQL Server 2000 is Microsoft's flagship database engine product. It's the follow-up version to Microsoft's most significant database release ever, SQL

Server 7.0. Microsoft committed to investing large amounts of money in support and marketing of SQL Server 7.0 and is showing the results of that support (and money) with SQL Server 2000. SQL Server 7.0 has been the premier database engine in the computing industry for the Windows NT/2000/XP platform, including 68 percent of the database market (all versions of SQL Server) according to Microsoft's Web site. SQL Server 2000 continues this trend and expands Microsoft's share of the database market. SQL Server 2000 has added significant amounts of functionality to SQL Server 7.0 and done a great job of rounding out features that had their groundwork laid in SQL Server 7.0.

SQL Server 2000 can run on either Windows NT 4.0 (with service pack 5 or later), Windows 2000, Windows XP, Windows 98, or Windows ME. A version of SQL Server 2000 also is available for the Windows CE platform. SQL Server's price/performance records have allowed many companies to have the power of a relational database management system (RDBMS) for a fraction of the cost of such a system just a few years ago. SQL Server 2000 has some of the best performance benchmarks in the world, according to the TPC-C database benchmarks at the time of this writing, and it also held the best records for price and performance. Microsoft SQL Server will continue to be enhanced for many years to come, making your career selection of working with the product a good one. For more information see Microsoft's Web site at: `www.microsoft.com/sql`.

Microsoft's SQL Server has sold millions of licenses since it was first introduced, including more than 10 million licenses in 1999 alone. The current version of the product, SQL Server 2000 (internally known as version 8.0), is the subject of this book. Before taking a closer look at SQL Server 2000 and learning how to use it, you'll find that the history of SQL Server is worth looking at.

For up-to-the minute news and support for Microsoft SQL Server, visit `http://www.microsoft.com/sql/`.

The History of SQL Server

New Term IBM invented a computer language back in the 1970s designed specifically for database *queries* (questions to the database) called SEQUEL, which stood for Structured English Query Language. Over time the language has been added to, so it's not just a language for queries but can also be used to build databases and manage security of the database engine. IBM released SEQUEL into the public domain, where it became known as SQL. Because of this heritage, you can pronounce it as *sequel* or spell it out as *S-Q-L* when talking about it.

Today's database engines use various versions of SQL. Microsoft SQL Server uses a version called Transact-SQL (T-SQL). Although you will use Transact-SQL in this book and learn the basics of the language, the emphasis in this book is on installing, maintaining, and connecting to SQL Server. Sams Publishing also published a book titled *Teach Yourself Transact-SQL in 21 Days, Second Edition*, which has more details on the language and its usage.

Microsoft initially developed SQL Server (a database product that understands the SQL language) with Sybase Corporation for use on the IBM OS/2 platform. Oh, what a tangled web we weave! When Microsoft and IBM split, Microsoft abandoned OS/2 in favor of its new network operating system, Windows NT Advanced Server. At that point, Microsoft decided to further develop the SQL Server engine for Windows NT by itself. The resulting product was Microsoft SQL Server 4.2, which was updated to 4.21. After Microsoft and Sybase parted ways, Sybase further developed its database engine to run on Windows NT (currently known as Sybase Adaptive Server Enterprise), and Microsoft developed SQL Server 6.0…then SQL Server 6.5, which also ran on top of Windows NT. SQL Server 7.0 introduced the capability to run on Windows NT as well as on Windows 95 and Windows 98.

SQL Server 7.0 was a major break of the Sybase code for the Microsoft database team. Previous releases were still very closely related to Sybase. However, with SQL Server 7.0, Microsoft dramatically rewrote and modified the Sybase code. The company rearchitected the core database engine and introduced a sophisticated query optimizer and an advanced database storage engine. SQL Server 2000 enhances this new code line, adding significant new features. It also enhances the scalability, reliability, and availability of the product; and makes your life easier as a database administrator.

Note

> Although you can run SQL Server 2000 on a Windows 9*x* system, you don't get all the functionality of SQL Server. When running it on the Windows 9*x* platform, you lose the capability to use multiple processors, Windows NT/2000 security, New Technology File System (NTFS) volumes, and much more. We strongly urge you to use SQL Server 2000 on Windows NT or Windows 2000 rather than on Windows 9*x*. Windows NT/2000 has other advantages as well. The NT platform is designed to support multiple users. Windows 9*x* isn't designed this way, and your SQL Server performance degrades rapidly as you add more users. This book will assume that you are running on Windows 2000.

SQL Server 2000 is implemented as a service on Windows NT Workstation, Windows NT Server, or any version of Microsoft Windows 2000 and Windows XP. When installed on Windows 98 or Windows ME, SQL Server runs as an application under the currently logged-in user. The included utilities, such as the SQL Server Enterprise Manager, operate as ordinary client/server applications, allowing you to run them from just about anywhere to control your SQL Server databases.

NEW TERM A *service* is an application that Windows NT/2000/XP can start either automatically when booting up or manually on demand. Services on Windows NT/2000/XP have a generic application programming interface (API) that can be controlled programmatically. Services allow you to run applications such as Microsoft SQL Server without requiring that a user be logged in to the server computer.

What Is a Database?

NEW TERM SQL Server uses a type of database called a relational database. In *relational databases*, data is organized into tables. Tables are organized by grouping data about the same subject and contain columns and rows of information. The tables are then related back to each other by the database engine when requested. Tables are closely related to something called a *relation,* or *entity* in proper theory books, but we're trying to be practical here.

You can generally think of a database as a collection of related data. In some earlier database products, a database was usually just a file—something like `employee.dbf`, which contained a single table of data. Inside the `employee.dbf` file were columns relating to employee data, such as salary, hire date, name, Social Security number, and so on. The file contained a row for each person in the company, with corresponding values in the appropriate columns. Indexes, used to speed data access, were in a separate file, as was any security-related item.

In SQL Server 2000, a database isn't necessarily tied to a single file; it's more of a logical concept based on a collection of related objects. For example, a database in SQL Server contains not only the raw data, but it also contains the structure of the database, any indexes, the security of the database, and perhaps other objects such as views or stored procedures related to that particular database.

Relational Database Objects

NEW TERM As you just read, a relational database is composed of different types of objects. These objects are all described in more detail in the particular day's lesson that applies to them. The following are some of the more common objects:

- *Tables* are the objects that contain the data types and actual raw data. Tables are the focus of Day 9, "Data Types and Creating Tables."
- *Columns* are the parts of the table holding the data. Columns must be assigned a data type and unique name within the scope of the table.
- *Data types* are the base storage type of your data. You can choose from various data types, such as character, numeric, or date. A single data type is assigned to each column within a table.
- *Stored procedures* are like macros in Transact-SQL code that can be written and stored under a name. By executing the stored procedure, you actually run the T-SQL code within the procedure. One use would be to take the T-SQL code that runs a weekly report, save it as a stored procedure, and from then on, just run the stored procedure to generate the report. You can also use stored procedures as security mechanisms.
- *User-defined functions* are Transact-SQL code that's very similar to stored procedures. However, functions can be called in your database queries either to modify a column of data you want to view or to act as tables, even though they're built programmatically and dynamically. An example might be that you could write your own date functions to modify columns of the datetime data type.
- *Triggers* are stored procedures that activate either before or after data is added, modified, or deleted from the database. They ensure that business rules or other data integrity rules are enforced in the database. For example, a trigger can ensure that every book in a bookstore has a valid publisher assigned to it.
- *Views* are basically SELECT queries stored in the database that can reference one or many tables. You can create and save them so that you can use them easily in the future. Views usually either exclude certain columns from a table or link two or more tables. You can also use them as security mechanisms.
- *Indexes* can help organize data so that queries run faster. Day 13, "Indexing for Performance," covers indexes in detail.
- *Primary keys*, although not objects per se, are essential to relational databases. They enforce uniqueness among rows, providing a way to uniquely identify every item you want to store.
- *Foreign keys* are one or more columns that reference the primary keys or unique constraints of other tables. SQL Server uses primary and foreign keys to relate the data back together from separate tables when queries are performed.
- *Constraints* are server-based, system-implemented data-integrity enforcement mechanisms.

- *Rules* are assigned to columns so that data being entered must conform to standards you set. For example, you can use rules to make sure that a person's phone number contains only numbers. Rules have been functionally replaced by `CHECK` constraints in SQL Server 2000.
- *Defaults* can be set on fields so that if no data is entered during an `INSERT` operation, default values are used. An example is setting the area code for the area where most of your customers come from, which saves you from entering the area code for local customers. Defaults have been functionally replaced by `DEFAULT` constraints in SQL Server 2000.

Designing Relational Databases

This section on designing relational databases is important for two reasons:

- You might be called on to design a relational database.
- You might have been given a relational database but want to understand why certain design decisions were made.

As a SQL Server administrator, you will likely be given a relational database that has been designed by someone else; using such a database doesn't mean you can be clueless when it comes to designing a relational database. Knowing some do's and don'ts about designing databases and knowing about normalization can only help you in your job.

Although the process of designing a good relational database could fill a book by itself, the following are some basic steps to consider:

- Analyze the situation to gather information about the proposed database.
- Decide on columns, data types, and lengths of data.
- Normalize the data into tables.
- Create the database and tables.

When you organize related data into related tables, you are following normalization rules, which you will learn about shortly.

The design process should start with a good look at the business situation and what the customer is trying to accomplish. Brainstorming about different variables and how they all fit together into tables is the next step. The process then moves to designing reports and queries that will benefit the users, as well as other pieces of the design, including access to Web pages.

The following do's and don'ts will help you during the design process. Remember, in the end you're building a solution to solve a business problem, so you need to remain focused on the problem you're solving and not get too worried about using the perfect technical terms to describe it.

Do	Don't
DO ask the users what they need.	**DON'T** ignore the users (also known as *customers*).
DO create a list of objects.	**DON'T** create objects you will never use.
DO keep object names short yet descriptive.	**DON'T** use complex names, names with spaces, or names with unusual characters because they are harder to type.
DO organize properties of objects into correct groupings.	**DON'T** have a column that contains more than one value.
DO create identically named columns in different tables to relate them back together. These columns become your primary and foreign keys.	**DON'T** create tables with a huge number of columns.
DO test your design with some sample data.	**DON'T** assume that because your design works well with 5 rows, it will perform well with 500,000 rows.
DO create at least one index for tables that will be queried.	**DON'T** create a lot of indexes (more than five) per table.
DO design your tables with security in mind.	**DON'T** forget to set up security on your data.
DO document table names, column names, and primary and foreign keys.	**DON'T** lose your documentation.
DO follow a standardized naming convention for your database objects. Following this convention can greatly simplify working with your objects. We like to use prefixes. For example, use `tblEmployees` for a table object named Employees and `ix_LastName` for an index based on last name.	

The exercise at the end of this lesson goes through a simulated interview with a customer and proceeds into the design of a relational database.

Interviewing the Customer

A good database design starts with a thorough understanding of the customer's situation and desired outcome. That's why the people who design new systems are called *analysts*—they analyze the problem in detail and try to think of ways to solve the problem.

Sometimes an old-fashioned interview is the best way to find out exactly what the customer wants, especially if you don't fully understand what the current situation is and what the goal is. Use questions like these to probe for your customer's needs:

- What is working for you now?
- What parts of the current system would you most like to replace?
- Do you have additional reports you want to be able to generate?
- What items would you most like to keep track of?
- Is the data private or public?
- Who needs access to the data, and what kind of access should each user or group have?
- Do you want the data posted on the Internet?
- Do you want the public to be able to look up information via the Internet?
- Do you have sufficient hardware in place to run both the database server and client software?
- If money and technology were no object, what would you want incorporated into the new system?

By asking these kinds of questions, you can quickly build a sense of why a database is needed. Although you might not be able to provide everything (given the limitations of the assigned budget, time frame, and hardware allowances), you will have the start of a long-term plan for growth and expansion of the database.

Organizing the Objects

After the interview (you did take good notes, didn't you?), it's best to brainstorm about possible objects, including their names, types, and lengths. After you decide on the objects, you can group them into related tables.

SQL Server supports several different data types, including those for characters, numbers, dates, and money. More detail on data types is provided on Day 9.

After you decide on your tables, specify the properties (columns) within these tables. Keep column names simple yet descriptive. Column lengths should satisfy all but the most extreme cases. When you're dealing with names, your limitation might be how many characters can fit onto a mailing label—not how many to store.

Normalizing the Data

NEW TERM Now that you've decided on the columns, you must organize the data into related tables, which is referred to as *normalizing* the data. Normalization is the process of organizing data into related tables.

By normalizing the data, you are attempting to eliminate redundant data. Suppose that the same customer buys two cars. In a single-table database, you have to enter his information twice. What's worse, if the customer moves, you have to change his address in both places, or your data isn't internally consistent. By entering his information once in a customer table and linking his record to any car purchase, you not only eliminate redundant (and sometimes conflicting) data, you now can change his record in only one location. Figure 1.1 shows an example of how these tables might look. Notice that separate tables for customers and cars have been created. In the Cars table, the CustID field represents a single customer ID. As you can see, Ann owns two cars, and Bob owns a single car. Cathy doesn't own any cars yet, but because of the database model you can accurately record this fact. You can also keep track of multiple cars for Ann while keeping only one copy of her address.

FIGURE 1.1

Organizing variables into a relational database.

Customer

CustID	Name	Address	City	etc...
1	Ann	123 AnyStreet	Redmond	
2	Bob	947 Main	Seattle	
3	Cathy	1010 1st Avenue	Bellevue	

Cars

CarID	Make	Model	Year	CustID
111AAA	Ford	Explorer	1999	1
222ABC	Honda	Civic	2000	1
112ADE	Toyota	Corolla	1998	2

NEW TERM Rules are established for the normalization of data. These rules are known as first, second, and third normal forms. There is a fourth and fifth normal form as well, but these are not generally used in practice but are great for a relational design theory class at your local college or university.:

- *First normal form (FNF or 1NF)* states that a column can't contain multiple values. For example, a person's name must be broken down into last name, middle name, and first name to follow FNF.
- *Second normal form (SNF or 2NF)* states that every non-key column must depend on the entire key, and not just a part of the primary key. For example, if you are using a customer ID and part number for a key, all the columns in that table must apply only to a particular customer and part number together. So, a `part_description` wouldn't belong in this table. A table must also comply with first normal form to be in second normal form.

- *Third normal form (TNF or 3NF)*, much like the SNF, states that all non-key columns must not depend on any other non-key columns. For example, if you have a table with addresses in it, the ZIP code must not depend on another non-key field such as state. It should depend on the entire primary key. Of course, the table must also comply with second normal form. The TNF is often violated for the sake of convenience.

Creating the Database and Tables

Because tables are the building blocks of databases, it's apparent that well-designed tables (and, thus, the columns within the tables) are critical to the success of databases. As with most things, planning and designing are the hard part; actually creating the database and tables is the easy part. A table is composed of columns that store the properties of a table. Day 4, "Creating and Administering Databases and Data Files," covers databases and their creation in more detail; Day 9 covers tables in greater detail.

SQL Server and the Client/Server Model

Microsoft's SQL Server is a client/server database engine, so it's important for you to understand the client/server model.

NEW TERM You can define a *client/server* application as one that's split into two parts: one that runs on a server and one that runs on workstations. The server side of the application provides security, fault tolerance, performance, concurrency, and reliable backups. The client side provides the user interface and can contain empty reports, queries, and forms. The idea is to have the best of both worlds by taking advantage of both and pairing them together.

SQL Server is the server part of the equation; various clients to choose from can connect to SQL Server, including the utilities that come with SQL Server, such as the SQL Server Query Analyzer. SQL Server provides the following advantages for both clients and servers:

Client Advantages	*Server Advantages*
Easy to use	Reliable
Supports multiple hardware platforms	Concurrent
Supports multiple software applications	Sophisticated locking
Familiar to the user	Fault tolerant
	High-performance hardware
	Centralized control

In client/server computing, when a query is run, the server searches the database and sends only matching rows to the client. This process not only saves bandwidth, but it can be faster than having the workstations perform the query, as long as the server is a powerful enough machine.

Summary

The material presented in today's lesson introduces you to this book, as well as to basic concepts of relational databases (including SQL Server). Microsoft's SQL Server is capturing more and more market share and is a client/server-based relational database management system. SQL Server 2000 uses Transact-SQL as its dialect of the SQL language. Note that SQL Server 2000 supports the ANSI SQL-99 standard as well.

A relational database is composed of tables, which contain columns and rows of data. The process of breaking a database into related tables is called *normalization*.

Designing a good database starts with understanding the client's requirements for the database. The data can then be grouped into tables.

Q&A

Q Do I need to know all this Transact-SQL stuff?

A If you are a developer, you should know it. If you plan mostly on administering existing databases, SQL Enterprise Manager provides a graphical interface you can use to perform most tasks. Familiarity with T-SQL can only help you, because you must enter some commands as T-SQL code, and everything in SQL Server Enterprise Manager is actually entering T-SQL commands.

Q How similar is SQL Server to Sybase, Oracle, or Access?

A Earlier versions of SQL Server (4.*x* and 6.*x*) closely resembled Sybase. Since Microsoft and Sybase went their separate ways, each of their products has become more unique, and SQL Server 2000 is now very different from current Sybase offerings. SQL Server least resembles Oracle, although administrators coming from an Oracle background tend to pick up SQL Server quickly because the concepts of relational databases are similar. Access is a single-computer database, although it can act as a server for small implementations (fewer than 20 users, or performance really suffers). Access makes a great front end to SQL Server, but the Jet database engine that supports earlier versions of Access just isn't as powerful a database engine as SQL Server.

Access 2000 includes the Microsoft Data Engine (MSDE 1.0), the core technology of SQL Server 7.0. SQL Server 2000 adds MSDE 2000 which can allow you to upgrade MSDE 1.0 to MSDE 2000.

Workshop

This section provides quiz questions to help you solidify your understanding of the concepts presented today. In addition to the quiz questions, exercises are provided to let you practice what you've learned today. Try to understand the quiz and exercise answers before continuing on to tomorrow's lesson. Answers are provided in Appendix A, "Answers to Quiz Questions."

Quiz

1. What is the building block of a relational database?
2. What are some of the objects held in a database?
3. Who is responsible for backing up SQL Server databases?

Exercises

1. Try to design a database on your own. Go through a simulated interview, and then try to make some sense out of the interview by creating variables and organizing them into tables. You can also see one way of doing it. Remember, in this case, there isn't just one right answer—just different ways of doing the same thing.
2. Imagine that your Uncle Joel has had a used car lot for practically as long as you can remember. You've helped him set up his computers and network, and now he calls you into his office.

   Joel: Glad you could come by. My lot has grown so big I'm having a hard time keeping track of everything. Sue almost sold a car I don't have, and Larry practically gave one away because he wrote down the wrong price. I need to get organized.

   You: Have you considered some sort of database?

   Joel: You're the computer expert. Just design me something I can use to keep track of my cars. I'm also having a hard time keeping track of my salespeople and how much they've sold. It wasn't that hard when I had a small lot, but now it takes too much of my time.

You: Would you want the database to print reports based on monthly activity by salesperson and other such reports?

Joel: That would help a lot.

You: Do you want the database to have pictures with it?

Joel: Can you do that? That would be really neat! I've also been reading about this Internet stuff, and I think it would be great if I could have my cars on it.

You: Just what were you thinking?

Joel: I don't know. You're the computer expert.

You: Do you want people to be able to look at your cars and prices on the Internet?

Joel: Can you do that? That would be neat! Can we show color pictures, too?

You: Yes, we can put pictures and prices and features on the Web page. What exact information do you want to put in the database?

Joel: I would want the year, make, model, color, mileage, and features such as air conditioning, four-wheel drive, radio/CD player, blue-book price, and retail price for everyone to see. I'd also want people to see a picture of the car and be able to compare the different cars I have. I'd want additional stuff that only my salespeople would see, such as the actual cost and any notes about the car, such as how eager we are to get rid of it and when the car came on the lot.

You: That should be enough to start with. Do you have a budget in mind?

Joel: Well, I can't blow the whole budget on it, but I've got to get something or my salespeople will be losing money on deals if I'm not careful.

You: I'll come up with some ideas and get back to you.

What you got out of the interview is that not only does Uncle Joel need a database that will keep track of cost and sales information, but the database should link to a Web page so that anyone can access public data about the various cars available for sale.

WEEK 1

DAY 2

Installing Microsoft SQL Server 2000

In yesterday's lesson, you learned a little bit about SQL Server 2000 and relational databases in general. Microsoft SQL Server is a mature product, but the 2000 release consists of a large amount of new functionality. You also looked at the reasons a typical developer or database administrator might need a relational database—customers demand it. They need to keep track of objects and properties that translate rather nicely to tables with rows of data, divided into columns.

Today's lesson examines how to install SQL Server 2000. Although running the setup program isn't very difficult, you need to make critical decisions that affect your entire development, and undoing any mistakes can be quite time consuming later. You also must understand issues such as hardware and software prerequisites so you can choose the best environment for SQL Server.

What Kinds of SQL Servers Are Available?

A great first question to ask yourself is, "Which SQL Server do I need?" Microsoft is simultaneously releasing six editions of SQL Server 2000. After you examine their requirements or needs, it should be obvious which one to use. However, the most important point to remember is that, regardless of the edition of SQL Server you choose, they are all built on a common code base (except for the version for Windows CE), so the same rules, conditions, and administration apply.

Standard Edition

The Standard Edition is what most people mean when they refer to SQL Server 2000. This version of the product supplies full functionality and is intended to run on Windows NT Server 4.0 (SP5) or later, as well as a Windows 2000 Server computer. It also runs on the Enterprise Edition of Windows NT 4.0 and Windows 2000 Advanced Server and Data Center. This version supports up to four central processing units (CPUs) and up to 2GB of random access memory (RAM).

Enterprise Edition

The Enterprise Edition of SQL Server 2000 is for very high-end installations or installations that require the best performance from SQL Server. It runs on Windows NT Server 4.0 (SP5 or later), or Windows 2000 Server, Advanced Server, or Data Center Server, and provides features such as large memory support (up to 64GB of RAM), Microsoft Clustering support (high-availability support for up to four cluster nodes), and support for up to 32 CPUs. Support for each of these features also depends on which operating system the product is installed. This book was developed using Service Pack 2 of the Enterprise Edition of SQL Server 2000, running on Windows 2000 Advanced Server. However, the material covered in the book also applies to the other versions of the product.

A 64-bit version of the Enterprise Edition is expected late in 2002, built around the Intel Itanium chip and the Windows.net 64-bit Advanced Server operating system.

Personal Edition

The Personal Edition runs on Windows 98 and Windows ME (Millennium Edition)—Windows 9*x* henceforth—and Windows NT Workstation 4.0, Windows 2000 Professional, or Windows XP Professional or Home Edition (or the server editions of any of the Windows NT family of products). It is meant as a development and remote SQL Server installation to support a central server. It can support several users simultaneously, but it's typically meant for fewer than five concurrent workloads (simultaneous queries). No limit is placed on database size, but Windows NT Workstation/Windows 2000 Professional/Windows XP Professional supports only two processors, and Windows 9*x* supports only one processor, so the personal edition will only work with two processors maximum.

The Personal Edition supports most of the features of SQL Server, but it doesn't allow you to publish in transactional replication (you'll examine replication on Day 16, "Understanding Replication Design Methodologies"). Running on the Windows 9*x* platform involves several additional restrictions, which are detailed later today. However, most of them aren't visible to a database developer, so you can develop with the Desktop Edition and then deploy to the Standard or Enterprise Edition and know that your code is 100 percent compatible.

Developer Edition

The Developer Edition of SQL Server 2000 is the Enterprise Edition in terms of feature set, with licensing restrictions to use it only for development and testing. Therefore, if you use the developer version of the product, you are actually using the Enterprise Edition. However, the developer edition works on the Windows NT/Windows 2000/Windows XP Professional operating systems as well.

Evaluation Edition

The Evaluation Edition of SQL Server 2000 is also the Enterprise Edition, with a 120-day time limit (from the day you install the product). Therefore, if you use the evaluation version of the product, you are actually using the Enterprise Edition. Note that it will NOT run on the desktop editions of the operating systems.

Microsoft SQL Server 2000 Desktop Edition (MSDE)

The MSDE version of SQL Server 2000 is a limited version of the full product. It's built from the same code base, but restrictions have been placed on the product, such as replication restrictions. It doesn't have a user interface (that is, tools), so it's meant as a back-end data store for your applications. You typically get MSDE through the purchase of Microsoft Visual Studio or Microsoft Office XP Professional. You can then develop applications and redistribute MSDE as an embedded part of your application.

If you're using this book to learn MSDE, much of this chapter won't apply to you (in particular, everything graphical about setup, but the pre-requisites below are the same). Please turn to Appendix C for detailed steps on how to install MSDE, as well as for some specific product differences that are unique to MSDE.

SQL Server Requirements

Understanding the prerequisites is critical before you begin the installation of SQL Server 2000. Physical requirements (hardware and software) as well as licensing requirements must be met. Also, when you're running SQL Server on Windows NT or Windows 2000 computers, you must deal with a few additional considerations, such as hardware and software options, Windows NT/2000 options, and licensing options.

Hardware and Software Options

Perhaps the first issue to consider is whether your computer can even run SQL Server 2000. As with most new Microsoft software releases, SQL Server 2000 requires more horsepower than previous releases. In general, the more powerful your computer, the happier you will be with SQL Server 2000's performance.

Supported Hardware

The lowest-powered CPUs supported are Pentium 166 processors. Pentium, Pentium Pro, Pentium 2, Pentium 3, and Pentium 4 computers were available at the time this lesson was written. Of course, Pentium instruction-set–compatible systems are also supported. You need at least 64MB of RAM, although the Personal Edition and MSDE requires only 32MB of RAM on Windows 98, Windows ME, or Windows NT 4.0.

> Although a Pentium 166 is the lowest-powered configuration supported, SQL Server 2000 will probably work (albeit run more slowly) on any Pentium-based computer. It can't run on a 486 or any processor that doesn't support the *full* Pentium instruction set.

The amount of disk space required varies based on which software components you choose to install. A minimal installation requires at least 65MB of space on your hard drive, and a full installation requires about 270MB of hard drive space. Any additional SQL Server components, such as Microsoft English Query (examined shortly), require more space in addition to the numbers mentioned here. English Query requires 80MB, and Microsoft SQL Server Analysis Services can require up to 130MB of disk space.

A CD-ROM installation (a local CD-ROM drive) is recommended; however, if you have access to a network, you can install a copy of SQL Server 2000 from a network share copied from a CD-ROM. This setup could be very practical if you want to perform automated unattended installations of SQL Server components.

Supported Operating System Choices

When you have the supported hardware, you must select or consider which operating systems are supported. SQL Server 2000 can run on a Windows NT computer (version 4.0 or later with service pack 5 or later), any version (Workstation, Server, Small Business Server, or Server Enterprise Edition). SQL Server 2000 can also run on any version of Windows 2000 and on a Windows 98 or Windows ME computer. SQL Server 2000 Developer or Personal editions will run on Windows XP Professional as well. You must consider some restrictions for the Windows platforms, however.

Windows 9*x* Restrictions The client components of SQL Server run unchanged on the Windows 9*x* platform. However, the Personal Edition of SQL Server behaves differently on the Windows 9*x* platform because of restrictions built into the operating system:

- Named Pipes, Banyan VINES, and AppleTalk network libraries aren't supported.
- Windows Authentication Mode (also known as integrated security) isn't available.
- Server-side multi-protocol encryption isn't supported.
- Asynchronous input/output (I/O) and scatter-gather I/O aren't available.
- SQL Server components don't run as services because Windows 9*x* doesn't support services. They run as applications, just like any other program you can run.
- Performance monitor and event viewer aren't available.
- Memory tuning is optimized for minimal memory usage.

Some of these terms might not mean much now, but before your 21 days are up, you will understand all these restrictions and their implementation details. However, you won't notice most of them.

Windows NT/Windows 2000/Windows XP Options Now that you have examined some issues with the Windows 9*x* platform, it's time to examine some of the Windows NT, Windows 2000, and Windows XP-specific features. Windows 2000 or Windows XP is definitely the recommended platform because all product features are available. Personally, we recommend Windows 2000 or Windows XP, because it's so much more reliable and even has better security than Windows NT 4.0.

The most important Windows NT/2000/XP options are security and the NTFS file system. Therefore, you will briefly examine each here. However, you might choose Windows NT/2000/XP for several other reasons. This book assumes that all features are available on most platforms but highlights features available only on Windows NT/2000/XP. Because it would be too confusing to reference all operating system features specific to each version, we have also chosen to use Windows 2000. Therefore, all parts of the book that reference operating system components assume Windows 2000 unless otherwise stated.

NEW TERM

Security Options Perhaps the most important option available with Windows NT/2000/XP is security. Windows NT, Windows 2000 and Windows XP are secure operating systems, allowing you to restrict who can do what to files as well as control access rights with Windows NT/2000/XP security accounts. This feature, known as *Windows Authentication Mode* or *integrated security*, allows you to use Windows user and group accounts directly in SQL Server. You'll examine this feature in detail on Day 5, "Setting Up Login and User Security."

The other security-related issue is whether to install SQL Server 2000 on a domain controller. From a SQL Server perspective, it's best to isolate SQL Server on its own computer, so you'll see better performance by keeping SQL Server on a member (or standalone) server. To take advantage of SQL Server's integrated security with Windows NT/2000/XP, you must install SQL Server on a computer that has access to accounts in your domain. This means (for Windows NT 4.0 networks) that you should install SQL Server on a computer that's a member of a domain that trusts your master account domains. For Windows 2000 networks, install SQL Server so that it's either within your backward-compatible domain structure or as a computer that's a member of your Active Directory.

Note

> If you don't understand the preceding paragraph, refer to your Windows NT, Windows 2000, or Windows XP documentation, or find your network administrator. He will be able to help you place SQL Server on the right computer in your network.

File System Options You can use the file allocation table (FAT), FAT32 (Windows 2000 only), or NTFS file systems with SQL Server 2000. I strongly recommend using the NTFS file system for security and reliability. If you install with the NTFS file system, SQL Server setup secures your installation files, including your system database files. NTFS is also much faster in terms of new database creation. With Windows 2000, you can also take advantage of the Encrypted File System (EFS) support to encrypt your database files so that no one can copy them without having the username and password of the SQL Server service account.

Licensing Options Two types of licenses are available in SQL Server 2000: per-seat licensing and per-processor. Per-seat licensing requires you to purchase a license for each computer that will access a SQL Server. However, after you purchase a per-seat license, you can connect to any number of SQL Servers in your network.

Per-processor licensing licenses each CPU in your computer separately. So, if you have an eight-CPU box and want to use all the available processors for SQL Server, you need to buy eight per-processor licenses.

Caution

> The right to install the Personal Edition of SQL Server 2000 is given only to users who have per-seat client access licenses. Therefore, don't choose the per-processor license if you want to install the Personal Edition of SQL Server.

With both licensing options, and with the Enterprise Edition of SQL Server 2000, you can install up to 16 instances of SQL Server on a single machine. For the Standard Edition, you must purchase each instance you want to install separately, again with a maximum number of instances set to 16.

Neither of us authors is a lawyer, and neither of us plays one on TV. Rely on your legal counsel for advice on licensing SQL Server properly. The outline in this book is just for informational purposes. Licenses might be subject to change or subject to special conditions your company has negotiated.

Installing SQL Server 2000

Now that you've figured out your licenses and selected your platform (hardware and operating system choices), it's time to begin the installation process. This book was written on Windows 2000 Advanced Server on a Pentium 3-1000 with 396MB of RAM. SQL Server 6.5 (with service pack 5A) is also installed, simply to show you the available screen shots and menu items for the upgrade options. All the screen shots in this book are from this system. Again, we'll point out platform-specific issues as they come up later.

Beginning the Installation Process

To begin the installation, insert the CD-ROM into your CD-ROM drive. You are presented with the autoplay dialog if that feature is enabled on your system (see Figure 2.1). If this dialog (or something similar) isn't presented when you insert your CD, use Windows Explorer to locate your CD-ROM drive, and run the `autorun.exe` program in the root directory.

The Autoplay Menu

You can make several choices right away on the automenu. Your best first step is to click Read the Release Notes, which brings up the file `readme.txt` from the CD. Choosing this option starts Notepad and allows you to view the last-minute information that didn't make it into the manuals. The `readme` file might contain quite a bit of information, but you should focus on just the relevant parts for installation before continuing. We don't know what's in the `readme.txt` file, by its very nature, until SQL Server ships. Therefore, reviewing this file just in case is a wise precaution.

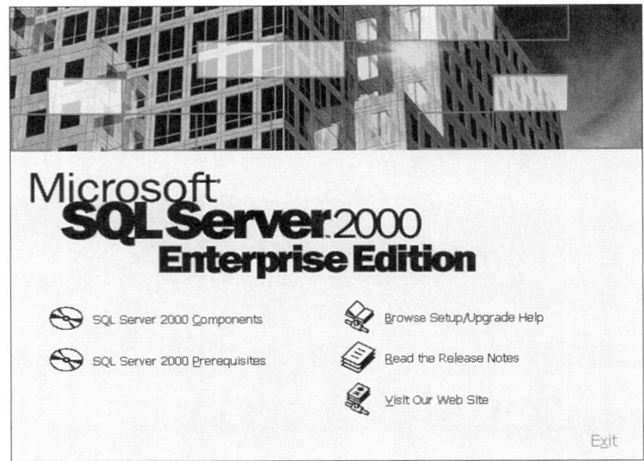

FIGURE 2.1
The Microsoft SQL Server 2000 automenu.

If you want to browse the online manuals for setup help, you must first have Internet Explorer 5.0, or later, installed to be able to view them. This way, you can read the installation manual if you don't have a paper copy before you install SQL Server. However, this lesson covers anything you need to know to install SQL Server 2000. You can also find a shortcut to the Microsoft SQL Server Web site (`http://www.microsoft.com/sql`), where you can get additional information and utilities for SQL Server 2000. The second line down refers to SQL Server 2000's prerequisites.

Prerequisites Based on Operating System

The prerequisites depend on the operating system on which you are installing SQL Server. For Windows 95, you must install the Winsock 2 update, as well as the Common Controls Library update. Windows 95 supports only the SQL Server management tools, and not any edition of the SQL Server product. Although Internet Explorer 5.0 (or later) isn't available from the SQL Server automenu, it is also required before you can install SQL Server or the client tools for SQL Server. This requirement doesn't stop you from using another Web browser (such as Netscape Navigator), but you must install the Internet Explorer minimal installation before you can continue. Windows 2000 already has the right version of Internet Explorer integrated. For Windows NT 4.0 computers, you must have service pack 5 installed as well. Both components (Internet Explorer and the Windows NT Service Pack) must be in place before you can begin installing SQL Server.

2

Installing SQL Server 2000 (Full Product)

After you install the prerequisite software (or if you don't need to), you can begin installing SQL Server 2000. From the main autoplay menu, select the option SQL Server 2000 Components. Figure 2.2 shows the menu that appears.

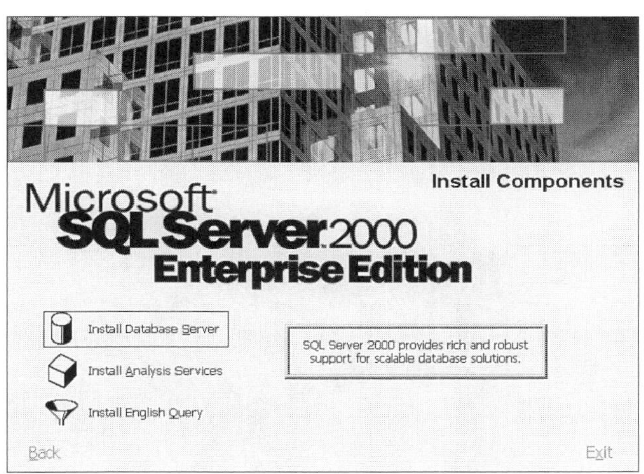

FIGURE 2.2
Install Components for SQL Server 2000.

You can choose to start an installation of the SQL Server product, or install either Analysis Services or English Query. Analysis Services will be covered on Bonus Day 22, "An Overview of Analysis Services." You can install it if you want (simply accept all the defaults), but you won't use it until Day 22. English Query is very similar, except that you'll examine it on Bonus Day 23, "An Overview of English Query."

> **Tip** The Personal Edition, included with SQL Server 2000, can run on any supported computer: Windows 98, Windows ME, Windows NT Workstation, Windows 2000 Professional, Windows NT Server, Windows 2000 Server, and even the Enterprise Edition of Windows NT Server. If you really want to, you can also run it on Windows 2000 Advanced Server or Windows 2000 Data Center Server.

This lesson walks you through the setup of the full product (the Enterprise Edition of SQL Server 2000). However, the setup is virtually identical for the Personal Edition. Setup of the Enterprise Edition, when failover clustering is involved, requires several special considerations and is beyond the scope of this book.

To continue the setup process from the menu shown in Figure 2.2, follow these steps:

1. Click Install Database Server. SQL Server setup welcomes you to the setup process. Click Next. You are presented with the option of installing SQL Server either on a remote computer or on your local computer (see Figure 2.3). Accept the default of installing on your local computer, and click Next.

> You use the Virtual Server option when installing SQL Server 2000 in a failover cluster.

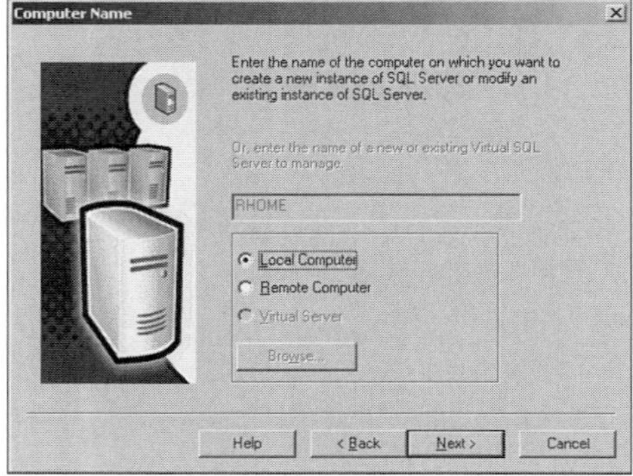

FIGURE 2.3
Local or remote setup?

2. Setup searches your computer to determine whether SQL Server was previously installed (including a previous release). After this determination (assuming that SQL Server isn't already installed), you are presented with the Installation Selection dialog (see Figure 2.4).
3. Accept the default selection to create a new instance of SQL Server, and click Next. In the User Information dialog (see Figure 2.5), enter your name and company name, and click Next. You then see the license agreement (see Figure 2.6). You should read the license agreement. If you don't like what you see and click No (that you don't agree), setup terminates and you should return SQL Server to wherever you purchased it. Because, of course, you won't choose No, simply click Yes, you agree.
4. Click Next. You then are presented with the dialog in Figure 2.7, into which you must enter the 25-character CD license key. This is the same kind of licensing you see in Office 2000 and Windows 2000. It should be on the yellow sticker of your CD liner notes or sleeve. If you don't have a valid SQL Server license key, you can't continue with setup.

FIGURE 2.4

Installation selection.

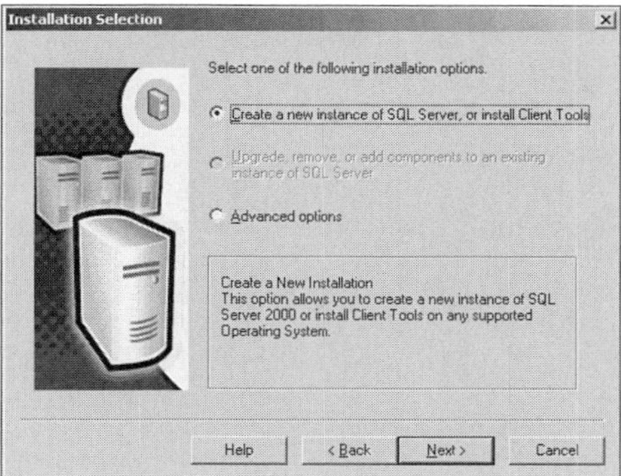

FIGURE 2.5

Gathering user information.

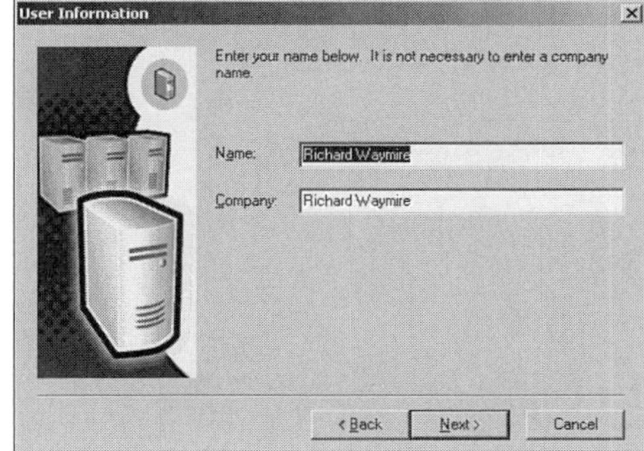

FIGURE 2.6

The SQL Server 2000 license agreement.

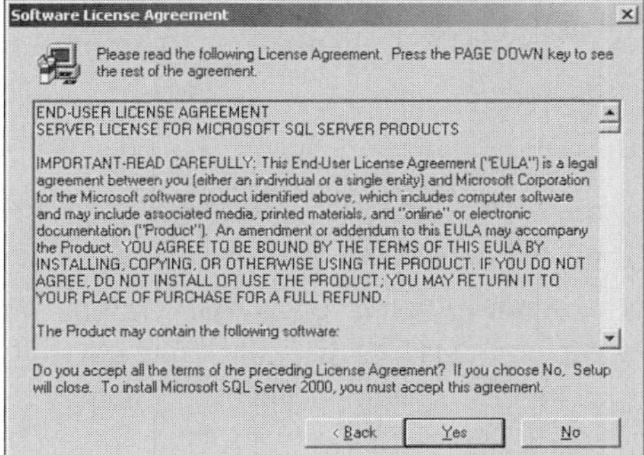

5. After you enter the proper license ID, click Next to move to the Installation Definition dialog (see Figure 2.8).

   To install all of SQL Server (the server software and the client tools), accept the default of Server and Client Tools. If you want to install just the SQL Server tools, you can do so by selecting the top option, Client Tools Only. Finally, if all you want is the updated data access components (also known as MDAC 2.6) that come with SQL Server 2000, select the last option, Connectivity Only.

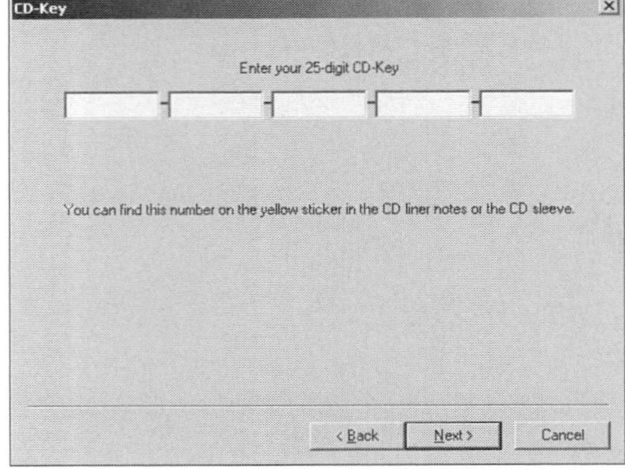

FIGURE 2.7
Specify your CD license key.

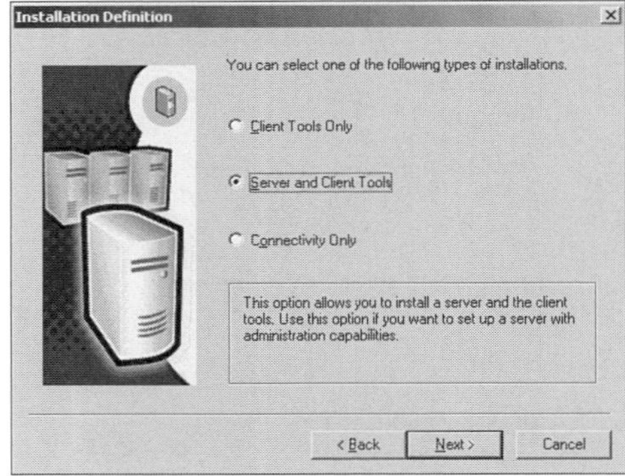

FIGURE 2.8
Select the installation type.

6. Select the default option, and click Next. You then see the Instance Name dialog (see Figure 2.9).

   For now, accept the default option to install a default instance of SQL Server. You will examine what a named instance is later today and will come back later and install a named instance of SQL Server.

7. Click Next to move to the Authentication Mode dialog (see Figure 2.10).

   Change the default from Windows Authentication Mode to Mixed Mode. Set a strong password for the sa login account. Optionally you can leave the (more secure) default to Windows Authentication Mode, but may have to change it later with SQL Enterprise Manager for some of the examples to match the book. Whatever you do, don't select the blank password option. Your SQL Server is easily compromised and hacking tools will likely find your computer.

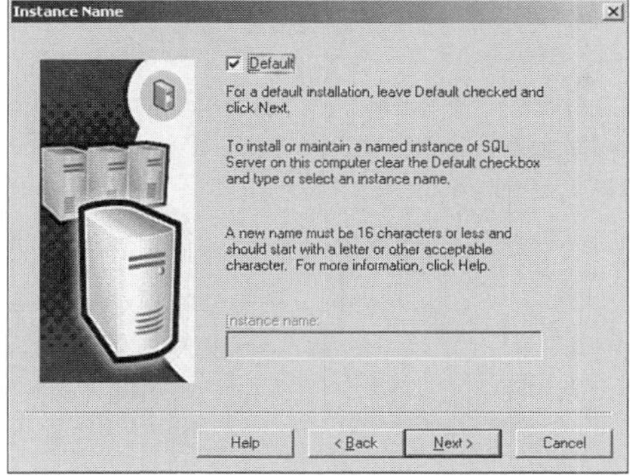

FIGURE 2.9

Select the instance name.

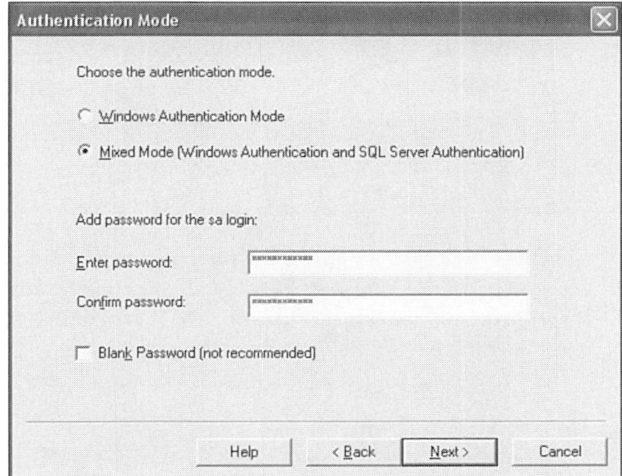

FIGURE 2.10

Select the Authentication Mode.

8. Click Next to move to the Setup Type dialog (see Figure 2.11).

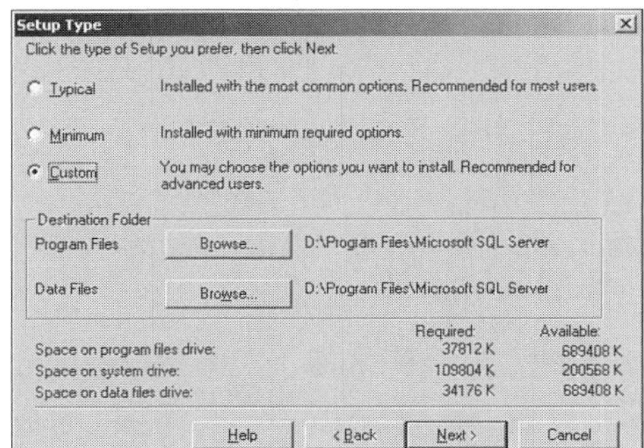

FIGURE 2.11

Select the setup type.

If you select Typical, all default options are taken, and setup jumps to the dialog in Figure 2.16. All components except the development tools and code samples are installed; however, you get the Transact-SQL Debugger by default. A Minimum installation follows the same path in terms of the screens you see but installs only the client-access components (ODBC and so on) and the SQL Server core services. It doesn't install any management tools or the Books Online.

As you can see in Figure 2.11, I've selected a Custom setup. This type of setup allows you to see each setup option and select it for yourself. This lesson also identifies which components on each screen are installed by default during a typical or minimum installation.

After selecting the setup type, you can change the setup location for SQL Server's program files (the programs needed to run SQL Server) and SQL Server's data files (the system databases, explained shortly, and the default location for your databases). The space requirements are listed at the bottom of the dialog. I don't have enough room to install on my C drive, so I plan to install SQL Server on the D drive of my computer. Most people choose to accept the default drive, C.

I recommend that you leave the directory as the default `\Program Files\Microsoft SQL Server`, even if you choose a different hard drive. This default is well understood to be a SQL Server directory and should make people think before they start deleting files later. It also helps make SQL Server 2000 Windows 2000 logo compliant.

Navigating the Custom Setup

When you click Next, you then can select the components you want to install for SQL Server 2000. The amount of disk space you use depends greatly on which components you choose to install. Your choices here also affect what you can do with your SQL Server installation down the road.

Select Components

Your first step is to select the components you want to install (see Figure 2.12). You need to make several key decisions here. You even have the possibility of performing a client-tools–only installation. Each selection possibility is described next.

Server Components Under Server Components, the following options are available:

- *SQL Server* is the core database engine and the management support service (known as SQL Server Agent—both are examined shortly). This option is enabled by default.

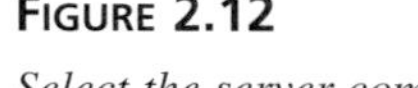

FIGURE 2.12

Select the server components to install.

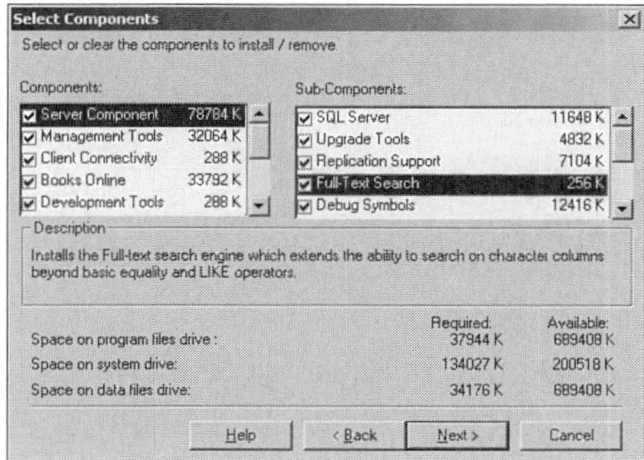

Tip

For the purposes of going through this book, select all available options.

- *Upgrade Tools* is the database upgrade support, so you can run the Version Upgrade Wizard to upgrade a SQL Server 6.5 installation. You don't need to have SQL Server 6.5 installed on the same computer as SQL Server 2000 to be able to migrate data to the server, but the computer must be running the Windows NT or Windows 2000 operating system. This option is enabled by default.
- *Replication Support* should be left enabled (as it is by default) if you plan to use replication.
- *Full-Text Search* uses technology from Microsoft Index Server to build indexes on textual data. This option is examined further on Day 13, "Indexing for Performance." Unlike in SQL Server 7.0, this option is installed by default. It's also available only on Windows NT and Windows 2000 operating system-based computers. Also, unlike SQL Server 7.0, SQL Server 2000 fully supports full-text search in a failover cluster configuration.
- *Debug Symbols*, enabled by default, provides debug files should you ever need to troubleshoot SQL Server with Microsoft Product Support. You should leave this option enabled.
- *Performance Counters* should be left enabled (as it is by default) if you want the ability to monitor SQL Server's performance with the performance monitor utility that Windows provides.

Management Tools Under Management Tools, the following options are available and are all enabled by default (see Figure 2.13):

- *Enterprise Manager* is the graphical management interface for both development and administration of SQL Server.

- The SQL Server *Profiler* is a great tool for monitoring SQL Server activities, including queries and how these queries are run. It also provides performance measurements.
- *Query Analyzer* is what you use to enter and run Transact-SQL statements. You can also view how SQL Server will optimize and run your queries. Experienced T-SQL developers tend to use this tool.
- *DTC Client Support* allows you to use the Distributed Transaction Coordinator to run data modification queries across multiple systems.
- *Conflict Viewer* is the conflict resolution wizard for merge replication.

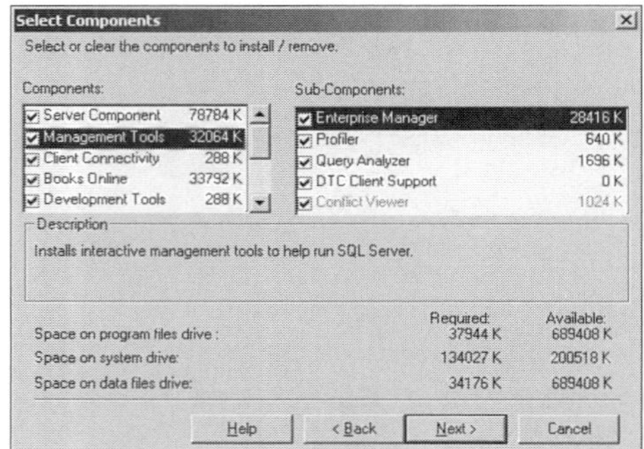

FIGURE 2.13
Select the management tools to install.

Client Connectivity Client Connectivity is the set of components that allow you to talk to SQL Server. This set includes components for Open Database Connectivity (ODBC), Object Linking and Embedding Database (OLE DB), and DB-Library. Each library allows you to write or use programs that connect to SQL Server. Without them, you can't do much of anything, so as you would expect, they're enabled by default. Collectively, they are known as MDAC (the Microsoft Data Access Components).

Books Online Here, you can choose to install the Books Online onto the local hard drive, add shortcuts in Windows to your SQL Server CD-ROM for the Books Online (to save disk space), or not install them. I strongly recommend you always install Books Online at every instance of SQL Server. Nothing is more frustrating than working on a server and not being able to view the manuals when you need them most. Also, note that unlike previous versions, all SQL Server tools use the Books Online as their help system now.

Tip

> An updated version of the books online is now available for download. When setup of SQL Server 2000 is complete, go to `http://www.microsoft.com/sql`, select downloads, and then search for the updated books online. Follow the instructions to download this version of the online documentation to make sure you have the latest, most up-to-date information about SQL Server 2000.

Development Tools You have the following options when installing the development tools (see Figure 2.14):

- *Headers and Libraries* are the include and library files for C/C++ that you need to develop SQL Server programs.
- *MDAC SDKs* are the Software Development Kits for XML and the Microsoft Data Access Components. These SDKs allow you to develop programs by using XML and MDAC.
- *Backup/Restore API* includes a sample program, necessary C/C++ files, and documentation on how to build backup and restore programs.
- *Debugger Interface* installs the components necessary to allow Microsoft Visual Studio components and the SQL Server Query Analyzer utility the capability to debug stored procedures. This option is selected by default.

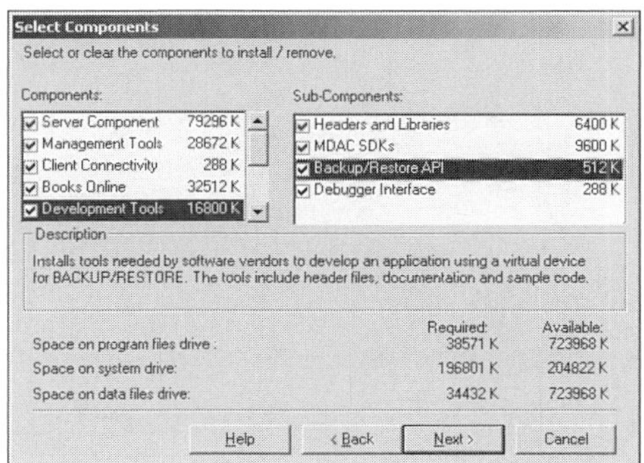

FIGURE 2.14
Select the development tools to install.

Code Samples None of the code samples are installed by default. However, you have the following options (see Figure 2.15):

- *ADO* includes programming examples for ActiveX Data Objects (ADO).
- *DBLIB* includes programming examples for the DB-Library API. DB-Library was the native Database Application Programming Interface (API) of SQL Server in

earlier releases, and is supported in SQL Server 2000 for backward compatibility only.

- *Desktop* includes code samples on setting up unattended install operations for the Microsoft SQL Server Desktop Engine (MSDE).
- *DTS* includes programming examples for data transformation services (DTS). DTS provides a way to move data from one source to another.
- *ESQLC* includes the programming examples for Embedded SQL for the C programming language.
- *MSDTC* includes the programming examples for the Microsoft Distributed Transaction Coordinator.
- *ODBC* includes the programming examples for the open database connectivity programming API in SQL Server.
- *ODS* includes the programming examples for the open data services (ODS) API for SQL Server.
- *OLE Automation* includes the programming examples to support OLE Automation for SQL Server.
- *Replication* includes the programming examples for SQL Server replication.
- *SQLDMO* includes programming examples for the SQL-Distributed Management Objects administrative programming interface.
- *SQLNS* includes programming examples for the SQL NameSpace administrative programming interface.

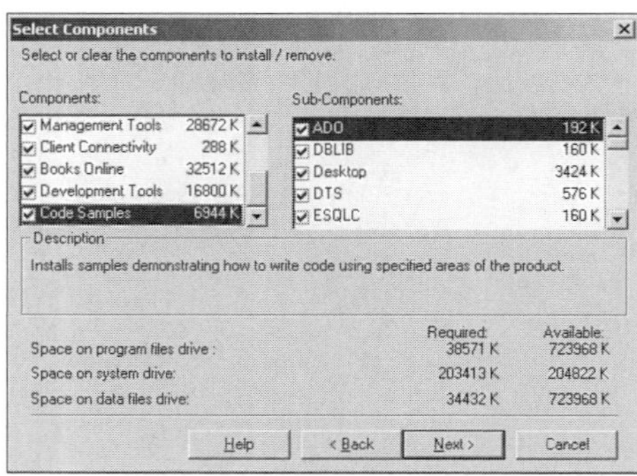

FIGURE 2.15

Select the code samples to install.

The Services Accounts Click Next after you select the components you need; you then move to the Services Accounts dialog (see Figure 2.16). This dialog appears on

Windows NT/2000 computers only. Windows 9*x* doesn't support the concept of services, so SQL Server on Windows 9*x* always runs in the context of the logged-in user. However, because SQL Server on Windows NT/2000 runs as a background service, it doesn't require anyone to log in to the computer to enable SQL Server services. However, even services must log in to the operating system to function.

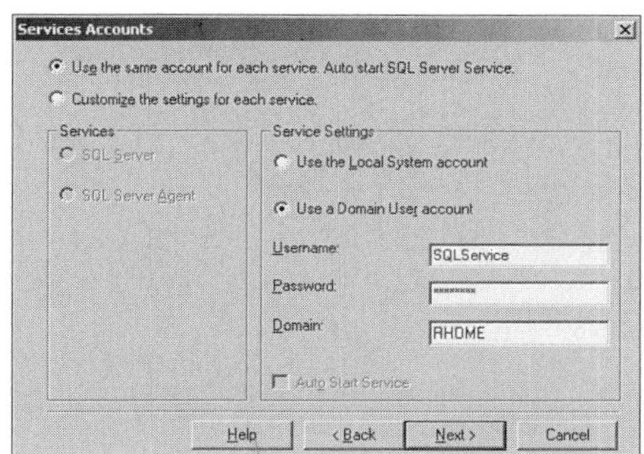

FIGURE 2.16
Select the services accounts.

In Windows NT/2000, the Local System account is generally understood to mean the operating system itself. Selecting the Local System account always works. However, this account has no network access rights. Therefore, if you want to integrate more than one SQL Server on your network or integrate SQL Server with other BackOffice services such as Microsoft Exchange Server, you should run the SQL Server services under a user account.

> You might hear that the Local System account has network access when running under Windows 2000. This statement is true, but only in pure Windows 2000 networks talking to other Windows 2000-based computers.

Setup selects the account of the user running setup by default. This choice is rarely correct. You should create a special user account to use for the SQL Server services. After you create the account, you may want to make it a member of the local administrator's group on the computer. If you don't grant the service account administrator rights, you will need to use setup to add the account to SQL Server or use the Enterprise Manager interfaces to change the service's accounts – never change the services to a non-administrator account using Windows Control Panel -> Administrative Tools -> Services or your SQL Server may not start.

If you are concerned about granting the service account membership in the administrator's group, see the SQL Server Books Online for more information about how to run SQL Server without using administrative rights.

The other choice here is to use the same account for both default SQL Server services (explained later today). You can use separate accounts for each service, but accepting the default configuration is much easier. If you are on your own personal SQL Server, use the administrator's account or create a custom account (as shown in Figure 2.17) with User Manager or User Manager for Domains in Windows NT 4.0, or Computer Management in Windows 2000 (Active Directory Users and Computers if in a Windows 2000 domain). If you are on an organized corporate network, have an appropriate account created for your use.

Make sure that the account you use has the following characteristics in addition to being for an administrator:

- Password never expires
- All logon hours allowed

This will prevent your SQL Server from stopping working arbitrarily. Your company may require your passwords to expire periodically. Figure 2.16 shows this configuration for Windows 2000 using the Computer Management interface.

FIGURE 2.17

Create or configure the services account(s).

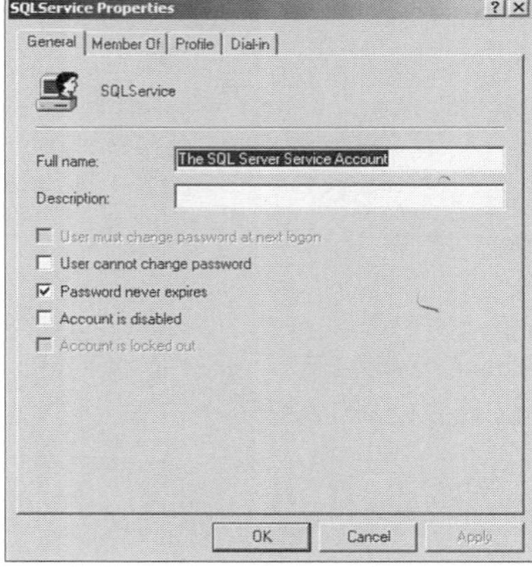

The Authentication Mode Click Next after you enter the proper username and password for your service accounts; you then move to the Authentication Mode dialog (see Figure 2.18). This dialog appears on all operating system platforms, but Windows

Authentication Mode isn't available on Windows 9*x* systems. For all Windows NT/2000 computers, Windows Authentication Mode is enabled by default.

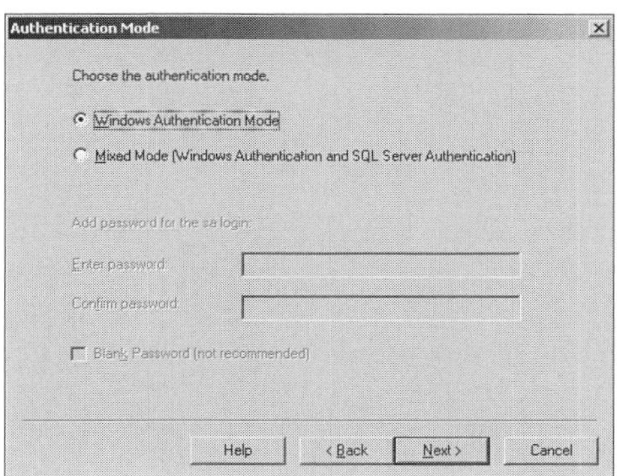

FIGURE 2.18

Select the authentication mode.

Authentication mode determines whether SQL Server depends on the operating system to create and manage user accounts (the default configuration is yes), or allows a combination of operating system accounts and accounts you create within SQL Server 2000. You will examine these options in detail on Day 5. For now, accept the default.

Note

If you change to Mixed Mode, you must specify a password for the system administrator (sa) login within SQL Server. If you really insist, you can check the check box to set a blank password. This dialog was added because too many SQL Server systems were put on the Internet with a blank sa password. If you're fortunate, your system uses Windows Authentication. If not, at least you have a password on your sa login.

Collation Settings

If you want to change your collation settings after you install SQL Server 2000, you have to rebuild your `master` database. However, unlike you do in previous releases, you don't have to reload your data and rebuild your indexes, because SQL Server 2000 supports data-specific (and even column-specific) collation settings.

Click Next to continue to the Collation Settings dialog, in which you make another critical decision about your SQL Server installation (see Figure 2.19). You must choose in what character set non-Unicode data is to be stored, how it will be sorted when returned from SQL Server, and what type of Unicode collation you want (how Unicode data will be sorted and returned to the user).

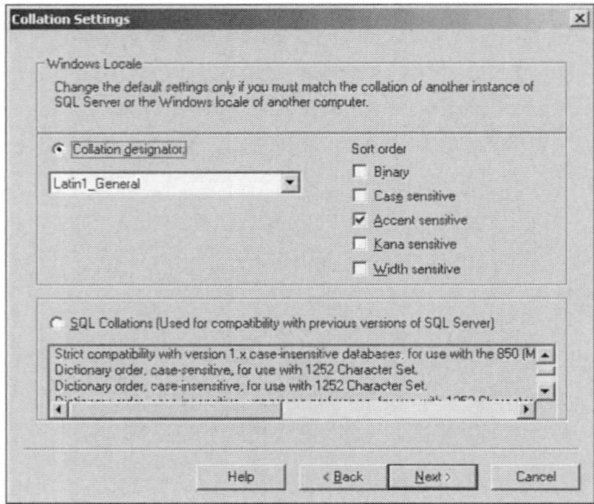

FIGURE 2.19
The Collation Settings dialog.

> **Note**
>
> What is Unicode? That's a great question. Traditional computer storage allows 1 byte of storage for each character you see onscreen. However, this storage system works out to allowing only 256 choices of characters. The first 128 characters are typically the same, and the last 128 characters vary, based on the character set (also known as the *code page*) you select.
>
> From a global perspective, not nearly enough characters are available to represent all languages. Unicode is a way to allow computers to keep 2 bytes per character. Although you double your storage space requirements, you can now keep data in any language in your server, and it never needs to be translated—it's always stored correctly. For any kind of international effort when multiple languages are involved, Unicode solves a very difficult problem—letting Germans store their data in German, Chinese store data in Chinese, and so on, but all within a single column in your database.

The default collation designator is Latin1_General. This collation should best support U.S. English, as well as most Western European languages. You should select this character set unless you have a compelling reason not to do so (for example, you're in China and want the Chinese default character set). You also can specify how data will be sorted:

- For Latin1_General, Accent Sensitive means that if you ask SQL Server to sort a list of names, the results are returned in the same order as they appear in the dictionary but are sensitive to accents. So, for example, *é* isn't equivalent to *E* or *e*.

- Many application vendors use the binary sort order (meaning results are returned in their ASCII sequence). Then the application assumes the responsibility of sorting. You would set that by checking the Binary sort order.
- Another option is to use a case-sensitive server, so that *S* and *s* are sorted in different groups. You can then choose whether upper- or lowercase letters come first. However, this choice has a profound side effect. In SQL Server, if you create a table called Sales, it's not the same table as SALES. You've therefore forced your users (and yourself) to be very precise. Also, a search for my last name, Waymire, would fail unless the first letter was capitalized. So, if you enter **`waymire`**, you won't find that information. Again, to enable this option, simply check the Case Sensitive sort order.
- Kana Sensitive determines whether SQL Server treats the two Japanese kana character sets (Hiragana and Katakana) as equal. If you select this option, they are treated as distinct; otherwise, they are treated as equal.
- Some languages can have the same character represented in a single byte or in a two-byte representation. If you select the Width Sensitive option, SQL Server treats these as separate characters when comparing them; if you leave it deselected, SQL Server treats these characters as identical. If you're not working with double-byte languages, don't worry about this setting.

You might also choose an alternative collation to maintain backward compatibility with previous installations of SQL Server that used a different character set and sort order (the terms used in previous releases). In that case, select the SQL Collations option, and then your choice depends on your previous or existing installations of SQL Server 7.0 or earlier.

If you think your previous installation accepted the defaults, more than likely you should select Dictionary Order, Case Insensitive, which is backward compatible with the 1252 Character Set. This option was the default in SQL Server 6.5 and SQL Server 7.0.

> SQL Server exports the Unicode features to the Windows 9*x* platform, even though you don't usually have Unicode support in these operating systems.

Network Libraries Click Next after accepting your collation settings, and you are presented with the Network Libraries dialog (see Figure 2.20). Here you need to choose the available network libraries to support for SQL Server. They are the network libraries that client computers can use to talk to your copy of SQL Server. The default for Windows NT/2000 computers is to install Named Pipes and Transmission Control

Protocol/Internet Protocol (TCP/IP) Sockets. For Windows 9*x* computers, only TCP/IP Sockets is selected by default.

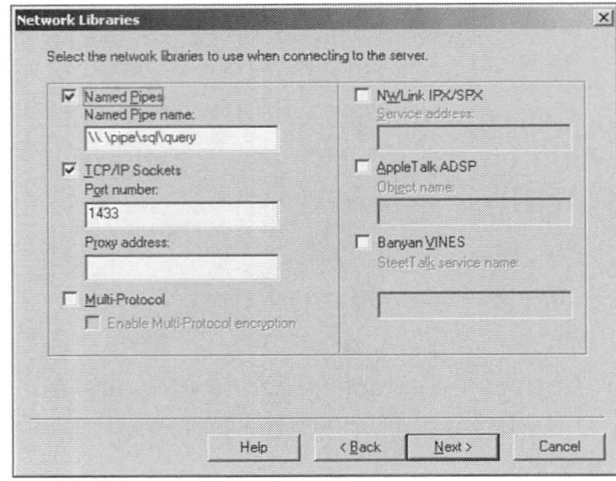

FIGURE 2.20
Select the network libraries to install.

It's a good idea to have an understanding of each network library before you continue.

Named Pipes Named Pipes is actually a file-system approach to network communications. When you connect to a file share, you specify a Universal Naming Convention (UNC) path to a file server: `\\FILESERVER\Sharename`. To connect to a named pipe, you connect to a share that is of the form `\\COMPUTER\pipe\sql\query`. You can change the named pipe on which you want SQL Server to listen, but you shouldn't do so unless you are an advanced SQL Server administrator and understand the implications.

Named Pipes is required for Windows NT/2000 systems and shouldn't be removed. It has been the traditional network library for the last several releases of SQL Server, so if you have SQL Server 6.*x* clients on your network, they most likely use Named Pipes when they try to connect to your server. As of this release, Named Pipes is being replaced as the primary communications mechanism for SQL Server—it's replacement is TCP/IP Sockets.

Named Pipes isn't available (on the server side) for Windows 9*x* systems. You can use it to connect to a server, but the server part of Named Pipes isn't available, so the option isn't available during a desktop SQL Server installation on the Windows 9*x* environments.

TCP/IP Sockets TCP/IP Sockets connect to SQL Server by using TCP/IP's sockets network capabilities. The default assigned socket for SQL Server is 1433. You use sockets every day (using socket 80 for Web browsing). This protocol is available and supported on all operating systems and is the default network library on all new installations of SQL Server 2000 software.

If you install a named instance (explained later today), the socket number is set to 0 (which means dynamic). Each time your named instance of SQL Server starts, it queries Windows for an available socket. If it can use the one it used the last time it started, it does so. If for some reason you want your sockets fixed, you can override the default setting here and type the number of a socket you know to be available on your server.

Note

> Why didn't Microsoft just use 1434 or some other number? The answer is that each number is assigned by an Internet numbering authority, and Microsoft SQL Server has only two: 1433 and 1434. Although SQL Server does own 1434, port 1434 UDP (as opposed to port 1434 TCP) is used by SQL Server to locate and query SQL Server installations on a network. So, because no other numbers are assigned to SQL Server, the issue is left up to Windows to arbitrate (or you if you manually select a port).

Multi-Protocol Multi-Protocol supports any available communications method between computers using Remote Procedure Calls (RPCs). The key advantage to the multiprotocol network library in previous releases was the option to enable encryption of all traffic over the network. For any kind of secure environment (banks, government, and so on), this option is great to use to protect your data while it crosses the network.

Multi-Protocol is no longer installed by default, for two reasons:

- All network libraries support encryption in SQL Server 2000 (you'll explore how tomorrow when you examine the server network utility).
- Multi-Protocol doesn't work against named instances of SQL Server. Multiprotocol encryption isn't available for SQL Servers running on Windows 9*x*.

NWLink IPX/SPX NWLink IPX/SPX is used to support legacy Novell environments. Don't use this option unless you are still using IPX/SPX only to connect by using Novell client software.

AppleTalk ADSP AppleTalk (as the name implies) supports communications over Macintosh- and Apple-computer–based networks. You must also install the services for Macintosh software for Windows NT/2000 before this network library can function. This library is no longer being enhanced and will eventually be phased out in favor of TCP/IP sockets. It also doesn't work with named instances of SQL Server 2000.

Banyan VINES Banyan VINES is used (surprisingly enough) in a Banyan VINES network environment. If you are on a Banyan StreetTalk network, select this option. Again, additional software components are necessary for Windows NT/2000 to enable this functionality. As with AppleTalk, this network library is no longer being enhanced and will eventually be phased out in favor of TCP/IP sockets. It also doesn't work with named instances of SQL Server 2000.

Finishing Setup

After you select the network libraries, click Next to get to the dialog in Figure 2.21 showing you that setup is ready to begin copying files.

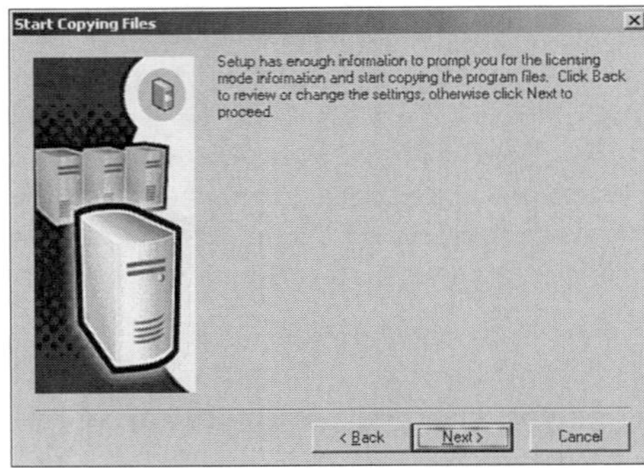

FIGURE 2.21
Setup is ready to begin copying files.

When you are ready to continue, click Next and you are presented with the licensing mode dialog for SQL Server (see Figure 2.22). You can choose per-seat or per-processor licensing for your SQL Server. You looked at licensing at the beginning of today's lesson. After you select the type of licensing you want to use, click Next, and setup will begin copying files.

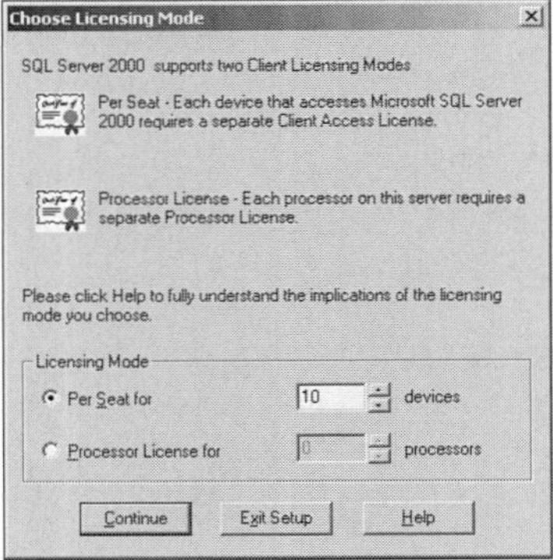

FIGURE 2.22
Choose your licensing mode.

SQL Server setup installs the components you selected. It first installs the client connectivity components, referred to as Microsoft Data Access Components (MDAC). The Full-Text Search engine is then installed; then, if needed, the Microsoft Management Console

(MMC)—the shell that contains SQL Server Enterprise Manager—is installed. MSDTC (explained shortly) is then installed (if needed), followed by the Hypertext Markup Language (HTML) help engine. Then the SQL Server program files are copied onto your computer. SQL Server copies only the files it needs to comply with the installation options you selected earlier.

When setup is complete, you might be prompted to restart your computer. You get such a request if this is the first time you've installed MDAC 2.6 components on your computer or if key files were in use during setup. If you are requested to do so, restart your computer.

Installing Other SQL Server Optional Components

After you install SQL Server 2000, you can install three additional services: the Microsoft Search Service, the Microsoft SQL Server Analysis Services, and Microsoft English Query. Although you can install the Microsoft Search Service (full-text indexing) during the default setup of SQL Server, you can also install the two other services after the initial setup is complete. You can also install these other two services independently of SQL Server if you want.

Microsoft SQL Server Analysis Services

Microsoft SQL Server Analysis Services (known as OLAP services in SQL Server 7.0) comprise a set of technologies to extend data warehousing into SQL Server. The Server Analysis Services help you build OLAP (OnLine Analytical Processing) data to perform detailed trend analysis in many ways, as well as support data mining. The services provide the capability to build and control these cubes, and a user interface to build, administer, and query these cubes is also installed. The server side installs only on Windows NT 4.0 or Windows 2000. The client components and user interface are also available in Windows 9*x*. For a brief overview of analysis services, see Bonus Day 22.

Microsoft English Query

Microsoft English Query allows an administrator to configure a database schema and allows end users to run their database queries in English instead of Transact-SQL. This capability is particularly beneficial for Internet-based applications that don't want to force users to run SQL statements. For example, you can say, "Show me the number of books sold for each author this year," rather than use a complicated SQL statement. You can install English Query on any supported platform for SQL Server 2000. You'll learn more about English Query on Bonus Day 23.

Postinstallation: What Did You Get?

So now that you've installed SQL Server 2000, what did you get for your time? You have a set of services (or applications, if you look at them on Windows 9*x*), a set of tools, and a set of manuals. You also have several files installed on your computer, and modifications have been made to your Windows Registry. Several default SQL Server databases were also installed, and the default security configuration was set up.

The SQL Server Services

The following is the complete list of SQL Server services that might have been installed:

- *MSSQLServer* is the actual database server. When you stop or start SQL Server, it typically means you have stopped the MSSQLServer service.
- *SQLServerAgent* provides support for scheduled jobs, alerts, event management, and replication. You'll examine this service further on Day 18, "Scheduling Jobs with SQL Server Agent."
- *MSDTC* (Distributed Transaction Coordinator) supports distributed transactions across multiple servers. You'll examine distributed transactions on Day 12, "Using Transact-SQL Extensions."
- *Microsoft Search* supports indexing of text fields in SQL Server.
- *MSSQLServerOLAPService* supports Microsoft SQL Server Analysis Services, as described earlier today.
- *MSSQLServerADHelper* supports Microsoft SQL Server's Active Directory Integration. This service won't be examined further in this book and doesn't require any administrative control (nor is it even running most of the time).

Each service can potentially be controlled in several different ways. By far, the easiest is to use the Service Manager utility or the SQL Server Enterprise Manager. You will learn how to use both in tomorrow's lesson when you examine the SQL Server tools and utilities. You can also use various Windows NT tools, such as the services applet under Administrative Tools in Windows 2000, or the Server Manager utility.

My favorite method is still the good old command prompt. The `NET START` and `NET STOP` commands can stop or start any service, but I use them most frequently for the SQL Server services. Open a command prompt (Start, Programs, Command Prompt) and type **`NET START`** to see the list of running services (see Figure 2.23).

In this list, to stop the SQL Server Agent service, type **`NET STOP SQLServerAgent`**. To start the service, type **`NET START SQLServerAgent`**. You start the other services similarly.

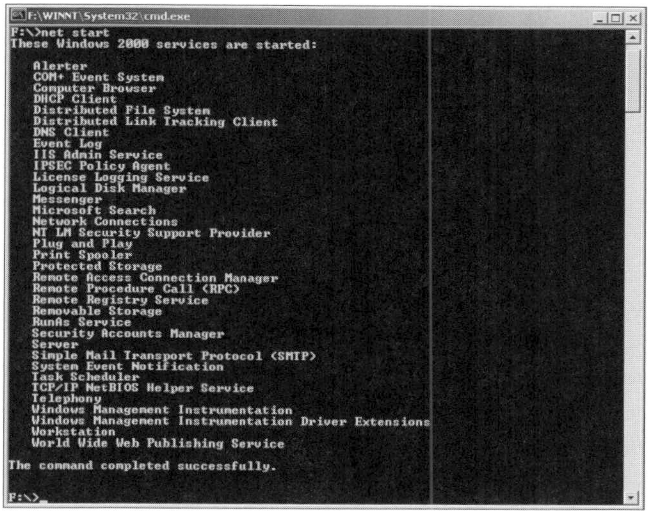

FIGURE 2.23
The list of services showing all SQL Server services.

Installation Folders

Two sets of installation folders are installed when you install your first copy of SQL Server 2000. One is for the instance of SQL Server you installed, whereas the other is for tools, utilities, and COM components common to all copies of SQL Server 2000 installed on your computer.

Installation Folders for Your Default Instance

Table 2.1 shows the folders created on your system and what's installed in each (prefix `D:\Program Files\Microsoft SQL Server\` to all the file locations listed).

TABLE 2.1 The SQL Server Folders for the Default Instance

File Location	*What's Installed*
`\MSSQL`	All other SQL Server and SQL Server Agent service support files, as well as the uninstall support files and the `readme.txt` file
`\MSSQL\Backup`	SQL Server backups (the folder is empty by default)
`\MSSQL\Binn`	All SQL Server program files and supporting DLLs, except the SQL Server tools
`\MSSQL\Data`	SQL Server data files (the system databases, as well as your databases)
`\MSSQL\FTData`	Microsoft Search Service indexes
`\MSSQL\Install`	SQL Scripts, which are run during setup, as well as the `.OUT` files reporting their success or failure

TABLE 2.1 continued

File Location	*What's Installed*
`\MSSQL\Jobs`	The folder in which jobs save data to a temporary location that is empty by default
`\MSSQL\Log`	SQL Server error logs
`\MSSQL\ReplData`	A folder used extensively during replication but is empty until replication is used
`\MSSQL\Upgrade`	All programs and files needed to upgrade from a previous release of SQL Server to SQL Server 2000
`\Program Files\OLAP Services`	Analysis Services components
`\Program Files\Microsoft English Query`	English Query components

Installation Folders for Your Tools and Utilities

Table 2.2 shows the folders created on your system and what's installed in each (by default according to the setup you just ran, prefix `D:\program files\Microsoft SQL Server\80\` to all the file locations listed).

TABLE 2.2 The SQL Server Tools Folders

File Location	*Tools Installed*
`\Tools\Binn`	All SQL Server tools program files and supporting DLLs
`\Tools\Books`	Books Online–compiled HTML files
`\Tools\DevTools`	Developer support tools (C header files, for example)
`\Tools\Html`	All HTML files used by the MMC
`\Tools\Scripts`	Transact-SQL scripts available for the tools and for you if you're interested
`\Tools\Templates`	Template files for building queries or traces in SQL Server Profiler and SQL Server Query Analyzer
`\COM`	The COM files used by all SQL Server instances installed, as well as by the SQL Server tools and utilities
`\COM\Resources\1033`	Language-specific DLL extensions

Windows Registry Entries

Your Registry was modified in quite a few places to install the SQL Server services, to register with the Windows NT/2000 performance monitor and event viewer applications, and to support the needed startup locations for the services. The most important location for you to know about is the key `HKEY_LOCAL_MACHINE\Software\Microsoft\MSSQLServer`. If you start up `regedit.exe` (or `regedt32.exe` on Windows NT/2000 computers, although `regedit.exe` works), you can navigate to this key. Figure 2.24 shows my Registry keys.

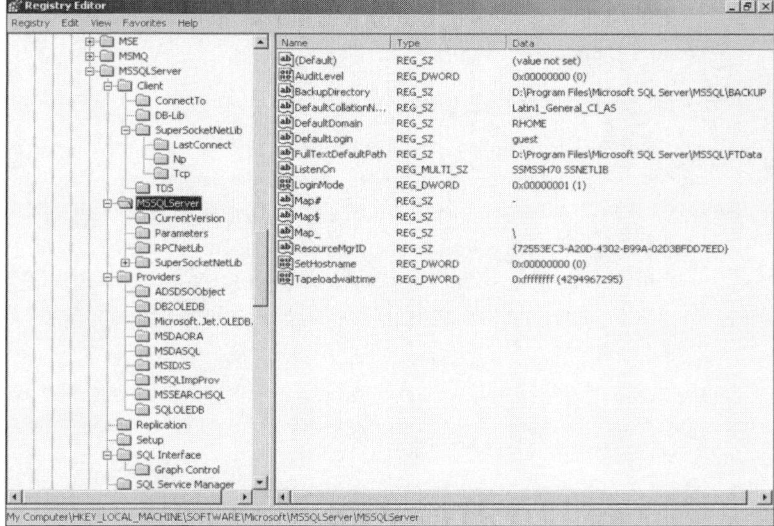

FIGURE 2.24
The SQL Server Registry keys.

I hope you never need to change anything here, but it's a good idea to know where these entries are, just in case. You can also find Registry configuration options stored in `HKEY_CURRENT_USER\Software\Microsoft\MSSQLServer` for your individual user preferences for the client utilities as well.

Services are stored under `HKEY_LOCAL_MACHINE\System\CurrentControlSet\Services\`*`servicename`*.

The SQL Server Default Databases

After you install SQL Server 2000, the databases discussed in the following sections (`master`, `model`, `tempdb`, MSDB, `pubs`, and Northwind) are installed. You can add your own later, but these databases are guaranteed to be there. Some of them (`master`, `model`, `tempdb`, and MSDB) are system databases—you can't drop one of these databases without causing serious harm to SQL Server. The other two, `pubs` and Northwind, are simply samples to help you learn SQL Server. You can safely drop them on your production SQL Servers.

The `master` Database

As just mentioned, the `master` database is the key database for running SQL Server. It contains a pointer to the primary data file for every other database installed on your system, as well as key serverwide information. This serverwide information includes such items as systemwide error messages, login information, system stored procedures, and connected or linked servers. The `master` database can be recovered only in the event of a disaster with special techniques examined on Day 8, "Restoring Your Databases." It's about 12MB after installation.

The `model` Database

The `model` database is best thought of as a template database. Each time you create a new database, the `model` database is actually copied, and then the size and other changes you requested for your new database are applied. Therefore, any object that exists in the `model` database is copied to the new database as it's created. For example, you can place a table or a username in this database right after you install SQL Server. Each time a database is created after that, the table and your username appear in every database.

The `model` database is about 768KB after installation. Because the `model` is copied to create each new database, no database can be smaller than the `model`.

The `tempdb` Database

The `tempdb` database is the place where sorts, joins, and other activities that require temporary space are performed. It's approximately 2MB after installation, but as is the case with all databases in SQL Server 2000 by default, it can grow as you need more space. The `tempdb` database is reinitialized each time SQL Server (the SQL Server service) is restarted.

The MSDB Database

The MSDB database supports the SQL Server Agent service, including storing information about jobs, alerts, events, and replication. A history of all backup and restore activity is also kept in this database. The MSDB database is about 12MB by default.

The `pubs` Database

The `pubs` database is meant to be a learning tool. It contains a sample database about a publisher, including information about authors, books, and sales. Most of the examples in the SQL Server Books Online (and this book) are based on the `pubs` database. Most database features are highlighted via their implementation in the `pubs` database. `pubs` is just under 2MB in size after installation.

The Northwind Database

The Northwind database is an alternative learning database to the pubs database. Northwind has been the sample database supplied with Microsoft Access for some time now. Because more and more Microsoft Access users are migrating to SQL Server, the Northwind database was brought over to assist them in learning the features of the product with a familiar database. Northwind is about 3.5MB by default.

2

SQL Server Default Login IDs

Strangely enough, one of the first things you'll want to do after you install SQL Server is to log in. Because you went with the default and selected Windows Authentication Mode, you simply select the Windows NT Authentication option on any dialog that asks you to connect to SQL Server. If you chose to use Mixed Mode, you could either do that or use the default login for SQL Server, sa (lowercase on case-sensitive sort-order servers). The letters *sa* stand for system administrator.

sa

The sa login is a member of the sysadmin fixed server role. As a member of this role, sa can do anything in SQL Server. The sa account always exists and can't be dropped. However, you can't use it when you are in Windows Authentication Mode. If you are in Mixed Mode, you can select to log in using this account. It's more likely you'll use the next option, logging in via your membership in your local administrators group.

Windows NT/2000 Local Administrators Group

If you are on a Windows NT/2000 computer and are a member of the local administrators group, you don't have to use SQL Server authentication. During setup, SQL Server 2000 adds the local Windows NT/2000 Administrators group to the sysadmin role, just as sa is added. As a result, all local administrators are made SQL Server administrators by default. On Windows 9*x* computers, Windows authentication isn't available, so you must use sa. Password control isn't necessary in SQL Server when you're using Windows authentication; SQL Server simply uses your Windows NT/2000 login credentials.

Named Versus Default Instances

SQL Server 2000 has introduced the capability to run multiple, independent copies of the database server on a single Windows-based computer. Microsoft supports up to 16 copies of SQL Server 2000 installed on a single computer. A couple of terms get used in reference to instances that should be explained: named versus default.

The Default Instance

You can connect to the default instance of SQL Server 2000 (you can have only one per machine) by specifying only the servername when connecting using an application program. People connected to SQL Server this way in all previous versions: They specified the name of the computer on which SQL Server was installed as the name of the SQL Server they wanted to talk to. For instance, my computer is named RHOME, so to connect, I would specify to connect to the SQL Server named RHOME when prompted for a SQL Server name.

The default instance is installed in the directories noted earlier in Tables 2.1 and 2.2 and has its Registry keys (for the most part) in the same location as SQL Server 6.5 and SQL Server 7.0. This means that most of the relevant Registry keys are at `HKEY_LOCAL_MACHINE\SOFTWARE\Microsoft\MSSQLServer`. The program files install to the default path of `\MSSQL`. The service names for the actual SQL Server services line up as follows:

Service Type	*Service Name*
SQL Server	MSSQLServer
SQL Server Agent	SQLServerAgent

Only one copy of the default instance of SQL Server can actually be running at any given moment, regardless of version. So, on my computer where I have 6.5 installed, I can't have SQL Server 6.5 running at the same time as my default instance of SQL Server 2000. I can, however, run named instances of SQL Server 2000 at the same time as my single default instance.

A Named Instance

A named instance of SQL Server 2000 is one that you name during setup. When you want to connect to a named instance, you specify both the servername and the instance name you entered during setup. For instance, in a few moments I'll ask you to install an instance named Trade on your computer. On my computer, when I then wanted to connect to that instance of SQL Server, I would specify RHOME\Trade as the servername. This tells SQL Server to talk to the computer named RHOME and look for an instance named Trade on the machine.

Named instances are Windows 2000 logo compliant. They use the Registry key home of `HKEY_LOCAL_MACHINE/SOFTWARE/Microsoft/Microsoft SQL Server/InstanceName`. They install into the program file path of `\MSSQL$InstanceName` instead of just `\MSSQL`. Hence, they are completely separate from both the default instance and every other named instance because no two instances on the same computer can have the same instance name. The services are created with unique names as well:

Service Type	*Service Name*
SQL Server	`MSSQL$InstanceName`
SQL Server Agent	`SQLAgent$InstanceName`

Common Components

Some components are shared between installations of SQL Server 2000; they don't really belong to either the default or any of the named instances you may have installed on your computer. They include the SQL Server tools, as well as system components such as MDAC 2.6.

2

> If you choose to install a named instance of SQL Server 2000, and have SQL Server 7.0 installed (it's a default instance by definition), your 7.0 tools are replaced with the SQL Server 2000 tools, and your SQL Server 7.0 tools are deleted. The SQL Server 2000 toolset works correctly when pointed to a SQL Server 7.0 installation.

Installing a Named Instance

Go ahead and install a named instance at this time. Select the instance named Trade (the default option should be grayed out when you select to install a new instance because one already exists on your computer). Do a typical setup, but change the security dialog. Rather than accept the default of Windows Authentication Mode, select Mixed Mode, and set your password (for the rest of the book, I set the password to *password*). Use the same service account that you used earlier. You will refer to the named instance occasionally throughout this book.

Upgrading from a Previous Version of SQL Server

If you are upgrading from SQL Server 7.0, when you begin setup, rather than select to create a new instance of SQL Server (refer to Figure 2.4), select to upgrade, remove, or add components to an existing instance of SQL Server; select the default instance; and then choose to upgrade your existing installation. Follow the prompts; they are similar to those presented previously for a new installation. The upgrade is an in-place upgrade, and when it's completed, you will have upgraded your 7.0 installation to SQL Server 2000. Your tools are replaced with the SQL Server 2000 Tools.

Upgrading from SQL Server 6.5

If you are upgrading from SQL Server 6.5, the process is a little bit different. You first install a default instance of SQL Server 2000, just as you did here. When you are done, you will have a new menu item, Microsoft SQL Server – Switch, in your Start menu. This menu contains an option to switch back to SQL Server 6.5, run the SQL Server Upgrade Wizard, or uninstall SQL Server 6.*x*.

Version Switching

You can switch your default instance to run either SQL Server 6.5 or SQL Server 2000. After you install a default instance of SQL Server 2000, your SQL Server 6.5 installation is disabled. You can switch back to it by selecting this menu item to disable your default instance of SQL Server 2000 and restart SQL Server 6.5. Your SQL Server 6.5 tools again appear in the Start menu (they're actually just marked hidden when you switch away and then unmarked when you switch back to 6.5).

You can switch back again by coming back to this menu. However, when you do so, the program entry is now named Microsoft SQL Server 2000, and selecting it disables your SQL Server 6.5 installation and returns your SQL Server 2000 default instance.

In general, switching back and forth manually isn't a good thing to do. Version switching was built for the express purpose of supporting your ability to run the upgrade wizard, explained next.

Running the Upgrade Wizard

The SQL Server Upgrade Wizard upgrades a SQL Server 6.5 installation to SQL Server 2000. After you install your default instance, you should start this program entry. The wizard migrates all your databases, as well as your system settings, into SQL Server 2000. For detailed information about upgrades, see the topic "Upgrading to SQL Server 2000" in the SQL Server Books Online.

Uninstalling SQL Server 6.5

After you upgrade your SQL Server 6.5 system to SQL Server 2000, you must manually remove it. You do that by selecting this program entry. It's imperative that you not run SQL Server 6.5 setup to uninstall SQL Server 6.5; it breaks your SQL Server 2000 default instance. This special version of uninstall was written to remove SQL Server 6.5 carefully while preserving SQL Server 2000's default instance.

Troubleshooting Your Installation

Setup of SQL Server is a relatively straightforward adventure. However, in the unlikely event something goes wrong, you should gather information on what failed so that you can take corrective action. Installation failures have been extremely rare with SQL Server 2000, so I hope you'll never need to use the following information.

sqlstp.log

In your Windows directory (`f:\winnt` on my system), you can find the `sqlstp.log` output log from the setup program. Any problems that occur should be logged to this file. If you encounter a problem, search this file for a report of what failed. Typically, you would find the failure information close to the bottom of the report.

2

*.OUT Files

In the `\MSSQL\install` folder, several setup scripts might have been run. If the `sqlstp.log` file indicates a failure in one of them, you can find the results of the run in the `.OUT` files in this directory. Usually, the message is straightforward, such as `Failed to create` *`xxx`*.

SQL Server Error Log

If SQL Server (the SQL Server service) was started, and some kind of failure occurred, it's likely you can find something useful in the SQL Server error log. These files are located in the `\MSSQL\Log` directory and are numbered from newest to oldest. The current error log is a file called `Errorlog.` (with a dot but no extension). The next oldest is `Errorlog.1`, then `Errorlog.2`, and so on.

Windows NT/2000 Application Event Log

If you are running Windows NT/2000, you might want to also check your error logs in the Windows Event Viewer. To open it, select Start, Programs, Administrative Tools, Event Viewer. Three different logs appear in the event viewer application: the system error log, the security error log, and the application error log. Switch to the application error log by selecting Application from the Log menu. Look for any errors with a red stop sign next to them. If you see any, examine them for additional troubleshooting information.

Removing SQL Server

If, for some reason, you need to remove SQL Server, it's very easy. In Control Panel, select Add/Remove Programs, and SQL Server 2000 will be in the list of programs—just like any other application on your computer. Selecting this option removes all files and Registry keys related to SQL Server but doesn't remove shared components that were installed, such as the MDAC components. Also, if this isn't the last instance of SQL Server to be removed, the tools remain. When you remove the last instance of SQL Server 2000, the tools are also removed.

You need to deal with one important issue if you upgrade to SQL Server 2000 on a computer with SQL Server 6.5 installed. When you are sure that you no longer want to use SQL Server 6.5, don't run the 6.5 setup program to remove the previous release of SQL Server. It can damage your SQL Server 2000 installation. Microsoft wrote a special uninstall program for SQL Server 6.5 and placed a shortcut to it in your Microsoft SQL Server Switch menu. It's called, surprisingly enough, Uninstall SQL Server 6.*x*.

Apply the Latest Service Pack

You typically will want to be running with the latest service pack for SQL Server. You can download the service pack for free from `http://www.microsoft.com/sql`. At the time of the update to this book, Service Pack 2 was current and Service Pack 3 was under development. It's critical that you not only apply the latest service packs to get whatever updates to the product have occurred (not to mention bug fixes), but that you're also current on all security patches. Also note that if you're using MSDE and/or Analysis Services, there's a separate service pack you must download and install. They don't come with the download for SQL Server.

For the purposes of the book, we'll walk through an SP2 setup, but if a later service pack is available, you should install that one instead. The setup should be basically the same.

Navigate to the SQL Server website, select downloads, then select the latest service pack. Additionally, create a directory on your hard drive to download the service pack to (in my case, I chose E:\Download\SQL2kSP2).

Once you've downloaded the service pack to your hard drive, run the .EXE file that you downloaded (SQL2kSP2.EXE, in my case), to expand the service pack directory c:\sql2ksp2 in my case (see Figure 2.25).

FIGURE 2.25

Service Pack root directory selection.

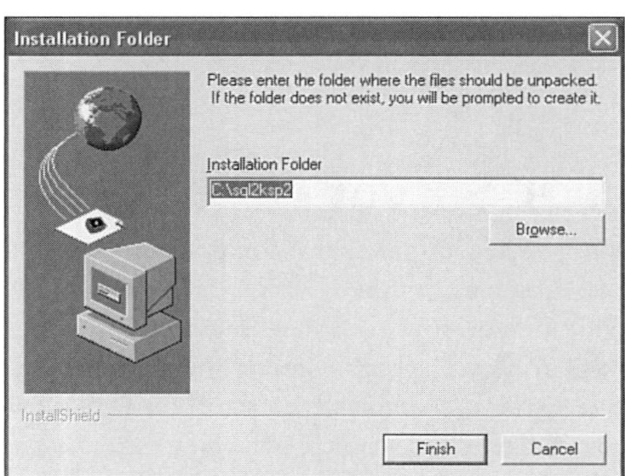

Once you've downloaded the service pack to your hard drive, run the .EXE file that you downloaded (SQL2kSP2.EXE, in my case), to expand the service pack directory. For service pack 2, the default is c:\sql2ksp2. When the extraction is complete, the message "The Package has been delivered successfully." will pop up. Click OK to finish the service pack file extraction.

Switch to the expanded directory (c:\sql2ksp2, in my case), and double-click the readme.htm file (sp2readme.htm for service pack 2). Read the directions carefully and thoroughly, and make all the backups that are recommended.

Then, start a command prompt (Start -> Run -> Cmd on Windows NT/2000/XP, or Start -> Run -> Command on Win9x systems), switch to the service pack directory, and run setup.bat.

Note: For some reason you can't simply double-click the setup.bat file – you must run the file from a command prompt.

You will be presented with Figure 2.26. Select Next, then read and accept the license agreement.

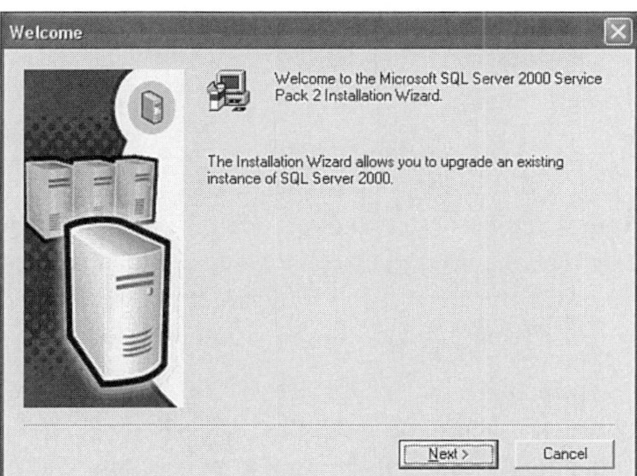

FIGURE 2.26
Service Pack Setup begins.

Just as in an ordinary setup of SQL Server, you will be presented with the instance selection dialog (same as Figure 2.9). Select the instance you'd like to patch with the service pack (you must apply the service pack to each instance one at a time).

Next, select the login you will use to connect to SQL Server to apply the service pack (See Figure 2.27). You will need to use the sa account if you are running on Windows 9x, otherwise, use Windows Authentication. Setup will assume you are a syadmin role member, otherwise installation will fail (see Chapter 5 for more details). By default if you're a local administrator of your computer, you are considered a sysadmin role member.

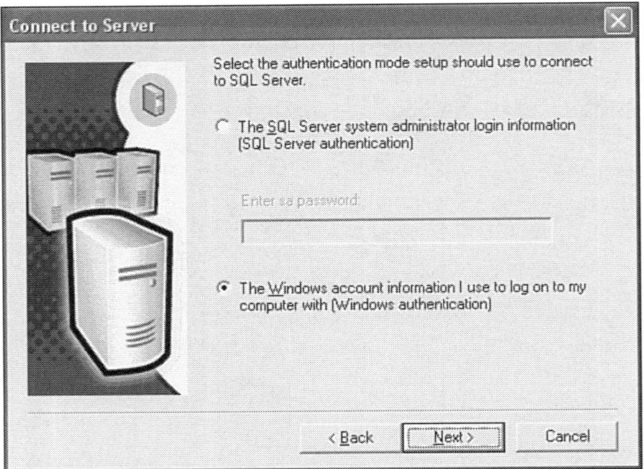

FIGURE 2.27
Service Pack Authentication.

If everything's ready, you'll be prompted to click Next. Do so, and the service pack will be applied. Setup will run for a few minutes, and then you'll be running the selected service pack on top of SQL Server 2000.

Summary

SQL Server 2000 is very easy to install and update. The hard part is making the correct decisions during setup, because you have to live with them for the rest of the time you are using the product. Setup starts the automenu program when you insert the CD and then helps you install the prerequisite software, if needed. You need to have Internet Explorer 5.0 on all systems if you want to install SQL Server 2000.

You must select which version of SQL Server 2000 you want to install. You can select the Standard Edition if you're running Windows NT Server. You can also select the Enterprise Edition, particularly if you want to be able to use all features of Microsoft SQL Server. You might also find yourself using the Developer or Evaluation versions of the product, which should be the same as using the Enterprise Edition (except for licensing). Finally, the Personal Edition runs on Windows 98, Windows ME, Windows NT Workstation (4.0 or later), or Windows 2000 or Windows XP Professional.

After you complete the prerequisites, you can begin the setup of SQL Server. If you are willing to accept the defaults (now that you know them), perform a typical installation. The rest is basically automatic. Do remember to create and use a service account if you are installing on Windows NT/2000/XP, if you ever intend to link your SQL Server with other SQL Servers or with other Microsoft Server components.

Q&A

Q Which setup option takes the least amount of space on my hard drive?

A A minimal setup.

Q How do I perform a client-tools–only installation?

A Perform a custom setup, and then uncheck the server components.

Q Which network libraries are installed by default on Windows NT?

A Named Pipes, Multi-Protocol, and TCP/IP Sockets.

Q Which file should I review before I begin setup?

A The `readme.txt` file; a shortcut appears on the SQL Server automenu.

Workshop

This section provides quiz questions to help you solidify your understanding of the concepts presented today. In addition to the quiz questions, exercises are provided to let you practice what you've learned today. Try to understand the quiz and exercise answers before continuing to tomorrow's lesson. Answers are provided in Appendix A, "Answers to Quiz Questions."

Quiz

1. What sort order should you use if you want data returned in ASCII order?
2. What does the Unicode Collation affect?
3. What component installs the OLE DB and ODBC drivers?
4. Which account should you use to control your SQL Server services?
5. How can you start SQL Server if it isn't running?
6. Which file system is recommended for SQL Server when running on Windows NT?
7. How do you get the Microsoft Search service installed?

Exercises

1. Set up SQL Server 2000 if you haven't already done so. Select a custom setup, and then install as many components as your version allows.
2. Look at your error log and the `sqlstp.log` file in your Windows directory. Also examine the `.OUT` files in your `\MSSQL\install` directory to look for any problems.
3. Install Microsoft SQL Server Analysis Services. You might find this product (discussed on Bonus Day 22) quite useful.
4. Verify the SQL Server Registry keys so that you know where they are in case you need to use them.

WEEK 1

DAY 3

Working with SQL Server 2000 Management Tools and Utilities

Yesterday you learned how to install SQL Server 2000. As you quickly discovered, running the setup program isn't very difficult—in fact, it's almost trivial. It's understanding the critical selections you are making during setup that requires effort. After you make these selections, changing your collation is a significant effort, but it's alleviated somewhat in SQL Server 2000 because you can set collations from the database level down to the individual columns of each table. Changing other settings has generally been simplified by the management utilities that come with the product.

Today's lesson focuses on the tools and utilities you installed, assuming that you installed all of them. In this lesson, you examine not just the utilities that appear in your Start menu, but also the command-line utilities and utilities that simply don't have Start menu shortcuts. These utilities might be a bit hidden, but you shouldn't underestimate their value.

The Microsoft SQL Server Program Group

The best place to start when you're examining the available tools is the SQL Server 2000 program group in your Start menu. To open it, click Start, Programs, Microsoft SQL Server (see Figure 3.1). Note that only one copy of the tools is installed, no matter how many instances of SQL Server itself you install. Also, note that if you upgraded from SQL Server 7.0, the SQL Server 2000 tools completely replace your 7.0 tools, and the SQL Server 2000 tools are guaranteed to work against SQL Server 7.0.

FIGURE 3.1

The Microsoft SQL Server program group.

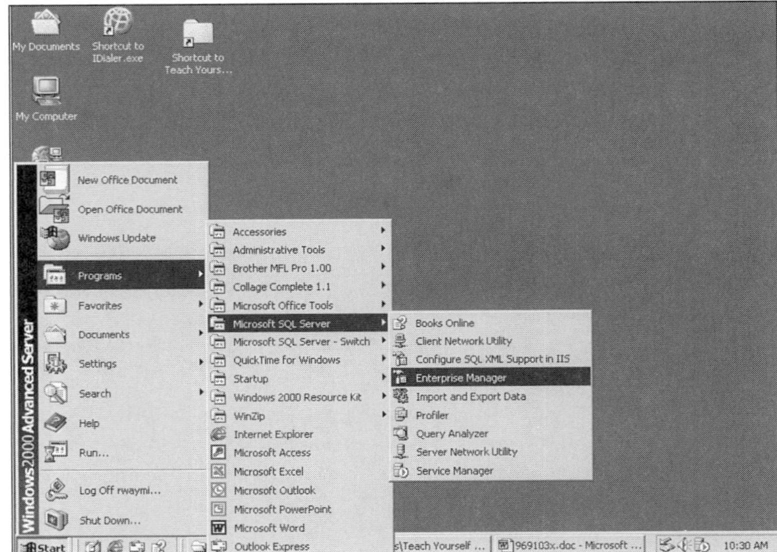

This is the main group of tools you work with when building SQL Server database applications or when administering SQL Server. You must be familiar with each tool in this program group because you will almost certainly end up using every one of them before your 21-day adventure into SQL Server is over. Today's lesson examines them in the order you will probably want to look at them—not in the order they appear in your Start menu.

Note

> MSDE does not include any of the graphical tools. The Client Network Utility is installed as part of the MDAC components, and osql.exe is your primary command line query interface to SQL Server. The graphical tools generally work with MSDE, but there are licensing restrictions and you should consult the MSDE license agreement or contact Microsoft to fully understand what license is required to use the administrative tools (Enterprise Manager, Query Analyzer, etc.) against an MSDE instance.

The `readme.txt` File

A great place to start is with the `readme.txt` file. This file contains important information you should read before you install, as well as information that didn't quite make it into the manuals before the product shipped. You should review this file once to make sure there's nothing you must do or change before moving on with SQL Server 2000. Of course, you did this yesterday before you installed the product, right?

Books Online

The SQL Server Books Online is your primary reference source for information (except, of course, for this book!). When you have a question about SQL Server, you can go to Books Online. Books Online is shipped in lieu of actual paper manuals, although you can order hard copies from Microsoft. The books ship as a compiled set of HTML pages, so you can view them within the context of Microsoft Internet Explorer 5 or later. Figure 3.2 shows the SQL Server Books Online utility.

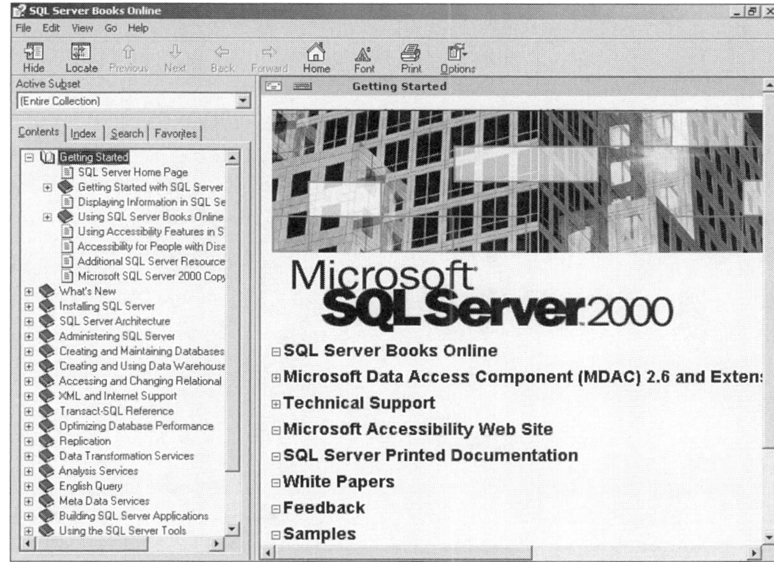

FIGURE 3.2
The SQL Server 2000 Books Online.

Books Online gives you the functionality you would expect from a set of manuals—the ability to view information, search for that information, and print paper copies. To print any topic, simply right-click the topic and select Print. You are prompted to print either the single page you are looking at or the page and all subpages.

Unless you want to kill lots of trees, be careful not to print from the top-level books.

The left pane of the Books Online is broken into four tabs by default:

- *Contents* shows every SQL Server Book as if you had paper copies of the manual. If you know what book a topic is in, simply expand the book (by clicking the plus [+] sign) to view the contents. Most books have several levels you need to drill down into to find a particular topic of interest.
- *Index* is a sorted list of just about every keyword in the Books, arranged alphabetically. Simply type the name of the word you are looking for, and the index scrolls to the closest index entry. To then display the contents (or, if multiple entries are listed for a keyword, an option to select which entry to go to), double-click the entry in the index.
- *Search* is the place where you usually end up. Simply type the concept, command, or option you want to know more about, and click List Topics. The results of your search are then displayed. Again, simply double-click an entry to have the entry displayed on the right half of your screen.
- *Favorites*, as in Internet Explorer, enables you to keep a list of favorites in the Books so you can simply click the entries here rather than search for items over and over. When you are viewing a topic, click the Add button (see Figure 3.3). When you want to go back to that topic, simply double-click the entry in your Favorites list.

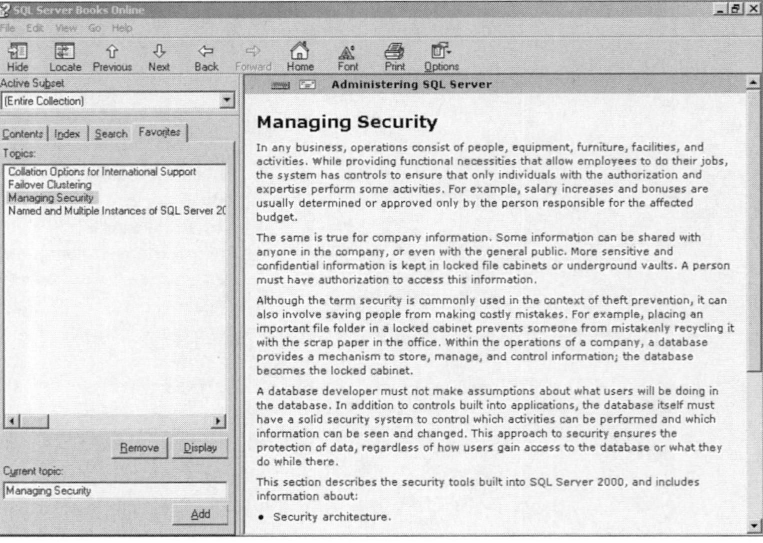

FIGURE 3.3

The Books Online Favorites tab.

The SQL Server Books Online is further broken into several "books", which you see on the Contents tab. Each book is explained in the following sections.

Getting Started

This book provides links to the rest of the books; documentation conventions (so you can understand the syntax statements and other formatting options); a list of the tools, wizards, and other features of SQL Server; and information on contacting SQL Server Technical Support. This book also includes information for people with disabilities and on backward compatibility. Everyone should read this book—it's quite short but very helpful in using the Books Online later.

What's New

This book includes a brief overview of product features that are new to people who have used previous releases of SQL Server. If you have used earlier versions of SQL Server, you should review this book to see what's changed.

Installing SQL Server

This book includes detailed information about setting up a new instance of SQL Server 2000. Because you've already read the lesson for Day 2, "Installing Microsoft SQL Server 2000," you don't need to read this book.

SQL Server Architecture

This book gives a detailed look at SQL Server 2000's architecture. It provides many details on how SQL Server works and how everything fits together. You will encounter most of the information in the *SQL Server Architecture* book on your 21-day adventure, but a great section to look at is "Implementation Details," where you can find all of SQL Server's documented limits. For example, you can find how big a database can be, how many tables can be in a database, and other detailed information.

Administering SQL Server

This book documents how to administer SQL Server. Because *Sams Teach Yourself Microsoft SQL Server 2000 and MSDE 2000 in 21 Days* teaches you everything you need to know to perform the basics (and some advanced options) of SQL Server administration, you have little need to review this Books Online book.

Creating and Maintaining Databases

This book documents how to create databases and all the objects to be contained in your databases. Again, *Sams Teach Yourself Microsoft SQL Server 2000 in 21 Days* teaches you everything you need to know on a day-to-day basis, so reading *Creating and Maintaining Databases* is also unnecessary.

Creating and Maintaining Data Warehouses

This book documents how to create data warehouses, a specialized type of relational database. The process of creating and maintaining data warehouses has become a specialty in its own right, separate from general database construction. If you intend to build or support data warehouses, you should review this book. Data warehousing typically builds on a basic understanding of building "ordinary" databases, so knowing the rest of SQL Server will give you a strong foundation should you want to pursue data warehousing. Data warehousing, although briefly mentioned on Day 22, "An Overview of Analysis Services," is beyond the scope of this book.

Accessing and Changing Relational Data

This book explains how to query and modify data in SQL Server. As with the other topics, *Sams Teach Yourself Microsoft SQL Server 2000 in 21 Days* has everything you need, so you don't need to review this Books Online book either.

XML and Internet Support

This book documents SQL Server 2000's support for XML. We will cover this topic extensively on Day 21, "Using XML with SQL Server 2000," but as with many topics, some advanced details are left to Books Online.

Transact-SQL Reference

This reference covers the precise syntax on how to call any object in SQL Server. If you can't remember the syntax for a T-SQL command, stored procedure, or function, you can look it up here. As you might expect, you'll examine all the important day-to-day commands in this *Sams Teach Yourself* book, but this part of Books Online is always available when you want to quickly look up something.

Optimizing Database Performance

This book presents performance tuning information for SQL Server. Day 20, "Performance Monitoring Basics and Tools," will help you with some performance tuning and monitoring basics, and you will encounter additional performance tuning information throughout your 21-day odyssey. However, performance tuning is a huge topic, so you might want to read this Books Online book (after you complete this 21-day book). I also recommend the *Microsoft SQL Server 2000 Unleashed* book from Sams Publishing for additional performance tuning information.

Replication

This book explains SQL Server 2000 replication. Day 16, "Understanding Replication Design Methodologies," and Day 17, "Implementing Replication Methodologies," fully cover SQL Server replication. So again, you don't need to review this part of the Books Online. See what a bargain this *Sams Teach Yourself* book is?

Data Transformation Services

The data transformation services (DTS) tool is explained in this Books Online book. Day 19, "Migrating Data Between Database Servers," covers most of what you need to use DTS. However, DTS is a very sophisticated tool and could be an entire 21-day book by itself. Therefore, for advanced transformations, you might choose to reference this book. You also can review *Microsoft SQL Server 2000 Data Transformation Services (DTS)* from Sams Publishing.

Analysis Services

This Books Online book explains Analysis Services, known as OLAP Services in SQL Server 7.0. We have chosen to include a brief overview of Analysis Services on Bonus Day 22, "An Overview of Analysis Services." Otherwise, you should review this Books Online book in detail.

English Query

Microsoft English Query is explained in this Books Online book. Again, we've chosen to include a brief overview of English Query on Bonus Day 23, "An Overview of English Query."

Meta Data Services

The Meta Data Services tool (known as Microsoft Repository in SQL Server 7.0) is explained in this book of the Books Online. We have chosen to include a very brief overview of Meta Data Services on Bonus Day 22.

Building SQL Server Applications

This book is huge! It contains all the programming references for various client and server technologies. The good news is that what you need to know about SQL Server commands is already interspersed throughout this *Sams Teach Yourself* book. This Sams book doesn't attempt to be a client programming reference, so some topics in the Books Online book are useful—particularly if you are writing client programs using open database connectivity (ODBC), Object Linking and Embedding Database (OLE DB), or ActiveX Data Objects (ADO). SQL Distributed Management Objects (SQL-DMO), which is the programmatic administrative interface for SQL Server, is also documented here.

Using the SQL Server Tools

This Books Online book covers basically what you're doing today—exploring each SQL Server tool. You will continue to use each tool for the rest of this book and by the end of your 21 days will be very adept at using most of the SQL Server toolset.

Troubleshooting

This book explains the most common problems and how to resolve them. After your 21 days, you should understand and be able to resolve most problems without ever referring to Books Online. This book is available just in case.

Glossary

The *Glossary* explains terms used throughout the SQL Server Books Online. For your convenience, a glossary of terms is also included in this book.

How To

This book explains how to perform specific actions using Transact-SQL, SQL Server tools and utilities, and other programming interfaces. You won't typically go directly to this book; hyperlinks (jumps) throughout the other books take you to the appropriate *How To* topic.

Service Manager

The SQL Server Service Manager utility enables you to control the SQL Server–related services on your computer (or any SQL Server computer on your network). When you start this utility, you see something similar to Figure 3.4.

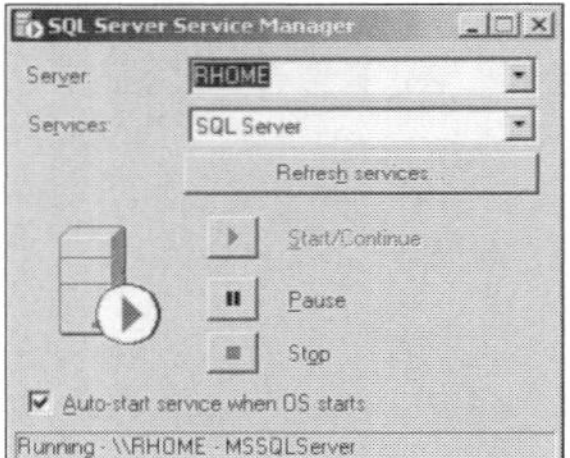

FIGURE 3.4
The SQL Server Service Manager utility.

The Server field contains the name of the server you are monitoring. The Services box shows which service you are examining, and the utility also contains a graphical representation of the state of the service. When a service is running, the green arrow is shown to indicate that, in this case, the SQL Server service is now running. As you learned on Day 2, the Service Manager is the main service that runs SQL Server.

In SQL Server 7.0, the actual service names, such as MSSQLServer and SQLServerAgent, were shown in this utility. With the introduction of multiple instances in SQL Server 2000, the SQL Server team decided it would be easier to always say "SQL Server" and "SQL Server Agent" in this dialog. Thus, if you are controlling a default instance of SQL Server, the service name is MSSQLServer for SQL Server, and SQLServerAgent for the Agent service. However, for named instances, starting or stopping SQL Server is really controlling the MSSQL$Instancename service, just as you learned yesterday.

You can also stop or pause a service. Some services don't support being paused, and those that do vary in their behavior. For example, the SQL Server service continues to function when paused, but new connections aren't allowed.

Note

The Service Manager utility also contains an option to autostart each service when the operating system starts. This option is especially handy on Windows 9*x* computers because they don't have services that can be configured to start automatically. Simply make sure that the check box next to Auto-start service when OS starts is checked for each service you want started automatically.

The Services drop-down list shows which services can be controlled from this utility. They include the SQL Server service, SQL Server Agent, Distributed Transaction Coordinator, and Microsoft Search. You can use the Server drop-down list to select another server. Named instances are also shown in the drop-down list, for example, on my system (as shown in Figure 3.5, RHOME\TRADE is shown separately).

FIGURE 3.5

Named instances in the SQL Server Service Manager utility.

Note

The Distributed Transaction Coordinator and Microsoft Search services show up in Service Manager for every named instance, as well as the default instance. They appear just for convenience; you still have only one copy of each service running on your computer, being shared by all instances of SQL Server on that machine.

The list can be somewhat unreliable, and the utility is flexible enough to allow you to simply type the name of the server (or `servername\instancename`) you want to examine. After you type a server name, click the drop-down list for Services. Service Manager then attempts to connect to the remote server and enumerate the installed services.

All the functionality of this application is also available from SQL Server Enterprise Manager. However, Service Manager runs from your taskbar and can be more convenient to access.

At this point, your security will be checked. You must be a Windows NT/2000 administrator or server operator on the server you are connecting to in order to control services (if the remote computer is a Windows NT/2000 computer). SQL Server permissions have no effect on your Windows 2000 permissions, so being a SQL Server administrator doesn't guarantee that you can control SQL Server services.

The SQL Server Service Manager has a somewhat hidden functionality. Click the icon in the upper-left corner of the application, and the normal application menu shows up with a couple of additions (see Figure 3.6). Notice that two additional menu choices are available: Connect and Options.

FIGURE 3.6

The additional features of the SQL Server Service Manager utility.

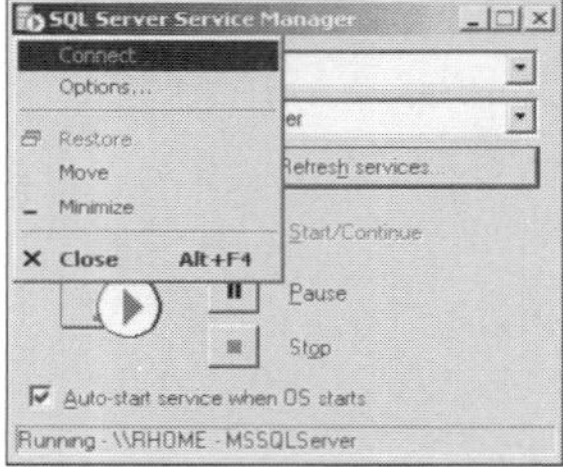

Connect

If you typed or selected a remote computer name under the Server list box, you can connect from the menu rather than click the Services list box. These two techniques perform the same action—attempting to connect to the remote computer to determine the state of the SQL Server services.

Options

When you choose Options, you see the dialog in Figure 3.7. In this dialog, you set the options for the Service Manager, such as the default service.

FIGURE 3.7

The SQL Server Service Manager Options dialog.

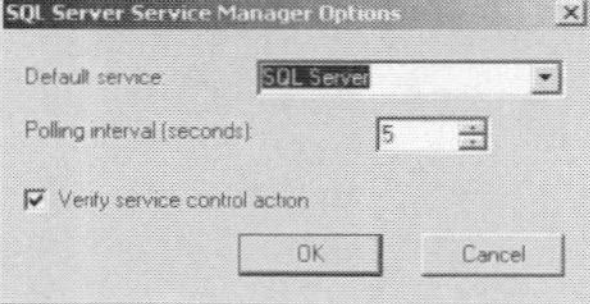

Setting the Default Service

The default service determines which SQL Server service is monitored (and shown in your taskbar) by default when you start the Service Manager application (typically when you log in). If you were more interested in monitoring the SQL Server Agent service than the SQL Server service, you could change the default setting here.

Setting the Polling Interval

The polling interval determines how often Service Manager checks for the state of the services you are monitoring. The default interval is five seconds. This means that every five seconds the utility queries the server for the state of all SQL Server–related services.

Verifying Your Service Control Actions

The Verify Service Control Action option is enabled by default. When you click the appropriate icon, the action you've requested is taken, but only after you are prompted with an Are You Sure…? dialog (see Figure 3.8). To turn off this verification and simply have services stopped and started when you double-click the appropriate graphic, uncheck the check box in the SQL Server Service Manager Options dialog.

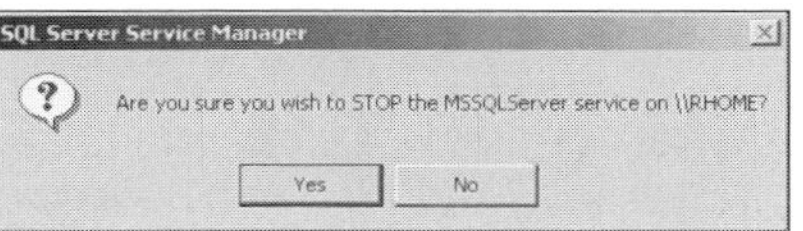

FIGURE 3.8
SQL Server Service Manager's Are you sure…? dialog.

Client Network Utility

The Client Network utility isn't difficult to use, but it has a tremendous impact on client computer connectivity to your SQL Server. When you start the utility, you see a dialog that looks like Figure 3.9.

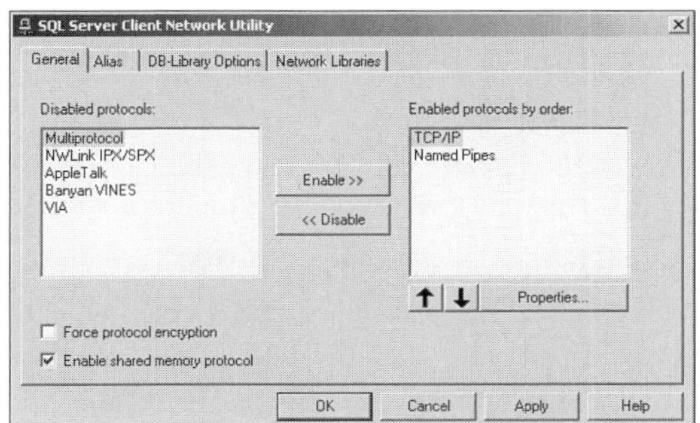

FIGURE 3.9
The SQL Server Client Network utility.

This dialog tells you which network library you use by default when you try to connect to any SQL Server through SQL Server client software. Think of it as a language. If your server speaks only English and French and you attempt to speak German, the server doesn't understand you and can't respond. SQL Server 2000 changes the default network library to always use the TCP/IP (Transmission Control Protocol/Internet Protocol) Sockets network library, regardless of operating system.

In SQL Server 7.0, the choice of client network library depended on your operating system: On Windows NT computers, the default was to use the Named Pipes network library, whereas on Windows 9*x* computers, the default was to use the TCP/IP Sockets network library.

Yesterday's lesson discussed each network library during installation. Simply select the one that makes the most sense for your environment. The "universal" network library is TCP/IP Sockets, so accepting that option should allow you to connect to any SQL Server, regardless of which Windows operating system it's running on. Named Pipes is required on Windows NT/2000 computers, so you know it will work as well. However, Microsoft is moving away from Named Pipes, so sticking with TCP/IP Sockets is the wise choice for the future.

When you're connecting with a server name of (local) or (.) (a single dot), you bypass the default network library and connect to the locally installed default instance. For a named instance, use `.\Instancename`. When you use this option, you (by default) use the shared memory network library. With SQL Server 2000's client tools installed, bypassing the network libraries and using shared memory should happen automatically, even if you use the `servername` or `servername\instancename` syntax to connect. If you've used SQL Server before, however, you are probably in the habit of using the single dot to connect locally.

If you select a network library that's not supported by a server, your connection attempt results in the error `Specified SQL Server Not Found`. This error could mean that the SQL Server service isn't running on the remote computer, but it could also mean that the server doesn't support the network library with which you are attempting to connect.

Two other options at the bottom of this dialog are Force Protocol Encryption and Enable Shared Memory Protocol. The shared memory protocol is used to connect to a local installation of SQL Server, but you can turn it off if you want. You should get superior performance when connecting locally with the shared memory protocol.

The Force Protocol Encryption option requires that any connection from your client computer negotiate encryption with the SQL Server you're trying to connect to. Because SQL Server versions before SQL Server 2000 don't have this kind of network encryption, you can't connect to any earlier version, nor can any application running on your computer. Even for SQL Server 2000 computers, the server must have a certificate for the server installed. You'll examine certificates a bit more when you look at the server network utility later today.

The Alias Tab

You can also override the default settings and connect to a named server with a specific network protocol. For example, if you have a server named Sales, and the server's copy of SQL Server supports only the NWLink IPX/SPX Net Library but the rest of your servers use TCP/IP Sockets, you can add an entry on this screen. Click the Alias tab and then Add to see a dialog like the one in Figure 3.10. Select NWLink IPX/SPX (or whatever network library you want to use), type the name of the server alias (in this case, **SALES**), and configure any additional fields provided (such as the service name). Each network library supports different configuration options. Click OK to add the server with the selected protocol. After you do so, whenever you type **SALES** as a server name in any SQL Server application or utility from this computer, you will use the NWLink IPX/SPX Net Library.

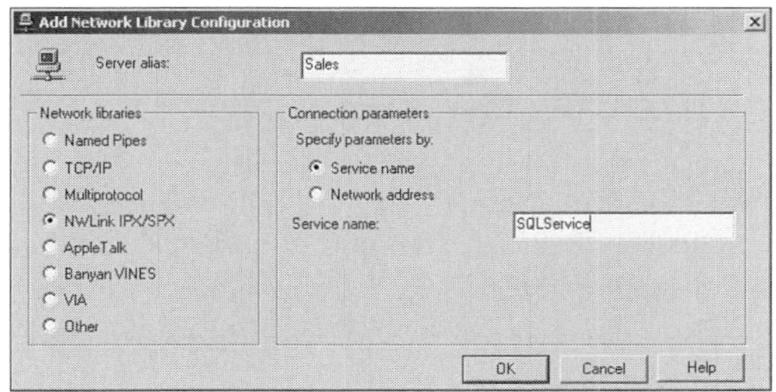

FIGURE 3.10
The Add Network Library Configuration dialog.

Yesterday you read that to connect to a named instance of SQL Server 2000, the client computers must have MDAC 2.6 installed (the version that comes with SQL Server 2000). However, you can use a workaround—an alias. For example, to connect to the named instance TRADE on my computer (RHOME), the named pipe name is `\\rhome\pipe\MSSQL$Trade\sql\query`. So, enter an alias for some servername (such as NAMEDINST), specify Named Pipes as the protocol, and then enter this pipe name. Now, whenever you type **`NAMEDINST`**, you'll go to the Named Pipe of the named instance and connect to your named instances. This solution is very handy if, for some reason, you're not allowed to update the client software on your computers but still want to connect to a named instance.

The DB-Library Options Tab

When you click the DB-Library Options tab, you see the dialog in Figure 3.11. Note that DB-Library is supported in SQL Server 2000 for backward compatibility only. ODBC and OLE DB technologies are the preferred mechanisms to connect to SQL Server 2000. All the client utilities that ship with SQL Server 2000 (except `isql.exe`) use ODBC. `isql.exe` still uses DB-Library, and older, user-written applications might still use this network library.

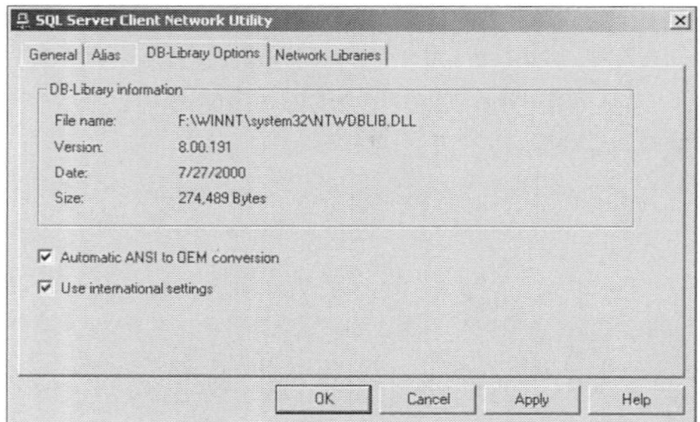

FIGURE 3.11
The DB-Library Options tab.

This tab tells you which version of the DB-Library dynamic link library (DLL) you are using on your system. It indicates where the file is physically located, the date and size of the DLL, and the name of the DLL. You also have two options available: Use International Settings and Automatic ANSI to OEM Conversion.

- International Settings uses certain settings, such as date and time formats, from Windows 9*x*, Windows NT, and Windows 2000. For example, if you're using Windows 2000 and have enabled a non-United States setting, your local settings are used in favor of the SQL Server settings.
- The ANSI to OEM conversion translates data coming back from SQL Server into the local code page used by your client.

Generally, you shouldn't disable either of these options.

The Network Libraries Tab

The Network Libraries tab shows each network library installed on your computer, as well as the filename, version, file date, and file size. This information is most useful when you need support. The versions tell your support vendor which service packs and network library releases you're using. All network libraries are installed on your computer by default.

Server Network Utility

The Server Network utility looks and feels like the Client Network utility. They are, as you might guess, closely related. Unlike the Client Configuration utility, which controls how your applications connect to SQL Server, the Server Network utility reflects which network libraries SQL Server 2000 listens on (see Figure 3.12). Using the language comparison already described, this utility presents the list of languages your server knows how to speak. If you try to connect by using any other network library, your SQL Server can't hear you.

FIGURE 3.12

The Server Network utility.

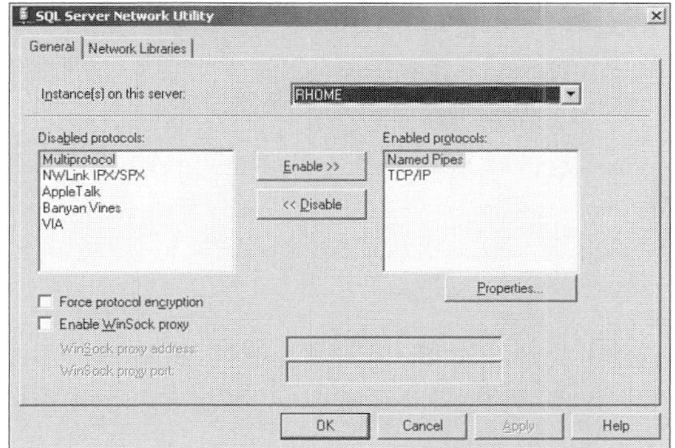

Simply click the Enable button to have SQL Server listen on an additional network library. To reconfigure a network library, click the Properties button. To disable a network library, highlight the library and click the Disable button. The changes you make will take effect the next time the SQL Server service is restarted.

Take a quick look at Figure 3.13. Notice that, just as discussed yesterday, only a subset of network libraries is supported with named instances of SQL Server 2000 (TCP/IP Sockets, Named Pipes, NWLink IPX/SPX). Support for the other network libraries is in a state similar to DB-Library in that no enhancements, including named instance connectivity, will happen from this point forward.

FIGURE 3.13
The Server Network utility for a named instance.

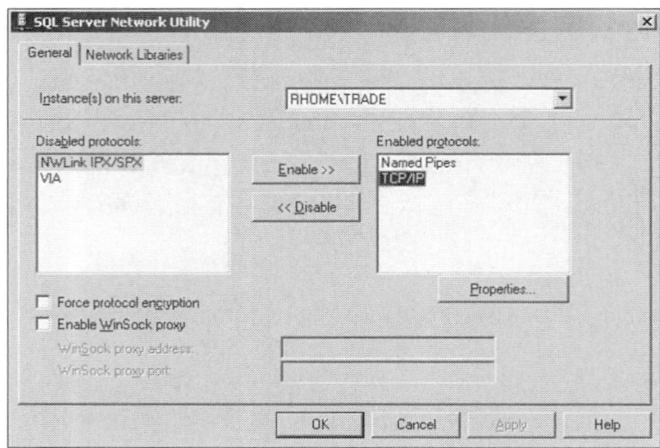

The Network Libraries tab is exactly the same as the Network Libraries tab of the Client Network utility, so we won't examine it further here.

Force Protocol Encryption

When you check this option, the server *forces* encryption on all connection attempts. If encryption can't be agreed on between the client and server, no connections can be made. Encryption in SQL Server 2000 is significantly different from that in SQL Server 7.0, which depended on the multiprotocol network library.

SQL Server 2000 uses Secure Sockets Layer/Transport Level Security (SSL/TLS) to encrypt all SQL Server traffic (if you want it to). This capability can be very handy if your SQL Server holds sensitive data, and you want to prevent someone from viewing your data as it goes across a network.

Sounds interesting, but how do you make it work? First, get a public key certificate for your server. It needs to be in the name of your computer's fully qualified DNS name. Then you need to install the certificate on the SQL Server machine through Internet Explorer. If SQL Server finds a certificate that matches the servername, it simply uses this certificate. The certificate must come from a certificate authority that's trusted by your client computers.

If you're using certificates inside your company or organization, you should show this page of the book to your certificate administrator, and he can help you get the right certificate and install it. Companies often have their own certificate infrastructure, so the following directions won't work for you.

If you're doing this procedure yourself, simply get a certificate from a certificate authority, such as VeriSign (`http://www.verisign.com`), that's trusted by your Internet Explorer clients (VeriSign even gave a trial certificate for free at the time this book was written). To figure out the DNS name of your machine, look in the Network

Identification tab by right-clicking your My Computer icon on the server's desktop. There, you can find the full name of your computer (if not, click Properties and you will see it there). For instance, my computer name might be RHOME.COMPUTERS. MYNETWORK.COM. Then ask for either a "server identity" certificate or a "Web server certificate." When you have it, use Internet Explorer to install the certificate (Tools, Internet Options, Content, Certificates in IE 5.0), and select Import to load the certificate emailed to you by VeriSign. Assuming that everything worked correctly, encryption should automatically start working the next time you start your SQL Server service.

If, for whatever reason, encryption doesn't work, you get a very specific message on the client that you were unable to negotiate encryption with the server. This message typically means that the certificate isn't trusted by the client. You can see the names of certificate authorities (companies) trusted by Internet Explorer by looking at the same location as before (Tools, Internet Options, Content, Certificates in IE 5.0), except now click Trusted Root Certificate Authorities. We chose VeriSign because it's been around a long time and is in all the lists of trusted certificate authorities.

Enable WinSock Proxy

The Enable WinSock Proxy option allows you to have a proxy server forward SQL Server requests from the Internet (or any other network) to SQL Server. Click Enable WinSock Proxy option, and then fill in the TCP/IP address of the proxy server machine, as well as the port you want to have act as a proxy for your SQL Server. This option allows requests to the proxy server to be rerouted to SQL Server and for SQL Server to respond to these requests. Most SQL Server computers being used for Internet e-commerce are the back end for Web sites and don't need to be exposed directly on the Internet. If you want to do so, however, the option is available.

Query Analyzer

The SQL Server Query Analyzer is your primary interface for running Transact-SQL queries or stored procedures. You will be using this utility throughout the rest of your 21 days, and it's a good idea to get comfortable with several available options. This said, it's worth noting that many features of this application are somewhat sophisticated, and you will explore them as you progress through this book.

Because you will use this application frequently, you might choose to simply click Start, Run, and type the application name. For historical reasons, this application's name is `ISQLW.exe`. So click Start, Run, and type **`isqlw`** to start the Query Analyzer.

As you will learn on Day 5, "Setting Up Login and User Security," every operation in SQL Server is secure. Therefore, you must first log in and identify yourself to any SQL

Server to which you want to connect (see Figure 3.14). As we mentioned in the discussion of the Client Network utility, you can enter **`(local)`** or **`.`** to connect to your local default instance of SQL Server. You can also leave the server name blank. The Query Analyzer figures out what you mean and connects to your default instance SQL Server. If you are at the computer running the SQL Server to which you want to connect, the default local network connection (TCP/IP Sockets) is used. Otherwise, whatever client network library you have configured is used. To connect to a named instance, simply type the ***`SERVERNAME\InstanceName`*** combination in the SQL Server text box.

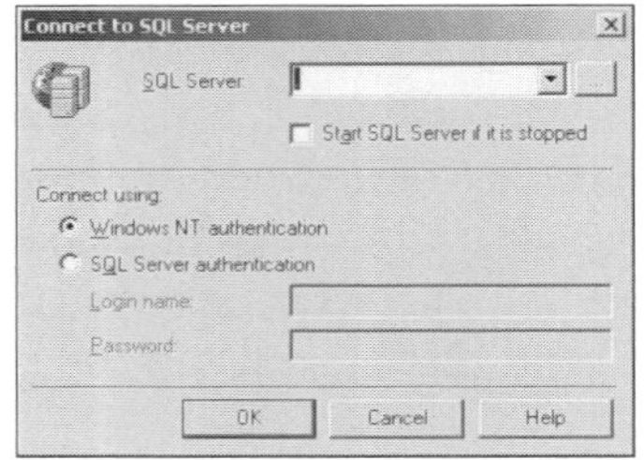

FIGURE 3.14
The Connect to SQL Server dialog of the SQL Server Query Analyzer.

If you like, you can have SQL Server automatically start if you attempt to connect and the SQL Server service isn't running. This option is fine for local or Windows 9*x* computers, but make sure you think it through when you're connecting to production servers. Why is the server down? Is it for maintenance, which you will harm if you restart the SQL Server service prematurely?

You also need to provide login information. If you are on a Windows 9*x* computer, you can use only the SQL Server Authentication option. Use a login name of sa and the password you selected during setup. On case-sensitive servers, the login is also case sensitive, so be sure to enter it in the proper case. If you are on a Windows 2000 computer or connecting to a copy of SQL Server running on Windows NT/2000, select the Windows NT Authentication option to log in using your Windows NT/2000 security credentials. If you can do so, using Windows NT authentication is much simpler. By default, members of the Windows NT/2000 local administrator's group can log in to SQL Server. In either case, you are logging in as a system administrator or superuser to SQL Server. There's nothing you can't do, so be careful.

After you click OK or press Enter, you are logged in to the appropriate instance of SQL Server (assuming that you've typed valid login ID and password information or your Windows NT/2000 credentials allow you to connect). You then see a screen that looks like Figure 3.15.

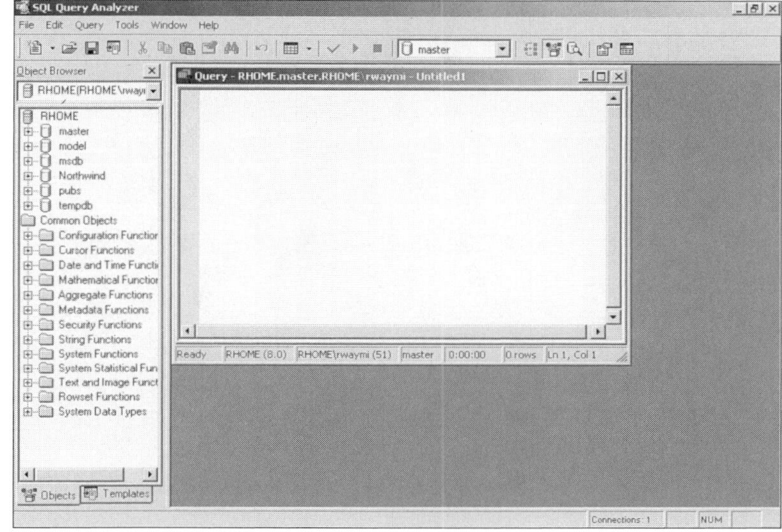

FIGURE 3.15
The SQL Server Query Analyzer.

If your login doesn't go smoothly, you might see a dialog similar to Figure 3.16. Usually, you see this dialog if you've mistyped your password. Simply try again. You should also verify that you've typed your login name properly. If you've changed the sa password, be sure to type the newest one in the connection dialog in Figure 3.14. You can easily produce this error if you followed along in Day 2 by trying to connect to RHOME\Trade (or whatever you installed as a named instance) with an incorrect sa password.

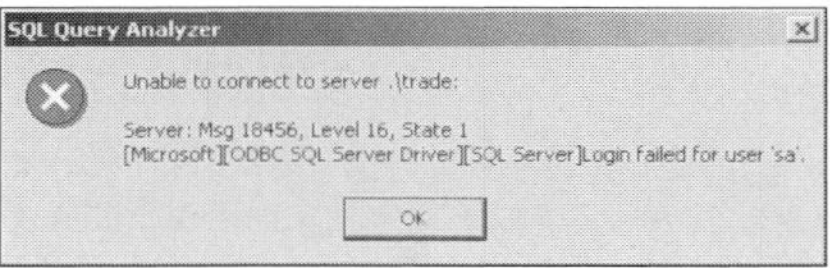

FIGURE 3.16
Login failed dialog.

You might also see a dialog like Figure 3.17, indicating that you tried to connect with SQL Server Security credentials. In this case, the server (your default instance) doesn't support anything but Windows Authentication Mode (also called integrated security), and this error is letting you know that. Go back to your login dialog and change to Windows NT Authentication; the connection should work then.

Figure 3.18 shows another error you might get. If you receive this error, you must look for several things. First, verify that the SQL Server service is running on the computer you are trying to log in to. If it is, the problem might be with your client configuration (see the Client Network utility discussion earlier today). Otherwise, make sure that you typed the server name correctly. To see a list of servers on the network, rather than type a server name, click the three dots next to the SQL Server name box to see a list of the active SQL Server machines on your network. I have had mixed success with this list. Don't be alarmed if your server doesn't show up here; you can still connect to a server that isn't visible by typing its computer name here. In this case, I tried to connect to a server named random, which doesn't exist on my network.

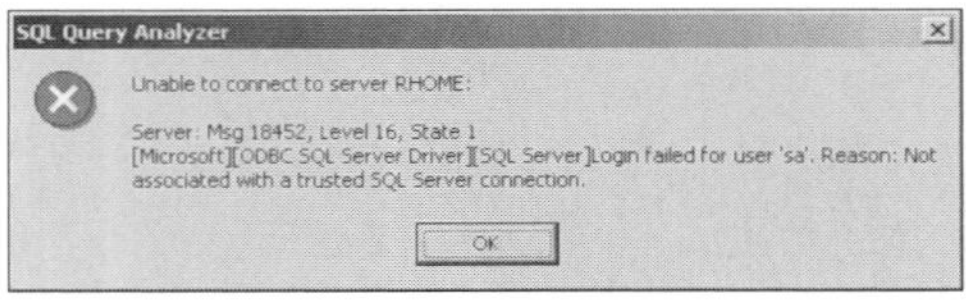

FIGURE 3.17 *Login failed—not using a trusted connection.*

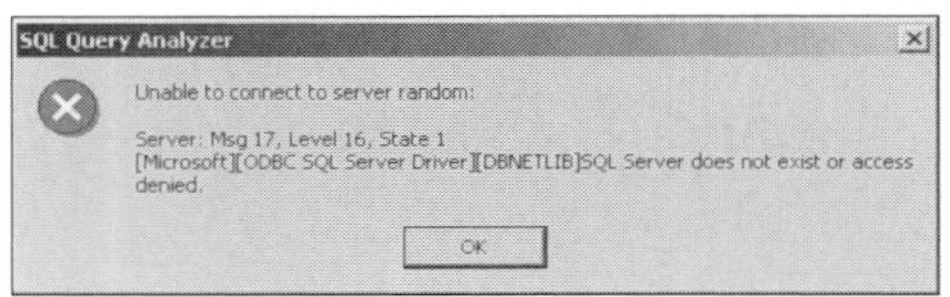

FIGURE 3.18 *Network connectivity problems.*

Figure 3.19 shows another blank query analyzer, but there are a few things worth noticing. Two separate connections are actually open here. Each connection has a title bar that identifies the following:

- Which computer you are logged in to
- Which database you are currently using
- Which login you used to connect
- The title of any query you have opened (examined shortly)
- Which window number is being displayed

As you might guess, having this information in the title bar when you have 40 or 50 connections open can be extremely handy. So, in Figure 3.19, you see one connection as the user sa and one using my Windows security credentials, RHOME\rwaymi. Both are connected to my computer, RHOME, in the master database, and each one is connected to a separate instance. There's no reason they couldn't both be connected to a single instance, except that our default instance supports only Windows authenticated connections.

The Query Toolbar

After you successfully log in, you can start running Transact-SQL queries (you will learn how to program these queries starting on Day 10, "Retrieving Data with the `Select` Statement").

The Query Toolbar is now available and has icons that represent shortcuts to the most commonly used functionality.

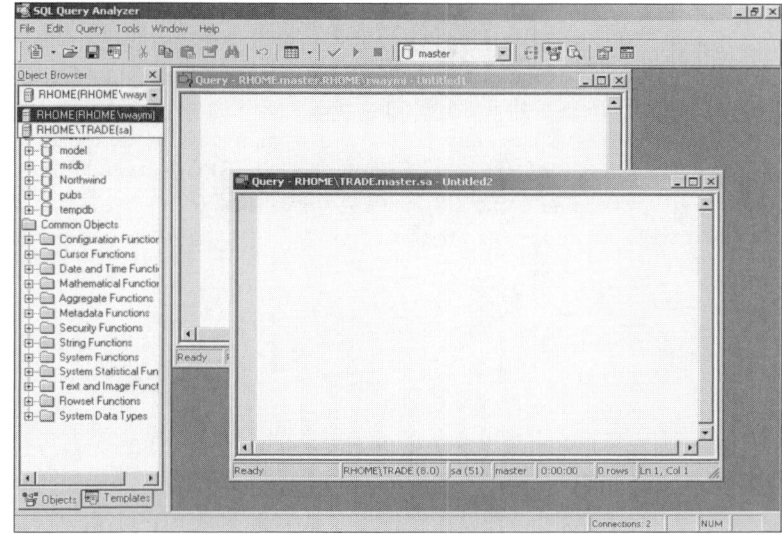

FIGURE 3.19
Multiple connections in a single instance of the Query Analyzer.

You can open multiple windows inside the Query Analyzer by selecting the New Query button (the leftmost button on the toolbar in Figure 3.20). Notice that this isn't the same as having multiple connections because each one could have been to a different computer. Each new query window you open is a separate connection to SQL Server; if you open too many, you might be wasting resources on your SQL Server.

FIGURE 3.20
The Query Analyzer toolbar.

Selecting the second button (which looks like a standard Windows File Open button) opens a standard dialog to find Transact-SQL scripts (which, by default, have a `.SQL` extension). The next button, the Save Query/Result button, either saves the text in your query window to a file or, if you have run a query and selected (or clicked in) the results window, saves the results of a query you have run. The next button loads a "template" SQL query, so you can quickly develop variations of work you've done before. The next several buttons are the Windows standard Cut, Copy, and Paste buttons. They are followed by a button to clear the contents of the current query window, followed by the standard Windows Find button. They become enabled when appropriate. The next button gives you the option of undoing whatever it was you just did (such as undo a deletion of some text you just accidentally wiped out).

The Execute Mode button is next, and it's pretty powerful. When you click the down-arrow next to this button, you are presented with a drop-down list of options that determine how and where your results will appear when you run a query. The default option, Results in Grid, can be very nice because many names in SQL Server 2000 can be 128 Unicode characters long. The default of displaying the text usually pads out all 128 characters with spaces if the names aren't fully used. The Grid option typically leaves enough space only for the widest data column to be displayed. You can also switch to Results in Text, which can be nice when you want to look at all that long text. You can even automatically have the results of your queries routed directly to a file. Figure 3.21 shows each option.

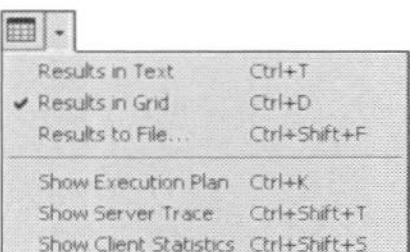

FIGURE 3.21
Query mode selection.

The next option on the menu in Figure 3.21 is Show Execution Plan. This option shows you the methods and indexes SQL Server uses to find the data you request with your queries. Unlike the text, grid, or file options, where you either have one or the other turned on, the Show Execution option is either on or off, regardless of the grid, text, or file options.

You will then see the next option, Show Server Trace. This option, available only to SQL Server system administrators, shows you all the underlying commands and several statistics about those commands from within SQL Server. It is basically a mini-version of the SQL Server Profiler, which you will examine later today.

The final option is Show Client Statistics. This option shows you everything that Query Analyzer learned from SQL Server when it ran your last command, as well as some averages over time as you run additional commands.

Enable each of these three Show options so you can see what each one produces. Unfortunately, you have to do so one at a time to set each one. When all three are on, verify that you are still in the default mode to return Results in Grid.

The easiest way to understand these options is to look at an example. Type the following text in your query window:

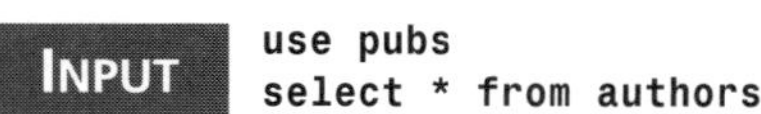

INPUT
```
use pubs
select * from authors
```

ANALYSIS This query is straightforward when you understand what these commands mean. The first statement, `use pubs`, tells the server to switch to the `pubs` database, a sample database installed on all SQL Servers. The second statement, `select * from authors`, requests that SQL Server return all rows and all columns of data from a table or view named authors (and, because you switched to the pubs database, you know it's in pubs). So, in English, these statements mean

Switch to the pubs database

Return all data about authors

After you type the two preceding commands, you can verify that you entered them correctly. Notice that several options on the toolbar are now available. Click the blue check mark on the toolbar to verify that you've typed everything correctly. SQL Server parses your query—meaning it checks that the query is syntactically correct. If the query works okay, you get back

OUTPUT

```
The command(s) completed successfully.
```


Now, to actually run the query, click the next button over—the Play button. You can also select Query, Execute; press F5 on your keyboard; or (my favorite) press Alt+X. After you run the query, the results pane appears with all information about authors in the pubs database (see Figure 3.22).

FIGURE 3.22

Your query results.

Notice that while your query was executing, the Stop toolbar button (the square) became available. Using it, you can cancel a query while it's still running. Your queries should run so fast that you'll never get a chance to cancel them, though.

Now, back to the Text versus Grid option. Click the Current Mode button on the toolbar, and switch to Results in Text. You can also press Ctrl+T to set this option. Now rerun the query and examine your results pane. Notice that all the same tabs are listed below, but your query results are formatted a little differently.

To take this example a step further, add another line of code so that your query pane contains the following Transact-SQL commands:

INPUT

```
use pubs
select * from authors
select * from titles
```

Run these queries again (using one of the methods examined earlier), and notice that Query Analyzer simply stacks up the results in the same, single results window. For each query you run, by default, Query Analyzer simply builds a new grid or separates out the text within the same window.

Moving on to the rest of the toolbar, the next option is a drop-down box that provides a list of the installed databases on the server to which you are connected. If you change the value here, the SQL script you run uses this database unless you specify a different database in the SQL script itself. When you do specify a different database in your script, when the script is finished running, the changed database is reflected in this list box.

The next button shows you how SQL Server estimates it will run your queries internally (as opposed to the previous option you set, Show Execution Plan, which shows you how the query actually ran). Why two options? What if a query takes multiple hours to run, but all you want to see is how SQL Server thinks it will execute the query? You'll look at this feature in more detail on Day 13, "Indexing for Performance."

The next option is the Object Browser on/off toggle. You can see the Object Browser turned on in the previous figures on the left side of the screen. By using it, you can easily browse all database objects for each connection. It's much more powerful than it first appears. You can drag and drop any object into your query window. That's pretty handy, but look what happens when you right-click the object and drag it into your query window. A pop-up appears (see Figure 3.23), allowing you to choose a number of different SQL statement options, such as writing a create table script or select query script—very powerful stuff. You may well find yourself using this feature frequently as you progress through the next few days.

Getting tired of all these great new features yet? Just wait, there are more! The next option is the object search. Click it to bring up the dialog in Figure 3.24. Can't remember where you put the table that had the salary column? Just use this feature, and the Query Analyzer searches everywhere you ask to find that table. This feature can be *very* handy when you're working on large or complex systems, or systems you haven't seen in a while.

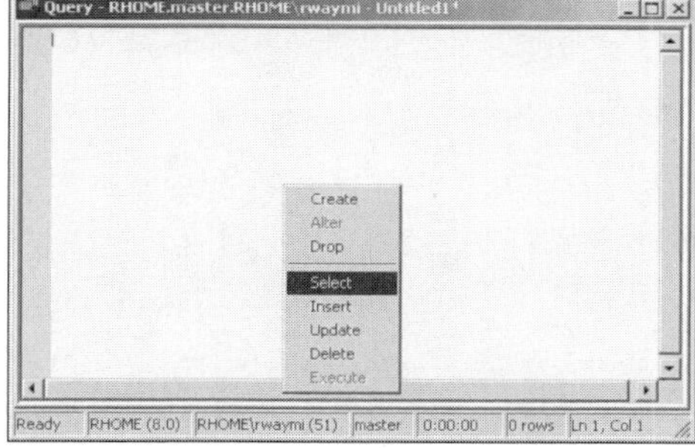

FIGURE 3.23

Drag and drop from the Object Browser.

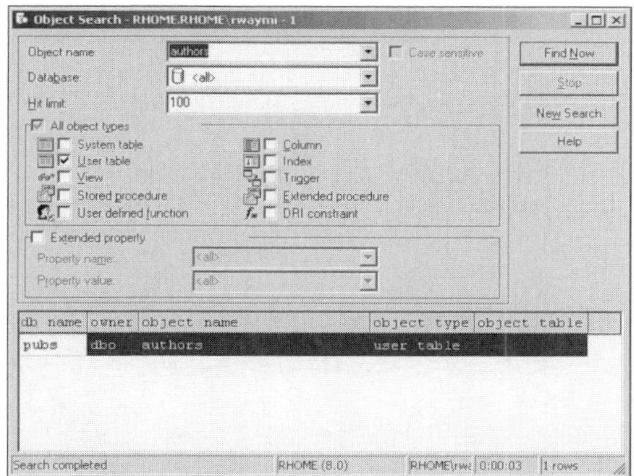

FIGURE 3.24

The Object Search dialog.

Skip over the next button for a moment. The last option on the toolbar simply allows you to always see the results window, even when you haven't run a query yet.

Configuring SQL Server Query Analyzer Options

The button with a hand holding a piece of paper (the one you skipped over a minute ago) displays the Query Analyzer Current Connection Properties dialog (see Figure 3.25). You can see the same dialog by selecting Query, Current Connection Properties.

Until you begin working with advanced SQL Server features, you shouldn't need to change any of these options, but at least you'll know where they are if you do need to change them.

You can configure and change Query Analyzer options in yet another place. You reach the dialog shown in Figure 3.26 by selecting Options from the Tools menu. A significant number of options are exposed here. SQL Server's Books Online explains each of them in detail, but you won't set most of them until you become a much more advanced SQL Server programmer or administrator.

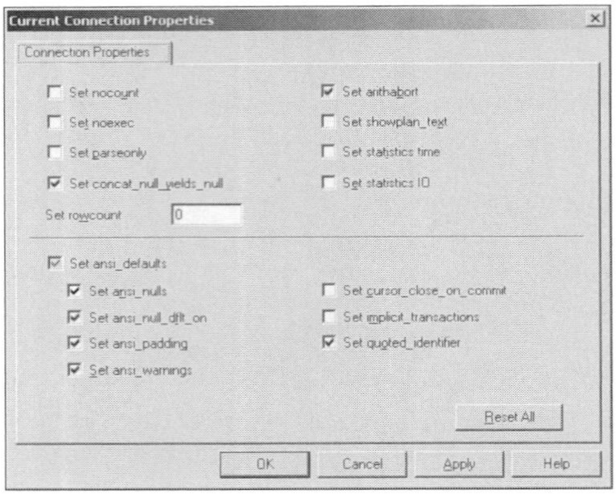

FIGURE 3.25

The Current Connection Properties dialog.

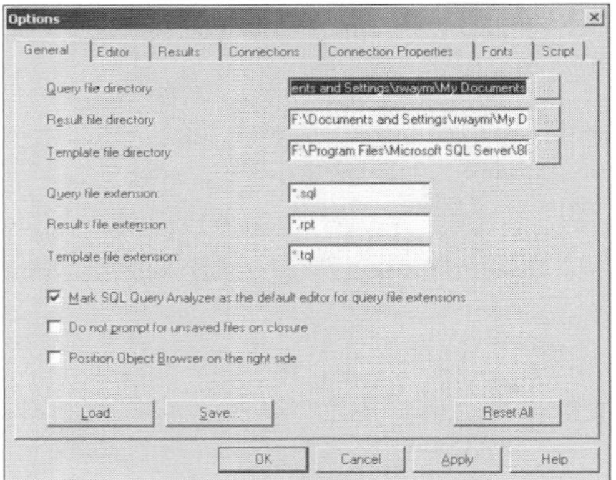

FIGURE 3.26

The Query Analyzer Options dialog.

NEW TERM We will sometimes note that you are running a script. A Transact-SQL *script* is any set of SQL commands stored and executed together. In fact, the File, Open and File, Save options allow you to save a query (or set of queries) and then run them again later. By default, scripts have the file extension `.SQL`. You can change that extension on the General tab, but changing it isn't recommended. You can also reset the default locations to search for scripts, as well as reset options for the locations of your results from running queries and the default extensions for those saved results.

On the Editor and Results tabs, you can reconfigure your development environment to whatever settings you are most comfortable with. The Fonts tab lets you change the default fonts used to display queries and results in the user interface. The Connection Properties tab shows you the same connection properties you saw a minute ago for your current connection (the defaults set for all connections).

The Connections tab allows you to configure how long Query Analyzer will wait when attempting to log in to SQL Server. You can also configure how long to wait for long-running queries (0 means wait forever; any other value is a number of seconds), as well as set language and other international settings.

Choose these options carefully; they can really change your output, and you might easily forget you have set any options here.

Help Options

The last option to examine here is Help. If you can't remember the syntax of a command (the right way to type a command or a list of options), highlight a keyword and press Shift+F1. Help for the command should pop up in a window. Help is built in for just about every Transact-SQL command. Unlike in previous releases of SQL Server, SQL Server 2000 help always launches Books Online, taking you to the most appropriate topic for the help you requested. This feature should assure you the most accurate help by having only one definitive source of information about syntax and query options.

Another really useful option is Alt+F1. If you highlight the name of a SQL Server object, such as a table, the default help is provided in the results window. The exact type of help you receive depends on the type of object you're asking for help with, but the help typically shows you useful properties about an object.

Tip

> If you highlight a command in the query window and then execute the query, just the highlighted text is run. This way, you don't have to execute every statement in a window.

Enterprise Manager

As you can see, Query Analyzer is a *very* powerful tool. It has been greatly enhanced in SQL Server 2000 to be the programmer's and the database administrator's best friend. However, you still have SQL Server Enterprise Manager, which is meant to be SQL Server's primary graphical administrative and development interface. There's very little SQL Server Enterprise Manager can do that you can't accomplish by using a Transact-SQL command in Query Analyzer. However, using the Enterprise Manager is sometimes more convenient, especially when you are new to SQL Server.

SQL Server Enterprise Manager is an MMC snap-in. MMC stands for the Microsoft Management Console, a common utility that Microsoft and third-party vendors can use as the common administrative interface to their respective products. All Microsoft BackOffice products, as well as system components within Windows 2000 and Windows XP, use the MMC as their primary administrative interfaces.

Registering a Server

When you start SQL Server Enterprise Manager, you might need to register a server. If you are sitting at a computer with SQL Server installed, your local SQL Server is registered for you during setup. If you have an earlier release of SQL Server installed on the Windows 2000 computer on which you installed SQL Server 2000, you might also see a SQL Server 6.*x* group. To register a server, expand the Microsoft SQL Servers option, and you should see the default group, SQL Server Group. Highlight the SQL Server Group option, and then from the Action menu, select New SQL Server Registration. The Register SQL Server Wizard then appears (see Figure 3.27).

FIGURE 3.27

The Register SQL Server Wizard.

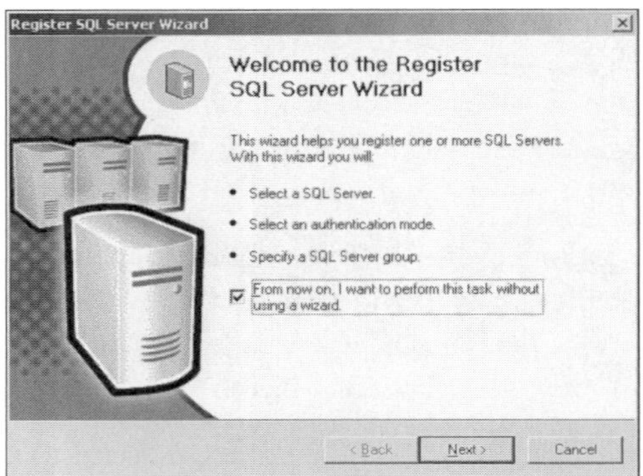

I recommend that you check the box to not use the wizard in the future because registering a SQL Server is one of the easier tasks you can perform. Click Next, and you are presented with the default dialog to register a SQL server (see Figure 3.28).

FIGURE 3.28

The Registered SQL Server Properties dialog.

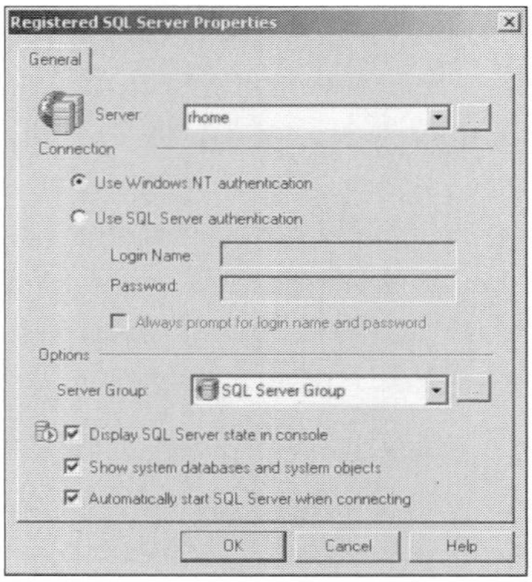

Enter your computer name as I've done in Figure 3.28, and then select the security mode you want to use. You can use Windows NT security mode (if the SQL Server is running on Windows NT), or you can specify a SQL Server security login (which works only on Windows 9*x* by default). Select the SQL Server login option, and complete your SQL Server login credentials if you select to use SQL Server Authentication. Because you previously installed your default instance in Windows Integrated Mode, you must select Use Windows NT Authentication.

Notice that you can also choose to be prompted for your login and password every time you try to connect (if you choose to use SQL Server authentication). Use this option on a Windows 9*x* computer to protect your security. If you are concerned about security, you should probably be using Windows 2000, which is much more secure than the Windows 9*x* operating systems.

You can select to add this server under the default grouping of servers or to create a new grouping in the Server Group text box near the bottom of the dialog. This grouping is used strictly as an organizational tool for your desktop. The SQL Server computers on your network have no knowledge of this grouping. You can also change several options such as to automatically start SQL Server when you use SQL Server Enterprise Manager and try to connect to the server and view the system databases. For the purposes of this book, make sure that you check all available options.

Now click OK—that's it! You've configured your first registration for Enterprise Manager.

Note

> Of course, you just got an error that says `A Server with this name already exists`, didn't you? When you install SQL Server, the setup program automatically registers your local installations in your copy of Enterprise Manager. So, for your local copies, you don't need to register them; they are already there. For any remote copies, however, you need to go through this registration process.

Examining How Enterprise Manager Works

Close the registration dialog by clicking the Cancel button. You see that your servers are already registered in the left pane of Enterprise Manager when you expand the SQL Server Group and then expand each server (see Figure 3.29). You can tell when you are connected by the presence of the red lightning bolt through your server icon. In Figure 3.29, you can see that I'm connected to both my default instance and my named instance of SQL Server, both installed on my local computer (RHOME). Note: You may have to select View -> Taskpad to get this view on your screen. Taskpads are turned off by default to make Enterprise Manager run faster.

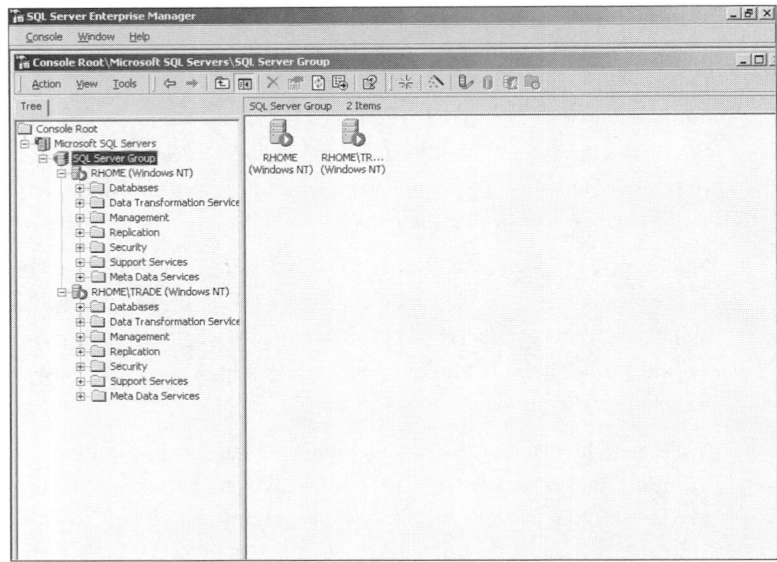

FIGURE 3.29

Enterprise Manager with the servers registered.

Within each server, the Databases folder lists the databases installed on your server. The Data Transformation Services folder shows any DTS "packages" that you've set up, as well as Meta Data Services packages. The Management folder shows administrative management features of SQL Server. The Replication folder shows any replication configuration changes that you've made to your server. The Security folder allows you to configure security in SQL Server. The Support Services folder enables you to control other SQL Server-related services on your computer, such as the Distributed Transaction Coordinator and full-text search. Figure 3.30 shows an expanded view of each folder. When you highlight your server, information about that server is displayed as an HTML page on the right side of the screen.

Now expand the `pubs` database folder, and then highlight the `pubs` database in the left pane. Notice how a new Web page is then displayed on the right (see Figure 3.31). This is how Enterprise Manager works: Container objects are typically shown on the left, and the contents of the container objects, or other information, are displayed on the right.

NEW TERM Some dialogs also open separate windows or dialogs for you to work with. For example, right-click the `pubs` database folder on the left, and select Properties from the pop-up menu. Notice that a new dialog opens on top of Enterprise Manager (see Figure 3.32). *Property sheets* (dialogs with the descriptions of properties of an object) often appear in these separate dialogs. Click Cancel to dismiss the `pubs` database's property sheet without making any changes.

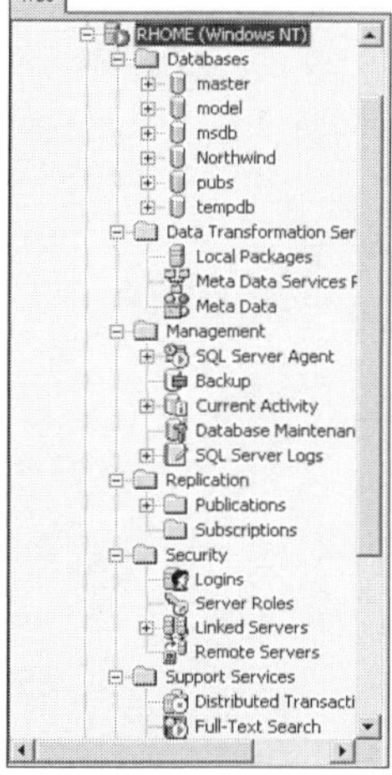

Figure 3.30

The left pane of Enterprise Manager with expanded folders.

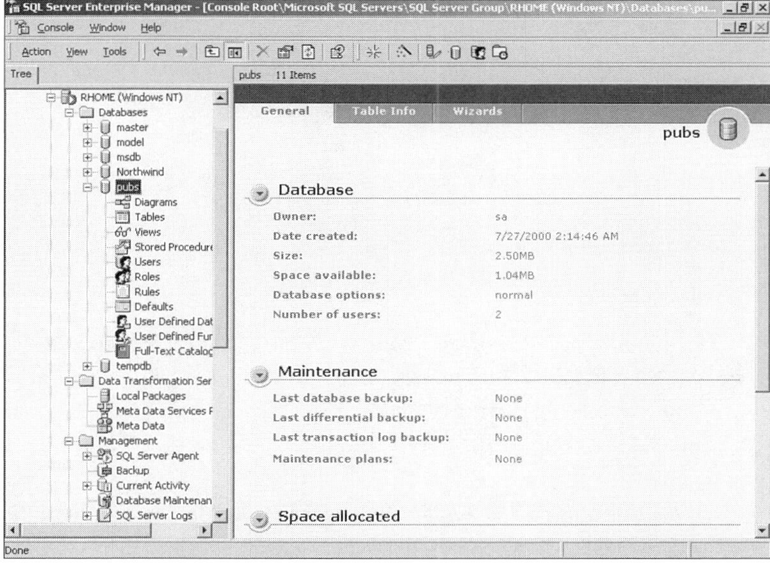

Figure 3.31

The pubs *database.*

Another feature that's worth examining is the menu options. The options available change depending on what you've highlighted. For example, you see the options in Figure 3.33 if you click the Tools menu with the pubs database highlighted. Don't be intimidated; you will learn what every option here does as you progress through the rest of your 21-day journey into SQL Server 2000.

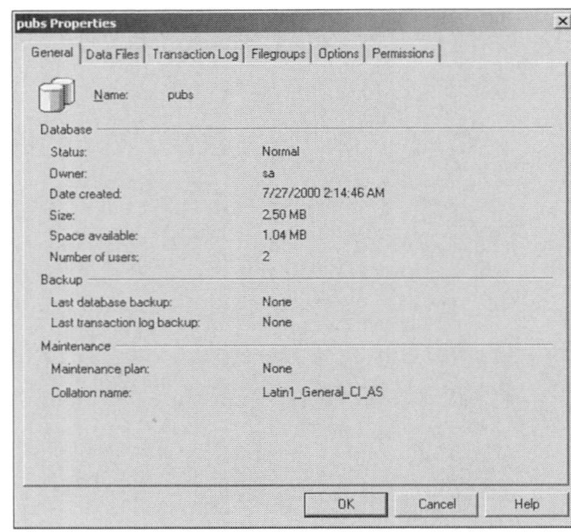

FIGURE 3.32

The properties of the pubs *database.*

FIGURE 3.33

Menu options in SQL Server Enterprise Manager.

Explanations of Enterprise Manager could literally fill another 20 to 30 pages. However, you should know enough now to begin using the tool as you move on. You will use Enterprise Manager every single day, so by Day 21 you will be an Enterprise Manager expert!

Import and Export Data

The Import and Export Data choice in the Microsoft SQL Server program group starts the DTS Wizard. You will examine DTS in greater detail on Day 19.

Configure SQL XML Support in IIS

By using the Configure SQL XML Support in IIS option, you can set up your Web server to allow direct queries into SQL Server using Extensible Markup Language (XML). You will examine this option and more on Day 21.

Profiler

The SQL Server Profiler utility enables you to monitor all activity on your SQL Server. You can also use the Profiler to perform performance tuning activities, such as examining the execution plan that SQL Server will use to run your queries. The Profiler has sophisticated filtering mechanisms to let you keep track only of specific users, applications, or types of commands. You can monitor more than 100 different events from SQL Server 2000. You'll examine the Profiler on Day 20.

The Microsoft SQL Server–Switch Program Group

The second program group, available only on Windows NT and Windows 2000 installations of SQL Server 2000, contains three possible options. These options are the SQL Server Version Upgrade Wizard, the uninstall utility, and possibly a SQL Server 6.*x* switch.

SQL Server Version Upgrade Wizard

You examined the Version Upgrade Wizard yesterday when you learned about installing SQL Server 2000. SQL Server Version Upgrade on Windows NT computers enables you to upgrade SQL Server 6.5 databases and server properties. You can upgrade a single database, multiple databases, or server and scheduled job properties from a previous release of SQL Server.

SQL Server versions 6.5 and 7.0 are the only releases supported for upgrade. No other previous releases are supported. SQL Server 7.0 can upgrade in place, so no upgrade wizard is required. You will find the version upgrade utility only on Windows NT/2000 systems because version 6.5 of SQL Server ran only on Windows NT or Windows 2000.

The version upgrade process leaves your SQL Server 6.5 database files in place. When you upgrade, the data is exported from SQL Server 6.5 into SQL Server 2000, and new databases and files are created in SQL Server 2000. You can upgrade your previous installation of SQL Server on the same computer, or you can install SQL Server 2000 on a second computer and then upgrade into the new SQL Server 2000 computer.

Microsoft SQL Server 6.*x* Switch

The Microsoft SQL Server 6.*x* Switch program group entry is present only on systems that had SQL Server 6.5 installed. When you click this option, you switch back to your SQL Server 6.5 installation. Your Start menu changes to reflect the SQL Server 6.5

utilities (although your SQL Server 2000 tools are also available), and the previous release of SQL Server is available to run. When you run SQL Server 6.5, the entry in the Switch menu is renamed to Microsoft SQL Server 2000. When you select it again, you return to SQL Server 2000, and your SQL Server 6.5 tools are again hidden.

These options apply only to switching between SQL Server 6.5 and a default instance of SQL Server 2000. As we noted yesterday, you can have SQL Server 6.5, SQL Server 7.0, or SQL Server 2000 as a default instance, with as many named instances as you want to install always running (up to 16 total).

Uninstall SQL Server 6.*x*

The Uninstall SQL Server 6.*x* program group entry is present only on systems with a previous release of SQL Server installed. When you click this option, you uninstall your previous release of SQL Server. This custom uninstall program safely removes your previous release of SQL Server.

Don't run setup to remove your old release of SQL Server 6.5. Using the custom uninstaller installed with SQL Server 2000 is the only safe way to remove the previous release without potentially damaging your SQL Server 2000 installation.

Other SQL Server Tools/Utilities

Several utilities that don't have shortcuts on your Start menu are available. These utilities, however, can be very useful. They are grouped into connectivity tools, server diagnostics, and maintenance utilities.

Connectivity Tools

Connectivity tools are the command-line utilities that provide a query interface or are network testing utilities. The first two tools you examine, OSQL and ISQL, allow you to connect to SQL Server and run Transact-SQL commands. They are the command-line equivalents of the SQL Server Query Analyzer. The second two sets of utilities, makepipe/readpipe and ODBCPing, let you test the network connectivity to your SQL Server.

OSQL

The OSQL.exe utility provides an ODBC-based query interface to SQL Server. This utility uses ODBC to connect to SQL Server. You can use this utility to run batch queries to support production tasks. You can also easily script Windows command files to run OSQL and run Transact-SQL commands to add new data, change data, or remove data from your databases. You can also create scripts (as you saw for the SQL Server Query Analyzer) and then run them without having to use a graphical interface. OSQL can be called with two different sets of options:

SYNTAX

```
osql [-L]| [-?]
```

In this simple syntax,

- -L shows a list of all SQL Servers found on the network.
- -? is the standard request for this syntax list.

3

SYNTAX

```
osql {{-U login_id [-P password]} | [-E]} [-S server_name] [-e] [-p] [-n]
[-I] [-b] [-O] [-u] [-R] [-d db_name] [-q "query"] [-Q "query"]
[-c cmd_end][-h headers][-w column_width] [-s col_separator] [-t time_out]
[-m error_level] [-r {0 | 1}] [-H wksta_name] [-i input_file]
[-o output_file] [-a packet_size] [-l time_out] [-D DSN]
```

In this more complete syntax,

- -U is your SQL Server login ID.
- -P is the SQL Server login password. If you don't enter it, OSQL prompts you to enter it when the program runs. If you've set an environment variable named OSQL-PASSWORD, this password is attempted before prompting you for a password.
- -E requests a Windows Authentication Mode connection, so you don't need to specify the -U or -P parameters.
- -S tells OSQL which server to connect to, in the form *SERVER\Instance*. If a server isn't specified, OSQL connects to the local default instance.
- -e echoes each statement you run in the output from that statement.
- -p prints out performance information for your queries.
- -n removes the numbers and the > prompt that OSQL normally includes in each row when you enter a set of commands.
- -I specifies that QUOTED_IDENTIFIER should be turned on for your connection. This will determine whether items in quotes are taken as string constants ("hello there") or as column or table names.
- -b tells OSQL to set the DOS error level when an error occurs. OSQL returns 1 when an error message with a severity level higher than 10 occurs.

- `-O` tells OSQL to emulate ISQL for backward compatibility.
- `-u` tells OSQL that the results of your query in your output file should be in Unicode.
- `-R` allows client-side conversion when converting money and date time values from SQL Server.
- `-d` specifies which database to switch to when you connect.
- `-q` tells OSQL to run the query you enclose in quotation marks when it starts. OSQL continues to run after running the query. If you must specify quotation marks within the query, use double quotes around the query and single quotes in your query.
- `-Q` tells OSQL to run the query you enclose in quotation marks when it starts and then quit `osql.exe`.
- `-c` sets the batch separator indicator. In SQL Server scripts, the word `GO` tells SQL Server to submit your queries to SQL Server as a group (known as a *batch*). However, you can override this and use your own indicator to OSQL to submit your queries to SQL Server. You shouldn't override this option.
- `-h` indicates to OSQL how many rows to print between your column headings and your query results. If you specify `-h-1`, no headings are produced for your queries.
- `-w` allows you to override the width of your output from the default of 80 characters.
- `-s` allows you to override the default column separator of a blank space.
- `-t` tells OSQL how long to wait before it considers your connection to the server to be a failure.
- `-m` changes error message reporting. The syntax is `-m` *`n`*, where *`n`* is the severity level of errors. Day 20 explains error severity.
- `-r` indicates that error messages should go to the stderr device. If this is set to `0`, only severity 17 or higher messages are sent to the stderr device. A setting of `1` indicates that all messages go to the stderr device.
- `-H` is your computer name if you want to send it to SQL Server.
- `-i` is the pathname and filename of the Transact-SQL script you want run.
- `-o` is the file in which you want your results from your script to be stored. The output file is in Unicode if your input file was in Unicode.
- `-a` indicates the packet size to use on the network.
- `-l` (that's a lowercase letter *L*, not a number 1) tells OSQL the login timeout (how long before it's assumed that your server isn't running).

- `-D` tells OSQL the name of a SQL Server Data Source Name defined in the Data Sources (ODBC) program in your administrative tools folder (or those that were created programmatically). This option works only for SQL Server data sources.

To run the commands you ran earlier for the SQL Server Query Analyzer, you would see the following in your command prompt:

> For this (and most) command-line tools, you can specify parameters with either a `-` or a `/`. So, for the servername parameter, you could run either `OSQL /S` or `OSQL -S`. They mean the same thing.

```
C:\>osql /E
1> use pubs
2> select * from authors
3> go
```

Then you would see your query results displayed, ending in the following:

OUTPUT

```
893-72-1158 McBadden                                    Heather
707 448-4982 301 Putnam
Vacaville            CA    95688        0
899-46-2035 Ringer                                      Anne
801 826-0752 67 Seventh Av.
Salt Lake City       UT    84152        1
998-72-3567 Ringer                                      Albert
801 826-0752 67 Seventh Av.
Salt Lake City       UT    84152        1
...
(23 rows affected)
1>
```

ANALYSIS The `GO` keyword tells OSQL to begin running the command(s) you've specified. The `1>` at the end of the output indicates that OSQL is ready to accept a new Transact-SQL command. Two other commands worth noting are `Reset` and `Exit`:

- `Reset` stops any command and returns you to the `1>` prompt.
- `Exit` leaves OSQL.

A batch file might look like this:

```
osql -E -I"D:\program files\Microsoft SQL Server\mssql\runquery.sql"
➥ -oc:\results.txt
```

The input file would contain your queries, and the results would show up in the `results.txt` file. This command would make a Windows authenticated connection to

SQL Server. You could then run this batch file any time and even schedule this batch file to run at some scheduled time in the future.

ISQL

`ISQL.exe` is the command-line query tool from previous releases of SQL Server. It uses the DB-Library network library to connect to SQL Server. Because it's based on DB-Library, it doesn't understand or can't work with SQL Server's new features, including Unicode. For this reason, you should discontinue using this utility if you have batch jobs already set up, and you should definitely not start using this tool now. It's only mentioned here for the sake of completeness as you may run into it from earlier installations of the product.

SYNTAX

```
isql -U login_id [-e] [-E] [-p] [-n] [-d db_name] [-q "query"]
[-Q "query"] [-c cmd_end] [-h headers] [-w column_width]
[-s col_separator] [-t time_out] [-m error_level] [-L] [-?]
[-r {0 | 1}] [-H wksta_name] [-P password] [-S server_name]
[-i input_file] [-o output_file] [-a packet_size]
[-b] [-O] [-l time_out] [-x max_text_size]
```

Many of these parameters are similar to OSQL.exe, but you really shouldn't use this utility in SQL Server 2000 except to support jobs that ran in previous releases.

Makepipe/Readpipe

You use the makepipe and readpipe utilities to verify the integrity of the Named Pipes file system. Because SQL Server 2000 doesn't use Named Pipes by default anymore, these utilities aren't installed by default. If you are having problems with Named Pipes, you can copy them from the `x86\binn` directory from your installation CD into your `\binn` directory for your SQL Server. You can find further directions on using these utilities in the SQL Server Books Online.

ODBCPing

ODBCPing enables you to verify that ODBC is working successfully from a client to a connection to SQL Server.

SYNTAX

```
odbcping [-?] | [{-Sserver | -Ddatasource} [-Ulogin] [-Ppassword]]
```

In this syntax,

- `-S` is the server to which you want to connect.
- `-D` is the name of an ODBC data source.
- `-U` is the login ID you're using to connect to SQL Server.
- `-P` is the password for the login ID you've chosen.

SQL Server 2000 doesn't install this program by default. However, it's in the `x86\binn` directory on your SQL Server 2000 CD. Copy the utility into your `\binn` directory (`d:\Program Files\Microsoft SQL Server\mssql\binn` for your default instance following our installation instructions), and then try the following to test that connection.

Go to a command prompt and enter the following to connect to your copy of SQL Server; specify your server name instead of mine (RHOME\Trade):

INPUT

```
odbcping -Srhome\trade -Usa -P
```

The server should respond with output similar to this:

OUTPUT

```
F:\>odbcping -Srhome\trade -Usa -Ppassword

CONNECTED TO SQL SERVER

ODBC SQL Server Driver Version: 2000.80.0100

SQL Server Version: Microsoft SQL Server  2000—8.00.100 (Intel X86)
        Apr 18 2000 01:19:00
        Copyright (c) 1988-2000 Microsoft Corporation
        Enterprise Edition on Windows NT 5.0 (Build 2195: )
```

3

This output means that ODBC is working fine. You can also connect to an ODBC DSN (Data Source Name), which is a preset configuration to a server you configure with the Data Sources (ODBC) application in your Administrative Tools folder.

> The ODBCPing tool doesn't support integrated security connections, so you can't use it against a default installation of SQL Server that's in integrated security–only mode (such as your default instance).

Server Diagnostics/Maintenance Utilities

The Server Diagnostic/Maintenance utilities are a set of utilities and tools you use at various times after you install SQL Server 2000.

SQLServr.exe

`SQLServr.exe` is the actual program that runs SQL Server (for a default instance, the MSSQLServer service). However, if you want to, you can run SQL Server from a command prompt. You would usually run it this way if you had to start SQL Server in what's known as single-user mode. You'll examine this procedure in more detail on Day 8, "Restoring Your Databases," because that's when you typically must run SQL Server in single-user mode.

SYNTAX

```
sqlservr [-sinstancename] [-c] [-f] [-dmaster_path] [-lmaster_log_path]
[-m] [-n][-eerror_log_path] [-pprecision_level] [-Ttrace#]
[-v] [-x] [-g number] [-O] [-y number]
```

In this syntax,

- `-s` specifies the instance name that you are starting. Leave off this parameter when you're manually starting a default instance of SQL Server. Otherwise, you must specify this option, even when you are calling `SQLServr.exe` from the `\binn` directory of a named instance.
- `-c` indicates that SQL Server should run as a program, and not as a Windows 2000 service. Using this parameter makes SQL Server start more quickly in a command window.
- `-f` indicates that SQL Server should start in a "minimal" configuration. You would specify this option when you manually set a configuration setting that prevents SQL Server from starting normally. It's an emergency mode meant to allow you to fix any mistakes you make.
- `-d` indicates the pathname and filename of your master database file. If you don't specify this option, the default you set during setup is found in your Registry and used. The default location is `D:\Program Files\Microsoft SQL Server\mssql\data\master.mdf`, or whatever drive on which you chose to install SQL Server.
- `-l` indicates the pathname and filename of your master database transaction log file. If you don't specify this option, the default you set during setup is found in your Registry and used. The default location is `D:\Program Files\Microsoft SQL Server\mssql\data \master.ldf`, or whatever drive on which you chose to install SQL Server.
- `-m` indicates that SQL Server will start in single-user mode, and only one user is allowed to connect to SQL Server at any time with a single connection. You can set this method during recovery situations after losing critical data files (such as recovering your master database from a backup).
- `-n` turns off error logging to the Windows NT/2000 Event Log (not recommended).
- `-e` is the pathname and filename of the SQL Server error log. It defaults to `D:\Program Files\Microsoft SQL Server\mssql\log\errorlog`, or whatever drive on which you chose to install SQL Server.
- `-p` is the maximum precision to allow for the decimal and numeric data types. By default, SQL Server allows these data types to hold up to 38 digits of precision. However, you can change this default by specifying a number here, from 1 to 38. Specify this option if you don't want to allow such large numbers in SQL Server or for backward compatibility with a previous release (such as SQL Server 7.0) that didn't support that much precision by default.

- `-T` specifies a trace flag to use in SQL Server. A *trace flag* is a numeric switch that tells SQL Server to enable special (nonstandard) behavior. You would typically use these flags only when directed to do so by SQL Server Product Support. To specify more than one, use multiple `-T` options.
- `-v` displays the version number of `sqlservr.exe`.
- `-x` turns off SQL Server performance statistics (not recommended).
- `-g` specifies the amount of memory you want to reserve for applications (such as extended stored procedures) running in process with SQL Server. You shouldn't modify this advanced configuration option unless instructed to do so.
- `-O` turns off DCOM and distributed queries. Set this option if you know you never want to run distributed queries.
- `-y` takes an error number as a parameter. When specified, this option writes the stack dump to your SQL Server error log when this error number is encountered. Again, you shouldn't use this option unless instructed to do so by a SQL Server support engineer.

For example, stop SQL Server with the SQL Service Control Manager or SQL Server Enterprise Manager, and then open a command prompt. Switch to your default instance's `\binn` directory and type the following:

INPUT

```
D:\Program Files\Microsoft SQL Server\MSSQL\Binn>sqlservr.exe -c
```

SQL Server runs in that command window and looks like Figure 3.34 when it's ready for you to begin logging in with a query tool.

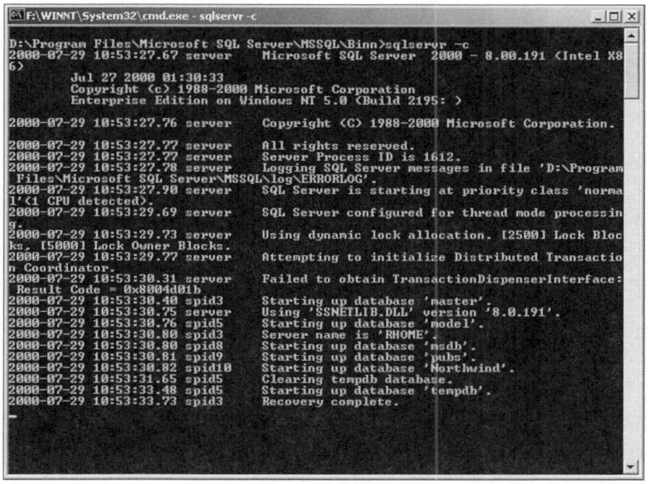

FIGURE 3.34

SQL Server when running in a command window.

To stop `sqlservr.exe`, press Ctrl+C with the command window selected, and you are prompted with

```
Do you wish to Shutdown SQL Server (Y/N)?
```

Type **Y**, and SQL Server stops. You can then restart SQL Server as a service.

The Rebuild Master Utility

The Rebuild Master utility rebuilds your master database, as well as the `msdb`, `model`, `tempdb`, `pubs`, and Northwind databases. You would run this utility for the following reasons:

- You lose a hard drive and don't have any backups.
- You want to change the default collation settings.
- Your master database has become corrupt.

When you run the Rebuild Master utility, new copies of each database are made from your SQL Server 2000 CD, and then the collation choice you've made is applied. Any databases (in addition to those just mentioned) defined in your previously running SQL Server are no longer defined, and you need to re-create all your databases, or "reattach" the databases to your SQL Server.

You typically rebuild the master in a disaster recovery scenario, which is where you will examine the utility further on Day 8.

The Registry Rebuild Option

You can use the Registry Rebuild option when your Windows Registry becomes corrupted for some reason or when you are instructed to do so by Microsoft SQL Server Product Support. Registry Rebuild simply re-creates all the Registry keys that were built during your previous setup.

To run Registry Rebuild, rerun setup, select to maintain your existing installation, specify the instance name if you're working against a named instance, and then select Advanced Options. Select Registry Rebuild from the menu, and then follow through setup. Select exactly the same options you chose during your initial setup to return the Registry to a usable state.

`SQLMaint.exe`

The `SQLMaint.exe` command supports routine system maintenance, including backup, consistency checking, and index maintenance. A wizard in SQL Server Enterprise Manager, called the Database Maintenance Plan Wizard, helps you configure maintenance plans and backups for your databases without having to know a lot about what's going on behind the scenes. The wizard is actually configuring automated jobs to call this utility. You have many options here, most of which won't make much sense now. However, by Day 18, "Scheduling Jobs with SQL Server Agent," when you learn to configure the SQL Server Agent, including setting up scheduled jobs, you should review this syntax and look at how to use this program to automate much of your server database maintenance. The basic syntax is examined here, but as you can see by the number of parameters, manual configuration of `SQLMaint.exe` can be a little tricky:

SYNTAX

```
sqlmaint [-?] | [ [-S server] [-U login_ID [-P password]]
{ [ -D database_name | -PlanName name | -PlanID guid ]
[-Rpt report_file [-DelTxtRpt time_period] ] [-To operator_name]
[-HtmlRpt report_file [-DelHtmlRpt time_period] ]
[-RmUnusedSpace threshold_percent free_percent]
[-CkDB | -CkDBNoIdx] [-CkAl | -CkAlNoIdx] [-CkCat]
[-UpdSts] [-UpdOptiStats sample_percent]
[-RebldIdx free_space] [-WriteHistory]
[ {-BkUpDB [backup_path] | -BkUpLog [backup_path] }
{-BkUpMedia  {DISK [ [-DelBkUps time_period]
[-CrBkSubDir ] [ -UseDefDir ]]
| TAPE }}
[-BkUpOnlyIfClean]
[-VrfyBackup] ] } ]
```

In this syntax,

- `-S`, as with the other utilities, is the name of the server you're running against (or *`server\instancename`* for a named instance).
- `-U` is the login name you're using to run the utility.
- `-P` is the password for the login name you just specified. If you leave off the `-U` and `-P` option, a trusted (Windows Integrated) connection is made to SQL Server.
- `-D` specifies the name of the database you are maintaining.
- `-Rpt` is the parameter that identifies where to put such information as the output file reporting errors from running this utility. It should be a full pathname and filename.
- `-To` is the name of an email account to which you want to have a copy of the report sent. You will examine email integration (called SQLMAIL) on Day 19.
- `-HtmlRpt` is the parameter that identifies where to put such information as the output file (in the form of a Web page) reporting errors from running this utility. It should be a full pathname and filename.
- `-RmUnusedSpace` is the parameter that tells `SQLMaint.exe` to remove any free space on databases larger than the *`threshold_percent`* parameter if the database is set to grow automatically (the default). The database shrinks, leaving some percentage of free space, specified in the *`free_percent`* parameter. Therefore, if you had a 100MB database, but only 50MB were used, and you had a *`free_percent`* of 10,

the database would only shrink to 55MB (because 10 percent of the 50MB used is 5MB, the database would have 5MB of free space remaining).

- `-CkDB | -CkDBNoIdx` parameters run the DBCC `Checkdb` command. This command is examined further on Day 7, "Backing Up Your Databases."
- `-CkAI | -CkAlNoIdx` parameters run the DBCC `Checkalloc` command. See Day 7 for more details.
- `-CkTxtAl` is the DBCC `Textall` command. Again, see Day 7.
- `-CkCat` is the DBCC `CHECKCATALOG` command. Is this getting familiar?
- `-UpdSts` runs the `Update Statistics` command. You'll examine statistics on Day 13.
- `-UpdOptiSts` runs the `Update Statistics` command with an optional parameter. You'll examine statistics on Day 13.
- `-Rebldldx` runs the DBCC `DBREINDEX` command to re-establish your fillfactors on your indexes—again, Day 13.
- `-WriteHistory` records that the maintenance plan was run in a system table in the MSDB database (the `sysdbmaintplan_history` table).
- `-BkUpDB | -BkUpLog` is the place where your backups will be placed. You can back up either the full database or just the transaction log. Backups will be examined on Day 7.
- `-BkUpMedia` indicates that you're backing up to either disk or tape.
- `-DelBkUps` indicates how long you want to keep your backups if you save them to disk. The *time_period* is specified as *number*`[minutes | hours | days | weeks | months]`.
- `-BkUpOnlyIfClean` indicates that the database should be backed up only if it's not corrupt. This is the most powerful feature of this utility and is discussed further on Day 7.
- `-VrfyBackup` verifies that the backup is readable after it has been made. Again, this parameter is examined on Day 7.

For example, you could run

```
sqlmaint -S rhome -D master -CkDB -Rpt d:\maint.txt
```

to get a DBCC `CHECKDB` command run in the master database for your default instance of SQL Server, with a report placed in the file `main.txt` in the root of your D drive.

> We're not trying to hide anything; it's just that most of these options will mean a lot more to you when you're finished reading the book than they do right now. That's why we keep saying "You'll learn more about this on Day *x*."

SQLDiag.exe

The SQLDiag utility prepares for a call to SQL Server Product Support. SQLDiag gathers your error logs, your server configuration information, and the version of SQL Server (including any service packs that have been applied), operating system information, computer system information, and other useful troubleshooting information, and places it all into a single file. This file, named `SQLDIAG.txt`, is placed in your `\mssql\log` directory by default.

3

SYNTAX

```
sqldiag [-S server] [-U login_ID] [-P password] [-E] [-O outputfile]
```

In this syntax,

- `-S`, as with the other utilities, is the name of the server you're running against (or *`server\instancename`* for a named instance).
- `-U` is the login name you're using to run the utility.
- `-P` is the password for the login name you just specified. If you leave off the `-U` and `-P` options, a trusted (Windows Integrated) connection is made to SQL Server.
- `-E` specifies that you want to connect using integrated security.
- `-O` specifies the pathname and filename that you want the report to go to.

Print out this text file (or copy it somewhere safe) because it contains so much valuable information about your system. Running this utility and having the information available to Microsoft's Product Support team will speed up any support call you make.

BCP: In a Class by Itself

BCP stands for the Bulk Copy Program. This utility loads data from a file into SQL Server or exports data from SQL Server to a file. You'll learn the details of this utility, including its syntax, on Day 19.

Summary

SQL Server 2000 ships with the best toolset yet from Microsoft. You can easily administer your entire organization from a single graphical management console. You have tools to run queries, examine performance information, and monitor your SQL Server services.

You can configure your network connectivity and even have network connectivity troubleshooting tools already installed on your system. Some tools are available via your Start menu, whereas others are available only from the command prompt in your `\mssql\binn` directory. Either way, you will end up using all these tools and utilities at one time or another—most likely in the remaining 18 days of this book.

Q&A

Q Which SQL Server utilities can I use to control the SQL Server-related services on my server?

A The SQL Server Service Manager and SQL Server Enterprise Manager

Q Which utilities allow me to run queries against SQL Server 2000?

A SQL Server Query Analyzer, `osql.exe`, and `isql.exe`

Q Which tool provides most of the functionality I need to support SQL Server as an administrator (or a developer, for that matter)?

A SQL Server Enterprise Manager

Q Which tool contains syntax help if I can't remember the exact way to type a command?

A SQL Server Books Online or Help in the SQL Server Query Analyzer

Workshop

This section provides quiz questions to help you solidify your understanding of the concepts presented today. In addition to the quiz questions, exercises are provided to let you practice what you have learned today. Try to understand the quiz and exercise answers before continuing to the next day's lesson. Answers are provided in Appendix A, "Answers to Quiz Questions."

Quiz

1. How do you prevent someone from logging in to SQL Server with your security credentials in Enterprise Manager?
2. Where would you set the default network library for your client computer?
3. Where would you add the NWLink IPX/SPX Network Library for your server?
4. Which utilities would you use to gather performance information about SQL Server 2000?
5. Which utility would you run before calling Microsoft Product Support?

Exercises

1. Explore Books Online, looking for additional information about the utilities you examined today.
2. Change your client network utility default setting to a setting not supported by your server, and attempt to connect using the SQL Server Query Analyzer.
3. Explore Enterprise Manager, examining what happens when you click some objects and seeing what menu options are available. Try to get accustomed to right-clicking an object and exploring the pop-up menus and the options that are available. The more comfortable you are with Enterprise Manager, the easier the rest of your time with SQL Server will be.

DAY 4

Creating and Administering Databases and Data Files

On Day 3, "Working with SQL Server 2000 Management Tools and Utilities," you learned about the different tools and utilities that come bundled with SQL Server 2000. You learned about the SQL Server Enterprise Manager, a utility within the Microsoft Management Console (MMC). You will use the SQL Server Enterprise Manager and the SQL Server Query Analyzer utilities to do much of the work described today.

This lesson shows you how to create, alter, and drop a database. When you create a database, it is stored in at least two separate files. One file contains the data, system tables, and other database objects; the other file stores the transaction log. In SQL Server 2000, you can make your database grow dynamically by specifying database and/or transaction log file growth options.

NEW TERM Filegroups are a tricky subject, and you will learn the basics of their use in this lesson as well. Essentially, a *filegroup* enables you to explicitly place database objects such as tables and indexes onto a specific database file (or group of files). Filegroups can improve database maintenance by allowing you to back up just the filegroup rather than an entire database. Filegroups provide advantages for both the administration and maintenance of the database, as well as potentially improve performance for larger instances of SQL Server.

In this lesson, you also look at the different database configuration options and how they affect your databases.

Creating a Database

To create a new database in SQL Server 2000, you can use one of three methods:

- The Database Creation Wizard
- The SQL Server Enterprise Manager
- The `CREATE DATABASE` statement

When you create a new database, you are really just making a copy of the model database. Remember that everything in the model database, including any database options that you may have set, will show up in any new databases you create. After you create the database by copying the model database, it expands to whatever size you've requested and fills the additional space with empty storage pages.

Databases need files to store their data physically on disk. When you create a new database, you should specify at least one file to store data and system tables, and a separate file to hold your transaction log. Your database and transaction log can span multiple files, as shown in Figure 4.1. The Trade database in this example has three separate data files and one file for its transaction log.

FIGURE 4.1

A database and transaction log can span multiple database files.

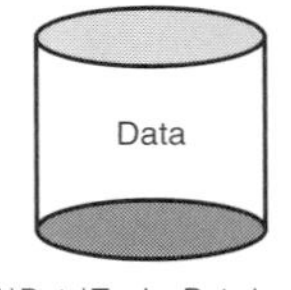

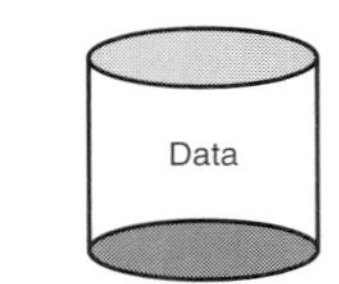

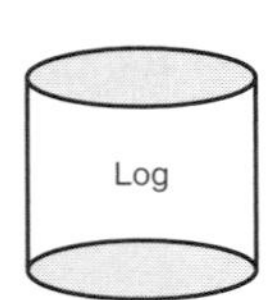

Note

> The database files you create can't be shared by any other database or transaction log.

In this section, you will break down the `CREATE DATABASE` statement and learn what each different parameter means. When you understand what's being accomplished, you will see how to create a database using the SQL Server Enterprise Manager. The `CREATE DATABASE` statement is as follows:

SYNTAX

```
CREATE DATABASE database_name
[ON {[PRIMARY]
(NAME = logical_name,
FILENAME ='physical_name'
[,SIZE = size]
[,MAXSIZE = max_size | UNLIMITED]
[,FILEGROWTH = growth_increment])
}[,...n]]
[LOG ON
{(NAME = logical_name,
FILENAME = 'physical_name'
[,SIZE=size | UNLIMITED]
[,MAXSIZE = max_size | UNLIMITED]
[,FILEGROWTH = growth_increment])}
[,...n]]
[,COLLATE collation_name]
[FOR LOAD | FOR ATTACH]
```

4

In SQL Server 2000, the only parameter that you need to include to create a database is the database's logical `NAME`. Although creating the database this way is possible in SQL Server 2000, it's not recommended. We suggest that you include the following parameters at a minimum: logical database name, filename and size for the data file, and transaction log filename and size. The following list describes the available `CREATE DATABASE` parameters:

- *`database_name`* refers to the database as a whole.
- `ON PRIMARY` specifies to which filegroup this database file is a member. The default filegroup is `Primary`. Filegroups will be discussed later today.
- `NAME` specifies the logical name you will use within SQL Server to refer to the physical database file on the hard disk.
- `FILENAME` is the pathname and filename pertaining to the location of the data on hard disk. It must be a local hard drive.
- `SIZE` specifies how big the database file should be. This value can be expressed in megabytes or kilobytes. The default size is the size of the Model file. To specify

megabytes or kilobytes, attach the `MB` or `KB` suffix to your size parameter. For example, `10MB` would create a 10 megabyte file.

Note

Megabytes can be specified only as whole numbers. To create a 2.5 megabyte database, you must use kilobytes, as in `2560KB`.

- `MAXSIZE` specifies the maximum size to which the database can dynamically grow. If you don't specify a size here and the autogrowth option is turned on, your database could grow to fill your entire hard disk. This parameter is also expressed in either megabytes or kilobytes.
- `FILEGROWTH` specifies which increments are used for the autogrowth of this database file. It can be expressed as either a number of megabytes or kilobytes, or as a percentage of the size of the file at the time of the growth. The default, if not specified, is `1MB`. The `FILEGROWTH` option can't exceed the `MAXSIZE` parameter.
- `LOG ON` describes where the transaction log files are located and what size they are.
- `COLLATE`, new to SQL Server 2000, specifies the collation sequence used for this particular database. It must be either a SQL Server collation name or a Windows collation name. If you don't specify this parameter, it defaults to the SQL Server 2000 instance's collation name. Collation sequences can also be specified at the table and individual column level.
- `FOR LOAD` marks the database for DBO Use Only. The option is provided for backward compatibility with SQL Server 6.5 only, and it shouldn't be used in SQL Server 2000.
- `FOR ATTACH` reattaches a set of files that make up a database. The files for the database must have been previously created and then detached from SQL Server 2000. You will examine this option later today.

Listing 4.1 shows the code necessary for creating a database that starts out reserving 25MB—20MB for the data portion of the database and 5MB for the transaction log. The files could grow to a total of 115MB—100MB for data and 15MB for the transaction log. It also uses the default SQL Server 2000 collation sequence. Open up the SQL Server Query Analyzer tool to enter this code.

Tip

With SQL Server 2000, it might be better for you to specify the amount of space needed right now to store your data and logs rather than reserve the total amount of disk space you might need in the future. You can then take advantage of the `FILEGROWTH` and `MAXSIZE` parameters to let the database grow as needed and conserve hard disk space now.

INPUT **LISTING 4.1** Creating a Database Reserving 25MB

```
USE master
GO
CREATE DATABASE Frogger ON PRIMARY
( NAME = FroggerData,
 FILENAME =
      'D:\Program Files\Microsoft SQL Server\MSSQL\Data\FroggerData.mdf',
 SIZE = 20MB,
 MAXSIZE = 100MB,
 FILEGROWTH = 10MB  )
LOG ON
( NAME = FroggerLog,
 FILENAME =
      'D:\Program Files\Microsoft SQL Server\MSSQL\Data\FroggerLog.ldf',
 SIZE = 5MB,
 MAXSIZE = 15MB,
 FILEGROWTH = 1MB )
GO
```

OUTPUT

```
The CREATE DATABASE process is allocating 20.00 MB on disk
'FroggerData'.
The CREATE DATABASE process is allocating 5.00 MB on disk
'FroggerLog'.
```


Listing 4.2 shows how to create a database that spans multiple files for both the data and the log. Notice that the logs and data files use the suggested Microsoft extensions. The first data file should have an `.MDF` extension, and subsequent data files have the `.NDF` extension. Log files should use the `.LDF` extension. Again, the default SQL Server 2000 collation sequence is used.

INPUT **LISTING 4.2** Creating a Database That Spans Multiple Files

```
USE master
GO
CREATE DATABASE Leap ON PRIMARY
( NAME = LeapData1,
  FILENAME =
    'D:\Program Files\Microsoft SQL Server\MSSQL\Data\LeapData1.mdf',
  SIZE = 5,
  MAXSIZE = 20,
  FILEGROWTH = 1 ),
( NAME = LeapData2,
  FILENAME =
    'D:\Program Files\Microsoft SQL Server\MSSQL\Data\LeapData2.ndf',
  SIZE = 5,
```

continues

LISTING 4.2 CONTINUED

```
  MAXSIZE = 20,
  FILEGROWTH = 5 )
LOG ON
( NAME = LeapLog1,
  FILENAME =
     'D:\Program Files\Microsoft SQL Server\MSSQL\Data\LeapLog1.ldf',
  SIZE = 2,
  MAXSIZE = 20,
  FILEGROWTH = 1 ),
( NAME = LeapLog2,
  FILENAME =
     'D:\Program Files\Microsoft SQL Server\MSSQL\Data\LeapLog2.ldf',
  SIZE = 2,
  MAXSIZE = 10,
  FILEGROWTH = 2 )
GO
```

OUTPUT

```
The CREATE DATABASE process is allocating 5.00 MB on disk
            ➥     'LeapData1'.
The CREATE DATABASE process is allocating 5.00 MB on disk
'LeapData2'.
The CREATE DATABASE process is allocating 2.00 MB on disk
'LeapLog1'.
The CREATE DATABASE process is allocating 2.00 MB on disk
'LeapLog2'.
```

When you specify the use of multiple data files, SQL Server automatically stripes information across all the data files specified. Striping can help reduce database contention and hotspots in your data. Note that SQL Server never stripes log files. The log files fill up with information sequentially, and when one log file is full, the data moves on to the next transaction log file.

> **Tip** If you aren't using RAID 5 (redundant array of inexpensive disks) or higher, it's strongly suggested that you place your transaction logs on separate physical hard disks. Setting them up this way allows for greater recoverability in the event of a hard disk failure. An additional benefit is that writes to the transaction log don't interfere with writes to the data files. This generally gives better performance.

Listing 4.3 shows how to create a database that uses a collation sequence specified with the `COLLATE` command. In this case, you specify that SQL Server 2000 create a database that uses the Latin1 code page or code page 1251, dictionary sort order (General), case insensitive (CI), and accent insensitive (AI).

INPUT

LISTING 4.3 Creating a Database That Uses a Nondefault SQL Server 2000 Collation Sequence

```
USE master
GO
CREATE DATABASE Swim ON PRIMARY
( NAME = SwimData,
  FILENAME =
     'D:\Program Files\Microsoft SQL Server\MSSQL\Data\SwimData.mdf',
  SIZE = 20MB,
  MAXSIZE = 100MB,
  FILEGROWTH = 10MB  )
LOG ON
( NAME = SwimLog,
  FILENAME =
     'D:\Program Files\Microsoft SQL Server\MSSQL\Data\SwimLog.ldf',
  SIZE = 5MB,
  MAXSIZE = 15MB,
  FILEGROWTH = 1MB )
COLLATE Latin1_General_CI_AI
GO
```

OUTPUT

```
The CREATE DATABASE process is allocating 20.00 MB on disk 'SwimData'.
The CREATE DATABASE process is allocating 5.00 MB on disk 'SwimLog'.
```


You can also use the SQL Server Enterprise Manager to create a new database. Follow these steps to create a new database:

1. Start the SQL Server Enterprise Manager by selecting Start, Programs, Microsoft SQL Server 2000, Enterprise Manager.
2. Connect to an instance of SQL Server.
3. Expand your Databases folder, as shown in Figure 4.2.
4. Right-click either the Databases folder icon or in the whitespace in the right pane, and choose New Database from the context menu.
5. You should now be on the General tab of the Database Properties dialog. Specify a database name. (I used Croak.) Now switch to the Data Files tab (see Figure 4.3) to see the new database file named `Croak_Data` with an initial size of 1MB in the default `...\Data` folder. In the File Properties section at the bottom of the dialog, notice that the Automatically Grow File option is turned on and that File Growth properties have been set. Also, the maximum file size is set to Unrestricted File Growth.
6. To change the properties of the database files, simply click the appropriate box and make your modifications. (I chose the defaults.) You can add additional database files if you go to the next box under File Name and add additional file properties.

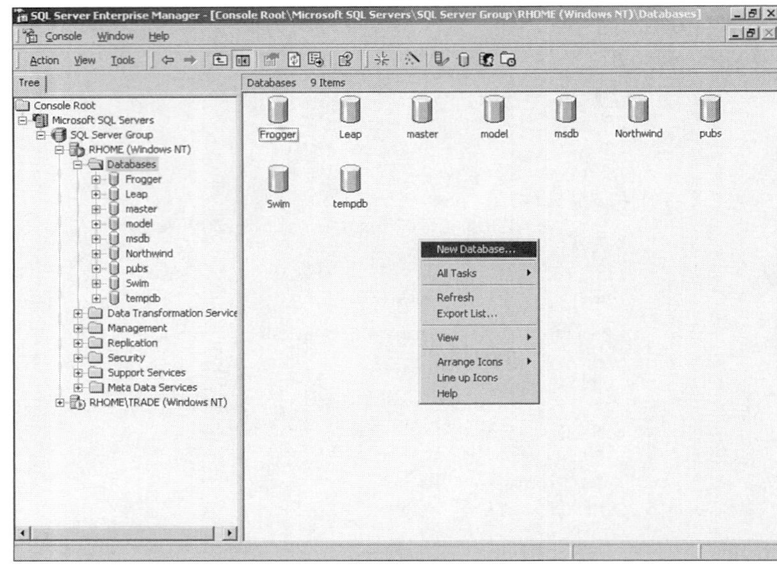

FIGURE 4.2

The right pane of the SQL Server Enterprise Manager shows the databases, and the pop-up menu lets you arrange icons or perform tasks.

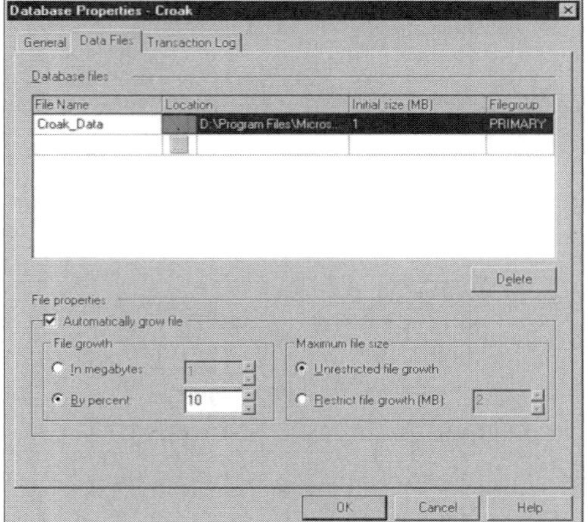

FIGURE 4.3

Use this tab to see the properties of a database, such as the name, size, and filegroup.

7. Click the Transaction Log tab. Notice that it has a default name of `Croak_Log` and is 1MB.
8. Click OK when you are finished. You should now have a screen similar to Figure 4.4. If you don't see your Frogger, Leap, or Croak databases, right-click the Databases folder, and choose Refresh from the pop-up menu.

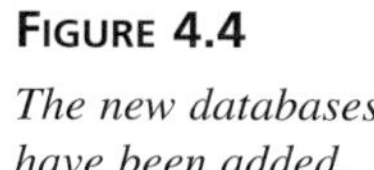

FIGURE 4.4

The new databases have been added.

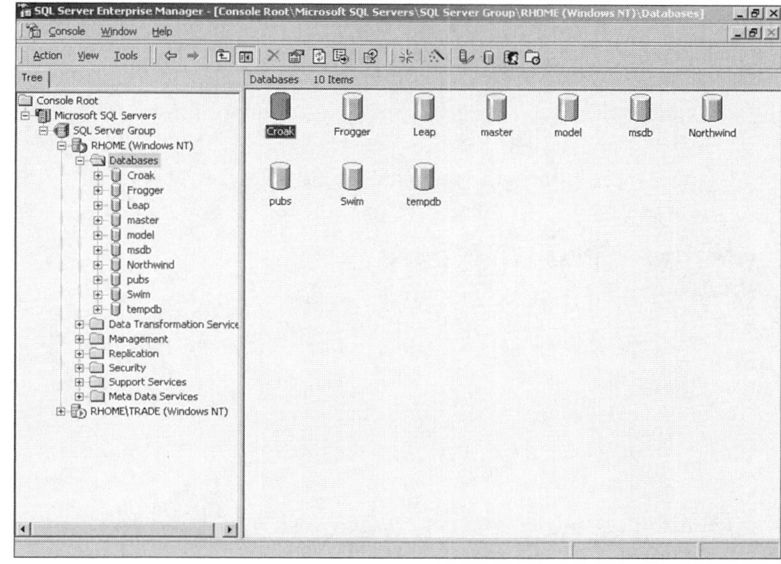

Gathering Database Information

As you might have suspected, you can gather information about your databases in several ways. You can use the SQL Server Enterprise Manager, or you can use the SQL Server Query Analyzer utility and run some system stored procedures.

You can use the `sp_helpdb` system stored procedure to examine an individual database or gather summary information on all databases in SQL Server. If you run `sp_helpdb` without specifying a database, you get summary information on all databases in SQL Server.

Note

> The following example is only part of the data returned. In addition to the information given here, you also get much more information including recoverability, update ability, and collation sequence, to name a few.

INPUT/OUTPUT

```
EXEC sp_helpdb
name     db_size  owner  dbid Created
-------- -------  -----  ---- -------
Croak     2.00 MB sa     9    Jan 14 2000
Frogger  25.00 MB sa     7    Jan 14 2000
Leap     14.00 MB sa     8    Jan 14 2000
master    9.25 MB sa     1    Nov 13 1999
model     1.50 MB sa     3    Jan 13 2000
msdb      8.75 MB sa     4    Jan 13 2000
```

```
Northwind 3.94 MB sa     6    Jan 13 2000
pubs      1.74 MB sa     5    Jan 13 2000
tempdb    8.50 MB sa     2    Jan 14 2000
```

As you can see, sp_helpdb gives you summary information about the databases in SQL Server. For example, the Frogger database is 25MB and is owned by the sa login. To gather more information about a single database, specify it in the sp_helpdb statement as follows:

INPUT/OUTPUT

```
EXEC sp_helpdb Croak

name   Db_size   Owner   dbid  Created
------ --------- ------- ----- -----------
Croak  2.00 MB   sa      9     Apr 14 1998

Name         Fileid   Filename
------------ -------- ---------------------------------------
Croak_Data   1        D:\PROGRAM FILES\MSSQL\data\Croak_Data.MDF
Croak_Log    2        D:\PROGRAM FILES\MSSQL\data\Croak_Log.LDF
```

In addition to what you get for the Croak row shown previously, you also get information about the files and how they are allocated. For example, the output from the preceding statement shows the file Croak_Data is 2MB and is used for data only. Croak_Log is 1MB and is used for the transaction log only.

You can also use the SQL Server Enterprise Manager to gather information about your databases. Open the SQL Server Enterprise Manager, and expand the Databases folder. Double-click a database to bring up the editing screens shown earlier. You can also gather information about a database by single-clicking it in the left pane, as shown in Figure 4.5. Figure 4.5 shows general information on the Leap database. You can gather additional levels of detail by choosing some of the options under the Database, Maintenance, or Space Allocated icons. Figure 4.6 shows the options available under the Database icon in the right pane.

Setting Database Options

Now you will learn a little more about the database options you can apply to your databases. As usual, you can modify database options with stored procedures in the SQL Server Query Analyzer or through the SQL Server Enterprise Manager.

In general SQL Server Enterprise Manager uses the SQL-DMO interface to work with SQL Server. The SQL-DMO is a programming interface for administering a SQL Server. The interface itself takes the programming calls and converts them to stored procedures or other TSQL calls which it then runs for you.

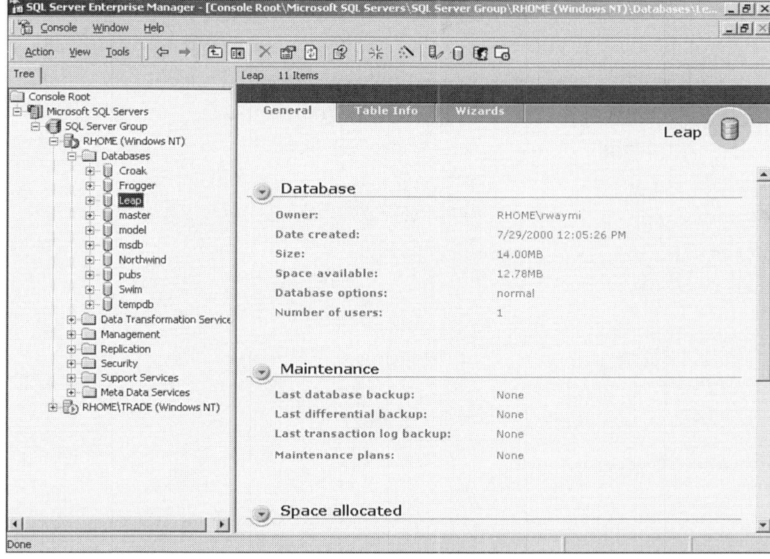

FIGURE 4.5

General information on the Leap database.

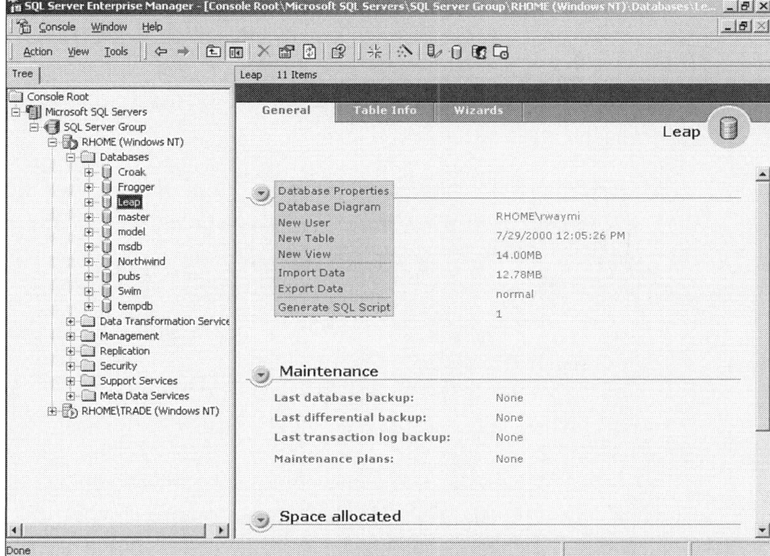

FIGURE 4.6

Additional database-related options.

4

To view and modify database options using the SQL Server Enterprise Manager, simply drill down until you find the database with which you want to work (pubs in this example). After you locate the database, you can double-click the database or right-click it and choose Properties from the context menu to bring up the pubs Properties sheet. Click the Options tab to view the database options, as shown in Figure 4.7.

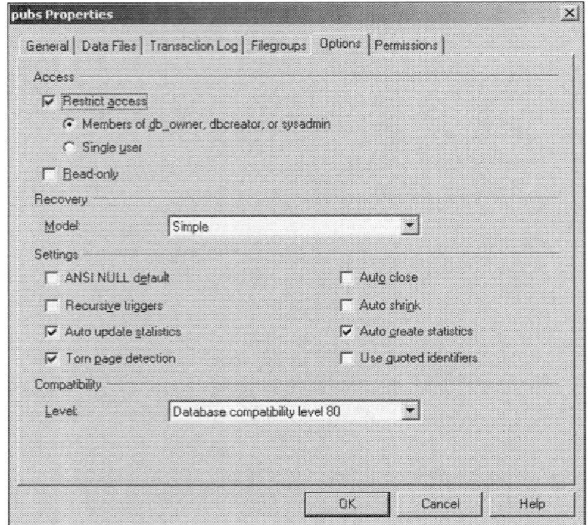

FIGURE 4.7

The Options tab of the pubs *database properties.*

As you can see, the database options are broken into three categories: Access, Settings, and Compatibility. Here's what each setting means:

- *Members of db_owner, dbcreator, or sysadmin* specifies that only members of the db_owners fixed database role can use the database. This option is often set when a database administrator is performing maintenance and doesn't want ordinary users working in a database. (This setting is also known as DBO Use Only.)
- *Single User* specifies that only one user at a time can access this database. This option actually allows only a single user connection to the database. It is most often used during a database restore.
- *Read-Only* marks the database as read-only, and no changes are allowed.
- *ANSI NULL Default*, when selected, defines new table columns as null by default (or NOT NULL). You will learn more about tables and columns on Day 9, "Data Types and Creating Tables."
- *Recursive Triggers* allows for (no surprise) recursive triggers. A *recursive trigger* occurs when a data modification on one table (I'll call it TableA) fires an update in TableB, which fires the trigger in TableB. TableB's trigger then makes a new update to TableA which in turn fires TableA's trigger again. This is known as indirect recursion. Direct recursion is also supported and occurs when TableA is

modified, fires its trigger which makes another modification to TableA which in turn fires its trigger again. SQL Server 2000 supports recursion only up to 32 levels of nesting.

- *Torn Page Detection* detects when a partial page write has occurred to disk (a form of corruption of your data). In prior versions of SQL Server, this problem occurred more often than we had hoped. Since SQL Server 7.0, torn pages haven't been a problem.
- *Auto Close* conserves resources on your server for a database that isn't used frequently. The database automatically closes when the last user exits from it.
- *Auto Shrink* automatically shrinks data and log files. Log files automatically shrink after a backup of the log is performed. The database files shrink when a periodic check on the database finds that the database has more than 25 percent of its assigned space unused. The autoshrink process shrinks your database to a size that has 25 percent of the space unused. Note that the autoshrink process doesn't shrink a database to a size smaller than its original size.
- *Auto Create Statistics* automatically generates statistics on the distribution of values in a column of data. This information is used by the SQL Server Query Optimizer to generate a query plan based on the cost of using different columns. We suggest that you enable this option.
- *Auto Update Statistics* works with Auto Create Statistics. Over time, the information in your columns will change; however, the statistics on those columns won't. To alleviate this problem, you must occasionally update your statistics. The Auto Update Statistics option does this job for you automatically. We suggest that you enable this option as well.
- *Use Quoted Identifiers* enables you to use double quotation marks as part of a SQL Server identifier. An *identifier* is the name of an object; it can be a variable, table, or something else. Quoted identifiers are useful when you have an identifier that also happens to be a SQL reserved word or an identifier that has a space in it—for example, the table `"Order Details"` or a table named `"Table"`. If you choose not to use Quoted Identifiers, then you must use SQL Server's square brackets to tell SQL Server that these are identifiers rather than reserved words or two word. Using the default properties, you would use [Order Details] and [Table].
- *Compatibility Level* enables you to specify what level of backward compatibility this database should support. The level 80 is for SQL Server 2000 (SQL Server version 8.0); 70 is for SQL Server 7.0; and 65 and 60 are for SQL Server 6.5 and 6.0, respectively.

You can also accomplish these same tasks by using the SQL Server Query Analyzer utility and the `sp_dboption` system stored procedure. For example, to restrict access to the pubs database to members of *db_owner, dbcreator,* or *sysadmin*, you would run the code shown in Figure 4.8. The code is

```
EXEC sp_dboption pubs, 'DBO Use Only', True
```

FIGURE 4.8

The code to mark the pubs *database as DBO Use Only.*

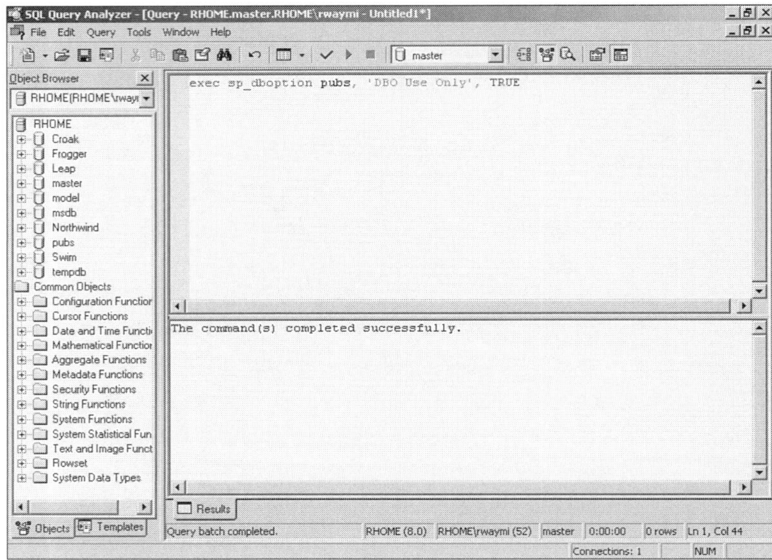

After running the preceding command, you can check to see whether it was really applied by running the `sp_dboption pubs` system stored procedure (see Figure 4.9). Notice the status section in the result set; it shows `dbo use only`. The `trunc. log on chkpt.` option is also set (which is the system default after installation), as well as a few others.

To turn off the DBO Use Only status, simply run the following code:

```
EXEC sp_dboption pubs, 'DBO Use Only', False
```

When you use the `sp_dboption` stored procedure, you can use an additional seven options that aren't available through the Enterprise Manager:

- *Concat NULL Yields NULL* works a lot like multiplying by zero. Multiplying by zero always results in a zero. Concat NULL Yields NULL says that anything you concatenate a `NULL` with results in a `NULL`—for example, `'Hello World' + NULL = NULL`.
- *Cursor Close on Commit* specifies that any open cursors are closed when the transaction is complete. A cursor is the result set from a query. Developers might recognize cursors as a type of recordset.

FIGURE 4.9

The results grid shows the change and status.

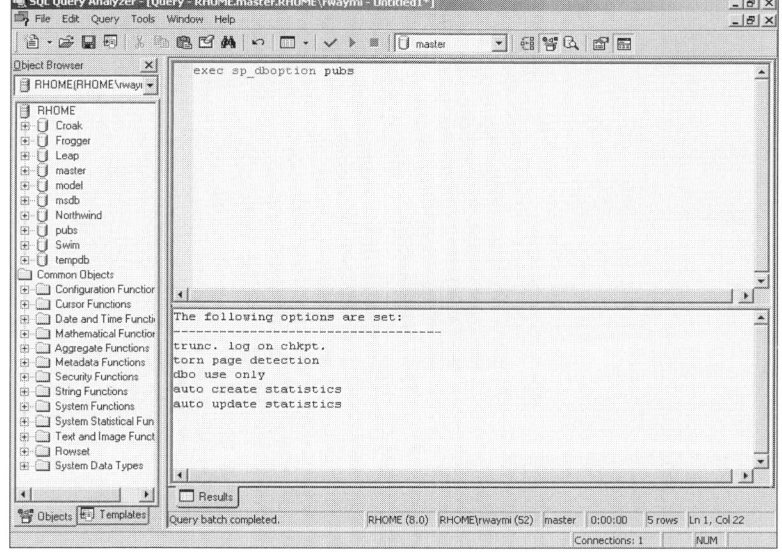

- *Default to Local Cursor* specifies that when a cursor is created without the `GLOBAL` keyword, it's available only to the local batch, trigger, stored procedure, and so on, that generated the cursor.
- *Merge Publish* enables the database to be used as a publisher in a merge replication scenario. Replication scenarios are covered on Day 16, "Understanding Replication Design Methodologies."
- *Offline* closes and shuts down the database. After a database is taken offline, it can be moved or copied to removable media (CD-ROM for example) and distributed.
- *Published* allows a database to publish articles for replication.
- *Subscribed* specifies that this database is the recipient of published data.

Resizing Your Database

To change the file definitions and size settings for a database, use the `ALTER DATABASE` statement or the SQL Server Enterprise Manager. To shrink a database, you must use the `DBCC SHRINKDATABASE` or `DBCC SHRINKFILE` commands. To add filegroups to your database, you can use the `ALTER DATABASE` statement. In this section, you will first examine the `ALTER DATABASE` statement and make some modifications to the databases already created in this lesson; you then will see how to shrink a database with the `DBCC SHRINKDATABASE` command. You will finish this section with a short lesson on filegroups.

> **Note:** You must have CREATE DATABASE permissions to use the ALTER DATABASE statement.

The syntax for the ALTER DATABASE statement is as follows:

SYNTAX

```
ALTER DATABASE database
{
  ADD FILE File_specification [,...n] [TO FILEGROUP filegroup_name]
| ADD LOG FILE File_specification [,...n]
| REMOVE FILE logical_name
| ADD FILEGROUP filegroup_name
| REMOVE FILEGROUP filegroup_name
| MODIFY FILE File_specification
| MODIFY NAME = new_dbname
| MODIFY FILEGROUP filegroup_name, filegroup_property
| SET optionspec, ...n WITH termination
| COLLATE collation_name
}

File_specification
(NAME = logical_name,
FILENAME ='physical_name'
[,SIZE = size]
[,MAXSIZE = max_size |UNLIMITED]
[,FILEGROWTH = growth_increment])
```

In this syntax,

- *database* is the name of the database to be altered.
- ADD FILE specifies a data file to be added.
- All the *File_specification* options are the same specifications listed earlier in the CREATE DATABASE examples.
- TO FILEGROUP specifies the filegroup to add this file to. If none is specified, the file is added to the default filegroup (PRIMARY).
- ADD LOGFILE adds a new log file to the database.
- REMOVE FILE removes a file from the database. The file must be empty before removal. You can use the DBCC SHRINKFILE with the EMPTYFILE option to empty a file, as covered later today.
- ADD FILEGROUP adds a new filegroup. You must also specify the new filegroup name.

- REMOVE FILEGROUP removes a filegroup as well as deletes all files that are members of the filegroup. The files in the filegroup must be empty. You can use the DBCC SHRINKFILE with the EMPTYFILE option to empty files, as covered later today.
- MODIFY FILE allows you to modify the properties of a file, including its *physical_name*, FILEGROWTH, and MAXSIZE options. If you modify the MAXSIZE parameter, the new size must be larger than the current size. You can change the FILENAME parameter only for files that reside in tempdb; this change doesn't take effect until you restart SQL Server.

Note

> Although you can specify a size less than the current size of the file, you can't shrink a file from here. You must use the DBCC SHRINKDATABASE or DBCC SHRINKFILE command.

- MODIFY NAME renames the database.
- MODIFY FILEGROUP allows you to change filegroup properties, including the READONLY, READWRITE, and DEFAULT properties.
- SET allows you to specify READONLY, READWRITE, and DEFAULT. The termination parameter specifies when a rollback occurs—either ROLLBACK AFTER *n* SECONDS or ROLLBACK IMMEDIATE.
- COLLATE specifies the collation used for the database. It must be the SQL Collation name. If the collation is not specified, it defaults to the SQL Server 2000 collation sequence.

4

Expanding Your Database

You can expand your databases by adding additional files for growth. You can add files to the data portion as well as the log portion of the database. Unless you specifically turned off your database's autogrow features, the database files automatically grow until you run out of disk space. Remember that data stored across multiple files in a database automatically stripes the information across those multiple files. You might be asking yourself, "If the database file automatically grows as needed, why in the world would I want to create multiple files for my data to live on? This would appear to make the maintenance of my database more cumbersome." The answer is yes, creating multiple files would make the maintenance a little bit more cumbersome, but it does present advantages as well:

- You can place files on separate physical hard disks.
- You can improve performance, because reads and writes to the database have a better chance of going to separate disk controllers.
- Database files can be backed up independently of each other.
- If you use filegroups, specific portions of your data can be placed in specific files. For example, the payroll table could be placed in its own filegroup in its own file.

Caution

> You should specify a maximum size for your database and transaction log. If you don't specify a maximum size and didn't specifically restrict autogrowth, your database could fill the entire hard disk. When a hard disk partition in Windows becomes full, Windows generates errors and might not continue to operate until you release space on the affected partition.

Listing 4.4 shows how to add a new data file to the Croak database from the SQL Server Query Analyzer.

INPUT

LISTING 4.4 Adding a New Data File to the Croak Database

```
ALTER DATABASE croak
ADD FILE
( NAME = CroakData2,
  FILENAME =
     'D:\Program Files\Microsoft SQL Server\MSSQL\Data\CroakData2.ndf',
  SIZE = 2,
  MAXSIZE = 10,
  FILEGROWTH = 2)
```

OUTPUT

```
Extending database by 2.00 MB on disk 'CroakData2'.
```

You can now run the following `sp_helpdb` system stored procedure to verify that your database was successfully enlarged:

```
sp_helpdb croak
```

Your database should be 4MB with files of `Croak_Data`, `Croak_Log`, and `CroakData2`.

Now you can extend the database log file:

INPUT

```
ALTER DATABASE croak
ADD LOG FILE
( NAME = CroakLog2,
  FILENAME =
     'D:\Program Files\Microsoft SQL Server\MSSQL\DATA\CroakLog2.ndf',
  SIZE = 2,
  MAXSIZE = 10,
  FILEGROWTH = 2)
```

OUTPUT

```
Extending database by 2.00 MB on disk 'CroakLog2'.
```

Verify your results by running the `sp_helpdb Croak` procedure now. Your database should now be 6MB.

You can accomplish much the same result by using the SQL Server Enterprise Manager. Follow these steps to modify the Frogger database created earlier:

1. Start SQL Server Enterprise Manager.
2. Expand your Databases folder, and open the Properties dialog for the Frogger database. (You can do so by right-clicking the Frogger database and choosing Properties from the context menu.)
3. In the Data Files tab under the Frogger Properties dialog, click the empty box under `FroggerData`, and add `FroggerData2`, as shown in Figure 4.10.
4. In the Location column, specify the new filename `D:\Program Files\Microsoft SQL Server\MSSQL\DATA\FroggerData2.NDF`, or you can take the default value of `FroggerData2_data.ndf`. (Your drive letter and path might be different.)
5. In the Space Allocated (MB) column, enter the number **2**.
6. Leave the Filegroup as `PRIMARY`.
7. In the File Properties section, make sure that Automatically Grow File is checked.
8. Set the File Growth option to In Megabytes, and set it to 2.
9. In the Maximum File Size section, set the Restrict File Growth (MB) option to 4.
10. Now that you've added a data file, extend the transaction log as well. Rather than add a new log file, just change the space allocated from 5MB to 10MB.
11. Click OK when you are finished.
12. To verify that Frogger was modified, click the Frogger database in the left panel under the Databases folder in the Enterprise Manager. In the right panel, look at the Space Allocated section, as shown in Figure 4.11.

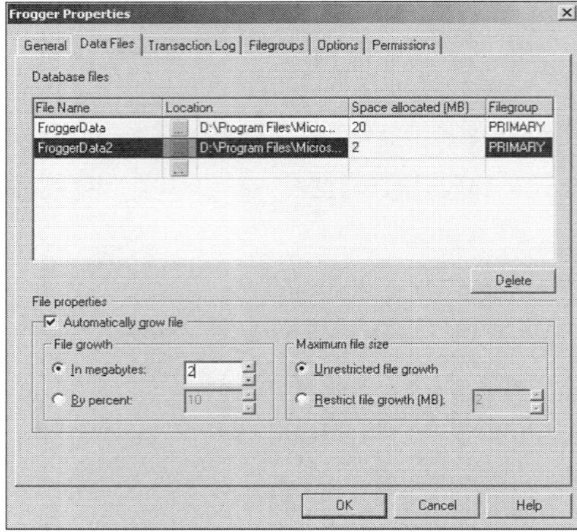

FIGURE 4.10

Adding `FroggerData2` *in the database files with a space allocation of 2.*

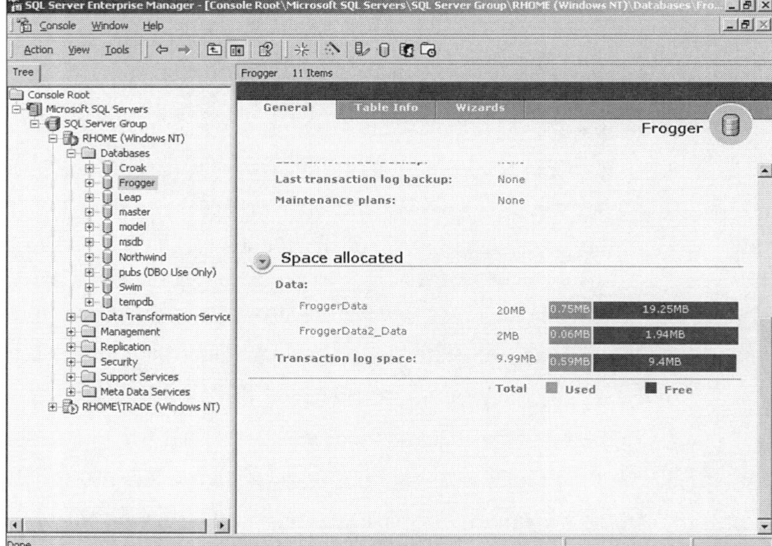

FIGURE 4.11

Verifying that the database has the space you allocated.

Shrinking Your Database

To shrink an entire database, you can use the `DBCC SHRINKDATABASE` command with the following syntax:

SYNTAX

```
DBCC SHRINKDATABASE {
(database_name
[, target_percent]
[,{NOTRUNCATE | TRUNCATEONLY}])
}
```

In this syntax,

- *database_name* is the name of the database to be shrunk.
- *target_percent* is the percentage of free space left in the database after you shrink it.
- NOTRUNCATE forces freed file space to be retained in the database files. The *target percent* is ignored. The default is to release the freed space back to the operating system.
- TRUNCATEONLY forces unused space in the data files to be released to the operating system. When you choose TRUNCATEONLY, the *target_percent* parameter is ignored, and all free space is released back to the system.

What exactly does this command do? How does all this work, and what's really going on? Essentially, the SHRINKDATABASE statement attempts to shrink all data files in the database, leaving your target percentage as free space. Used pages at the end of your data files are relocated below your percentage threshold. For example, if you have a 10MB database with only 5MB of data stored in it, you could set your target percentage to 20. This means that you want to leave 20 percent of your database as free space. All rows located in the database are relocated, clearing up any free space at the beginning of the database. This process is similar to defragmenting your disk drives. Because you have only 5MB of actual data and want to leave 20 percent of the database as free space, 20 percent of 5MB is 1MB. So, your database is resized to 6MB, and the other 4MB are released back to the operating system.

4

Note

> You can't shrink your database smaller than what's needed to store your data, nor can you shrink your database smaller than the model database. You also can't shrink your database smaller than the original size specified in your CREATE DATABASE command. To do so, you must use the DBCC SHRINKFILE command.

If you choose the NOTRUNCATE option, data is relocated to free up space at the end of the file, but the newly freed space is retained by the database rather than released to the operating system.

The TRUNCATEONLY option frees up all unallocated space without moving any data around. Any empty pages at the end of a file are released back to the system.

You can shrink individual files within your database by using the DBCC SHRINKFILE statement. DBCC SHRINKFILE can be used to modify individual files rather than all files in a database as the DBCC SHRINKDATABASE does. The syntax for the DBCC SHRINKFILE statement is as follows:

SYNTAX

```
DBCC SHRINKFILE {
(file_name | file_id }
[, target_size]
[, {EMPTYFILE | NOTRUNCATE | TRUNCATEONLY}])
}
```

When you use the DBCC SHRINKFILE statement, you must specify either a database filename or its *file_id*. You can find the *file_id* by running the sp_helpdb system stored procedure, as you saw earlier in this lesson.

The *target_size* is used in the same manner as the SHRINKDATABASE statements earlier. The TRUNCATEONLY and NOTRUNCATE statements are also the same as described earlier. The EMPTYFILE parameter is interesting in that it relocates any used data pages in the current database file to other database files in the filegroup. After all pages are moved, the database file is marked as empty, and you aren't allowed to store any data there. This capability can be useful if you want to use the REMOVE FILE or REMOVE FILEGROUP parameter in the ALTER DATABASE statement, because it requires the file to be empty.

Listing 4.5 empties the FroggerData2 file and uses the REMOVE FILE option to remove it from the Frogger database.

INPUT

LISTING 4.5 Emptying the File and Using *REMOVE FILE*

```
USE frogger
GO
DBCC SHRINKFILE (FroggerData2,EMPTYFILE)
GO
ALTER DATABASE Frogger REMOVE FILE FroggerData2
```

OUTPUT

```
DBCC execution completed. If DBCC printed error messages,
contact your system administrator.
The file 'FroggerData2' has been removed.
```

As you can see, FroggerData2 is first emptied using the EMPTY FILE option. You then run the second half of the batch statement where you alter the database and drop the file. To verify that the file has been dropped, you can run EXEC sp_helpdb Frogger:

INPUT

```
EXEC sp_helpdb Frogger
```

OUTPUT

```
name     Db_size   Owner     dbid  Created      status
-------  --------- --------- ----- -----------  ----------
Frogger  30.00 MB  sa        7     Jan 14 1999  no options set

Name        Fileid Filename                                   Filegroup
----------- ------ ------------------------------------------ ---------
FroggerData 1      D:\PROGRAM FILES\MSSQL\data\FroggerData.mdf PRIMARY
FroggerLog  2      D:\PROGRAM FILES\MSSQL\data\FroggerLog.ldf  NULL

/...size      maxsize     growth     Usage
/...-----     ---------   -------    -----
/...20480 KB  102400 KB   10240 KB   Data only
/...10240 KB  15360 KB    1024 KB    Log only
```

Notice that FroggerData2 is no longer associated with the Frogger database. If you use Explorer and navigate to your ...\DATA folder, you will find that the FroggerData2.ndf file has also been removed from your system.

4

Renaming a Database

Sometimes you might want to rename a database. You might do so because of an organizational change, such as merging the accounting and finance departments, or you might be moving a development database into the production environment. For whatever reason you want to change your database name, doing so is relatively straightforward.

To rename a database, you must execute the sp_renamedb system stored procedure:

```
EXEC sp_renamedb 'old_name', 'new_name'
```

Keep these restrictions in mind when you rename a database:

- You must be a member of the sysadmin fixed server role to rename a database.
- Some SQL scripts might depend on the database name to run correctly. You might want to check your database for them.
- The database must be in single-user mode.

- The database filenames and filegroup names aren't affected by a name change.
- You must be in the master database to execute the `sp_renamedb` system stored procedure.

In this example, you will rename the Frogger database to TsingWa (*Tsing Wa* is Chinese for frog):

INPUT
```
USE master
GO
EXEC sp_dboption Frogger, 'Single User', True
EXEC sp_renamedb 'Frogger', 'TsingWa'
EXEC sp_dboption TsingWa, 'Single User', False
GO
```

OUTPUT
```
sp_dboption command succeeded
The database name 'TsingWa' has been set.
sp_dboption command succeeded
```

To verify that the name has been changed, run `sp_helpdb`:

INPUT/OUTPUT
```
EXEC sp_helpdb

name      db_size owner dbid created     status
--------- ------- ----- ---- ----------- ------
Croak      6.00 MB sa    9    Jan 14 2000 no options set
Leap      14.00 MB sa    8    Jan 14 2000 no options set
master     9.25 MB sa    1    Nov 13 1999 trunc. log on chkpt.
model      1.50 MB sa    3    Jan 13 2000 no options set
msdb       8.75 MB sa    4    Jan 13 2000 trunc. log on chkpt.
Northwind  3.94 MB sa    6    Jan 13 2000 select into/bulkcopy, trunc. log
                                          ➥on chkpt.
pubs       1.74 MB sa    5    Jan 13 2000 trunc. log on chkpt.
tempdb     8.50 MB sa    2    Jan 14 2000 select into/bulkcopy, trunc. log
                                          ➥on chkpt.
TsingWa   30.00 MB sa    7    Jan 14 2000 no options set
```

Working with Database Filegroups

Filegroups enable you to explicitly place database objects such as tables and indexes onto a specific set of database files. Doing so can be useful for administration as well as performance. For example, if you aren't using RAID 5 technology, you can place files in a filegroup onto separate physical disk drives and then place specific tables, indexes, and other database objects onto the files that are members of that filegroup. This approach can improve performance, because reads and writes to the database can be running on separate physical disk drives at the same time. An administrative advantage is that you can back up and restore individual files in a filegroup, or the entire filegroup. For example, if you had a 50GB database spread over five filegroups (10GB each), you could back up a different filegroup every evening rather than the entire database and still maintain recoverability.

SQL Server uses two types of filegroups: `PRIMARY` (the default) and user-defined. The `PRIMARY` filegroup must contain the primary data file and any other files that aren't in another filegroup. You create user-defined filegroups when you alter your database and add files to a specific filegroup.

Keep in mind a few rules when working with filegroups:

- A file can't be a member of more than one filegroup.
- The primary data file must reside in the `PRIMARY` filegroup.
- You can allocate tables, indexes, text, ntext, and image data to a filegroup.

> **Note**
> The terms *ntext*, *nchar*, and *nvarchar* refer to Unicode data types. Unicode uses multiple bytes (usually 2) to represent each character displayed, whereas ASCII (char, varchar, and text) uses only 1 byte to store each character. You will learn more about data types on Day 9.

- All system files must reside in the `PRIMARY` filegroup on the primary file.
- If the `PRIMARY` filegroup runs out of space, new data pages aren't automatically allocated to the user-defined filegroups.

In the following examples, you will create a new filegroup and then add a data file to it. You will then alter your database again, modify the filegroup property, and make it part of the default filegroup. The default filegroup, `PRIMARY`, is created when you create your database. Only one filegroup can be the default in your database. When you mark a new filegroup as the default filegroup, new files added to the database are placed there if you don't specify `PRIMARY`. You will finish the examples by removing the filegroup.

To create a new filegroup, run the following:

```
ALTER DATABASE Leap
ADD FILEGROUP LeapGroup1
GO
```

```
The command(s) completed successfully
```

To verify that the filegroup is part of the Leap database, run the following procedure:

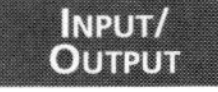

```
use Leap
GO
EXEC sp_helpfilegroup
```

```
Groupname           Groupid     Filecount
-----------         -------     ---------
PRIMARY             1             2
LeapGroup1          2             0
```

Now alter the database, and add a new file to the filegroup:

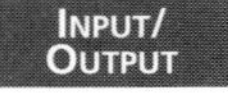

```
ALTER DATABASE Leap
ADD FILE
(Name = LeapDataG1,
 FILENAME =
     'D:\PROGRAM FILES\Microsoft SQL Server\MSSQL\DATA\LeapDataG1.ndf',
 SIZE = 2)
TO FILEGROUP LeapGroup1
GO
```

```
Extending database by 2.00 MB on disk 'LeapDataG1'.
```

Rerun the `sp_helpfilegroup` stored procedure again. You should have something similar to this:

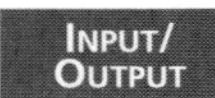

```
USE Leap
GO
EXEC sp_helpfilegroup
```

```
Groupname       Groupid        Filecount
----------      --------       ---------
PRIMARY           1              2
LeapGroup1        2              1
```

You can make the user-defined filegroup `LeapGroup1` part of the default filegroup by modifying its filegroup property. You can also mark the filegroup as `READONLY` or `READWRITE`. See the SQL Server Books Online for more information on `READONLY` and `READWRITE` options.

To mark your new filegroup as the default filegroup, run the following:

```
USE Leap
GO
ALTER DATABASE Leap
MODIFY FILEGROUP LeapGroup1 DEFAULT
```

```
The filegroup property 'DEFAULT' has been set.
```

To test your new default filegroup, add a new data file without specifying a filegroup:

INPUT/OUTPUT

```
USE Leap
GO
ALTER DATABASE Leap
ADD FILE
(NAME = LeapDataTest,
     FILENAME = 'D:\PROGRAM FILES\Microsoft SQL Server\MSSQL\DATA\
     ➥LeapDataTest.ndf',
 SIZE = 2)
GO
```

```
Extending database by 2.00 MB on disk 'LeapDataTest'.
```

To view which files reside in which groups, run the `sp_helpfile` stored procedure.

To remove a filegroup, first make the default filegroup the `PRIMARY` filegroup. Then empty the files in the old filegroup. After you empty the files, you can safely remove the files and then the filegroup, as in this example:

INPUT

```
USE Leap
GO

ALTER DATABASE Leap
MODIFY FILEGROUP [PRIMARY] DEFAULT
GO

ALTER DATABASE Leap
REMOVE FILE LeapDataG1
Go

ALTER DATABASE Leap
REMOVE FILE LeapDataTest
GO

ALTER DATABASE Leap
REMOVE FILEGROUP LeapGroup1
GO
```


You should see messages to the effect that your filegroup `LeapDataG1` and the files contained in that filegroup are also deleted. You can rerun `sp_helpfile` to verify that the filegroup and the files have been successfully removed.

You can also accomplish this result through the SQL Server Enterprise Manager in much the same way that you created files. Follow these steps to create a new database file and add it to a new filegroup:

1. Drill down to the Croak database, and open its property sheet to the Data Files tab.
2. To create a filegroup and add a file to it, click the empty box below `CroakData2`, and add `CroakDataG1`.

3. Fill in the location as `D:\Program Files\Microsoft SQL Server\MSSQL\Data\CroakDataG1.ndf`.
4. In the Space Allocated (MB) column, type **1**.
5. In the Filegroup box, add `CroakGroup1`, as shown in Figure 4.12.

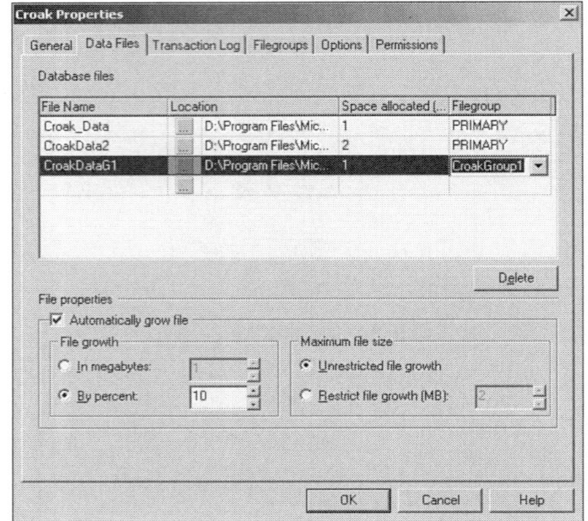

FIGURE 4.12
Select the filegroup in the properties for the database.

6. Click OK when you are finished.
7. To verify, open the property sheet again for the Croak database, and click the Filegroups tab. You should see `CroakGroup1` listed as well as `Primary`.

This section provides just an overview of what filegroups are and how they are created. Filegroups can be very complex and aren't covered further in this book. For more information on filegroups, look at the SQL Server Books Online or *Microsoft SQL Server 2000 Unleashed*, published by Sams Publishing. After you complete your study with this 21-day book, your skills should be somewhere between intermediate and advanced with SQL Server 2000. To take your SQL Server education further, we strongly suggest that you pick up a copy of the *Unleashed* book.

Removing a Database

Sometimes you might need to remove a database from your system. Perhaps you no longer need the database. In any event, removing a database from SQL Server is relatively straightforward. As you might have already guessed, you can remove it from both the SQL Server Enterprise Manager and through Transact-SQL.

Before you actually drop a database, keep in mind a few things:

- Dropping a database removes the database information from the system tables and removes the data and log files from the system.
- A dropped database can be re-created only by restoring it with a backup.
- No users can be in the database at the time you drop it.
- You must be a member of the db_owner database role (or the sysadmin server role) to drop your database.
- You must be in the master database when you issue the `DROP DATABASE` statement.

SYNTAX

Now look at the `DROP DATABASE` syntax and an example:

```
DROP DATABASE database_name, database_name2...
```

The `DROP DATABASE` statement enables you to drop multiple databases at one time. In this example, you will drop both the TsingWa (formerly Frogger) and the Croak databases. Run this code from the SQL Server Query Analyzer:

INPUT

```
USE MASTER
GO
DROP DATABASE TsingWa, Croak
GO
```

OUTPUT

```
Deleting database file
➥'D:\PROGRAM FILES\Microsoft SQL Server\MSSQL\data\Croak_Data.MDF'.
Deleting database file
➥'D:\PROGRAM FILES\ Microsoft SQL Server\MSSQL\data\Croak_Log.LDF'.
Deleting database file
➥'D:\PROGRAM FILES\ Microsoft SQL Server\MSSQL\data\CroakData2.ndf'.
Deleting database file
➥'D:\PROGRAM FILES\ Microsoft SQL Server\MSSQL\data\CroakLog2.ldf'.
Deleting database file
➥'D:\PROGRAM FILES\ Microsoft SQL Server\MSSQL\data\CroakDataG1.NDF'.
Deleting database file
➥'D:\PROGRAM FILES\ Microsoft SQL Server\MSSQL\data\froggerdata.mdf'.
Deleting database file
➥'D:\PROGRAM FILES\ Microsoft SQL Server\MSSQL\data\froggerlog.ldf'.
```

As you can see, all the data files associated with these two databases are deleted, and the databases are removed from the system. To verify, you could run `sp_helpdb`.

You can also use the SQL Server Enterprise Manager to drop a database. Follow these steps:

1. Start the SQL Server Enterprise Manager, and drill down to the Databases folder.
2. Right-click the Leap database, and choose Delete from the context menu.
3. In the Delete Database confirmation box, click Yes.

That's all there is to it. The database is no longer part of your system. The database and log files are also deleted.

Summary

Today you learned how to create, alter, and drop a database as well as how to set different database options. When you create a database, the database is stored in at least two separate files. One file contains the data, system tables, and other database objects, and the other file stores the transaction log. In SQL Server 2000, you can have your database dynamically grow by specifying database or transaction log file growth options. You also learned a little bit about filegroups and how they can be used for administration and performance benefits. The lesson ended with a discussion on dropping a database.

To create a database, you can use the SQL Server Enterprise Manager or the `CREATE DATABASE` statement. When you create a database, you should specify a logical name as well as a physical filename. You should also include the logical and physical names of the transaction log associated with that database. You also learned about file growth options that enable you to specify how a file can be automatically made larger when it runs out of space, how much larger it will grow, as well as a maximum size that it can be grown.

You then learned how to add additional files to your database and transaction log. Included in this was the capability to modify the parameters of existing files. You used the `ALTER DATABASE` statements to do so.

Database options determine how a particular database behaves, whether it's marked for single-user access or whether it's marked for read-only access. To set these options, you can use the Database Properties dialog in Enterprise Manager or the `sp_dboption` stored procedure.

You rename a database by using the `sp_renamedb` stored procedure. Remember that when you rename a database, you must be in the sysadmin user role and the database must be in single-user mode.

You create filegroups either through the SQL Enterprise Manager in the Database Properties dialog or through the `ALTER DATABASE` statements. With a filegroup, you can add data files that can have tables and indexes explicitly placed into them. Adding data files can benefit performance and administration.

The lesson concluded with a look at removing a database from the SQL Server. To accomplish this task, you can use the SQL Server Enterprise Manager, right-click the database you want to drop, and choose the Delete context menu item. From the SQL Server Query Analyzer, you must make sure that you are in the master database. When you get there, you can issue the `DROP DATABASE` statement to remove the database information from the system tables and delete the database files from the operating system.

Q&A

Q Will I create a lot of databases in the real world?

A The answer depends on the type of business you're running. In my consulting business, I've found that I don't create many databases. The databases I do create tend to be development databases in which I can store test data and do development work. When that database is ready, I re-create it in the production environment and let it run.

Q Should I use the SQL Server Enterprise Manager or the SQL Server Query Analyzer to create and modify my databases?

A If the database is going into the production environment or might need to be re-created several times, I tend to use the Query Analyzer. This approach is an advantage for me because the Query Analyzer enables me to save my script files for easy reuse. If the database I'm working with is for development and I can quickly and easily re-create it, I will most likely use the Enterprise Manager in those instances.

Q How big should I make my database and transaction logs?

A The initial size of your database should be large enough to hold all the data you are planning to place in it, including the amount of data in each row and the number of rows that will fit on a single data page. Don't forget that indexes can take up a lot of data space as well. You will learn more details about database size on Day 9, when you will learn how much space different data types require and how they are stored. The transaction log size depends on how much change will take place in your database. If your database is read-only, your transaction log can be very small—perhaps 5 percent of the size of your data files. If your database will be undergoing many updates, deletes, and inserts, you might want to make a larger transaction log. I suggest a log in the vicinity of 25 percent to 30 percent of the total size of your data files. For normal database usage, I recommend a log size somewhere between 10 percent and 15 percent of data file size.

Q Should I have a bunch of small data files in my database or just a few large ones?

A The choice is really up to you. Having more data files means more complex administration. With complexity, you do gain certain advantages. For example, rather than back up one huge data file, you can back up several smaller data files.

Q Which database options are changed the most often?

A Again, the answer depends on what you are doing with your database. For example, I have several databases that are loaded with data from a text file generated by an AS400 every night. The quickest way to get those files into the database tables is to set the Select Into/Bulk Copy parameter to True and then run a bulk copy script. Sometimes you will use the DBO Use Only option as well. Throughout this book, you will see examples illustrating when these different options are required.

Q How important are filegroups?

A Filegroups are mainly an optimization tool. Most databases run just as well without any additional user-defined filegroups.

Q Why would I want to remove a database, and how often does that occur?

A You can probably think of many reasons to drop a database from the system. I can think of all kinds of scenarios. The two most common reasons I have removed databases are to get rid of test/development databases and to remove corrupted databases so that I can re-create them.

Q Should I use the autogrowth feature or disable it?

A The autogrowth feature is one of SQL Server 2000's greatest strengths. It allows for dynamic sizing of your database with very little overhead. If you decide to use autogrowth, I suggest that you also specify the maximum size to which your database can grow.

Workshop

This section provides quiz questions to help you solidify your understanding of the concepts presented today. In addition to the quiz questions, exercises are provided to let you practice what you have learned today. Try to understand the quiz and exercise answers before continuing to tomorrow's lesson. Answers are provided in Appendix A, "Answers to Quiz Questions."

Quiz

1. What is the SQL code needed to create the following database?

   Database: Accounting

   FileSize: 20MB with a maximum of 40MB growing by 2MB

   LogSize: 5MB with a maximum of 10MB growing by 1MB

2. What does the following code do?

```
ALTER DATABASE Test
ADD FILE
```

```
(NAME = TestData2,
 FILENAME =
 'C:\Program Files\Microsoft SQL Server\MSSQL\data\TestData2.ndf',
SIZE = 10)
```

3. What's the code used to drop the following four databases: Von, Ron, Don, and Christina?

Exercises

This exercise is only one question long with several different pieces. The next piece of the exercise requires that you successfully complete the previous pieces. Please read the entire set of instructions for each step before attempting the next step.

1. Create a new database called Frog with the following characteristics:
    - Two data files named `FrogData1` and `FrogData2`. These data files should be 3MB at initial creation. The data files should be able to grow to a maximum size of 20MB, each growing 2MB each time.
    - Two log files named `FrogLog1` and `FrogLog2`. These log files should be 1MB each at initial creation. The maximum size of the log files should be 5MB each.
    - Use the default growth increment.
2. Add an additional data file named `FrogData3` with default properties for all other values.
3. Shrink the database by 20 percent.
4. Empty the `FrogLog2` log file.
5. Remove the `FrogLog2` file.
6. Rename the database to TreeFrog.
7. Drop the database.

WEEK 1

DAY 5

Setting Up Login and User Security

Yesterday you examined how to create databases, along with their files. You also learned how and when to use file groups with SQL Server 2000. You will rarely need to use file groups, but it's good to understand the basics of their operation. Everything you do in SQL Server is authenticated, including when you created the databases and files yesterday. Understanding SQL Server security is critical to the successful operation of your SQL Server. In today's lesson, you examine how SQL Server authenticates connections to the SQL Server and to individual databases, and you learn how Windows 2000 authentication works. The Windows 98 platform doesn't have all the security mechanisms available to Windows 2000 users, so a brief examination of the differences is provided. You'll examine permissions on individual objects within each database on Day 6, "Establishing Database Permissions."

The SQL Server Security Access Model

Connecting to SQL Server 2000 so far has been relatively easy. You've been using SQL Server Mixed Mode Authentication Security (which you overrode to select during setup) and logging in with your Windows login credentials as a member of your local administrators group. As you connect, several things are happening that might not be obvious at first.

When you are running SQL Server under Windows 2000, security is checked in three different places as you attempt to connect to SQL Server 2000 (see Figure 5.1). You might be validated by Windows 2000, SQL Server itself (in the form of a SQL Server login), and then at the individual database level (in the form of a database username).

> Having a login doesn't say anything about which databases you can access; only a database username sets that policy. Also, you haven't actually attempted to access any database objects yet; that requires permissions, which you'll examine in tomorrow's lesson.

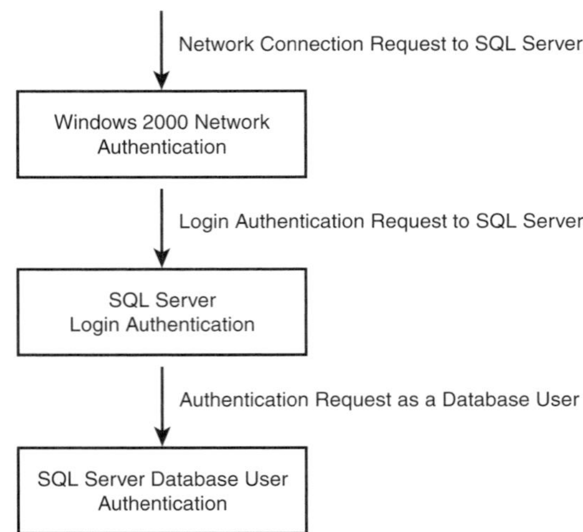

FIGURE 5.1
Network and SQL Server security authentication layers.

Windows Authentication

When you connect from your client computer to a Windows NT/2000 computer running SQL Server 2000, Windows might require validation of your network connection. Whether it does depends on your SQL Server network library. If you are using Named

Pipes or Multiprotocol as your SQL Server network library, you must be validated as an authorized Windows 2000 connection before you are allowed to talk to SQL Server.

As you can see in Figure 5.2, both Named Pipes and Multiprotocol pass through the Windows 2000 Server service, which performs network validation of a user's connection request. Hence, you must have a valid set of Windows 2000 security credentials to connect to the Windows 2000 server computer. Because the Transmission Control Protocol/Internet Protocol (TCP/IP) Sockets network library doesn't go through the Server service, you don't need a valid Windows account to connect to SQL Server 2000. Starting in SQL Server 2000 (as noted earlier in the week), TCP/IP Sockets is the default network library, so this issue isn't as critical as it was if you're connecting to previous releases. However, if you have clients with SQL Server 7.0 (or earlier) client-side software on their computers, they probably are still defaulting to Named Pipes as their network library.

FIGURE 5.2
SQL Server network communications.

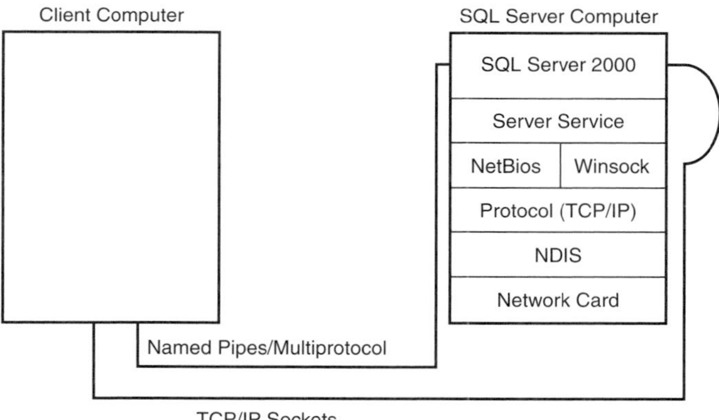

5

Note

Windows 98/ME doesn't authenticate network connections in the same way as Windows NT/2000, so security checks start at the SQL Server login stage for SQL Servers running on a Windows 9*x* computer. Also, Windows 9*x* doesn't support running Named Pipes for server applications, so you can't connect to a Windows 9*x* server by using that protocol.

Note

Understanding this security architecture can be useful when you're troubleshooting. If you get the infamous `Specified SQL Server Not Found` message, perhaps you are being denied permission to connect to the Windows

2000 computer on which SQL Server is installed. To see whether this is the problem, create a share on the SQL Server computer, and attempt to connect to the server (or attempt to connect to an existing share if one exists). If you can't connect or are prompted for a user ID/password, you can't connect to SQL Server. To verify for certain that you have this problem, finish the connection to the aforementioned share, and then try to connect again to SQL Server.

If you can then connect, you must modify the security settings on your Windows 2000 computer. You can do so in one of three ways:

- Enable the guest account (not recommended). If you enable the guest account, you compromise Windows 2000 security to some extent. To keep your system secure, create an individual account for every user.
- Create a local Windows 2000 account with the Computer Management interface, using the same password as the account you are currently logged in with (a last resort).
- Have your server join a domain that's either a member of or trusts the domain where your network account resides (a better option), or that's within the same forest in Active Directory. This option is the best one available. If using this option is possible on your network, you should do so. Consult with your network administrator or refer to a book on Windows 2000 Active Directory to examine Windows 2000 domains, the Active Directory, and security in more detail.

With the switch to the default network library of TCP/IP Sockets, connecting shouldn't be much of a problem, but if for some reason you are forced to use Named Pipes, the preceding rules apply.

SQL Server Login Authentication

You must provide a valid SQL Server login name and password to connect to SQL Server (or have a valid Windows Integrated connection). You will see the details on how to do so shortly. If your login credentials are valid, you are connected to SQL Server. If your credentials aren't valid, you are denied access—even if Windows network authentication (your network connection to the Windows 2000 Server) succeeded.

SQL Server Database Username

To use each database on your system, you must explicitly be allowed to enter each database. You can get access to a database in various ways, all of which will be discussed later today. If you don't have a database username, you are denied access to the database you are attempting to connect to.

Permissions

The final layer of security is permissions. After you successfully log in to SQL Server and switch to a database, you must then be given the explicit right to access database objects (either for read-only or modification). Tomorrow's lesson examines permissions in great detail.

The Security Modes of SQL Server (Including Logins)

SQL Server 2000 provides two different security modes: Windows Integrated Mode and Mixed Mode (both Windows Integrated and SQL Server authentication). The security mode determines whether Windows or both Windows and SQL Server are responsible for validating SQL Server connection requests. This validation is completely independent of the Windows network connection authentication that you examined previously. It's critical that you understand the differences so that you can properly implement SQL Server security.

Mixed Mode Security

In SQL Server 2000 Mixed Mode security, a user can connect to SQL Server using either Windows Integrated Mode or SQL Server Authentication Mode. Mixed Mode is the best selection for backward compatibility, and it provides the greatest amount of connectivity with non-Windows–networked computers, such as Novell NetWare users. To understand both of these authentication modes, you must examine them closely. It's easiest to start with an understanding of SQL Server Authentication Mode, which, for historical reasons, has been the way SQL Server connectivity was provided.

5

SQL Server Authentication Mode

SQL Server Authentication Mode is the mode in which SQL Server accepts a login ID and password from a user and validates the credentials, without any help from Windows. This method is always used on a Windows 9*x* computer and is optional on a Windows 2000 computer. This mode isn't as secure as Windows Integrated Mode and isn't recommended for any SQL Server storing sensitive information. Information about logins is kept inside SQL Server (in the `master` database, in the `sysxlogins` system table). Releases of SQL Server before SQL Server 7.0 used a mode of SQL Server authentication called Standard Security, which is equivalent to SQL Server Authentication Mode. So, if you see any documentation that uses the old term, don't be confused; just map it to the new terminology.

If you've connected using the login, you've been using SQL Server Authentication Mode. Therefore, the `sysxlogins` system table contains an entry for the sa login ID, as well as a password if you've assigned one (our setup set the password to `password`). After you install SQL Server 2000, only the sa standard SQL Server login exists. On a Windows 2000 computer, the local administrators group is also added as the equivalent of sa (as members of the sysadmin security role).

> The sa login is added by default even if you accept the default installation and are in Windows Integrated Mode. However, you won't be able to actually connect unless you're in Windows Integrated mode.

Passwords

SQL Server Authentication Mode login passwords are kept in the password column of the `sysxlogins` table in the `master` database. To look at the entries in the `sysxlogins` table, start the SQL Server Query Analyzer, and run this query (you must be logged in as a member of the sysadmin role, explained later, to run it):

INPUT

```
SELECT  substring(name,1,25) AS name,
        substring(password,1,20) as password, language
        FROM sysxlogins
```

OUTPUT

```
name                    password                              language
----------------------- ------------------------------------- ----------
BUILTIN\Administrators  NULL                                  us_english
RHOME\SQLService        NULL                                  us_english
sa                      0x2131214A212C312939442439285B585D    NULL
NULL                    NULL                                  NULL
(4 row(s) affected)
```

> The row in the preceding result set for the BUILTIN\Administrators Windows 2000 group, as well as the SQL Server service account (SQLService), isn't present on a Windows *9x* SQL Server installation, as mentioned earlier.

The first row in the preceding output represents the local Windows administrators group; you'll examine Windows Integrated security in the following text. The next row represents the service account you selected for the SQL Server services during setup. The sa login ID, shown next, is installed with the password you selected during setup—in our case, `password`, represented by the encrypted text here. All SQL Server authenticated logins and passwords are kept in this system table. If the password is null, you see the `NULL` keyword in the password column. If a password is anything other than null, it is stored as encrypted text, and you see a hexadecimal representation of the encrypted text (as shown for sa here). For the purposes of comparison, it's safe to think of null as blank in the context of security logins.

Passwords that can be viewed with a query might seem a bit disconcerting to you at first. You need to consider a few facts, however, before worrying too much:

- Only a member of the sysadmin role (including the sa login) can view the password column. No other login or user can view it unless you explicitly give her the right to do so (which you'll learn how to do on Day 6).
- The encryption algorithm is one way. When a password is encrypted, it can't be decrypted. When you log in, the password you provide is encrypted and then compared to the encrypted password in the `sysxlogins` table. If they match, access is granted to the server. If they don't match, you get the `Login Failed` error message and can't connect. Also, if you're using a Windows Integrated security login, no passwords are ever stored in SQL Server.

> If you are concerned about security, particularly with passwords, the best solution is to use Windows Authentication.

Administering SQL Server Authentication Mode Logins

The first step in setting up your server for access is to create logins. You can add logins by using the `sp_addlogin` system stored procedure (as follows) or the SQL Server Enterprise Manager. Note again that if you're using Windows 2000, Windows Integrated Mode is the preferred method of security administration and will be examined later today.

5

SYNTAX

```
sp_addlogin [@loginame =] 'login' [,[@passwd =] 'password'
[,[@defdb =] 'database' [,[@deflanguage =] 'language'
[,[@sid =] 'sid' [,[@encryptopt =] 'encryption_option']]]]]
```

In `sp_addlogin`,

- *`login`* is the name you want the user to use when logging in. This name must be a valid SQL Server identifier (beginning with a letter or the characters `#`, `@`, or _, and the rest of the characters can be these characters or letters plus numbers—up to 128 Unicode characters).
- *`password`* is the password for this login. The password is null if you don't choose one at this time.
- *`database`* is the default database you want the user to be put into when he logs in. If you don't specify this parameter, the default database is set to `master`.

- *language* is the default language to be used for this user when she logs in. The default language is US_English if you don't specify this parameter.
- *sid* is the security identifier you specify for a user (this option isn't recommended since it's primarily used for advanced options importing logins).
- You can use the *encryption_option* to turn off password encryption (mentioned earlier). This feature allows you to extract an encrypted password from an earlier version of SQL Server and insert it directly into SQL Server 2000 so that a user's login password will work against this SQL Server as well. To turn off encryption, use the literal string skip_encryption here.

To add a login to your server, open the SQL Server Query Analyzer and log in. Run the following Transact-SQL (T-SQL) command:

INPUT
```
EXEC sp_addlogin 'yourname', 'yourpassword'
```

Note

I ran exec sp_addlogin 'richard', 'password'. If you want to follow along with exactly what's in this book, you should use this login name and password. Otherwise, whenever you see richard for a login, substitute your name.

If you rerun the query you ran earlier against the sysxlogins table, you see a new row with your name and an encrypted password. If you create a new connection to SQL Server, you can log in with the name and password you have just added.

The next thing you might want to do is change your password. You can do so either through the SQL Server Enterprise Manager or by using the sp_password system stored procedure:

SYNTAX
```
sp_password [[@old =] 'old',] {[@new =] 'new'}
[,[@loginame =] 'login']
```

In this procedure syntax,

- *old* is your old password.
- *new* is your new password.
- For *loginname*, if you are logged in as a member of either the sysadmin or securityadmin roles, you can change anyone's password. In fact, you don't need to know a person's old password; you can simply script the old password as null.

Tip

> One minor point that we'll mention again later is that securityadmin role members can change anyone's password *except* the sysadmin role member's passwords. Sysadmin role members really can change anyone's password, without exception.

An example of the `sp_password` system stored procedure looks like this:

```
EXEC sp_password NULL, 'newpass', 'richard'
```

Although you don't know Richard's old password, you can change it, because you're the system administrator. As a security precaution, ordinary users can't do this and must know their old password before they are allowed to change to a new password. This procedure shouldn't be hard because they have to log in first to run this command.

Changing your passwords regularly is a very good idea. Unfortunately, SQL Server 2000 doesn't have any way to enforce password restrictions and other security precautions. This is one reason you might choose to implement integrated security. Windows 2000 can specify minimum password lengths, frequency of change, and minimal password complexity rules.

You also might like to change the default database or the default language that a user is logged in with. You can do so from the SQL Server Enterprise Manager or by using the `sp_defaultdb` and `sp_defaultlanguage` system stored procedures:

SYNTAX

```
sp_defaultdb loginname, defdb
sp_defaultlanguage loginname [, language]
```

The parameters are the same as discussed previously. These options simply allow you to change various fields in the `sysxlogins` table (the default database or the default language).

5

You can use two additional system stored procedures to manage logins: `sp_helplogins` and `sp_droplogin`. The system stored procedure `sp_helplogins` enables you to get a report on the logins that have been created on your server. Figure 5.3 shows a sample run of this stored procedure.

In Figure 5.3, notice that the column `SID` shows up again; it was referenced earlier for `sp_addlogin`. The SID (security identifier) is the way SQL Server keeps track of logins and users within SQL Server. For SQL Server authenticated logins, it's a 16-byte binary value generated by SQL Server. For Windows Integrated users (examined shortly), it's the user's globally unique network identification number, which identifies the user on the Windows network.

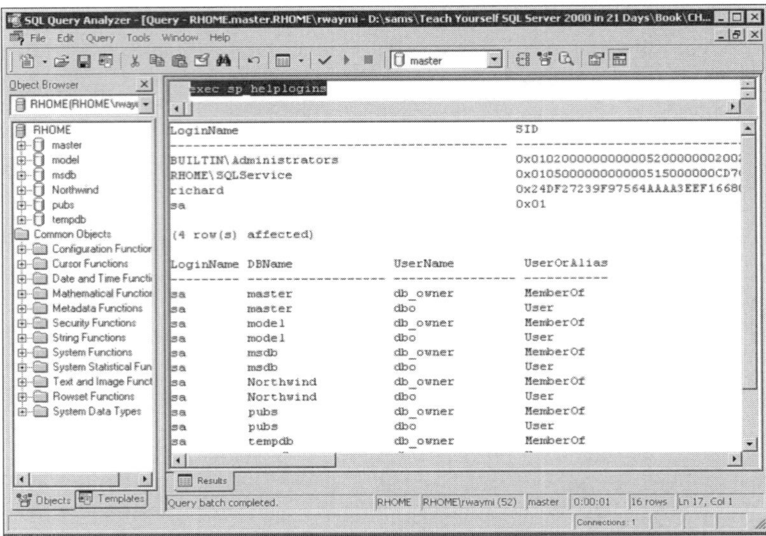

FIGURE 5.3
The results of `sp_helplogins`.

The system stored procedure `sp_droplogin` removes the login entry from the `sysxlogins` table. After an entry is deleted, the user can no longer log in to SQL Server:

SYNTAX

```
sp_droplogin login
```

For the `sp_droplogin` stored procedure, *`login`* has the same meaning as it does for each of these stored procedures.

At this point, you've learned how to accomplish SQL Server Authentication Mode login management by using the various system stored procedures. You will see how to manage security with the SQL Server Enterprise Manager later today.

Windows Authentication Mode in Mixed Security

NEW TERM Windows Authentication Mode is the other option in Mixed Mode security, but you will examine it later in the "Windows Authentication Mode" section, because these modes are identical in functionality and administration. One terminology note is in order before you examine Windows connections. A connection made via Windows authentication is said to be a *trusted connection*. So, when you see the term *trusted connection*, think of it as a Windows authenticated connection, which has been validated by either Windows NT or Windows 2000.

Windows Authentication Mode

In Windows Authentication Mode security, after you connect to SQL Server over the network, you must present SQL Server with your Windows security credentials (known as your *access token*). You build these credentials in the process of logging in to a Windows 2000 network. These security credentials are silently passed for you, so you don't need to do anything special to have your security passed. You can grant access to SQL Server via Windows 2000 security accounts directly, or indirectly via Windows 2000 groups.

The best part about Windows Authentication Mode is that users don't have to worry about logging in separately to SQL Server. This capability complies with the concept that users should have to log in to the network only once and remember only a single password. Not only that, but you also can take advantage of most of your users likely already having Windows login accounts, thus reducing the administrative overhead of managing login accounts for your SQL Server.

Setting Up Windows 2000 Groups and Users

The first step to configuring Windows Authentication Mode security isn't a SQL Server step at all—it's a visit to the Computer Management utility (or User Manager on Windows NT computers). First, create Windows 2000 groups for users, create the users (if they don't already exist) and add them to the new groups you just created, and then assign them permissions to log in to SQL Server. To do so, select Start, Programs, Administrative Tools, Computer Management to start the Computer Management console (if you're managing a domain, you use the Active Directory Users and Computers management console instead). Expand the Local Users and Groups option, as shown in Figure 5.4.

FIGURE 5.4
Computer Management: Local Users and Groups.

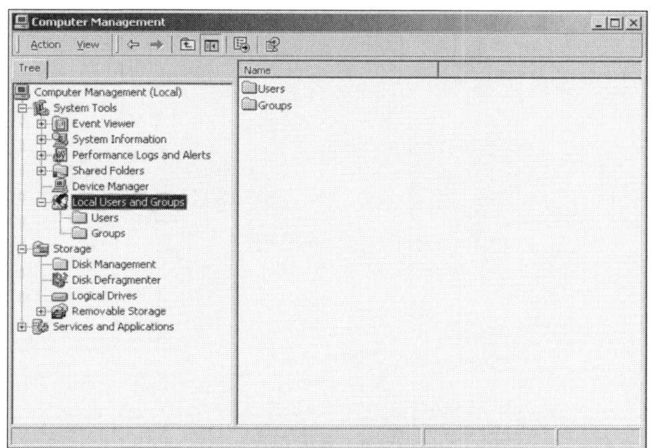

Of course, the Computer Management tool doesn't apply to Windows 9*x* installations. Also, on Windows NT computers, the application is named User Manager or User Manager for Domains.

You must add new local groups to the Windows security accounts manager (SAM) database of the machine on which SQL Server is running. It's a Windows 2000 internal database, not a SQL Server database. If you want to control a remote computer rather than the computer you are currently working on, simply right-click Computer Management (Local), select Connect to Another Computer, and then enter the name of the computer you want to administer. If you want to administer an Active Directory Domain, you must use the Active Directory toolset, as mentioned earlier.

As with most Windows 2000–related operations in the book, you must be logged in to the computer as a member of the local administrators group, or you can't perform the following operations.

Now create three new local groups to use with SQL Server: one group to contain users who can log in as SQL Server administrators (those Windows 2000 users who can fully administer SQL Server), another group for Sales people, and another for Marketing users. You can then assign users to each group as you want. You can determine what the users can do after they're logged in when you examine this topic later today and on Day 6.

The first group is for administrative access to SQL Server. Highlight the Groups folder, right-click it, and then select New Group. Fill in the Group Name and Description fields, as shown in Figure 5.5.

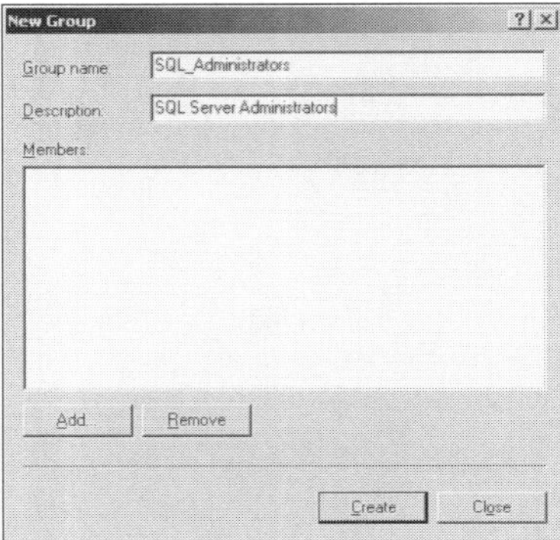

FIGURE 5.5

Adding a new local group for Windows 2000 security.

Now put your account into the group, as shown in Figure 5.6. Click the Add button to see a list of accounts you can add. The list is made up of the global groups and accounts from your default domain, or just the accounts if your SQL Server computer isn't a member of a domain.

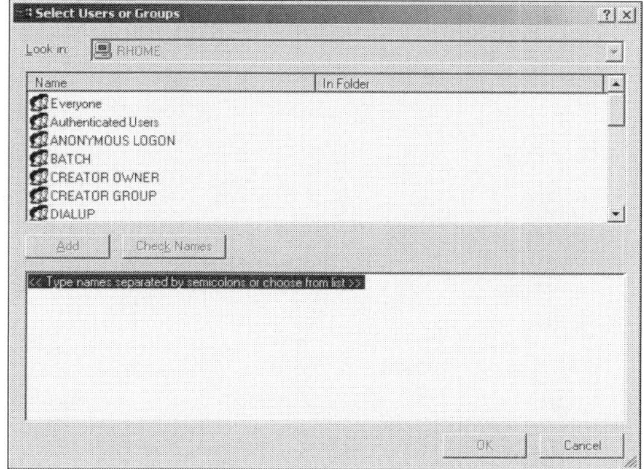

FIGURE 5.6
The Select Users or Groups dialog.

If you don't see your computer name in the List Names From pane, select it from the drop-down list. You then see your computer name, your default domain, and any trusted domains in the dialog. If you are using a domain, select your domain account to add to the list rather than create and add a duplicate local Windows 2000 account. Now that you're looking at the right list, add your username to the group by selecting your account name, clicking Add, and then clicking OK.

Note

You should also add the account you used for the SQL Server Agent service during setup (SQLService if you followed the setup on Day 2, "Installing Microsoft SQL Server 2000"). The SQL Server Agent service requires that it make a trusted connection to SQL Server to function properly. If you don't add the account, and the SQL Server Agent can't make a trusted connection to SQL Server, all functionality provided by that service fails, including jobs, alerts, and replication.

If you didn't use an account for the service (you selected the LocalSystem account option), you don't need to do anything special for that account here. You also don't need to do anything special if you choose to keep Windows 2000 administrators as SQL Server Administrators (the default configuration).

The completed group should look something like Figure 5.7.

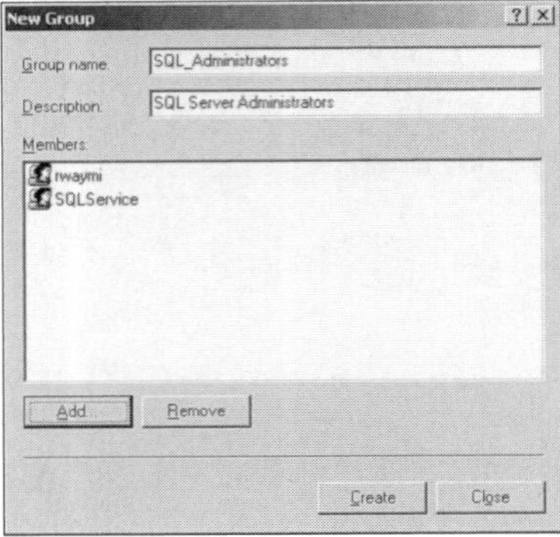

FIGURE 5.7

The completed New Group dialog.

Click Create, and then repeat the process to create a group called Sales. Then do it again to create the group Marketing. This time, however, add a different user or set of users. On my system, I set up three extra users—Ann, Bob, and Cat—for this purpose. I put Ann and Bob in Sales, and I put Bob and Cat in Marketing. I intentionally added Bob to both groups. If you've never added a user to a group in Windows 2000, highlight the group, right-click, select Add to Group, click Add as before, and select the users to add to the group. If you create the users now, remember to uncheck the User Must Change Password at Next Login option. I gave all users the same password, `password`.

> **Note:** If you're in a hurry, you can run a script to add the users, groups, and the membership of the users and groups. On the Sams Publishing Web site, double-click the file *PATH*`\CH05\Add Groups\Users.CMD`. This script adds Ann, Bob, and Cat as local users, as well as creates the groups Sales, Marketing, and SQL_Administrators and sets the membership for each group. It doesn't, however, add your account to the SQL_Administrators group.

Giving Windows 2000 Accounts Permission to Log In to SQL Server

After you set up the users and groups, it's time to grant those groups access to SQL Server. You can do so by using the system stored procedures `sp_grantlogin`, `sp_revokelogin`, and `sp_denylogin`. They function very much like `sp_addlogin` and `sp_droplogin`, which you examined earlier along with SQL Server Authentication Mode.

Give permission for logins to Windows groups first and then only as needed to individual users. This method of granting logins allows you to run the fewest commands and have the lowest administrative overhead, while still allowing individual control of login privileges. To grant permissions to log in, use the `sp_grantlogin` system stored procedure:

SYNTAX

```
sp_grantlogin [@loginame =] 'login'
```

In this syntax, *`login`* is the name of the Windows 2000 group or user to whom you grant the right to log in to SQL Server. The login should be in the form of *`SECURITY_DATABASE`*`\`*`Username`*—for example, `MYDOMAIN\Richard`.

For example, to grant the Sales group permissions to log in to SQL Server, you could run

INPUT

```
Exec sp_grantlogin 'RHOME\Sales'
```

replacing `RHOME` with your computer name (or domain name if you're running SQL Server on a domain controller). You should receive a message similar to this:

OUTPUT

```
Granted login access to 'RHOME\Sales'.
```

Now any Windows 2000 user who's a member of the Sales group can log in to SQL Server. You can test this capability by logging in to Windows 2000 as either Ann or Bob, starting the SQL Server Query Analyzer, and selecting the Windows NT Authentication option to force a trusted connection to SQL Server 2000. In the title bar of the query connection, you see your Windows 2000 username. Notice that you are connected as yourself in Windows 2000, even though the Sales group is the entity actually granted login rights to SQL Server. Connecting this way guarantees an audit trail and allows you much better permissions control later.

Note

> If you can't log in as Ann or Bob and get the message `The local policy of this system does not permit you to log on interactively`, don't panic . ☺. Log in as an administrator on your computer; select Start, Run; and enter **`GPEdit.msc`**. Under Computer Configuration expand the Windows Settings, Security Settings, Local Policies, and User Rights Assignment folders, and select the Log on Locally option. Right-click, select Security, and then click the Add button to add the Sales group to the list. You should see something like Figure 5.8. Click OK, and all users can log in locally to your computer.

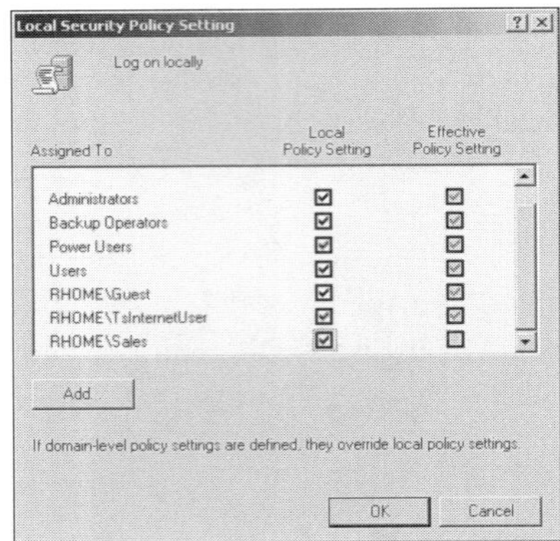

FIGURE 5.8
The Local Policy Settings dialog.

You can also take away a Windows 2000 user's or group's right to log in to SQL Server by using the `sp_revokelogin` system stored procedure:

SYNTAX

```
sp_revokelogin [@loginame =] 'login'
```

In this procedure, *`login`* is the name of the Windows 2000 group or user from which you want to remove the right to log in to SQL Server.

`sp_revokelogin` removes a previously granted login right. So, the following removes the ability of anyone in the Sales group to log in to SQL Server, because the Sales group was previously given this right:

INPUT

```
Exec Sp_revokelogin 'RWHOMENT\Sales'
```

However, the following has no effect because Marketing was not previously granted login rights to SQL Server:

```
Exec sp_revokelogin 'RWHOMENT\Marketing'
```

Also, note that, although you can revoke Ann's right to log in, such as the following, revoking this right doesn't affect any rights she receives from groups:

INPUT

```
Exec sp_revokelogin 'RWHOMENT\Ann'
```

Therefore, if the Sales group has the right to log in, and you've run the preceding statement, it doesn't change Ann's ability to log in to SQL Server.

If you want to specify that anyone in the Sales group can log in except Ann, you must use the `sp_denylogin` system stored procedure:

INPUT
```
sp_denylogin [@loginame =] 'login'
```

In this procedure, *login* is the name of the Windows 2000 group or user from which you want to deny the right to log in to SQL Server.

Try this code as an example (again substituting the correct security database name in place of RHOME):

INPUT
```
Exec sp_grantlogin 'RHOME\Sales'
Exec sp_denylogin 'RHOME\Ann'
```

Now log in to your Windows 2000 system as Ann and attempt to connect to SQL Server. You are denied login permissions. Log in to Windows 2000 as Bob, and connect to SQL Server, and the login works just fine. Ann has been denied permissions, but Bob, as a member of Sales, has been given permission to log in. Deny rights always supersede any other granted rights.

Note

SQL Server 2000 uses the Security Support Provider Interface (SSPI) to call into Windows 2000. Sometimes you might get an error referring to the SSPI context. This message means something went wrong when SQL Server tried to call Windows 2000; typically, it means that your domain controller can't be located.

Setting the Security Mode

So far, you've learned how to add SQL Server Authentication Mode users and Windows 2000 users and groups to SQL Server. However, you must know which security mode to use. To establish which security mode your server is now using, start the SQL Server Enterprise Manager, and right-click your server in the left pane of the tool. Select Properties from the pop-up menu, and click the Security tab.

If you are working on a Windows 2000 computer, you see the dialog shown in Figure 5.9 and can select either Windows NT/2000 Only (the default), or SQL Server and Windows NT/2000. On a Windows 9*x* computer, most of this dialog is grayed out because those systems have no Windows authentication. To change the security setting, simply click the option you want. The change doesn't take effect until you restart the SQL Server service (MSSQLServer for a default instance, MSSQL$*InstanceName* for a named instance).

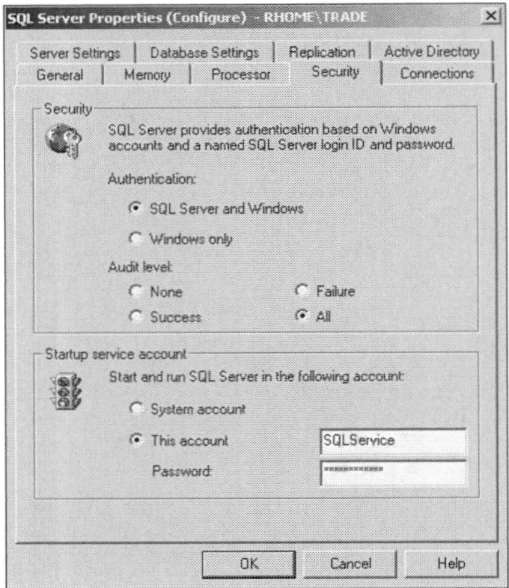

FIGURE 5.9

The security configuration dialog.

> You might want to enable auditing for your server. No auditing is turned on by default. You can audit Failure (failed logins to SQL Server), Success (logins to SQL Server that go through), or both (the All option). I recommend both, as you see in Figure 5.9. You can view these audits in both the SQL Server error log and the Windows NT Event Viewer application. You must stop and restart the SQL Server service for auditing to begin. Note that SQL Server 2000 includes much more extensive security auditing, which we'll examine on Day 20, "Performance Monitoring Basics and Tools," when we examine the SQL Server Profiler Utility in more detail.

The Startup Service Account frame allows you to change the account that SQL Server is using to run the SQL Server service. This option was addressed on Day 2.

After you make any changes in this dialog, you must stop and restart SQL Server for the changes to take effect. Because you are unlikely to make this kind of change more than once, stopping and restarting shouldn't be too big a problem.

Graphically Managed Logins

Now is a great time to examine what you've learned so far today. SQL Server has two kinds of logins:

- Windows NT/2000 logins, either via groups or individual user IDs
- SQL Server logins, stored in the `sysxlogins` system table in the `master` database

Each has its advantages. SQL Server logins can be used on the Windows 9*x* platform and don't require you to have organized Windows 2000 domains on Windows 2000 systems. Windows 2000 logins, however, are preferred if you are already on a properly configured Windows network, because they've already been created and uniquely identify each user in your organization. You've learned how to create each of them and how to allow logins to SQL Server. You did this through the use of system stored procedures such as `sp_addlogin` and `sp_password`. However, an easier way is to use SQL Server Enterprise Manager.

I didn't hold out on showing you SQL Server Enterprise Manager to be mean. It's just that you can create both types of logins easily from a single graphical interface, so you need to understand them both before examining this interface.

Figure 5.10 shows what my system looks like after running the code from earlier in today's lesson. I've granted permissions for the Windows 2000 Sales group to log in to SQL Server and explicitly denied the Windows 2000 user Ann from logging in. The BUILTIN\Administrators Windows 2000 group is added during setup, and the sa login is also created during setup. I've added myself as a standard (SQL Server) login.

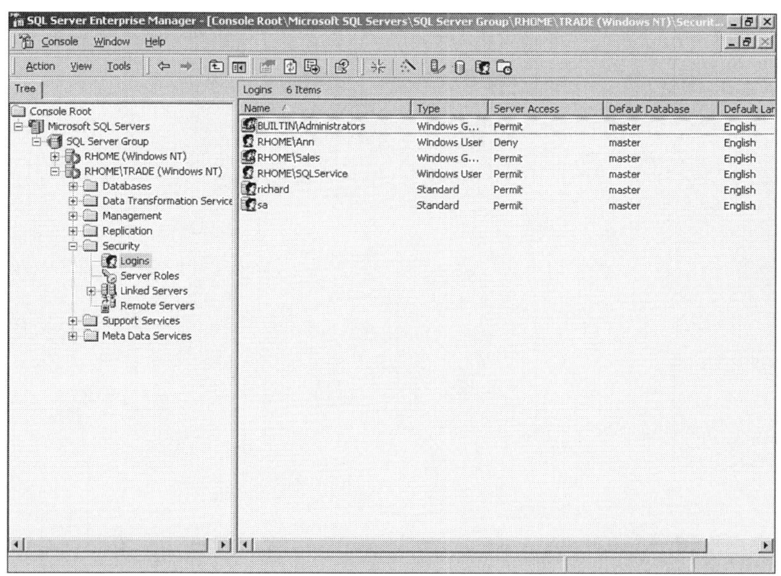

FIGURE 5.10

The logins information in SQL Server Enterprise Manager.

To add the Marketing group as a valid login, right-click anywhere in the right panel of the Enterprise Manager window, and select New Login. You are presented with the dialog in Figure 5.11. Complete the dialog as shown in the figure to add the Marketing group.

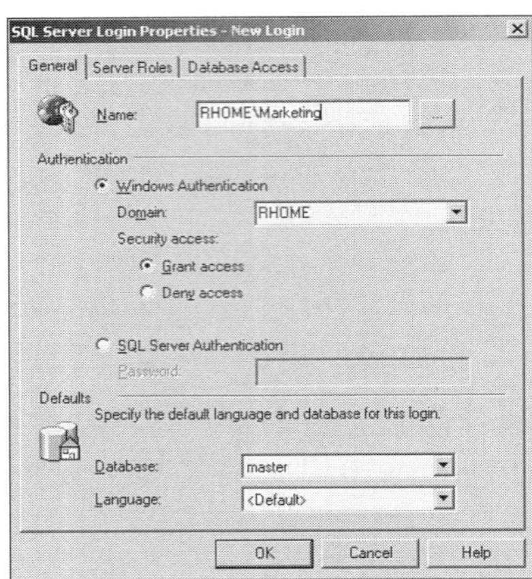

FIGURE 5.11
Adding a Windows 2000 login via Enterprise Manager.

Click OK to finish adding the login, and then do the same to add an account for Bob. (You don't really need to add an account for Bob, because Bob has been able to log in from either the Sales or Marketing groups.) Add a SQL Server login named Don, with a password of `password`. Figure 5.12 shows the configuration dialog. After you click OK, you have to confirm the password you've entered.

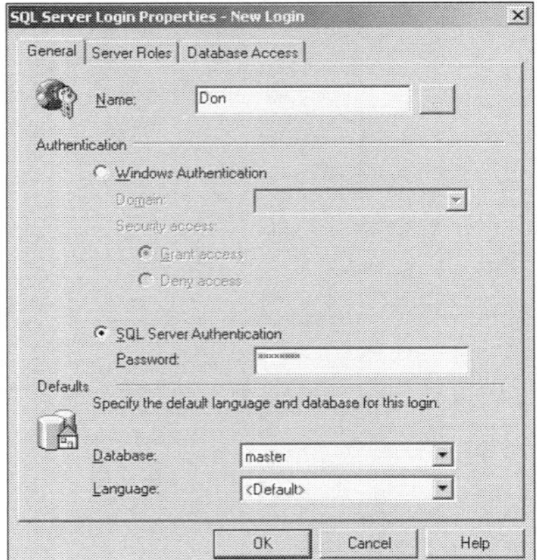

FIGURE 5.12
Adding a SQL Server login via Enterprise Manager.

All you must do to deny someone access is to select Deny Access. Choosing this option makes sense only for Windows 2000 logins. To deny access to a SQL Server login, simply don't create it.

To edit an existing login, right-click the login in the right panel, with the Logins folder highlighted, and select Properties from the pop-up menu. You've noticed by now that you've been working with two other tabs in the dialog: Server Roles and Database Access. They are the next two topics you'll examine.

Database Users

After you configure login security and establish your logins, you can begin to configure access to databases. Having a login to SQL Server doesn't give you access to any databases in the server. For that, you must have a database username.

Each database has a separate access path, which is stored in the `sysusers` system table in each database. Logins are essentially mapped to a username in each database the user needs to access. You can create that mapping or create a database user in a database by using the `sp_grantdbaccess` system stored procedure or the SQL Server Enterprise Manager.

> **Note**
>
> You might also find several system stored procedures to perform similar tasks. They include `sp_adduser`, `sp_dropuser`, `sp_addgroup`, `sp_dropgroup`, and `sp_changegroup`. These legacy system stored procedures are used in SQL Server releases before version 7.0. Although they still work to control SQL Server Authentication login to username mappings, they don't function properly to control Windows NT/2000 Authentication usernames and group names. Therefore, don't use them unless you have a server that has been upgraded from SQL Server 6.5 and were using them before. However, even in this instance, you should change over to the new system stored procedures at your earliest convenience.

Adding a User to a Database

To add a user to a database, run the `sp_grantdbaccess` system stored procedure:

SYNTAX

```
sp_grantdbaccess [@loginname =] 'login' [,[@name_in_db =]
➥'name_in_db'] OUTPUT
```

In this syntax,

- *`login`* is the login name you added earlier (either as a SQL Server login or a Windows NT/2000 login or group).
- *`name_in_db`* is the name you want an individual to have while he is in this database (the username). If you don't specify a name, it's set to the same as the login name.

I recommend that you set the username to the login name at every opportunity so that it's easier to follow security from logins to users in each database. You don't have to, but isn't it a bit confusing to log in as Richard but have a username of Bill in the `sales` database and Johnny in the `pubs` database? Keeping the names the same eliminates confusion (which is in everyone's best interest in a complex product like SQL Server). Of course, none of this is an issue if you use Windows users and groups.

For example, if you want Bob to be able to access the `pubs` database on your server, run

INPUT
```
Use pubs
EXEC sp_grantdbaccess 'RHOME\Bob'
```

In this case, you should get

OUTPUT
```
Granted database access to 'RHOME\Bob'.
```

You can do the same thing with a group:

INPUT
```
EXEC sp_grantdbaccess 'RHOME\Marketing'
```

Again, you should receive a success message. After you add a group, every member of the Windows group can access the database, but only the group has a database user—that is, an entry doesn't exist for every user of the group, but simply the group itself, just as was the case for logins.

To remove someone's database access, you would run the `sp_revokedbaccess` system stored procedure:

SYNTAX

```
sp_revokedbaccess [@name_in_db =] 'name_in_db']
```

In this stored procedure, *`name_in_db`* is the name of the database user to remove.

Only members of the db_accessadmin and db_owner roles (or the sysadmin fixed server role) can run either of these system stored procedures. You'll examine roles later today.

To see which users are in your database and which login they belong to, you can run the `sp_helpuser` system stored procedure:

SYNTAX

```
sp_helpuser [[@name_in_db =] 'username']
```

Here, *`username`* is optional and is either a username or role name.

If you don't specify a username, a report of all users and roles is produced. Otherwise, you get a report for a specific user or role.

When you create a database, one user is already there. One of these users is named dbo (for dataBase owner). The dbo user is mapped to the sa login by default. When you install SQL Server, the sa login is considered the owner of all databases. If another login were to create a database, that login would be the owner of the database. Within a database, there is nothing the dbo user can't do. This user is as powerful as the sysadmin role members within each database. However, only members of the sysadmin fixed server role (discussed later) have certain systemwide privileges.

Note

> In SQL Server 7.0, another user known as INFORMATION_SCHEMA existed by default in each database. This username exists as the owner of several views used to provide system catalog information compliant with the American National Standards Institute (ANSI) specification. In SQL Server 2000, the views owned by INFORMATION_SCHEMA exist only in the `master` database, although if you query them, they always show you information about the database you are currently working in.

Now try to create a user in the `pubs` database. If you've been following along, you should have a login named Don in your SQL Server. You created this user as a SQL Server login earlier today. Start the SQL Server Query Analyzer, and run the following T-SQL statements:

INPUT

```
USE pubs
EXEC sp_grantdbaccess 'Don'
```

This example adds the new user Don to the `pubs` database, mapped back to the login ID of Don in the `sysxlogins` table in the `master` database. You can verify it by running `sp_helpuser` in the `pubs` database (see Figure 5.13).

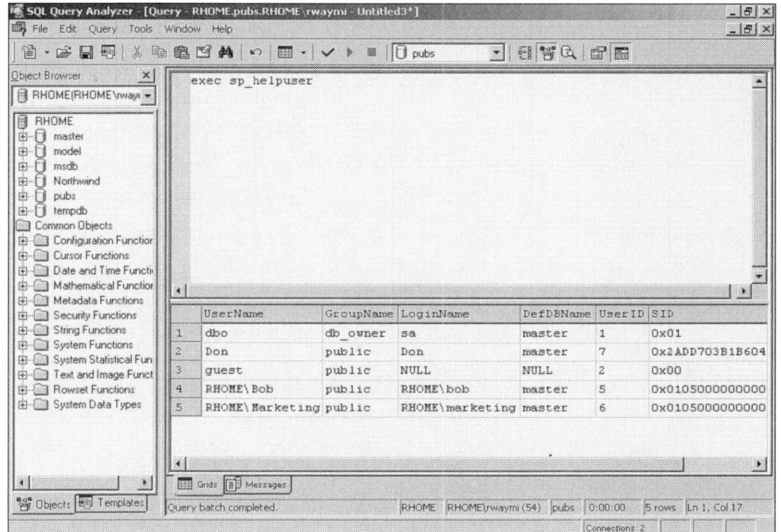

FIGURE 5.13

The results of `sp_helpuser`.

You can see that Don has been added as a user to the database, with a login name of Don. You can probably see why it would be confusing to use different names here. You can also see that the grants you ran earlier for Windows 2000 users and groups are also there, along with dbo and guest.

I said awhile back that a login doesn't allow you to access any databases, and yet when you log in, you can access all the system databases as well as the sample `pubs` and Northwind databases. How is this possible? You can do so because of the guest username.

Running `sp_grantdbaccess 'guest'` in a database adds a special user account known as guest to the database. Notice this guest account in the results of the `sp_helpuser` system stored procedure in Figure 5.13. You can also see that it's not mapped back to a login; it's mapped to a `NULL` login. It's a special user and not subject to normal rules. When a guest user account exists in a database, any login that requests access to the database and doesn't have a username specifically created in the database (either via group membership or an individual account) is allowed in as guest. Hence, during setup, a guest account is built into each default database on your server.

> **Note** You can't remove the guest username from the `master` or `tempdb` database. If you did, where would a user go when she had a login but no specific database access?

The Guest Username

If you log in with a login for which you haven't created a specific username in the `pubs` database, you access the database as the guest username. If you try to access a database in which you don't have a username, and no guest username exists, you get an error message. For example, if you try to use the Northwind database (either by selecting it in the Database text box in the SQL Server Query Analyzer or by running the Transact-SQL command `use Northwind`) after you remove the guest username (with `sp_revokedbaccess`), you receive a message similar to this:

```
Server: Msg 916, Level 14, State 1, Line 1
Server user 'don' is not a valid user in database 'Northwind'.
```

The error reports that your login isn't properly mapped to a user in the Northwind database and implies that no guest account exists. To fix this problem, either add the guest account by running the following, or more likely, add an appropriate login mapping to the database:

INPUT

```
Use Northwind
EXEC sp_grantdbaccess 'guest'
```

SQL Server 7.0 includes a guest account in every database (except `model`) by default, so you don't need to explicitly add the guest user here. However, after you remove it, you can reproduce this issue. If the guest user is in the `model` database, every new database you create will have a guest user.

So far, you've discovered two ways to access a database: by being mapped as a user from a login or by using the guest username. You can also be the dbo, meaning you're the login who actually created the database. Or you might be aliased to another user for historical reasons.

The following section on aliasing is provided strictly for backward compatibility. You shouldn't use aliases in SQL Server 2000. Roles provide a much cleaner solution, as you will see shortly.

Adding an Alias

NEW TERM You can add a *database username alias* by using the `sp_addalias` system-stored procedure. This alias allows a login to impersonate another database user rather than map his login to his own username or group name.

SYNTAX

`sp_addalias` *`login_name`*, *`username`*

In the `sp_addalias` syntax,

- *`login_name`* is the login name of the user you want to map.
- *`username`* is the database user whom you want to impersonate.

Aliasing was created to help streamline security in a database. You can alias as many logins as you want to a single username in a database. If a login already has a username mapped in the database, that login can't also be aliased to a user. Again, roles provide a much cleaner and better security model.

This database access option is typically used to map logins to the dbo user in a database. However, there can be only one "real" database owner at any time. Because most companies have more than one administrator, they might want more than one user to act as owner of the database. Roles take care of this problem.

If you should change your mind and decide to drop the alias, you can do so by using the sp_dropalias system stored procedure:

SYNTAX

```
sp_dropalias login_name
```

In this syntax, *login_name* is the login name of the user.

Aliases should exist only in a database that was upgraded from SQL Server 6.5 to SQL Server 2000 and should be removed as time and testing permit, because they won't likely be supported in future releases of Microsoft SQL Server.

Changing the Database Owner

You might want to change the owner of an existing database to assign responsibility for a database to a particular database administrator (DBA). If you want to make this change, the login must not exist in the database as a username.

To change the owner, run the sp_changedbowner system stored procedure:

SYNTAX

```
sp_changedbowner [@loginame =] 'login' [,[@map =] remap_alias_flag]
```

In this syntax,

- *login* is the SQL Server login ID to be mapped.
- *remap_alias_flag* is an optional parameter, which, if you don't provide it, causes all users aliased as dbo to be dropped when you change the database owner. If you specify the TRUE parameter, all those who are currently aliased to the old dbo are aliased to the new dbo.

You have examined four distinct ways to access a database after you successfully log in to SQL Server. They are checked in the following order:

- **sa**—The sa (or any member of the sysadmin server role) can always access a database and always appears to be dbo, even when you've assigned database ownership to another login with sp_changedbowner.
- **Database username**—The "normal" way to access a database is to use a username mapped to a SQL Server login ID (either a Windows 2000 username or group name). This also applies to Windows 2000 groups to which you might have granted access rights.
- **Alias**—You can be aliased to a valid database user. Inside the database, you emulate the other user in terms of permissions and privileges.
- **Guest**—If all other checks fail, SQL Server checks whether a guest account exists in the sysusers database system table. If one exists, access is granted as guest. Otherwise, access is denied.

Note

> You might find that Windows NT/2000 accounts aren't mapped back to logins. If a Windows user gets login and database access via membership in a Windows 2000 group, further mappings with an individual login would be redundant. You won't typically create this situation, but SQL Server might. For example, suppose you add a Windows 2000 group to a database, and then a user creates a table. To keep track of who owns the table, SQL Server creates a new user for the Windows 2000 user; but the user that SQL Server creates is only for tracking purposes and doesn't actually grant database access.

Roles

We've put off talking about roles until now because they tie everything else together in SQL Server 2000. You can think of roles as SQL Server groups. We don't use the term *groups* so that we won't confuse these options in SQL Server with Windows NT/2000 groups.

SQL Server roles allow you to combine database usernames into groupings. It doesn't matter whether the database usernames were derived from Windows 2000 groups, Windows 2000 users, or SQL Server logins. Roles can even contain other roles as members.

The Public Role

In each database, SQL Server 2000 contains one built-in role named public. All users, groups, and roles are members of the public role and can't be removed. Think of the public role as similar to the Everyone group from Windows 2000 (if you want to get technical, it's actually like the Authenticated Users group, because you've been validated by SQL Server first). Referring to all users without having to name them explicitly is a convenient shortcut. You'll see this approach used on Day 6's discussion of permissions. In Figure 5.13, you saw the role name of public displayed for most users.

Serverwide Roles

One point that keeps coming up in today's lesson is that the sa login is all-powerful and can do anything she wants on an instance of SQL Server. Although this is true, it's really because the sa login is a member of the serverwide role named sysadmin. SQL Server has eight serverwide roles. You can make a login a member of one or more of these serverwide roles at any time. You can't, however, remove from or add to the list of available serverwide roles. For example, you can't remove sa from the sysadmin serverwide role.

Available Serverwide Roles

The following list describes the complete set of available serverwide roles. Study them carefully so that you know when to use them:

- **sysadmin**—Members of this role can do anything to the SQL Server. They appear to be the dbo of every database (even if they're not). They essentially override the permissions and security systems.
- **serveradmin**—Members of this role can set configuration options with the `sp_configure` system stored procedure and can shut down the server. They can also configure the Full-Text service. Server operators are good candidates to be members of this role.

> Members of the serveradmin role can issue only the Transact-SQL `SHUTDOWN` command to shut down the server. Their permissions to control services are Windows 2000 rights, not SQL Server rights.

- **setupadmin**—Members of this role can install and configure linked servers and mark a stored procedure to run on startup.
- **securityadmin**—Members of this role can create and control server logins as well as permissions to create databases. They can configure linked server security settings. They can also reset the passwords of SQL Server Logins (except for sysadmin role members). Again, operators are candidates for this role, and most likely your help desk personnel would be members of this role.
- **processadmin**—Members of the this role can control processes running on the database server. This process typically involves "killing" runaway queries, and help desk personnel might need this right.
- **dbcreator**—Members of this role can create, alter, and drop databases on your server. They can also restore any database on your server. DBAs are good candidates for this role (if you don't want your DBA to be a member of the sysadmin role).
- **bulkadmin**—Members of this role can run the `BULK INSERT` statement. You will learn more about `BULK INSERT` on Day 19, "Migrating Data Between Database Servers."
- **diskadmin**—Members of this role can manage files and file growth on the server. However, the commands they can use are mostly for compatibility with SQL Server 6.5, so you probably won't use this role often. DBAs are good candidates for this role (if you don't want your DBA to be a member of the sysadmin role).

Assigning a Login to a Server Role

To assign a login to a specific server role, use either the SQL Server Enterprise Manager or the `sp_addsrvrolemember` system stored procedure:

SYNTAX

```
sp_addsrvrolemember [@loginame =] 'login' ,[@rolename =] 'role'
```

In this syntax,

- *`login`* is the SQL Server login ID to add to the role.
- *`role`* is the server role name you want to have the login assigned to.

A single login can belong to zero, one, or many roles. However, the sysadmin role encompasses all other roles—both serverwide and database-specific—so you don't need to assign any other role if you select the sysadmin role. To remove a login from a serverwide role, use the `sp_dropsrvrolemember` system stored procedure:

SYNTAX

```
sp_dropsrvrolemember [@loginame =] 'login' ,[@rolename =] 'role'
```

In this syntax,

- *`login`* is the SQL Server login ID removed from the role.
- *`role`* is the server role name from which you want to have the login removed.

As an example, to make RHOME\Bob a member of the server role securityadmin, you could run the following:

INPUT

```
Exec sp_addsrvrolemember 'RHOME\Bob','securityadmin'
```

In this case, you would see the following output:

OUTPUT

```
'RHOME\Bob' added to role 'securityadmin'.
```

To remove Bob from this role, you could then run

INPUT

```
Exec sp_dropsrvrolemember 'RHOME\Bob','securityadmin'
```

You would receive this success message:

OUTPUT

```
'RHOME\Bob' dropped from role 'securityadmin'.
```

To accomplish the same changes with the SQL Server Enterprise Manager, expand your server, expand the security folder, and then highlight the Server Roles menu item (the icon with the key next to it). The right pane contains the eight serverwide roles. Double-click Security Administrators to see the Server Role Properties dialog. Click Add, and you are presented with a list of valid logins. Select RHOME\Bob (or the equivalent on your server), click OK, and you should see something similar to Figure 5.14. After you click OK again, you will have essentially run the `sp_addsrvrolemember` system stored procedure, except you've used the graphical interface.

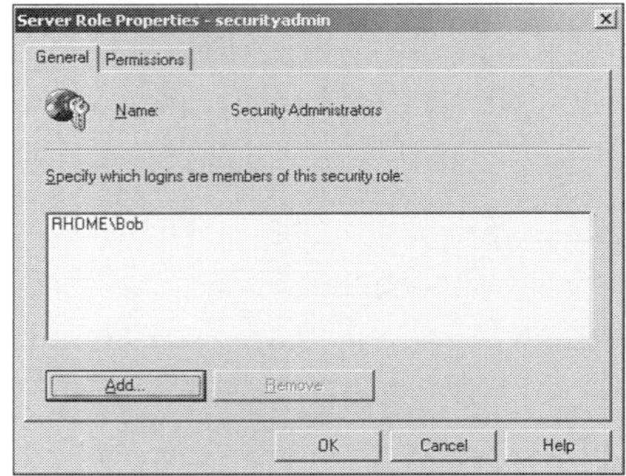

FIGURE 5.14
The Server Role Properties dialog for the Security Administrator role.

Database Roles

Each database also contains roles. Some of these roles are fixed, and you also can add your own roles (unlike serverwide roles). Keep in mind that database roles are database specific, so you can't have roles that affect more than a single database at any time. However, you can create the same roles in each database.

Database-Specific Fixed Roles

Each database also has a set of fixed database roles a username can be assigned to. There are nine by default, and these nine always exist (you can't delete any of them). Each database role, just like each server role mentioned earlier, assigns users specific permissions and capabilities. You'll learn more about permissions in tomorrow's lesson.

- **db_owner**—Members of this role can do anything they want—but only within their database. Being a member of the db_owner role gives a user mostly the same rights and permissions as the dbo user of a database (the owner). The exception involves the `restore` command. You will look at that exception much more closely on Day 8, "Restoring Your Databases," when you examine `restore`.
- **db_accessadmin**—Members of this role can add or remove users' access to the database (running the `sp_grantdbaccess` system stored procedure, for example).
- **db_securityadmin**—Members of this role can control all permissions, roles, role membership, and owners of objects in the database.

- **db_ddladmin**—Members of this role can create, modify, and drop all database objects, but they can't issue security-related commands (`grant`, `revoke`, `deny`). You'll learn more about these commands in tomorrow's lesson.
- **db_backupoperator**—Members of this role can issue selected DBCC commands, as well as the checkpoint and backup commands.
- **db_datareader**—Members of this role have the select permission on any table, view, or function in the database.
- **db_datawriter**—Members of this role have insert, update, and delete rights on any table or view in the database.
- **db_denydatareader**—Members of this role can't select data from any table, view, or function in the database.
- **db_denydatawriter**—Members of this role can't modify any data in the database with the `insert`, `update`, or `delete` statements on any table or view in the database.

User-Defined Database Roles

In addition to the fixed database roles available, you can create roles yourself and then assign users or roles to these newly created roles. You would create roles in a SQL Server database for the same reasons you would create a Windows 2000 group—to conveniently group users who perform similar functions. You should create as many roles as make sense. No restrictions are placed on how many roles a user can be a member of, and roles can be members of other roles.

5

To create a role, start with the `sp_addrole` system stored procedure:

```
sp_addrole [@rolename =] 'role' [,[@ownername =] 'owner']
```

In this syntax,

- *`role`* is the name you want to have for the new role.
- *`owner`* is the SQL Server username you want to own the role (each user can own his own roles). The default value is dbo, and it's likely that that's exactly what you want to happen.

Only members of the sysadmin serverwide role or db_owner or db_securityadmin database roles can add a new role to a database. This holds true for dropping roles as well. One oddity about roles: Although you can specify the owner name, the role name must still be unique in the database. Hence, you don't need to know the owner when you drop a role, because the name is unique in a database.

To drop a role from a database, run the `sp_droprole` system stored procedure:

SYNTAX

```
sp_droprole [@rolename =] 'role'
```

In this syntax, *role* is the name of the user-created role you want to delete.

You can't delete a role if it has any users or other roles as members of the role. You also can't delete the role if it owns any objects. You'll learn more about object ownership in tomorrow's lesson. This brings up another interesting question: How do you add users to a role? Use the `sp_addrolemember` system stored procedure to add users to user-defined or fixed database roles:

SYNTAX

```
sp_addrolemember [@rolename =] 'role', [@membername =] 'database_account'
```

In this syntax,

- *role* is the name of the role you want to add a user to.
- *database_account* is the username, group name, or role name you want to add to this role.

To remove a member from a role, run `sp_droprolemember`:

SYNTAX

```
sp_droprolemember [@rolename =] 'role', [@membername =]'database_account'
```

In this syntax,

- *role* is the name of the role from which you want to remove a user.
- *database_account* is the username, group name, or role name you want to remove from this role.

The following code shows how you might use these stored procedures. To add a new role in the `pubs` database and then assign a user to it, run this code:

INPUT

```
Use pubs
Exec sp_addrole 'Management'
Exec sp_addrole 'Operations'
Exec sp_addrolemember 'Management','Don'
Exec sp_addrolemember 'Operations','RHOME\Marketing'
```

You should see this output:

OUTPUT

```
New role added.
New role added.
'Don' added to role 'Management'.
'RHOME\Marketing' added to role 'Operations'.
```

Notice that if you try to drop a role with members, you get an error:

```
Exec sp_droprole 'Operations'
```

This error results in the following:

```
Server: Msg 15144, Level 16, State 1, Procedure sp_droprole, Line 53
The role has members. It must be empty before it can be dropped.
name
----------------
RHOME\Marketing
```

> You get the preceding results when SQL Server Query Analyzer is in Results in Text mode. If you are in the default mode, Results in Grid, the error message shows up on the Messages tab, and the list of users still in the role appears on the Grids tab.

SQL Server is even nice enough to tell you which members remain in the role. To clean up these members, run the following:

INPUT

```
Exec sp_droprolemember 'Operations','RHOME\Marketing'
Exec sp_droprole 'Operations'
```

This output indicates your success:

OUTPUT

```
'RWHOMENT\Marketing' dropped from role 'Operations'.
Role dropped.
```

Membership in each role is stored in a combination of the `sysusers` and `sysmembers` system tables. You can examine which roles exist by running the `sp_helprole` or `sp_helprolemember` system stored procedure. Both stored procedures take a single parameter: the role name in quotation marks.

5

You can achieve the same results by using SQL Server Enterprise Manager. Go back to the Logins folder for your server, and either double-click a login, or right-click and select Properties from the pop-up menu. I've selected RHOME\Bob for the following example. You can configure server roles here as well as on the Server Roles tab. However, for now, focus on the last tab, Database Access. Highlight the `pubs` database, and you should see a list of roles appear in the Database roles window, as shown in Figure 5.15.

Not only do all the fixed database roles appear, but your user-created roles do also. Scroll to the bottom of the list, and Management should be there. To make this database user a member of a role, simply check the box next to the role name. To remove it from the role, uncheck the box. It's that simple!

To create a new role with SQL Server Enterprise Manager, expand the databases folder, and then expand the database you're interested in working with. For this example, expand the `pubs` database. Then highlight the Roles folder, and the list of roles appears in the right pane. To add a new role, right-click in the whitespace in the right pane, and select New Database Role. Add a new role named Finance, with Don as a member of the role. When completed, the dialog should look like Figure 5.16. Click OK to finish creating the role. You'll learn more about the application role option in the next section.

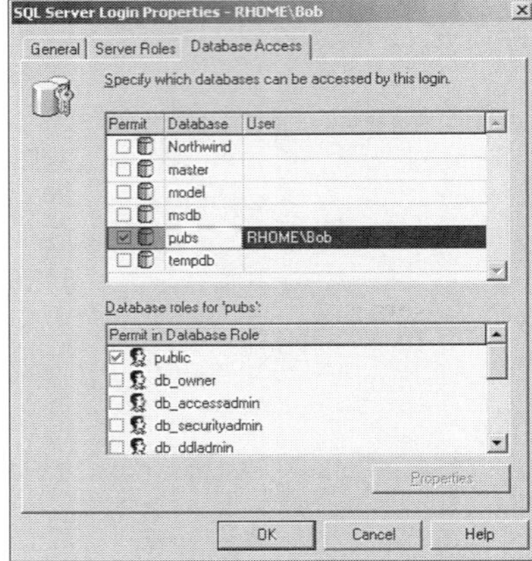

FIGURE 5.15

The SQL Server Login Properties showing the database access.

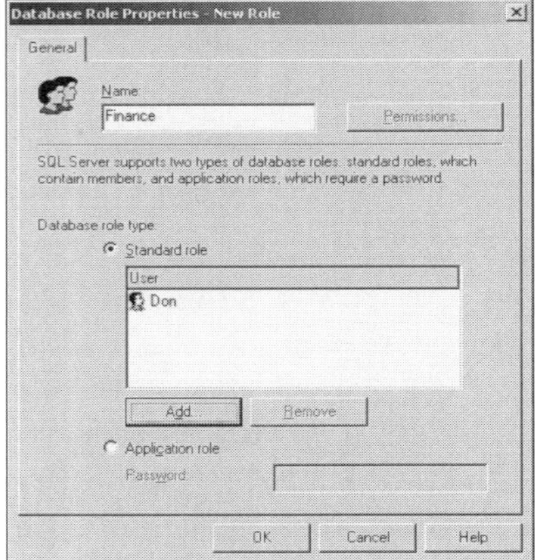

FIGURE 5.16

Adding a new database role.

Application Roles

Application roles are a very useful feature of SQL Server 2000. Although you can think of application roles as similar to other roles you've examined, they perform a different function from other roles.

Application roles serve some of the same purposes roles do; using them is a wonderful way to group users so that permissions can be applied at a higher level than maintaining them user by user. However, they are different in that application roles can be "turned on" by an application. After an application has enabled an application role, all the permissions of the user are suspended, and only the permissions of the role are enforced. Of course, the role requires a password to be enabled successfully (unless you don't want a password).

Imagine a payroll application as a great example of their use. Although all the administrators in the payroll department must update employee salary and bonus information periodically, you would rather have them use your application than directly query the SQL Server database themselves (with potentially disastrous consequences). When the application starts, you can have the users log in to SQL Server as themselves (either with SQL Server logins or preferably with their Windows 2000 credentials so they don't even know it's happening). Then run the appropriate code (the `sp_setapprole` system stored procedure) to turn on the payroll application role. From that moment on, until the application terminates its connection to the database, the permissions of the role are enforced and the permissions of the users are turned off. Therefore, if the payroll role has permissions to modify the payroll tables, but the payroll administrators don't, you can still have them run the application. Better yet, they can't knowingly (or unknowingly) go around any security or controls you've put in place with your application. The best part is that all activity is still audited with the users' login information.

Application roles tell a compelling story. Now examine how to implement them. I think you'll agree that they're relatively simple, given how powerful they are. You'll learn how to assign permissions to roles in tomorrow's lesson.

5

First, create an application role by using the `sp_addapprole` system stored procedure:

SYNTAX

```
sp_addapprole [@rolename =] 'role', [@password =] 'password'
```

In this syntax,

- *`role`* is the name of the role you want to create.
- *`password`* is the password the application must pass to enable the role.

To drop an application role, run the `sp_dropapprole` system stored procedure:

SYNTAX

```
sp_dropapprole [@rolename =] 'role'
```

In this syntax, *`role`* is the name of the role you want to remove.

To then use the role in your application, you would execute the `sp_setapprole` system stored procedure:

SYNTAX

```
sp_setapprole [@rolename =] 'role' ,
[@password =] {Encrypt N 'password'} | 'password'
[,[@encrypt =] 'encrypt_style']
```

In this syntax,

- *role* is the name of the role you want to enable.
- *password* is the password specified in the `sp_addapprole` execution.
- *Encrypt N 'password'* requests that the password be encrypted when sent over the network (if you just specify the password, it's sent over the network without encryption).
- *encrypt_style* specifies the type of encryption to use. Currently, you can choose from two available values: `none` and `odbc`. Open database connectivity (ODBC) is specified when you are using an ODBC-based client and means that the ODBC canonical encrypt function will be used to encrypt the password before it's sent over the network.

> If you are using an Object Linking and Embedding Database (OLE DB) client, the encryption capability is still available. Simply specify `odbc`, and the same type of encryption will take place.

To create and then use an application role, you can run the following script within the SQL Server Query Analyzer (an ODBC-based tool):

INPUT

```
Use pubs
Exec sp_addapprole 'Payroll','password'
Go
Exec sp_setapprole 'Payroll', {Encrypt N 'password'},'odbc'
```

You receive the following success messages:

OUTPUT

```
New application role added.
The application role 'Payroll' is now active.
```

From this point on, all permissions for this connection to SQL Server will use the permissions of the application role. Auditing of activity performed still shows up with an individual user's login information, not the application role. So, you can still tell what an individual is doing, even when she has enabled this group functionality. There is no way to turn an application role off, so you must end the connection to SQL Server to stop using the application role.

Tip

> One point of confusion with application roles occurs in regards to permissions. We'll say it again tomorrow, but it's important to note that when an

application role is enabled, it's still a member of the "public" role, so permissions assigned to the public role also work when an application role is enabled.

Summary

To access SQL Server data, you must pass through several layers of security. If you're using Named Pipes or Multiprotocol for your SQL Server network library, Windows 2000 validates your connection request at the network level, regardless of the security mode. If you are in Mixed Security Mode, either SQL Server or Windows NT/2000 validates your login. The `sysxlogins` system table in the `master` database is used if you request a SQL Server–authenticated connection. If you are in Windows Authentication Mode (the default), or when you request Windows validation in Mixed Mode, Windows 2000 is called via the SSPI interface to validate your login request and allow you access to SQL Server. Remember that connections that Windows have validated are sometimes referred to as *trusted connections*.

After you log in, you still need database access for each database you want to use. You must be a member of a Windows 2000 group that's been added to a database, have a username created for your login in a database, have an alias in a database, or have a guest username before you are allowed access to that database. This type of access has nothing at all to do with the rights (or permissions) you have when you are in the database. Rights and permissions are the subject of tomorrow's lesson.

You should use SQL Server roles when Windows 2000 groups aren't available or are otherwise inconvenient. Roles are database specific, so they contain users, not logins. You should use the fixed database roles whenever possible. Serverwide roles are available for permissions that cross multiple databases. Using application roles is a way to have an application provide database functionality that individual users don't have with their own security accounts.

Q&A

Q What's the difference between integrated and mixed security?

A Integrated security allows only trusted connections, whereas mixed security also allows SQL Server-authenticated connections if you request them.

Q What security mode is appropriate if I have mostly Windows 2000 clients but also a few UNIX computers that need access to SQL Server?

A You need mixed security because UNIX computers probably won't be logged in to your Windows 2000 domain.

Q What stored procedure activates application roles?

A The `sp_setapprole` system stored procedure.

Q If I have a login but not a username, why can I use the `pubs` database?

A Because the guest username exists in the `pubs` database.

Workshop

This section provides quiz questions to help you solidify your understanding of the concepts presented today. In addition to the quiz questions, exercises are provided to let you practice what you have learned today. Try to understand the quiz and exercise answers before continuing to tomorrow's lesson. Answers are provided in Appendix A, "Answers to Quiz Questions."

Quiz

1. How would you revoke the right of Windows 2000 administrators to log in to SQL Server as system administrators (sa)?
2. If you wanted someone to have all the rights of the owner of a database, but someone else was already the dbo, what would you do?
3. When would you need to create an individual SQL Server login for a Windows 2000 user instead of using a Windows 2000 group?

Exercises

1. Create the following logins in SQL Server. Also, add each login to a user-defined database on your server.
   - George
   - Henry
   - Ida
   - John
2. Now make John the dbo of the database you just referenced. Fix any errors you receive to make this change possible.

WEEK 1

DAY 6

Establishing Database Permissions

Yesterday, you examined SQL Server 2000's security model. SQL Server has two different security modes: Windows Authentication Mode (the default) and Mixed Mode Authentication. You can use either your Windows NT/2000 user/group account or a SQL Server security mode login to connect to SQL Server. Although you can log in to SQL Server this way, you must have a user account to connect to and use a database. A user account in a database can be a Windows group, Windows user, or SQL Server user, and all of them can be grouped with SQL Server roles. Application roles, which are also available, provide a powerful feature to help secure your database applications.

When you are in a database, however, you must have permissions to perform any action. SQL Server is an inherently secure system. If you want to perform some action, you must have been given permission to do so. Today you examine how permissions work, the difference between statement and object permissions, and how permissions are combined between roles and user accounts. You also examine ownership chains, exploring what they are and why you must understand them.

Why Use Permissions?

Until now, you've done all your work in SQL Server through the sa (system administrator) login or your Windows user account, which is a member of the local administrators group, and hence, a member of the sysadmin fixed server role in a default installation. The sa login is also a member of that role, as you learned on Day 5, "Setting Up Login and User Security." Therefore, when you examine the sysadmin fixed server role, you're also examining what the sa login can do. Members of the sysadmin fixed server role have no restrictions on what they can do in SQL Server, which is not only convenient but also necessary for many of the administrative tasks you might have to perform in SQL Server. Ordinary users, however, shouldn't be connecting to SQL Server either as the sa login or as members of the sysadmin fixed server role because they would have all permissions to the SQL Server—enough to delete all the databases and shut down the server!

By designing and implementing a good security plan for SQL Server, you can eliminate many problems before they happen rather than spend your time trying to figure out how your data (or SQL Server) became damaged. You can successfully restrict what data modifications can be made as well as what data a user is allowed to see. You can also restrict whether a user can back up a database, back up the transaction log for a database, or create and manipulate objects in a database.

Another benefit of enabling multiple logins, users, and permissions is that you can track what individual users are allowed to do and audit their activity. This capability is critical if you want to have any hope of determining what happened when something magically "disappears" from your database. You will examine SQL Server 2000 auditing on Day 20, "Performance Monitoring Basics and Tools."

Implementing Database Permissions

One critical point must be clear up front: All permissions in SQL Server are given to database users. So, when you examine permissions, you are always looking at a database user's permissions, not the permissions for a login. This means that permissions are database specific.

For every rule, there's an exception. Fixed server roles are granted to logins, not to database users. Granting these roles to logins makes sense, however, because being a member of one of these fixed server roles gives you permissions across the entire server.

For example, Sue has all permissions to the sales database. (She is a regional sales executive.) Sue might have SELECT (read) permissions on tables in the purchasing database. (She can see items on order, but only the purchasing department can buy new items.) Finally, Sue might have no permissions in the accounting database. (Only the accountants have permissions in the accounting database.)

In this example, Sue must connect to SQL Server with a SQL Server Authentication Mode login or use her Windows account credentials. Within each database, she has a separate user account (or she can use her Windows user account or group membership) to gain access. As you saw in yesterday's lesson, she might also use guest permissions, for example, in the accounting database (if a guest username exists). Keep in mind that each user in each database has separate permissions.

Note

The `syspermissions` database system table tracks security within a database. That's why security is database specific. There is also a view for backward compatibility with SQL Server 6.5, known as sysprotects. The table and view also exist in the `master` database. This table and view can be found in every database in SQL Server.

Types of Permissions

SQL Server 2000 uses three terms to indicate what action you are taking in reference to permissions: They are the GRANT, DENY, and REVOKE statements. You will examine these statements in detail later, but it's useful to begin with a brief example of the terminology.

To let a user perform an action, you must grant the user some kind of permission. To prevent a user from performing an action, you deny the user the right to perform an action. To remove a previously granted permission, you revoke the permission.

You can grant two types of permissions: statement level and object level. Statement-level permissions enable a user to run a particular Transact-SQL command, whereas object-level permissions allow a user to perform some operation: SELECT data (read), INSERT data, UPDATE data, or DELETE data.

Permissions Precedence

Understanding how permissions are applied is critical to understanding when a particular permission is in effect. All permissions in SQL Server are cumulative, except DENY, which overrides other permissions.

If you have the SELECT permission from your membership in Role1 and the INSERT permission from your membership in Role2, you effectively have the SELECT and INSERT permissions. If you then were to be denied SELECT permissions within either of these roles or within your individual account, you would no longer have the SELECT permission. DENY always overrides any other permission.

SQL Server's Special Permissions

SQL Server 2000 has several different levels of permissions. Most of these permissions are database specific. However, as we mentioned earlier, fixed server roles are tied to logins, not database users. As you saw on Day 5, each role implies a specific set of permissions. Also, sysadmin role membership implies its own particular set of permissions.

Within each database are fixed database roles, each of which is associated with a particular set of permissions. Each database also has a special user known as dbo (the database owner). Although you never see information directly in SQL Server about it, there's a concept of a database object owner. Special permissions are inherent for anyone who's in this conceptual role as well.

Later today, you will examine the public role and what permissions are implied with it. In this next section, you will learn more about the fixed server roles and their permissions.

Fixed Server Role Permissions

Each role has implicit permissions associated with it, and you can view them by running the system stored procedure `sp_srvrolepermission`:

SYNTAX

```
sp_srvrolepermission [[@srvrolename =] 'role']
```

In this syntax, *`role`* is the name of the fixed server role for which you want to see the permissions.

The results of running this system stored procedure are as follows. For example, if you run

INPUT

```
EXEC sp_srvrolepermission 'dbcreator'
```

you would see the following:

OUTPUT

```
ServerRole                          Permission
----------------------------------- -----------------------------------
dbcreator                           Add member to dbcreator
dbcreator                           ALTER DATABASE
dbcreator                           CREATE DATABASE
```

```
dbcreator                       DROP DATABASE
dbcreator                       Extend database
dbcreator                       RESTORE DATABASE
dbcreator                       RESTORE LOG
dbcreator                       sp_renamedb

(8 row(s) affected)
```

Each permission and server role is explained in the following sections.

sysadmin

Members of the sysadmin server role can do anything they want to SQL Server, literally. Members of this fixed server role are granted an extremely powerful set of permissions and should be considered carefully. The sa login is always a member of this role and can't be removed from the sysadmin role. Members of the sysadmin fixed server role are always considered to be the database owner of every database they use. Members of the sysadmin role can't be prevented from accessing any database on SQL Server.

A list of rights is provided by the user interface for sysadmin members; however, it's a little misleading because a sysadmin role member can do anything. Keep this point in mind when you're deciding whether to give someone membership in this role.

serveradmin

Server administrators who won't otherwise be administering databases or other objects are best suited to be members of the serveradmin role. Members of this role can perform the following operations:

- Add another login to the serveradmin fixed server role
- Run the `DBCC FREEPROCCACHE` command
- Run the `sp_configure` system stored procedure to change system options
- Run the `RECONFIGURE` command to install changes made with `sp_configure`
- Run the `SHUTDOWN` command to shut down SQL Server
- Run the `sp_fulltext_service` system stored procedure to configure the full text service of SQL Server 2000

6

setupadmin

Members of the setupadmin role are typically administrators who are configuring remote servers. Members of this role can perform the following operations:

- Add another login to the setupadmin fixed server role
- Add, drop, or configure linked servers
- Mark a stored procedure as startup

securityadmin

Members of the securityadmin role can perform any operation related to serverwide security in SQL Server. Help desk personnel (individuals who set up new accounts) are great candidates for membership in this role. Members of this role can perform the following operations:

- Add members to the securityadmin fixed server role
- Grant, revoke, or deny the `CREATE DATABASE` statement permission
- Read the SQL Server error log by using the `sp_readerrorlog` system stored procedure
- Run security-related system stored procedures, including `sp_addlogin`, `sp_droplogin`, `sp_password` (for all except sysadmins), `sp_defaultdb`, `sp_defaultlanguage`, `sp_addlinkedsrvlogin`, `sp_droplinkedsrvlogin`, `sp_dropremotelogin`, `sp_grantlogin`, `sp_revokelogin`, `sp_denylogin`, `sp_grantdbaccess`, `sp_helplogins`, and `sp_remoteoption` (update part)

Being a securityadmin member doesn't give you access to every database. Therefore, some stored procedures, such as `sp_helpdb` or `sp_droplogin`, might return an error if you try to access a database that you don't have permissions to see. The information you are allowed to see is still displayed and, in the case of `sp_droplogin`, logins are still dropped.

processadmin

Members of the processadmin role can control processes running on the database server. This role typically involves "killing" runaway queries, and help desk personnel might need this right. Members of this role can perform the following operations:

- Add members to the processadmin fixed server role
- Run the `KILL` command to end a SQL Server process

dbcreator

Members of the dbcreator fixed server role, which most likely includes senior database administrators, can perform operations relating to creating and modifying databases. The permissions of this role include being able to perform the following operations:

- Add members to the dbcreator fixed database role
- Run the `sp_renamedb` system stored procedure

- Run the `CREATE DATABASE`, `ALTER DATABASE`, and `DROP DATABASE` commands
- Restore a database or transaction log

diskadmin

Members of the diskadmin fixed server role can manage files. This role is mostly for backward compatibility with SQL Server 6.5. In general, most database administrators are better served with the dbcreator fixed server role. Members of the diskadmin fixed server role can perform the following operations:

- Add members to the diskadmin fixed server role
- Run the following `DISK` commands (used for backward compatibility): `DISK INIT`, `DISK REINIT`, `DISK REFIT`, `DISK MIRROR`, and `DISK REMIRROR`
- Run the `sp_diskdefault` and `sp_dropdevice` system stored procedures
- Run the `sp_addumpdevice` system stored procedure to add backup devices

sa

The sa login is worth separate mention here. In releases of SQL Server before version 7.0, all permissions for serverwide administration were associated with the sa SQL Server Authenticated login. No separate roles broke up these permissions. sa is still included for backward compatibility and still has all the permissions it had in previous releases. However, it has these capabilities because of the login's membership in the sysadmin fixed server role. You can't remove sa from this role. You also can't rename the sa login.

The sa login (and all members of the sysadmin fixed server role) always emulates being the dbo user in each database. You can't change this behavior. Emulating this user isn't the same thing as being a member of the db_owner fixed database role.

> With SQL Server 2000 and the move to Windows Authentication Mode security, the sa login is becoming much less relevant than in previous releases.

6

Fixed Database Roles

Members of fixed database roles are given specific permissions within each database. Unlike fixed server roles, however, they are specific to each database. Being a member of a fixed database role in one database has no effect on permissions in any other database. Now examine each of the nine fixed database roles. You can view these roles by running the `sp_dbfixedrolepermission` system stored procedure:

SYNTAX

```
sp_dbfixedrolepermission [[@rolename =] 'role']
```

In this syntax, *role* is the name of the fixed database role for which you want to see permissions.

The following sections describe the results of running this system stored procedure.

db_owner

Members of the db_owner fixed database role are the "owners" of a database. They have very broad permissions within a database and can do almost everything the actual database owner can do. Members of the db_owner fixed database role can perform the following operations within their databases:

- Add members to, or remove members from, any fixed database role except for db_owner
- Run any data definition language (DDL) statement, including `TRUNCATE TABLE`
- Run the `BACKUP DATABASE` and `BACKUP LOG` statements
- Run the `RESTORE DATABASE` and `RESTORE LOG` statements
- Issue a `CHECKPOINT` in a database
- Run the following Database Consistency Checker (DBCC) commands: `DBCC CHECKALLOC`, `DBCC CHECKFILEGROUP`, `DBCC CHECKDB`, `DBCC CHECKIDENT`, `DBCC CLEANTABLE`, `DBCC DBREINDEX`, `DBCC PROCCACHE`, `DBCC SHOW_STATISTICS`, `DBCC SHOWCONTIG`, `DBCC SHRINKDATABASE`, `DBCC SHRINKFILE`, and `DBCC UPDATEUSAGE`
- Grant, revoke, or deny the SELECT, INSERT, UPDATE, DELETE, REFERENCES, or EXECUTE permissions on every object (as appropriate for each object type)
- Add users, groups, roles, or aliases to a database by using the following system stored procedures: `sp_addalias`, `sp_addapprole`, `sp_addgroup`, `sp_addrole`, `sp_addrolemember`, `sp_adduser`, `sp_approlepassword`, `sp_change_users_login`, `sp_changegroup`, `sp_dropalias`, `sp_dropapprole`, `sp_dropgroup`, `sp_droprole`, `sp_droprolemember`, `sp_dropuser`, `sp_grantdbaccess`, and `sp_revokedbaccess`
- Rename stored procedures by using the `sp_recompile` system stored procedures
- Rename any object by using the `sp_rename` system stored procedure
- Modify some table-specific options by using the `sp_tableoption` system stored procedure
- Change the owner of any object by using the `sp_changeobjectowner` system stored procedure

- Configure full-text services within the database by using the following system stored procedures: sp_fulltext_catalog, sp_fulltext_column, sp_fulltext_database, and sp_fulltext_table

Note

> The db_owner fixed database role permissions specify that members of the role can "run any data definition language (DDL) statement except for GRANT, REVOKE, and DENY." This statement deserves a little explanation. By default, members of the db_owner role can grant, revoke, or deny permissions to any object in the database. However, the database object owner (dboo), examined later today, can take away the abilities of the dbo and members of the db_owner fixed database role for their objects.

Tip

> A difference still exists between being the one and only database owner (dbo) and being a member of the db_owner database role. The first difference involves object creation: The dbo's objects are owned by the user dbo, whereas members of the db_owner role show up with their username as the object owner. The other difference is that if a database is damaged or for some other reason needs to be restored but still exists, SQL Server uses the dbo user as recorded in the sysdatabases system table in the master database to determine your right to restore the database. It does so because it can't get into the database to determine who's a member of the db_owner role. You will examine restores, including security requirements, on Day 8, "Restoring Your Databases."

db_accessadmin

Members of the db_accessadmin fixed database role manage which logins can access a database. As with the securityadmin role, your help desk staff might be the best candidates for membership in this role. Members can perform the following operation:

- Run the following system stored procedures: sp_addalias, sp_adduser, sp_dropalias, sp_dropuser, sp_grantdbaccess, and sp_revokedbaccess

db_securityadmin

Members of the db_securityadmin fixed database role can administer security within a database, and they can perform the following operations:

- Run the GRANT, REVOKE, or DENY statements
- Run the following system stored procedures: sp_addapprole, sp_addgroup, sp_addrole, sp_addrolemember, sp_approlepassword, sp_changegroup,

`sp_changeobjectowner`, `sp_dropapprole`, `sp_dropgroup`, `sp_droprole`, and `sp_droprolemember`

db_ddladmin

Members of the db_ddladmin fixed database role can perform the following operations:

- Run any DDL command except `GRANT`, `REVOKE`, and `DENY`
- Grant the REFERENCES permission on any table
- Recompile stored procedures by using the `sp_recompile` system stored procedure
- Rename any object by using the `sp_rename` system stored procedure
- Modify some table-specific options by using the `sp_tableoption` system stored procedure
- Change the owner of any object by using the `sp_changeobjectowner` system stored procedure
- Run the following DBCC commands: `DBCC CLEANTABLE`, `DBCC SHOW_STATISTICS`, and `DBCC SHOWCONTIG`
- Control full-text services by using the `sp_fulltext_column` and `sp_fulltext_table` system stored procedures

db_backupoperator

Members of the db_backupoperator fixed database role can perform all operations related to backing up a database. They can do the following:

- Run the `BACKUP DATABASE` and `BACKUP LOG` statements
- Issue a `CHECKPOINT` in a database

db_datareader

Members of the db_datareader fixed database role have the SELECT permission on any table or view in a database. They can't grant permission to or revoke it from anyone else.

db_datawriter

Members of the db_datawriter fixed database role have the INSERT, UPDATE, and DELETE permissions on all tables or views in a database. They can't grant permission to or revoke it from anyone else.

db_denydatareader

Members of the db_denydatareader fixed database role can't run the `SELECT` statement on any table or view in the database. This option is useful if you want your database administrator (DBA) to set up your objects (as a member of the db_ddladmin fixed database role) but not be able to read any sensitive data in the database.

db_denydatawriter

Members of the db_denydatawriter fixed database role can't run the `INSERT`, `UPDATE`, or `DELETE` statement on any table or view in the database.

The Database Owner (dbo)

The dbo user has all the rights that members of the db_owner role have. Each database can have only one dbo.

If a user is the dbo, when he creates an object, the owner of the object is set to dbo, and the dbo user becomes the database object owner (dboo) as you would expect. This isn't true for members of the db_owner fixed database role (or any other user of the database). Unless he qualifies his object name with the dbo owner name, the owner's name is his username.

Note

If you issue a `create table` statement, the table is owned by dbo. If you are logged in via Windows security and are a member of the db_owner role, the table shows up with your Windows credentials as the owner. So, the table might be `dbo.mytable` if you are dbo or `[rhome\Richard].mytable` if you are logged in as a member of db_owner. This point is critical to you because, by default, any SQL statement that doesn't specify an object owner always looks for the object in the current user's name and then for one owned by dbo. For example, if you log in as [rhome\Joe] and then issue the query `Select * from mytable`, you are not telling SQL Server which table you want, so it looks for `[rhome\Joe].mytable` and then `dbo.mytable`.

The moral of the story: It's always better to qualify all SQL statements with the owner when referencing objects.

Tip

Replace RHOME with your computer name in all code examples.

6

You are considered the dbo of a database in any of the following four situations:

- You are the creator of a database. The login that created a database is the dbo. By default, the sa SQL Server login is the owner of every database when you install SQL Server 2000. This is true even if you select Windows Authentication Mode security when you install, because SQL Server switches to Windows Authentication only at the end of setup.

- You are assigned as the database owner. The owner of a database can later be assigned using the `sp_changedbowner` system stored procedure. You examined `sp_changedbowner` yesterday.
- You connect to SQL Server as any member of the sysadmin fixed server role. If you connect to SQL Server using either the sa login or any other member of the sysadmin fixed server role, you have all permissions in all databases because you impersonate the dbo in each database.
- You connect to a database with a login aliased to the dbo of a database. Only a single user can be the dbo at any given time. In previous releases of SQL Server, you could alias a login to another user in a database. This technique became obsolete in SQL Server 7.0; however, aliases are supported for backward compatibility in SQL Server 2000. You shouldn't use them. If you've upgraded from SQL Server 6.5 and had logins aliased to dbo, they emulate being the dbo for your database. You should add users to the db_owner role in SQL Server 2000 rather than use aliases.

Database Object Owner (dboo) Permissions

A user who creates a database object is the dboo of that object. By default, a user who creates an object is the owner of the object. Members of the db_owner and db_ddladmin fixed database roles can create objects as themselves or can qualify the object name as owned by the dbo. So, if you issue the following `create` statement while logged in as Joe, with a database username of Joe, the owner is Joe:

```
Use Pubs
Create table mytable (c1 int NOT NULL)
GO
```

To check the ownership of this object, you can run the following code:

```
EXEC sp_help mytable
```

You then see the following output:

```
Name              Owner      Type             Created_datetime
----------------- ---------- ---------------- ----------------------
mytable           joe        user table       2000-04-26 22:05:11.593

...

The object does not have any indexes.
```

```
No constraints have been defined for this object.

No foreign keys reference this table.

No views with schemabinding reference this table.
```

Notice that the owner is Joe.

However, if you have membership in the db_owner or db_ddladmin roles, you can run the following:

INPUT

```
Drop table mytable
GO
Create table dbo.mytable (c1 int)
GO
EXEC sp_help mytable
```

The output looks like this:

```
Name              Owner     Type            Created_datetime
----------------- --------- --------------- ----------------------
mytable           dbo       user table      2000-04-26 22:07:54.970

...

The object does not have any indexes.

No constraints have been defined for this object.

No foreign keys reference this table.

No views with schemabinding reference this table.
```

Notice that the object is no longer owned by Joe but by dbo when you run the `sp_help mytable` command (as expected).

It's a good idea to use objects only in production databases owned by the dbo user. You will examine the reasons when you look at ownership chains later today. If the owner is specified as dbo, the dbo user is the owner of the object, not the user who actually created the object. Hence, the user who creates an object with the owner qualified isn't the dboo of that object.

A user who owns a database object is automatically granted all permissions to that object. The appropriate permissions for each type of object are granted to the owner. For example, when a user creates a table, she is granted the SELECT, INSERT, UPDATE, DELETE, REFERENCES, and BACKUP permissions on that table. You can change the ownership of an object by using the `sp_changeobjectowner` system stored procedure:

SYNTAX

```
sp_changeobjectowner [@objname =] 'object', [@newowner =] 'owner'
```

In this syntax,

- `object` is the name of a database object (table, view, or stored procedure). The object can be qualified with the owner name if necessary (and it's a good idea to always do so).
- `owner` is the username, role name, or Windows NT user or group you want to own the object you specified with the `object` parameter.

So, to change the ownership of the dbo's table to Joe, run the following:

INPUT

```
EXEC sp_changeobjectowner 'dbo.mytable', 'Joe'
```

User Permissions

Most people who use your database will be ordinary users. The database user has no inherent rights or permissions (other than those given to the public role, examined in the next section). All rights must be explicitly granted or assigned to the user, the user's roles, or the public role.

Permissions granted to users can be categorized into statement and object permissions:

- *Statement permissions* allow users to create new databases, create new objects within an existing database, or back up the database or transaction log. Statement permissions allow you to run particular commands rather than operate on particular objects.
- *Object permissions* enable users to perform actions on individual objects. For example, users might have the ability to read (select) data from a table, execute a stored procedure, or modify data in a table or view (with INSERT, UPDATE, and DELETE permissions).

Details for both types of permissions, as well as how to grant them, are discussed in a little bit.

The Public Role

The public role exists in each database and can't be removed. It's mentioned here because it's extremely useful, but you must understand how to use it.

Every database user, role, Windows user, and Windows group within a database is a member of the public role and can't be removed from it. Therefore, public is a great role to use when you want everyone to have a permission.

An example of this use is already present on your SQL Server system. The SELECT permission, as well as the EXECUTE permission on many system stored procedures, is granted to public on all system tables in each database. This permission is required for successful operation of SQL Server and shouldn't be changed.

Be careful when you grant permissions to the public role. Remember, this means that everyone, including users who are added to the database later, will have these permissions.

Statement Permissions

Statement permissions allow a database user, database role, or Windows user or group to perform various tasks such as creating databases, creating objects, or backing up the database. Statement permissions allow a user to run a particular command (or set of commands) rather than merely manipulate a particular object.

You should carefully consider granting a user or role permissions to create an object. When a user creates an object, she becomes the owner of that object (unless the creator specifies the owner as dbo when she creates it) and has all the permissions associated with database object ownership. Later, you will see that having objects owned by different owners can create some difficult permission situations.

Statement permissions should be granted only when explicitly needed. The haphazard granting of statement permissions can leave a database with unnecessary and even unusable objects.

You can grant statement permissions to individual database users, Windows users/groups, or database roles, including the public role. The statement permissions that can be granted, revoked, or denied include CREATE DATABASE, CREATE TABLE, CREATE PROCEDURE, CREATE DEFAULT, CREATE RULE, CREATE VIEW, CREATE FUNCTION, BACKUP DATABASE, and BACKUP LOG.

You can grant these permissions individually or all at once (by using the keyword `ALL`). Each command has implications that must be considered before you use it.

The CREATE DATABASE Permission

The CREATE DATABASE permission enables users to create their own databases and thus become the dbo of those databases. Database ownership can later be changed with the `sp_changedbowner` system stored procedure. Only members of the sysadmin or dbcreator fixed server role are allowed to grant a user the CREATE DATABASE permissions. Because permissions are always granted to users (and never to logins), you must grant this permission in the `master` database only. This statement permission doesn't exist in any other database. The CREATE DATABASE permission also grants you rights to use the `ALTER DATABASE` command. In other words, you can't use `ALTER DATABASE` unless you have the CREATE DATABASE permission.

Using the dbcreator fixed server role is much better than granting the `CREATE DATABASE` statement permission. You usually need the other rights granted by the dbcreator fixed server role anyway, and figuring out who has what rights is easier when you take advantage of SQL Server roles.

The CREATE TABLE, VIEW, FUNCTION, PROCEDURE, DEFAULT, and RULE Permissions

CREATE TABLE, VIEW, FUNCTION, PROCEDURE, DEFAULT, and RULE permissions enable users to run the referenced statement to create objects in the database where the permissions were given. Programmers are frequently given these permissions to allow them to create the resources they need in a database during development.

All CREATE permissions include the right to alter or drop any objects created by a user. Giving this permission can cause serious problems in your database because a user can drop objects he is finished with, only to find that others were using the object. A user might also alter an object and make it unusable to some other user in the database. To check for these types of dependencies, you can run the `sp_depends` system stored procedure.

The BACKUP DATABASE and BACKUP LOG Statement Permissions

The BACKUP DATABASE and BACKUP LOG permissions can also be assigned to individual users, Windows users/groups, and roles. Although backing up the database and transaction logs is usually an automated process carried out by scheduled jobs created by the system administrator, some environments require that individual users be given the ability to perform these backups.

Tip

> Again, using the db_backupoperator fixed database role is much better than granting the BACKUP DATABASE and BACKUP LOG statement permissions. You usually need the other rights granted by the role membership anyway, and figuring out who has what rights is easier when you take advantage of SQL Server roles.

Assigning Statement Permissions

You can use Transact-SQL or SQL Server Enterprise Manager to grant, revoke, and deny statement permissions.

The GRANT Statement Permission Command

The GRANT command gives a user statement permissions:

SYNTAX

```
GRANT {ALL | statement_list} TO {account}
```

In this syntax,

- ALL stands for all possible statement permissions.
- *statement_list* is an enumerated list of the statement permissions you want to give to an account.
- *account* is the name of a database user, database role, Windows user, or Windows group.

The REVOKE Statement Permission Command

The REVOKE command takes away statement permissions already granted:

SYNTAX

```
REVOKE {ALL | statement_list} TO {account}
```

In this syntax,

- ALL stands for all possible statement permissions.
- *statement_list* is an enumerated list of the statement permissions you want to take away.
- *account* is the name of a database user, database role, Windows user, or Windows group.

6

The DENY Statement Permission Command

Unlike a REVOKE command, DENY explicitly takes away a statement permission. The permission doesn't have to be granted first to a user. For example, if Joe is a member of a database role, and that role has the CREATE TABLE statement permission, Joe can also create tables. However, if you don't want Joe to be able to create tables, even though he is a member of a role that has the permission, you can deny the statement permission from Joe. Therefore, Joe can't run the CREATE TABLE statement, even though his role would normally give him the right to do so.

SYNTAX

```
DENY {ALL | statement_list} TO {account}
```

In this syntax,

- ALL stands for all possible statement permissions.
- *statement_list* is an enumerated list of the statement permissions you want to deny from an account.
- *account* is the name of a database user, database role, Windows user, or Windows group.

Transact-SQL Permissions Examples

Working through a few examples is the easiest way to understand how to use these commands:

- To grant a windows user named Joe permission to create a view in a database, run

INPUT

```
GRANT CREATE VIEW TO [Rhome\Joe]
```

- To revoke the permission to create views and tables from Joe and Mary, run

INPUT

```
REVOKE CREATE TABLE, CREATE VIEW FROM [Rhome\Mary], [Rhome\Joe]
```

- To grant Joe all permissions in a database, run

INPUT

```
GRANT ALL TO [Rhome\Joe]
```

Note

If GRANT ALL is executed in the master database, the user specified is given all permissions in that database. If it's executed in any other database, the user is given all permissions except CREATE DATABASE because that particular permission can be granted only in the master database.

ANALYSIS Assuming that user Bob is a member of Role1 and Role2, what would the permissions be at the end of this set of statements?

```
EXEC sp_addrole 'Role1'
EXEC sp_addrole 'Role2'
GO
GRANT CREATE TABLE TO Role1
GRANT CREATE VIEW to Role2
GRANT CREATE DEFAULT to [Rhome\Bob]
REVOKE ALL FROM Role1
DENY CREATE VIEW to [Rhome\Bob]
```

At this point, Bob can create a default, and that's all. His CREATE TABLE permissions (given to Role1) were later taken away by the `REVOKE ALL FROM Role1` command. The CREATE VIEW permissions gained from Bob's membership in Role2 were lost when Bob was denied CREATE VIEW permission. Therefore, the only permission still in effect is the CREATE DEFAULT permission.

> **Tip:** Remember the difference between a revoke and a deny. Deny says you can NEVER perform an operation, revoke simply removes a previous GRANT or DENY right recorded by SQL Server. It doesn't necessarily prevent you from accessing an object if other permissions are still in effect.

Administering Statement Permissions with SQL Server Enterprise Manager

SQL Server Enterprise Manager provides a graphical interface for implementing statement permissions. To view or edit statement permissions in SQL Server Enterprise Manager, open the databases folder for your SQL Server. Right-click the database you want to view or modify, and select Properties. Click the Permissions tab to view the statement permissions for your database. You should see something similar to Figure 6.1, which shows the pubs database's permissions.

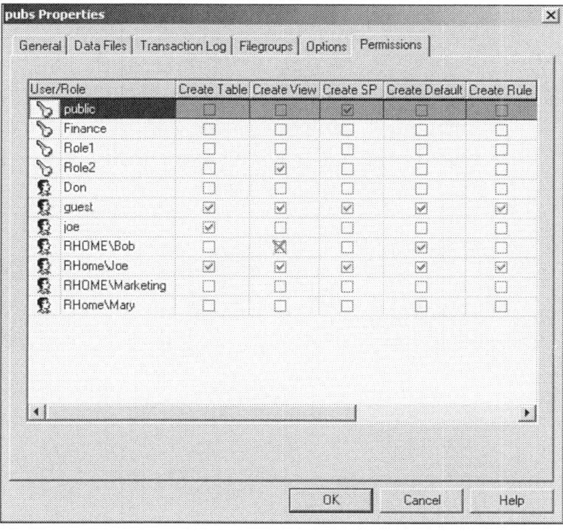

FIGURE 6.1
The Statement Permissions tab for pubs.

As you grant and revoke permissions, the boxes contain one of three indicators:

- A check mark indicates a statement permission that has been granted.
- A red X indicates a deny statement permission.
- A blank indicates no explicit permission assigned.

6

To grant a permission, check the appropriate box for an account. To deny a permission, click the box twice (to make the red X appear). If a permission has been previously granted, clicking the box once makes the red X appear. Remember that this is a deny permission. You must click again to clear the check box if you want SQL Server Enterprise Manager to send a REVOKE command to your server. Click OK to make your changes permanent.

If you look at statement permissions on any database other than the `master` database, the CREATE DATABASE permission isn't present because that right can be assigned only from the `master` database. Figure 6.2 shows the Statement Permissions tab for the `master` database.

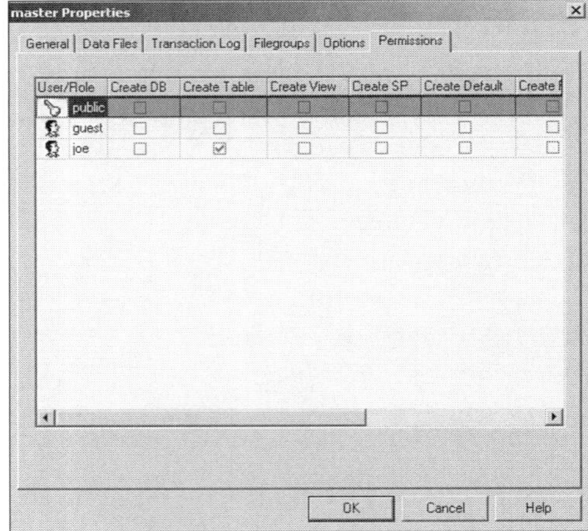

FIGURE 6.2
The Statement Permissions tab for `master`.

The ability to create objects in a database is a serious matter. Don't grant the permission to do so unless it's necessary for a user to perform her job.

Object Permissions

Object permissions allow a user, role, or Windows user or group to perform actions against a particular object in a database. The permissions apply only to the specific object named when granting the permission, not to all the objects contained in the entire database. Object permissions enable users to give individual user accounts the rights to run specific Transact-SQL statements on an object. Object permissions are the most common types of permissions granted.

These object permissions are available:

SELECT	View data in a table, view, or column.
INSERT	Add data to a table or a view.
UPDATE	Modify existing data in a table, view, or column.
DELETE	Remove data from a table or view.
EXECUTE	Run a stored procedure.
REFERENCES	Refer to a table with foreign keys (see Day 14, "Ensuring Data Integrity") or when creating a function or view with the `WITH` SCHEMABINDING option that references an object (see Day 15, "Creating Views, Triggers, Stored Procedures, and Functions").

Note

The REFERENCES permission (abbreviated to DRI, which means *declarative referential integrity* in SQL Server Enterprise Manager) allows users (or applications) to compare a value against values in another table without being able to actually see the data in the other table. For example, this permission can be used to let an application find a matching Social Security number without giving enough rights for the application to see the other Social Security numbers.

A new use in SQL Server 2000 is to allow something called *schema binding*, about which you'll learn more on Day 15. Basically, it prevents objects that you depend on from being changed if you're using them from views or functions.

Assigning Object Permissions

You can use Transact-SQL or SQL Server Enterprise Manager to grant, revoke, and deny object permissions.

6

Granting Object Permissions with Transact-SQL

The `GRANT` command gives someone one or more object permissions. It also removes a `DENY` permission.

SYNTAX

```
GRANT {ALL [PRIVILEGES] | permission_list [,...n]}
{
[(column[,...n])] ON {table | view}
| ON {table | view}[(column[,...n])]
| ON {stored_procedure | extended_stored_procedure}
| ON {user_defined_function}
}
TO account[,...n]
[WITH GRANT OPTION]
[AS {group | role}]
```

In this syntax,

- `ALL` stands for all possible object permissions that apply to a particular object type.
- *`permission_list`* is an enumerated list of the object permissions you want to give to an account.
- *`column`* is the level down to which object permissions can be granted (only for SELECT or UPDATE).
- *`account`* is the name of a database user, database role, Windows user, or Windows group.
- `WITH GRANT OPTION` allows the user who's the recipient of the grant also to give away the permission he has been granted to other users.
- `AS {`*`group`*` | `*`role`*`}` specifies which group or role you are using for a particular grant. If you have multiple roles or Windows groups that might have conflicting permissions, specify this option.

The REVOKE Object Permission Command

The `REVOKE` command takes away one or more object permissions that have already been granted. You don't receive an error message if you revoke a command that hasn't previously been granted; it just doesn't have any effect.

SYNTAX

```
REVOKE [GRANT OPTION FOR]
{ALL [PRIVILEGES] | [,...permission_list n]}
{
[(column[,...n])] ON {table | view}
| ON {table | view}[(column[,...n])]
| {stored_procedure | extended_stored_procedure}
| {user_defined_function}
}
FROM account[,...n]
[CASCADE]
[AS {group | role}]
```

In this syntax,

- `ALL` stands for all possible object permissions that apply to a particular object type.
- *`permission_list`* is an enumerated list of the object permissions you want to take away from an account.
- *`column`* stands for the column or columns from which you want to revoke permissions. Object permissions at the column level apply only to the `SELECT` or `UPDATE` commands.
- *`account`* is the name of a database user, database role, Windows user, or Windows group.
- `CASCADE` revokes permissions that were granted by a user who was previously given the WITH GRANT OPTION permission.

- `AS {group | role}` specifies which group or role you are using for a particular revoke. If you have multiple roles or Windows groups that might have conflicting permissions, specify this option.

The DENY Object Permission Command

Unlike a REVOKE command, DENY explicitly takes away an object permission. The permission doesn't have to first be granted to a user. For example, if Joe is a member of a database role and that role has the SELECT permission on the authors table, Joe can read data in the authors table. However, if you don't want Joe to be able to read data from the authors table, even though he is a member of a role that has the permission, you can deny Joe the permission. Therefore, Joe can't select data from the authors table, even though his role would normally give him the right to do so.

SYNTAX

```
DENY
{ALL [PRIVILEGES] | permission_list [,...n]}
{
[(column[,...n])] ON {table | view}
| ON {table | view}[(column[,...n])]
| ON {stored_procedure | extended_stored_procedure}
| ON {user_defined_function}
}
TO account[,...n]
[CASCADE]
```

In this syntax,

- `ALL` stands for all possible object permissions that apply to a particular object type.
- *`permission_list`* is an enumerated list of the object permissions you want to deny for an account.
- *`column`* is the column or columns to which you want to deny access. Object permissions at the column level apply only to the `SELECT` or `UPDATE` commands.
- *`account`* is the name of a database user, database role, Windows user, or Windows group.
- `CASCADE` denies permissions to an account as well as denies permissions to any account that has been previously granted the permission from a user who had the WITH GRANT OPTION permission.

6

Transact-SQL Permissions Examples

Working through a few examples is the easiest way to understand how to use these commands:

- To grant a user named Joe permission to select data from the `sales` table in the `pubs` database, run

INPUT

```
GRANT SELECT ON SALES TO [Rhome\Joe]
```

- To revoke Joe and Mary's permissions to select data from and insert data into the authors table, run the following:

INPUT
```
REVOKE SELECT, INSERT ON AUTHORS FROM [Rhome\Mary], [Rhome\Joe]
```

- To grant Joe column-level permissions to select data from the au_fname and au_lname columns in the authors table from the pubs database, run

INPUT
```
GRANT SELECT ON AUTHORS (AU_FNAME, AU_LNAME) TO [Rhome\Joe]
```

Note that the preceding is the same as

```
GRANT SELECT (AU_FNAME, AU_LNAME) on AUTHORS TO [Rhome\Joe]
```

Tip

Although you can grant permissions to accounts at the column level, it's a better idea to restrict access to tables by creating a view and then granting permissions on that view. A *view* is a predefined Transact-SQL statement or group of statements that can return data. For the preceding example, you can create a view called viewAuthorName, which selects the au_fname and au_lname fields from the authors table. You can then grant Joe permissions on that view. (You'll learn more about views on Day 15.)

This approach is more efficient because any user who references that table has to be checked for his column-level permissions. If you create a view rather than use column-level permissions, permissions must be checked only once on the view rather than on each column.

Caution

Column-level permissions, once invoked, remain in force. This can lead to an incorrect representation of the permissions in the Enterprise Manager Graphical Interface.

For example, if you have a table with two columns, and you grant select on a table, then deny select on column2, then revoke the deny on column 2, you will see in Enterprise Manager that you still have select on the table (implied that you have select on all columns). But, because the revoke only removed the deny on column2, you now have NO permission to column2, and therefore can't select * or column2. SELECT is explained further on Day 10, and you may want to re-read this note when you're done with Day 10.

Here's the code to demonstrate this caution:

INPUT
```
CREATE TABLE test (c1 int, c2 int)
GRANT SELECT ON test TO [Rhome\Joe]
DENY SELECT ON test (c2) to [Rhome\Joe]
REVOKE SELECT ON test (c2) from [Rhome\Joe]
```

> And now look at the permissions [Rhome\Joe] has on table test in Enterprise Manager and it will appear that Joe should be able to select from the table. Log in as Joe and you can verify that you are not able to run "select * from test" because you don't have permissions on column c2.

- To grant Ann the right to select and update the `publishers` table and give others the right to read and update the `publishers` table, run

INPUT
```
GRANT SELECT, INSERT ON PUBLISHERS TO [Rhome\Ann] WITH GRANT OPTION
```

- To then take the permissions away from Ann and from anyone Ann has given the permissions to, run

INPUT
```
REVOKE SELECT, INSERT ON PUBLISHERS FROM [Rhome\Ann] CASCADE
```

Granting Object Permissions with SQL Server Enterprise Manager

Object permissions are part of system administration. Granting and revoking these permissions are common tasks that you will perform daily.

SQL Server Enterprise Manager provides a fast, easy, and visual way to control object permissions. Permissions can be viewed based on objects or users. The ability to view the information in two different ways can make tracking down errors much easier.

Viewing Permissions for an Object

To view or modify object permissions in SQL Server Enterprise Manager, follow these steps:

1. Expand a database folder for a database you want to view or modify, and then highlight the icon for the object type you want to control.
2. Right-click the object, and select Properties.
3. Click the Permissions button. Figure 6.3 shows the resulting dialog for the `authors` table in the `pubs` database.

6

You can control whether you see all users, groups, and Windows users or groups available in the database as opposed to just a list of accounts that have already been given permissions on the object you are viewing. Note that implied permissions aren't shown here. This means two different things:

- dboo permissions aren't shown. So, if Joe creates a table, SQL Server Enterprise Manager (and the Transact-SQL help commands) doesn't show Joe's SELECT, INSERT, UPDATE, DELETE, and REFERENCES permissions, even though they are in place. Again, they aren't shown because they are implied by Joe's object ownership.

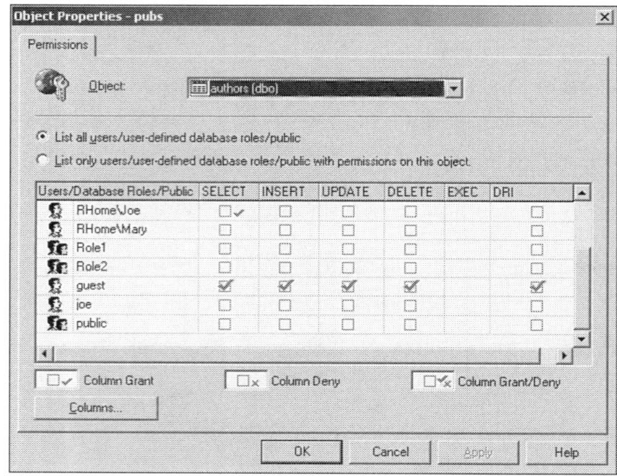

FIGURE 6.3

The Object Properties dialog showing permissions for a table.

- If Ann is a member of the accounting role and the accounting role has INSERT permissions for a table, the permissions don't show up for Ann because, again, the permissions are implied by her role membership. However, if you explicitly grant Ann permissions, they do show up here.

The Object Permissions tab works just like the Statement Permissions tab. To grant a permission, check a box. To deny a permission, place a red X in the box. To revoke a permission, clear the appropriate box. After you make the changes you want, click Apply or OK to make your changes take effect. To set column-level permissions, click the Columns button. Figure 6.4 shows this option for the `authors` table for user [Rhome\Joe].

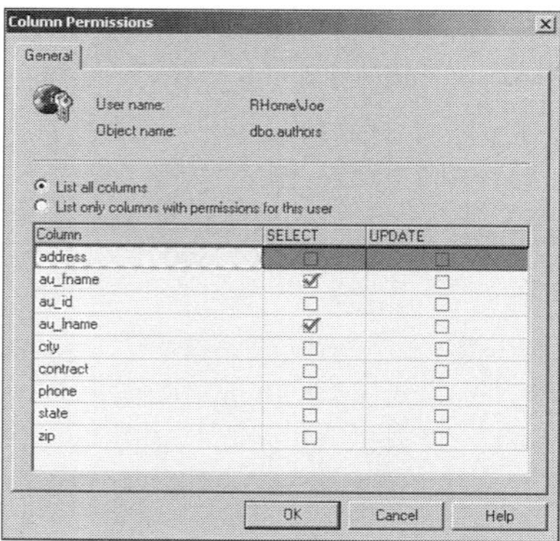

FIGURE 6.4

The Column Permissions dialog for the user [Rhome\Joe].

Notice that SQL Server Enterprise Manager is smart enough to present you with only the appropriate permissions options based on the type of object you have selected.

Viewing Permissions for a User or Database Role

You can also choose to view permissions for a user or role. To view or modify permissions in SQL Server Enterprise Manager on a user or role basis, follow these steps:

1. Expand a database folder for a database you want to view or modify; then highlight the icon for either Database Users or Database Roles.
2. Right-click the user or role, and select Properties.
3. Click the Permissions button. Figure 6.5 shows the resulting dialog for the database role Role1 in the pubs database.

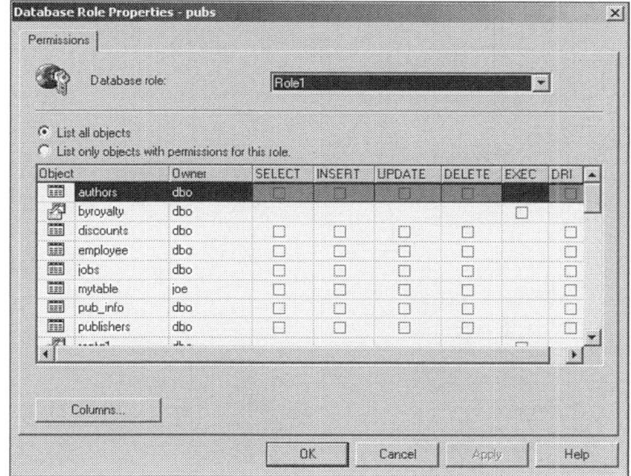

FIGURE 6.5
The Database Role Properties dialog.

4. Click the appropriate boxes to grant or revoke object permissions. When you finish setting your permissions, click Apply or OK to make your changes permanent.

Permissions on Views, Stored Procedures, and Functions

6

Views, stored procedures, and functions can help you administer permissions by allowing you to grant fewer permissions directly to the tables that hold your data. They can also help you avoid using column-level permissions, because such permissions can overly complicate your security administration model. Although you might not necessarily understand all the details about views and stored procedures (at least until Day 15), you can see how they help you restrict permissions.

Permissions on Views

The easiest way to think of a view is as a stored query that appears as a table to users. The stored query appears as a SELECT statement. To restrict certain users from accessing particular columns or rows, you can create a view that refers only to selected columns of a table. You can then assign permissions to the view for those users, and they won't have any rights to see the underlying table. They will be able to view data from the table only through the view. To illustrate this point, Figure 6.6 shows a table called `Employees`, with columns for first name, last name, address, and salary. Even if Mary is assigned the task of updating everyone's address, she won't have (and shouldn't have) permissions to access the salary column. You have two choices on how to accomplish this:

- Assign Mary permissions column by column (an awkward solution).
- Create a view based on only those columns you want her to be able to see and update (View_1, as shown in Figure 6.6).

FIGURE 6.6
Using a view to provide column-level security.

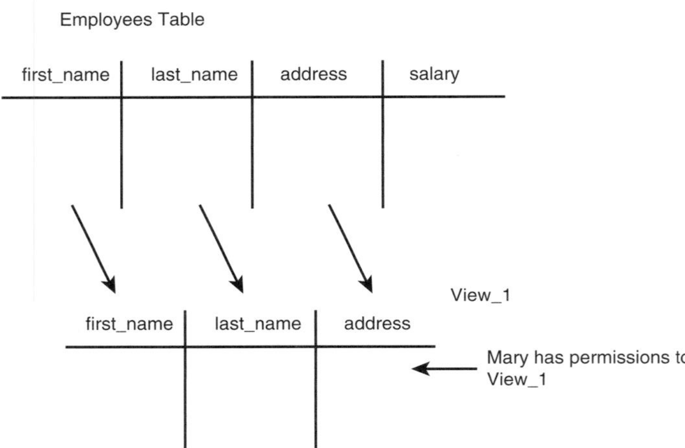

Permissions on Stored Procedures

Very much like permissions on views, permissions on stored procedures enable you to abstract users from the tables and not grant permissions directly on your tables. Unlike views, however, stored procedures can contain many statements and operations. In fact, in some ways, stored procedures are miniprograms. They can view or modify data in many tables or views and can gather data from other databases. In SQL Server 2000, they can even get data from other data sources. Therefore, they make nice containers in which to put many operations together. As you saw earlier today, a user needs only a single permission—EXECUTE—to run a stored procedure. It doesn't matter what the stored procedure does; users still need only that single permission. This is one of many reasons people use stored procedures extensively in SQL Server. You will examine stored procedures in great detail on Day 15.

Permissions on User-Defined Functions

Similar to permissions on stored procedures, permissions on functions allow you to abstract users from the tables and even views. User-defined functions can be nearly as complex as stored procedures.

However, user-defined functions can be a little weird in their permissions. If a function returns a scalar value (a single value), you need EXECUTE permissions to call the function. However, if the function returns a table data type, hence acting more like a view, you need SELECT permissions on the function. You'll examine both options for functions in great detail on Day 15.

Ownership Chains

Every object in SQL Server has an owner assigned to it. Although it's best if only the dbo user owns all the database objects, ordinary users can own objects in your database if you permit it.

NEW TERM For example, a user can create a view based on another user's tables and views. Users can also create stored procedures that use another user's tables, views, and stored procedures. These types of objects are called *dependent objects*. A large database can have a long series of dependencies and owners. This series is the *ownership chain*.

Consider this example. The dbo owns a table and gives Mary the right to select from his table. Mary creates a view based on the original table and gives Paul permission to select from her view. When Paul attempts to select information from Mary's view, the data is actually coming from the original (owned by the dbo) table. Did the dbo ever give Paul permission to select from the original table? Should Paul be allowed to view this data?

SQL Server handles these cases by looking at the ownership chain of objects and where permissions have been assigned.

The two distinct types of ownership chains are the single-owner chain and the broken ownership chain, in which more than one user owns objects in a dependency chain.

Single-Owner Chain

A single-owner chain is created when the same user owns all the dependent objects within a chain. In this case, SQL Server checks permissions only on the first object in the chain being accessed and doesn't check permissions on objects later in the chain.

6

For example, in Figure 6.7, the dbo owns all the objects in the chain. The dbo creates View1 based on the two tables (which are also owned by the dbo) and then creates a second view (View2) based on View1 (which is based on the tables). If the dbo gives Melissa SELECT permission from View2, permissions are checked only once—when Melissa attempts to SELECT on View2. SQL Server 2000 doesn't bother to check objects at a higher level, because the owner (dbo in this instance) is the same. SQL Server assumes that, if the owner is the same, the original owner would have granted permissions had SQL Server required it.

FIGURE 6.7

Example of a single-user ownership chain.

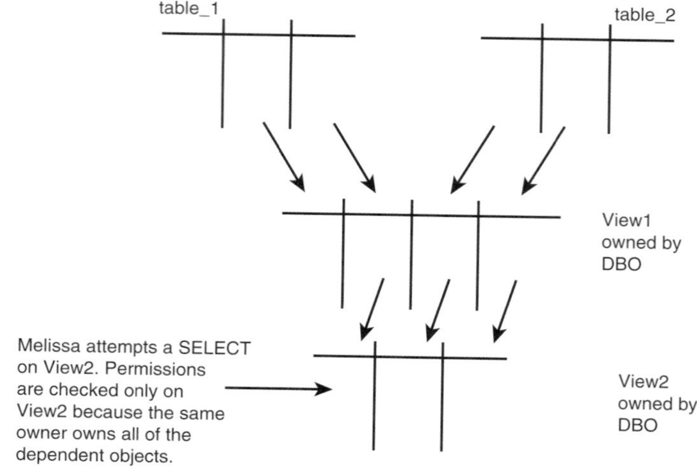

Broken Ownership Chains

When an object depends on other objects owned by different users, the ownership chain is broken. Permissions are checked on the first object and every object on which ownership has changed. In Figure 6.8, Melissa has created a view (View2) based on the dbo's View1. If Melissa gives Scott permission to select from her View2, permissions for Scott are checked on Melissa's View2 and then again on the dbo's View1. If Scott doesn't have permissions to select from the dbo's `View1`, he can't use the `SELECT` command on Melissa's view.

FIGURE 6.8

Example of a broken ownership chain.

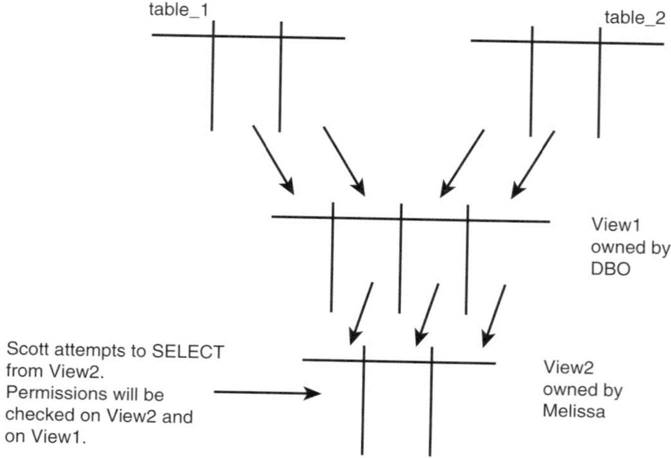

> Broken ownerships can become very complex very quickly. If you let users create objects, your database security will soon resemble a bowl of spaghetti. For this reason, all objects should be created by the dbo or users who are members of the db_owner or db_ddladmin role who have specifically set the object owner to dbo in their CREATE statements. Note that this Caution applies to production servers and might not apply to development servers (if you're not concerned about ownership chains).

Now imagine a chain of 10 or more objects. Trying to figure out which permissions are needed rapidly becomes a nightmare. Stick to single-owner chains whenever possible.

Designing a Permissions Strategy

Until now, today's lesson has focused on how to implement security. The following sections discuss why and when to implement a permissions scenario, as well as present a list of do's and don'ts.

Best Practices

SQL Server allows very flexible security, which can present a problem when you're trying to find the best way to secure your system. You should follow several rules, as well as general guidelines for assigning permissions. However, as usual in the computer industry, your situation might be different enough that the rules don't apply exactly.

If one person is in charge of the entire SQL Server, that person needs to connect as a member of the sysadmin fixed server role or as the sa login. If a user is in charge of a single database, she should be assigned as the dbo of that particular database (or a member of the db_owner role). If a user doesn't need special permissions to do her job, she should be treated as a normal database user and get permissions from the public role, from one or more roles of which she is a member, or from permissions directly assigned to her.

When you're assigning permissions, you can more easily maintain and document your security implementation if you

6

- Assign permissions that all users need to the public role
- Assign permissions that all members of a group of people need to that particular Windows group, or create a role and grant permissions to the role
- Assign individual permissions to users only if the permissions they need can't be assigned to a role or Windows group

Do's and Don'ts

The following are some general guidelines in the form of a Do/Don't list that can help you better manage your security. Most of these guidelines have to deal with the fact that users should have only the permissions they really need.

Do	Don't
DO grant users the permissions they need to do their jobs. For example, if all users need to see the data, be sure to grant SELECT permissions—probably to the public role.	**DON'T** grant users all permissions to fix a problem. Take the time to find out exactly which permissions they really need, and grant only those permissions. For example, you can easily solve issues caused by lack of permissions by making the user a member of the sysadmin or db_owner roles. Although this solution fixes the original security problem, it introduces new, more critical problems in that the user has too many permissions and can easily damage the database (or the entire server).
DO keep track of the permissions you've granted. Keep a log of what you do to your SQL Server. Another option is to generate scripts that document all the objects and permissions contained in the database. You'll learn how to generate scripts later today.	**DON'T** allow ordinary users to create databases or objects within databases. If you allow users to make databases and objects, you not only lose control over what SQL Server contains and where databases and objects reside, but also must deal with broken ownership chains. All objects within a database should be created by the dbo (or members of the db_owner or db_ddladmin roles specifying the object owner as dbo) and be documented.
DO assign a user to be the dbo of a database if he is responsible for that database. If other users need permissions associated with being the dbo user, you need to assign them membership in the db_owner role, because only one person can be assigned as the dbo.	**DON'T** grant permissions unless necessary. Users like to have permissions even when they don't need them. For example, if a certain user needs only SELECT permissions, grant only that permission, even though the user might request all permissions.

Another problem with granting users excessive permissions is that taking those permissions away later can often be difficult.

In a perfect world, all users could log in as members of the sysadmin role and would make changes only to the database to which they are supposed to make changes. Of course, because this isn't a perfect world, having everyone with sysadmin permissions is just asking for trouble sooner or later (usually sooner). Believe it or not, in some systems out there, everyone actually does indeed connect with the sa login.

In cases where excessive permissions exist, everything might be fine until one of the following occurs:

- Accidental user destruction of records
- Intentional user destruction of records
- Malfunctioning program destruction of records

A wise administrator guards against these situations through the judicious use of permissions.

Generating Scripts for Security

SQL Server can "reverse-engineer" database objects and security, as well as generate a script that can be run later to reconstruct objects and security. To access the scripting function from SQL Server Enterprise Manager, right-click a database and choose All Tasks, Generate SQL Scripts to open the dialog shown in Figure 6.9. (You may have to select the Show All button to see the same options as Figure 6.9.)

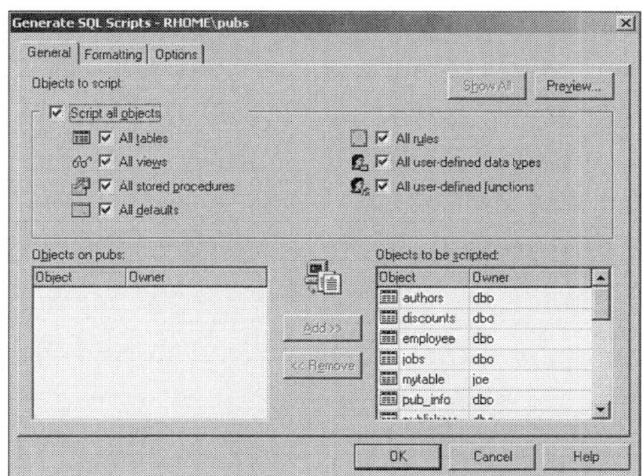

FIGURE 6.9

Selecting to generate SQL scripts.

When you are in the Generate SQL Scripts dialog, you can choose what kind of script to generate. The General tab contains the objects you are going to script. If you click the Formatting tab, notice that the default is to generate a script that drops and creates objects. Uncheck both of these options and any other option that's set on the Formatting tab. Click the Options tab to select the appropriate security scripting options (see Figure 6.10).

To do the actual scripting, click OK. You then are prompted for a filename and location for the script, or you can select the Preview button on the General tab, which causes the scripts to be generated in a preview window. If you choose Preview, you can copy the entire script into the Windows Clipboard by selecting the Copy button (see Figure 6.11).

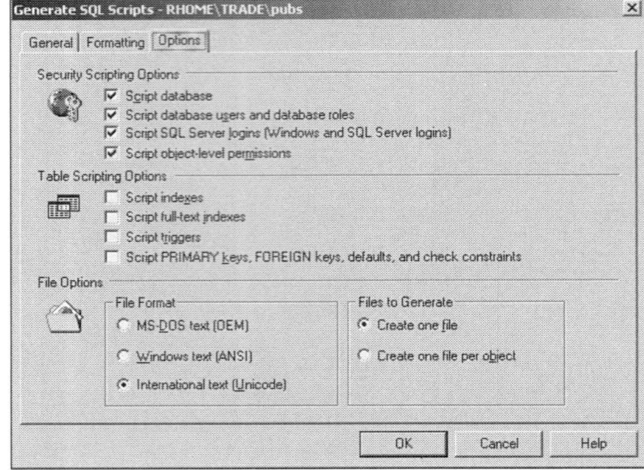

FIGURE 6.10

Selecting options to generate a script to re-create the security of a database.

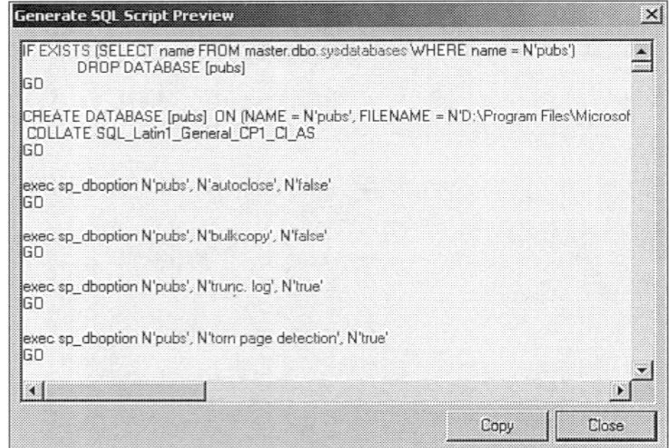

FIGURE 6.11

A preview of a script.

You can select different options from the main Generate SQL Scripts dialog, depending on your desired outcome.

Summary

SQL Server provides a secure environment through the use of permissions. A user connected to SQL Server might have certain rights based on the type of user she is. Security in SQL Server is hierarchical, with the sa account having all permissions, the dbo account having all permissions in its particular database, and the dboo having all permissions to the individual object it owns. Database users have no inherent permissions; they have only those permissions they have been granted.

The combination of statement and object permissions enables a system administrator to control exactly what occurs on the SQL Server. Statement permissions allow you to create objects and back up databases and transaction logs. Object permissions allow you to specify who can do what with the data contained in the objects. Common object permissions include SELECT, INSERT, UPDATE, and DELETE.

You can assign or revoke permissions by using Transact-SQL commands or the SQL Server Enterprise Manager.

Ownership chains demonstrate some of the challenges that can occur by allowing different users to create objects within a database.

Permissions must be implemented correctly and thoroughly to ensure the security and usability of your data.

SQL Server can reverse-engineer objects and permissions so you can save scripts that can easily and quickly reconstruct the security of a database.

Q&A

Q Establishing database permissions seems like a lot of work. Are permissions really that important?

A The answer depends. The more secure you want to keep your database, the more control and maintenance you have to perform using the permissions hierarchy.

Q Should I use roles, or should I just assign permissions to users directly?

A Roles and Windows groups are much easier to administer, because you can manage the permissions for hundreds or even thousands of users with a single command or click of a check box.

Q Must I use the built-in roles, or can I assign permissions without them?

A You don't have to use roles, but you are only hurting yourself by not using them. They provide convenient groupings of permissions for common administrative tasks.

Workshop

This section provides quiz questions to help you solidify your understanding of the concepts presented today. In addition to the quiz questions, exercises are provided to let you practice what you have learned today. Try to understand the quiz and exercise answers before continuing to tomorrow's lesson. Answers are provided in Appendix A, "Answers to Quiz Questions."

Quiz

1. How would you grant user Mary permission to read data from the table `MyTable`?
2. Mary created a table called `MaryTable` and gave Joe SELECT permissions on it. Joe created a view called JoeView. Joe wants Paul to have permission to `SELECT` from his view. Assuming that the users created their objects through their own owner IDs (not dbo), what permissions are necessary?
3. Joe is granted permission to `SELECT` on `dbo.MYTABLE`. Public is denied SELECT on `MYTABLE`. What are the effective permissions?
4. Joe is granted permission to `SELECT` on `dbo.MYTABLE`. Public is revoked SELECT on `MYTABLE`. What are the effective permissions?
5. What's the preferred way to prevent broken ownership chains?
6. You are the owner of a database. You want all users to be able to query the table `MYTABLE`. What command would you execute?
7. You execute the command `GRANT ALL TO JOE` in a user database. What permissions does Joe have?

Exercises

1. Create the following logins in SQL Server. Also, add each login to a user-defined database on your server: George, Henry, Ida, and John.
2. Now make John the dbo of the database you just referenced. Fix any errors you receive to make this change possible.

WEEK 1

DAY 7

Backing Up Your Databases

Yesterday you examined permissions and how to set them to secure your database. SQL Server 2000 is an inherently secure system; users can't do anything unless you explicitly grant them permissions to perform a particular action. You can easily give someone permissions and revoke any given permissions. Permissions are cumulative, so you should add up the permissions a user has, as well as any Windows groups and SQL Server roles of which the user is a member. If a deny permission is in effect, it overrides any other permissions.

Today and tomorrow you will turn to what's perhaps the most important but least glamorous aspect of supporting a relational database: backup and recovery. No matter how much work you do to make your database secure and your data available, data protection is the most critical aspect of your job. If your server crashes and all your data is lost, it's likely you've lost something else as well—your job! Today you will examine the backup process and the types of backup SQL Server supports. To lead off your examination of backup, you will look at the protection you can provide so that you don't lose disks and your SQL Server stays up and running.

Protecting Data with Mirroring, Duplexing, and Striping

To begin, you will examine fault-tolerance protection for disks on your server, SQL Server mirroring, and then backup and recovery. Implementing backup and recovery is all about preventing data loss; implementing fault tolerance for disks and devices also guards against data loss. Implementing fault tolerance, however, doesn't imply that you don't need to back up your databases.

NEW TERM It's best to start by defining some key terms. Two disks are said to be *mirrored* if they contain exactly the same data. When one disk is modified, the other is also modified (see Figure 7.1). *Duplexing* implies that the disks are mirrored, but a separate disk controller device (such as small computer system interface [SCSI] cards) controls each disk (see Figure 7.2). This configuration is different from mirroring because mirrored disks are assumed to be using the same disk controller, as Figure 7.1 illustrates. *Striped* disks distribute data evenly across multiple disks, with part of each logical piece of data on each disk in the striped set of disks (see Figure 7.3).

FIGURE 7.1
Disk mirroring.

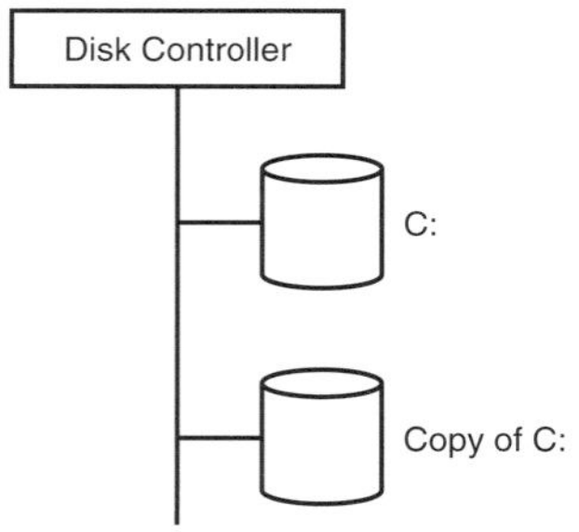

FIGURE 7.2
Disk duplexing.

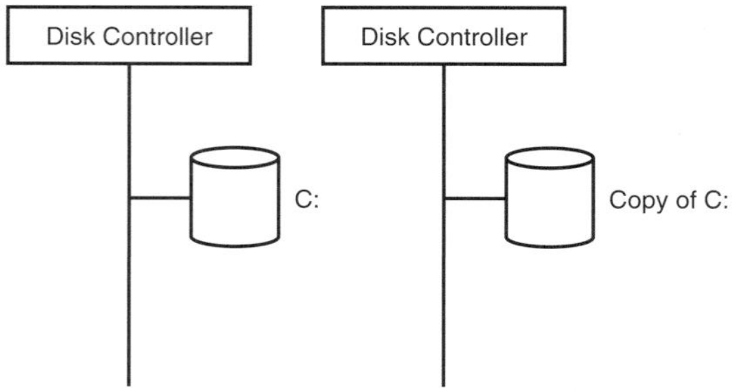

FIGURE 7.3
Disk striping.

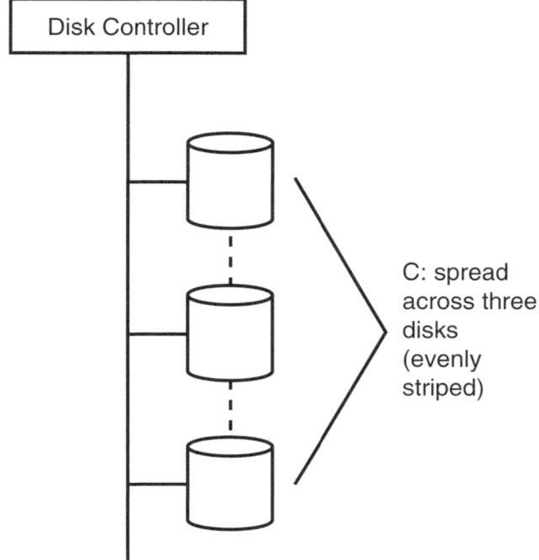

This discussion assumes that you are using SCSI disks. Although they aren't required—in fact, the servers we're using to write this book are using standard Integrated Development Environment (IDE) hard drives—SCSI disks generally provide superior performance and reliability when compared to non-SCSI disks.

RAID

Mirroring, duplexing, and striping all fit into a scheme known as Redundant Array of Inexpensive Disks (RAID). You configure disks into these RAID arrays to protect data on the disks and to provide high availability. If you can prevent your data from becoming unavailable, you can insulate your users from most hardware failures. The seven commonly accepted RAID levels are as follows:

RAID 0	Striped sets without parity information
RAID 1	Disk mirroring or duplexing
RAID 2, 3, 4	Iterations leading to RAID 5 (rarely implemented)
RAID 5	Striped sets with parity information evenly distributed within the stripe
RAID 10	Striped sets with parity mirrored across two controllers

RAID 10 (also called RAID 1+0) is becoming more widely deployed, but it's not typically included in a list of RAID options in most texts. It's included here because you will most likely run into this term when working with hardware vendors. RAID 10 isn't in wide use now because it requires nearly twice as much storage space as a RAID 5 system. Remember that RAID 10

> not only stripes information, but it also mirrors those stripe sets across multiple controllers. However, with RAID 10, unlike RAID 5, no parity information is kept.

RAID 0 provides no fault tolerance by itself, which means it isn't useful for fault tolerance. However, it can benefit performance. RAID 10 is a better option for fault tolerance while still providing superior performance.

RAID 1 is either mirroring or duplexing of data. With mirroring, however, if you lose the SCSI card controlling your mirrored disks, the data on those disks becomes unavailable. But you can still lose one of the disks and continue to access the data. If you duplex your disks, you can lose either a single disk or a disk controller card and still access your data. Therefore, duplexing is a superior fault-tolerance mechanism (but costs more because you need the additional disk controller card).

RAID levels 2, 3, and 4 were iterations of striping with parity that were functionally replaced with RAID 5.

RAID 5 is a set of three or more logically grouped disks. Each disk contains either a "stripe" or section of data or parity information. In RAID 5, the parity information for each stripe is distributed evenly throughout the set of disks. For example, if your RAID stripe set includes three disks, it might look like Figure 7.4.

FIGURE 7.4
RAID 5 striping of data with parity.

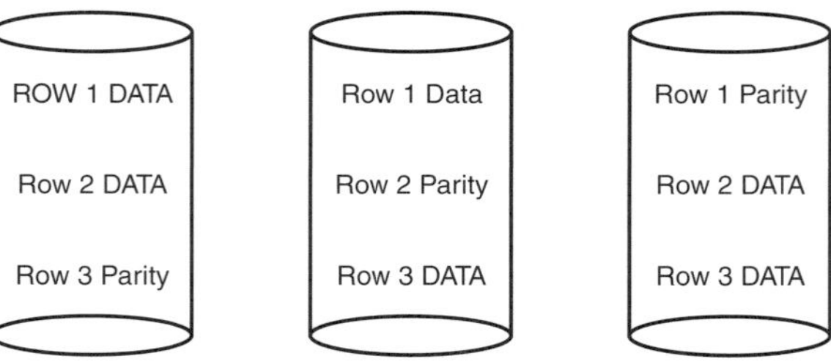

Parity information is a computed set of values that can be used to recalculate missing data. Current parity values are accurate to 1 in 2 billion. If you lose a single data disk and still have the rest of the data disks, as well as the parity disk, you can rebuild the missing data disk by using the parity information. If you lose the disk with the parity information on it, you still have all the data. Either way, you don't lose any data when using RAID with parity.

In row 1, half the data is on disk 1, the other half is on disk 2, and parity information (which, when combined with either of the disks, is enough information to rebuild the missing data) is on disk 3. Row 2 has half the data on disk 1, half on disk 3, and parity information on disk 2. Row 3 is similarly distributed. As you add additional disks to the set, it becomes more efficient in terms of overhead, with a higher risk of having more than one disk become unavailable at the same time (because the disk failure rate is theoretically constant for each disk). Although Figure 7.4 shows three disks, you can have as many disks as your hardware or software allows.

RAID 5 is generally accepted as the most inexpensive option because it has the least overhead—especially as you increase the number of disks. RAID 10 is generally considered the best solution for high-end installations of SQL Server, and if you can afford it, simply the best solution overall for performance, reliability, and availability. Mirroring or duplexing is considered to be fairly expensive, because it requires you to use double the amount of disk space to hold a given amount of information.

In the sample case here, you should have 54GB of data space available for your database server. You choose to implement a RAID 5 array using 18GB SCSI disks (the current industry standard as of this writing). You would need at least four disks: You are effectively losing one disk total for parity, leaving three disks available for data storage, and three disks × 18GB = 54GB. To implement the same amount of storage with mirroring, you would need six 18GB disks.

Hardware-Level RAID

Many computer companies implement hardware RAID solutions. These solutions tend to provide superior performance when compared with your other choice, Windows NT software RAID (examined next). Typically, hardware RAID is implemented with special controller cards and also often use external disk cabinets (either standalone or mounted on server "racks"). The downside of using hardware RAID is that these special controller cards—at least the good ones—are very expensive. You can buy a bunch of disks for the same price as one of these cards. Most people still buy these cards, however, because the performance is so much better than a purely software solution.

Software RAID with Windows 2000 Server

If you're running SQL Server 2000 on Windows 2000 Server (or Windows NT Server), you can take advantage of the operating system's built-in features to implement RAID across ordinary disks. RAID levels 0, 1, and 5 are implemented on Windows 2000's server products.

Other Supported Windows Platforms and RAID

Windows 98/ME, Windows NT Workstation, and Windows 2000 Professional don't support these software features but generally run just fine on hardware RAID implementations (because the operating system isn't aware that RAID has been implemented).

File System Choices

One other consideration when you're using RAID and disks in general is which file system to use for SQL Server. Currently, three file systems are supported for Windows 9*x*, Windows NT, and Windows 2000:

- *FAT*, the File Allocation Table, also known as FAT16, is the file system that has been around since early versions of MS-DOS. This file system has no security for files and doesn't support advanced options such as encryption. It's generally not recommended to hold SQL Server files.
- *FAT32* is the newer implementation of the FAT16 file system. It implements much more efficient storage of data on disk but has the same limitations as FAT in terms of security and encryption. FAT32 is implemented on later versions of Windows 95 (OSR2) and is fully supported on Windows 98 and Windows 2000. Note that FAT32 isn't supported on Windows NT 4.0.
- *NTFS*, the New Technology File System, supports many advanced features, including compression and encryption (in Windows 2000), neither of which should be used in most OLTP (Online Transaction Processing) environments. More importantly, NTFS supports permissions on individual directories and files. You therefore can secure access to the SQL Server data files to only the SQL Server service accounts (and Windows administrators).

How Backup Works

SQL Server 2000 backs up data *dynamically*. This means that you don't have to stop using a database to back it up. As always, running your backup at a time of relative inactivity is a good idea because doing so takes some resources. However, benchmarks have shown that the backup process has very little impact on the overall throughput of SQL Server's real work, your data queries and modifications.

SQL Server database backups are consistent at the point of the *completion* of a database backup. Therefore, if your backup finishes at 6 p.m., you know that you have an image of all your data as of that time.

Note

> In all releases of SQL Server before version 7.0, the backup was consistent with the *beginning* of the backup. This change might be insignificant, or it might affect any previously designed backup strategies you have. Either way, it's worth noting.

You can store database and transaction log backups in files dynamically, or you can preallocate storage locations on backup devices. A backup device can be a physical disk file, a tape, a remote physical disk file, or a Named Pipe. Named Pipes are typically used with third-party backup solutions. You will most likely back up your databases to disk or to tape.

A member of the sysadmin fixed server role or the db_owner or db_backupoperator database roles can back up a database or transaction log. As you saw on Day 6, "Establishing Database Permissions," you can grant others permissions to back up a database and a transaction log.

Caution

> SQL Server 2000 backups aren't compatible with any previous release of SQL Server. SQL Server 2000 can read backups made with SQL Server 7.0 but can't read backups taken with earlier versions of SQL Server. This issue is mostly an upgrade consideration but something you need to be aware of if you are administering SQL Server. The only way to read a SQL Server backup from releases before 7.0 is to install the earlier release and use the SQL Server Version Upgrade Wizard against the database if it's SQL Server 6.5, or export/import the data if it's an earlier release.

Backup Types

You can perform several kinds of backups in SQL Server 2000. You will examine full database backups, differential database backups, file and filegroup backups, and transaction log backups. For the context of the discussion here, all backups except transaction log backups will be referred to as *database backups*.

Tip

> For historical reasons, backups are sometimes referred to as *dumps* or *database dumps*.

The following is an overview of the different types of backups:

- A *full database backup* backs up an entire database, including all tables, indexes, system tables, and database objects (which are contained in those system tables). A database backup also backs up transaction log records but doesn't store empty pages or remove any transaction log records from a database.
- A *differential database backup* backs up all the data pages modified since the last full database backup. You might want to use differential backups because restoring them is faster than restoring transaction log backups. You'll examine the restoration process in tomorrow's lesson.
- A *file and/or filegroup backup* involves backing up only selected files or filegroups rather than the entire database. If you were to place one or more tables or indexes on separate filegroups rather than leave all data and indexes on the default filegroup, you could independently back up that data. The advantage here is that if an individual disk fails and you have a backup of just the files from the failed disk, you could restore the affected files without recovering the entire database. This type of backup should be faster than a full database backup. However, this procedure is getting beyond what the average SQL Server administrator is likely to do. This advanced backup mechanism is discussed in more detail in *Microsoft SQL Server 2000 Unleashed* by Sams Publishing.
- A *transaction log backup* contains a copy of the records of each change made to your database over time. It includes statements run by users, as well as background system activity, such as allocating space within your database. The log can then be "replayed" to restore all the activity (transactions) that has been recorded in the transaction log. Another nice feature of the transaction log is that you can replay your transactions to a specific point in time. You'll learn more about this type of backup on Day 8, "Restoring Your Databases."

Transactions and Checkpoints

Transactions (discussed in depth on Day 12, "Using Transact-SQL Extensions") are a logical set of operations that either all complete successfully or all fail. Each data modification statement you run against a database is, by default, a transaction and is recorded in the transaction log (a set of records in a separate database file) for each database. You can also explicitly request a transaction so that multiple statements are completed or they fail as though they were a single operation.

You can use the information recorded in the transaction log to recover changes to your database to a point in time other than when you have taken a full database backup. Other tasks, such as space allocation, are also written to the transaction log. Over time, the transaction log will fill up if you don't back it up or erase it (or it will fill the disk that the log file is on if you haven't disabled the file's autogrow feature). Autogrowth options were discussed on Day 4, "Creating and Administering Databases and Data Files." You can clean out completed transactions from the transaction log file by using the `BACKUP LOG` statement, examined later today. When a transaction is complete (all modifications to the data have been completed successfully), the transaction log records are written to disk immediately. This is part of what guarantees that your database can be recovered in the event of a failure. However, what writes the data pages to disk? The answer is the checkpoint process.

Checkpoints

NEW TERM Day 12 provides a full explanation of the checkpoint process, but a cursory examination is necessary here. A *checkpoint* is a periodic operation that copies out to disk data pages that have been modified in memory. Many events can also cause data pages and log records to be written to disk. However, checkpoints are the primary mechanism of synchronizing a database between what has occurred in memory and what has physically been written to your disks. The checkpoint itself is also a *logged transaction*, meaning that the checkpoint itself is also written to the transaction log and saved to disk.

Alternative Backup Strategies

Some administrators believe that an alternative way to back up SQL Server is to stop the SQL Server service and then back up all files associated with SQL Server (in particular, the files from your `\mssql\data` folder). However, this approach isn't as fully functional as it sounds because it might not allow you to recover databases individually and doesn't provide the ability to perform a point-in-time recovery. Therefore, it's strongly recommended that you use SQL Server backups and not back up the files directly. You should also note that "normal" Windows backups don't back up the device files for SQL Server while SQL Server is running, because the files are open when SQL Server is running.

Backup Terminology

NEW TERM SQL Server 2000 uses several terms in the documentation and user interface concerning backups. You have a *backup set* after you run a single backup command. It's the database backup that resides on a backup device (your backup media, examined later today). When you create a backup, you're also creating a *media set*. A media set is one or more backup devices used during a backup or set of backups. It is particularly handy when you look at SQL Server 2000's capability to back up to multiple devices. This feature, known as *parallel striped backup*, is also examined later today.

NEW TERM The other term to know is *media family,* which refers to all the tapes used for a single backup device. So, if performing a backup takes five tapes, those five tapes together are the media family for that backup. In that case, it's basically the same as a backup set. If you perform a parallel striped backup, each set of tapes from each tape drive involved in the backup is known as a media family.

Sound confusing? Maybe, but these terms are sprinkled throughout the Microsoft documentation on backups and restoring databases. The good news is that you can run plenty of backups and never use these terms. The bad news is that you might see them periodically, and it's good to have some idea what the documentation is talking about.

Backup Considerations

You should consider many questions when performing backups. How often should you back up your databases? Which databases should you back up? Where should you back them up to? How long should your backups be kept? Who's responsible for the backups, and how will you verify that they are good backups? Now examine these questions one at a time, starting with who's responsible.

Who's Responsible for the Backups?

I like to say, "If it's not someone's problem, it won't get done." When it comes to talking about backups, this statement is especially true. Backups are, well, boring. When it comes to glamour, this isn't it. It takes a lot of work to properly set up backups and test them regularly. Backup responsibility might very well fall on the database administrator or the system administrator. It's also entirely possible that the network administrator will want to help perform backups. Ultimately, however, the important point is that they be someone's responsibility and that they are performed.

How Will You Verify That the Backups Are Good?

If a database becomes corrupt, you might still be able to back it up. However, you might not. You might not even get a warning message about the corruption. You should run some checks before backup begins (you'll see them shortly), and SQL Server runs many checks internally to detect corruption (and possibly even fix it). But if you don't run the consistency checks or don't check the results first, you can't tell whether your backups are good until you attempt to restore them.

It's a really good idea to test your backups periodically by restoring one to a test server and ensuring that everything is working as expected. This way, you know whether your backups are good and can periodically test your restoration process. SQL Server 2000 includes the capability to verify the integrity of the backup after it is taken. Besides, who has ever heard of database administrators being fired because they were paranoid with their backup and recovery planning?

Which Databases Should You Back Up?

This advice might sound obvious, but you should back up all your user-defined databases. If creating the database and putting it on a server are important enough, backing it up is also important. What about system databases? You should back up `master` and MSDB. Having a backup of the `model` database might be useful, but you don't need to back up `tempdb`. If you are using replication, you should also back up your distribution database regularly. I recommend that you treat it like any other frequently modified user database.

Where Should You Back Up Your Databases?

As I mentioned previously, you can back up your databases to disk, tape, a network drive, or a Named Pipe. Tape is most people's preferred media but has some significant limitations, not the least of which is speed. Backups to disk are usually the fastest. An alternative is to back up your database to another server's disk over the network (of course, this would require that your SQL Server service account have security permissions on the remote server's file share). You should back up your disk backups to tape, whether those disk backups are to a local disk or to another server's disk. A typical scenario might be to back up to a network server over a fast network connection (100MB Ethernet, ATM, and so on) and then use Windows 2000's built-in backup program to back up the backup devices or files. An alternative is to purchase a third-party backup utility (which might or might not use the Named Pipe option). Most major brands of backup utilities include an add-in to back up SQL Server databases.

As tape speeds increase, they become the preferred media for backups. The limitation for SQL Server backups (in terms of speed) is typically the speed of the tape drives, not the speed of SQL Server.

How Often Should You Back Up Your Databases?

The answer to the question of how often you should back up depends on the size of your database, how quickly you want the recovery process to run, and how much data you're willing to lose. For databases smaller than a few gigabytes in size, the answer is usually a full database backup daily, with transaction log backups at some point during the day. At a minimum, you should back up your databases weekly, with at least daily transaction log backups. You'll examine shortly the special considerations for system databases.

As a database grows significantly larger, you might not have enough time to fully back it up daily. However, as tape drives become faster (or you take advantage of parallel backups), this limitation might disappear. Again, the SQL Server 2000 software typically isn't the limitation on the speed of your backups.

How Long Should You Keep Your Backups?

You might not need some backups as soon as you take the next one. It's usually a good idea, however, to have a few around in case one of the previous backups is found to be corrupt. Many sites choose to maintain the last two weeks' worth of backups as an arbitrary retention period. You might also maintain data for legal requirements, such as tax data needing several years of backups. You should investigate these requirements before determining your backup retention policies. The last thing in the world you want is to be criminally culpable for not storing backups long enough.

How Long Will It Take to Recover a Backup?

There's nothing worse than having a server crash, except possibly when your boss asks, "So, how long will it take to recover the server?" and you have absolutely no idea. Therefore, regularly testing the recovery of your backups can help you avoid embarrassment in a difficult situation and understand your recovery process better. You'll examine the recovery process tomorrow.

Do You Have a Disaster Recovery Plan?

One of the best things ever done in the mainframe era involved having a disaster recovery plan and occasionally running disaster "drills." I was once involved in such a drill. We grabbed our tapes, jumped on a plane, flew to a backup site, and got our mainframe up and running, as well as our databases. If you want to test a backup plan and verify that everything you need is being backed up, run one of these drills. It's amazing how many things you forget. Interesting questions might arise, such as does your backup site have the same brand/model of tape drive available? Did you remember to get the software you need in your backups?

Some typical items to consider including in your plan are the following:

- Windows NT/2000 on CD
- The appropriate service pack for Windows NT/2000
- A SQL Server 2000 CD, along with the appropriate service pack that you've applied to your server(s)
- Any application-specific software or external DLLs (extended stored procedures) you've incorporated into SQL Server, including third-party backup and recovery software (if used)
- *Your backups*
- *Any special configuration changes you've made that are not covered by the above items*

You don't necessarily have to jump on a plane if you have the discipline to make sure no one cheats and grabs that last file you need off the network or sneaks back to her desk. You can also ask yourself these questions:

- Do you know what drive SQL Server is installed on?
- Do you know what character set and sort order were used?
- Which network libraries are installed?
- Do you know the network account SQL Server was using?
- What drives and filenames are used for each database?
- What mail profile was used to automate email with SQL Server?

You get the idea. If you have more than one SQL Server, dealing with such a disaster can quickly become unmanageable without a plan. Perhaps this plan requires some serious thought before a disaster occurs. Remember that disasters can happen at any time. Floods, fire, ice storms, tornadoes, hurricanes, earthquakes, volcanoes, sabotage, and self-inflicted problems (a poorly written transaction, for example) are all real problems in various parts of the world, perhaps even in your area.

Where Do You Keep Your Backup Tapes?

Do you keep your backup tapes in your desk? On top of the server? In the tape drive on the server? I've heard all these answers before. If an earthquake has just leveled your building (and perhaps all the buildings around yours as well), can you still get to your building, let alone your backup tapes? You should invest in an offsite storage location for your tapes. Some companies simply have an employee rotate them to his house. A better solution for relatively small databases is to look into a safe deposit box at a bank. For larger backups, tape vault companies specialize in safe, secure offsite storage. Most reputable tape vault companies deliver and pick up tapes, and should even pick them out and bring them to you in an emergency (for a nominal fee). You should inspect the vault and verify that the company has taken adequate precautions (and security has been addressed) to protect one of your company's most valuable assets—its data.

Miscellaneous Tape Considerations

If you choose to back up to tapes, you should be aware of the following:

- SQL Server writes to tape using American National Standards Institute (ANSI) tape headers. This means that SQL Server can share tapes with Windows NT or Windows 2000 backups.
- SQL Server uses the console program to notify an operator when a tape needs to be changed (if the program is running).

- As you might expect, you can store more than one backup on a single tape.
- If you plan to take advantage of a particular tape drive's special features, such as hardware compression, make sure that the same model will be available when you need to recover using the tape. This is particularly true if you plan to keep the tapes around for a long time. Are you sure that you'll still have that brand of tape drive available in five years?

Backing Up User Databases

As we just stated, user-created databases should be backed up regularly. At a minimum, this means weekly for full database backups and daily for transaction log backups. Daily database backups are preferred, with periodic transaction log backups. Remember that a full database backup doesn't empty transactions from the transaction log of a database. A differential backup also doesn't remove entries from the transaction log.

The following are some reasons not to back up a database regularly:

- If the data is read-only, a single (verified) backup is probably sufficient.
- It's a test database, and the data either isn't significant or can be easily re-created.
- The data can be re-created quickly from an alternative source.

However, you should focus on the times you need to back up your databases. If you have a large database (bigger than a few gigabytes), you might want to back it up immediately after you create it.

Database Recovery Models and Backup

New Term SQL Server 2000 introduces *recovery models*, which allow you to configure how much transaction logging you want to have for your database. Setting a recovery model for your database dramatically changes the types of backups allowed and how you perform recovery. However, you must understand them so that you know what kind of backup to perform.

The reason for having these different recovery models is that you might need different levels of availability for restore on your database. One reason you might have different logging needs revolves around bulk operations (they were often referred to as *nonlogged operations* in previous releases). Operations such as loading in large amounts of data may mean that you would need to take your backup only before or after the load operation, but not during. The recovery models fully support this type of configuration via the bulk-logged recovery model.

Another common configuration is that you want to restore to only a full database backup. For instance, if your database changes only once a day and is otherwise read-only, the simple recovery model is for you.

Full Recovery Model

The full recovery model is probably what you'll run most databases with. The full recovery model allows all database backups (full, transaction log, differential, file/filegroup). You can recover to a point in time or to a "marked" transaction (which you'll examine later today). Basically, if you want 100 percent data protection (and job protection), set your database to the full recovery model and leave it there. This is the default setting for a new database created with the Standard and Enterprise Editions of SQL Server 2000.

Bulk-Logged Recovery Model

When you perform selected commands, such as `SELECT INTO`, `BULK INSERT`, `CREATE INDEX`, `WRITETEXT`, and `UPDATETEXT`, you typically write large amounts of data. In the full recovery model, every row you added to SQL Server is recovered fully in the transaction log. As you can imagine, that means your data is essentially written twice. That provides the maximum amount of recoverability but may be excessive for your needs.

In bulk-logged mode, the data modified by these commands isn't fully logged; images of the modified pages are logged after the page is loaded. Because of the method used to log your data in the database, point-in-time recoverability is lost. You can restore only to the end of a database backup or the end of a transaction log backup.

Caution

> The other issue with bulk-logged mode is what happens if you lose a data file. When you are set to full recovery mode, you simply back up the transaction log and then perform a database restore (you'll see how tomorrow). However, transaction log backups made while in bulk-logged mode require access to the database. If your database files are damaged, you can't back up your transaction log and may lose work. This situation might not be an issue for you (you may have a backup taken right before you began loading data into the database), but you definitely need to be aware of it.

Simple Recovery Model

The simple recovery model is the most restrictive. Basically, use this model when all you care about is getting back to your last full backup, or perhaps a differential backup. Transaction log backups aren't available, and your transaction log is periodically erased.

In SQL Server 7.0 and earlier releases, you set the database-level options Truncate Log on Checkpoint and Select Into/BulkCopy to get into the equivalent of the simple recovery model.

If your database is such that all you need to do in a failure is to recover to a single point in time (the time of your last full backup or differential backup), simple logging is for you. The least amount of information possible is logged in your transaction log, and the log is kept to the minimum size possible. Some transaction logging still occurs so that SQL Server itself can remain consistent internally and support objects such as triggers that use the transaction log.

Basically, *never* set the simple recovery model option on a database that you want to be able to run data modification queries against and expect to be able to recover the database. It's fine for sample databases, static databases that don't change, or databases in which you can easily redo any work that's run, but you should never use this mode on production databases where users are interactively adding, changing, or deleting data.

Viewing and Setting the Recovery Model

To view the recovery model your database is currently in, run

INPUT
```
Select DATABASEPROPERTYEX('mydb','recovery')
```

You get back either `FULL`, `BULK_LOGGED`, or `SIMPLE`.

The `pubs` and Northwind databases ship with recovery mode set to `SIMPLE`. However, the `model` database is set to `FULL`. Remember that creating a database involves first copying `model`, so you inherit `model`'s settings when you create a new database.

To change the recovery model, use the `ALTER DATABASE` statement. You run this command, for example, to change the `pubs` database to `FULL`:

INPUT
```
Alter Database pubs SET RECOVERY FULL
```

Backing Up System Databases

Next, you'll examine the system databases and how often you should back them up. System databases include `master`, `model`, MSDB, and `tempdb`. Their backup strategy is different from the backup strategy used for databases you create.

The `master` Database

The `master` database is a special system database. If you lose the `master` database for some reason, SQL Server 2000 can't function. Therefore, how and when you back up this database are critical.

Note

> Unlike SQL Server versions 6.*x* and earlier, the `master` database is kept on its own set of files, with the transaction log as a separate file. If you're upgrading from SQL Server 6.5 or earlier, note the changes here carefully.

Microsoft recommends that you back up the `master` database each time you modify it. As a practical matter, however, backing up each time isn't really possible in most environments. Consider the items found in the `master` database: databases, logins, system and user error messages, and more. Logins, for example, include passwords. It's not always practical to back up the `master` database each time someone changes her password. I recommend that you back up the `master` database daily. This means that any passwords changed after the last backup you've recovered aren't set properly. However, this applies only to logins created with SQL Server Authentication Mode security.

It's also critical to back up the `master` database after any significant changes are made to your server, such as configuration changes; creating, changing, or dropping databases; adding remote or linked servers; or enabling replication.

Caution

> By default, the `master` database is in simple recovery mode. You should probably leave this mode set because you can perform only full database backups of the master database. Differential, file, filegroup, and transaction log backups aren't available for the master database.

7

The MSDB Database

The MSDB database contains the support information for the SQL Server Agent service, as well as for replication operations. If you choose to take advantage of the SQL Server Agent service (and I suspect you will), you need to take regular backups of this database.

As a rule, MSDB should be backed up at least weekly, with log backups daily. Just as with user databases, more frequent backups might be justified. You might want to synchronize your backups with the `master` database. If you must rebuild the `master` database (likely in the event of a significant media failure), your MSDB database is reinitialized and therefore must be restored from backup as well.

For some reason, Microsoft shipped MSDB in simple recovery mode. I don't understand this choice and think you'll want to switch MSDB to `FULL`. Either that, or change the recommendation here to running full daily backups of MSDB.

The `model` Database

The `model` database probably won't change often. After you add custom tables, views, security, and stored procedures to the model database, they tend to remain there with few modifications over time. However, because an administrator's paranoia can be a very good thing, it's good to have a backup. If you have to rebuild your `master` database, the `model` database is also reset.

The `tempdb` Database

The `tempdb` database is reset after each restart of the MSSQLServer service. Therefore, you don't need to back up the `tempdb` database. You should leave `tempdb` in `SIMPLE` mode so that the transaction log doesn't grow unnecessarily.

The Distribution Database

If you're using replication, the distribution database stores replicated transactions. You'll examine replication in more detail on Day 17, "Implementing Replication Methodologies." You should treat the distribution database like any important user database; daily backups and occasional transaction log backups are recommended. Perform more frequent backups as time and maintenance overhead allow.

Preparing to Implement Backups

Now that you've gone over much of the theory of database backups, you can focus on the physical implementation of backups. You will examine full database backups, differential backups, and file and filegroup backups. You will also look at transaction log backups. Finally, you'll wrap up the section by examining a real-world server configuration and setting up a backup plan for the server.

Along the way, we've thrown in a few topics of interest that you need to know. You must store your backups somewhere, and you must verify the integrity of your backups and your databases.

Creating a Backup Device

The first step in preparing to back up your databases is to create a backup device. Although having pre-declared backup devices isn't technically necessary when you're performing backups, it can make your backup command syntax easier, as well as help out the poor administrator who must work on the system when you're finished with it.

A backup device is simply a pointer in the SQL Server system catalog (the `sysdevices` system table in the `master` database) that contains a logical name and a physical path to a local hard disk file, a local tape drive, or a remote file on another computer. Backups can't be performed using remote tape drives. When you specify the `BACKUP` command, you can reference this logical name rather than specify the full path and filename each time. This approach helps reduce the overhead of repeatedly typing all that information and is less error prone.

When you first install SQL Server 2000, no backup devices are defined on your system. One of your first steps is to create them. If you want to back up to a tape device, you typically create only a single backup device pointing to the tape drive. You might still create multiple "logical" devices, each one pointing back to the same tape drive. Of course, if this server has multiple tape drives, you should create one device per tape drive.

For disk (or network) backup devices, you would typically create one backup device for each database. A good place to start is to define backup devices for system databases that exist on your server.

Controlling Backup Devices with Transact-SQL

You create the backup devices by using the `sp_addumpdevice` system stored procedure:

SYNTAX

```
sp_addumpdevice [@devtype =] 'device_type',
[@logicalname =] 'logical_name',[@physicalname =] 'physical_name'
[, {[@cntrltype =] cntrltype |
[@devstatus =] 'device_status'}]
```

In this syntax,

- *`device_type`* is the type of device you want the backup device to point to. It's one of the following:

`Disk`	A pointer to a physical file on a local hard disk
`Tape`	A pointer to a local tape drive
`Pipe`	A pointer to a Named Pipe

7

- *logical_name* is the name you want to use in your backup and restore commands when referencing this physical backup location.
- *physical_name* is the physical location of the backup device. For disks, it would be the path and filename. For a tape, it's the pointer to the tape drive. For a Named Pipe, it's the network address of the Named Pipe.
- *cntrltype* is an obsolete parameter provided for backward compatibility.
- *device_status* determines whether the ANSI tape headers are ignored when writing to this backup device. If you specify a *device_type* of `Tape`, SQL Server assumes that you mean `NoSkip` here. This means that if a tape has header information about a previous backup on the tape, SQL Server doesn't automatically ignore it and reinitialize the tape. If you want this behavior (automatically initializing the tape even if it contains data), you can specify `Skip` here.

A brief mention of some details for the *physical_name* parameter in the syntax is necessary here. If you specify a local path, it must be fully qualified. An example might be

```
d:\program files\Microsoft SQL Server\mssql\backup\master_backup.bak
```

A network file must be in the form of a Universal Naming Convention (UNC) path, such as

```
\\remoteserver\backups\sql\master_backup.bak
```

Finally, you specify tape units by using the convention

```
\\.\tape#
```

starting at `0` for the first tape drive on your system. So, if you have a single tape unit, you would refer to it as

```
\\.\tape0
```

The following example creates a dump device that can be used for the `master` database. This command adds a new disk backup device called `master_backup` in the appropriate physical location:

```
EXEC sp_addumpdevice 'disk', 'master_backup',
➥'d:\program files\Microsoft SQL Server\mssql\backup\master_backup.bak'
```

Note

The term *dump device* is a throwback to earlier releases of SQL Server. It's still used here for backward compatibility with SQL Server 6.5. The same backward compatibility consideration applies to the stored procedures you'll work with later today, such as `sp_dropdevice`.

To drop a backup device, you run the `sp_dropdevice` system stored procedure:

```
sp_dropdevice [@logicalname =] 'logical_name', [@delfile =] 'delfile'
```

In this syntax,

- *`logical_name`* is the name you want to use in your backup and restore commands when referencing this physical backup location.
- *`delfile`*, if included, specifies that the physical backup file (if on disk) should be deleted.

So, if you want to drop the `pubs_backup` backup device, first create it with sp_addumpdevice, and then drop it with sp_dropdevice. The code to do this is:

```
EXEC sp_addumpdevice 'disk', 'pubs_backup',
➥'d:\program files\Microsoft SQL Server\mssql\backup\pubs_backup.bak'
```

```
EXEC sp_dropdevice 'pubs_backup'
```

To get rid of the backup file at the same time (assuming you're backing up `pubs` to disk), run the following:

```
EXEC sp_dropdevice 'pubs_backup','delfile'
```

You should receive output similar to this:

```
Successfully deleted the physical file 'd:\program files\Microsoft SQL
Server\mssql\backup\pubs_backup.dat'.

Device dropped.
```

To view a list of all devices on your system, run the `sp_helpdevice` system stored procedure:

```
sp_helpdevice [[@devname =] 'logical_name']
```

In this syntax, *`logical_name`* is the name you want to use in your backup and restore commands when referencing this physical backup location. For example, if you run

```
EXEC sp_helpdevice
```

you see the following output, which is broken here to fit the page:

```
device_name   physical_name
description                          status     cntrltype   size

master        D:\Program Files\Microsoft SQL Server\mssql\data\master.mdf
master_backup D:\Program Files\Microsoft SQL Server\mssql\backup\master...
mastlog       D:\Program Files\Microsoft SQL Server\MSSQL\data\mastlog...
modeldev      D:\Program Files\Microsoft SQL Server\MSSQL\data\model.mdf
modellog      D:\Program Files\Microsoft SQL Server\MSSQL\data\modellog...
```

```
tempdev        D:\Program Files\Microsoft SQL Server\MSSQL\data\tempdb.mdf
templog        D:\Program Files\Microsoft SQL Server\MSSQL\data\templog...

disk, backup device  16          2          0
special, physical disk, 1 MB     2          0          128
special, physical disk, 0.6 MB   2          0          80
special, physical disk, 0.8 MB   2          0          96
special, physical disk, 2 MB     2          0          256
special, physical disk, 0.5 MB   2          0          64
special, physical disk, 4 MB     2          0          512

(7 row(s) affected)
```

Notice that several are reported as `special, physical disk`, but one is reported as `disk, backup device`. That is your backup device. You need to sift through the results of `sp_helpdevice` to find your backup devices.

Controlling Backup Devices with SQL Server Enterprise Manager

You also can use SQL Server Enterprise Manager to create or remove a backup device. To do so, expand your server, expand the management folder, and highlight the Backup icon. Right-click the icon (or anywhere on the right side of the Enterprise Manager window), and select New Backup Device from the pop-up menu. You should see a dialog that looks like Figure 7.5. Notice again that no backup devices are defined when you first install SQL Server 2000 (notice, however, that the `master_backup` device added with Transact-SQL above is present).

FIGURE 7.5

The Backup Device Properties dialog.

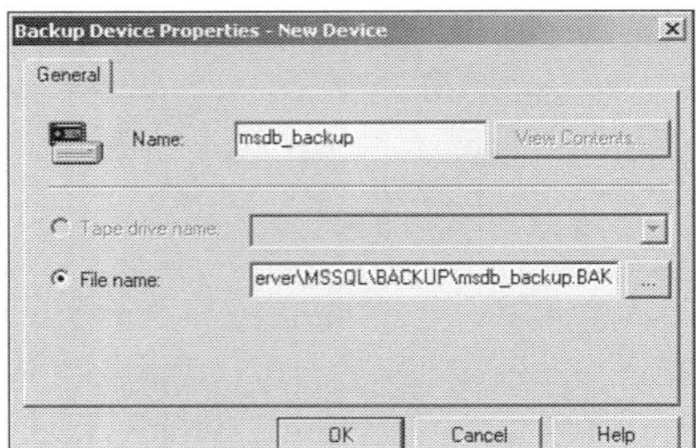

Just as you did before, you can create a backup device here to hold your database backups. I've created a backup device named `msdb_backup` as a container to hold the MSDB database. Notice that SQL Server Enterprise Manager fills in the filename for you when you type the device name and defaults, keeping the same name as the logical name of the device. Keeping the device's logical and physical names the same is an exceptionally good idea.

After you fill out the dialog, click OK to finish creating the device. If you want to change a device to point to a network location, enter the UNC path to that remote server in the

Name text box. Never use mapped drive letters, because getting them working is very complicated. Remember that when you create the backup device, you are simply creating a pointer in the system tables; no actual data is written to the device yet.

To remove a backup device with SQL Server Enterprise Manager, simply right-click the device in the Backup Devices folder, and select Delete from the pop-up menu. Confirm the deletion, and the device is removed from the SQL Server system tables. If the physical file has been created, your removal of the backup device in SQL Server Enterprise Manager doesn't delete it.

Verifying Database Consistency

When you have a backup device available, you are almost ready to begin backing up your databases. You might need to take an important step before you can start, however. As we just mentioned, a corrupt database backup is worthless. Therefore, you must verify that your backup is good. Microsoft provides two options for you to verify the integrity of your database and your backups. The backup command has an option to validate the backup after it's complete. A set of commands also provides the capability to verify your database's integrity.

For now, focus on the consistency-checking capabilities you have within your SQL Server database. If your database is okay before the backup, it's very likely that your backup itself is also okay. To verify the consistency of your database, use extensions of the Database Consistency Checker (DBCC) utility. Several different DBCC utilities check various aspects of database integrity. You're most likely to run the `DBCC CHECKDB` command:

SYNTAX

```
DBCC CHECKDB ( 'database_name' [, Noindex |
{ Repair_Allow_Data_Loss | Repair_Fast | Repair_Rebuild }] )
[With {[ALL_ERRORMSGS] | [NO_INFOMSGS],
[TABLOCK],[ESTIMATEONLY],[PHYSICAL_ONLY],[TABLERESULTS]] }]
```

In this syntax,

- *`database_name`* is the name of the database for which you want to check integrity.
- `Noindex` specifies that you don't want the utility to check the integrity of your nonclustered indexes. (You'll examine indexes on Day 13, "Indexing for Performance.")
- `Repair_Allow_Data_Loss` specifies that all repairs that would be performed by the `Repair_Rebuild` option will be done. It also "cleans up" broken pages and text/image pages, whether or not doing so causes data loss. The database must be in single-user mode to specify this option.

- `Repair_Fast` modifies corrupted indexes if it's safe to do so (no data can be lost using this option). It also makes only quick and easy repairs (such as corrupted index keys). The database must be in single-user mode to specify this option.
- `Repair_Rebuild` fixes corrupted indexes just like the `Repair_Fast` option but performs more time-consuming fixes such as re-creating corrupted indexes. The database must be in single-user mode to specify this option.
- `ALL_ERRORMSGS` returns all messages from the command. By default, SQL Server stops returning error messages after you receive 200 messages. I hope you never need this option.
- `NO_INFOMSGS` specifies that only significant error messages will be reported; no informational messages will be reported. You'll want to use this option most of the time.
- `TABLOCK` specifies that shared table locks should be used instead of the default of page locks. Using this parameter speeds up the `DBCC` command if your system is busy but hurts concurrent users who may be blocked by your `CHECKDB` command.
- `ESTIMATEONLY` specifies that you want to know how much space in `tempdb` is needed to run the command but without running `CHECKDB` itself.
- `PHYSICAL_ONLY` specifies that you want to check only the physical integrity of your database (not the logical integrity). This option runs faster and catches the most common types of corruption in SQL Server (such as problems with a disk, disk controller, and torn pages), but doesn't allow for the use of any repair options.
- `TABLERESULTS` specifies that you want the results of the `DBCC` command to be returned in the format of a `SELECT` statement (a "result" set). This option, new for SQL Server 2000, allows you to save the results of this command (and all other `DBCC` commands) into a table rather than have to pore over reports looking for interesting output.

SQL Server 2000 can repair consistency problems. You'll examine the repair options on Day 8. For now, check out this code sample of the command to check your database's consistency and integrity:

```
DBCC CHECKDB ('pubs') With NO_INFOMSGS, TABLERESULTS
```

```
The command(s) completed successfully.
```

If you omit `With NO_INFOMSGS` from this command, you see many rows (two for each table in your database) similar to Figure 7.6.

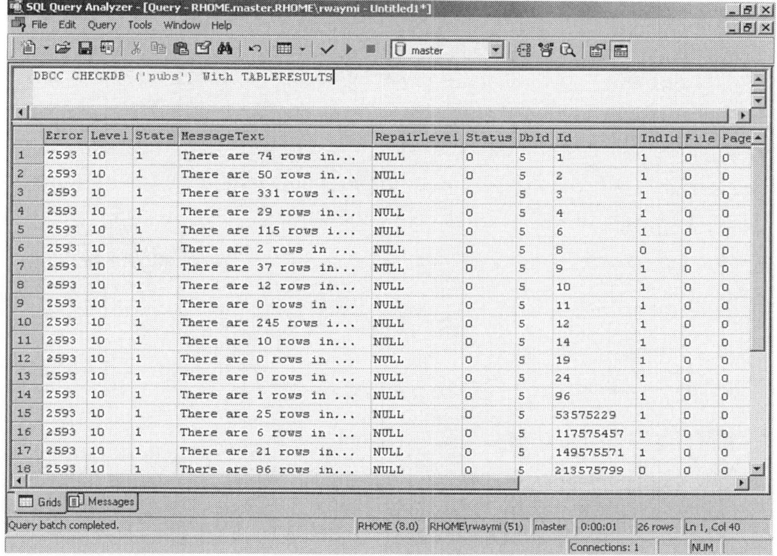

	Error	Level	State	MessageText	RepairLevel	Status	DbId	Id	IndId	File	Page
1	2593	10	1	There are 74 rows in...	NULL	0	5	1	1	0	0
2	2593	10	1	There are 50 rows in...	NULL	0	5	2	1	0	0
3	2593	10	1	There are 331 rows i...	NULL	0	5	3	1	0	0
4	2593	10	1	There are 29 rows in...	NULL	0	5	4	1	0	0
5	2593	10	1	There are 115 rows i...	NULL	0	5	6	1	0	0
6	2593	10	1	There are 2 rows in ...	NULL	0	5	8	0	0	0
7	2593	10	1	There are 37 rows in...	NULL	0	5	9	1	0	0
8	2593	10	1	There are 12 rows in...	NULL	0	5	10	1	0	0
9	2593	10	1	There are 0 rows in ...	NULL	0	5	11	1	0	0
10	2593	10	1	There are 245 rows i...	NULL	0	5	12	1	0	0
11	2593	10	1	There are 10 rows in...	NULL	0	5	14	1	0	0
12	2593	10	1	There are 0 rows in ...	NULL	0	5	19	1	0	0
13	2593	10	1	There are 0 rows in ...	NULL	0	5	24	1	0	0
14	2593	10	1	There are 1 rows in ...	NULL	0	5	96	1	0	0
15	2593	10	1	There are 25 rows in...	NULL	0	5	53575229	1	0	0
16	2593	10	1	There are 6 rows in ...	NULL	0	5	117575457	1	0	0
17	2593	10	1	There are 21 rows in...	NULL	0	5	149575571	1	0	0
18	2593	10	1	There are 86 rows in...	NULL	0	5	213575799	0	0	0

FIGURE 7.6

A DBCC CHECKDB *command with verbose output.*

Interpreting the results of your command is considerably easier if you use the NO_INFOMSGS option. Unless you're looking for a report on the number of rows and pages, there's no point in omitting NO_INFOMSGS.

If you do get some other kind of message, your database likely has some form of corruption. Troubleshooting errors from the DBCC CHECKDB command is outside the scope of this book, but you can find additional information in Microsoft's knowledge base (http://support.microsoft.com/support). If you can't repair any damage to your databases, you will most likely need to restore from your last backup. You'll examine how to perform recovery on Day 8.

The DBCC CHECKDB consistency check is more than adequate 90 percent of the time. In fact, with SQL Server 2000, you probably don't need to run DBCC commands. However, because paranoia is a good thing when your company's data is involved, a daily DBCC check is probably a good idea. Unless your database is very large (hundreds of gigabytes), you shouldn't encounter any problems with the time required to check the integrity of your databases. Only members of the sysadmin server role or db_owner database role can run the DBCC CHECKDB command.

Other Consistency Checks

The next three commands—DBCC CHECKCATALOG, DBCC CHECKALLOC, and DBCC CHECKTABLE—are subsets of DBCC CHECKDB. They run when you run DBCC CHECKDB, so you don't need to run them if you can use DBCC CHECKDB.

These three commands require that you be a member of the sysadmin server role or the db_owner database role (and db_backupoperator for CHECKCATALOG). The same cautions and usage of DBCC CHECKDB apply.

DBCC CHECKCATALOG

The DBCC CHECKCATALOG command checks the referential integrity of the system tables. You'll learn more about referential integrity on Day 14, "Ensuring Data Integrity."

SYNTAX

```
DBCC CHECKCATALOG ( 'database_name' ) [WITH NO_INFOMSGS]
```

In this syntax, *database_name* is the name of the database for which you want to check integrity.

Here's an example of the command in use:

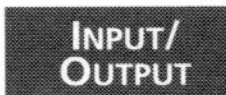

```
DBCC CHECKCATALOG('Pubs')
```

```
DBCC results for 'pubs'.
DBCC execution completed. If DBCC printed error messages,
➥contact your system administrator.
```

Notice that you get only two lines of output. For this command, the NO_INFOMSGS option eliminates only the first line:

```
DBCC Results for 'databasename'.
```

SYNTAX

DBCC CHECKALLOC DBCC CHECKALLOC checks that the database's allocation information (that is, which extents are owned by which tables) is correct.

```
DBCC CHECKALLOC ( 'database_name' [, NOINDEX |
{ REPAIR_ALLOW_DATA_LOSS | REPAIR_FAST | REPAIR_REBUILD }] )
[WITH {[ALL_ERRORMSGS | NO_INFOMSGS], [TABLOCK] [,ESTIMATEONLY]
[,TABLERESULTS]}]
```

All the options in this syntax are the same as for DBCC CHECKDB.

DBCC CHECKTABLE DBCC CHECKTABLE performs the same operations as DBCC CHECKDB but is restricted to a single table. This is very handy if you have one large table that you want to check but don't need to check the entire database.

SYNTAX

```
DBCC CHECKTABLE ( 'table_name' [, NOINDEX | index_id
| { REPAIR_ALLOW_DATA_LOSS | REPAIR_FAST | REPAIR_REBUILD }] )
[WITH {[ALL_ERRORMSGS | NO_INFOMSGS],
[TABLOCK],[ESTIMATEONLY],[PHYSICAL_ONLY].[TABLERESULTS]}]
```

In this syntax, all the options are the same as for DBCC CHECKDB, except these two:

- *table_name* is the name of the table for which you want to check integrity.
- *index_id* specifies that you want to check the integrity of a particular index. (You'll examine index IDs on Day 13.)

Backing Up a Database

Can you believe you've made it to the actual backup commands? You have a lot to do before you back up your databases. It's never a trivial pursuit, even on a small system. When you have your backup devices and have verified that your databases aren't corrupt, it's time to back up each database. The first step to examine is which backup devices you want to use and how you will use those backup devices.

Backup Device Options

You can back up to a single backup device or to multiple devices; or you can put multiple backups on a single device. Everywhere that you can specify a backup device, you can also specify a filename instead in the `BACKUP` command.

Single-Device Backups

A single-device backup is the default and the most often recommended way to perform a backup. If each database has a corresponding backup device, you can perform a one-to-one backup strategy. If you're backing up to disk backup devices, this approach is recommended. If you lose a file for some reason, you would lose only a single backup of a single database rather than multiple backups contained in a single file. If you're backing up to tape, backing up multiple databases to a single tape (backup device) is much more acceptable (and cost effective).

Parallel Striped Backups

A parallel striped backup allows you to back up a single database to multiple backup devices. You simply enumerate more than one backup device in the `BACKUP` command. SQL Server 2000 initiates a thread for each device you choose to use in your parallel striped backup, with up to 64 devices (and hence threads) possible.

The big advantage to using parallel striped backups is with tape backups. You can attach multiple tape drives to a single server and back up a database to multiple tapes at the same time. If you have a single database that takes three hours to back up and you purchase two additional tape drives (for a total of three), you can quite possibly finish your backup of that database in one hour. The news gets better: You don't need to have the same number of tape drives available when you're ready to restore from the backup. This point is particularly important for disaster recovery. There's no guarantee that you'll get the same number of tape drives in your recovery server. You still need all the tapes to recover your database, however.

After you use a tape in a parallel striped backup, you can't use it for anything but another parallel striped backup with the same number of tape drives until you reformat the tape.

Multiple Backups on a Single Device

You can also put multiple backups on a single backup device. If you think about it, this is the default configuration you want for a tape backup. It's likely that you'll want to put as many database backups on a single tape as possible. You can also do that with disk devices; however, I don't recommend this approach for disk devices—if the single file becomes corrupt or lost, all database backups on that device are lost.

The BACKUP DATABASE Command for Entire Databases

Backing up the database is the next logical step (finally). You do so by using the BACKUP command:

SYNTAX

```
BACKUP DATABASE {database_name | @database_var}
TO backup_device [, ...n]
[WITH [BLOCKSIZE = {blocksize | @blocksize_variable}]
[[,] DESCRIPTION = {text | @text_variable}]
[[,] DIFFERENTIAL]
[[,] EXPIREDATE = {date | @date_var}
| RETAINDAYS = {days | @days_var}]
[[,] PASSWORD = {pwd | @pwd_var}
[[,] FORMAT | NOFORMAT]
[[,] {INIT | NOINIT}]
[[,] MEDIADESCRIPTION = {text | @text_variable}]
[[,] MEDIANAME = {media_name | @media_name_variable}]
[[,] MEDIAPASSWORD = {media_pwd | @media_pwd_variable}]
[[,] [NAME = {backup_set_name | @backup_set_name_var}]
[[,] {NOSKIP | SKIP}]
[[,] {NOUNLOAD | UNLOAD}]
[[,] {NOREWIND | REWIND}]
[[,] [RESTART]
[[,] STATS [= percentage]]
```

where

```
backup_device :: =
{
{backup_device_name | @backup_device_name_var}
|
{DISK | TAPE | PIPE} =
{'temp_backup_device' | @temp_backup_device_var}
}
```

Here's what the myriad options mean. We won't repeat these descriptions unless they're specific to one of the other backup commands when you see them later, so you might need to refer to this description for the `BACKUP LOG` and `BACKUP FILE/FILEGROUP` options.

- *`database_name`* is the name of the database you want to back up.
- *`@database_var`* is the name of the database you want to back up, except it's expressed as a variable.
- *`backup_device`* is either the name of a backup device or a variable placeholder for the backup device. You can also specify just the name of the file, tape, or Named Pipe you want to use for the backup. Again, you can also specify it as a variable.
- *`blocksize`* specifies the block size you want to use if you are using a tape or Named Pipe. See your Windows 2000 documentation or tape drive hardware manual for recommended block sizes.
- `DESCRIPTION` is up to 255 characters describing this backup. Again, you can specify a variable for this parameter.
- `DIFFERENTIAL` deserves its own section for a complete description. See the following section.
- `EXPIREDATE` is the date that the tape can be overwritten. If you attempt to write to a tape before the `EXPIREDATE` for a backup has passed, you can't do so without specific override parameters.
- `RETAINDAYS` has the same effect as `EXPIREDATE`, except that you specify the number of days rather than a specific date.
- `PASSWORD` is the password you want specified for a restore from this backup to be possible.

Note

The backup is just password protected, not encrypted in any way.

- `FORMAT | NOFORMAT` allows you to request that your tape be reformatted. Any password protection or existing data is ignored. Using this parameter is the equivalent of specifying both the `INIT` and `SKIP` options.
- `INIT | NOINIT` specifies whether to initialize your backup device before writing this backup. `NOINIT` is the default, meaning that if your backup device already has another backup of some kind on it, the current backup request is appended to the tape or disk file. If the device doesn't contain a backup, it's initialized and then written to. `INIT` overwrites the existing content of the tape or disk file, while

retaining the media header information. For tapes, if the retention date hasn't expired or the backup MEDIANAME doesn't match, the tape isn't initialized. You must specify the SKIP option if that's your intention (and if that's what you want, you might as well use the FORMAT option).

- MEDIADESCRIPTION is another comment field for the backup, up to 255 characters long.
- MEDIANAME is a description of the backup set, up to 128 characters. This name is used for overwrite comparisons. If you plan to use a single tape to hold both Windows 2000 and SQL Server backups, you must specify a MEDIANAME.
- MEDIAPASSWORD is a password you want to use when you create backups as part of this media set, as well as the password you want to require when a backup is restored from this media set.
- NAME is yet another name for the backup set. Again, it can also be specified as a variable.
- NOSKIP | SKIP specifies whether to skip reading the tape header when writing to a tape. If NOSKIP is specified (the default), the tape header is read, and EXPIREDATE and MEDIANAME are checked to prevent accidentally overwriting a tape.
- NOUNLOAD | UNLOAD specifies whether the tape is ejected when the backup is complete.
- NOREWIND | REWIND specifies whether the tape is rewound when the backup is complete.
- RESTART lets you restart a backup if it was interrupted and you want to continue from wherever it left off. When you do, you must specify this parameter. RESTART is valid only when you're making a multi-tape backup.
- STATS = *percentage* specifies how frequently you will be notified of progress in your backup. The default is 10, meaning that each time 10 percent of your backup is completed, SQL Server will return a message telling you of its progress.

The BACKUP command can look very intimidating, so how about a sample? Sometimes there's nothing like a little code to clear things up. The following script creates a new backup device for the pubs database, checks the database's integrity, and then backs up the database.

INPUT/OUTPUT

```
exec sp_addumpdevice 'disk', 'pubs_backup',
'd:\program files\Microsoft SQL Server\mssql\backup\pubs_backup.bak'
go
use pubs
dbcc checkdb ('pubs') With NO_INFOMSGS
BACKUP DATABASE pubs to pubs_backup WITH INIT
```

```
(1 row(s) affected)

'Disk' device added.
Processed 208 pages for database 'pubs', file 'pubs' on file 1.
Processed 1 pages for database 'pubs', file 'pubs_log' on file 1.
BACKUP DATABASE successfully processed 209 pages in 0.639 seconds
(2.668 MB/sec).
```

See, that wasn't nearly as scary as it sounded. This next code segment backs up the `pubs` database, but this time you specify the local tape drive. You can't run it unless you have a tape drive installed on the computer running SQL Server 2000. This time, you specify that the tape will expire in 30 days, it should be formatted before it's written, and its block size is 8,192 bytes. The name of the backup will be `Pubs Backup Tape`.

INPUT

```
exec sp_addumpdevice 'tape', 'pubs_tape_backup', '\\.\tape0'
use pubs
dbcc checkdb ('pubs') With NO_INFOMSGS
BACKUP DATABASE pubs to pubs_backup WITH FORMAT,
Retaindays = 30, MediaName='Pubs Backup Tape',
Blocksize=8192
```

The DIFFERENTIAL BACKUP DATABASE Command

As you discovered earlier today, the differential backup copies all the modified pages in the database—meaning all pages that have changed since the last full backup. If a differential backup is taken, and then another differential backup is taken, the second differential backup contains everything that was on the first one plus all changed pages that happened after that first backup. Note, however, that a differential backup makes sense only as a follow-up to a full database backup.

Now make a differential backup of the `pubs` database. First, create a table and add one row to it (so you have something new to back up). You won't make a new backup device, but you will append the differential backup onto the same device that contained the database backup. You might want to specify `NOINIT` (as I have done) just to be clear, even though it's the default.

INPUT

```
use pubs
Create table backuptest (col1 int not null)
Insert backuptest values (1)
Go
BACKUP DATABASE pubs to pubs_backup WITH differential, NOINIT
```

You receive output looking like this:

OUTPUT

```
(1 row(s) affected)

Processed 48 pages for database 'pubs', file 'pubs' on file 2.
Processed 1 pages for database 'pubs', file 'pubs_log' on file 2.
```

7

```
BACKUP DATABASE WITH DIFFERENTIAL successfully processed 49 pages in
0.486 seconds (0.811 MB/sec).
```

You need a lot of information to use differential backups properly. However, that discussion is best left to Day 8.

Note

> The RESTART option is exciting if you have large database backups. If the backup fails for some reason, you don't have to start from the beginning; you can start where you left off and continue the backup. However, if you have only a single tape or are still on the first tape, you will start over from the beginning whether or not you specify the RESTART parameter.

Setting the Media Retention for Tape Backups

If you don't pass the EXPIREDATE or RETAINDAYS option to a tape backup, the retention date for the tape is set to the default media retention server configuration option. You can set this option like you would any other server configuration option by using the sp_configure system stored procedure (although it's an advanced option). For example, to set the default retention of tapes to 30 days, you can run the following code:

INPUT

```
exec sp_configure 'media retention',30
RECONFIGURE WITH OVERRIDE
```

You must restart SQL Server 2000 to make this change take effect. The default configuration of the media retention is 0 days (no retention period).

The BACKUP DATABASE Command for Files and Filegroups

The syntax for backing up files or filegroups is shown here for the sake of completeness. However, you should back up files or filegroups only if you can't accomplish a full database backup (or a combination of full and differential backups) in a reasonable amount of time. You might want to perform filegroup backups for other valid reasons, but that advanced topic is beyond the scope of this book.

Essentially, the BACKUP DATABASE command allows you to back up an individual file or set of files known as a *filegroup* (described on Day 4). You still need a transaction log backup if you want to use a file or filegroup backup to restore your database.

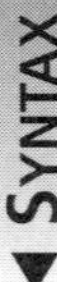


```
BACKUP DATABASE {database_name | @database_name_var}
file_or_filegroup [, ...n]
TO backup_device [, ...n]
[WITH
[BLOCKSIZE = {blocksize | @blocksize_variable}]
```

```
[[,] DESCRIPTION = {text | @text_variable}]
[[,] EXPIREDATE = {date | @date_var}
| RETAINDAYS = {days | @days_var}]
[[,] PASSWORD = {pwd | @pwd_var}]
[[,] FORMAT | NOFORMAT]
[[,] {INIT | NOINIT}]
[[,] MEDIADESCRIPTION = {text | @text_variable}]
[[,] MEDIANAME = {media_name | @media_name_variable}]
[[,] MEDIAPASSWORD = {mediapwd | @mediapwd}]
[[,] [NAME = {backup_set_name | @backup_set_name_var}]
[[,] {NOSKIP | SKIP}]
[[,] {NOUNLOAD | UNLOAD}]
[[,] {NOREWIND | REWIND}]
[[,] [RESTART]
[[, ] STATS [= percentage]]
]
```

where

```
file_or_filegroup :: =
{
FILE = {logical_file_name | @logical_file_name_var}
|
FILEGROUP = {logical_filegroup_name | @logical_filegroup_name_var}
}
```

In this syntax, most options have been covered except the following:

- `FILE` specifies the name of the single file (or a variable listing a single file path and name) that you want to back up.
- `FILEGROUP` specifies the logical name of the filegroup you want to back up. All files within the filegroup will be backed up.

The BACKUP LOG Command

You can also back up just the transaction log for a database by using the `BACKUP LOG` command:

SYNTAX

```
BACKUP LOG {database_name | @database_name_var}
{[WITH { NO_LOG | TRUNCATE_ONLY }] }
|
{TO backup_device [, ...n]
[WITH
[BLOCKSIZE = {blocksize | @blocksize_variable}]
[[,] DESCRIPTION = {text | @text_variable}]
[[,] EXPIREDATE = {date | @date_var}
| RETAINDAYS = {days | @days_var}]
[[,] PASSWORD = {pwd | @pwd_var}]
[[,] FORMAT | NOFORMAT]
[[,] {INIT | NOINIT}]
```

7

```
[[,] MEDIADESCRIPTION = {text | @text_variable}]
[[,] MEDIANAME = {media_name | @media_name_variable}]
[[,] MEDIAPASSWORD = {mediapwd | @mediapwd}]
[[,] [NAME = {backup_set_name | @backup_set_name_var}]
[[,] NO_TRUNCATE]
[[,] {NORECOVERY | STANDBY = undo_file_name}]
[[,] {NOSKIP | SKIP}]
[[,] {NOUNLOAD | UNLOAD}]
[[,] {NOREWIND | REWIND}]
[[,] [RESTART]
[[,] STATS [= percentage]]
]}
```

Most of these options have been covered except the following:

- `TRUNCATE_ONLY` and `NO_LOG` are identical. They remove committed transactions from the log but don't actually back up the entries. For example, after you back up a database that has had nonlogged operations run against it, the transaction log is no longer useful. You might want to issue `BACKUP LOG WITH TRUNCATE_ONLY` followed by a full database backup. That the log is truncated is in itself a logged operation. Also note that this option doesn't actually perform a backup; hence, the name of a backup device is unnecessary. Of course, if you want to do so, you might want to switch your database recovery mode to `SIMPLE`.
- `NO_TRUNCATE` makes a backup of the transaction log (just like a `BACKUP LOG` without any special options). However, it does something that an ordinary backup can't: It can back up the transaction log even if a database isn't available. Assume that you have a database in which the data file is on one physical disk and the transaction log is on a separate disk. If the data file is lost for some reason, you can run the `BACKUP LOG` statement with `NO_TRUNCATE` to capture all transactions that have occurred since the last backup of the transaction log. This way, you can recover your database right up to the point of disk failure.

You can back up the transaction log for a database only if you've previously made a full database backup. You can't make a transaction log backup if the database is in SIMPLE mode.

Transaction log backups are a sequence of backups. With these backups, unlike differential backups, no duplication occurs between one transaction log backup and the next. When you must restore the transaction logs, you need every single one you've made since your last full database backup. Tomorrow's lesson goes into greater detail on how to restore your database using transaction logs.

How often should you back up your transaction log? A typical scenario might look something like this (for a database used primarily during business hours):

6:00 a.m.	Perform daily full database backup with FORMAT
6:05 a.m.	Back up the transaction log with FORMAT
10:00 a.m.	Back up the transaction log again (NOINIT)
12:00 p.m.	Perform differential database backup (NOINIT)
2:00 p.m.	Back up the transaction log again (NOINIT)
6:00 p.m.	Back up the transaction log again (NOINIT)
8:00 p.m.	Perform differential database backup (NOINIT)
10:00 p.m.	Back up the transaction log (last time)

The script would look something like Listing 7.1 for the pubs database. Of course, this assumes your database is in FULL database recovery mode.

> The pubs database is in SIMPLE database recovery mode by default. When this mode is set, you can't back up the transaction log. So, if you want to run the code in Listing 7.1, you must set the database to FULL by running
>
> `Alter Database pubs SET RECOVERY FULL`

LISTING 7.1 Setting Up a Schedule

```
--SCRIPT BEGINS AT 6:00 AM
use pubs
go
dbcc checkdb ('pubs') With NO_INFOMSGS, TABLERESULTS
go
BACKUP DATABASE pubs to pubs_backup WITH FORMAT,
Retaindays = 30, MediaName='Pubs Backup Tape',
Blocksize=8192
Go

-- 6:05 AM
BACKUP LOG pubs to pubs_log_backup WITH INIT
Go
-- 10:00 AM
BACKUP LOG pubs to pubs_log_backup
Go
```

LISTING 7.1 continued

```
-- 12:00 PM
BACKUP DATABASE pubs to pubs_backup WITH DIFFERENTIAL,
NOINIT, NOSKIP, Retaindays = 30, MediaName='Pubs Backup Tape',
Blocksize=8192
Go

-- 2:00 PM
BACKUP LOG pubs to pubs_log_backup
Go

-- 6:00 PM
BACKUP LOG pubs to pubs_log_backup
Go

-- 8:00 PM
BACKUP DATABASE pubs to pubs_backup WITH DIFFERENTIAL,
NOINIT, NOSKIP, Retaindays = 30, MediaName='Pubs Backup Tape',
Blocksize=8192
Go

-- 10:00 PM
BACKUP LOG pubs to pubs_log_backup
Go
```

This script allows you to recover your database and not lose transactions (as long as you don't lose the backup devices). This example assumes two tape drives: one for the full/differential database backups and one for the transaction log backups.

Using SQL Server Enterprise Manager for Backups

As you would expect, SQL Server Enterprise Manager is fully functional in the area of backups. To begin, create two more backup devices: one for the `pubs` database (called `pubs_backup`) and another for the Northwind database (called `northwind_backup`). Set both databases to `FULL` recovery mode.

Now expand the Databases folder, right-click the database you want to back up, and select All Tasks, Backup Database. Figure 7.7 shows the resulting SQL Server Backup dialog.

Now that you've examined all the Transact-SQL backup syntax options, filling in this dialog should be a piece of cake. Fill in the appropriate details for the description of the backup (if you want), and select the backup type. Remember, if you want to back up the transaction log, you must have first made a full database backup, and the database must not be in `SIMPLE` mode.

FIGURE 7.7

The SQL Server Backup dialog.

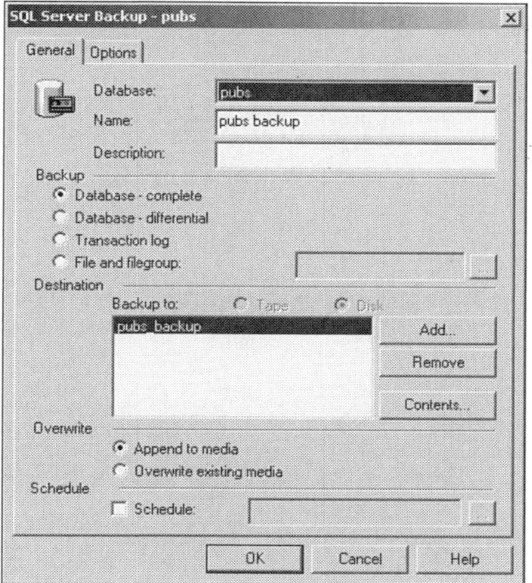

Under Destination, click Add to move to the Select Backup Destination dialog (see Figure 7.8). Here, you select a file location, a tape drive, a network location, a Named Pipe, or (the easy choice) a backup device. For the Backup Device option, pick `pubs_backup` from the list.

FIGURE 7.8

The Select Backup Destination dialog.

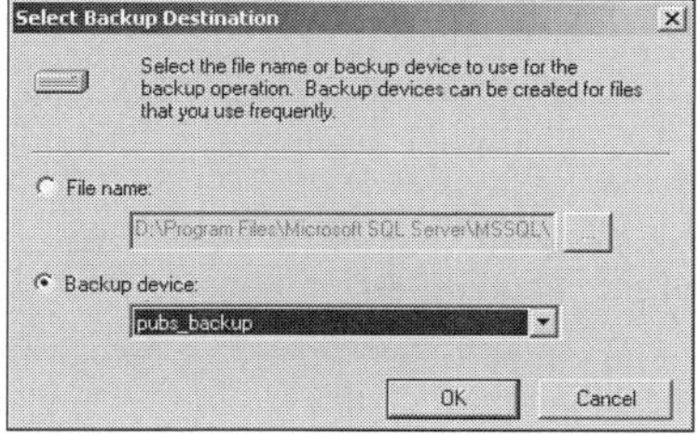

Click OK to finish selecting the backup device, and move on to the Overwrite section of the SQL Server Backup dialog. The default (as described earlier) is to append your back-up to any previous backups that might exist on a particular backup device or backup file. Choose the Overwrite Existing Media option if you want to wipe out the contents of the backup device before writing the current backup. This is the same as the FORMAT option for the BACKUP command.

The Schedule check box gives you an interface into the scheduling engine for SQL Server, which is provided by the SQL Server Agent service. Check this box if you want SQL Server to perform regular backups as scheduled jobs on whatever time basis you would like. You would most likely go through this user interface, set your backup the way you want it, check the Schedule option, and then configure the schedule. Because scheduling backups is just one use (a very important one) of the scheduling features of

SQL Server, these features are treated in depth on Day 18, "Scheduling Jobs with SQL Server Agent."

Now click the Options tab to see the dialog in Figure 7.9. Notice that the Verify backup upon completion option is checked. It verifies that your backup is intact and doesn't appear to be corrupted.

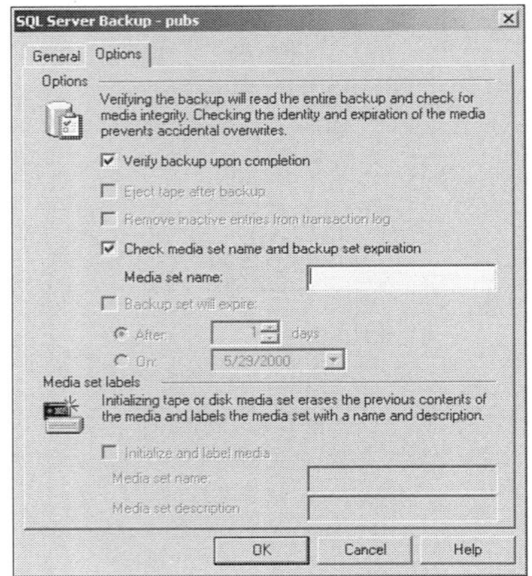

FIGURE 7.9

The SQL Server Backup Options tab.

The Verify Backup Upon Completion option isn't the same as `DBCC CHECKDB`. It doesn't check the integrity within the database; it just checks that the backup media itself isn't corrupted.

Each grayed-out option is simply unavailable for the type of backup you have selected—in this case, a full database backup to disk. If this were a transaction log backup, you would have available the option Remove Inactive Entries from Transaction Log, which specifies the default behavior of a log backup. If you want the equivalent of the `NO_TRUNCATE` option for the log backup, uncheck this option.

The rest of the options on this tab are specific to tape drives and are self-explanatory. To begin your backup, click OK. You then see a dialog like the one in Figure 7.10, showing you the progress of your backup. If you selected the Verify option, you also see the dialog in Figure 7.11 if the verification is successful.

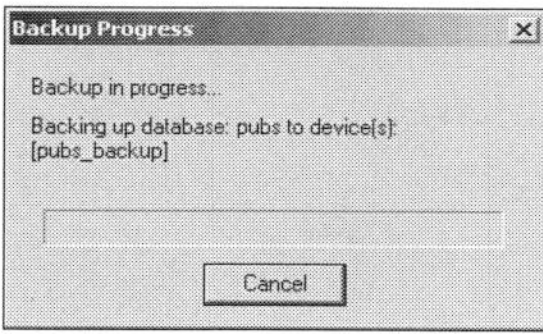

FIGURE 7.10
The Backup option in progress.

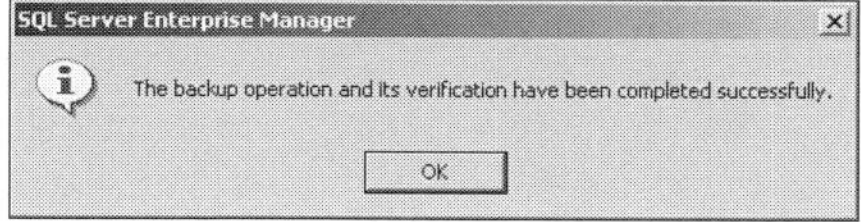

FIGURE 7.11
SQL Server verifies the backup's success.

Now, here's the best part about using backup devices instead of directly using files. Expand the Management folder in Enterprise Manager, click the Backup icon, and double-click the `pubs_backup` backup device. Click the now active View Contents button, and you are presented with a list of all the backups stored on that backup device, showing the type of backup and when it was completed. This information is very handy to keep around. In Figure 7.12, notice that both a full database backup and a transaction log backup are on the backup device.

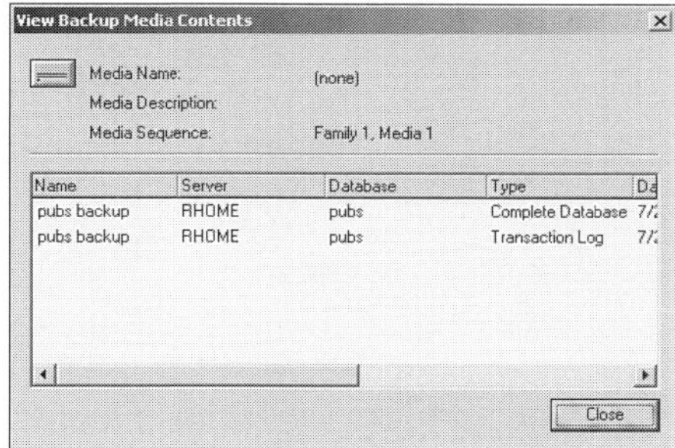

FIGURE 7.12
The View Backup Media Contents dialog.

That's it! Backing up your databases and transaction logs with SQL Server Enterprise Manager is that simple. Of course, understanding what you're doing and what all the options mean is a little bit of work, but I hope you agree that it is worthwhile.

Summary

Backing up and restoring are probably the most important parts of maintaining your SQL Server system. Backing up a database requires careful planning. You must determine which kinds of backups you need (full database backups, differential backups, log backups, and file/filegroup backups), and there's no right answer. The kind you choose depends on the size of your database and your restore requirements. Setting the database recovery mode is essential and determines the types of backups available. Only through careful planning and then the implementation of those plans will you know whether you have the right set of backups. Don't forget to plan for major disasters, as well as the "accidental" deletion of data that always seems to happen right before a holiday. Protect your servers with RAID so you have less need to use your backups. You will most likely want to schedule your backups rather than run them interactively. Scheduling backups (and any other command) is examined on Day 18.

Q&A

Q Can I back up a database to a new file dynamically?

A Yes. Simply specify the device as a file instead of the name of a backup device.

Q Which command do I use to create a backup device?

A `sp_addumpdevice` (or SQL Server Enterprise Manager).

Q Does RAID level 0 protect my data when a disk is lost?

A No. RAID level 0 is just striping of data and doesn't provide any fault tolerance.

Q When can't I back up my transaction log?

A When the database is in SIMPLE mode or a full database backup hasn't been made first.

Q Can I back up the transaction log of the `master` database?

A No. You can perform only a full database backup of the `master` database.

Workshop

This section provides quiz questions to help you solidify your understanding of the concepts presented today. In addition to the quiz questions, exercises are provided to let you practice what you have learned today. Try to understand the quiz and exercise answers before continuing to tomorrow's lesson. Answers are provided in Appendix A, "Answers to Quiz Questions."

Quiz

1. Which RAID option is preferred for holding transaction logs?
2. Can you back up to a device whose physical location is `\\myserver\sqlbackups\master_backup.dat`?

3. In the SQL Server Backup dialog, the Transaction Log backup option is unavailable. Can you explain why this might be the case?
4. Where should you keep your backup tapes?
5. Will a checkpoint interfere with your transaction log backups?

Exercises

1. Create backup devices and perform backups for each of your databases. Examine the database options that are set so you can see which databases can have their transaction logs backed up.
2. Perform differential database backups of your `pubs` and Northwind databases.
3. Back up the transaction log of the `pubs` database.

WEEK 1

In Review

It's time to take a quick refresher on what you covered this first week.

You were introduced to SQL Server 2000 on Day 1. You learned about relational databases, data warehousing, and some history of SQL Server and relational database design. If you did the exercises, you participated in an interview with a client and designed the tables for a simple database.

On Day 2, you went through the installation process and examined various components you can install with SQL Server. If you installed MSDE, you also turned to Appendix C to install MSDE.

On Day 3, you learned about the tools and utilities that come packaged with SQL Server. You examined when and how to use each tool.

On Day 4, you examined how storage is handled in SQL Server. More specifically, you developed an understanding of the relationship between databases and files. You also learned how to create, edit, and delete databases and database files.

By Day 5, you had installed the server and created databases and files. For anyone to be able to have access to your newly created databases, you needed to create some login IDs and user accounts. These accounts gave you access to the SQL Server and the databases, but they didn't allow you to do much of anything inside a database.

You might have created user accounts, logins, and roles, but your users will have some difficulty accessing data. Day 6 covered how to assign rights and database roles to your users so that they have permission to access your database objects.

Day 7 was the first of two presentations into the realm of the paranoid database administrator. On Day 7, you learned how to protect your job and your data by implementing various types of database and transaction log backups.

WEEK 2

At a Glance

During your second week, you will learn how to recover your databases, create tables, retrieve and modify data, create indexes, understand some internals of Transact-SQL (T-SQL), and ensure the integrity of your data.

Day 8 completes your trip to the realm of the paranoid administrator. You learn how to recover and restore the databases that you backed up on Day 7. Although this process isn't difficult, knowing when to back up your data and how to restore your data can be crucial.

On Day 9, you learn what different data types are available in SQL Server 2000. You also learn how to create your own user-defined data types. Now that you have data types, you can combine them into a table definition.

Day 10 covers the fundamentals of data retrieval. You learn about the `SELECT` statement and its syntax and use. Make sure that you understand this new construct, because the second half of Day 11 builds on it. You learn how to use more powerful statements to gather just the data you want and how to work with subqueries, aggregate functions, and many system functions. This lesson is long, but it's an excellent overview of a large piece of the Transact-SQL language.

After completing Day 11, you will be able to modify existing data in your database one record at a time or as an entire set of records. You will be able to add (insert), remove (delete), or modify (update) data.

Day 12 gives you a foundation in the programming concepts used in Transact-SQL, as well as transactions and locking.

All this data retrieval and modification that you learn can be optimized through the use of indexing. Day 13 covers indexing in detail, focusing on both clustered and nonclustered indexes. You also are introduced to full-text indexing.

Data retrieval and modification can still be rendered useless if the data in your database isn't sound. Day 14 covers data integrity. This lesson enables you to minimize the amount of bad data that can enter your database. You learn how to take advantage of declarative referential integrity.

This week looks long, but hang in there. You will cover some of the most difficult material in a database system, but by the end you will be two-thirds of the way though your 21 days and have a solid understanding of the material presented. Be sure to do the exercises at the end of the lessons, because everything in database development tends to build on what preceded it.

WEEK 2

DAY 8

Restoring Your Databases

Yesterday you examined backups in SQL Server. You saw how to use fault tolerance (in the form of hardware fault tolerance and Windows 2000 software fault tolerance) to prevent needing your backups. You learned about the types of backups available in SQL Server 2000, including full database backups, differential database backups, and transaction log backups. You saw how to implement these backups by using Transact-SQL and the SQL Server Enterprise Manager.

Today you will finish what's perhaps the most important but least glamorous aspect of supporting a relational database: recovery. No matter how much work you do to make your database secure and your data available, data protection is the most critical aspect of your job. If your server crashes and all your data is lost, it's likely you've lost something else as well—your job! Today you will examine the restore process and what types of restore scenarios SQL Server supports. To lead off your examination of restoration, you will look at the recovery mechanisms SQL Server 2000 uses, including automatic and manual recovery. Most of today's lesson deals with manual recovery—restoring a database to a consistent point in time.

Restoring Databases

Backups are good but not terribly useful in and of themselves. They're really handy, however, when you have problems with your server. If a disk quits functioning or a database file becomes corrupted, you need to restore any databases affected by the loss of the files.

Another reason to restore a database backup is to restore a database to a logically consistent point in time. Suppose that your boss deleted all the day's sales at 5 p.m. You can recover data from the previous full database backup and then apply all your transaction log backups (or any differential backups plus the transaction log backups) until the point in time right before your boss ran the delete command. This way, you can recover the data with a minimal loss of work.

SQL Server 2000 can restore backups made with SQL Server 7.0 but not from any release before 7.0. Also, note that SQL Server 2000 backups can't be read by any prior release of SQL Server, including SQL Server 7.0.

Before you examine recovery, you must understand that SQL Server has two different types of recovery: automatic and manual.

Automatic Recovery

Automatic recovery is the process SQL Server goes through each time the SQL Server service is started. You can't disable it and don't need to do anything special to make it occur—hence, the name *automatic*.

Each time SQL Server restarts, it goes through a particular set of steps that roll forward any committed transactions found in the transaction log that have occurred since the last checkpoint. Rolling forward transactions means that any committed transactions for a database are reapplied to that database. SQL Server then rolls back any transactions in the transaction log that haven't been committed. Rolling back means that any partially completed—but not committed—transactions are removed from the database. When the automatic recovery process finishes, each database is left in a logically consistent form, and a checkpoint is issued. You will examine transactions further on Day 12, "Using Transact-SQL Extensions."

The automatic recovery process guarantees that, no matter how or why SQL Server is stopped, it starts in a logically consistent state. Even if your server crashes suddenly, you can recover cleanly. Log pages for all committed transactions are written to disk immediately (known as a *synchronous write*). Therefore, any permanent changes to the database are successfully copied to disk and are used during this process.

Automatic recovery processes each database in a particular order. It does so by first locating the `master` database files (`master.mdf` and `mastlog.ldf`), seeking the database location in the Windows Registry. You can find this information in the Registry key `HKEY_LOCAL_MACHINE\Software\Microsoft\MSSQLServer\MSSQLServer\Parameters` for a default instance, or `HKEY_LOCAL_MACHINE\Software\Microsoft\Microsoft SQL Server\`*`INSTANCENAME`*`\MSSQLServer\Parameters` for a named instance (substitute your instance name for *`INSTANCENAME`*). Here, you can find the location where SQL Server believes it will find your `master` database files. You can see a sample of my (Windows 2000) Registry key set in Figure 8.1. The Registry location is the same for all Windows platforms.

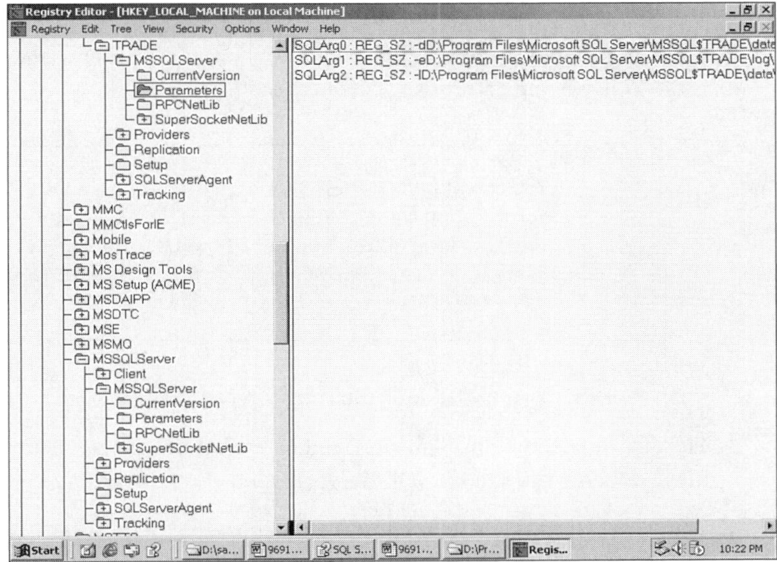

FIGURE 8.1

The SQL Server Registry keys for service startup.

After SQL Server locates the `master` database files, it loads and recovers the `master` database. You must load and restore the `master` database first because it contains the references to the primary data file (the `.mdf` file) for the rest of the databases in the `sysdatabases` system table in the filename column. After it recovers the `master` database, SQL Server can begin the process of locating, opening, and recovering the rest of the databases. Each database keeps track of which files are associated with it by storing that information in its `sysfiles` and `sysfilegroups` system tables.

Before SQL Server can recover any other databases, it must recover the `model` database. The `model` database, remember, is the template database. You must recover this database before you can continue because your next step is to create the `tempdb` database. You need the `tempdb` database to perform a wide variety of queries or stored procedures in SQL Server. The `tempdb` database is re-created every time you start SQL Server. SQL Server creates the database by making a copy of the `model` database and then expanding it to the appropriate size you previously specified.

The MSDB database is restored next, followed by the distribution database (if it exists), the `pubs` and Northwind databases, and finally any user databases (the ones you care about).

You can examine this entire process by looking at the SQL Server Error Log:

1. Start SQL Server Enterprise Manager if it's not already open, connect to your server, expand the Management folder, and expand the SQL Server Logs option. You then see a list with the current error log and typically the last six error logs as well.
2. Highlight the error log you want to view so that it appears in the right pane of the SQL Server Enterprise Manager (see Figure 8.2).

Note

> You can also view these files directly by using an editor such as Notepad. You can find these files in the `\mssql\log` directory, with the name `errorlog.*`, where `*` is the number of the backup. The current error log's filename is `errorlog.` (with a dot but no extension). The previous logs are named `errorlog.1`, `errorlog.2`, and so on.

3. Start by finding the entry Starting Up Database Master.

The error log shown in Figure 8.2 indicates that the `master` database is being opened (the files are being opened by SQL Server) and then recovered to a consistent logical point.

The `model` database is then opened and recovered; then MSDB and your user-created databases (including `pubs` and Northwind) are recovered. Next, `tempdb` is cleared (copied from `model`) and started. You will know that recovery was successful when you see the `Recovery Complete` entry in the error log (the highlighted line in figure 8.2).

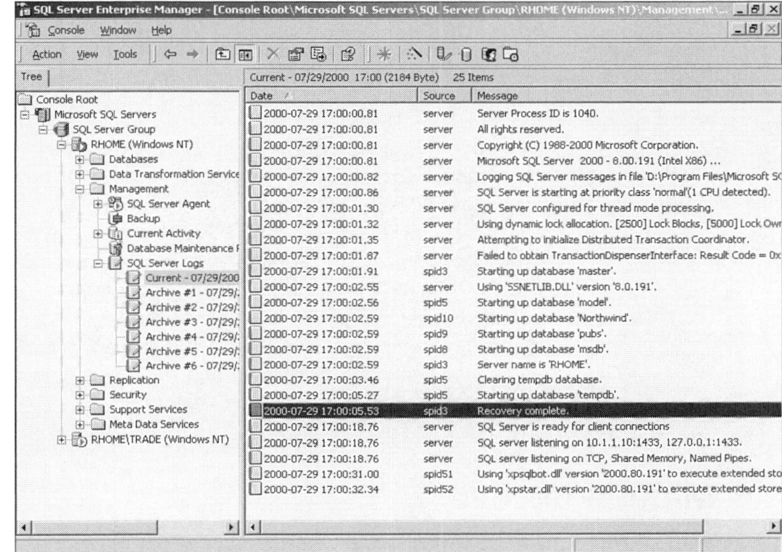

FIGURE 8.2
The server error log view in Enterprise Manager.

Configuring Automatic Recovery

The most important thing you can do to configure automatic recovery is to configure the Recovery Interval option. This option specifies the maximum amount of time that SQL Server will take to perform automatic recovery on each database. The default value is `0`, meaning that SQL Server will automatically configure how frequently it decides to issue a checkpoint.

This configuration parameter affects how often checkpoints occur. A *checkpoint*, remember, is the process that copies data pages and log records that have been modified in memory onto your disks. After a checkpoint is completed, transactions committed before the checkpoint must no longer be rolled forward (recovered) on disk in the event of a server restart.

You configure the recovery interval by using the `sp_configure` system stored procedure. For example, to change the recovery to three minutes, run the following Transact-SQL code:

INPUT

```
Exec sp_configure 'Recovery Interval',3
Go
Reconfigure with Override
Go
```

Unless you are experiencing a performance degradation based on too many checkpoints, you shouldn't change the recovery interval from the default automatic configuration.

The recovery interval doesn't help if you have a very long-running transaction. Suppose that you have a system process that begins a transaction and then begins to run a series of updates that last hours, and at some point your server crashes. If you don't have enough memory to hold all the changes in memory, and some of these changes are written to disk, you need to roll back these changes from your database. If you previously configured your recovery interval to three minutes (as in the preceding code segment), recovering the database will probably still take more than three minutes. To avoid this problem, keep the size of your transactions small so that you can recover quickly if a problem occurs.

Manual Recovery

Manual recovery—the topic of the rest of today's lesson—is the process of recovering a database. This process might include recovering from a full database backup, possibly recovering a differential database backup, or restoring one or more transaction log backups from your backup devices. The details of the recovery process vary depending on the reasons for the recovery.

You can recover a database and then apply the transaction logs to restore fully a lost database or recover to a point in time to undo a change to your database. You can even restore to a named (also called a *marked*) transaction. You can also use the differential database backups (if you've made them) to help restore fewer transaction logs. SQL Server 2000 even has an option to restore just a set of filegroups (to perform partial restores).

Restoring a database from a backup has the following restrictions:

- The database can't be in use. A database is in use if anyone has issued the `USE` command and pointed to the database, or is running any query against that database.
- You must have the proper permissions. Only members of the sysadmin or dbcreator serverwide role or the dbo user in a database can recover a database. The right to do so can't be given away. Restoring a database is an extremely powerful right. In addition, if the database doesn't currently exist on the system you must have CREATE DATABASE permissions as well.
- You must restore the transaction logs in the sequence in which they were created. Each transaction log has a sequence number associated with it. You must restore

the transaction log backups in the proper order, or the recovery will fail. You'll examine many considerations today before you begin restoring your transaction log backups.

If you're trying to recover because you've lost a hard drive, you must first replace the disk that failed (including re-establishing mirroring or other RAID configurations) and then drop any affected databases. You can then re-create the databases or have the databases re-created as part of the restore operation.

If you perform a restore against an existing database, the default results in the existing database's contents being wiped out in favor of your backups (with some important considerations you will examine later).

Restoring from the Files (Reattaching a Database)

Before you examine the restore processes, consider one possible restore option. You can reattach a database if you have a copy of all the data files associated with it. SQL Server 2000 can detach and then reattach databases by using Transact-SQL system stored procedures and the `CREATE DATABASE` option with the `FOR_ATTACH` option.

First, create the database to be used for the detach/attach. This code sample shows a `create` database that has two database files, `test_data.mdf` and `test_log.ldf`:

INPUT

```
create database test
on (name='test_data',filename = 'd:\program files\Microsoft SQL
Server\mssql\data
                  ➥\test_data.mdf')
log on (name='test_log',filename = 'd:\program files\Microsoft SQL
Server\mssql\data
                      ➥\test_log.ldf')
```

This sample should return the following:

OUTPUT

```
The CREATE DATABASE process is allocating 0.75 MB on disk 'test_data'.

The CREATE DATABASE process is allocating 1.00 MB on disk 'test_log'.
```

You can then use the `sp_attach_db` system stored procedure to detach the database you just created. Run the `sp_detach_db` system stored procedure as follows:

INPUT

```
Exec sp_detach_db 'test'
Go
```

You should see something similar to the following:

OUTPUT

```
The command(s) completed successfully.
```

This procedure detaches your test database from your server. You can then send your database files to anyone you want, and the recipient can run the following (or you can as well):

```
EXEC sp_attach_db @dbname = 'test',
@filename1 = 'd:\program files\Microsoft SQL Server\mssql\data\test.mdf',
@filename2 = 'd:\program files\Microsoft SQL Server\mssql\data\test_log.ldf'
```

Notice that the `sp_attach_db` system stored procedure essentially issues a `CREATE DATABASE FOR ATTACH` command. No functional difference exists in the two options, except that CREATE DATABASE can handle attaching more than 16 files at a time (the `create` database or the `sp_attach_db` options). Also, notice in the code sample that if you simply issue the command

```
create database test
```

the database is created with the filenames shown in the example. If you use different filenames, you need to make the necessary substitutions in the path of the files in the call to `sp_attach_db`.

Reattaching databases isn't a good backup-and-restore policy. It is simply a way for you to easily move databases around. For a backup strategy, you should make full database backups, differential backups, and transaction log backups as described on Day 7, "Backing Up Your Databases." As you will see later today, you are severely restricting your recovery options by not using SQL Server's built-in backup-and-restore capabilities.

Finding the Right Backup Set

Your first step is to find the correct backup set. You can proceed in two different ways here: the hard way and the easy way. You should start (as always) with the hard way because that's how you learn what's really going on. You can use these three Transact-SQL commands to find out (to various degrees) what's on your backup devices:

- `RESTORE LABELONLY` supplies a single line of summary information about the entire backup set.
- `RESTORE HEADERONLY` supplies summary information about each item in the backup set.
- `RESTORE FILELISTONLY` supplies a list of the databases and logs backed up on a particular backup device.

RESTORE LABELONLY

When you run the RESTORE LABELONLY command, the media header of your backup device (you would typically use this command for tapes) is read and summed up as a single row. That row describes the name of the media you specified during your backup, the description you entered when you backed up the database, and the last date of a backup on the backup device. Other information is also returned, but unless you're working on an advanced backup strategy, you don't need to explore this information.

SYNTAX

```
RESTORE LABELONLY FROM backup_device
[WITH {NOUNLOAD | UNLOAD }][[,] MEDIAPASSWORD = {mediapwd | @mediapwd_var}]
```

In this syntax,

- *backup_device* is the name of a backup device or variable placeholder for the backup device. You can also specify just the name of the file, tape, or Named Pipe you want to use for the restore (and, again, can specify it as a variable). Refer to yesterday's BACKUP syntax for a detailed description of what can go in the *backup_device* placeholder.
- NOUNLOAD | UNLOAD specifies whether the tape is ejected when RESTORE LABELONLY is complete.
- MEDIAPASSWORD is used when you create the backup (if one is used at all). If you don't have the password and the backup media is password protected, you cannot run this command. Having a password on individual backups doesn't prevent RESTORE LABELONLY; only passwords on the media itself prevent the command from completing successfully unless you have the proper password.

RESTORE HEADERONLY

RESTORE HEADERONLY gets information about every backup on a backup device. The command returns one row for each backup that exists on a database backup, because unlike the RESTORE LABELONLY command, RESTORE HEADERONLY reads information from each backup on a backup device one at a time. This process could be time consuming if you have several backups on a tape. For disk backup files, this command usually runs very quickly.

SYNTAX

```
RESTORE HEADERONLY FROM backup_device
[WITH {NOUNLOAD | UNLOAD}] [[,] FILE = file_num]
[[,] PASSWORD = { pwd | @pwd_var }]
[[,] MEDIAPASSWORD = {mediapwd | @mediapwd_var } ]
```

This syntax uses the same options as RESTORE LABELONLY, except for the following:

- FILE specifies which backup set on the tape to examine. For example, if the tape contains two backup sets, you can specify either 1 (the first set) or 2 (the second set).
- PASSWORD is the password you specified when making the backup set.

The results of this command include the names of the backups (as well as the descriptions) and the time the backups are set to expire. They include who created the backup, what server the backup came from, which database was backed up, how big the backup is, and when the backup began and was completed. The results also include the code page and sort order (used in SQL Server 7.0), the collation (the SQL Server 2000 equivalent of the sort order/code page/Unicode LocaleID), the database compatibility mode, and version of SQL Server used to make the backup. The information also includes internal information about log sequence numbers (which are beyond the scope of this book).

RESTORE FILELISTONLY

The `RESTORE FILELISTONLY` command returns a list of the database and log files that were backed up on the specified backup device. You can get information about only one backup at a time, so if a backup device contains multiple backups, you must specify which one you want to know about.

This information is particularly handy in disaster recovery situations. If you want to restore a database and don't know where the files were previously, you can find out by running `RESTORE FILELISTONLY`:

SYNTAX

```
RESTORE FILELISTONLY FROM backup_device
[WITH {NOUNLOAD | UNLOAD}] [[,] FILE = file_num]
[[,] PASSWORD = { pwd | @pwd_var }]
[[,] MEDIAPASSWORD = {mediapwd | @mediapwd_var } ]
```

This syntax uses the same options as `RESTORE HEADERONLY`.

If you don't know the file number you want to examine, run `RESTORE HEADERONLY` to get a list of file numbers and which backup each applies to. If you don't specify the `FILE` parameter, it's assumed to be the first backup on the backup device.

Establishing That Your Backup Set Is Usable

Assume for a minute that you ran the appropriate `DBCC` checks on your database before you ran your backup. Also, assume that you took advantage of the Verify option available during backup. Does that mean your backup is ready to restore?

If you (like us) can't immediately say yes, you aren't alone. Microsoft had this feeling as well, because it provided the `RESTORE VERIFYONLY` command. This command simply checks that all your tapes or disk files are available for a restore and that all the information needed can be read. It doesn't run the database `DBCC` checks on your backup; it simply checks that the tape/disk files can be read.

SYNTAX

```
RESTORE VERIFYONLY FROM backup_device [,...n]
[ WITH [FILE = filen_um] [[,] { NOUNLOAD | UNLOAD } ]
[[,] LOADHISTORY ] [[,] { NOREWIND | REWIND } ]
[[,] PASSWORD = { pwd | @pwd_var } ]
[[,] MEDIAPASSWORD = { mediapwd | @mediapwd_var } ]
]
```

This syntax uses the same options as discussed earlier, except for the following:

- `LOADHISTORY` specifies that the information about the backup that you examine be added to the backup history tables in the MSDB database. You will examine these tables shortly.
- `NOREWIND | REWIND` specifies whether the tape should be rewound when `RESTORE VERIFYONLY` is complete.

The MSDB Backup History Tables

A minor diversion is in order before you continue examining the actual restore commands. Every time you perform a SQL Server backup, the details of that backup are stored in the MSDB database in the following system tables:

- `Backupfile` contains information about file backups.
- `BackupMediaFamily` contains information about media families. You got a brief introduction to media families yesterday. Remember that they're typically used for parallel striped backups.
- `BackupMediaSet` contains information about media sets. Again, media sets are typically discussed when used with parallel striped backups, but every backup is part of a media set.
- `Backupset` contains information about each backup you make.
- `Restorefile` contains information about each restore of a file.
- `Restorefilegroup` contains information about each restore of a filegroup.
- `Restorehistory` contains information about every restore you run.

Every time you create any kind of backup or perform a restore operation, it's recorded in these system tables as necessary. It doesn't matter whether the backup or restore is performed using Transact-SQL statements or SQL Server Enterprise Manager. The implication, however, is that you need to back up your MSDB database frequently to save this information in case you lose either the MSDB or `master` database.

Performing a Full Database Restore

A full database restore takes a full database backup (you might think of it as a "normal" backup) and lays that backup down on your server, simply replacing all your data pages.

It uses the transaction log that was backed up with the database backup to recover the database, rolling forward any committed transactions and rolling back any uncommitted transactions, as of the time the database backup was complete. As with the backup commands, the Transact-SQL `RESTORE` command has more functionality than that of the SQL Server Enterprise Manager, and the SQL Server Enterprise Manager dialogs are much easier to understand when you see the commands running on SQL Server.

Several options are available when you restore a database. You can

- Move files around from where they were when the database was backed up.
- Set the `RESTRICTED_USER` database option during your restore in case you're not finished yet or want to restrict access to your database.
- Choose to recover or not recover to a consistent point in time (depending on whether you want to apply transaction log backups) or to a marked transaction entry.
- Create a standby file. You would create such a file in case you wanted to continue applying transaction log backups but wanted to examine the state of a database in a "read-only" mode between restoring those backups. You'll learn about this situation shortly.
- Restart a restore that was interrupted at some point (for example, if a power failure occurred during your restore operation).

Performing a Full Database Restore with Transact-SQL's `RESTORE` Command

You use the `RESTORE` command to recover a database from a full database backup. First, look at the syntax of the command:

SYNTAX

```
RESTORE DATABASE databasename FROM backup_device [, ...n]
[WITH [RESTRICTED_USER] [[,] FILE = file_num]
[[,] PASSWORD = { pwd | @pwd_var } ]
[[,] MEDIANAME = {media_name | @media_name_var}]
[[,] MEDIAPASSWORD = { mediapwd | @mediapwd_var } ]
[[,] MOVE 'logical_file_name' TO 'new_file_name'][,...n]
[[,] KEEP_REPLICATION]
[[,] {NORECOVERY | RECOVERY | STANDBY = undo_file_name}]
[[,] {NOUNLOAD | UNLOAD}] [[,] REPLACE] [[,] RESTART]
[[,] { NOREWIND | REWIND }]
[[,] STATS [= percentage]]]
```

In this syntax,

- *`databasename`* is the name of the database you want to restore.
- *`backup_device`* is the name of either a backup device or a variable placeholder for the backup device. You can also specify just the name of the file, tape, or Named Pipe you want to use for the restore—again, as a variable.

- `RESTRICTED_USER` specifies that only members of the sysadmin or dbcreator fixed server roles or db_owner fixed database role can have access to the database after the restore is complete. This option is used with the RECOVERY option.
- `FILE` specifies which backup on the backup device you want to restore.
- `PASSWORD` is the password you specified when making the backup set.
- `MEDIANAME` specifies that the backup's stored media name is compared to the specified media name. If they don't match, the restore fails.
- `MEDIAPASSWORD` is a password you used when you created the backup (if one was used at all). If you don't have the password and the backup media is password protected, you can't run this command.
- `MOVE` specifies that for each logical filename you reference, the restore operation should find that logical file in the backup set and restore it to the alternative pathname and filename you indicate.
- `KEEP_REPLICATION` tells restore to keep the replication configuration of a database. This option is available to support log shipping, an advanced availability technique that isn't described further in this book.
- `RECOVERY` indicates that the restore should roll back any uncommitted transactions and bring the database to a consistent state. After you use the `RECOVERY` option, you can't restore any transaction log backups or differential backups to the database. This option is the default if no other recovery option (`NORECOVERY` or `STANDBY`) is specified.
- `NORECOVERY` indicates that the restore shouldn't roll back any uncommitted transactions and that the restore won't bring the database to a consistent point. Use this option during the restore of your database when you want to apply transaction log backups or differential backups to the database after a full database restore.
- `STANDBY` specifies the pathname and filename of an undo file, which keeps enough information to restart transactions rolled back during the recovery process. Use `STANDBY` when you want to examine a database (in read-only fashion) between differential or transaction log restores. If the file you specify doesn't exist, SQL Server creates it for you.
- `NOUNLOAD | UNLOAD` specifies whether the tape is ejected when `RESTORE DATABASE` is complete.
- `REPLACE` indicates that the restore should replace any database with the same name that currently exists on your server. A normal restore without this option specifies that if the database name is different from the name of the backed-up database, or the set of files doesn't match from the backup to the existing database, the restore will fail. This is a safety check.

- `RESTART` restarts your backup from the place it last left off. As we indicated earlier today, this option applies only when you're recovering from a multiple-tape backup, when you are on the second tape or later.
- `NOREWIND | REWIND` specifies whether the tape should be rewound when `RESTORE` is complete.
- `STATS` indicates that you want a status report every specified percentage of the restore operation's progress. The default, just like in backups, is to let you know about the restore progress every 10 percent that is completed.

To restore the `pubs` database, which was backed up onto the `pubs_backup` backup device, accepting all defaults, you would run the following command:

INPUT
```
RESTORE DATABASE PUBS FROM PUBS_BACKUP
```

Tip

You may get an error that the database is in use. This is most likely because you've either got the database or something inside the database highlighted in Enterprise Manager or Query Analyzer (including a query window in Query Analyzer with the database set to the database you are attempting to restore). Simply click on another database in either tool to no longer be considered using the database you're attempting to restore, and re-try the command.

If three backups were stored on the `pubs_backup` backup device, and you wanted to restore the third of these full database backups, you would run two sets of commands. The first step is to verify that you really want file number three on the backup device:

INPUT
```
RESTORE HEADERONLY from pubs_backup
```

The second step actually performs the restore:

INPUT
```
RESTORE DATABASE PUBS FROM PUBS_BACKUP WITH FILE = 3
```

To restore your `pubs` database, but store the `pubs.mdf` file on your computer's D drive after the restore, leave the database in a standby state, restore from file number three, and provide notification of the restore's progress after every 25 percent of the restore is complete. You would run the following command:

INPUT
```
RESTORE DATABASE PUBS FROM PUBS_BACKUP
WITH MOVE 'pubs' TO 'D:\pubs.mdf',
FILE = 3,
```

```
STANDBY = 'd:\standby.dat',
STATS = 25
```

You should get output similar to this:

```
26 percent restored.
53 percent restored.
76 percent restored.
100 percent restored.
Processed 208 pages for database 'PUBS', file 'pubs' on file 3.
Processed 1 pages for database 'PUBS', file 'pubs_log' on file 3.
RESTORE DATABASE successfully processed 209 pages in 0.807 seconds
(2.112 MB/sec).
```

At this point, you would need to apply a transaction log or differential database backup to complete the recovery of your database, so you might run

INPUT

```
restore log pubs from pubs_backup with file = 4, RECOVERY
```

where file number four was a transaction log backup that occurred after your full database backup. In this case, you would get something like this from your command:

```
Deleting database file 'd:\standby.dat'.
Processed 5 pages for database 'pubs', file 'pubs_log' on file 4.
RESTORE LOG successfully processed 5 pages in 0.048 seconds
(0.853 MB/sec).
```

Notice that SQL Server deletes your standby file and finishes recovering the log. Now that it's no longer needed, you need to delete the standby file.

The `MOVE` Option

The `MOVE` option enables you to perform easy migrations of data from one server to another. If your production server has drive letters H and I, for example, and they contain SQL Server data or log files, you can restore these backups to your development server. This is true even if that server has only drives C, D, and E. You simply specify the logical filenames from the old backup and provide the new location on the new server for each logical file.

> Remember that you can find the list of files in a backup set by using the `RESTORE FILELISTONLY` command.

This option also helps in a disaster recovery situation. It's possible, but not likely, that the server you end up with after a disaster won't have the same drive letters, so it's good to know how to use the `MOVE` option.

Just in case you think I'm emphasizing disasters a little too much, consider this event on the Internet that happened when we were writing the 7.0 version of this book. I visited a Web site that apologized for its lack of content because its servers were stolen during a burglary. Still think it can't happen to you?

The REPLACE Option

The REPLACE option is useful because it tells you about some checks that are normally running during a restore. If the database name you backed up (for example, Accounting) isn't the same as the one you're attempting to restore (for example, Sales), a normal restore operation isn't allowed. This behavior is meant to help prevent you from sounding like Homer Simpson and letting out a big "Doh!" after a restore (is that résumé ready to go?).

It also helps you if the set of files doesn't match. If both the backed-up database and the database you want to restore to are named Accounting, but the production (currently running) accounting database consists of 20 1GB files and the backup is the wrong one (say, your test database of 20MB), SQL Server notices and prevents the restore.

You can override this behavior in both instances by specifying the REPLACE option, which basically tells SQL Server to butt out—you know what you are doing.

Be very sure before you specify the REPLACE option. If you get a failure because of one of the conditions referenced here, it's usually time to step back, take a deep breath, and put a little thought into what you're doing. It's better to wait a minute than try to explain why you deliberately recovered the wrong database into production.

Restoring with Differential Backups

Restoring a differential backup works just like restoring a full database backup. There's no syntactical difference. Simply specify the correct file number from your backup devices.

You can restore a differential backup only after you restore a full database backup. You must also have specified either the STANDBY or NORECOVERY options during your full database restore to be able to apply your differential backups.

Your differential backups are cumulative, so if you've made three differential backups since your last full database backup, you must restore only the last of these differential backups.

Restoring from a Transaction Log

Restoring from a transaction log is relatively straightforward, as long as you keep the rules in mind. You can restore the transaction logs only in the sequence in which they were backed up. Unlike differential backups, transaction log backups aren't cumulative, so you need all of them to be intact to be able to recover completely.

With transaction log restores, unlike database or differential backup restores, which let you recover only to the point in time the backup was taken, you can restore to a chosen point in time when recovering backups, as well as restore to a named mark in your transaction log.

Using Transact-SQL to Restore Transaction Logs

You specify the RESTORE LOG command to recover a transaction log backup:

SYNTAX

```
RESTORE LOG databasename FROM backup_device [, ...n]
[WITH [RESTRICTED_USER] [[,] FILE = file_num]
[[,] PASSWORD = { pwd | @pwd_var } ]
[[,] MEDIANAME = {media_name | @media_name_var}]
[[,] MEDIAPASSWORD = { mediapwd | @mediapwd_var } ]
[[,] MOVE 'logical_file_name' TO 'new_file_name'][,...n]
[[,] KEEP_REPLICATION]
[[,] {NORECOVERY | RECOVERY | STANDBY = undo_file_name}]
[[,] {NOUNLOAD | UNLOAD}] [[,] { NOREWIND | REWIND }]
[[,] RESTART] [[,] STATS [= percentage]]
[[,] STOPAT = datetime]
| [,] STOPATMARK = 'markname' [AFTER datetime]
| [,] STOPBEFOREMARK = 'markname' [AFTER datetime]]]
```

This syntax uses the same options as a full database restore, except for the following:

- STOPAT indicates the date and time you want to choose as your point of consistency during the restore of the transaction log. Any transactions that were active (not committed) at this time are rolled back.
- STOPATMARK indicates a named mark (specifying the marked entry name) at which to stop.
- STOPBEFOREMARK allows you to stop just before the named mark.

After you recover from your full database backup (and specify the STANDBY or NORECOVERY option), you apply a transaction log like this (assuming that the pubs_log_backup backup device exists and contains one or more transaction log backups):

```
RESTORE LOG pubs from pubs_log_backup
```

That's it. You've restored the log. The complete recovery of both the full backup and log backup looks like this:

```
RESTORE DATABASE pubs FROM pubs_backup WITH NORECOVERY
RESTORE LOG pubs from pubs_log_backup WITH RECOVERY
```

RECOVERY is the default option, so you don't need to provide it on the transaction log restore, but I included it here for clarity.

Now, for the sake of argument, assume that you made your database backup and then made three transaction log backups (file numbers 1, 2, and 3 on the pubs_log_backup backup device). You would run the following command sequence to restore the database and recover all your transaction log backups:

INPUT

```
RESTORE DATABASE pubs FROM pubs_backup WITH NORECOVERY
RESTORE LOG pubs from pubs_log_backup WITH FILE = 1, NORECOVERY
RESTORE LOG pubs from pubs_log_backup WITH FILE = 2, NORECOVERY
RESTORE LOG pubs from pubs_log_backup WITH FILE = 3, RECOVERY
```

You see results like this:

OUTPUT

```
Processed 208 pages for database 'pubs', file 'pubs' on file 1.
Processed 1 pages for database 'pubs', file 'pubs_log' on file 1.
RESTORE DATABASE successfully processed 209 pages in 0.744 seconds
(2.291 MB/sec).
Processed 2 pages for database 'pubs', file 'pubs_log' on file 1.
RESTORE LOG successfully processed 2 pages in 0.066 seconds
(0.186 MB/sec).
Processed 1 pages for database 'pubs', file 'pubs_log' on file 2.
RESTORE LOG successfully processed 1 pages in 0.110 seconds
(0.032 MB/sec).
Processed 1 pages for database 'pubs', file 'pubs_log' on file 3.
RESTORE LOG successfully processed 1 pages in 0.053 seconds
(0.019 MB/sec).
```

Restoring to a Point in Time To restore a point in time, restore as you did previously, except for transaction log within the time range at which you want to stop. You can use the RESTORE HEADERONLY command to explore the time ranges covered by each transaction log backup. So, for the exact same commands you ran before, but stopping at a particular time during the third log restore, run the following:

INPUT

```
RESTORE DATABASE pubs FROM pubs_backup WITH NORECOVERY
RESTORE LOG pubs from pubs_log_backup WITH FILE = 1, NORECOVERY
RESTORE LOG pubs from pubs_log_backup WITH FILE = 2, NORECOVERY
RESTORE LOG pubs from pubs_log_backup WITH FILE = 3, RECOVERY,
STOPAT = 'Jun 3, 2002 4:53 PM'
```

The restore brings your database to what would have been a consistent state at exactly 4:53 p.m. on June 3, 2002.

Restoring to a Marked Transaction Log Entry As we mentioned earlier, you can also recover to a marked point in your transaction log. The trick here is that you restore to the transaction name, not the mark name (which is really just a comment so you know what the transaction was later). Consider this example (Which will work when the database is in FULL recovery mode):

```
exec sp_dropdevice 'pubs_backup','DELFILE'
exec sp_dropdevice 'pubs_log_backup','DELFILE'
```

```
go
exec sp_addumpdevice 'disk','pubs_backup','d:\program files\microsoft sql
➥server\mssql\backup\pubs_backup.bak'
exec sp_addumpdevice 'disk','pubs_log_backup','d:\program files\microsoft sql
➥server\mssql\backup\pubs_log_backup.bak'
--create backup file #1 (full database backup)
backup database pubs to pubs_backup with init
go
use pubs
create table table3 (c1 int not null)
BEGIN TRANSACTION tran1 WITH MARK 'My first Mark'
insert table3 values (1)
COMMIT TRANSACTION tran1
-- create backup file #1 (tran log backup)
backup log pubs to pubs_log_backup with noinit
create table table4 (c1 int not null)
insert table4 values (1)
-- create backup file #2 (tran log backup)
backup log pubs to pubs_log_backup with noinit
insert table3 values (2)
BEGIN TRANSACTION tran2 WITH MARK 'My Second Mark'
insert table3 values (3)
insert table4 values (3)
COMMIT TRANSACTION tran2
-- create backup file #3 (tran log backup)
backup log pubs to pubs_log_backup with noinit
```

This script creates a backup file for a transaction log and a database backup, backs up the database, creates some objects, and in the middle creates two "marked" transactions: tran1 and tran2. You can restore to one of these marked points just as you did before, as in this example:

INPUT

```
RESTORE DATABASE pubs FROM pubs_backup WITH NORECOVERY
RESTORE LOG pubs from pubs_log_backup WITH FILE = 1, NORECOVERY
RESTORE LOG pubs from pubs_log_backup WITH FILE = 2, NORECOVERY
RESTORE LOG pubs from pubs_log_backup WITH FILE = 3, RECOVERY,
STOPATMARK = 'tran2'
```

And you would see something like this:

OUTPUT

```
Processed 144 pages for database 'pubs', file 'pubs' on file 1.
Processed 1 pages for database 'pubs', file 'pubs_log' on file 1.
RESTORE DATABASE successfully processed 145 pages in 0.629 seconds
(1.877 MB/sec).
Processed 2 pages for database 'pubs',  file 'pubs_log' on file 1.
RESTORE LOG successfully processed 2 pages in 0.064 seconds
(0.224 MB/sec).
Processed 1 pages for database 'pubs', file 'pubs_log' on file 2.
RESTORE LOG successfully processed 1 pages in 0.052 seconds
(0.068 MB/sec).
```

```
Processed 1 pages for database 'pubs', file 'pubs_log' on file 3.
RESTORE LOG successfully processed 1 pages in 0.049 seconds
(0.020 MB/sec).
```

Restoring Transaction Log and Differential Database Backups

If you want to combine restoring differential database backups with transaction log backups, remember that you need all the transaction logs that were active from the time of the differential backup forward. For example, if in the previous example you had taken a differential database backup after the second transaction log backup, you could run the following set of code:

```
RESTORE DATABASE pubs FROM pubs_backup WITH FILE = 1, NORECOVERY
RESTORE DATABASE pubs FROM pubs_backup WITH FILE = 2, NORECOVERY
RESTORE LOG pubs from pubs_log_backup WITH FILE = 1, RECOVERY
```

You would see something like the following output:

```
Processed 144 pages for database 'pubs', file 'pubs' on file 1.
Processed 1 pages for database 'pubs', file 'pubs_log' on file 1.
RESTORE DATABASE successfully processed 145 pages in 0.599 seconds
(1.971 MB/sec).
Processed 48 pages for database 'pubs', file 'pubs' on file 2.
Processed 1 pages for database 'pubs', file 'pubs_log' on file 2.
RESTORE DATABASE successfully processed 49 pages in 0.312 seconds
(1.263 MB/sec).
Processed 3 pages for database 'pubs', file 'pubs_log' on file 1.
RESTORE LOG successfully processed 3 pages in 0.070 seconds
(0.307 MB/sec).
```

Your database is now restored using the full database backup, then applying the differential backup, and finally applying the only transaction log backup made after the differential backup: transaction log backup number 3.

Restoring Files or Filegroups

You can also restore individual files or a filegroup if you want. Today's lesson includes the syntax and an example for completeness. Although file and filegroup backups and restores are very powerful features of SQL Server, they require sophisticated planning to ensure you use them successfully, and they are beyond the scope of this book.

SYNTAX

```
RESTORE DATABASE databasename file_or_filegroup [, ...n]
[FROM backup_device [, ...n]]
[WITH [RESTRICTED_USER] [[,] FILE = file_num]
[[,] PASSWORD = { pwd | @pwd_var }]
[[,] MEDIANAME = {media_name | @media_name_var}]
[[,] MEDIAPASSWORD = { mediapwd | @mediapwd_var } ]
[[,] NORECOVERY] [[,] {NOUNLOAD | UNLOAD}] [[,] {NOREWIND | REWIND}]
[[,] REPLACE][[,] RESTART] [[,] STATS [= percentage]]]
```

In this syntax,

```
file_or_filegroup :: =
{FILE = {logical_file_name | @logical_file_name_var} |
FILEGROUP = {logical_filegroup_name | @logical_filegroup_name_var}}
```

The only difference between this and the full database restore syntax is that you can specify either a file or filegroup name in the command.

If you had backed up the `test_data` file of a database named `test` to the backup device `test_file_backup`, you could restore it by using the following commands:

```
RESTORE DATABASE test FILE = 'test_data'
FROM test_file_backup WITH NORECOVERY
RESTORE LOG test
FROM test_log_backup WITH RECOVERY
```

Note

> You can't restore a file or filegroup backup without next applying a transaction log restore to bring the database to a consistent state. This example is just a hint at the complexity of a file or filegroup backup strategy.

Restoring with SQL Server Enterprise Manager

You made it! Now that you understand what's really going on behind the scenes, it's time to examine how easily you can restore a database by using the SQL Server Enterprise Manager.

Expand the Databases folder, right-click the database you want to recover, and select All Tasks, Restore Database. Now a good question should pop into your head: What if the database you want to restore doesn't exist?

After you connect to your server, select Restore Database from the Tools menu. You end up in the same place in both cases—the Restore Database dialog (see Figure 8.3 for the `pubs` database on my system).

As you can see in Figure 8.3, SQL Server Enterprise Manager makes database restoration a trivial affair. SQL Server, as you learned earlier today, remembers when backups are made by storing information in system tables in the MSDB system database. That information is what you see reflected in the restore dialogs. For each box checked, SQL Server restores that backup item. In Figure 8.3, you can see that a restore from a full database backup would have occurred (the first checked box), followed immediately by a restore of a transaction log (the next two checked boxes). The full database restore happens with the `NORECOVERY` option, because you apply a transaction log restore next. The transaction log restore occurs with the `RECOVERY` option, and your database is then available.

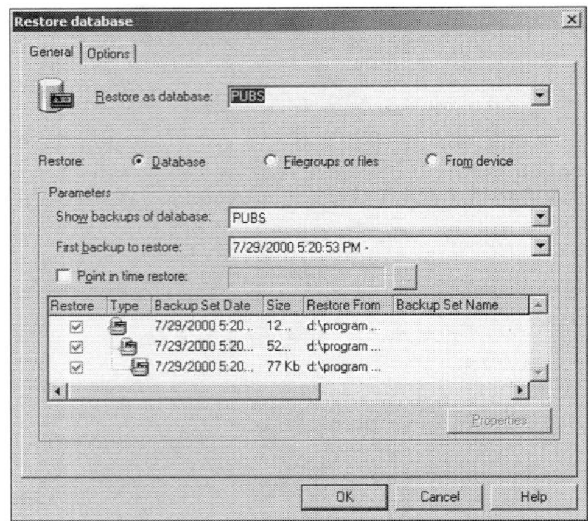

FIGURE 8.3

The Restore Database dialog.

To perform a file or filegroup restore, simply click that option. To perform a point-in-time restore (assuming that you're restoring one or more transaction logs), simply check the Point in Time Restore box.

If you click the Restore From Device option, the dialog morphs into the one shown in Figure 8.4.

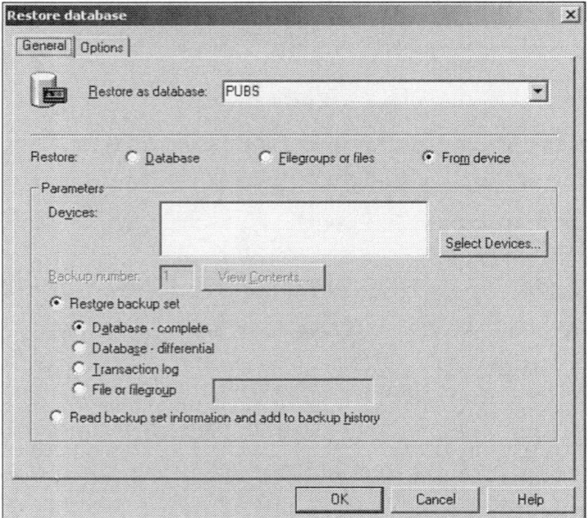

FIGURE 8.4

The Restore Database dialog (using a device).

To choose a backup device, click the Select Devices button. Then, click the Add button to see the dialog in Figure 8.5. Select a file containing a database or transaction log backup, or select a backup device.

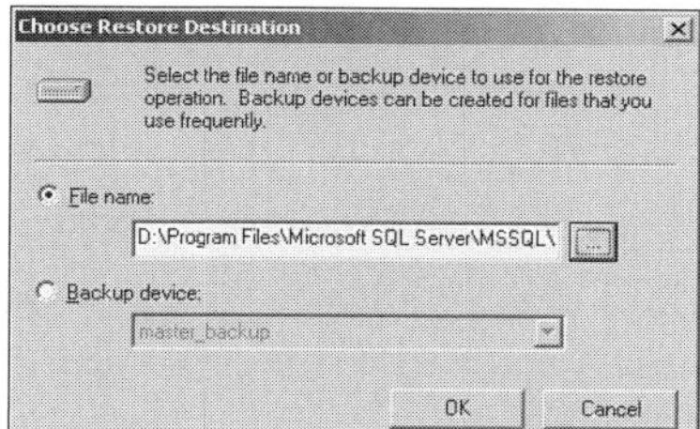

FIGURE 8.5

The Choose Restore Destination dialog.

After you return to the Restore Database dialog, specify the kind of backup you want to restore. Then select the Backup number (the `FILE` parameter from the `RESTORE` command). Another nifty feature here is that you can click the View Contents button to see the equivalent of the `LOAD HEADERONLY` command. However, here you can choose to restore the contents of the backup device, if multiple backups (for example, multiple transaction log backups) are contained on the device (see Figure 8.6).

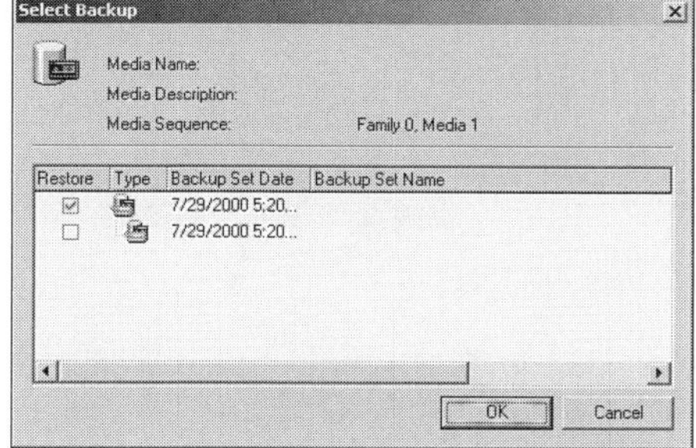

FIGURE 8.6

The Select Backup dialog.

Finally, when you are in the Restore Database dialog, notice the option at the bottom that allows you to update the backup history information in SQL Server's MSDB database, "Read backup set information and add to backup history."

To change other restore options in the Restore Database dialog (as if you haven't examined enough yet), click the Options tab (see Figure 8.7). The following options are available on this tab:

- Eject Tapes (If Any) After Restoring Each Backup does as indicated and ejects your tapes when the restore is done.
- Prompt Before Restoring Each Backup allows you to be notified between each restore you've selected on the General tab.
- Force Restore Over Existing Database issues the `REPLACE` option for the `RESTORE DATABASE` statement.

- For each file in your backup set, you can rename it in the Restore Database Files As section. This is the same as the MOVE option from the RESTORE DATABASE statement.
- Recovery Completion State has three options. The first, the default, is to leave your database operational (which is the same as specifying the RECOVERY option on the final restore).

  Use the middle option button when you want to continue applying differential or transaction log restores. This option specifies the NORECOVERY option on the final transaction log restore (or full database/differential restore if you choose not to apply any logs).

  The final option is the same as specifying the STANDBY option in a restore statement. As with the Transact-SQL RESTORE command, you must specify the location and filename of the undo file.

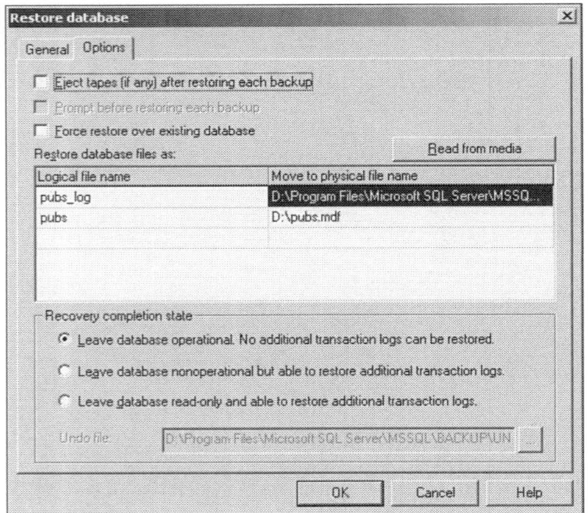

FIGURE 8.7
The Restore Database Options tab.

When you're ready to begin the restore operation, click OK. SQL Server Enterprise Manager then submits the appropriate RESTORE commands that you've graphically specified.

Recovery Scenarios

Perhaps the most important thing you can do is look at how to apply the backup and restore techniques you examined yesterday and today.

Recovery After Losing a Disk

One of the most common recovery scenarios is to restore databases after a disk is lost on the server. Perform the following steps to recover your database:

1. Verify that you have all the information you need to restore the devices and databases.
2. Capture the transaction log if it's still available.
3. Drop the affected databases.
4. Replace the failed disk.
5. Restore the databases and transaction logs as appropriate.

Now explore each of these steps in detail.

Verify That You Have All the Information You Need to Restore a Database

You should have the `CREATE DATABASE` statements to re-create any databases affected by the lost disk. The good news is that with SQL Server 2000, as long as you can find your backups (or the backup tape), you can figure out what's on it by using the commands you've examined today (`RESTORE HEADERONLY`, `RESTORE FILELISTONLY`). All the information you need to recover your backups is contained in your backups now with SQL Server 2000.

Capture the Transaction Log If It's Still Available

If your database files are damaged somehow, and the transaction log files are available (on another disk), you can run the `BACKUP LOG` command with the `NO_TRUNCATE` option. The idea here is that you back up the transaction log entries that have occurred since your last backup so that you can recover those log entries when you are ready to restore your database.

Drop the Database

Because the database is suspect or partially lost, you can drop the database and then prepare for the restore. You run the `DROP DATABASE` command to drop the database and any files from your server. The `DROP DATABASE` command works even if the database is marked suspect.

Replace the Failed Disk

This step should be obvious. Before restarting Windows 2000, however, you need to reset any RAID configurations. If you're using Windows 2000 RAID, you need to configure the RAID setup in the Disk Administrator program before the next step. Refer to your Windows 2000 documentation if you are using Windows 2000 RAID, or your hardware documentation otherwise.

Re-Create the Lost Databases (Optional)

If you want, you can re-create the database. This step is optional. The restore process can re-create the database for you.

Restore the Full Database Backup, Any Differential Backup, and Transaction Log Backups As Needed

After all you've learned in today's lessons, this step should also be self-explanatory. Recover your full database backup and your last differential backup (if it exists), and then apply your transaction log (including the last log backup you made after the disk failed).

Run `DBCC CHECKDB` to Verify a Good Restore (Optional)

This step is optional, but a very good idea. Run `DBCC CHECKDB` on every database you've recovered to verify that your backup and restore operation returned you to a good state. If it didn't for some reason, you need to go to your previous backup and try the restore again.

> As you can see, recovering databases is not rocket science, but it's sufficiently scary that you should practice recovery occasionally so that you are comfortable with each step when it's your production server with the problem instead of your test server.

Recovery After Losing the `master` Database

The `RESTORE` procedure works fine as long as you didn't lose your `master` database. What if you do? There are really two ways you can be affected by a lost master database. They relate to what you can do to repair the damage.

If you have the database or log file that has been corrupted or have logical problems (someone deleted all your logins, or something like that) but can still get SQL Server running, you can simply restore the `master` database. Frankly, the more likely scenario is that when the `master` database fails, it will take your server with it. That's why it's such a good idea (as you will examine on Day 20, "Performance Monitoring Basics and Tools") to mirror the disks that hold your `master` database and transaction log files.

Restoring the `master` Database

First, the easy scenario: To restore your `master` database from your full database backup, start SQL Server in single-user mode. The easiest way to do so is from a command prompt on the server running SQL Server 2000. Open a command prompt, and run the following sequence of commands:

INPUT
```
NET STOP MSSQLSERVER
```

This command shuts down the MSSQLServer service (for a default instance). To shut down a named instance, substitute MSSQL$*InstanceName* (for example, MSSQL$TRADE for our named instance "trade") to stop your named instance.

Next, start SQL Server with the single-user mode switch (`-m`):

INPUT
```
SQLSERVR.EXE -m
```

This command starts SQL Server as an application running in the command window. Don't type in or close the command window; that's really SQL Server! When SQL Server quits spitting out text (which, not coincidentally, looks like the error logs you examined earlier today), it's ready for you to use.

To start a named instance, you must start it by using the `-s` option as described on Day 2, "Installing Microsoft SQL Server 2000." So, to start the instance named TRADE, you would run

INPUT
```
SQLSERVR.EXE -m -STRADE
```

Next, start your favorite query tool (or SQL Server Enterprise Manager), and restore your `master` database as you would any other full database backup. When the restore operation is complete, SQL Server stops itself. Simply start the service to return to normal operations. You can use the following command to restart the service:

INPUT
```
NET START MSSQLServer
```

or

INPUT
```
NET START MSSQL$TRADE
```

Note

> You can restore the `master` database only when you are in single-user mode. If you aren't, SQL Server Enterprise Manager and the query tools prevent you from doing so, and you receive a message like this:
>
> ```
> Server: Msg 3108, Level 16, State 1, Line 2
> RESTORE DATABASE must be used in single user mode
> when trying to restore the master database.
> Server: Msg 3013, Level 16, State 1, Line 2
> RESTORE DATABASE terminating abnormally.
> ```
>
> You must finish restoring the `master` database and restart SQL Server normally before you can restore any other databases.

You need to apply manually any changes that you've made to your `master` database since your last full database backup—another fine reason to make frequent backups of your `master` database.

Rebuilding the `master` Database

The other scenario is that your `master` database isn't available and functioning, and you basically have a dead server. As one of my favorite authors always says, "Don't panic!" You can make it through this situation and maybe even be a hero at the office.

When SQL Server doesn't start because your `master` database is dead, it usually means that you've lost the disk (or disks) that held any of the `master` database files. The first step is to run the Rebuild Master utility (`rebuildm.exe`), located in your `\Program Files\Microsoft SQL Server\80\tools\binn` directory.

This utility assumes that SQL Server isn't running. When it starts, you are presented with the Rebuild Master dialog (see Figure 8.8).

FIGURE 8.8

The Rebuild Master dialog.

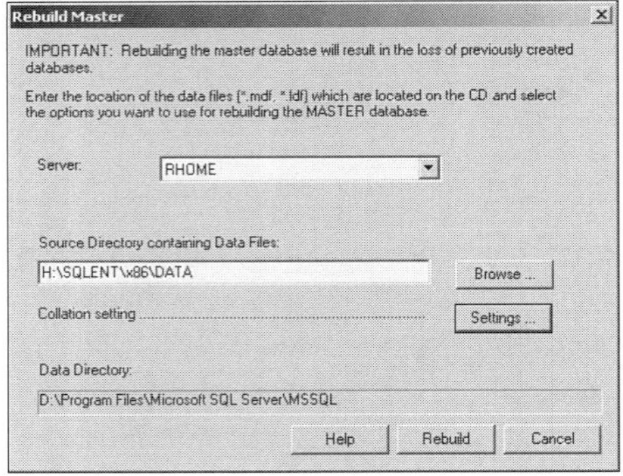

Click the Browse button to locate your `\data` directory from your installation CD. Click the Settings button to change the Collation settings (see Figure 8.9) if you didn't accept the defaults when you installed SQL Server.

After you set these options, click OK. In the Rebuild Master dialog, click the Rebuild option to make SQL Server copy the original database files from your CD. They include all the files for `master`, MSDB, `model`, `pubs`, and Northwind. Rebuild Master then starts SQL Server, which re-creates your `tempdb` database, and completes any conversions needed, depending on your collation choices. When finished, it tells you that the rebuild is complete.

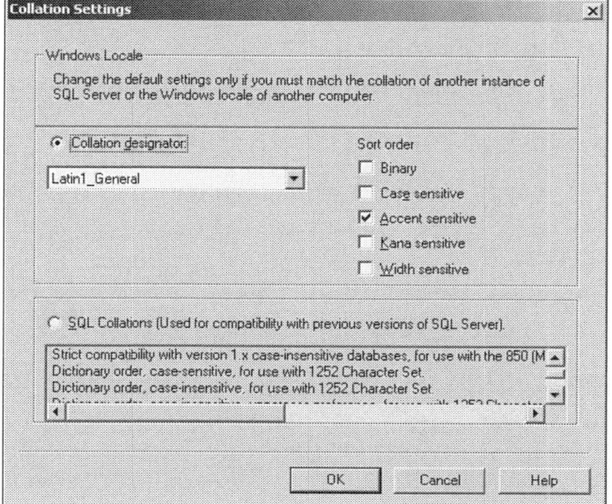

FIGURE 8.9
Selecting the appropriate rebuild options.

Restore `master` and Then Other System Databases

After you rebuild your server, restore your `master` database backup as just described. Then you need to restore your `model` database (if you've changed it), the MSDB database, and your distribution database if this server is a distribution server used in replication.

Attach or Restore Databases, If Necessary

Finally, restore any other affected databases. If you still have the database files, use the `CREATE DATABASE FOR ATTACH` command or `sp_attach_db` system stored procedure to reattach the databases to SQL Server.

Perform DBCCs on the Entire Server

Finally, because you live in the land of the paranoid, after a crash like this, run `DBCC CHECKDB` on every database to verify that your server is up and running without any corruption.

Summary

The backup and recovery process is probably the most important part of maintaining your SQL Server system. As you saw today, restore can be very straightforward when you're using SQL Server Enterprise Manager, or it can get a bit complicated when you're rebuilding or restoring the master database. The only advice I can give you is to test your backup and restore routines on a regular basis. It's the only way you will ever feel comfortable with this process.

Q&A

Q Which command would I use to restore a database from a backup?

A The `RESTORE DATABASE` command.

Q Which command would I use to restore a differential backup of the `master` database?

A You can't make a partial restore on the master database, so it's not an issue. You can make only full database backups of the `master` database.

Q Which command would I use to restore a transaction log but leave the database in an unrecovered state?

A The `RESTORE LOG WITH NORECOVERY` command.

Workshop

The Workshop section provides quiz questions to help you solidify your understanding of the concepts presented in this lesson. In addition to the quiz questions, exercises are provided to let you practice what you have learned in this lesson. Try to understand the quiz and exercise answers before continuing on to the next day's lesson. Answers are provided in Appendix A, "Answers to Quiz Questions."

Quiz

1. If you rebuild the master database, what other database must be recovered?
2. If you specify the `RESTORE FILELISTONLY` command, what will you get as a result?
3. Can you restore a backup made with multiple tapes onto a server with a single tape drive?
4. What configuration option is used to tune automatic recovery?
5. If your manager accidentally dropped the payroll table, how would you recover it?

Exercises

1. Create a test database, back it up, and then test the restoration procedures. Try this procedure for a full database backup, and then also test recovering transaction logs. Make changes to your database, such as creating a table, between each transaction log backup. When you restore, apply each transaction log, and verify that only the appropriate changes are recovered with each restore.
2. Back up your database, make some changes, and then make a differential backup. Finally, make a transaction log backup after making additional changes. Restore

from the backups using Transact-SQL commands only, and verify that the restores were successful.

3. Repeat exercise 2. This time stop after the full database backup by using the `STANDBY` option after each restore, and examine the state of your database to see what's happening and verify that your changes really are being rolled forward and back. Of course, perform a `WITH RECOVERY` on the final transaction log restore.

WEEK 2

DAY 9

Data Types and Creating Tables

Yesterday you learned how to restore your databases from backups. You looked at the different recovery mechanisms that SQL Server 2000 uses, including automatic and manual recovery. You learned how to restore a single database, as well as apply transaction log backups to bring your database to a specific point-in-time with certain recovery options. Now that you know how to handle your backups and restoration plans, you can learn how to create tables and add data to your database.

Today you will learn how to add tables to your database. First, you are presented with an overview of tables and then a look at the different data types used to create your tables. Next, you learn how to put all the information together to create and modify tables in your database using code. Then you see how Microsoft has simplified the code process by enabling you to create tables graphically with the SQL Server Enterprise Manager.

Tables

Tables store all the data in your database and are organized into rows and columns (records and fields, known in relational theory as tuples and attributes). Each column in your table can store a specific type of information, or data type.

A single table represents an entity in your database. Each row in the table represents an occurrence of that entity. The columns in your table describe the attributes of that logical entity. For example, you might create a table of employees (in which employees are a logical entity or group). A single row in your employees table represents a single instance of an employee. The columns that make up that table describe the employee. Some columns you might include are EmployeeID, FirstName, LastName, and SSN (Social Security number).

Columns

Each column (field) in your table must be assigned a name, a data type, a length (optional), collation (optional), and a nullability status. You can place columns in any order in your table definition. Each column must also have a unique name within the table and follow the rules for SQL Server identifiers (discussed in the following section).

A single database can have up to 2 billion tables in it, with each table holding up to 1,024 columns. If you have anywhere near this number of tables, or columns within a table, you may need to take another look at your design. The maximum length of any row is 8,192 bytes, minus overhead inherent in the physical storage of rows in SQL Server. That overhead varies depending on many factors beyond the scope of this book. Needless to say, the maximum amount of storage space for data is 8,060 bytes per row.

The maximum length for a single column is 8,000 bytes, and you can have up to 1,024 columns in a row; however, a row can't exceed a data page (8,192 bytes) for data and overhead. The exception is for the text and image data types, which allow up to 2GB of textual or binary information. They aren't physically stored as part of a table row, so they don't count against the restriction that a data row fit in a single data page. You'll learn more details about column lengths and table and row overhead later today.

The maximum amount of storage space in a data page for data is 8,060 bytes. In other words, the minimum amount of overhead on any given data page is 132 bytes.

SQL Server Identifiers

All SQL Server table names, as well as column names and any other object name, must follow these rules for SQL Server identifiers:

- Identifiers can be from 1 to 128 Unicode Standard 2.0 characters long, including letters, symbols, and numbers.
- The first character must be a letter (either lower or upper case) or one of the following symbols: `@`, `#`, or _ (underscore). `@` and `#` have special meanings in SQL Server.
- You can use the following symbols after the first character: `#`, `$`, and _.
- Identifiers that begin with the `@` symbol are used as local variables. The `@` symbol can appear only as the first character in an identifier.
- Identifiers that begin with the `#` symbol are used to signify that the objects you are creating are temporary and can be referenced by the user during the session.
- Identifiers that begin with `##` signify that the objects you are creating are global temporary objects and can be referenced by all users in the database.
- You can use embedded spaces in your identifiers, but to reference those objects you must encapsulate them in either double quotation marks (“”) or square brackets ([]). For example, a table named Employee Pension would need to be referenced as `"Employee Pension"` or `[Employee Pension]` in the database. Using the square bracket syntax is preferable (if you insist on using spaces in your identifier names) so as not to confuse constant strings with SQL Server identifiers. You must take the same approach if you use SQL Server reserved words as identifiers. For example, a table name PRINT or SELECT.

> Although using symbols and embedded spaces in identifiers is allowed in SQL Server, most developers avoid their use because they can lead to confusing SQL statements.

Table 9.1 shows some examples of valid and invalid identifiers.

TABLE 9.1 Valid and Invalid Identifiers

Identifier	*Comments*
`1001ArabianNights`	Invalid identifier. Identifiers must begin with a letter.
`@Addresses`	This identifier is valid only for creating a variable.
`Table@Address`	Invalid identifier. The `@` symbol can only be the first character in an identifier.
`#tblCities`	This identifier is valid only if you are creating a local temporary object. A local temporary object is available only to the user who created it.
`##tblCities`	This identifier is valid only if you are creating a global temporary object, which is available to all users.
`tblEmployee`	Valid identifier. Although prefixing identifiers (`tbl` for table) isn't necessary, it does make your SQL statements easier to read because the prefix denotes what the identifier represents. Other common identifiers are `qry` for query, `tr` for trigger, `sp_` for system-stored procedures, and so on.
`Titles`, `[Author_Review]`, `AuthorReview`	These identifiers are valid.

Data Types

The data type specifies what kind of information (numeric, character, and so on) and how much space that information takes up in a particular column. Some data types have a variable length, whereas others have a fixed length. SQL Server data types can be broken down into the following groups: string, Unicode data, binary, integer, approximate and exact numeric, special, date and time, money, autoincrementing, synonyms, user-defined, and computed column. Table 9.2 lists the different data types allowed in SQL Server 2000.

TABLE 9.2 SQL Server 2000 Supported Data Types

Category	*Data Type*	*Comments*
String	`char(`*n*`)`, `varchar(n)`	Stores character strings.
Binary	`binary(`*n*`)`, `varbinary(n)`	Stores binary information in 2-byte pairs.
Integer	`int`, `smallint`, `bigint`, `tinyint`	Stores integer values.

TABLE 9.2 continued

Category	*Data Type*	*Comments*
Approximate numeric	`float`, `real`	Stores approximate numeric information.
Exact numeric	`decimal`, `numeric`	Stores exact numeric information.
Special	`bit`, `text`, `image`, `sql_variant`, `table`, uniqueidentifier	Stores a single bit, character information greater than 8,000 bytes, or image data. `sql_variant` stores just about anything, and `table` stores tables.
Date and Time	`datetime`, `smalldatetime`	Stores dates and times.
Money	`money`, `smallmoney`	Stores currency values.
Auto-incrementing	`rowversion` (formerly `timestamp`)	Stores values that are data types automatically incremented or set by the SQL Server.
Synonyms	(See Table 9.9)	Maps ANSI data types to SQL Server data types.
User-defined		You can create your own data types to store information.
Unicode data	`nchar`, `ntext`, `nvarchar`	Stores data in a Unicode (double byte per stored character) format.
Computed columns		Stores the expression used to compute the column. It doesn't store the data, just the expressions used to create it.

9

Nullability

NEW TERM The *nullability* of a column refers to whether an entry is required for that column. If you want to allow a column to indicate that the value is unknown, specify `NULL`. If you want to insist that each row have an entry in that column, specify `NOT NULL`. If you don't specify `NULL` or `NOT NULL`, the default value for the database (or the SQL Server connection) is used. When you first install SQL Server, the default in each database is that columns are created with the `NOT NULL` option. As with most options in SQL Server, this default can be modified, even on a connection-by-connection basis. Therefore, it's an extremely good idea to always specify whether you want a column to have the `NULL` or `NOT NULL` attribute.

Collate

You can also specify a collation for an individual column of data in your table. If you don't specify a collation name, SQL Server uses the database default collation.

Strings

Strings contain character data made up of letters, numbers, and symbols. You can store character data in either a fixed-length or variable-length format by using the `char(n)` or `varchar(n)` keywords. You can store a maximum of 8,000 characters in these data types.

When you create a fixed-length field (by using the char or nchar datatype), you are specifying that this field will always contain *n* bytes of information. If the data you entered in the field is less than *n*, the field is padded with spaces so that it always takes up *n* bytes. If you try to put more than *n* bytes of data in the field, your data is truncated. Table 9.3 shows some examples of entering data into a field declared as `Fname char(8)`. (The symbol * denotes a space in this example.)

TABLE 9.3 Fixed-Length Character Fields

Data Entered	`Fname` *Contains*
Lawrence	Lawrence
Mark Anthony	Mark Ant
Denise	Denise**

When you use variable-length fields (by using the varchar or nvarchar datatype), you specify the maximum length that the field can be. But unlike fixed-length fields, the variable-length fields aren't padded with spaces. Using this type of field might make your database more memory efficient, but you pay a small price in performance. When a field is declared as variable length, SQL Server must determine where the field stops and the next field begins. Additional overhead is associated with variable-length fields in the form of bytes added to the rows and the table. `varchar` is useful when you are expecting a wide variation in data size, or you are going to allow null values in your field.

When you enter character data into SQL Server, you must enclose the data in single or double quotation marks. Single quotation marks are preferable so that there's no confusion between string constants and SQL Server identifiers. To enter `NULL` into a field in SQL Server, use the `NULL` keyword without quotation marks.

Listing 9.1 shows an example of creating a table using the `char` and `varchar` keywords.

LISTING 9.1 Using `char` and `varchar`

```
CREATE TABLE Customers
(
CustID char(8) NOT NULL,
CustName varchar(30) NOT NULL,
Email varchar(50) NULL
)
```


Binary Data

The binary data type stores binary data. Binary data is stored as a series of 1s and 0s, which are represented on input and output as hexadecimal pairs. These hexadecimal pairs are made up of the characters 0 through 9 and A through F. For example, if you create a field such as `SomeData binary(20)`, you are specifying that you are going to have 20 bytes of binary data.

As with the string data types, you can specify a maximum of 8,000 bytes for both the `binary(n)` and `varbinary(n)` data types. If you use the `binary(n)` data type, information you enter is padded with spaces (`0x20`). The `varbinary(n)` data type doesn't pad. If you try to enter data longer than the specified maximum length, the data is truncated.

To enter data into a binary data type, precede the string with `0x`. For example, to enter the value `10` into a binary field, you would prefix it like this: `0x10`.

Consider these sample declarations:

```
MyIcons varbinary(255)

MyCursors binary(200)

binTinyWav varbinary(255)
```

Integers

The four kinds of integer data types are `bigint`, `int`, `smallint`, and `tinyint`, which store exact, scalar values. The difference between the integer data types is the amount of storage space they require and the range of values they can store. Table 9.4 lists the integer data types and their ranges.

TABLE 9.4 Integer Data Types

Data Type	*Length*	*Range*
`tinyint`	1	0–255
`smallint`	2	±32,767
`int`	4	±2,147,483,647
`bigint`	8	±2^63

Consider these sample declarations:

```
EmployeeAge tinyint NULL

EmployeeID smallint NOT NULL

CustomerID int NOT NULL

WebOrderID bigint NOT NULL
```

Integer data types perform better (in terms of storage, retrieval, and mathematical calculations) than any other data type. If you can use an integer data type, it is the best way to go. SQL Server supports a default maximum precision of 38 digits to ensure compatibility with the limits of front-end development tools such as Microsoft Visual Basic and PowerBuilder.

Approximate and Exact Numeric Data Types

NEW TERM SQL Server allows both approximate data types (`float` and `real`), as well as exact numeric data types (`decimal` and `numeric`). When you declare approximate data types, you specify a precision that's the maximum number of digits allowed on both sides of the decimal point. When you declare an exact data type, you must also specify a *scale*, which is the total number of digits allowed on the right side of the decimal point.

Table 9.5 lists the precision values allowed for approximate and exact numeric data types and the number of storage bytes required.

TABLE 9.5 Precision and Storage Requirements

Precision	*Storage*
1–9	5
10–19	9

TABLE 9.5 continued

20–28	13
29–38	17

Approximate Numeric Data Types

The approximate numeric data types are `float` and `real`. The numbers stored in these data types are made up of two parts: the mantissa and the exponent. The algorithm used to produce these two parts isn't exactly precise. In other words, you might not get back exactly what you put in. This becomes a problem only when the precision of the number stored approaches the precision specified by the data type. For example, the precision allowed for floats is up to 53 digits. Floats and reals are useful for scientific and statistical data for which absolute accuracy isn't necessary, but where your values range from extremely small to extremely large numbers.

Reals have a precision of seven digits and require 4 bytes of data storage. If you declare a float and specify a precision of less than 7, you're really creating a real data type. Floats can have a precision from 1 to 53. By default, a float has a 15-digit precision if no value is specified. You can perform all calculations on a float with the exception of modulo (which returns the integer remainder of integer division). Suppose that you create the following data type:

```
SomeVal real
```

You can store the numbers 188,445.2 or 1,884.452, but not the values 188,445.27 or 1,884.4527 because they are longer than the default precision of seven digits. To hold these larger values, you should create a float variable with a precision large enough to hold all the digits. Because 8 bytes of storage are required, you declare your data type like this:

```
SomeVal float(8)
```

Exact Numeric Data Types

Exact numeric data types are `decimal` and `numeric`. Accuracy is preserved to the least significant digit. When you declare an exact numeric data type, you should specify both a precision and a scale. If you don't specify a precision and scale, SQL Server uses the default values of 18 and 0.

If you specify a scale of 0, you're creating the equivalent of an integer data type because 0 digits can appear to the right of the decimal point. Using a scale of 0 is useful because you can have very large, very precise numeric values that are bigger than ±2 billion. The `IDENTITY` property, which automatically generates a new value when a new record is added, requires an integer data type. If you are going to have more than 2 billion records, you can use an exact numeric data type with a scale of 0.

If a column is declared as `decimal(7,2)`, it can hold the number 1000.55 and 11000.55, but not the numbers 11110000.55 or 1100.5678. If you attempt to place a number larger than is allowed by the precision and scale, the number is truncated. Listing 9.2 shows an example of using exact numeric data types.

LISTING 9.2 Using Numeric Data Types

```
CREATE TABLE Gold
(
AtomicWeight decimal(8,4),
MolesPerOunce numeric(12,6),
Density numeric(5,4)
)
```

In general, avoid using float and real data types. If you can store the information you need in the decimal and numeric data types, you should do so. Calculations using float and real data types can lead to interesting and confusing results.

Special Data Types

Several data types just don't fall well into any category. I've added them here in the "Special Data Types" section. You will learn about the `bit` data type and the two BLOB (binary large object) data types, `text` and `image`, as well as the `RowGUID` data type (often pronounced as *ROW-goo-id*).

bit

The `bit` data type is a logical data type used to store Boolean information. Boolean data types are used as flags to signify things such as on/off, true/false, and yes/no. The values stored here are either 0 or 1.

Bit columns can be `NULL` (unknown) but can't be indexed. `bit` data types require a single byte of storage space. If you have several bit columns defined in a table, SQL Server automatically groups up to eight bit fields together into a single byte of storage space. If there are more than eight bit fields but less than 17 in a table (i.e. 9 – 16), SQL Server stores this as 2 bytes. Similarly if there are between 17 and 24 bit columns these are stored as 4 bytes, and so on. Consider these examples of using the `bit` data type:

```
Gender bit NOT NULL

Paid bit NULL

Printed bit NOT NULL
```

text, ntext and image

You use the `text` and `image` data types when storage requirements exceed the 8,000-character column limitations. These data types are often referred to as BLOBs. The `text` and `image` data types can store up to 2GB of binary or text data per declaration.

When you declare a `text` or `image` data type, a 16-byte pointer is added to the row. This 16-byte pointer points to a separate 8KB data page where additional information about your data is stored. If your data exceeds an 8KB data page, pointers are constructed to point to the additional pages of your BLOB.

The storage and retrieval of text and image data can hamper your database performance because large amounts of data are applied to your transaction logs during inserts, updates, and deletes. You can get around this problem by using the `WRITETEXT` command, because it applies changes to the data without making a corresponding entry to the transaction log.

Caution

When you use nonlogged operations, back up your database immediately, because the recoverability of your database is now an issue (as you examined on Day 7, "Backing Up Your Databases").

An alternative to the large storage requirements of `text` and `image` data types is to store these items as separate files and then store the path to those files in your database. You could also create an additional table with a char(8000) column.

The following are some sample declarations of the `text` and `image` data types:

```
EmployeePhoto image

ScannedContracts image

Description text

Comments text
```

RowGUID

When you use merge replication, as discussed on Day 16, "Understanding Replication Design Methodologies" and Day 17, "Implementing Replication Methodologies," each column in your replicated tables must have a unique identifier. You accomplish this by creating a column in every replicated table as a `uniqueidentifier` data type. This `uniqueidentifier` data type has a property called `ROWGUIDCOL`. When the `ROWGUIDCOL` property is turned on, a globally unique identifier (GUID) can be assigned to the column. In this way, columns in one version of the replicated table have the same GUID as in another version of the same table. If you make a change to a row in a replicated table with a `ROWGUIDCOL`, the `ROWGUIDCOL` is modified by SQL Server. In this way, replicated rows from two databases can be tracked separately.

You can initialize GUIDs in two ways:

- Use the `NEWID` function.
- Convert a string constant into a hexadecimal digit in the form of *`xxxxxxxx-xxxx-xxxx-xxxx-xxxxxxxxxxxx`*. Now, consider this example of a valid `RowGUID`: `8FE17A24-B1AA-23DA-C790-2749A3E09AA2`.

You can use the following comparison operators with your `uniqueidentifier` data types: `=`, `<>`, `IS NULL`, and `IS NOT NULL`. Here is an example using the uniqueidentifier data type.

```
MyPrimaryKey uniqueidentifier

TrackingCol uniqueidentifier
```

sql_variant

The sql_variant data type is similar to the Visual Basic variant data type. The sql_variant data type allows you to store just about any other base SQL Server data type within it. The exceptions are ntext, timestamp, and itself (sql_variant).

You can use these data types within columns, as variables in a DECLARE command, as parameters, and as the results of user-defined functions. (User-defined functions will be discussed on Day 15, "Creating Views, Triggers, Stored Procedures, and Functions.")

Some special rules apply when you are comparing the sql_variant data types. Each data type in SQL Server is placed within a data type family, as shown in Table 9.6.

TABLE 9.6 Data Type Families

Data Type	*Family*
sql_variant	sql_variant
datetime, smalldatetime	datetime
float, real	Approximate numeric
bigint, bit, decimal, int, money, smallint, smallmoney, tinyint	Exact numeric
char, nchar, nvarchar, varchar	Unicode
binary, varbinary	Binary
uniqueidentifier	Unique identifier

One special rule applies to the sql_variant data type: When you compare two sql_variant data types from different families, the family with the base data type listed higher in Table 9.6 is considered the higher value. For example, if you stored a float in a sql_variant data type and a binary value in another, when you do your comparison, the float value always evaluates to a higher value than the binary value.

The sql_variant data type is so new that it's hard to define exactly when and where it should be used. Many rules and details associated with this data type are beyond the scope of this book. For additional information on the sql_variant data type, see the SQL Server Books Online, or *Microsoft SQL Server 2000 Unleashed*, by Sams Publishing.

table

The `table` data type is generally used to store result sets for later use. Using it is similar to creating a temporary table. The real power of the `table` data type is that it can be used like an ordinary table, or it can be used like a local variable in functions, batches, and stored procedures. We will take a much more detailed look at this new data type on Day 15.

Date and Time Data Types

Date and time data can be stored in a `datetime` or `smalldatetime` data type. Notice that date and time are always stored together in a single value.

Date and time data can take several different formats. You can specify the month using the full name or an abbreviation. The case is ignored, and commas are optional.

Consider these examples using the alpha formats for April 15, 2001:

"Apr 15 2001"

"Apr 15 01"

"Apr 01 15"

"15 Apr 01"

"2001 April 15"

"2001 15 April"

NEW TERM You can also specify the ordinal value for the month. The *ordinal value* of an item is the positional value within a list of items. In the preceding examples, April is the fourth month of the year, so you can use the number 4 as its designation. These examples use the ordinal value for April 15, 2001:

4/15/01 (mdy)

4-15-01 (mdy)

4.15.01(mdy)

4/01/15 (myd)

15/01/04 (dym)

01/15/04 (ymd)

15/04/01 (dmy)

You can also use several different time formats. The following are some examples:

16:30 (4 hrs, 30 mins)

16:30:20:999 (4 hrs, 30 mins, 22 seconds, 999 milliseconds)

4:30PM

Dates stored in the `datetime` data type are stored to the millisecond. In this case, 8 bytes are used—4 for the number of days since January 1, 1900, and 4 for the number of seconds past midnight. (Dates before this are stored as negative numbers, making the range of dates 1/1/1753 to 12/31/9999.) The accuracy of these dates is within 3.33 milliseconds.

Tip

Internally, the integer values are the number of days and numbers to the right of the decimal are the number of milliseconds. Because of this, you can add whole numbers to dates as days.

Tip

Don't use `datetime` to store partial dates like just the month, day, or year. If the only data you need is the year, `smallint` or `tinyint` would be much more efficient. If you don't store dates this way, you have to parse the date yourself every time you want to insert, update, or otherwise work with the information.

The `smalldatetime` data type uses 4 bytes. Dates stored this way are accurate to the minute. Internally, the number of days is an integer value and the seconds since midnight are to the right of the decimal. The range for a `smalldatetime` is from 1/1/1900 to 6/6/2079.

Tip

Use `smalldatetime` for current dates in databases, especially those that are transitory in nature. They would be dates that you aren't going to be using for more than a few years.

Table 9.7 delineates the `datetime` data types.

TABLE 9.7 Date and Time Data Types

Data Type	*Storage*	*Range*
`datetime`	8	1/1/1753–12/31/9999
`smalldatetime`	4	1/1/1900–6/6/2079

Examples:

```
BirthDay smalldatetime
ExpirationDate datetime
```

Money

The two money data types are `money` and `smallmoney`. Both have a scale of four, meaning they store four digits to the right of the decimal point. These data types can store information other than dollar values for international use, but no monetary conversion functions are available in SQL Server. When you enter monetary data, you should precede it with a dollar sign. Table 9.8 shows the money data types, their requirements, and their ranges.

TABLE 9.8 Money Data Types

Data Type	*Storage*	*Range*
`money`	8	±922,337,203,685,447.5807
`smallmoney`	4	±214,748.3647

As you can see, `smallmoney` can hold up to 10 digits with a scale of four. The `money` data type is large enough to hold the U.S. national debt (or Bill Gates's annual income), with values in the hundreds of trillions.

These sample declarations use the money data types:

```
AccountsReceivable money

AccountsPayable smallmoney
```

The Auto-incrementing rowversion (timestamp) Data Type

rowversion is the new name for the timestamp data type. Timestamps are still supported in SQL Server and comply with the ANSI SQL-99 standard. For the rest of this discussion, we will use the rowversion keyword rather than timestamp. Every time you add a new record to a table with a rowversion field, time values are automatically added. If you make an update to a row, the rowversion also automatically updates itself.

The rowversion data type creates a SQL Server–generated, unique, automatically updated value. Although the rowversion looks like a datetime data type, it's not. Rowversions are stored as binary(8) for NOT NULL columns or varbinary(8) if the column is marked as allowing null values. You can have no more than one rowversion column per table.

The timestamp/rowversion data type doesn't reflect the system time. It's simply a constantly increasing counter value.

You can use the rowversion data type to track the order in which items are added and modified in your table. These examples use the timestamp/rowversion data types:

```
LastModified rowversion NOT NULL
```

```
PhoneCall timestamp NOT NULL
```

Working with ANSI and Unicode

To ensure that SQL Server data types map to American National Standards Institute (ANSI) data types, you can use the ANSI data types in place of the SQL Server data types. Table 9.9 lists the ANSI data types and their SQL Server equivalents.

TABLE 9.9 SQL Server Synonyms

ANSI Data Type	*SQL Server Data Type*
character	char
character(*n*)	char(*n*)

TABLE 9.9 continued

`char varying`	`varchar`
`character varying(n)`	`varchar(n)`
`binary varying`	`varbinary`
`dec`	`decimal`
`double precision`	`float`
`float(n) n = 1 - 7`	`real`
`timestamp`	`rowversion`
`integer`	`int`

Unicode data uses the Unicode UCS-2 character set, which is a multibyte character set. When you use normal ANSI characters, 1 byte of data is required to store any given character. As a result, ANSI is sometimes referred to as "narrow." Unicode is known as a "wide," or multibyte, character set. The UCS-2 Unicode character set uses 2 bytes to represent a single character. It is especially useful when you are dealing with databases that have different languages represented within them. For example, the English and Spanish languages have few enough letters that a single-byte character set can easily represent all letters in the alphabet. Now think of a language like Japanese. Even standard Japanese (Kana) has more than 1,000 characters in it. A standard 8-bit byte can represent only 256 characters, whereas a 2-byte Unicode character can represent 65,536 characters.

You can use the `nchar`, `nvarchar`, and `ntext` data types to represent your Unicode information. `nchar` and `nvarchar` have a maximum limit of 8,000 bytes or 4,000 characters. For example, `nchar(4000)` is valid, but `nchar(6000)` represents 12,000 characters and doesn't fit on a single data page. Your `nchar(6000)` should either be broken into two separate `nchar` data types or a single `ntext` data type. The `ntext` data type can support up to 2.14GB of data.

Unicode data types are an extremely powerful feature of SQL Server 2000. If you have any plans for internationalization or using SQL Server in countries that don't use U.S. English, storing your data with the Unicode data types is an excellent solution. Look for Unicode to become more of the standard storage mechanism as Windows NT and SQL Server provide better support for international solutions.

Creating User-Defined Data Types

You can create user-defined data types for a specific database or for placing in the model database. Remember, the model database is a template for creating new databases. By creating user-defined types, you can have them available in all subsequent databases.

To create a user-defined data type, you must base them on the system-provided data types. For example, you can create a new data type called `EmployeeID` and define it as character or integer, but not as some nonexistent data type such as `column_id`.

You must create the user-defined data type before you add it to a table. To create a user-defined data type, you can use the SQL Server Enterprise Manager or the `sp_addtype` system stored procedure. You'll learn more details about user-defined data types on Day 14, "Ensuring Data Integrity."

To create user-defined data types using SQL Server, use the `sp_addtype` system-stored procedure. For example, to add the same three user-defined data types to the `pubs` database, run the following SQL:

INPUT
```
EXEC sp_addtype EmpID, 'char(9)', 'NULL'
EXEC sp_addtype ID, 'varchar(11)', 'NULL'
EXEC sp_addtype TID, 'varchar(6)', 'NULL'
```

After you declare a user-defined data type, you can use it as often as you would like in your database. For example, you can use the following `CREATE TABLE` statement:

INPUT
```
CREATE TABLE Employee
(
EmployeeId EmpID NOT NULL,
Fname char(15) NOT NULL,
Lname char(20) NOT NULL,
PensionPlan ID NOT NULL
)
```

To add user-defined data types with the SQL Server Enterprise Manager, follow these steps:

1. Open the SQL Server Enterprise Manager.
2. Drill down to your `pubs` database.
3. Drill down to the User Defined Datatypes folder.
4. Right-click the folder, and choose New User Defined Data Type.

5. Fill in the name, data type, length, and any rules or defaults it's bound to.
6. Click OK.

To drop user-defined data types, you can use the SQL Server Enterprise Manager or the `sp_droptype` system-stored procedure. In the SQL Server Enterprise Manager, follow these steps:

1. Expand your database, and highlight the User Defined Data Types folder.
2. In the right panel, right-click the user-defined data type you want to drop, and click Delete.

That's all there is to it. In Transact-SQL, you can run the `sp_droptype` system stored procedure like this:

INPUT
```
EXEC sp_droptype EmpID
```

> A user-defined data type can't be dropped if it's still in use in a table or is bound to a rule or default. You'll examine what these terms mean on Day 14.

Working with Computed Columns

NEW TERM A *computed column* is a great feature in SQL Server 2000. A computed column doesn't store computed data; rather, it stores the expression used to compute the data, similar to an Excel spreadsheet. For example, I might create a computed column called Total on my table with an expression of `Total AS Price * Quantity`.

The expressions you store can be created from a noncomputed column in the same table, such as constants, functions, variables, and even names. Your computed column automatically computes the data when it's called in the `SELECT`, `WHERE`, or `ORDER BY` clauses of a query (which you'll examine on Day 10, "Retrieving Data with the `SELECT` Statement"). You can also use them with regular expressions.

You must follow a few rules when you're dealing with computed columns:

- Columns referenced in the computed-column expression must be in the same table.
- The computed-column expression can't contain a subquery.
- Computed columns can be used as part of an index, but there are certain restrictions that you need to keep in mind. (See the BOL for more information.)

- A computed column can't have a `DEFAULT` constraint attached to it.
- Computed columns can't receive `INSERT` or `UPDATE` statements.

Now, consider some examples using computed columns:

```
CREATE TABLE Order (
OrdID int NOT NULL,
Price money NOT NULL,
Qty smallint NOT NULL,
Total AS Price * Qty
)
```

This first table has a computed column called `curTotal`, which is made up of the `Price * Qty` fields.

```
CREATE TABLE PrintInvoice (
InvoiceID int NOT NULL,
InvDate datetime NOT NULL,
PrintDate AS DateAdd(day,30, InvDate)
)
```

In this example, a computed column called `PrintDate` uses the `DateAdd` function to add 30 days to the `InvDate` column.

If only the last two digits of the year are given, SQL Server interprets values of less than 50 as 20*yy*, whereas numbers greater than or equal to 50 are interpreted as 19*yy*. For example, April 15 03 would be interpreted as April 15, 2003.

Creating Tables

Now that you've seen all the data types available in SQL Server 2000, it's time to put them all together with the `CREATE TABLE` statement. As with most things in SQL Server, you can create tables in two ways: by using the SQL Server Enterprise Manager or Transact-SQL scripts. You will first learn more about the `CREATE TABLE` statement.

Using the `CREATE TABLE` Statement

The `CREATE TABLE` statement is used to create new tables in SQL Server 2000. Creating tables can be accomplished through code or the Enterprise Manager. You will first look at using code to generate our tables, and then have an opportunity to work with the Enterprise Manager. The following is the syntax of the `CREATE TABLE` command:

```
CREATE TABLE [database.[owner.]table_name
(
column_name datatype [Identity|constraint|NULL|NOT NULL|Collate]
[...]
)
```

In this syntax,

- `table_name` is the name of the new table following the rules for identifiers. It must also be unique within the database for its owner. This means that if two users have permission to create tables within a database, the tables themselves might have the same name, but are still considered unique because the owner's name forms part of the table name.
- `column_name` is the column name and must follow the rules for identifiers.
- `datatype` is the data type of the column.
- The last piece is optional. You can specify the `Identity` property, field constraints, and nullability.
- `Collate` is also optional. This property allows you to override the database collation sequence for this column.

> The `CREATE TABLE` syntax shown here is significantly simplified from what you would find in the SQL Server Books Online. Many of the additional options are specific to ANSI constraints, which you'll examine in great detail on Day 14.

Listing 9.3 shows a sample `CREATE TABLE` statement. It creates an employee table with the ability to capture information about the employees' names, addresses, and start dates.

LISTING 9.3 Creating a Table

```
CREATE TABLE Employee
(
Emp_id tinyint IDENTITY NOT NULL,
Fname char(15),
Lname char(20) NOT NULL,
Address1 varchar(30),
Address2 varchar(30),
City varchar(30),
State char(2),
ZipCode char(10),
StartDate datetime
)
```

Creating Tables with SQL Server Enterprise Manager

With the SQL Server Enterprise Manager, you can visually create your tables. To do so, follow these steps:

1. Connect to your SQL Server, expand your databases folder, and then expand the database you want to work with. Then click the Tables folder.
2. Right-click in the right pane and choose New Table, as shown in Figure 9.1.

FIGURE 9.1

In the Tables folder, select the database where you want to add a table.

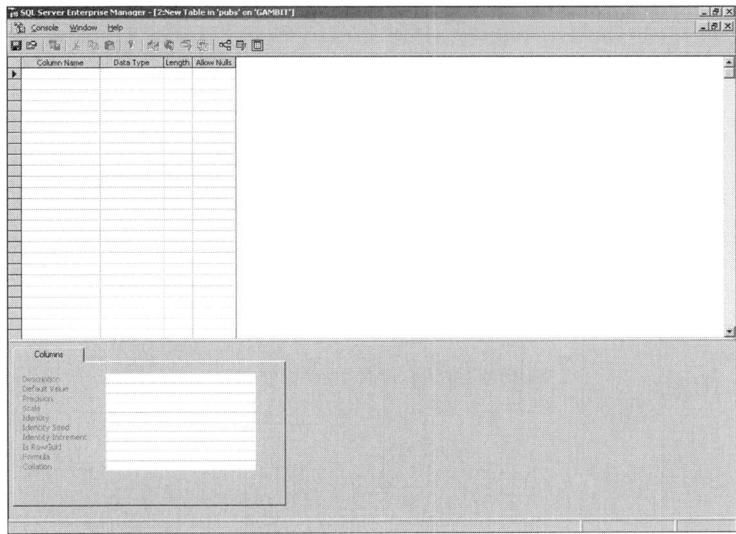

3. Add information to Column Name, Data Type, Length, and Allow Nulls. In the lower half of the screen, you can set column properties such as description and default values scale. If you want to create an identity field, set the `Identity` property in the Columns tab to Yes, and then choose an identity seed and increment. You'll learn more details about `Default` and `IsRowGUID` on Day 14. As you can see in Figure 9.2, I've added several fields to my `Employee` table.
4. When you are finished, click the Save icon to save your table and give it a name, and then close the dialog.

Dropping Tables

You can drop tables in SQL Server Enterprise Manager by right-clicking the table and selecting Delete from the context menu. To drop a table by using Transact-SQL, run the `DROP TABLE` statement. For example, to drop the `Employee` table, run

INPUT

```
DROP TABLE Employee
```

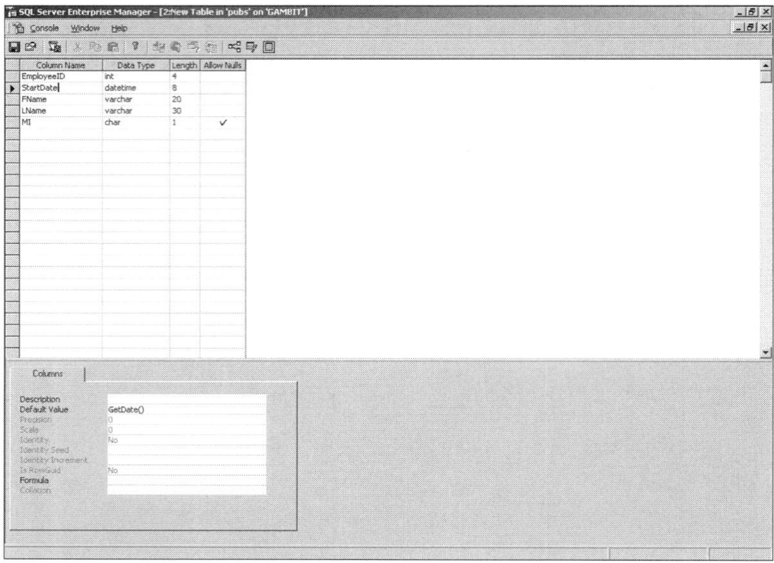

FIGURE 9.2

You can use the grid to specify the fields and properties rather than use code.

Note

System tables can't be dropped.

To drop a table by using the SQL Server Enterprise Manager, follow these steps:

1. Drill down to the Tables folder, and right-click the table you want to drop.
2. Choose Delete from the context menu. You get a dialog similar to the one shown in Figure 9.3.

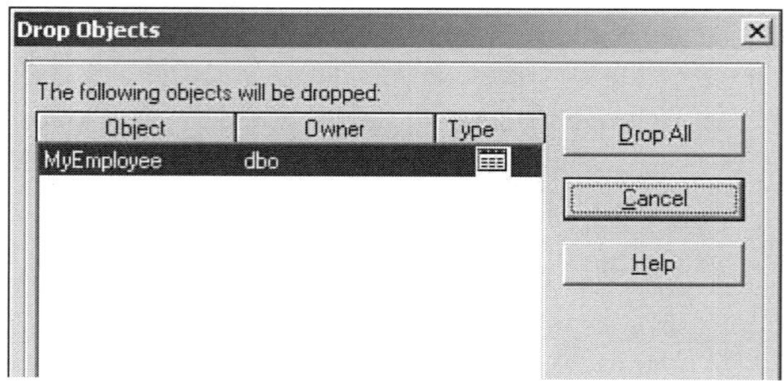

FIGURE 9.3

You can drop the tables listed in this dialog or check for dependencies.

3. If you want to see any dependencies on this table, click the Show Dependencies button. When the table is no longer participating in any primary key/foreign key relationships, you can click the Drop All button to remove the table. (Again, these relationships are described in detail on Day 14.)

Summary

SQL Server has many native data types, which you can use to create columns within your tables. You must choose the data type for each column carefully because your choice can affect performance and the need for storage space. You also can't change the data type without dropping and re-creating the table.

SQL Server also enables you to create user-defined data types by using the `sp_addtype` system-stored procedure or the SQL Server Enterprise Manager. They must be based on a native data type and be defined before they're used in a table.

You can create tables by using the SQL Server Enterprise Manager table editor or the `CREATE TABLE` statement.

Q&A

Q Do I need to use user-defined data types?

A No. User-defined data types aren't required, but they can make your columns and `CREATE TABLE` statements more readable. They also enable you to create a data type that you can reuse in multiple locations.

Q What are some general rules to follow when I'm dealing with numeric values?

A Integer data types are the fastest data types in SQL Server and also require a smaller amount of storage space. If you can save your information in an `int`, `tinyint`, or `smallint`, do so. For larger numbers, or numbers that require a decimal point, use the exact numeric data types `decimal` and `numeric` rather than `float` and `real`. Floats and reals don't have the precision of the exact numeric data types.

Q What are some general rules when I'm dealing with character data?

A The answer really depends on the type of character data you are dealing with. If you have columns that vary in length only a little (5 to 10 characters), using a fixed-length column is probably a better choice than using a variable-length field. Variable-length fields add about 2 bytes of overhead per row to your database and are slower to process than fixed-length fields. If your fixed-length fields vary greatly (20–100 characters), a variable-length field might be a better choice. You really must weigh the speed of one type over another versus the amount of storage space lost on fixed-length data.

Q You said that I could have as many as 2 billion tables in my database. How many tables should I have?

A The number really depends on the business scenario you are trying to model. If you have anything near 100,000 tables in your database, you might need to rethink your design. A typical database of 5–10GB has anywhere from 20 to 75 tables. Larger systems might have more.

Q Because `text` and `image` data types take up so much room in my database and aren't logged when added, deleted, or modified, what are some other ways I can handle these BLOBs?

A Many companies have found it useful to put their BLOBs in a separate directory on a fast file server somewhere on the network. They then store the path to the file in the SQL Server database as a `varchar` column. This approach has some advantages and disadvantages. The main disadvantage is consistency. If someone moves or deletes the file, how is SQL Server going to be notified of the update? On the upside, if you have thousands of documents or images, you aren't using valuable storage space in your database.

Q What's the most important point to remember about creating tables?

A The three rules of real estate are location, location, location. The three rules of database are design, design, design. Coming from a programming background, I always want to jump right in and start coding the project. I have found that, in the long run, this approach creates a lot of spaghetti code and tables in my database and an exponentially increasing lack of efficiency. Spend the time designing your tables, relationships, user-defined data types, and constraints before you implement them. Keep printed documentation of your design somewhere as well. It's an invaluable tool for anyone who must prepare to maintain your SQL Server system.

Workshop

This section provides quiz questions to help you solidify your understanding of the concepts presented today. In addition to the quiz questions, exercises are provided to let you practice what you have learned today. Try to understand the quiz and exercise answers before continuing to tomorrow's lesson. Answers are provided in Appendix A, "Answers to Quiz Questions."

Quiz

1. When should you choose the `char` data type over the `varchar` data type?
2. When should you choose the `varchar` data type over the `char` data type?
3. What are your alternatives to the `text` data type? When should you use each of them?

4. What are the best practices for using data types in SQL Server?
5. Which data type would you use for the following data (be sure to add any characteristics such as number of items in the string or the precision or scale):
    a. ZIP code
    b. Birth date
    c. Year of car manufacture
    d. Vehicle identification number
    e. Store ID, where 95 percent of the stores require a 10-digit alphanumeric entry. The other 5 percent vary in size, but none require more than 10 digits. The company owner is thinking of requiring all stores to have a 10-digit store number.
    f. Company name, where the name varies in length from 10 to 50 characters.
    g. A date value in a short-term database. Dates will range over a period of 10 years.
    h. Money, where you need to account for a scale of six.
6. You've created a table using the following `CREATE TABLE` statement. What's the maximum size of a row in this table?

```
CREATE TABLE table1
(
ID char(10),
FName char(15) NULL,
LName char(15) NOT NULL,
Comment varchar(255)
)
```

7. Can the following `CREATE TABLE` statement be implemented? Why or why not? What's the maximum row size?

```
CREATE TABLE phooey
(ID char(10) NOT NULL,
FName char(15) NULL,
LName char(15) NOT NULL,
Comment varchar(255),
Notes text,
Directions varchar(255),
HousePicture image)
```

Exercises

Write down the answers to the following questions. When you are sure your answers are correct, create these objects in the database:

1. How would you create the following user-defined data types?

   `zip_code`

   `phone_number`

   `store_id`

   `fax`

   `email`

2. What's the T-SQL required to create a table to hold information about stores? Data should include store identification, name, address, city, state, ZIP, owner, contact, fax, and email.
3. What's the T-SQL required to create a table to hold information about store sales? Data should include store identification, sales date, total sales, total returns, and deposit.

WEEK 2

DAY 10

Retrieving Data with the SELECT Statement

Once you have information in your database, it's time to learn how to extract just the data you want and to make modifications to that data. You begin today's lesson with a simple statement and learn how to grab specific columns. You then expand on this simple SELECT with data manipulation and conversion techniques. You then learn how to select information from specific rows in tables and eliminate duplicate data. You finish the lesson by learning advanced query topics such as subqueries, joins, and data correlation.

Today is long but very important. Take your time today because SQL is a fundamental language used with nearly every relational database management system. In other words, you can use most of the statements presented here with little or no modification in any database. Let's start with a simple SELECT statement.

SQL Server 2000 supports both the ANSI SQL '92 syntax standards and its own Microsoft SQL Server 2000 flavor, which you've seen referred to throughout this book as Transact-SQL (T-SQL).

Writing Simple SELECT Statements

You can create queries to retrieve information from your database by using the SQL Server Query Analyzer inside or outside the SQL Server Enterprise Manager as well as command-line utilities such as `osql`. You also can use other utilities, including the MSQuery program and the SQL Server English Query utility. Other tools and third-party utilities are available as well. In this book, you will concentrate on using the SQL Server Query Analyzer.

The `SELECT` statement has three basic components: `SELECT`, `FROM`, and `WHERE`. Its basic syntax is as follows:

SYNTAX

```
SELECT column_list
FROM table_list
WHERE search_criteria
```

The `SELECT` portion of the statement specifies the columns you want to retrieve. The `FROM` clause specifies the tables from which the columns are to be retrieved. The `WHERE` clause limits the rows returned by your query.

The complete syntax for the `SELECT` statement is as follows:

```
SELECT [ ALL | DISTINCT ][ TOP n [PERCENT] [ WITH TIES] ]
select_list
[ INTO new_table ]
[ FROM table_sources ]
[ WHERE search_condition ]
[ GROUP BY [ALL] group_by_expression [,...n]
[ WITH { CUBE | ROLLUP } ]]
[ HAVING search_condition ]
[ ORDER BY { column_name [ ASC | DESC ] } [,...n] ]
[ COMPUTE { { AVG | COUNT | MAX | MIN | SUM } (expression) }
➥[,...n] [ BY expression [,...n] ]
[ FOR BROWSE ] [ OPTION (query_hint [,...n) ]
```

`SELECT * FROM table_name` is the most basic of all queries. Using an asterisk (`*`) for the `column_list` retrieves all columns from the table. Inside SQL Server, the `*` is turned into a list of all the table's columns.

In the pubs database, you can run this query to select all columns and rows from the employee table:

INPUT/OUTPUT

```
SELECT *
FROM employee

emp_id    fname    minit lname      job_id    job_lvl
--------- -------- ----- ---------- --------- -------------------
PMA42628M Paolo    M     Accorti
PSA89086M Pedro    S     Afonso
VPA30890F Victoria P     Ashworth
H-B39728F Helen          Bennett
L-B31947F Lesley         Brown
F-C16315M Francisco      Chang
[...]                    [...]
GHT50241M Gary     H     Thomas
DBT39435M Daniel   B     Tonini

43 row(s) affected)
```


To select specific columns, you must separate each column with a comma (,). However, you shouldn't place a comma after the final column:

```
SELECT column_name[, column_name...]
FROM table_name
```

The following query selects the first name, last name, and employee ID for each employee from the employee table:

INPUT/OUTPUT

```
SELECT fname, lname, emp_id
FROM employee

fname      lname     emp_id
---------- --------- ---------------
Paolo      Accorti   PMA42628M
Pedro      Afonso    PSA89086M
Victoria   Ashworth  VPA30890F
Helen      Bennett   H-B39728F
Lesley     Brown     L-B31947F
Francisco  Chang     F-C16315M
[...]      [...]     [...]
Gary       Thomas    GHT50241M
Daniel     Tonini    DBT39435M

43 row(s) affected)
```

When you execute a query with SELECT *, the column order is the same as the column order specified in the CREATE TABLE statement. When you select columns from a table, the *column_list* order doesn't have to be the same as the table column order. You can rearrange the column order in your query output by rearranging the columns in the *column_list*.

You also can rearrange the column order from the preceding query. The same information is returned, but it's displayed in a different column order:

```
SELECT emp_id, lname, fname
FROM employee

emp_id         lname        fname
-------------- ------------ ----------
PMA42628M      Accorti      Paolo
PSA89086M      Afonso       Pedro
VPA30890F      Ashworth     Victoria
H-B39728F      Bennett      Helen
L-B31947F      Brown        Lesley
F-C16315M      Chang        Francisco
[...]          [...]        [...]
.GHT50241M      Thomas       Gary
DBT39435M      Tonini       Daniel

43 row(s) affected)
```

Changing Column Headings

When query results are displayed, the column headings are the names used in the *`column_list`*. Rather than use column headings, such as `lname` and `fname`, you can produce more readable column headings, such as `FirstName` and `LastName`, by aliasing the column headings. You can alias column headings using either SQL Server 2000 syntax or American National Standards Institute Structured Query Language (ANSI SQL) syntax.

You can alias columns with SQL Server in these two ways. The first example uses SQL Server 2000 (T-SQL) syntax:

SYNTAX

```
SELECT column_heading = column_name
FROM table_name
```

This example uses the ANSI standard:

```
SELECT column_name AS 'column_heading'
FROM table_name
```

If the alias you use has spaces or is a SQL Server keyword, you must enclose the alias in single quotation marks or the SQL Server identifier delimiters (`[]`). This example uses spaces and square brackets:

```
SELECT lname AS 'Last Name', fname AS [First Name]
FROM employee
```

The following example uses a SQL keyword:

```
SELECT 'count' = Count(*)
FROM employee
```

You can rewrite your query by using the following SQL Server 2000 statement:

```
SELECT EmployeeID = emp_id, LastName = lname, FirstName = fname
FROM employee
```

You can also rewrite it by using ANSI SQL:

```
SELECT emp_id AS EmployeeID,  lname AS LastName,  fname AS FirstName
FROM employee
```

> The AS keyword isn't required. For example, the following statement returns the same information shown in the preceding query:
>
> ```
> SELECT emp_id AS EmployeeID, lname AS LastName, fname AS FirstName
> FROM employee
> ```


Both queries have the same results:

OUTPUT

```
EmployeeID    LastName    FirstName
------------ ---------- --------------
PMA42628M     Accorti     Paolo
PSA89086M     Afonso      Pedro
VPA30890F     Ashworth    Victoria
H-B39728F     Bennett     Helen
L-B31947F     Brown       Lesley
F-C16315M     Chang       Francisco
[...]         [...]       [...]
GHT50241M     Thomas      Gary
DBT39435M     Tonini      Daniel

43 row(s)  affected)
```

Using Literals

NEW TERM You can also use literals to make output more readable. A *literal* is a string enclosed in single or double quotation marks included in the *column_list* and displayed as another column in the query result. In the results, a label is placed in the column next to your results.

SYNTAX

The syntax for including a literal value is as follows:

```
SELECT 'literal'[, 'literal'...]
```

The following query returns first name, last name, a column containing the literal string Employee ID, and the employee IDs for all employees from the employee table:

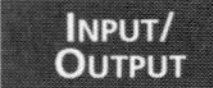

```
SELECT fname, lname, 'Employee ID:', emp_id
FROM employee

fname      lname                     emp_id
---------- ---------- -------------- ----------
Paolo      Accorti    Employee ID:   PMA42628M
Pedro      Afonso     Employee ID:   PSA89086M
Victoria   Ashworth   Employee ID:   VPA30890F
Helen      Bennett    Employee ID:   H-B39728F
[...]      [...]      [...]          [...]
Gary       Thomas     Employee ID:   GHT50241M
Daniel     Tonini     Employee ID:   DBT39435M

    (43 row(s) affected)
```

Manipulating Data

You can manipulate data in your query results to produce new columns that display computed values, new string values, converted dates, and more. You can manipulate your query results by using arithmetic operators, mathematical functions, string functions, datetime functions, and system functions. You can also use the `CONVERT` and CAST functions to convert from one data type to another for easier data manipulation.

Arithmetic Operators

You can use arithmetic operators on the following data types: `bigint`, `int`, `smallint`, `tinyint`, `numeric`, `decimal`, `float`, `real`, `money`, and `smallmoney`. Table 10.1 shows the arithmetic operators and the data types you can use with them.

TABLE 10.1 Data Types and Arithmetic Operations

Data Type	*Addition* +	*Subtraction* –	*Division* /	*Multiplication* *	*Modulo* %
`bigint`	Yes	Yes	Yes	Yes	Yes
`decimal`	Yes	Yes	Yes	Yes	No
`float`	Yes	Yes	Yes	Yes	No
`int`	Yes	Yes	Yes	Yes	Yes
`money`	Yes	Yes	Yes	Yes	No
`numeric`	Yes	Yes	Yes	Yes	No
`real`	Yes	Yes	Yes	Yes	No
`smallint`	Yes	Yes	Yes	Yes	Yes
`smallmoney`	Yes	Yes	Yes	Yes	No
`tinyint`	Yes	Yes	Yes	Yes	Yes

Operator Precedence

With arithmetic operations, two levels of precedence exist: *data type precedence* and *operator precedence*.

- Data type precedence is used when arithmetic operations are performed on different data types. When you use different data types, the smaller data type is converted to the higher data type. For example, if you multiply a `smallint` by an `int`, the result is an `int`. The only exception to this rule occurs when you use the `money` data type, in which case the result is always of data type `money`.
- Operator precedence is used when multiple operators are used. Operators follow the normal rules for operator precedence in which modulo is always evaluated first, followed by multiplication and division, followed by addition and subtraction—as read from left to right.

As with normal arithmetic operations, you can change the order of precedence by placing expressions within parentheses. The innermost expressions (most deeply nested expressions) are evaluated first. You can also use parentheses to make the arithmetic operation more readable. For example,

5 + 5 * 5 = 30 (Multiplication is performed first.)

but

(5 + 5) * 5 = 50 (The nested expression is performed first.)

In general, enclosing your arithmetic operations within parentheses improves the readability and clarity of your Transact-SQL code.

Mathematical Functions

Mathematical functions enable you to perform commonly needed operations on mathematical data. You can return mathematical data by using the following syntax:

SYNTAX

```
SELECT function_name(parameters)
```

Table 10.2 lists the mathematical functions with their parameters and results. These examples include such operations as finding the absolute value, finding trigonometric function values, deriving square roots, and raising values to an exponential power. Table 10.3 shows some additional examples.

TABLE 10.2 Mathematical Functions

Function	*Result*
`ABS(numeric_expr)`	Absolute value
`ACOS | ASIN | ATAN(float_expr)`	Angle in radians whose cosine, sine, or tangent is a floating-point value
`ATN2(float_expr1, float_expr2)`	Angle in radians whose tangent is between `float_expr1` and `float_expr2`
`COS | SIN | COT | TAN(float_expr)`	Cosine, sine, or tangent of the angle (in radians)
`CEILING(numeric_expr)`	Smallest integer greater than or equal to the specified value
`DEGREES(numeric_expr)`	Conversion from radians to degrees
`EXP(float_expr)`	Exponential value of specified value
`FLOOR(numeric_expr)`	Largest integer less than or equal to specified value
`LOG(float_expr)`	Natural log
`LOG10(float_expr)`	Base-10 log
`PI()`	Constant 3.141592653589793
`POWER(numeric_expr,y)`	Value of *numeric_expr* to the power of *y*
`RADIANS(numeric_expr)`	Conversion from degrees to radians
`RAND([seed])`	Random float number between 0 and 1
`ROUND(numeric_expr,len)`	*numeric_exp* rounded to the specified length in an integer value
`SIGN(numeric_expr)`	Positive, negative, or zero
`SQUARE(float_expr)`	Square of the specified value
`SQRT(float_expr)`	Square root of the specified value

TABLE 10.3 Mathematical Functions and Results

Statement	*Result*
`SELECT SQRT(9)`	3.0
`SELECT ROUND(1234.56, 0)`	1235
`SELECT ROUND(1234.56, 1)`	1234.60
`SELECT ROUND($1234.56, 1)`	1,234.6000
`SELECT POWER (2,8)`	256
`SELECT FLOOR(1332.39)`	1332
`SELECT ABS(-365)`	365

Tip

When you use mathematical functions with monetary data types, always precede the data type with a dollar sign ($). Otherwise, the value is treated as a `numeric` data type with a scale of 4.

Caution

When using the `float` data type, you might get unexpected results from the SQL Server Query Analyzer and other tools. For example, if you run

```
SELECT ROUND(12.3456789E+5,2)
```

you get back

```
1234567.8899999999
```

This result is a function of open database connectivity (ODBC). SQL Server is still performing the rounding, but by definition, `float` data types are imprecise and don't necessarily return what you expect. In general, you are better served by avoiding the `float` data type.

String Functions

When dealing with character information, you can use various string functions to manipulate the data (see Table 10.4). Because most string functions manipulate only `char`, `nchar`, `varchar`, and `nvarchar` data types, other data types must first be converted. You can return character data by using the following syntax:

SYNTAX

```
SELECT function_name(parameters)
```

TABLE 10.4 String Functions

Function	*Result*
`'expression' + 'expression'`	Concatenates two or more character strings
`ASCII(char_expr)`	Returns the ASCII code value of the leftmost character
`CHAR(integer_expr)`	Returns the character equivalent of the ASCII code value
`CHARINDEX(pattern, expression, start_position)`	Returns the starting position of the specified pattern
`DIFFERENCE(char_expr1, char_expr2)`	Compares two strings and evaluates their similarity; returns a value from 0 to 4, 4 being the best match
`LEFT(char_expr, integer_expr)`	Returns a character string starting from the left and preceding `integer_expr` characters
`LEN(char_expr)`	Returns the length of a string of characters

Table 10.4 continued

Function	*Result*
`LOWER(char_expr)`	Converts to lowercase
`LTRIM(char_expr)`	Returns data without leading blanks
`NCHAR(integer_expr)`	Returns the Unicode character corresponding to the *integer_expr*
`PATINDEX('%pattern%',expression)`	Returns the starting position of the first occurrence in *expression*
`QUOTENAME('string1', 'quote_char')`	Returns a Unicode string (`nvarchar(129)`) with valid SQL Server delimiters
`REPLACE('string1', 'string2', 'string3')`	Replaces all occurrences of *string2* with *string3* in *string1*
`REPLICATE(char_expr, integer_expr)`	Repeats *char_expr integer_expr* number of times
`REVERSE(char_expr)`	Returns the reverse of *char_expr*
`RIGHT(char_expr, integer_expr)`	Returns a character string starting *integer_expr* characters from right
`RTRIM(char_expr)`	Returns data without trailing blanks
`SOUNDEX(char_expr)`	Returns a four-digit (`SOUNDEX`) code to evaluate the similarity of two character strings
`SPACE(integer_expr)`	Returns a string of repeated spaces equal to *integer_expr*
`STR(float_expr [, length[, decimal]])`	Returns character data converted from numeric data; *length* is the total length and *decimal* is the number of spaces to the right of the decimal
`STUFF(char_expr1, start, length, char_expr2)`	Deletes *length* characters from *char_expr1* at *start* and inserts *char_expr2* at *start*
`SUBSTRING(expression,start, length)`	Returns part of a character or binary string
`UNICODE('nchar_string')`	Returns the Unicode integer value of the first character of *'nchar_string'*
`UPPER(char_expr)`	Converts to uppercase

For example, you can submit the following to return a column aliased as `Name`, which is a concatenation of last name, first initial, and employee ID:

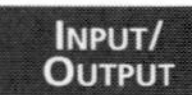


```
SELECT lname + ', ' + SUBSTRING(fname,1,1) + '.'
AS Name, emp_id as EmployeeID
FROM employee
```

```
Name           EmployeeID
-------------- --------------
Accorti, P.    PMA42628M
Afonso, P.     PSA89086M
Ashworth, V.   VPA30890F
Bennett, H.    H-B39728F
[...]          [...]
Sommer, M.     MFS52347M
Thomas, G.     GHT50241M
Tonini, D.     DBT39435M

(43 row(s) affected)
```

Table 10.5 lists some more examples of string functions.

TABLE 10.5 More String Functions

Statement	*Result*
SELECT ASCII('G')	71
SELECT LOWER('ABCDE')	abcde
SELECT PATINDEX('%BC%','ABCDE')	2
SELECT RIGHT('ABCDE',3)	CDE
SELECT REVERSE ('ABCDE')	EDCBA

Date Functions

You can manipulate `datetime` values by using date functions. You can use date functions in the *`column_list`*, the `WHERE` clause, or wherever an expression can be used. To do so, use the following syntax:

SYNTAX

```
SELECT date_function (parameters)
```

You must enclose `datetime` values passed as parameters between single quotation marks or double quotation marks. Some functions take a parameter called a *`datepart`*. Table 10.6 lists the *`datepart`* values and their abbreviations.

TABLE 10.6 *datepart* Values

datepart	*Abbreviation*	*Values*
day	dd	1–31
day of year	dy	1–365
hour	hh	0–23
millisecond	ms	0–999

TABLE 10.6 continued

datepart	*Abbreviation*	*Values*
minute	`mi`	0–59
month	`mm`	1–12
quarter	`qq`	1–4
second	`ss`	0–59
week	`wk`	0–53
weekday	`dw`	1–7 (Sun–Sat)
year	`yy`	1753–9999

Table 10.7 lists the date functions, their parameters, and their results. Table 10.8 shows some date function examples.

TABLE 10.7 Date Functions

Function	*Result*
`DATEADD(`*`datepart, number, date`*`)`	Adds the number of *`dateparts`* to the *`date`*
`DATEDIFF(`*`datepart, date1, date2`*`)`	Returns the number of *`dateparts`* between two dates
`DATENAME(`*`datepart, date`*`)`	Returns the ASCII value for a specified *`datepart`* for the *`date`* listed
`DATEPART(`*`datepart, date`*`)`	Returns the integer value for a specified *`datepart`* for the *`date`* listed
`DAY(`*`date`*`)`	Returns an integer value representing the day
`GETDATE()`	Returns the current date and time in internal format
`GETUTCDATE()`	Returns the current date and time in the Universal Time Coordinate Coordinate (UTC) formally known as Greenwich Mean Time (GMT)
`MONTH(`*`date`*`)`	Returns an integer value representing the month
`YEAR(`*`date`*`)`	Returns an integer value representing the year

TABLE 10.8 Date Function Examples

Function	*Result*
`SELECT DATEDIFF(mm, '1/1/00', '12/31/02')`	`35`
`SELECT GETDATE()`	`Apr 29, 2000 2:10AM`
`SELECT DATEADD(mm, 6, '1/1/00')`	`Jul 1, 2000 2:10AM`
`SELECT DATEADD(mm, -5, '10/6/00')`	`May 6, 2000 2:10AM`

Note that you may get slightly different results depending on your language settings in Windows and your collation sequence in SQL Server.

Now look at a more complex query that involves many of the different pieces you have learned so far:

INPUT/OUTPUT

```
SELECT emp_id AS EmployeeID,  lname + ', ' + SUBSTRING(fname,1,1) +
➥'.' AS Name,
'Has been employed for ', DATEDIFF(year, hire_date, getdate()), ' years.'
FROM employee
```

```
EmployeeID   Name
------------ -------------- ------------------------------------
PMA42628M    Accorti, P.    Has been employed for     8    years.
PSA89086M    Afonso, P.     Has been employed for     10    years.
VPA30890F    Ashworth, V.   Has been employed for     10    years.
H-B39728F    Bennett, H.    Has been employed for     11    years.
[...]        [...]          [...]
MFS52347M    Sommer, M.     Has been employed for     10    years.
GHT50241M    Thomas, G.     Has been employed for     12    years.
DBT39435M    Tonini, D.     Has been employed for     10    years.

(43 row(s) affected)
```

10

System Functions

You can use several built-in system functions to get information from the system tables. To return data, you can use the following syntax:

SYNTAX

SELECT *function_name*(*parameters*)

You can use system functions in the `column_list`, WHERE clause, and anywhere else an expression can be used.

Table 10.9 lists some system functions, their parameters, and their results.

TABLE 10.9 System and Metadata Functions

Function	*Result*
COALESCE(expression1, expression2, ...expressionN)	Returns the first non-NULL expression
COL_NAME(*table_id*, *column_id*)	Returns the column name
COL_LENGTH('*table_name*', '*column_name*')	Returns the column length
DATALENGTH('*expression*')	Returns the actual length of *expression* of any data type
DB_ID(['*database_name*'])	Returns a database ID
DB_NAME([*database_id*])	Returns a database name

TABLE 10.9 continued

Function	*Result*
`GETANSINULL(['database_name'])`	Returns the default nullability of the database
`HOST_ID()`	Returns the host workstation ID
`HOST_NAME()`	Returns the host computer name
`IDENT_INCR('table_name')`	Returns an increment value specified during creation of the identity column
`IDENT_SEED('table_name')`	Returns the seed value specified during creation of the identity column
`INDEX_COL('table_name', index_id, key_id)`	Returns an indexed column name
`ISDATE(variable | column_name)`	Checks for a valid date format; returns `1` if valid, or else it returns `0`
`ISNULL(expression, value)`	Returns a specified value in place of `NULL`
`ISNUMERIC(variable | column_name)`	Checks for a valid numeric format; returns `1` if valid, else returns `0`
`NULLIF(expression1,expression2)`	Returns `NULL` if *`expression1`* = *`expression2`*
`OBJECT_ID('object_name')`	Returns a database object ID
`OBJECT_NAME(object_id')`	Returns a database object name
`STATS_DATE(table_id, index_id)`	Returns the date that index statistics were last updated
`SUSER_ID(['server_username'])`	Returns a server user's ID
`SUSER_NAME([server_id])`	Returns a server user's name
`USER_ID(['username'])`	Returns a database user's ID
`USER_NAME([user_id])`	Returns a database user's name

The following query uses two system functions to return the name of the second column of the `employee` table:

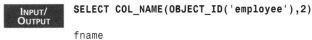

```
SELECT COL_NAME(OBJECT_ID('employee'),2)

fname
(1 row(s)  affected)
```

Data Conversion

Because many functions require data in a certain format or data type, you might need to convert from one data type to another. You use the `CONVERT()` or `CAST()` function to modify your data types. You can use the `CONVERT()` function anywhere expressions are allowed; it has the following syntax:

```
CONVERT(datatype[(length)], expression[, style])
```

Table 10.10 lists the style parameter associated with its standard and the format of the output.

TABLE 10.10 Using the *CONVERT()* Function for the *DATETIME* Data Type

Style Without Century yy	*Style with Century yyyy*	*Standard*	*Date Format Output*
—	0 or 100	Default	`mon dd yyyy hh:mi AM` (or `PM`)
1	101	USA	`mm/dd/yy`
2	102	ANSI	`yy.mm.dd`
3	103	British/French	`dd/mm/yy`
4	104	German	`dd.mm.yy`
5	105	Italian	`dd-mm-yy`
6	106	—	`dd mon yy`
7	107	—	`mon dd, yy`
8	108	—	`hh:mi:ss`
—	9 or 109	Default + milliseconds	`mon dd, yyyy hh:mi:ss:ms AM` (or `PM`)
10	110	USA	`mm-dd-yy`
11	111	Japan	`yy/mm/dd`
12	112	ISO	`yymmdd`
—	13 or 113	Europe default + milliseconds	`dd mon yyyy hh:mi:ss:ms` (24h)
14	114	—	`hh:mi:ss:ms` (24h)

You can submit the following query to convert the current date to a character string of eight and a date style of ANSI (yy.mm.dd):

INPUT/OUTPUT

```
SELECT CONVERT(CHAR(8),GETDATE(),2)

--------
00.07.06

(1 row(s) affected)

SELECT emp_id AS EmployeeID,  lname + ', ' + SUBSTRING(fname,1,1) + '.'
AS Name, 'Has been employed for ' + CONVERT(CHAR(2),
(DATEDIFF(year, hire_date, getdate()))) + ' years.'
FROM employee
```

```
EmployeeID   Name
------------ ------------ ------------------------------
PMA42628M    Accorti, P.   Has been employed for 8  years.
PSA89086M    Afonso, P.    Has been employed for 10  years.
VPA30890F    Ashworth, V.  Has been employed for 10  years.
H-B39728F    Bennett, H.   Has been employed for 11  years.
[...]        [...]         [...]
MFS52347M    Sommer, M.    Has been employed for 10  years.
GHT50241M    Thomas, G.    Has been employed for 12  years.
DBT39435M    Tonini, D.    Has been employed for 10  years.

(43 row(s)affected)
```

ANALYSIS This example is built on the query you ran earlier in the "Date Functions" section. In this example, you combine the last three columns into one column by using the `CONVERT()` function and string concatenation.

Choosing Rows

You've looked at various ways to retrieve, format, and manipulate the columns in a query's result set. Now you will learn how to specify which rows to retrieve based on search conditions. You can do so by using the `WHERE` clause of your `SELECT` statement. Search conditions include comparison operators, ranges, lists, string matching, unknown values, combinations, and negations of these conditions.

The basic syntax for specifying which rows to retrieve follows:

SYNTAX

```
SELECT column_list
FROM table_list
WHERE search_conditions
```

Comparison Operators

You can implement search conditions by using comparison operators (see Table 10.11). You can select rows by comparing column values to a certain expression or value. Expressions can contain constants, column names, functions, or nested subqueries. If you're comparing two different character data types (such as `char` and `varchar`) or comparing date data types (such as `datetime` and `smalldatetime`), you must enclose them in single quotation marks. Double quotation marks are acceptable, but single quotation marks maintain ANSI compliance.

TABLE 10.11 Available Comparison Operators

Operator	*Description*
=	Equal to
>	Greater than
<	Less than

TABLE 10.11 continued

Operator	*Description*
`>=`	Greater than or equal to
`<=`	Less than or equal to
`<>`	Not equal to (preferred)
`!=`	Not equal to (not ANSI SQL-92 compliant)
`!>`	Not greater than (not ANSI SQL-92 compliant)
`!<`	Not less than (not ANSI SQL-92 compliant)
`()`	Order of precedence

10

The syntax for the `WHERE` clause using comparison operators follows:

SYNTAX

```
SELECT column_list
FROM table_list
WHERE column_name comparison_operator expression
```

The following query returns the employee ID, last name, and first name for all employees employed by the publisher with a pub_id of `0877`:

```
SELECT emp_id, lname, fname
FROM employee
WHERE pub_id = '0877'

emp_id      lname      Fname
----------- ---------- -----------
PMA42628M   Accorti    Paolo
VPA30890F   Ashworth   Victoria
H-B39728F   Bennett    Helen
[...]       [...]      [...]
M-R38834F   Rance      Martine
DBT39435M   Tonini     Daniel

(10 row(s)  affected)
```

Note

> If you're using arithmetic operators (+, -, *, /, mod) joined by logical operators (AND, OR, etc.), arithmetic operators are processed first. Of course, you can always change the order of precedence by using parentheses.

Ranges

You can retrieve rows based on a range of values by using the `BETWEEN` keyword. As with the comparison operator, if you are specifying ranges based on character data types (such as `char` and `varchar`) or date data types (such as `datetime` and `smalldatetime`), you must enclose them in single quotation marks.

The syntax for the WHERE clause using comparisons is as follows:

```
SELECT column_list
FROM table_list
WHERE column_name [NOT] BETWEEN expression AND expression
```

The following query returns the last name and employee ID for all employees hired between 10/1/92 and 12/31/92:

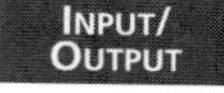

```
SELECT lname, emp_id
FROM employee
WHERE hire_date BETWEEN '10/1/92' AND '12/31/92'

lname      emp_id
---------- --------------
Josephs    KFJ64308F
Paolino    MAP77183M

(2 row(s) affected)
```

In this example, the BETWEEN clause is inclusive. This means that both 10/1/92 and 12/31/92 are included as potential hire dates. Notice that the smaller value must come first in the BETWEEN clause.

Lists

You can retrieve rows with values that match those in a list by using the IN keyword. If you are specifying ranges based on character data types (such as char and varchar) or date data types (such as datetime and smalldatetime), you must enclose these types in single quotation marks.

The syntax for the WHERE clause using comparisons is as follows:

```
SELECT column_list
FROM table_list
WHERE column_name [NOT] IN (value_list)
```

If you want to find employees who work for publishers with a pub_id of 0877 or 9999, submit the following query:

```
SELECT emp_id, lname, fname
FROM employee
WHERE pub_id IN ('0877', '9999')

emp_id      lname      fname
----------- ---------- ----------
PMA42628M   Accorti    Paolo
VPA30890F   Ashworth   Victoria
H-B39728F   Bennett    Helen
[...]       [...]      [...]
```

```
A-R89858F     Roulet       Annette
DBT39435M     Tonini       Daniel

(17 row(s) affected)
```

You also can retrieve rows not in the list by using the `NOT` operator. If you want to find all employees who don't work for publishers with a pub_id of `0877` or `9999`, you can submit the following query:

INPUT/OUTPUT

```
SELECT emp_id, lname, fname
FROM employee
WHERE pub_id NOT IN ('0877', '9999')

emp_id      lname        fname
----------- ------------ --------------
PSA89086M   Afonso       Pedro
F-C16315M   Chang        Francisco
PTC11962M   Cramer       Philip
A-C71970F   Cruz         Aria
AMD15433F   Devon        Ann
[...]       [...]        [...]
CGS88322F   Schmitt      Carine
MAS70474F   Smith        Margaret
HAS54740M   Snyder       Howard
MFS52347M   Sommer       Martin
GHT50241M   Thomas       Gary

(26 row(s)  affected)
```

Try using positive search conditions whenever possible. Avoid using `NOT` because the query optimizer doesn't always recognize negative search conditions. In other words, SQL Server must do a lot more work to return your result set when you use `NOT`. You can rewrite the preceding query using `BETWEEN` and `AND` statements. You could also use > and < symbols.

Character Strings

You can retrieve rows based on portions of character strings by using the `LIKE` keyword. `LIKE` is used with `char`, `varchar`, `nchar`, `nvarchar`, `text`, `datetime`, and `smalldatetime` data. You can also use four wildcard characters in the form of regular expressions.

The syntax for the `WHERE` clause using the `LIKE` keyword follows:

SYNTAX

```
SELECT column_list
FROM table_list
WHERE column_name [NOT] LIKE 'string'
```

The available wildcards are

%	String of zero or more characters
_	Single character
[]	Single character within the specified range
[^]	Single character not within the specified range

When you use the LIKE clause, be sure to enclose the wildcard characters in single quotation marks.

You can submit the following query to return the title_id and title of all books with computer anywhere in the title from the titles table:

INPUT/ OUTPUT

```
SELECT title_id, title
FROM titles
WHERE  title LIKE '%computer%'

title_id  title
--------- -------------------------------------------------------
BU1111    Cooking with Computers: Surreptitious Balance Sheets
BU2075    You Can Combat Computer Stress!
BU7832    Straight Talk About Computers
MC3026    The Psychology of Computer Cooking
PS1372    Computer Phobic AND Non-Phobic Individuals: Behavior Variations

(5 row(s) affected)
```

You can submit the following query to return the au_id, au_lname, and au_fname of all authors whose names begin with B or M from the authors table. To display names that begin with a B or an M, use the LIKE clause with both letters inside the square brackets:

INPUT/ OUTPUT

```
SELECT au_id, au_lname, au_fname
FROM authors
WHERE au_lname LIKE '[BM]%'

au_id        au_lname           au_fname
-----------  ------------------ ----------
409-56-7008  Bennet             Abraham
648-92-1872  Blotchet-Halls     Reginald
724-80-9391  MacFeather         Stearns
893-72-1158  McBadden           Heather

(4 row(s) affected)
```

Unknown Values

NEW TERM A *null* value isn't the same as a blank character string, nor is it the same as a 0 when you're dealing with numeric data. A NULL occurs when a value isn't assigned to a field. This is another way of saying that NULL is equivalent to the value "unknown." In such cases, a NULL fails all comparisons to blanks, zeros, and other NULLs (when you use the > or < comparison operator). So how do you find rows based on NULL values? You can discriminate between rows in your tables containing NULL values by using the IS NULL and IS NOT NULL keywords.

The syntax for the WHERE clause using the IS NULL and IS NOT NULL operators is as follows:

SYNTAX

```
SELECT column_list
FROM table_list
WHERE column_name IS [NOT] NULL
```


For example, you can submit this query to find all books that have no sales:

INPUT/OUTPUT

```
SELECT title_id, title
FROM titles
WHERE ytd_sales IS NULL

title_id    title
----------- ------------------------------------------------
MC3026      The Psychology of Computer Cooking
PC9999      Net Etiquette

(2 row(s) affected)
```

In contrast to the preceding query, you can use the IS NOT NULL clause to find all books that do have ytd_sales values by submitting the following query:

INPUT/OUTPUT

```
SELECT title_id, title
FROM titles
WHERE ytd_sales IS NOT NULL

title_id   title
---------- -------------------------------------------------------
BU1032     The Busy Executive's Database Guide
BU1111     Cooking with Computers: Surreptitious Balance Sheets
BU2075     You Can Combat Computer Stress!
BU7832     Straight Talk About Computers
[...]      [...]
TC3218     Onions, Leeks, and Garlic: Cooking Secrets of the
➥Mediterranean
TC4203     Fifty Years in Buckingham Palace Kitchens
TC7777     Sushi, Anyone?

(16 row(s)  affected)
```

Using Multiple Criteria to Retrieve Rows

You've looked at selecting rows based on specific values, ranges, lists, string comparisons, and unknown values. You will now look at retrieving rows using multiple search criteria.

You can combine multiple search criteria using the logical operators AND, OR, and NOT. Using AND and OR allows you to join two or more expressions. AND returns results when all conditions are true; OR returns results when any of the conditions are true.

When more than one logical operator is used in the WHERE clause, the order of precedence can be significant. NOT is followed by AND and then OR.

The syntax for a WHERE clause using multiple criteria follows:

SYNTAX

```
SELECT column_list
FROM table_list
WHERE [NOT] expression {AND|OR} [NOT] expression
```

Query 1

Consider the following: You want to retrieve the title ID, title, and price for all books with a pub_id of 0877 or the word computer in the title, and for which the price is NOT NULL.

```
SELECT title_id, title, price, pub_id
FROM titles
WHERE title LIKE '%computer%' OR pub_id  = '0877' AND price IS NOT NULL

title_id title                                             price   pub_id
-------- ------------------------------------------------- ------- ------
BU1111   Cooking with Computers: Surreptitious Balance ... 11.95     1389
BU2075   You Can Combat Computer Stress!                    2.99      736
BU7832   Straight Talk About Computers                     19.99     1389
MC2222   Silicon Valley Gastronomic Treats                 19.99      877
MC3021   The Gourmet Microwave                              2.99      877
MC3026   The Psychology of Computer Cooking               (null)      877
PS1372   Computer Phobic AND Non-Phobic Individuals: Be... 21.59      877
TC3218   Onions, Leeks, and Garlic: Cooking Secrets of ... 20.95      877
TC4203   Fifty Years in Buckingham Palace Kitchens         11.95      877
TC7777   Sushi, Anyone?                                    14.99      877

(10 row(s) affected)
```

Query 2

Now run the query again and see whether you can get rid of that NULL value in your price field:

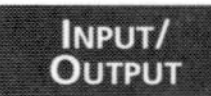

```
SELECT title_id, title, price, pub_id
FROM titles
WHERE (title LIKE '%computer%' OR pub_id  = '0877') AND price IS NOT NULL
```

```
title_id title                                                     price   pub_id
-------- --------------------------------------------------------- ------- ------
BU1111   Cooking with Computers: Surreptitious Balance ... 11.95      1389
BU2075   You Can Combat Computer Stress!                    2.99       736
BU7832   Straight Talk About Computers                     19.99      1389
MC2222   Silicon Valley Gastronomic Treats                 19.99       877
MC3021   The Gourmet Microwave                              2.99       877
PS1372   Computer Phobic AND Non-Phobic Individuals: Be... 21.59       877
TC3218   Onions, Leeks, and Garlic: Cooking Secrets of ... 20.95       877
TC4203   Fifty Years in Buckingham Palace Kitchens         11.95       877
TC7777   Sushi, Anyone?                                    14.99       877

(9 row(s)affected)
```

Notice that this query returns the desired results by changing the order of precedence.

Eliminating Duplicate Information

When selecting certain information from a table, you might receive duplicate rows of information. You can eliminate duplicates by using the `DISTINCT` clause in the `SELECT` portion of the `SELECT` statement. If you don't specify the `DISTINCT` clause, all rows that meet the `WHERE` clause criteria are returned.

The syntax for the `DISTINCT` clause is as follows:

SYNTAX

```
SELECT DISTINCT column_list
FROM table_name
WHERE search_conditions
```

Distinctness is determined by the combination of all the columns in the *`column_list`*. Because `NULL` values are treated as duplicates of each other, only one `NULL` is returned.

Table 10.12 shows some `SELECT` statements with the `DISTINCT` clause. Query1 lists states in which authors live without listing duplicates. Query2 lists cities in which authors live without listing duplicates. Query3 lists distinct combinations of cities and states.

TABLE 10.12 Each Query Shows Distinct Results

Query1	*Query2*	*Query3*
`SELECT DISTINCT state FROM authors`	`SELECT DISTINCT city FROM authors`	`SELECT DISTINCT city,state FROM authors`
State	*City*	*City and State*
CA	Ann Arbor	Ann Arbor, MI
IN	Berkeley	Berkeley, CA
KS	Corvallis	Corvallis, OR
MD	Covelo	Covelo, CA

TABLE 10.12 continued

Query1	*Query2*	*Query3*
MI	Gary	Gary, IN
OR	Lawrence	Lawrence, KS
TN	Menlo Park	Menlo Park, CA
UT	Nashville	Nashville, TN
	Oakland	Oakland, CA
	Palo Alto	Palo Alto, CA
	Rockville	Rockville, MD
	Salt Lake City	Salt Lake City, UT
	San Francisco	San Francisco, CA
	San Jose	San Jose, CA
	Vacaville	Vacaville, CA
	Walnut Creek	Walnut Creek, CA

If you just want to list the different cities where authors live, why not just use Query2 because it gives you the same cities Query3 does? To answer this question, suppose that two authors in your database live in Portland. If you run Query2, it would return Portland as one of the distinct values. However, one author lives in Portland, Oregon; the other, in Portland, Maine. Obviously, they are two distinct locations. So, submitting Query3 using the `DISTINCT` combination of city and state returns both Portland, Oregon, and Portland, Maine.

Notice that the results in all three queries are sorted. This might be by chance. Past versions of SQL Server sorted the values first, so the first value could be compared to the next value to make it easier to remove duplicate values. SQL Server 2000 uses a more complex hashing algorithm to gather its information. This algorithm increases speed and efficiency, but you might lose the sorting. To guarantee that your data is sorted, include an `ORDER BY` clause in your queries.

Now take a closer look at Query3:

INPUT

```
SELECT DISTINCT city, state
FROM authors
```

The results returning Portland, OR, and Portland, ME, would look like this. Note, these are hypothetical values in the authors table. They do not exist there now:

OUTPUT

```
city                 state
-------------------- -----
Portland             ME
Portland             OR

(2 row(s) affected)
```

Sorting Data Using the ORDER BY Clause

You can sort your query results by using the ORDER BY clause in your SELECT statement. The basic syntax for using the ORDER BY clause is as follows:

SYNTAX

```
SELECT column_list
FROM table_list
[ORDER BY column_name | column_list_number [ASC|DESC]]
```

You can have any number of columns in your ORDER BY list as long as they are no wider than 900 bytes. You can also specify column names or use the ordinal number of the columns in the *column_list*.

These queries return the same ordered result sets:

Query1

```
SELECT title_id, au_id
FROM titleauthor
ORDER BY title_id, au_id
```

Query2

```
SELECT title_id, au_id
FROM titleauthor
ORDER BY 1, 2
```

10

You can use column names and ordinal numbers together in the ORDER BY clause. You can also specify whether you want the results sorted in ascending (ASC) or descending (DESC) order. If you don't specify ASC or DESC, ASC is used.

If you sort results based on a column with NULL values and ASC order is used, the rows containing NULLs are displayed first.

When you use the ORDER BY clause, the sort order of your SQL Server can make a difference in your result sets. The default sort order for SQL Server is dictionary order and case insensitive. A case-sensitive sort order can affect the ordering of your result sets, because a capital A isn't considered the same as a lowercase a.

To find out what your server's current sort order (or collation sequence) is, you can execute the system stored procedure sp_helpsort.

Note

> You can't use ORDER BY on columns that are of text or image data types. This is true for text data types because they're stored in a different location in your database and can range from 0 to 2GB in length. SQL Server doesn't allow you to sort on a field this size. Image data types are also stored in their own separate 8KB data pages and aren't sortable. A workaround is used to create a related table that has summary information about your image or text.

Midday Review

You've had to digest quite a bit so far today, so let's take a break to review what you've covered so far.

You've built a foundation for data retrieval by using the `SELECT` statement. You learned how to change your column headings (aliasing) and add string literals to your output by using

```
SELECT col_name AS new_col_name
```

to change a column heading and

```
SELECT string_literal, col_name
```

to add a string literal. You then expanded on your understanding of the `SELECT` statement by using arithmetic operators, mathematical functions, string functions, and date and time functions. You then learned about system functions such as `GETDATE` to further manipulate your data and gain access to system resources.

Often the data you want to work with isn't expressed in the format and data type you must use. You learned how to use the data conversion command `CONVERT` to alter your data from one data type to another.

You then continued expanding on the `SELECT` statement with a discussion and examples of choosing different rows of information by applying comparison operators, ranges of values, lists, and character strings.

You learned how to eliminate rows with `NULL` values. You also learned how to select distinct rows of information.

You finished with this latest section on sorting your results by using the `ORDER BY` clause.

Now that you've had a breather, you can continue learning how to work with some more advanced `SELECT` statements. You will now work with "advanced features" such as producing summary information with the `GROUP BY` and `HAVING` aggregate functions, as well as the `COMPUTE` and `COMPUTE BY` statements. You will also learn how to correlate data and perform subqueries. You will finish with a look at some other advanced queries that involve selecting data from more than one table.

Just because these queries are advanced doesn't necessarily mean they will be too difficult for you. They simply tend to take a little more practice to master than the simple `SELECT` statements you've worked with already.

Aggregate Functions

Aggregate functions can return summary values for an entire table or for groups of rows in a table. Aggregate functions are normally used with the GROUP BY clause and in the HAVING clause or the *column_list*. This information might seem a little overwhelming at first, but bear with me. You will see each piece in its basic form, and then you will learn how to add additional pieces, one at a time. Table 10.13 lists the aggregate functions with their parameters and results.

TABLE 10.13 Aggregate Functions

Function	*Result*
AVG([ALL | DISTINCT] *column_name*)	Returns the average of the values in the numeric expression, either all or distinct.
BINARY_CHECKSUM()	Returns the binary checksum value computed over the row of a table. Used to detect changes to a row or table.
CHECKSUM()	Returns a checksum over a row or a list of expressions. Used to building hash indices.
CHECKSUM_AGG()	Returns checksum values in a group. Nulls are ignored.
COUNT(*)	Returns the number of selected rows.
COUNT([ALL | DISTINCT] *column_name*)	Returns the number of values in the expression, either all or distinct.
COUNT_BIG()	Works like COUNT, but returns a BIGINT.
GROUPING()	Returns a Boolean value to determine if the NULL value associated with a row of data is from an aggregate calculation, or is part of the actual data.
MAX(*column_name*)	Returns the highest value in the expression.
MIN(*column_name*)	Returns the lowest value in the expression.
STDEV(*column_name*)	Returns the statistical standard deviation of all values in the column name or expression.
STDEVP(*column_name*)	Returns the statistical standard deviation for the population of all values in the given column name or expression.
SUM([ALL | DISTINCT] *column_name*)	Returns the total of the values in the numeric expression, either all or distinct.
TOP *n* [PERCENT]	Returns the top *n* values or *n*% values in your result set.
VAR(*column_name*)	Returns the statistical variance of values listed in the column name or expression.
VARP(*column_name*)	Returns the statistical variance of a population of values listed in the column name or expression.

For example, this query returns a count of the total number of rows in the employee table:

INPUT/ OUTPUT

```
SELECT COUNT(*)
FROM employee

-----------------
       43

(1 row(s) affected)
```

This query selects the maximum value found in the ytd_sales column from the titles table:

INPUT/ OUTPUT

```
SELECT MAX(ytd_sales)
FROM titles

---------------
22246

(1 row(s) affected)
```

This query selects all the values in the qty column of the sales table and adds them:

INPUT/ OUTPUT

```
SELECT SUM(qty)
FROM sales

---------------
493

(1 row(s)  affected)
```

GROUP BY and HAVING

The GROUP BY clause groups summary data, that meets the WHERE clause criteria, to be returned as single rows. The HAVING clause sets the criteria to determine which rows will be returned by the GROUP BY clause. For example, you could find out which books have more than one author and then return the book title and the authors for each book.

The syntax for the GROUP BY and HAVING clauses follows:

SYNTAX

```
SELECT column_list
FROM table_list
WHERE search_criteria
[GROUP BY [ALL] non_aggregate_expression(s)
[HAVING] search_criteria]
```

The HAVING clause has the same effect on the GROUP BY clause as the WHERE clause has on the SELECT statement. For example, the following query finds all books that have more than one author and returns the title_id and number of authors for each book:

INPUT/ OUTPUT

```
SELECT title_id, count(title_id) AS Number_of_Authors
FROM titleauthor
GROUP BY title_id
HAVING count(title_id) > 1
```

```
title_id   Number_of_Authors
-------    ------------------
BU1032     2
BU1111     2
MC3021     2
PC8888     2
PS1372     2
PS2091     2
TC7777     3
```

The GROUP BY ALL clause returns all groupings, including those not meeting the WHERE clause criteria.

If you want to find all books with year-to-date sales of $4,000 or more and list all title IDs, you can submit the following query:

INPUT/OUTPUT

```
SELECT title_id, ytd_sales
FROM titles
WHERE (ytd_sales>=4000)
GROUP BY ALL title_id, ytd_sales
```

```
title_id     ytd_sales
--------     ---------
BU1032            4095
BU1111            3876
BU2075           18722
BU7832            4095
MC2222            2032
MC3021           22246
MC3026          (null)
PC1035            8780
PC8888            4095
PC9999          (null)
PS1372             375
PS2091            2045
PS2106             111
PS3333            4072
PS7777            3336
TC3218             375
TC4203           15096
TC7777            4095
```

Notice that all books that don't meet the WHERE clause criteria are still listed.

The GROUP BY and HAVING clauses must meet certain requirements to comply with ANSI standards. One of these requirements is that the GROUP BY clause must contain all nonaggregate columns from the SELECT *column_list*. Another is that the HAVING clause criteria columns return only one value.

COMPUTE and COMPUTE BY

The COMPUTE and COMPUTE BY clauses produce new rows of summary and detail data. They use the aggregate functions specified earlier. The COMPUTE clause returns detail rows and a grand total summary row. The COMPUTE BY clause returns new rows of summary data, much like the GROUP BY clause, but returns the rows as subgroups with summary values.

The syntax for the COMPUTE and COMPUTE BY clauses is as follows:

SYNTAX

```
SELECT column_list
FROM table_list
WHERE search_criteria
[COMPUTE] aggregate_expression(s)
[BY] column_list
```

The following examples compare the COMPUTE BY and GROUP BY clauses:

```
SELECT type, SUM(ytd_sales)
FROM titles
GROUP BY type

type         ytd_sales
------------ ---------
business         30788
mod_cook         24278
popular_comp     12875
psychology        9939
trad_cook        15471
UNDECIDED         NULL
```

This query returned the sum of the year to date sales of businesses grouped by the type of business.

If you use the COMPUTE BY clause, you must also include the ORDER BY clause. If your ORDER BY clause is

```
ORDER BY title_id, pub_id, au_id
```

your COMPUTE BY clause can be one of the following:

- COMPUTE *aggregate_function* (*column_name*)
  BY title_id, pub_id, au_id
- COMPUTE *aggregate_function* (*column_name*)
  BY title_id, pub_id
- COMPUTE *aggregate_function* (*column_name*)
  BY title_id

As you can see, the columns listed in the COMPUTE BY clause must be the same as, or a subset of, the columns in the ORDER BY clause. The order of the columns in COMPUTE BY must be the same as those in ORDER BY, and you can't skip columns. Now enter the following and look at the results:

INPUT/ OUTPUT

```
SELECT type, ytd_sales
FROM titles
ORDER BY type
COMPUTE SUM(ytd_sales) BY type

type       ytd_sales
---------- ---------
business        4095
business        3876
business       18722
business        4095

    sum
    =========
    30788

type       ytd_sales
---------- ---------
mod_cook        2032
mod_cook       22246

    sum
    =========
    24278

type            ytd_sales
------------ ---------
popular_comp      8780
popular_comp      4095
popular_comp    (null)

    sum
    =========
    12875

type        ytd_sales
----------- ---------
psychology       375
psychology      2045
psychology       111
psychology      4072
psychology      3336

    sum
    =========
    9939

type       ytd_sales
---------- ---------
trad_cook        375
trad_cook      15096
trad_cook       4095
```

```
    sum
    =========
    19566

type       ytd_sales
---------- ---------
UNDECIDED     (null)

    sum
    =========
    (null)

(24 row(s) affected)
```

Because the COMPUTE and COMPUTE BY operators produce new rows of nonrelational data, you can't use them with the SELECT INTO statement. Also, you can't use COMPUTE and COMPUTE BY operators with text or image data types because they are nonsortable.

Super Aggregates (ROLLUP and CUBE)

To produce additional summary rows, referred to as *super aggregates*, use the ROLLUP and CUBE operators. You use these operators with the GROUP BY clause.

The following is the syntax for the ROLLUP and CUBE operators:

SYNTAX

```
SELECT column_list
FROM table_list
WHERE search_criteria
[GROUP BY [ALL] nonaggregate_expression(s)
[WITH {ROLLUP | CUBE}]]
```

The ROLLUP operator is typically used to produce running averages or running sums. You do so by applying the aggregate function in the SELECT *column_list* to each column in the GROUP BY clause moving from left to right. What does that mean? You'll understand most easily by looking at an example:

INPUT/OUTPUT

```
SELECT type, pub_id,
SUM(ytd_sales) AS ytd_sales
FROM titles
GROUP BY type, pub_id
WITH ROLLUP

type           pub_id  ytd_sales
-------------- ------- ---------
business       736         18722
```

```
business       1389        12066
business       (null)      30788
mod_cook       877         24278
mod_cook       (null)      24278
popular_comp   1389        12875
popular_comp   (null)      12875
psychology     736          9564
psychology     877           375
psychology     (null)       9939
trad_cook      877         19566
trad_cook      (null)      19566
UNDECIDED      877        (null)
UNDECIDED      (null)     (null)
(null)         (null)      97446

(15 row(s) affected)
```


ANALYSIS The ROLLUP operator produces a row in your output for each row in the titles table with a single type and pub_id. It then lists the ytd_sales for each item and produces an additional row for each type with summary information. In this example, the rows with (null) in the pub_id field display the sum of all the ytd_sales for that group of types.

Let me put this explanation into English for you. The titles table contains two rows that have both a business type and a unique pub_id (the real table contains a total of four books of type business, with one author [pub_id] writing three books and another author writing the fourth). Each author who wrote business books has ytd_sales of 18,722 and 12,066, respectively.

The ROLLUP operator then creates a subtotal field that sums all the business type books (18,722 + 12,066 = 30,788). The query then does the same thing for each group of book types and authors in the table and gives you a grand total (97,446) signified by a (null) value in the type and pub_id fields.

The CUBE operator produces super-aggregate rows by using every possible combination of the columns in the GROUP BY clause. Like the ROLLUP operator, the CUBE operator produces the running averages and running sums but also cross-references columns to return additional summary rows. Now consider this example:

INPUT/ OUTPUT

```
SELECT type, pub_id,
SUM(ytd_sales) AS ytd_sales
FROM titles
GROUP BY type, pub_id
WITH CUBE

type           pub_id  ytd_sales
-------------- ------- ---------
business       736         18722
```

```
business       1389       12066
business       (null)     30788
mod_cook       877        24278
mod_cook       (null)     24278
popular_comp   1389       12875
popular_comp   (null)     12875
psychology     736         9564
psychology     877          375
psychology     (null)      9939
trad_cook      877        19566
trad_cook      (null)     19566
UNDECIDED      877       (null)
UNDECIDED      (null)    (null)
(null)         (null)     97446
(null)         736        28286
(null)         877        44219
(null)         1389       24941

(18 row(s) affected)
```

ANALYSIS The CUBE operator produces a row in your output for each row in the titles table with a single type and pub_id. It then lists the ytd_sales for each item and produces an additional row for each type with summary information and another row for each pub_id. In this example, the rows with (null) in the pub_id field display the sum of all the ytd_sales for that group of types; the rows with (null) in the type field display the sum of all the ytd_sales for that group of pub_ids.

When ROLLUP or CUBE is used, some restrictions are placed on the GROUP BY clause. You can have a maximum of 10 columns in the GROUP BY clause, the sum of the sizes of those columns can't exceed 900 bytes in size, and you can't use the GROUP BY ALL clause.

The ROLLUP and CUBE operators produce new rows of relational data. Relational results are preferred to the free-form results you get when using the COMPUTE and COMPUTE BY statements.

Also, keep in mind that you can't use the ROLLUP and CUBE operators with text or image data types because they are nonsortable.

Data Correlation

In the following sections, you will look at implementing joins to retrieve data from two or more tables. The results will appear as a single table with columns from all the tables specified in the SELECT *column_list* and meeting the search criteria. You will see how to implement joins (inner joins, cross joins, outer joins, and self joins) using both ANSI and SQL Server syntax.

Implementing Joins

To join tables, you must compare one or more columns from a table to one or more columns in one or more tables. The result of the comparison produces new rows by combining the columns in the SELECT *column_list* from the joined tables that meet the join conditions. When you join tables, you can use either the older SQL '89 ANSI syntax, or the newer SQL '99 ANSI join syntax.

Note The result sets for these two syntaxes will be identical in most queries. The only time there's a difference is when an outer join is performed. Under the older SQL '89 syntax, a query compiler might look at the query and decide that the outer join is unnecessary and perform a simple inner join between the two tables. Under the newer SQL '99 standard, this doesn't happen.

SQL '99 ANSI Join Syntax

The join statements for the newer ANSI syntax show up in the FROM clause of the SELECT statement:

SYNTAX

```
SELECT table_name.column_name[, ...]
FROM {table_name [join_type] JOIN table_name
ON search_criteria}[, ...]
WHERE search_criteria
```

The WHERE clause selects rows from the joined rows to be returned. You can choose three types of ANSI join statements: INNERJOIN, OUTERJOIN, and CROSSJOIN.

SQL '89 Join Syntax

Although SQL Server 2000 still supports the older SQL '89 syntax, we suggest you use the newer ANSI standard syntax instead:

SYNTAX

```
SELECT table_name.column_name[, ...]
FROM table_list
WHERE table_name.column_name
join_operator table_name.column_name[, ...]
```

If you use earlier versions of the syntax, the FROM clause lists the tables involved in the join. The WHERE clause includes the columns to be joined and can include additional search criteria that determine the rows to be returned. The join operators for SQL Server syntax are the following: =, >, <, >=, <=, <>, !>, and !<.

Inner Joins

Joins connect two tables based on a join condition producing results as a new table, with the rows that satisfy the join condition. Inner joins produce information when matching information is found in both tables. The most common types of inner joins are equi-joins and natural joins. In an *equi-join*, column values are compared for equality, and redundant columns are displayed as columns in the result set. In a *natural join*, the redundant columns aren't displayed twice.

Look at the following example to clarify this explanation. In this example, the `SELECT` statement selects all columns from the `publishers` and `pub_info` tables when the pub_id columns for the joined tables are equal. Notice the redundant pub_id column.

Older ANSI Statement

INPUT

```
SELECT publishers.pub_id, pub_name, pr_info
FROM publishers, pub_info
WHERE publishers.pub_id = pub_info.pub_id
```

The Preferred ANSI Statement

```
SELECT publishers.pub_id,  pub_name, pr_info
FROM publishers
INNER JOIN pub_info ON publishers.pub_id = pub_info.pub_id
```

```
pub_id pub_name             pr_info
------ -------------------- ------------
736    New Moon Books       This is sample text data for New Moon...
877    Binnet & Hardley     This is sample text data for Binnet & ...
1389   Algodata Infosystems This is sample text data for Algodata...
1622   Five Lakes Publishing This is sample text data for Five Lakes...
1756   Ramona Publishers    This is sample text data for Ramona...
9901   GGG&G                This is sample text data for GGG&G...
9952   Scootney Books       This is sample text data for Scootney...
9999   Lucerne Publishing   This is sample text data for Lucerne...

(8 row(s) affected)
```

Natural Joins

In a natural join, column values are compared for equality, but redundant columns are eliminated from the columns in the result set. In the following example, the `SELECT` statement selects all columns from the `publishers` table and all columns except pub_id from the pub_info table.

Older ANSI Statement

INPUT

```
SELECT publishers.*, pub_info.logo, pub_info.pr_info
FROM publishers, pub_info
WHERE publishers.pub_id = pub_info.pub_id
```

Preferred ANSI Statement

INPUT

```
SELECT publishers.*, pub_info.logo, pub_info.pr_info
FROM publishers
INNER JOIN pub_info ON publishers.pub_id = pub_info.pub_id
```

OUTPUT

```
pub_id pub_name             city       state country ...
------ -------------------- ---------- ----- ------- ...
736    New Moon Books       Boston     MA    USA     ...
877    Binnet & Hardley     Washington DC    USA     ...
1389   Algodata Infosystems Berkeley   CA    USA     ...
1622   Five Lakes Publishing Chicago   IL    USA     ...
1756   Ramona Publishers    Dallas     TX    USA     ...
9901   GGG&G                München    NULL  GER     ...
9952   Scootney Books       New York   NY    USA     ...
9999   Lucerne Publishing   Paris      NULL  FRA     ...

(8 row(s) affected)
```

10

Cross or Unrestricted Joins

Cross or unrestricted joins return a combination of all rows of all tables in the join as the result set. You create a cross or unrestricted join not by using the WHERE clause in the SQL Server join of two or more tables, but by using the CROSS JOIN keyword for the ANSI join.

NEW TERM Combining all rows from all tables involved in the join yields a *Cartesian product*. In most cases, this type of result set is unusable unless your intention is to find every possible combination, such as some type of statistical or mathematical analysis. To put it another way, if you look at each table as a matrix and then multiply the matrices, you get a new matrix with all combinations (see Figure 10.1). Each row from Table1 is added to each row in Table2. If you add the number of columns from both tables, you get the resulting number of columns. If you multiply the number of rows in Table1 by the number of rows in Table2, you get the total number of rows returned by your query.

Note

Tables can't be joined on text or image columns. You can, however, compare the lengths of text columns from two tables by using a WHERE clause, but you can't compare actual data.

FIGURE 10.1

Creating a Cartesian product.

A	B
C	D
E	F

Table 1 is a 2x3

1	2	3
4	5	6
7	8	9

Table 2 is a 3x3

A	B	1	2	3
C	D	1	2	3
E	F	1	2	3
A	B	4	5	6
C	D	4	5	6
E	F	4	5	6
A	B	7	8	9
C	D	7	8	9
E	F	7	8	9

When you perform a cross join, you will get a 5x9 result set.

As an example of creating a Cartesian product by using the cross join or an unrestricted join, say that you want to list all book titles and their authors' IDs. To do so, you submit the following query:

Older ANSI Syntax

```
SELECT titles.title, titleauthor.au_id
FROM titles, titleauthor
```

Preferred ANSI Syntax

INPUT

```
SELECT titles.title, titleauthor.au_id
FROM titles CROSS JOIN titleauthor
```

OUTPUT

```
title                                   au_id
--------------------------------------  -----------
The Busy Executive's Database Guide     172-32-1176
The Busy Executive's Database Guide     213-46-8915
[...]                                   [...]
Sushi, Anyone?                          998-72-3567
Sushi, Anyone?                          998-72-3567

(450 row(s) affected)
```

ANALYSIS The results of the query you submitted yield 450 rows, with 18 rows in the `titles` table and 25 rows in the `titleauthor` table. Because an unrestricted or cross join returns all possible combinations, you get 18×25 = 450 rows—not quite the desired result, right?

To avoid submitting an unrestricted join, you should subtract 1 from the number of tables you are joining. $N - 1$ indicates the number of join clauses needed, where N is the number of tables involved in the join (that is, three tables, $3 - 1 = 2$, two join clauses). You might have more join clauses if you are joining based on a composite key.

Outer Joins

You can restrict rows from one table while allowing all rows from another table as your result set by using outer joins. One of the most common uses for this type of join is to search for orphan records. The outer join operators and keywords for ANSI syntax are as follows:

`LEFT OUTER JOIN`	Includes all rows from the first table and only the matching rows in the second table
`RIGHT OUTER JOIN`	Includes all rows from the second table and only the matching rows in the first table
`FULL OUTER JOIN`	Includes all nonmatching rows from both tables as well as the matching rows

Suppose that you have a table of customers and a table with orders. These two tables are related by a CustomerID field. With an equi-join or a natural join, you return records only when the CustomerID field has a match in both tables. Outer joins can be handy to get a customer list, and if a customer happens to have an order, that order information also shows up. If the customer doesn't have an order, the information from the orders table shows up as `(null)`.

If you do a left outer join on these tables and specify the customers table first, the desired results are returned. If you specify a right outer join, your results show all orders. If an order happens to have a CustomerID that doesn't match a CustomerID in the customers table, the customer information is `(null)`. (If you follow the rules of referential integrity, you should never have an order without a valid CustomerID. If this is the case, your right outer join will have the same results as an equi-join or a natural join—all orders and customers when a match occurs on CustomerID.)

The left and right outer joins can return the same results, depending on the table order. For example, these two joins return the same information:

```
Customers.CustomerID *= Orders.CustomerID
```

and

```
Orders.CustomerID =* Customers.CustomerID
```

In releases of SQL Server before version 7.0, you could use the following SQL '89 syntax:

- *= includes all rows from the first table and only the matching rows in the second table (left outer join).
- =* includes all rows from the second table and only the matching rows in the first table (right outer join).

Unfortunately, these operators aren't guaranteed to produce the correct results. Problems can occur when NULL values are present. Therefore, when using OUTER joins, always use the newer ANSI SQL '99 outer join syntax.

If you want to find all the titles, whether they have sold any copies, and the number of copies sold, you can submit the following query using the newer SQL '99 syntax:

INPUT

```
SELECT titles.title_id, titles.title, sales.qty
FROM titles LEFT OUTER JOIN sales
ON titles.title_id = sales.title_id
```

OUTPUT

```
title_id title                     qty
-------- ------------------------- ----
BU1032   The Busy Executive's D... 5
BU1032   The Busy Executive's D... 10
BU1111   Cooking with Computers... 25
BU2075   You Can Combat Compute... 35
BU7832   Straight Talk About Co... 15
MC2222   Silicon Valley Gastron... 10
MC3021   The Gourmet Microwave     25
[...]    [...]                     [...]
TC4203   Fifty Years in Bucking... 20
TC7777   Sushi, Anyone?            20

(23 row(s) affected)
```

Self Joins

As the name suggests, a *self join* correlates rows of a table with other rows in the same table. Comparison queries for the same information are used the most for self joins. For example, if you want to list all authors who live in the same city and ZIP code, you compare city and ZIP by executing the following query:

Older ANSI Syntax

INPUT

```
SELECT au1.au_fname, au1.au_lname,
au2.au_fname, au2.au_lname,
au1.city, au1.zip
FROM authors au1, authors au2
WHERE au1.city = au2.city
```

```
AND au1.zip = au2.zip
AND au1.au_id < au2.au_id
ORDER BY au1.city, au1.zip
```

Preferred ANSI Syntax

INPUT

```
SELECT au1.au_fname, au1.au_lname,
au2.au_fname, au2.au_lname,
au1.city, au1.zip
FROM authors au1
INNER JOIN authors au2 ON au1.city = au2.city
AND au1.zip = au2.zip
WHERE au1.au_id < au2.au_id
ORDER BY au1.city, au1.zip
```

OUTPUT

```
au_fname  au_lname  au_fname  au_lname  city           zip
--------- --------- --------- --------- -------------- ---
Cheryl    Carson    Abraham   Bennet    Berkeley       94705
Dean      Straight  Dirk      Stringer  Oakland        94609
Dean      Straight  Livia     Karsen    Oakland        94609
Dirk      Stringer  Livia     Karsen    Oakland        94609
Ann       Dull      Sheryl    Hunter    Palo Alto      94301
Anne      Ringer    Albert    Ringer    Salt Lake City 84152

(6 row(s)  affected)
```


Notice that when you perform a self join on a table, you create an alias for the table name. You use the alias so that one table is treated logically as two tables.

> A table alias is useful any time you do a multitable join operation. It allows you to create a more readable and shorter query statement because you reference the table alias instead of the table name.

Working with Subqueries

A SELECT statement nested inside another SELECT statement is commonly referred to as a *subquery*. Subqueries can produce the same results as a join operation. In the following sections, you will look at how the subquery is used, the types of subqueries, subquery restrictions, and correlated subqueries.

How to Use a Subquery

A SELECT statement can be nested within another SELECT, INSERT, UPDATE, or DELETE statement. If the subquery returns a single value, such as an aggregate, it can be used anywhere a single value can be used. If the subquery returns a list, such as a single column of many values, it can be used only in the WHERE clause.

In many cases, a join operation can be used instead of a subquery; however, some instances can be processed only as a subquery. In some cases, a join operation can yield better performance than a subquery, but generally you'll notice little performance difference.

The subquery is always enclosed within parentheses and, unless you're doing a correlated subquery, it concludes before the outer query is processed. A subquery can contain another subquery, and that subquery can contain a subquery, and so on. There's no practical limit to the number of subqueries that can be processed other than system resources.

The syntax for a nested SELECT statement is as follows:

SYNTAX

```
(SELECT [ALL | DISTINCT] subquery_column_list
[FROM table_list]
[WHERE clause]
[GROUP BY clause]
[HAVING clause])
```

Types of Subqueries

A subquery can return a single column or single value anywhere a single value expression can be used and can be compared against using the following operators: =, <, >, <=, >=, <>, !>, and !<. It can return a single column or many values that you can use with the IN list comparison operator in the WHERE clause. A subquery can also return many rows that you can use for an existence check by using the EXISTS keyword in the WHERE clause.

To find all authors who live in the same state as the bookstore that sells their publishers' books, you can run either of the following queries:

INPUT

```
SELECT DISTINCT au_fname, au_lname, state
FROM authors
WHERE state IN
(SELECT state FROM stores)
```

or

INPUT

```
SELECT DISTINCT au_fname, au_lname, state
FROM authors
WHERE EXISTS
(SELECT * FROM stores
WHERE state = authors.state)
```

OUTPUT

```
au_fname             au_lname           state
-------------------- ------------------ ------
Abraham              Bennet             CA
Akiko                Yokomoto           CA
Ann                  Dull               CA
Burt                 Gringlesby         CA
```

```
[...]                    [...]               [...]
Sheryl                   Hunter              CA
Stearns                  MacFeather          CA

(16 row(s) affected)
```

Some restrictions are placed on what you can do with subqueries. You can create and use a subquery by following these rules:

- It must be in parentheses.
- If used when a single-value expression is used, it must return a single value.
- It can't be used in the `ORDER BY` clause.
- It can't contain an `ORDER BY`, `COMPUTE`, or `SELECT INTO` clause.
- It can't have more than one column in the *`column_list`* if used with the `IN` clause.
- It must have `SELECT *` if used with the `EXISTS` clause.
- Text and image data types aren't allowed in the select list (except for the use of `*`).
- It can't include the `GROUP BY` and `HAVING` clauses if used with an unmodified comparison operator (one without an `ANY` or `ALL` keyword).

10

Correlated Subqueries

NEW TERM A *correlated subquery* references a table from the outer query and evaluates each row for the outer query. In this aspect, a correlated subquery varies from a normal subquery because the subquery depends on values from the outer query. A normal subquery is executed independently of the outer query.

In the following example, the join query is rewritten as a correlated subquery. The queries return the same information. The queries answer the following instruction: Show me authors who live in the same city and ZIP code.

Using a `JOIN`

INPUT

```
SELECT au1.au_fname, au1.au_lname,
au2.au_fname, au2.au_lname,
au1.city, au1.zip
FROM authors au1, authors au2
WHERE au1.city = au2.city
AND au1.zip = au2.zip
AND au1.au_id < au2.au_id
ORDER BY au1.city, au1.zip
```

OUTPUT

```
au_fname  au_lname  au_fname  au_lname  city           zip
--------- --------- --------- --------- -------------- ------
Cheryl    Carson    Abraham   Bennet    Berkeley       94705
Dean      Straight  Dirk      Stringer  Oakland        94609
Dean      Straight  Livia     Karsen    Oakland        94609
```

```
Dirk       Stringer  Livia     Karsen    Oakland        94609
Ann        Dull      Sheryl    Hunter    Palo Alto      94301
Anne       Ringer    Albert    Ringer    Salt Lake City 84152

(6 row(s) affected)
```

Using a Correlated Subquery

INPUT

```
SELECT au1.au_fname, au1.au_lname, au1.city, au1.zip
FROM authors au1
WHERE zip IN
(SELECT zip
FROM authors au2
WHERE au1.city = au2.city
AND au1.au_id <> au2.au_id)
ORDER BY au1.city, au1.zip
```

OUTPUT

```
au_fname  au_lname  city           zip
--------- --------- -------------- ---------
Abraham   Bennet    Berkeley       94705
Cheryl    Carson    Berkeley       94705
Livia     Karsen    Oakland        94609
Dirk      Stringer  Oakland        94609
Dean      Straight  Oakland        94609
Sheryl    Hunter    Palo Alto      94301
Ann       Dull      Palo Alto      94301
Albert    Ringer    Salt Lake City 84152
Anne      Ringer    Salt Lake City 84152

(9 row(s) affected)
```

Notice that the same data is returned, even though the row count is higher in the second query; it's just formatted differently and is more readable.

SELECT INTO

The SELECT INTO statement enables you to create a new table based on query results. The new table is based on the columns you specify in the select list, the tables you name in the FROM clause, and the rows you choose in the WHERE clause. You can create two types of tables with a SELECT INTO statement: permanent and temporary. The syntax for the SELECT INTO is as follows:

SYNTAX

```
SELECT column_list
INTO new_table_name
FROM table_list
WHERE search_criteria
```

When creating a permanent table, you must set the SELECT INTO/BULKCOPY database option (only in SQL Server v7.0). Using the SELECT INTO statement, you can define a table and put data into it without going through the usual data definition process. The new table's name must be unique within the database and must conform to the rules for SQL Server naming conventions.

If columns in the *column_list* of your SELECT statement have no titles, such as derived columns like aggregate functions, the columns in the new table will have no names. This result poses two problems:

- Column names within a table must be unique; therefore, if more than one column has no header, the SELECT INTO fails.
- If the new table contains a column with no header, the only way to retrieve that column is to use SELECT *.

For these reasons, it's good practice to create column aliases for derived columns. Also, because using SELECT INTO is generally a nonlogged operation (unless your database is in FULL mode), you should back up your database immediately following this operation. You can also use the SELECT INTO statement to create temporary tables.

The two types of temporary tables are as follows:

- A *local* temporary table is available only during the current user session to SQL Server and is deallocated when the session is terminated. You create a local temporary table by preceding the new table name with the # symbol.
- A *global* temporary table is available to all user sessions to SQL Server and is deallocated when the last user session accessing the table is terminated. You create a global temporary table by preceding the new table name with two ## symbols.

These temporary tables reside in the tempdb database. The following example creates a temporary table called #tmpTitles with a list of title IDs, the title itself, and its selling price:

INPUT

```
SELECT title_id, title, price
INTO #tmpTitles
FROM titles
GO
SELECT * FROM #tmpTitles
GO
```

OUTPUT

```
title_id title                                          price
-------- ---------------------------------------------- -----
BU1032   The Busy Executive's Database Guide             19.99
BU1111   Cooking with Computers: Surreptitious ...      11.95
BU2075   You Can Combat Computer Stress!                  2.99
[...]    [...]                                           [...]
TC3218   Onions, Leeks, and Garlic: Cooking Secrets ... 20.95
TC4203   Fifty Years in Buckingham Palace Kitchens       11.95
TC7777   Sushi, Anyone?                                  14.99

(18 row(s)  affected)
```

Tip

The SELECT INTO statement creates a new table. If you want to add rows to a preexisting table, use INSERT or INSERT INTO, both of which you will learn about tomorrow.

UNION Operator

You can combine the results of two or more queries into a single result set by using the UNION operator. By default, duplicate rows are eliminated; however, using UNION with the ALL keyword returns all rows, including duplicates. The UNION operator takes the following syntax:

SYNTAX

```
SELECT column_list [INTO clause]
[FROM clause]
[WHERE clause]
[GROUP BY clause]
[HAVING clause]
[UNION [ALL]
SELECT column_list
[FROM clause]
[WHERE clause]
[GROUP BY clause]
[HAVING clause]...
[ORDER BY clause]
[COMPUTE clause]
```

The following are the rules for using the UNION operator:

- All *column_lists* must have the same number of columns, same column order, and similar data types.
- If you use an INTO clause in one of the queries, you must use it in the first query.
- You can use GROUP BY and HAVING clauses only within individual queries.
- ORDER BY and COMPUTE clauses are allowed only at the end of the UNION statement to define the order of the final results or to compute summary values.
- Column names come from the first SELECT *column_list*.

In the following example, you can use the UNION operator to pull data from two separate queries and combine the two result sets into a single result set:

INPUT

```
SELECT title, stor_name, ord_date, qty
FROM titles, sales, stores
WHERE titles.title_id = sales.title_id
AND stores.stor_id = sales.stor_id
UNION
SELECT title, 'No Sales', NULL, NULL
```

```
FROM titles
WHERE title_id NOT IN
(SELECT title_id FROM sales)
ORDER BY qty
```

```
title                          stor_name            ord_date        qty
------------------------------ -------------------- --------------- ------
Net Etiquette                  No Sales             (null)          (null)
The Psychology ...             No Sales             (null)          (null)
Is Anger the Enemy?            Eric the Read Books  Sep 13 1994...  3
[...]                          [...]                [...]           [...]
Onions, Leeks, and Garlic: ... News & Brews         Jun 15 19...    40
Secrets of Silicon Valley      Barnum's             May 24 1993...  50
Is Anger the Enemy?            Barnum's             Sep 13 1994...  75

(23 row(s) affected)
```

10

Summary

Today you built a foundation for data retrieval by using the SELECT statement. You then learned how to change your column headings and add string literals to your output. You expanded on your understanding of the SELECT statement by using arithmetic operators, mathematical functions, string functions, and datetime functions. You also learned about system functions that can be used to further manipulate your data.

Often, the data you want to work with isn't expressed in the format and data type you must use. You learned how to use data conversion to alter your data from one data type to another.

You expanded on your knowledge by learning how to pull certain rows of information out of your database by applying comparison operators, ranges, lists, and character strings. You also learned how to eliminate rows with null values. You then studied methods of removing duplicate information by using the DISTINCT keyword.

Next, you sorted your results by using the ORDER BY clause with your data. You then learned about some of the advanced features you can apply in SQL Server, including aggregate functions such as SUM and AVG and how to use them in a SELECT statement.

Recall that the aggregate functions can return summary values for an entire table or for groups of rows in a table and are normally used with the GROUP BY or HAVING clause or in the *column_list*. GROUP BY clauses group summary data that meet the WHERE clause criteria to be returned as single rows. HAVING clauses can also be used to set the criteria to be returned by the GROUP BY clause.

The ORDER BY clause sorts your results. Remember that SQL Server sometimes returns results in sorted order, but that order isn't guaranteed unless you specify the ORDER BY clause.

You also learned about the `COMPUTE` and `COMPUTE BY` clauses, which can produce new rows of summary and detail data. The `COMPUTE` clause is useful because it returns detail rows and a grand total summary row. The `COMPUTE BY` clause returns rows as subgroups with summary values.

To produce additional summary rows that are often called super aggregates, you learned about the `ROLLUP` and `CUBE` operators, which are used with the `GROUP BY` clause. The `ROLLUP` operator is typically used to produce running averages or running sums. The `CUBE` operator produces super-aggregate rows by using every possible combination of the columns in the `GROUP BY` clause.

You also learned how to join tables by using both the ANSI syntax and the SQL Server syntax. The join statements for the ANSI syntax show up in the `FROM` clause of the `SELECT` statement (FROM Table1 LEFT JOIN Table2 ON Table1.Col1 = Table2.Col1, whereas the `WHERE` clause is used for the ANSI '89 syntax (WHERE col1 *= col2). You examined the three types of ANSI join statements: `INNER JOIN`, `OUTER JOIN`, and `CROSS JOIN`. Inner joins, which are either equi-joins or natural joins, return information when values in two tables are identical. Outer joins can show all the information from one table; if the associated table has values that match, they are displayed as well. Cross or unrestricted joins return a combination of all rows of all tables in the join as the result set.

You also learned about creating subqueries. They occur when you nest a `SELECT` statement inside another `SELECT` statement. Subqueries can produce the same results as a join operation.

The `SELECT INTO` statement allows you to create a new table based on query results. You can create either permanent or temporary tables. When you create a permanent table, you must have the `SELECT INTO/BULKCOPY` option set to true for the database. To create temporary tables, you prefix the table name with a `#` for a local temporary table or a `##` for a global temporary table.

Finally, you learned how to combine the results of two or more queries into a single result set by using the `UNION` operator.

Q&A

Q It looks like `SELECT` statements can get pretty long. Is there a limit to how big they can be?

A Yes, queries are limited to 64KB in length.

Q Where can I find SELECT statements?

A You can often find SELECT statements in front-end applications such as Visual Basic and PowerBuilder. You can also find SELECT statements embedded in views, stored procedures, triggers, events, alerts, and many other locations in your SQL Server.

Q When should I use ANSI syntax, and when should I use SQL Server syntax?

A In general, try to use the ANSI syntax, because this implementation is a standard, the code is much more portable, and you experience little or no performance gain/loss.

Q What does the following statement do?

```
SELECT SUM(qty) FROM sales
```

A It returns the sum of the qty field in the sales table.

Q Is it a good idea to use COMPUTE and COMPUTE BY?

A Using these statements is okay, but remember that the data they return is nonrelational.

Workshop

This section provides quiz questions to help you solidify your understanding of the concepts presented today. In addition to the quiz questions, exercises are provided to let you practice what you've learned today. Try to understand the quiz and exercise answers before continuing on to tomorrow's lesson. Answers are provided in Appendix A, "Answers to Quiz Questions."

Quiz

1. What do these queries return?

   a.

```
SELECT * FROM authors
WHERE au_lname LIKE 'M%'
```

   b.

```
SELECT emp_id AS EmployeeID,
    lname AS LastName,
    fname AS FirstName
    FROM employee
```

c.

```
SELECT ROUND ($7725.53, 1)
```

d.

```
SELECT lname + ', ' + SUBSTRING(fname,1,1) + '.' AS Name,
emp_id AS EmployeeID
FROM employee
```

2. Can you run a subquery as a join and vice versa?
3. *True or False:* `ROLLUP` and `CUBE` don't supply summary information.
4. Can you use a `SELECT INTO` statement to build a temporary table that everyone has access to?

Exercises

1. You want to retrieve title_id, title, and price for all books that have a publisher ID of `0877` or the word *computer* in the title, and when the price is `NOT NULL`. What Transact-SQL would you use? (*Hint:* Use the `titles` table.)
2. Write a query to find all books in the `titles` table that have price values that are `NOT NULL`.
3. Write a query to list all book titles and prices in the `titles` table in descending order based on price.
4. Create a query that returns the average of the ytd_sales figures from the `titles` table in the `pubs` database.
5. Using the `GROUP BY` and `HAVING` clauses, create a query that will find all books with more than one author. (*Hint:* Use the `titleauthor` table.)
6. Using the `COMPUTE BY` clause, create a query that will report the stor_id and a running sum of the quantity of books ordered. Use the `sales` table.
7. Create a query using joins (either a SQL Server join or an ANSI join) to show an author's first name, last name, and book titles. (Use the au_fname and au_lname fields from the `authors` table and the title field from the `titles` table.) (*Hint:* You must do two joins—one from `authors` to `titleauthor` and one from `titles` to `titleauthor`.)
8. Create a subquery to find authors who live in the same states as any of the stores.
9. Create a temporary table containing all the information from the `employee` table. Test the existence of your new table by selecting data from it.

WEEK 2

DAY 11

Modifying Data

Yesterday you looked at retrieving data by using the `SELECT` statement. You saw how you could retrieve only some columns in a table and use the `WHERE` clause to restrict the rows to be returned. You looked at manipulating the data with numeric, string, and date functions. You also learned how you could summarize the data returned by using the super-aggregates `GROUP BY`, `ROLLUP` and `COMPUTE`. Finally, you looked at using the `SELECT` statement to retrieve data from more than one table by using the join operation or by writing subqueries.

Today's lesson focuses on modifying the data in your SQL Server tables by using the `INSERT`, `UPDATE`, and `DELETE` statements. However, before you learn about the actual statements, you will look at the relationship between data modifications and transaction logging.

Transaction Logging

SQL Server keeps track of changes to a database by logging almost every change made to the database and placing it in the transaction log. You learned about placement and management of the transaction log on Day 4, "Creating and Administering Databases and Data Files." As you are modifying your data, be aware that every change is being written to the transaction log. When you perform an INSERT, a copy of the entire new row is written to the transaction log; when you run a DELETE, a copy of the entire deleted row is written to the transaction log.

With the UPDATE operation, the result is not so straightforward. For some UPDATE operations, SQL Server just logs the bytes being changed. For many other UPDATE operations, SQL Server must make two entries into the log: the entire old (deleted) version of the row and then the entire new (inserted) version of the row. Examining the rules for when SQL Server just logs the bytes being changed rather than when it adds before and after entries to the transaction log is beyond the scope of this book. The amount of data written to the transaction log is also affected by the number of indexes you have, as you will learn on Day 13, "Indexing for Performance."

Some exceptions apply to the logging requirements just discussed, such as the BCP (Bulk Copy Program) utility (see Day 19, "Migrating Data Between Database Servers"), which is equivalent to multiple INSERT commands. If you run the fast version of BCP, the individual rows aren't written to the transaction log as they are inserted into the table; for tables with indexes on them, however, every single new row is written to the transaction log. However, some logging to the transaction log takes place for the recording of the space being allocated during the BCP operation, whether or not it's a "fast" BCP. On Day 10, you learned about the SELECT INTO operation, which also isn't logged (with the previously noted exception about space allocation). Today you will learn about TRUNCATE TABLE, which is equivalent to a DELETE without the logging of every deleted row.

Now that you have some familiarity with how the transaction logging process works, it's time to look more closely at the statements that force logging to occur. You will begin with an inspection of the INSERT statement.

Before going any further, take a minute to copy some of your data to backup tables so that later you can refresh the tables you are working with. Run the following queries to create copies of your publishers and sales tables. If you are using SQL Server 7.0, be sure to turn on the Select Into/Bulk Copy database option before you attempt to run these statements.

INPUT

```
USE pubs
GO
SELECT * INTO tmpPublishers FROM publishers
SELECT * INTO tmpStores FROM stores
SELECT * INTO tmpTitles FROM titles
SELECT * INTO tmpSales FROM sales
GO
```

Inserting Data

The basic INSERT statement adds one row at a time to a table, table variable, or through a view into a base table. By using variations of the basic INSERT statement, you can add multiple rows by selecting data from another table or view or by executing a stored procedure or function. In any of these cases, you must know something about the structure of the table into which you are inserting. The following information is useful to know:

- The number of columns in the table
- The data type of each column
- The name of the columns for some INSERT statements
- Constraints and column properties such as identity, uniqueidentifier, or quantity > 20.

You'll learn about constraints and identity columns on Day 14, "Ensuring Data Integrity." The following is the syntax for the INSERT statement:

SYNTAX

```
INSERT [INTO]
   {table_or_view}
   {{[(column_list)]
VALUES
    ({DEFAULT |
    constant_expression} [,...n]) |
    select_statement |
    execute_statement} |
    DEFAULT VALUES}

table_or_view :: =
{ table_name | view_name
| rowset_function
}[,...n]
```


The simplest method for finding out the number of columns, along with their names and data types, is to use the Table Properties dialog in Enterprise Manager (see Figure 11.1). Follow these steps to open this dialog:

1. Select a database from the Databases folder.
2. Select a table from the Tables folder.
3. Right-click the table and choose Properties.

If you don't have SQL Server Enterprise Manager readily available, you can execute the sp_help system stored procedure to get the same information:

INPUT

```
USE pubs
go
EXEC sp_help publishers
go
```

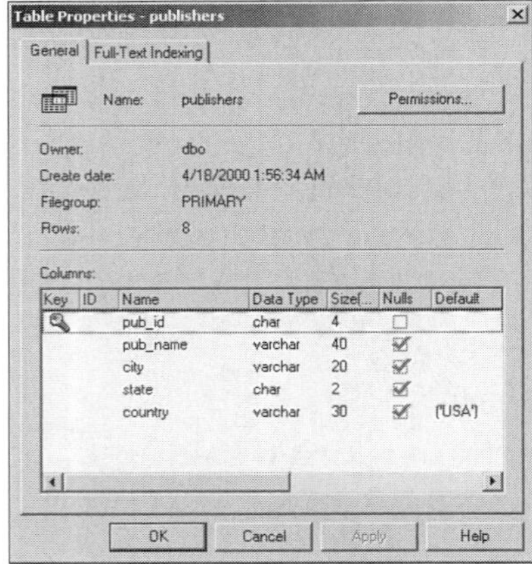

FIGURE 11.1
The Table Properties dialog.

Part of the results should look similar to the following:

```
Column_name     Type       Computed     Length
----------      --------   --------     ----------
pub_id          char         no          4
pub_name        varchar      no          40
city            varchar      no          20
state           char         no          2
country         varchar      no          30
```

This output shows you the column name, the data type, and the position of each column. You need this information when building your `INSERT` statements.

You can also use the `INFORMATION_SCHEMA` views to gather information. For example, to find out the column names and data types in the preceding example, you could run the following query:

```
USE pubs
GO
SELECT * FROM INFORMATION_SCHEMA.Columns
WHERE TABLE_NAME = 'publishers'
GO
```

Using the `INSERT VALUES` Statement

The simplest form of the `INSERT` statement requires a value for every column of the table, in the order the columns were defined. This order was shown in the preceding examples. To insert a single row into the `tmpPublishers` table, you can execute the following command:

INPUT

```
USE pubs
GO
INSERT INTO tmpPublishers
VALUES('9956', 'A New Publisher', 'Poulsbo', 'WA', 'USA')
```

If you have permission to INSERT into this table and aren't violating any constraints, you should get the following message back from the SQL Server:

Output

```
(1 row(s) affected)
```

> **Note**
>
> Because the columns are all character data types, all values are enclosed in quotation marks. Numeric values aren't enclosed in quotation marks.

> **Note**
>
> Unbound grid-type controls used in the visual front-end tools don't automatically add data to the database. You would need to write some code to loop through all the values changed in the grid and then use INSERT/VALUES to place those rows into the database.

The simplest form of the INSERT statement requires that you explicitly supply a value for each column, and each value must be in the correct sequence. If you want to supply the values in a different order or don't want to supply an explicit value for a column, you can use another variant of the INSERT statement.

The following INSERT statement has a list of column names before the VALUES clause, and that list includes only a subset of the column names in the table. The values list then needs to have values only for the columns listed.

```
INSERT INTO tmpPublishers(state, pub_id)
VALUES('AK', '9932')
```

> **Note**
>
> When client applications such as Microsoft Visual Basic or PowerBuilder connect to a database and add data, they use the INSERT/VALUES statements you just looked at.

So what happens to the columns not mentioned in the column list? If you insert a new row, every column must have some value. If you don't supply a value, SQL Server must be able to determine one. For SQL Server to be able to determine a value, every column not mentioned in the list of columns must meet one of the following criteria:

- The column has a default value attached to it.
- The column is an identity column.

- The column allows nulls.
- The column is of type `rowversion` (formerly called `timestamp` in prior versions of SQL Server).

Defaults and identity columns are discussed on Day 14. You learned about nulls and `rowversion` columns on Day 9, "Data Types and Creating Tables."

In the preceding `INSERT` statement, no value is supplied for the publisher name, the city, or the country. In the `publishers` table, the publisher name and city columns both allow nulls, and the country has a default value of USA. After executing the `INSERT` statement, you can run the following query to see the row you have just inserted:

INPUT
```
SELECT * FROM tmpPublishers
WHERE pub_id = '9932'
```

Notice the null values and the default value for country:

OUTPUT
```
Pub_id  Pub_name          City          state   country
------  ----------------  ------------  ------  -------
9932    (null)            (null)        AK      USA
```

If you try to execute an `INSERT` statement but leave out values for columns that didn't meet one of the listed criteria, you get an error.

This `INSERT` doesn't supply a value for the pub_id column:

INPUT/OUTPUT
```
INSERT INTO tmpPublishers(pub_name, city, state)
VALUES('The Best Books', 'New Orleans', 'LA')
```

```
Server: Msg 515, Level 16, State 2, Line 1
Cannot insert the value NULL into column 'pub_id',
➥table 'pubs.dbo.tmpPublishers';
column does not allow nulls. INSERT fails.
The statement has been terminated.
```

Notice that the error message isn't entirely complete. Part of the problem is that the pub_id column doesn't allow nulls, but it also doesn't have a default value and isn't an identity column.

DEFAULT VALUES

You can use one more variation of the simple, single-row `INSERT` statement when you don't want to include a list of column names but do want SQL Server to use default values when they exist (this also includes nulls and identity values). You can use the keyword `DEFAULT` in the actual values list as a way of telling SQL Server that it should determine what value should be used. Consider this example:

```
INSERT INTO tmpPublishers
VALUES('9950', DEFAULT, DEFAULT,'AK', DEFAULT)
```

If every column in a table has some kind of default value that SQL Server can determine, you can use one more variation. You can simply tell SQL Server to use all default values by using the keywords `DEFAULT VALUES`, as in the following `INSERT` statement:

```
INSERT INTO tmpPublishers DEFAULT VALUES
```

Of course, this `INSERT` statement will fail though, due to the same reasons as described earlier.

Inserting Data Using SELECT

All the preceding `INSERT` statements inserted a single row into a table. If you want to insert more than one row at a time, you must have a source where those rows already exist. That source is typically another table or a join between two or more other tables, or a view. In this form of the `INSERT` statement, you use a subquery to determine the rows of data to be inserted. (You learned about subqueries on Day 10, "Retrieving Data with the `SELECT` Statement.") The subquery's result set becomes the set of rows to be inserted. The number of columns in the subquery's result set must match the number of columns in the table, and the columns must have compatible data types. In this first example, you will create a table to keep track of addresses:

INPUT/OUTPUT

```
CREATE TABLE AddressList
([Name] varchar(50) not null,
Address varchar(50) not null,
City varchar(20) not null,
State char(2)  )
```

```
This command completed successfully.
```

This table has four character fields, so any `SELECT` statement you use to populate it must return four character columns. Here's an example:

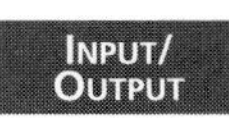

```
INSERT INTO AddressList
SELECT stor_name, stor_address, city, state
FROM tmpStores
```

```
(6 row(s) affected)
```

Note: Unlike the subqueries you read about yesterday, the subquery used with an `INSERT` statement doesn't have parentheses around it.

The column names used in the subquery are ignored; the table already has column names associated with each field.

You can execute another `INSERT` statement to add more rows to your `AddressList` table. Suppose that you want to add names and addresses from the `authors` table. Instead of just a single name, the `authors` table has a first name column (au_fname) and a last name column (au_lname). The `address_list` table is expecting just a single value for its name column, so you can concatenate the last and first names together. You can include a comma and space in the concatenated result.

```
INSERT INTO AddressList
SELECT au_lname + ', ' + au_fname, address, city, state
FROM authors

(23 row(s) affected)
```

This last example creates a table to keep track of the names of all the publishers and the titles of all the books each publisher has published:

```
CREATE TABLE PublisherList
(PubName varchar(40) NULL,
Title varchar(80) NULL)
```

To populate this table, you need to join the `tmpPublishers` and `tmpTitles` tables. Use an outer join so that those publishers that don't currently have any books published are included.

```
INSERT INTO PublisherList
SELECT pub_name, title
FROM tmpPublishers LEFT OUTER JOIN tmpTitles
ON tmpPublishers.pub_id = tmpTitles.pub_id
```

Using Stored Procedures to Insert Data

SQL Server has one more option for inserting rows into a table. If a stored procedure returns a single result set, and you know the number and type of columns that the result set contains, you can `INSERT` into a table using the results returned when calling that stored procedure.

If the system stored procedure returns more than one result set, make sure that all the results have the same number of columns and return the same type of data in the corresponding columns.

You'll write your own stored procedures on Day 15, "Creating Views, Triggers, Stored Procedures, and Functions," but for now you can use a system stored procedure. The `sp_spaceused` system stored procedure returns information about the space usage of a single table. You can create a table to hold the results of running this procedure and `INSERT` a row into this table at regular intervals. By doing so, you can monitor the growth of the table over time.

Look at the output of the sp_spaceused system stored procedure (your results might vary slightly):

INPUT/OUTPUT

```
EXEC sp_spaceused tmpPublishers
Name            Rows   Reserved    Data    index_size    unused
-------------   ----   --------    ----    -----         ---------
TmpPublishers   11     32 KB       2 KB    4 KB          26 KB
```

This procedure returns six columns, all of which are character strings. Although the second column looks numeric, it really isn't. You can determine the type by either examining the code for the sp_spaceused system stored procedure (you'll see how to do that on Day 15) or trying to create the table with an integer column. Notice the error message you get when you try to insert a row.

The following table should be able to hold the results:

```
CREATE TABLE SpaceUsage
(TableName varchar(30) not null,
[Rows] varchar(9),
Reserved varchar(10),
Data varchar(10),
IndexSize varchar(10),
Unused varchar(10)  )
```

To insert into this table, you can execute the system stored procedure sp_spaceused:

INPUT

```
INSERT INTO SpaceUsage
EXEC sp_spaceused 'tmpPublishers'
```

One very nice extension of this capability to insert rows from a system stored procedure is the capability to insert rows from a remote stored procedure. If you have a stored procedure on a remote (linked) server that returns rows from a table, you can execute that remote procedure to copy all the rows from the remote server to the local one. To run a remote procedure, you must specify the following in your remote procedure call: server name, database name, procedure owner name, and procedure name.

For example, if you have a SQL Server named Wildlife with a database named Water and a procedure named Fish with an owner of dbo, you can run the following query:

```
INSERT INTO LocalTable
EXEC Wildlife.Water.dbo.Fish
```

You must take into account a few additional considerations when inserting data into a table with an identity column. These issues are covered on Day 14, which also covers restrictions that you might encounter when you attempt to insert values where check constraints or referential integrity constraints appear in the table.

11

Deleting Data

When you use the DELETE command, you can remove one or more rows from a table:

```
DELETE [FROM] {table_name | view_name}
[WHERE clause]
```

The word FROM is optional, as is the WHERE clause. However, for these DELETE commands to be transportable, you should use the FROM within the statement.

The following DELETE statement removes all rows from the tmpSales table:

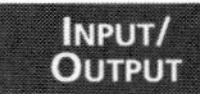

```
DELETE FROM tmpSales

(21 row(s) affected)
```

To remove only a subset of rows in a table, you must use the WHERE clause, which allows you to qualify the rows to be removed. The WHERE conditions can include any conditions you learned about on Day 10, such as relational operators (<, >, =); and the keywords IN, LIKE, and BETWEEN.

The following DELETE statement removes all books with a pub_name of "New Moon Books" from the tmpPublishers table:

```
DELETE FROM tmpPublishers
WHERE pub_name = 'New Moon Books'
```

Performing a DELETE Using a Lookup Table

A single DELETE statement can remove rows from a single table only. However, SQL Server enables you to include another table in your DELETE statement to be used as a lookup table. Often, the lookup table appears in a subquery. In this next example, you'll remove all titles published by New Moon Books. The tmpTitles table is the one to be modified, but it contains only the publisher ID, not the publisher name. You must look in the publishers table to find the publisher ID for New Moon Books (we already deleted the ID from the tmpPublishers table), which then determines the rows to remove from the tmpTitles table.

```
DELETE FROM PublisherList
WHERE PubName =
(SELECT pub_name FROM tmpPublishers
WHERE pub_id = '9956')

(1 row(s) affected)
```

The subquery accesses the `tmpPublishers` table and returns a single value for `pub_name`. That value is then used to determine which rows in `publisher_list` you are going to delete—that is, all rows with a pub_name equal to the returned value. Keep in mind that no more than one row will be returned because pub_id is the primary key of the `publishers` table. If the subquery could return more than one row, you would have to use the `IN` keyword instead of the equal (=) sign.

The preceding query could have been written more efficiently as a `JOIN`. When you use a `JOIN` with a `DELETE` command, you specify two `FROM` keywords: one to specify the table to delete records from and one to specify the join table. This example performs the same delete shown earlier:

```
DELETE FROM PublisherList
FROM PublisherList pl INNER JOIN tmpPublishers p
ON pl.PubName = p.pub_name
AND p.pub_id = '9956'
```

The next example uses a lookup table that returns more than one value. You'll remove all rows from the `tmpSales` table that indicate the sale of business books. The `tmpSales` table holds the title_id value of the book sold, but not its type. You must access the `tmpTitles` table to find which title_ids correspond to business books. Because you deleted the information in the `tmpSales` table earlier today, you need to repopulate the table. Remember that when you started this lesson, you copied all the sales information to another table. Now drop the `tmpSales` table, and then re-create and repopulate it by using a `SELECT INTO` statement:

11

INPUT

```
USE pubs
GO
DROP TABLE tmpSales
GO
SELECT * INTO tmpSales
FROM Sales
GO
```

Now remove all rows from the `tmpSales` table that are of type "business":

INPUT/OUTPUT

```
DELETE FROM tmpSales
WHERE title_id IN
(SELECT title_id FROM tmpTitles
WHERE type = 'business')

(5 row(s) affected)
```

The subquery accesses the `tmpTitles` table and returns a list of title_id values. Those values are then used to determine which rows in `tmpSales` to delete—that is, all rows with a title_id equal to any of the returned values.

You can use a Transact-SQL extension to write DELETE statements using a FROM clause containing multiple tables. This approach makes the DELETE appear as a join operation, although only one table has rows deleted. The functionality provided is the same as using subqueries. The second table is used only as a lookup table.

The following example shows how the DELETE statements use multiple tables in a FROM clause:

```
DELETE FROM tmpSales
FROM tmpSales s INNER JOIN tmpTitles t
ON s.title_id = t.title_id
WHERE t.type = 'business'
```

ANALYSIS The choice of whether to use the subquery or join method depends mainly on personal preference. I usually prefer the subquery method because there's no confusion as to which table is being modified and which is being used only as a lookup table. You should also be aware that the join method is non-ANSI standard. The upside of the join method is that SQL Server usually processes joins more efficiently than it does subqueries.

Using TRUNCATE TABLE

Earlier today, you saw an example of a DELETE statement with no WHERE clause that would delete every row in the table. If you really want to remove all data from a table while leaving the table structure intact, you can resort to another alternative:

```
TRUNCATE TABLE tmpSales
```

Unlike the DELETE statement, this statement doesn't return a message about the number of rows affected. The following are some other differences between DELETE with no WHERE clause and TRUNCATE TABLE:

- DELETE logs every row as it's deleted; TRUNCATE TABLE only writes the page and extent deallocations to the transaction log.
- DELETE maintains the indexes by removing pointers one at a time and logging each index adjustment; TRUNCATE TABLE shrinks the indexes in a single step and again only writes the page deallocations to the transaction log.
- TRUNCATE TABLE can be executed only by the table owner, a member of the db_owner database role, or the sysadmin server role; DELETE can be executed by any user who has been given appropriate permissions on the table.
- A DELETE trigger isn't fired when a table is truncated but is fired when rows are deleted (see Day 15 for more information about triggers).
- TRUNCATE TABLE resets any identity value back to the seed; DELETE doesn't affect the next identity value to be used.

Updating Data

The third data modification statement you will look at today is the UPDATE statement, which allows you to change column values within an existing row.

Before you go any further, now is a good time to make sure that you have fresh data. Run the following queries to refresh the tmpSales, tmpPublishers, tmpStores, and tmpTitles tables:

INPUT

```
USE pubs
GO
DROP TABLE tmpSales
DROP TABLE tmpPublishers
DROP TABLE tmpStores
DROP TABLE tmpTitles
GO
SELECT * INTO tmpPublishers FROM publishers
SELECT * INTO tmpSales FROM sales
SELECT * INTO tmpStores FROM stores
SELECT * INTO tmpTitles FROM titles
GO
```

11

Using the UPDATE Statement

The UPDATE statement uses the following syntax:

SYNTAX

```
UPDATE
    {table_name | view_name}
SET
    column_name1 = {expression1 | NULL | (select_statement)}
    [, column_name2 = ...]
[WHERE search_conditions]
```

The SET clause specifies the columns to be updated. Here, as with the DELETE statement, the WHERE clause is optional.

The following UPDATE statement changes the ytd_sales column in the tmpTitles table to 0 for every row. You might want to update this column at the beginning of every year.

INPUT/OUTPUT

```
UPDATE tmpTitles
SET ytd_sales = 0

(18 row(s) affected)
```

Without a WHERE clause, this statement changes the value of the ytd_sales column to 0 in every row in the table.

The following example updates the city column for the publisher Algodata Infosystems:

INPUT/OUTPUT

```
UPDATE tmpPublishers
SET city = 'El Cerrito'
WHERE pub_name = 'Algodata Infosystems'
```

```
(1 row(s) affected)
```

An UPDATE statement can make the new value in the column dependent on the original value. The following example changes the price of all psychology books to 10 percent less than the current price:

INPUT/ OUTPUT

```
UPDATE tmpTitles
SET price = price * 0.90
WHERE type = 'psychology'

(5 row(s) affected)
```

An UPDATE statement can change more than one column. The word SET occurs only once, and the different columns to be changed are separated by commas. The following UPDATE statement increases the price of all popular computing books by 20 percent and appends the string (price increase) to the notes field of the same rows:

INPUT/ OUTPUT

```
UPDATE tmpTitles
SET price = price * 1.2, notes = notes + ' (price increase)'
WHERE type = 'popular_comp'

(3 row(s) affected)
```

Performing an UPDATE Using a Lookup Table

A single UPDATE statement can change rows from a single table only. However, SQL Server allows you to include another table in your UPDATE statement to be used as a lookup table. Usually, the lookup table appears in a subquery, which can appear in either the WHERE clause or the SET clause of the UPDATE statement. In this next example, you'll change the publisher of all business books to New Moon Books:

INPUT/ OUTPUT

```
UPDATE tmpTitles
SET pub_id =
(SELECT pub_id FROM tmpPublishers
WHERE pub_name = 'New Moon Books')
WHERE type = 'business'

(4 row(s) affected)
```

The publisher name appears only in the tmpPublishers table, but the tmpTitles table must be modified. The subquery accesses the tmpPublishers table and returns the publisher ID for New Moon Books. This value is used as the new value in the pub_id column of tmpTitles.

Just as you can do with the DELETE statement, you can use a Transact-SQL extension to write UPDATE statements using a FROM clause containing multiple tables. This approach makes the UPDATE appear as a join operation, although only one table has rows modified.

The functionality provided is the same as that is used for subqueries; the second table is used only as a lookup table.

The following example shows how you can rewrite the previous UPDATE statement by using multiple tables in a FROM clause:

```
UPDATE tmpTitles
SET tmpTitles.pub_id = p.pub_id
FROM tmpTitles t INNER JOIN tmpPublishers p
ON t.pub_id = p.pub_id
WHERE p.pub_name = 'New Moon Books'
AND type = 'business'
```

The choice of whether to use the subquery method or the join method depends mainly on personal preference. Just like in the DELETE statement, the subquery method seems much clearer as to which table is modified, what the new value of pub_id is to be, and which rows are changing. Also, remember that the join method in an UPDATE statement is non-ANSI standard.

Some UPDATE statements are also quite a bit more complicated to write using the join method. One such case is if the UPDATE statement uses subqueries for both the SET clause and the WHERE clause.

This example changes the publisher of all psychology books published by New Moon Books to Binnet & Hardley:

INPUT/OUTPUT

```
UPDATE tmpTitles
SET pub_id =
    (SELECT pub_id FROM tmpPublishers
     WHERE pub_name = 'Binnet & Hardley')
WHERE type = 'psychology' AND pub_id =
    (SELECT pub_id FROM tmpPublishers
     WHERE pub_name = 'New Moon Books')

(4 row(s) affected)
```

ANALYSIS Again, the publisher name appears in the tmpPublishers table only, but it's the tmpTitles table that needs to be modified. The first subquery accesses the tmpPublishers table and returns the publisher ID for Binnet & Hardley. This pub_id value is used as the new value in the pub_id column of tmpTitles. The second subquery accesses the tmpPublishers table again to return the pub_id value for New Moon Books. This pub_id is used to determine which rows in the tmpTitles table need to be updated.

This UPDATE statement would be much more difficult to write using the join method because the tmpPublishers table would need to appear twice: once for determining the new value of pub_id and once for determining the pub_id of the rows to be changed. This is just another reason I prefer the subquery method over the join method.

Summary

Today you learned the SQL statements used to modify data in your SQL Server tables. You can add new rows to a table by using the `INSERT` statement. You can add them either one row at a time, or you can insert many rows that are coming from another table. You can remove rows from a table by using the `DELETE` statement, and you can change values in existing rows by using the `UPDATE` statement.

Whenever you are modifying data, remember the logging that SQL Server does. Every new row is written to the transaction log, every deleted row is written to the transaction log, and with most updates, two versions of the row are written to the log: the row before the changes are made and the row after the changes are made. The only exceptions are the `SELECT INTO` operation, which doesn't log the new rows in a table, and the `TRUNCATE TABLE` operation, which doesn't log the deleted rows. There's no magic switch to turn off logging for the server.

Q&A

Q How do I undo a `DELETE` or `UPDATE` operation after it's executed?

A By default, when a change is made to a table, it's committed and permanent. SQL Server has no `UNDO` command. However, you can execute a `DELETE` or `UPDATE` within a transaction, and then you can roll back the entire transaction. Transaction control is covered on Day 12, "Using Transact-SQL Extensions."

Q What does the following statement do?

```
INSERT INTO Publishers DEFAULT VALUES
```

A This statement adds a row to the `publishers` table and uses the default values for each column if they are defined. If they aren't defined, it adds null values.

Workshop

This section provides quiz questions to help you solidify your understanding of the concepts presented today. In addition to the quiz questions, exercises are provided to let you practice what you've learned today. Try to understand the quiz and exercise answers before continuing onto tomorrow's lesson. Answers are provided in Appendix A, "Answers to Quiz Questions."

Quiz

1. What happens if you execute a `DELETE` statement without a `WHERE` clause?
2. *True or False*: You must supply a value for every column in a row when inserting a new row.
3. What do joins in a `DELETE` or `UPDATE` statement allow you to do?

Exercises

The exercises assume your `tmpTitles` table in the `pubs` database is in its initial condition. If you've been modifying the table to practice the statements in this lesson, you need to rebuild the `pubs` database. To do so, run the `instpubs.sql` script in your `...\MSSQL\Install` folder. You should also re-create the `tmpTitles` table as the following:

```
USE pubs
GO
DROP TABLE tmpTitles
GO
SELECT * INTO tmpTitles
FROM titles
GO
```

1. Create a temporary table containing the title ID, title, publisher ID, and price of all modern cookbooks (`type = 'mod_cook'`). Use this table for the remaining exercises.
2. Insert the title ID, title, publisher ID, and price from all the traditional cookbooks (`type = 'trad_cook'`) into the temp table.
3. Update the price of all books by 20 percent.
4. Decrease the price of all books published by Binnet & Hardley by 10 percent.
5. Delete all books with a price less than $10.
6. Delete all books with year-to-date sales greater than 10,000.

WEEK 2

DAY 12

Using Transact-SQL Extensions

On Day 11 you looked at modifying your data by using the INSERT, UPDATE, and DELETE commands. These commands shouldn't be taken lightly, especially DELETE. We rarely, if ever, give our database users DELETE permissions. It's far too easy for accidents to happen with this kind of power. What we like to do is create stored procedures that do a delete and ensure that data integrity is maintained. You will learn more about stored procedures on Day 15, "Creating Views, Triggers, Stored Procedures, and Functions."

Today's lesson focuses on the programming features of the Transact-SQL (T-SQL) language. You start off by learning about batches and scripts. You then examine transactions in SQL Server. The next section focuses on control-of-flow language elements, such as IF...ELSE blocks and WHILE statements. You then examine the different types of locking used in SQL Server for concurrency control.

Batches

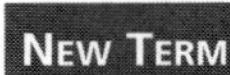

A *batch* is a set of T-SQL statements interpreted together by SQL Server. The statements are submitted together, and the GO statement marks the end of the batch. This example shows a batch run from the SQL Server Query Analyzer:

```
USE PUBS
SELECT au_id, au_lname FROM authors
SELECT pub_id, pub_name FROM publishers
INSERT publishers VALUES ('9998','SAMS Publishing', 'Seattle', 'WA','USA')
GO
```

Batches follow several rules:

- All the SQL statements are compiled as a group.
- If a syntax error occurs anywhere in the batch, the entire batch is canceled.
- Some statements can be combined in a batch, although other statements are restricted. The following CREATE statements can be bound within a single batch:

  ```
  CREATE DATABASE
  CREATE TABLE
  CREATE INDEX
  ```

  These statements can't be combined with others in the same batch:

  ```
  CREATE RULE
  CREATE TRIGGER
  CREATE PROCEDURE
  CREATE DEFAULT
  CREATE VIEW
  ```

  If you try to combine them, you receive error 111, which looks like this:

  ```
  Server: Msg 111, Level 15, State 1
  'CREATE VIEW' must be the first statement in a query batch.
  ```

- You can't alter a table and then use the new columns within the same batch.
- SET statements take effect immediately, except the QUOTED_IDENTIFIER and ANSI_NULLS options.

Keep in mind a few other points when you're working with batches. As we noted earlier, when a batch is submitted for processing, it's parsed, resolved, optimized, compiled, and then executed. During execution, if any single statement fails, the batch continues with the next statement until it finishes processing. For example, if your batch has five CREATE TABLE statements in it and statement 3 causes an error, SQL Server creates tables 1, 2, 4, and 5. Table 3, however, isn't created.

Scripts

New Term A *script* is a set of one or more batches that are saved as a group. Scripts typically are executed as part of some unit of work that needs to be accomplished, such as a data load or database maintenance. Listing 12.1 shows an example of a script.

Listing 12.1 An Example of a Script

```
USE PUBS
SELECT au_id, au_lname FROM authors
SELECT pub_id, pub_name FROM publishers
INSERT publishers VALUES ('9997','SAMS Publishing', 'Seattle', 'WA','USA')
GO

SELECT * FROM stores
GO

DELETE publishers WHERE pub_id = '9997'
GO
```

Batches and scripts don't necessarily have anything to do with transactions, which you will learn about shortly. Microsoft ships various scripts in the `...\MSSQL\INSTALL` directory that you can use as examples. Look for files that end in `.SQL`—these scripts are excellent examples of how you should do your T-SQL scripting.

Transactions

New Term A *transaction* is a unit of work in which all statements are processed successfully or none of the statements are processed. Transactions are constantly being used, but you might not be aware of them. For example, a bank teller transfers $50 from a checking account to a savings account. Her code might debit checking $50 and then credit savings $50. What would happen if she forgot to put the money into savings? Most people would be pretty upset by that. They expect that if the money comes out of checking, it goes into savings. That's a transaction. The unit of work completes all commands successfully, or it fails and undoes everything that it has done. We've come to expect transactions in our daily lives, but as a SQL Server developer, you must manually program transactions for them to work properly. As an administrator, you need to understand transactions because they can cause your transaction logs to fill up if they are used improperly.

Transactions are made up of the following four properties, which, when put together, are called the *ACID properties*:

- **Atomic**—A transaction is said to be *atomic* when it either concludes in its entirety or aborts completely. If any one statement fails, all the statements that are part of the transaction fail.
- **Consistent**—A transaction is said to leave the database in a *consistent* state after it concludes or fails. The changes made by a transaction are consistent from one state to another.
- **Isolated**—A transaction is said to be *isolated* when it doesn't interact or conflict with any other transaction in the database.
- **Durable**—A transaction is said to be *durable* if the work is guaranteed to remain completed regardless of anything that happens to the database after the transaction concludes successfully. If the power fails and the database server crashes, the transaction is guaranteed to still be complete when the server restarts.

NEW TERM Transactions guarantee that the work being performed can succeed or fail completely, as described in the preceding list. Locks provide part of that guarantee. During a transaction, no other transaction can modify data your transaction has changed until you decide whether the change is permanent. While you're modifying the data, you hold an *exclusive lock* on the data that you are working with. Conversely, you can't read another transaction's data if it's in the process of modifying that data. You are requesting a *shared lock* on the other data, but the other transaction is using an *exclusive lock* on its data that prevents you from reading it. You will examine locks in more detail later.

Transaction Types

You use three types of transactions: explicit, implicit, and automatic (often referred to as *autocommit*).

Explicit Transactions

NEW TERM *Explicit transactions* are ones that you manually configure. Reserved words are used to indicate the beginning and end of explicit transactions. These reserved words include `BEGIN TRAN[SACTION]`, `COMMIT TRAN[SACTION]`, `COMMIT WORK`, `ROLLBACK TRAN[SACTION]`, `ROLLBACK WORK`, and `SAVE TRAN[SACTION]`.

To begin an explicit transaction, type **`BEGIN TRAN`** (or **`BEGIN TRANSACTION`** if you're in the mood to type more). To tell SQL Server that your transaction is complete and all work should be saved, enter **`COMMIT TRAN`** (or **`COMMIT WORK`**). Hence, a typical transaction might look like this:

```
BEGIN TRAN

    UPDATE authors
    SET city = 'San Jose' WHERE au_lname = 'Smith'
```

```
    INSERT titles
    VALUES ('BU1122','Teach Yourself SQL Server 2000 in 21 days',
     'business','9998',$35.00, $1000.00,10,4501, 'A great book!', '8/1/2000')
    SELECT * from titleauthor

COMMIT TRAN
```

You also need to cancel transactions. To do so, you use `ROLLBACK TRAN` (or `ROLLBACK WORK`). Now consider this example of the `ROLLBACK TRAN` statement:

```
BEGIN TRAN
    Delete sales where title_id = 'BU1032'
    IF @@ERROR > 0
        ROLLBACK TRAN
    ELSE
        COMMIT TRAN
```

NEW TERM The `ROLLBACK TRAN` statement cancels the transaction completely. Any work done in the transaction up to that point is *rolled back*, or canceled. You also can create *savepoints* (discussed later today) within a transaction and then selectively roll back to those points. Again, a code example illustrates this usage best:

```
BEGIN TRAN
    UPDATE table1 SET col1 = 5 WHERE col2 = 14
    SAVE TRAN savepoint1
    INSERT table2 values (3,16)
    IF @@error > 0
        ROLLBACK TRAN savepoint1
        DELETE table3 WHERE col1 > 2
    IF @@error > 0
        ROLLBACK TRAN
    ELSE
        COMMIT TRAN
```

12

Notice that the `SAVE TRAN` command has a name after it, known as the *savepoint name*. By including the savepoint name in the first rollback, you are expressing that, rather than roll back the entire transaction from the beginning, you want to roll back to a particular named point—in this case, `savepoint1`. The `INSERT` into table2 would be canceled if the first rollback were issued, but the transaction itself would continue. Essentially, the `INSERT` would be "removed" from the transaction. Because no name is given to roll back to in the later rollback, `ROLLBACK TRAN` goes all the way back to the `BEGIN TRAN` statement.

Now take a closer look at the `TRANSACTION` statements, beginning with `BEGIN` and `COMMIT`.

SYNTAX

```
BEGIN TRAN [transaction_name]
COMMIT TRAN [transaction_name]
COMMIT [WORK]
```

You can assign the optional *transaction_name* to the transaction. The *transaction_name* must be a valid SQL Server identifier. You can substitute a variable wherever you see *transaction_name*, as long as it resolves to a valid transaction name. You don't need to name a transaction except the outermost `BEGIN` statement in your transaction. With the `COMMIT WORK` statement, you aren't allowed to specify a transaction name. COMMIT WORK is for ANSI (an international standards body) compliance and is rarely used in applications I've seen.

> Transactions can be nested, although this nesting is strictly syntactical in nature. Transactions can't truly be nested. You might have multiple transactions appear to occur within a script, but in fact only one actual transaction is being used.

SYNTAX

Here is the syntax for the `SAVE TRANSACTION` command:

```
SAVE TRAN [savepoint_name]
```

savepoint_name indicates a safe point to abort some amount of work in a transaction without canceling the entire transaction. The *savepoint_name* must be a valid SQL Server identifier.

SYNTAX

Here is the syntax for the `ROLLBACK TRANSACTION` command:

```
ROLLBACK TRAN [transaction_name | savepoint_name]
ROLLBACK [WORK]
```

Refer to the earlier discussion of `BEGIN/COMMIT TRAN` and `SAVE TRAN` statements for a description of the optional names. Again, the `ROLLBACK WORK` statement doesn't allow you to specify either a transaction name or a savepoint name. Again, the ROLLBACK WORK statement exists for ANSI compliance purposes.

The `@@trancount` Global Variable

A global variable, `@@trancount`, applies directly to these transactions. When you issue a `BEGIN TRAN`, `@@trancount` is incremented by one. A `SAVE TRAN` has no effect on `@@trancount`. A `ROLLBACK TRAN` can have several effects, depending on whether a transaction name is specified. If no transaction name is specified, `@@trancount` is reset to `0` (all work is undone). If the last transaction name is specified, `@@trancount` is decremented by one. A `ROLLBACK WORK` statement always resets `@@trancount` to `0`, as well as cancels all work that was done from the first `BEGIN TRAN`. Examine this code to see how it works:

```
SELECT @@TRANCOUNT -- It should return 0.
BEGIN TRAN t1
SELECT @@TRANCOUNT -- It should return 1.
```

```
SAVE TRAN savepoint1
SELECT @@TRANCOUNT -- It still is set to 1.
ROLLBACK TRAN savepoint1
SELECT @@TRANCOUNT -- It still is set to 1.
BEGIN TRAN t2
SELECT @@TRANCOUNT -- It should return 2.
ROLLBACK TRAN
SELECT @@TRANCOUNT -- It's back to 0.
```

As you can see, you can increase the value of @@trancount with multiple BEGIN TRAN statements, but when it comes to rolling back a transaction, there is in fact only one real transaction (hence the jump from @@trancount of 2 to @@trancount of 0).

Allowed and Disallowed Statements

Some statements aren't allowed as part of explicit transactions, including the following:

`ALTER DATABASE`	`RESTORE DATABASE`
`DROP DATABASE`	`CREATE DATABASE`
`RECONFIGURE`	`RESTORE LOG`
`BACKUP LOG`	`UPDATE STATISTICS`

Other statements can appear together inside a transaction, although this doesn't change any of the rules you learned about earlier.

Savepoints

There's no published limit on the number of savepoints within a transaction. Once the transaction is committed, there's no way to roll it back, so savepoints are only useful within the context of a transaction.

12

You might have duplicate savepoint names within a single transaction; however, only the final instance of the savepoint name is actually used if you roll back to that savepoint. For example, the following `ROLLBACK TRAN transave1` statement goes back only as far as the second `transave1` savepoint. The first savepoint is ignored after the name is reused.

```
BEGIN TRAN
    INSERT
    UPDATE
    SAVE TRAN transave1
    DELETE
    INSERT
    SELECT
    SAVE TRAN transave1
    INSERT
    DELETE
    IF @@ERROR <> 0
         ROLLBACK TRAN transave1
    ELSE
        COMMIT TRAN
```

When you issue a ROLLBACK TRAN statement within a trigger and no savepoint name is specified, the entire transaction is rolled back and the rest of the batch isn't executed. However, processing might continue with the next batch. You need to test for this in your code and verify that you handled this particular kind of rollback gracefully. It might be wise to simply return some kind of error in a trigger back to the calling routine and rely on the calling routine to properly deal with the state of a transaction. This approach is certainly much safer.

Remote Stored Procedures

Calls to remote stored procedures aren't normally considered part of a transaction:

```
BEGIN TRANSACTION
UPDATE table1 SET col1 = 5 WHERE col1 = 1
DELETE table1 WHERE col1 = 5
EXEC server2.pubs..usp_insertpublisher parm1 parm2 parm3
COMMIT TRAN
```

If the `pubs..usp_insertpublisher` stored procedure on server2 were to issue a `ROLLBACK TRAN` statement, it wouldn't affect the local transaction.

However, a server configuration option called `REMOTE_PROC_TRANS`, normally set to `0` (off), controls whether remote stored procedures are automatically enrolled (distributed). To enable automatic enrollment of remote stored procedures in transactions, run the following:

```
EXEC sp_configure "REMOTE_PROC_TRANS", 1
RECONFIGURE WITH OVERRIDE
```

This example affects all executions of remote stored procedures on the server, so enable it with caution. You'll learn about distributed transactions later today in the section, "Distributed Transactions."

Automatic Transactions

Even when transactions don't appear to be used, they are lurking behind the scenes. Any execution of a data modification statement in SQL Server is an *implied transaction*.

In the following batch, each SQL statement is a separate transaction. Thus, this batch is actually three separate transactions. If any one of the statements fails, it doesn't affect the others. Each statement succeeds or fails on its own, regardless of the other statements in the batch.

```
INSERT table1 VALUES (1,'abcde')
UPDATE table1 SET col1 = 5 WHERE col1 = 1
DELETE FROM table1 WHERE col1 = 5
GO
```

Transactions can also provide performance benefits. By not writing the transaction log entries to disk until the transaction is completed, SQL Server can provide more efficient utilization of the disk. Therefore, it's beneficial to group statements. If you group the preceding statements into the following transaction, only five log entries are written, instead of nine.

```
BEGIN TRAN
INSERT table1 VALUES (1,'abcde')
UPDATE table1 SET col1 = 5 WHERE col1 = 1
DELETE FROM table1 WHERE col1 = 5
COMMIT TRAN
```

As you increase the grouping of statements, transactions can dramatically increase the efficiency of your data modification statements.

Implicit Transactions

Implicit transactions are provided for American National Standards Institute (ANSI) compliance. When implicit transactions are enabled, selected T-SQL statements automatically issue a `BEGIN TRAN`. You must commit or roll back these statements explicitly by issuing a `COMMIT` or `ROLLBACK TRAN` statement.

You enable implicit transactions at the session level by issuing the following statement:

```
SET IMPLICIT_TRANSACTIONS ON
```

For the rest of that session, the following statements need to be explicitly committed (or rolled back):

ALTER TABLE	GRANT	REVOKE
CREATE	DROP	DELETE
SELECT	INSERT	UPDATE
TRUNCATE TABLE	FETCH	OPEN

To turn off implicit transactions, you run

```
SET IMPLICIT_TRANSACTIONS OFF
```

For example, the following two code snippets are identical (in terms of transactions). Note that you can verify this usage by using the `@@trancount` variable.

```
CREATE TABLE table1 (col1 int not null)
BEGIN TRAN
INSERT table1 VALUES (1)
SELECT @@trancount -- returns a value of 1
COMMIT TRAN
```

```
SET IMPLICIT_TRANSACTIONS ON
INSERT table1 values (2)
SELECT @@trancount -- returns a value of 1
COMMIT TRAN
```

Enabling the `IMPLICIT_TRANSACTIONS` option requires that you remember to commit or roll back every transaction. Forgetting to do so is easy—and if you do forget, you will tend to leave transactions open and hold locks (discussed later) far longer than you might want to. I recommend that you not enable this option unless you are very sure that you will remember to commit your transactions.

How Do Transactions Work?

Now that you've looked at explicit, implicit, and automatic transactions, consider a step-by-step description of what happens inside SQL Server during a transaction, using the set of SQL statements in Listing 12.2 as an example.

LISTING 12.2 Stepping Through a Set of Transactions

```
BEGIN TRAN
    INSERT table1 values (1,'abcde')
    UPDATE table1 SET col1 = 5 WHERE col1 = 1
    DELETE FROM table1 WHERE col1 = 5
COMMIT TRAN
```

ANALYSIS The following occurs in this listing:

1. When the `BEGIN TRAN` statement is sent to the database, the SQL Server parser detects the request to begin an explicit transaction. However, SQL Server 2000 is smart enough that it doesn't allocate a log record in memory until any actual work is done, so a transaction technically isn't started yet.
2. The `INSERT` statement runs. SQL Server creates a log record in memory and allocates a transaction ID to associate with this new transaction. The new row is recorded in the transaction log, and then the data page for `table1` is modified in memory (see Figure 12.1). If the needed page isn't in memory, it's retrieved from disk.
3. The next statement runs similarly. The `UPDATE` statement is recorded in the transaction log, and then the data page is modified in memory (see Figure 12.2).

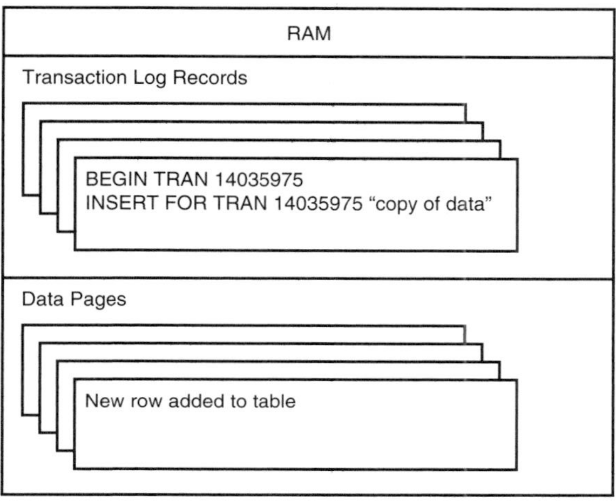

FIGURE 12.1
Step 2 of the transaction process.

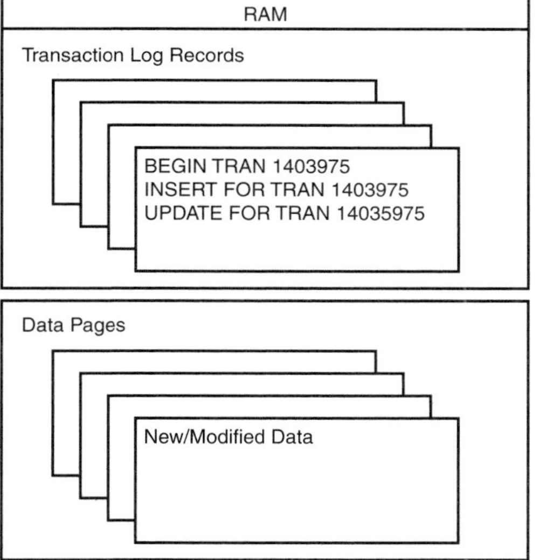

FIGURE 12.2
Step 3 of the transaction process.

12

Note

In this example, a single row is listed in the log for the update. Most of the time it is probably true that the log actually shows a delete followed by an insert rather than a single modify record. It would require an *update in place* to get a single modify record to be written into the log. The various conditions required to get an update in place to occur are covered in detail in Sams Publishing's *Microsoft SQL Server 2000 Unleashed*.

4. When SQL Server receives the `COMMIT TRAN`, the log record is written to the transaction log file for the database (see Figure 12.3). This is your guarantee that the transaction can be recovered. Because the log changes are written to disk, it guarantees that the transaction is recoverable—even if power is lost or the database crashes before the data page is written to disk.

FIGURE 12.3
Step 4 of the transaction process.

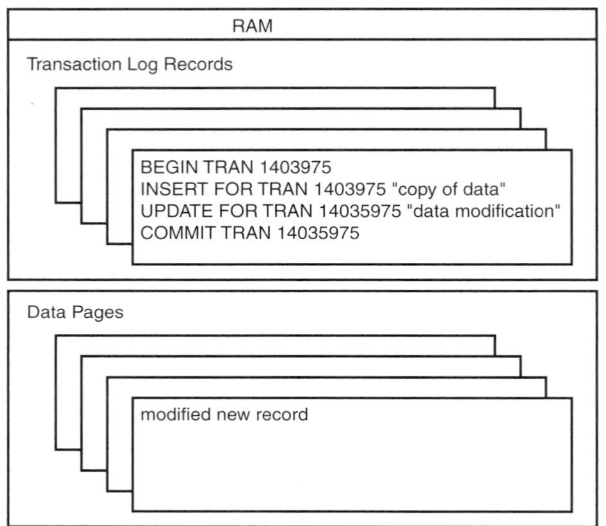

Note

There's a product called Lumigent Log Explorer that you can download from `http://www.lumigent.com`. If you'd like to peek directly into the transaction log, this is a great utility. It allows you to view, and in some cases, modify your transaction log. Generally I think it's interesting to see in the log, but you will rarely need to use this for more than to satisfy your own curiosity about the product (but it's still cool!).

In SQL Server 2000, log records are written in a separate file (or set of files) and aren't accessible with T-SQL. Microsoft doesn't provide a utility to access the transaction log (other than the advanced `DBCC LOG` command, which is too advanced to cover in this book). Only SQL Server internal processes, such as backup and recovery, need to access the transaction log.

The `CHECKPOINT` Process

NEW TERM After the discussion of transactions, you might be wondering when the data pages get written to disk. The log records get written when the `COMMIT TRAN` statement is run. So when does the data get written to disk? The answer is in the `CHECKPOINT` process, an internal process that SQL Server uses to *flush* (copy) the data pages from memory to disk.

The checkpoint helps assure that recovery of committed transactions doesn't take an excessive amount of time. After a checkpoint occurs, a log entry is written to indicate that all modified pages in memory have been written to disk. This entry gives the SQL Server recovery process a point in the transaction log where it's assured that no earlier committed transactions must be looked at to guarantee a complete recovery.

The two kinds of checkpoints used in SQL Server are automatic and manual. The automatic checkpoint process occurs based on internal SQL Server calculations. You configure how often the checkpoint process will occur by using the `RECOVERY INTERVAL` configuration option. This option specifies, in minutes, the maximum amount of time required to recover each database in your system. If SQL Server determines it would take that much time or longer to recover a database, it issues the automatic checkpoint. When this happens, all modified data pages (for this database) in memory are written to disk, and all log records for this database are also written to disk. The automatic checkpoint process wakes up every 60 seconds and cycles through each database, determining whether the database needs to be checkpointed. The default setting for the `RECOVERY INTERVAL` option is `0`, meaning SQL Server decides when a checkpoint is needed.

An automatic checkpoint also occurs in two other circumstances. The first occurs when you run the `sp_dboption` system stored procedure to change a database option. SQL Server automatically issues a checkpoint for you. The second occurs when you shut down SQL Server. You can either issue the Transact-SQL command `SHUTDOWN` or shut down the MSSQLServer service.

12

To force a manual checkpoint at any time, type the T-SQL command **`CHECKPOINT`**. You must be a member of the db_owner role of a database to execute this command. When a manual checkpoint is issued, all modified pages in memory are flushed to disk, in the same way as during the automatic checkpoint process.

Note

> For databases with the Truncate Log on checkpoint option set, the automatic checkpoint process truncates committed transactions from the log periodically (or when the transaction log fills up). A manual checkpoint has no effect on the transaction log (other than copying log records to disk), whether or not the Truncate Log on checkpoint database option is set.

Distributed Transactions

All the transactions that you've considered so far have been on only one server. SQL Server 2000 can support transactions that involve more than one server. This capability is supported with the Microsoft Distributed Transaction Coordinator (MSDTC) service.

You can use distributed transactions in three different ways:

- You can program distributed transactions by using the DB-Lib, open database connectivity (ODBC), or object linking and embedding (OLE) DB application programming interface (API). ActiveX Data Objects (ADO) also allow you to use distributed transactions. These options are beyond the scope of this book.
- You can use the T-SQL syntax `BEGIN DISTRIBUTED TRANSACTION`.
- You can use the `SET REMOTE_PROC_TRANSACTIONS` option to enable distributed transactions for a single session.

Now let's examine the last two methods more closely. To enlist the MSDTC service in your transaction and have it coordinate activity across multiple servers, you must issue the `BEGIN DISTRIBUTED TRANSACTION` statement in exactly the same way you used the `BEGIN TRAN` statement. The earlier discussion about transactions mentioned that remote stored procedures operate outside the current transaction from which they are called. With distributed transactions, the remote stored procedures are now included within the transaction. A failure on the remote server also affects the calling server or servers. In the following code example, if a failure occurred in the stored procedure called from server2, the transaction on your server would be affected as well:

```
BEGIN DISTRIBUTED TRANSACTION
UPDATE table1 SET col1 = 5 WHERE col1 = 1
DELETE table1 WHERE col1 = 5
EXEC server2.pubs..usp_insertpublisher parm1 parm2 parm3
COMMIT TRAN
```

SQL Server 2000 can also query remote servers as part of any T-SQL statement. So, the following code segment is also a valid distributed transaction in SQL Server 2000 (assuming you've set up a linked server named remoteserver):

```
BEGIN DISTRIBUTED TRANSACTION
INSERT remoteserver.pubs..remotetable (col1, col2) VALUES (1,2)
UPDATE localtab SET col2 = 5 WHERE col1 = 1
COMMIT TRAN
```

The third method is to use the `SET REMOTE_PROC_TRANSACTIONS` statement. When it is set in a session, all remote stored procedures called during the statement are considered part of the transaction. You can also set the same configuration option with `sp_configure`, and the option is set for all sessions from that time on. Before you set it as a serverwide configuration option, make sure that you've tested the implications of this use on any existing remote stored procedures.

SQL Server 2000 allows you to connect remotely with two types of remote databases: remote servers and linked servers. The remote server option is provided for backward compatibility, and the linked server option has been improved in SQL Server 2000.

Remote Servers

Remote servers enable you to execute stored procedures on remote SQL Server databases. Depending on whether you used the `BEGIN DISTRIBUTED TRANSACTION` or `SET REMOTE_PROC_TRANSACTIONS ON` Transact-SQL statement, remote stored procedures might or might not be part of a transaction. To allow remote stored procedures to be run, you must set up the remote server as follows:

1. Add the name of the remote server to the `sysservers` system table on your SQL Server. Do so by running `exec sp_addserver` *`remoteserver`*.
2. Add your server to the `sysservers` table in the remote SQL Server database. Again, run `exec sp_addserver` *`yourserver`*.
3. On your server, run the following T-SQL statements:
   ```
   EXEC sp_addremotelogin remoteserver, sa, sa
   EXEC sp_remoteoption remoteserver,sa, sa, trusted, true
   ```
4. On the remote server, run the code from step 3, but reference your server.

You can now run remote stored procedures while logged in as sa. To set up other logins, you need to rerun the previous stored procedures. To reference the remote stored procedure, use the four-part name—*`servername.dbname.owner.procname`*—with the execute statement. For example, if you were referencing the `byroyalty` stored procedure in the `pubs` database on server gizmo, you would run the following code:

```
Exec gizmo.pubs.dbo.byroyalty 10
```

This approach is very useful but isn't as flexible as using linked servers.

12

Linked Servers

Microsoft improved linked servers in SQL Server 2000. Linked servers enable you to open an OLE DB rowset against a remote server. Unlike remote servers already mentioned, linked servers enable you to get data from non-SQL Server data sources. You can access any OLE DB data source in this fashion. Hence, you can access data from Oracle, Microsoft Access, Microsoft Excel, or any other OLE DB data source.

Perhaps an even more powerful use of linked servers is going well beyond what's allowed with remote servers. You can still execute remote stored procedures, but you can also join remote tables. To set up a linked server, use the `sp_addlinkedserver` and `sp_addlinkedsrvlogin` system stored procedures:

```
Exec sp_addlinkedserver 'remoteserver','SQL Server'
Exec sp_addlinkedsrvlogin 'remoteserver','TRUE'
```

> You must run the script `instcat.sql` from the SQL Server 2000 install directory against any SQL Server 6.5 servers if you want to run distributed queries or remote stored procedures with the linked server options.

The preceding code adds the remote server on your SQL Server and specifies that, when you attempt to connect to the remote server, you should log in with whatever credentials you've used on the local server.

Now you can run queries like the following, which joins the `titles` table from your local server with the `publishers` table from a remote server:

```
Select t1.title, t2.pub_name
From pubs..titles t1 -- This is the local table
Inner Join remoteserver.pubs..publishers t2 -- This is the remote table
On t1.pub_id = t2.pub_id
```

As you might have guessed, you might need a lot of additional information to implement linked servers—particularly if you decide you need to join SQL Server tables with non-SQL Server data using the OLE DB heterogeneous data capabilities. Such topics are beyond the scope of this book, and I recommend that if you need further information about linked servers, you reference Sams Publishing's *Microsoft SQL Server 2000 Unleashed*.

Control-of-Flow Language Elements

When a batch of statements is submitted to SQL Server for execution, the normal flow is for the commands to be executed in the order they are given. The T-SQL language provides several commands that allow you to change the sequence of command execution. They are most useful in transactions, triggers, functions, and stored procedures.

`BEGIN...END` Block

Several control-of-flow commands that will be presented require a single statement as part of their syntax. Whenever a single statement is expected, you can use just a single statement. If you need multiple statements to be executed together, you must enclose them between the keywords `BEGIN` and `END`. You will see this construct used in some of the following examples.

`PRINT` Statement

Up to this point, the only way you have been able to return any information from SQL Server to your client program was to use a `SELECT` statement. SQL Server also provides a `PRINT` statement, but it's fairly limited:

SYNTAX

```
PRINT {'Any ASCII text' | @local_variable | @@global_variable}
```

All that you can print is an ASCII string (string constant) or variable of type character (either fixed or variable length), as in this example:

```
PRINT "Hello"
PRINT @@version
```

If you want to print something more complex, you must build the string in a character variable and then print that variable.

The following example uses `@msg` to build one big string to print. You can't use concatenation operations and numeric variables in a `PRINT` statement, but you can use them in an assignment `SET` or `SELECT` and then print the result.

INPUT/ OUTPUT

```
USE pubs
DECLARE @msg varchar(50),
@numWA tinyint
SELECT @numWA = COUNT(*) FROM stores
WHERE state = 'WA'
SELECT @msg = 'There are ' + convert(varchar(3), @numWA) +
' stores in Washington'

PRINT @msg

(1 row(s) affected)
(1 row(s) affected)
There are 2 stores in Washington.
```

IF...ELSE Block

12

An `IF...ELSE` block allows a statement to be executed conditionally. The word `IF` is followed by an expression that must be either true or false. If the expression is true, the next statement is executed. The optional `ELSE` keyword introduces an alternative statement that's executed when the expression following `IF` is false.

SYNTAX

```
IF Boolean_expression
{sql_statement | statement_block}
ELSE [Boolean_expression]
{sql_statement | statement_block}
```

For example, this statement calls the procedure `uspWeeklyReport` if today is Friday; otherwise, it calls the uspDailyReport:

```
IF(datename(dw,getdate()) = 'Friday')
    BEGIN
    PRINT 'Weekly report'
    EXEC uspWeeklyReport
    END
ELSE
```

```
BEGIN
PRINT 'Daily Report'
EXEC uspDailyReport
END
```

Notice that no specific keyword marks the end of the `IF...ELSE` block. Also notice that the Boolean expression that follows the `IF` can include a `SELECT` statement. If that `SELECT` statement returns a single value, it can then be compared with another value to produce a Boolean expression.

In the following example, if the average book price is greater than $15, you want to print one message; if the average book price is less than or equal to $15, you want to print a different message:

```
IF (SELECT avg(price) FROM titles) > $15
    PRINT 'Hold a big sale'
ELSE
    PRINT 'Time to raise prices'
```

If the `SELECT` statement that follows the `IF` returns more than one value, you can use a special form of `IF`—`IF EXISTS`:

SYNTAX

```
IF EXISTS (SELECT statement)
    {sql_statement | statement_block}
[ELSE
    {sql_statement | statement block}]
```

`IF EXISTS` returns true if the ensuing `SELECT` statement returns any rows at all and returns false if the `SELECT` statement returns no rows. The following example returns all the information about any book published by the publisher with ID 9933:

```
IF EXISTS
(SELECT * FROM titles WHERE pub_id = '9933')
BEGIN
    PRINT 'Here are the books: '
    SELECT * FROM titles WHERE pub_id = '9933'
END
ELSE
    PRINT 'No books from that publisher'
```

This query has the same results but asks the opposite question:

```
IF NOT EXISTS
(SELECT * FROM titles WHERE pub_id = '9933')
BEGIN
    PRINT 'No books from that publisher'
    RETURN
END
ELSE
```

```
BEGIN
    PRINT 'Here are the books'
    SELECT * FROM titles WHERE pub_id = '9933'
END
```

In some cases, IF EXISTS provides better performance than alternative methods because SQL Server can stop processing as soon as the first row is found.

Caution

Don't use IF EXISTS with aggregates because aggregates always return data, even if the value of that data is 0. If you want to see whether publisher 9933 has published any books, the following does *not* work:

```
IF exists
(SELECT COUNT(*) FROM titles WHERE pub_id = '9933')
```

This SELECT statement always returns one row. If the database contains no books by this publisher, that one row has the value 0, but IF EXISTS returns true.

CASE Expressions

Programmers often want the ability to apply a conditional expression within another statement. The CASE expression allows T-SQL expressions to be simplified for conditional values. It allows the statement to return different results depending on the value of a controlling value or condition.

A simple CASE expression has this syntax:

SYNTAX

```
CASE expression
    WHEN expression1 THEN expression1
    [[WHEN expression2 THEN expression2] [...]]
    [ELSE expressionN]
END
```

You can use a searched expression as well. Here is that syntax:

```
CASE
    WHEN boolean_expression1 THEN expression1
    [[WHEN boolean_expression2 THEN expression2] [...]]
    [ELSE expressionN]
END
```

A simple CASE expression compares an initial expression with each expression in the list and returns the associated result expression. If none of the expressions match, the result expression after the word ELSE is returned.

12

Let's look at some CASE expressions in use. In the following example, for each row in the titles table, the value in the type column is compared to each value in the CASE list. The first matching value determines what expression will be returned. A searched case expression returns the expression associated with the first Boolean expression in the list that evaluates to true. If none of the expressions evaluate to true, the result expression after the ELSE is returned.

INPUT

```
SELECT title_id, type = CASE type
    WHEN 'business' THEN 'Business Book'
    WHEN 'psychology' THEN 'Psychology Book'
    WHEN 'mod_cook' THEN 'Modern Cooking Book'
    WHEN 'trad_cook' THEN 'Traditional Cooking Book'
    WHEN 'popular_comp' THEN 'Popular Computing Book'
    WHEN 'undecided' THEN 'No type determined yet'
    END
FROM titles
```

Your results should look similar to the following:

OUTPUT

```
title_id    type
---------   --------------------------
BU1032      Business Book
BU1111      Business Book
BU2075      Business Book
BU7832      Business Book
MC2222      Modern Cooking Book
MC3021      Modern Cooking Book
MC3026      No type determined yet
PC1035      Popular Computing Book
PC8888      Popular Computing Book
PC9999      Popular Computing Book
PS1372      Psychology Book
PS2091      Psychology Book
PS2106      Psychology Book
PS3333      Psychology Book
PS7777      Psychology Book
TC3218      Traditional Cooking Book
TC4203      Traditional Cooking Book
TC7777      Traditional Cooking Book
```

In this next example, for each row in the titles table, multiple expressions are evaluated. In this case, you're comparing the value of price against different values. The first expression that's true determines what expression will be returned.

INPUT

```
SELECT title_id, cost = CASE
    WHEN price < 10 THEN 'Cheap'
    WHEN price BETWEEN 10 and 20 then 'Midrange'
    ELSE 'Expensive'
    END
FROM titles
```

Your output should look similar to the following:

```
title_id  cost
--------  ----------
BU1032    Midrange
BU1111    Midrange
BU2075    Cheap
BU7832    Midrange
MC2222    Midrange
MC3021    Cheap
MC2025    Expensive
PC1035    Expensive
PC8888    Midrange
PC9999    Expensive
PS1372    Expensive
PS2091    Midrange
PS2106    Cheap
TC3218    Expensive
TC4203    Midrange
TC7777    Midrange
```

Notice that the first CASE example was really just a special version of the searched CASE expression. You could have rewritten the first example as follows and received the same result:

```
SELECT title_id, type = case
    WHEN type = 'business' THEN 'Business Book'
    WHEN type = 'psychology' THEN 'Psychology Book'
    WHEN type = 'mod_cook' THEN 'Modern Cooking Book'
    WHEN type = 'trad_cook' THEN 'Traditional Cooking Book'
    WHEN type = 'popular_comp' THEN 'Popular Computing Book'
    ELSE 'No type determined yet'
    END
FROM titles
```

You can use the simple form of the CASE expression whenever all the conditions test for equality. You also can use two other functions instead of CASE: COALESCE and NULLIF.

12

Using the COALESCE Function

Sometimes a CASE expression has the following form:

```
CASE
    WHEN expr1 IS NOT NULL THEN expr1
    [[WHEN expr2 IS NOT NULL THEN expr2]
    [...]]
    [ELSE exprN]
END
```

Here, the value returned by the expression is the first non-NULL value in the list of values. An equivalent way of writing this expression would be to use the COALESCE function.

In this example, a wages table includes three columns with information about an employee's yearly wage, hourly wage, salary, and commission. However, an employee receives only one type of pay and only one of the three columns has a value in it. The other two columns are NULL. You could run the following code to create a sample table with some sample data:

```
USE pubs
GO
CREATE TABLE tblWages (
intEmpID int NOT NULL,
curHourly money NULL,
curSalary money NULL,
curCommission money NULL,
bigNumSales bigint NULL)
GO
INSERT tblWages VALUES (111, NULL, 52000, NULL, NULL)
INSERT tblWages VALUES (112, 14, NULL, NULL, NULL)
INSERT tblWages VALUES (113, NULL, NULL, 0.15, 50000)
INSERT tblWages VALUES (114, NULL, 73000, NULL, NULL)
INSERT tblWAGES VALUES (115, 4.90, NULL, NULL, NULL)
INSERT tblWages VALUES (116, NULL, 28500, NULL, NULL)
GO
```

After this table is created and loaded with data, you can determine the total amount paid to all employees by using the COALESCE function to receive only the non-NULL value found in the hourly, salary, and commission columns, as in this example:

```
SELECT intEmpID as "Employee ID", "Total Salary" = Convert(money,
(COALESCE(curHourly * 40 * 52, curSalary, curCommission * bigNumSales)))
FROM tblWages

Employee ID Total Salary
----------- --------------------
111         52000.0000
112         29120.0000
113         7500.0000
114         73000.0000
115         10192.0000
116         28500.0000

(6 row(s) affected)
```

Using the NULLIF Function

Sometimes a CASE expression has the following form:

```
CASE
    WHEN expr1 = expr2 THEN NULL
    [ELSE expr1]
    END
```

Here, the value returned by the expression is `NULL` if the two expressions are equivalent; otherwise, the value of the first expression is returned.

Suppose that you have a table similar to the one in the preceding example—a `tblWages` table that includes the data in the previous example, except that the `NULL` values are now stored as 0s. You can run the following code and reset the values to `0` instead of `NULL`:

```
USE pubs
GO
UPDATE tblWages
    SET curHourly = ISNULL(curHourly, 0),
    curSalary = ISNULL(curSalary, 0),
    curCommission = ISNULL(curCommission, 0),
    bigNumSales = ISNULL(bigNumSales, 0)
```

To use the `NULLIF` expression, you need a scenario. If you need to write a `SELECT` statement that returns how many employees receive an hourly wage, how many receive a salary, and how many work on a commission, the following code does *not* work:

```
SELECT Hourly = COUNT(curHourly),
    Salary = COUNT(curSalary),
    Commission = COUNT(curCommission)
FROM tblWages
```

The `COUNT` function counts how many values occur in a column, and 0 counts as a value. The only thing not included in the `COUNT` function is `NULL` values. So, you can use the `NULLIF` function to turn the 0s into `NULL`s and leave non-`NULL` values as they are. To get the correct answer to the previous example, you could run the following code:

```
SELECT Hourly = COUNT(NULLIF(curHourly, 0)),
    Salary = COUNT(NULLIF(curSalary, 0)),
    Commission = COUNT(NULLIF(curCommission, 0))
FROM tblWages
```

12

Using the `WHILE` Command

The T-SQL language has a `WHILE` construct that allows repetitive execution until some condition is met. The use for this construct is limited in many cases because, by its nature, SQL works with sets of rows. For example, you don't need a `WHILE` statement to loop through each row in a table; the `SELECT` statement itself steps through all the rows, testing your `WHERE` criteria for each row.

In certain situations, you need to repeat actions. You can repeat them inside a transaction (not suggested, as transactions should be small and fast), within a stored procedure, or within a SQL function. `WHILE` statements can be useful when you navigate through a cursor.

A `WHILE` construct repeats as long as a specified condition remains true. Just like with `IF...ELSE`, if the condition includes a `SELECT` statement, the entire `SELECT` must be in parentheses.

The following example repeatedly checks the average price of all books. As long as that average is less than $20, the price of every book is updated. The repetition stops when the average price is greater than or equal to $20.

```
WHILE (SELECT AVG(price) FROM titles) < $20
BEGIN
    UPDATE titles SET price = price * 1.1
    PRINT 'all prices have been increased by 10%'
END
```

As in any programming language, there's always the chance that the repetition could continue indefinitely. It's up to the programmer to make sure this doesn't happen.

In the example, the repetition continues as long as the price is less than a specified amount, so some action is required inside the loop to raise the price; eventually, the price will no longer be less than that specified amount. (The only way this won't be true is if all prices are $0.00.) If the `UPDATE` in this example were decreasing the price of books (price = price * 0.90), you would have an infinite loop.

Locking

Locking usually comes up in a negative context. Locking helps provide concurrency within the database. Often you hear someone talk about locking problems, but rarely do you hear about positive benefits; however, there are many. Without locking, SQL Server would have no mechanism to prevent multiple users from updating data at the same time.

In general, you can use four types of locks in SQL Server:

- You can place a *shared lock* (also called a *read lock*) on data you are reading. A shared lock prevents other users from changing the data while you are looking at it. Shared locks are compatible with other shared locks, meaning many users can have shared locks on an object at the same time.
- You can use an *exclusive lock* when you want to change data. It prevents other users from viewing or modifying the data you're working on until you release the lock. Exclusive locks aren't compatible with other locks.
- You use an *update lock* much like an exclusive lock. Update locks prevent others from modifying data while you are in the process of changing the data.

- An *intent lock* is used on a "higher" level object to indicate that a lock (one of the types of locks described) is being taken within that object. You will learn more about intent shortly.

> Update locks are necessary when a query goes through two phases to modify data: a search phase and a modify phase. If SQL Server uses a shared lock during the search phase, another user could also acquire a shared lock on the same object. When the searching transaction tries to modify the data, it needs an exclusive lock. The other transaction might have already attempted to get an exclusive lock, and SQL Server doesn't give you an exclusive lock. Hence, a blocking or deadlock situation might occur. To prevent this situation, you can use an update lock, which prevents another transaction from getting exclusive locks on the object that has been locked for update.

Lock Types

Different levels or types of objects can be locked:

- *RID* is another term for a row-level lock. RID stands for Row Identifier. When a RID lock is taken, only one row at a time is locked.
- *Key* is a row-level lock that's taken within an index. The key lock locks either a single key value or multiple key values (known as a key range lock). This lock type can help serialize transactions within an index.
- *Page* is the standard 8KB unit in SQL Server. A page lock locks all the contents on a single page, which can be one or many rows.
- An *extent* lock is acquired when no more pages are available for a particular object and more data must be added. It indicates that a new set of eight pages (an extent) is being acquired for this object.
- You can acquire a *table* lock either automatically via the escalation process (examined later), or you can request one explicitly. All pages in the table are locked as a unit.
- An *intent* lock is a way to indicate at the table level that there are page or row locks, or to a page that a row lock is in place. For example, if a single shared page lock is taken within a table, an intent shared lock is taken at the table level.

In SQL Server 2000, locking is completely dynamic. In releases of SQL Server before version 7.0, page-level locking was the default. However, SQL Server 2000 decides which lock type to take when a query is optimized. For selects that access a very small amount of data, or small inserts, updates, or deletes, row-level locks (and/or key range locks) are likely taken. For very large selects (such as `SELECT * FROM tblLargeTable`), using page- or even table-level locking might be more efficient.

Row-level locking involves locking a single row at a time instead of a page or table. Row-level locking can be useful because a single page might contain many rows. Generally speaking, the smaller the unit of locking, the better the concurrency (the ability of multiple users to access data simultaneously). The trade-off, however, is that taking 5,000 row locks requires more resources, and hence more time, than does taking a single table lock. Because locking involves compromises, and it isn't always obvious which lock type you should take, it's best to leave the locking decisions up to SQL Server.

Controlling Locking

Normally, you don't need to be concerned with controlling locking. For `INSERT`, `UPDATE`, and `DELETE` operations, SQL Server obtains an exclusive lock. However, SQL Server can configure locks query by query by using locking hints for the `SELECT` statement. You specify them after the name of the table in your query. Occasionally, you have to change the default locking behavior because of problems with transactions conflicting or blocking each other.

For example, to force an exclusive table lock on the `authors` table so that no one can modify the table while you examine it, you can run this query:

```
SELECT *
FROM authors (TABLOCKX)
```

You can use these different parameters in place of `TABLOCKX`:

- `NOLOCK` requests that no locking be used. (This type of read is also referred to as a *dirty read*.) Using this optimizer hint allows a query to read data that has been locked for exclusive use. This usage introduces the possibility that data that has been changed, but not necessarily committed, could be read as part of the query. Although this option is useful in some circumstances, you shouldn't use it unless you fully understand the ramifications.
- `READUNCOMMITTED` is the same as `NOLOCK`.
- `READPAST` specifies that if some rows are locked, and you are reading several rows, including some that would normally stop you from continuing (you would be "blocked" until the locks were freed up), those rows are skipped. Be very cautious in using this option because your result set could be missing data.
- `REPEATABLEREAD` specifies that locking should comply with the `REPEATABLE READ` transaction isolation level. This generally means that when you're reading data, the locks you take aren't released until you finish your transaction; hence, none of the

rows of data that you have read can be modified by other transactions until you're finished with it. Therefore, updates and deletes are prevented, but inserts are allowed.

- `HOLDLOCK` requests that the lock you've taken be held for the duration of a transaction. Normally, during a select statement, shared locks are acquired and released as soon as the next needed row or page is acquired. With this option, those shared locks aren't released until the current transaction is either committed or rolled back. Locks also are taken in such a way that inserts aren't allowed either. This behavior is generally implemented with key range locks.
- `SERIALIZABLE` is the same as `HOLDLOCK`.
- `UPDLOCK` requests an update lock rather than a shared lock. This option isn't normally used.
- `ROWLOCK` forces the use of row-level locks.
- `PAGLOCK` requests a shared page lock.
- `TABLOCK` requests a table-level shared lock rather than locks individual pages or rows.
- `TABLOCKX` requests an exclusive table lock.

Lock Escalation

Lock escalation is the process of changing a lower-level lock (such as a row or page lock) to a higher-level lock (such as a table lock). SQL Server escalates locks when it determines the need to do so. You have no control over when this process occurs.

The `LOCKS` Option

One other configuration option is available for locks—surprisingly enough, the `LOCKS` option. It's an advanced configuration option. The default value of `0` means that SQL Server adjusts the number of locks as the system's needs change. By default, SQL Server assigns 2 percent of the memory it uses to locks. You can set the number of locks manually if you want; however, if you run out of locks, SQL Server puts error messages in both the Windows NT Application Event Log and the SQL Server error log. All activities that require locks on the system pause until more locks become available. Each lock requires a small amount of memory, so don't manually assign locks or set the parameter arbitrarily high unless you understand the impact of this change.

Observing Locks

To see locks as they occur, you can run the `sp_lock` or `sp_processinfo` stored procedures. The following is an example of `sp_lock` on my system:

INPUT/ OUTPUT

```
EXEC sp_lock
GO
```

```
spid   dbid   ObjId       IndId  Type Resource    Mode   Status
------ ------ ----------- ------ ---- ----------- ------ ------
1      1      0           0      DB               S      GRANT
6      1      0           0      DB               S      GRANT
7      1      0           0      DB               S      GRANT
7      2      0           0      DB               S      GRANT
7      5      0           0      DB               S      GRANT
7      2      0           0      EXT  1:80        X      GRANT
7      1      117575457   0      TAB              IS     GRANT
8      1      0           0      DB               S      GRANT

(8 row(s) affected)
```

As you can see from the results of the sp_lock query, interpreting the results can be difficult. You need to interpret the results by looking up the dbid (database IDs) from the sysdatabases table in the master database and the ObjID (object ID) from the sysobjects table in the appropriate database. You might need to look up the IndId (Index ID) from the sysindexes table in that database as well. The Type column explains what kind of object is locked—database, table, extent, key, page, or row (RID). The Resource column indicates what's locked depending on the type of lock:

- EXT (extent) is in the form *fileno*:*Extent*. For example, 1:80 means an extent lock is on file number 1 of the database, in extent 80.
- PAG (page) is in the form *fileno*:*pageno*. For example, 1:2401 would be a page lock on page number 2401 in file number 1 in the database.
- RID (row) is in the form *fileno*:*pageno*:*rowid*. So 1:32:16 indicates file number 1, page 32, row 16 on that page is locked.
- KEY (key range) shows internal information from SQL Server that users can't interpret.

The Mode column indicates the type of lock (S for shared, X for exclusive, I for intent, and so on).

The information in the Status column is what you're most likely looking for. GRANT means the lock is now being used. WAIT indicates that the lock can't be taken because of another user holding an incompatible lock (lock compatibility is discussed next). CNVT shows that a lock is being converted to another lock (most likely, it's escalating). From a blocking perspective, you can treat CNVT much like a WAIT status.

Using the SQL Server Enterprise Manager's Current Activity windows to view locks might be easier. To see the Current Activity dialogs, expand your servername, expand the Management folder, and then expand the Current Activity option. Here, you can view which processes (users) are running, which locks are held by process, and which locks are held by object. Figure 12.4 shows a sample of what that window might look like.

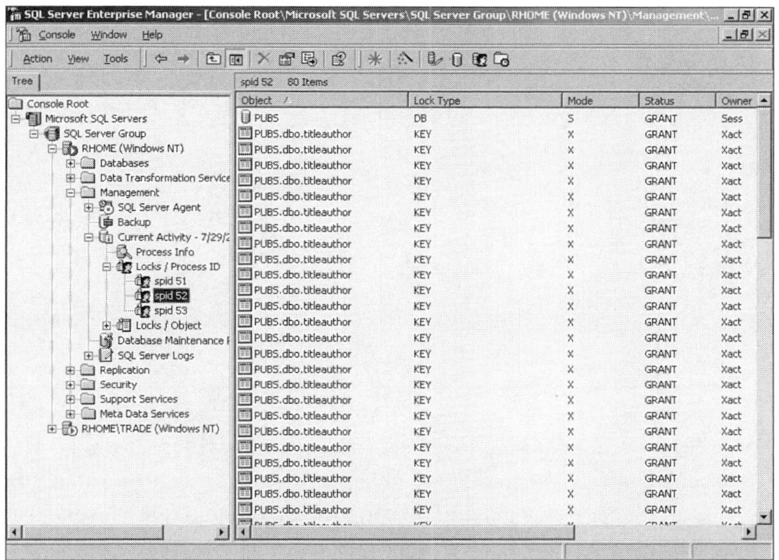

FIGURE 12.4

The Locks/Process ID Current Activity window.

If you expand the Locks/Object option, you can observe the locks in place for each object (see Figure 12.5).

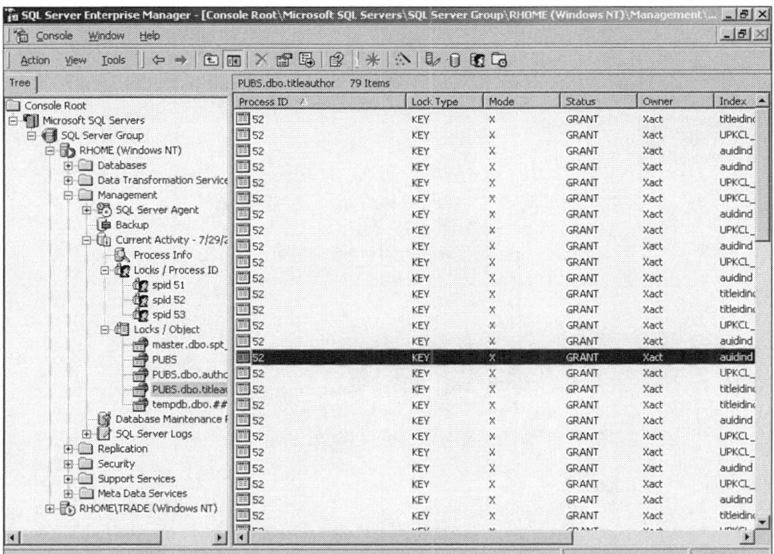

FIGURE 12.5

The Locks/Object Current Activity window.

Lock Compatibility

Locks might or might not be compatible with other locks. Table 12.1 shows a compatibility matrix for locks.

TABLE 12.1 Lock Compatibility

	IS	*S*	*U*	*IX*	*SIX*	*X*
Intent Shared (IS)	YES	YES	YES	YES	YES	NO
Shared (S)	YES	YES	YES	NO	NO	NO
Update (U)	YES	YES	NO	NO	NO	NO
Intent Exclusive (IX)	YES	NO	NO	YES	NO	NO
Shared With Intent Exclusive (SIX)	YES	NO	NO	NO	NO	NO
Exclusive (X)	NO	NO	NO	NO	NO	NO

Notice that exclusive locks are incompatible with everything. If you think about this, it makes sense. When you are changing data, you don't want anyone else changing the exact same data. Shared locks, on the other hand, are reasonably flexible. When you're reading data, it's okay if other people are reading the same data.

Deadlocks

NEW TERM A *deadlock* is a situation in which two transactions conflict with each other and the only resolution is to cancel one transaction. An example provides the easiest way to understand deadlocks:

1. Create the two tables shown here using the Query Analyzer, and populate them with data:

INPUT

```
USE pubs
GO

CREATE TABLE tblChecking
(intAcctNum INT NOT NULL,
 strLastName CHAR(30) NOT NULL,
 curBalance MONEY NOT NULL
)
GO
CREATE TABLE tblSavings
(intAcctNum INT NOT NULL,
 strLastName CHAR(30) NOT NULL,
 curBalance MONEY NOT NULL
)
GO
```

```
INSERT tblChecking VALUES (1,'smith', $500.00)
INSERT tblChecking VALUES (2,'Jones', $300.00)
INSERT tblSavings VALUES (1,'smith', $100.00)
INSERT tblSavings VALUES (2,'Jones', $200.00)
GO
```

2. Open a second Query Analyzer window (from the File menu, select Connect). In the first window, run

INPUT
```
use pubs
GO
BEGIN TRAN
    UPDATE tblChecking
    SET curBalance = curBalance + $100.00
    WHERE intAcctNum = 1
```

You should get back

OUTPUT
```
(1 row(s) affected)
```

3. In the second window, run

INPUT
```
USE pubs
GO
BEGIN TRAN
    UPDATE tblSavings
    SET curBalance = curBalance - $100.00
    WHERE intAcctNum = 2
```

with the same results. So far, so good.

4. Now, in the first window, run

INPUT
```
UPDATE tblSavings
SET curBalance = curBalance - $100.00
WHERE intAcctNum = 1
```

Notice that the transaction is still running, while the other query window is blocking it. The results of running `sp_lock` in a third window follow:

```
spid   dbid   ObjId       IndId  Type Resource         Mode     Status
------ ------ ----------- ------ ---- ---------------- -------- ------
51     5      0           0      DB                    S        GRANT
51     5      773577794   0      TAB                   IX       GRANT
51     5      773577794   0      RID  1:141:0          X        GRANT
51     5      789577851   0      RID  1:143:1          U        WAIT
51     5      789577851   0      RID  1:143:0          X        GRANT
51     5      789577851   0      PAG  1:143            IX       GRANT
51     5      773577794   0      PAG  1:141            IX       GRANT
51     5      789577851   0      TAB                   IX       GRANT
54     5      789577851   0      PAG  1:143            IX       GRANT
54     5      789577851   0      TAB                   IX       GRANT
54     5      789577851   0      RID  1:143:1          X        GRANT
54     5      0           0      DB                    S        GRANT
55     1      85575343    0      TAB                   IS       GRANT
```

12

Notice that one spid shows the word `WAIT` under Status, indicating that the process is waiting to get a lock and can't run until another spid releases its lock on the required resource.

5. In the second window, run

INPUT
```
UPDATE tblChecking
SET curBalance = curBalance + $100.00
WHERE intAcctNum = 2
```

and you should get a message like this:

OUTPUT
```
Server: Msg 1205, Level 13, State 50, Line 1

Your transaction (Process ID 54) was deadlocked on {lock} resources
with another process and has been chosen as the deadlock victim. Rerun
your transaction.
```

6. The original query is now complete. Run the following clean-up code in the first window:

INPUT
```
COMMIT TRAN
GO
DROP TABLE tblChecking
DROP TABLE tblSavings
GO
```

Deadlock avoidance is important because time and resources are wasted when a deadlock occurs. One way to avoid deadlocks is to always access tables in the same order. In the preceding example, if both transactions had started with the same table, the deadlock wouldn't have occurred. One transaction would have waited for the other to complete before it began. When you do get a deadlock, it's generally a good idea to wait a second or two and then resubmit your transaction.

> **Note**
>
> One common myth is that deadlocks don't occur when row-level locking is in effect. As you can see from the preceding example, deadlocks don't have as much to do with row-level locking as they do with just needing the wrong locks at the wrong time. It's important to run thorough testing to eliminate as many deadlocks as you can from your applications.
>
> For details on troubleshooting locking and deadlocking, please look at Microsoft Knowledge Base Article Q298475 `http://support.microsoft.com/default.aspx?scid=kb;en-us;Q298475` at the time of this writing).

Transaction Isolation Levels

Transaction isolation levels affect the default kinds and duration of locks taken during a `SELECT` statement. As you saw earlier, the types of locks taken can be overridden query by query. The isolation level performs similarly but can be overridden on a session-level basis (meaning that all queries that run during a single session have this setting take effect). To do so, use the `SET TRANSACTION ISOLATION LEVEL` statement:

SYNTAX

```
SET TRANSACTION ISOLATION LEVEL
    {READ COMMITTED | READ UNCOMMITTED | REPEATABLE READ | SERIALIZABLE}
```

- With `READ COMMITTED`, the default, a select query sees only data that the query can get a shared lock on (it doesn't do dirty reads).
- `READ UNCOMMITTED`, which is the same as the optimizer hint `NOLOCK`, allows dirty reads on all queries during a particular session. Be careful with this option because you can view data that hasn't yet been committed in the database.
- `REPEATABLE READ` doesn't release shared locks until the transaction has been completed and is equivalent to the `HOLDLOCK` hint described earlier. It prevents updates and deletes of data you've read.
- `SERIALIZABLE` prevents not just updates and deletes of data you have read, but also prevents inserts within the key range of any data you have read.

Both `REPEATABLE READ` and `SERIALIZABLE` have dramatic effects on concurrency, so you should be very careful that you understand the consequences of using each of them before you implement them.

To view which isolation level is in force, use the `DBCC USEROPTIONS` command. Without having run the `SET TRANSACTION ISOLATION LEVEL` statement, you would see the following:

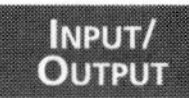

```
DBCC USEROPTIONS
GO

Set Option                 Value
-----------------------    ----------
textsize                   64512
language                   us_english
dateformat                 mdy
datefirst                  7
ansi_null_dflt_on          SET

(5 row(s) affected)

DBCC execution completed. If DBCC printed error messages,
 contact your system administrator.
```

12

Notice the difference after turning on dirty reads with the `READ UNCOMMITTED` option:

```
SET TRANSACTION ISOLATION LEVEL READ UNCOMMITTED
GO
DBCC USEROPTIONS
GO
```

```
Set Option              Value
----------------------- ----------
textsize                64512
language                us_english
dateformat              mdy
datefirst               7
ansi_null_dflt_on       SET
isolation level         read uncommitted

(6 row(s) affected)

DBCC execution completed. If DBCC printed error messages,
contact your system administrator.
```

Summary

Today you learned about transactions, distributed transactions, locks, batches, and scripts. You saw how batches are used from the SQL Server Query Analyzer. You also examined scripts.

You saw how to use transactions and distributed transactions to accomplish "units of work" with SQL Server. You examined the ACID properties of a transaction to understand why they provide reliable and durable data consistency. You also examined the three types of transactions: implicit, explicit, and automatic. (Remember, implicit transactions can be dangerous if you're not prepared for them.) The checkpoint process is used to copy data periodically from memory to disk. You can let SQL Server control the recovery interval, or you can adjust it yourself.

You also learned about locks, including the types of locks available in SQL Server 2000, and examined the syntax for locks, how to override SQL Server's decision about when to use a particular kind of lock, and when the use of lock overrides is appropriate. Remember, most of the time SQL Server picks the correct choice, and you should be very conservative in overriding locks.

You also learned how to observe locks through T-SQL and SQL Server Enterprise Manager. Finally, you learned how to create a deadlock situation and avoid them in the future.

Q&A

Q Is this a valid example of a batch?

```
BEGIN TRAN
    SELECT * FROM titles
    UPDATE titles set PRICE = $12.99 WHERE TITLE_ID = 'BU1032'
```

```
    ROLLBACK TRAN
    SELECT * FROM titles
COMMIT TRAN
```

A No. If you were to run the preceding set of SQL statements, you would end up with the following error message:

```
Server: Msg 3902, Level 16, State 1
The COMMIT TRANSACTION request has no corresponding BEGIN TRANSACTION.
```

You get this message because the transaction is rolled back by the time the `COMMIT TRAN` is run.

Q True or false: The `COMMIT TRAN` writes all modified pages in memory to disk.

A False. The `CHECKPOINT` process writes modified pages from memory to database files in SQL Server (both data pages and log records). The `COMMIT TRAN` statement writes the modified LOG records for each transaction to the transaction log files for each database.

Q What kinds of locks are compatible with a shared lock?

A Shared locks are compatible with shared locks and update locks. It doesn't matter whether they're row, page, or table locks. Extents and databases don't really get shared locks.

Q What is it called when two transactions have an exclusive lock on a resource and each of the other transactions needs to lock the resource the other transaction has locked?

A A deadlock. You can avoid deadlocks by accessing tables in the same sequence when you write separate processes—preferably in stored procedures.

Workshop

This section provides quiz questions to help you solidify your understanding of the concepts presented today. In addition to the quiz questions, exercises are provided to let you practice what you've learned today. Try to understand the quiz and exercise answers before continuing onto tomorrow's lesson. Answers are provided in Appendix A, "Answers to Quiz Questions."

Quiz

1. What `CREATE` statements are allowed within a single batch?
2. What locks will be held at the time of the `COMMIT TRAN` from the following batch?
3. How do you enable remote stored procedures to automatically be part of a distributed transaction at all times?

4. How do you cancel a transaction that you began with implicit transactions?
5. If you roll back a transaction from within a trigger on `table1` in the code listed here, will `SELECT * FROM AUTHORS` be run?

```
BEGIN TRAN
INSERT table1 VALUES (3)
GO
SELECT * FROM AUTHORS
COMMIT TRAN
```

Exercise

1. You've added a new book to your inventory (*How to Surf the Net in 3 Easy Steps*). Not only is the title new, but also the publisher (Waycool Publishers) and the two authors (Ann Jackson and Bob Greene). Write a script to add all this information so that it all concludes or fails together.

DAY 13

Indexing for Performance

On Day 12, you looked at the programming extensions to SQL Server and Transact-SQL, as well as transactions. Transactions allow you to logically group database modifications and have these logical groupings either fully change or fully abort as a single unit of work. You also examined locking and how it's used to protect a relational database and make it appear as though it's a single-user system.

Today's lesson focuses on indexes. Indexes provide a set of logical pointers to your data, much like an index in the back of a book helps you find things you're looking for. Although all the queries you examined earlier this week work without indexes (`SELECT`, `INSERT`, `UPDATE`, `DELETE`), they usually run faster with indexes.

Today you'll start by justifying why you want indexes and then examine some of the basics of B+-tree indexes (the type of index SQL Server implements). You will then look at the syntax of the `CREATE INDEX` statement. You will be introduced to several options and performance issues associated with indexes. You will also examine indexes on views and why they can be *very* helpful. Then you will examine some of the `DBCC` commands that you can use with indexes, as well as other maintenance issues. You will finish by looking at SQL Server 2000's full-text indexing capabilities.

Why Use Indexes?

NEW TERM You might want to index for many reasons, the most obvious being the one I just mentioned—speed. Without indexes, SQL Server accesses data by reading every page of data on each table you've specified in your SQL statement. This *table scan* (reading every page of the data) can be an excellent method of data retrieval. For example, if a table is small, or if you are accessing a large portion of the table, a table scan might very well be the best plan to access the data. However, quite frequently data access is much faster with an index. It can also speed up joins between tables.

Another reason to create an index is to enforce uniqueness. Having two identical rows in a table isn't an error condition. However, that's probably not how most people want to store data. Imagine a system that keeps track of customers. If you can't tell your customers apart, you might have difficulty keeping customers when you bill them incorrectly. You have several options to uniquely identify your customers. You could give them numbers, use their names and birthdates together, use their credit card numbers, or use some other value or set of values. Regardless of the choice you make, the way to tell SQL Server about your choice is to use a *unique* index. Day 14, "Ensuring Data Integrity," will discuss another way to enforce uniqueness—the unique constraint—but even then SQL Server is still creating a unique index as its enforcement mechanism.

Index Structures

An index typically consists of a set of pages known as a *B+ tree*. A B+ tree looks something like the illustration in Figure 13.1.

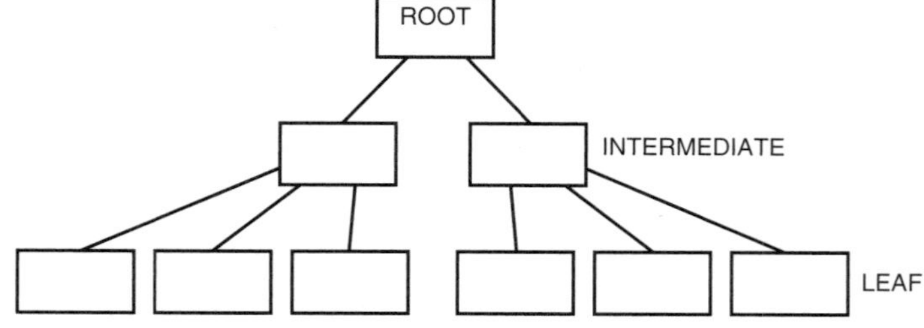

FIGURE 13.1
A B+ tree.

As we mentioned previously, an index helps find data quickly. To find an individual row of data, you navigate the B+ tree to find that row and then move to the individual data row. You start with the root page. A pointer to the root page is located in the `sysindexes` system table (oddly enough, in the column named root for *nonclustered* indexes). The root page contains index entries (the data for the column or columns you've indexed), as well as pointers to each page below the root page. Each index might have one or more intermediate levels. Again, each entry has an index value and a pointer to the next page below.

NEW TERM On the leaf pages (the lowest level in the tree), what you find depends on whether a table has a *clustered index*. Logically speaking, you would find an entry for every row in the table being indexed, as well as a pointer to the data page and row number that has the actual data row. If the table also has a clustered index, any nonclustered indexes contain the key values from the clustered index rather than the data page and row number information. Clustered and nonclustered indexes will be explained later, but for now think of a clustered index as a way to presort the actual data. Tables without a clustered index are called *heaps*, and nonclustered indexes are separate index structures that don't directly sort the data.

The data itself is stored on pages called *data pages* (no sense in making this hard). Each page is 8,192 bytes in size, with a header of 96 bytes. Hence, each page has 8,096 bytes available for storage. Each page has the same basic structure.

Figure 13.2 shows an example of what an index might look like. This index is on a first-name column.

FIGURE 13.2

A sample B+ index.

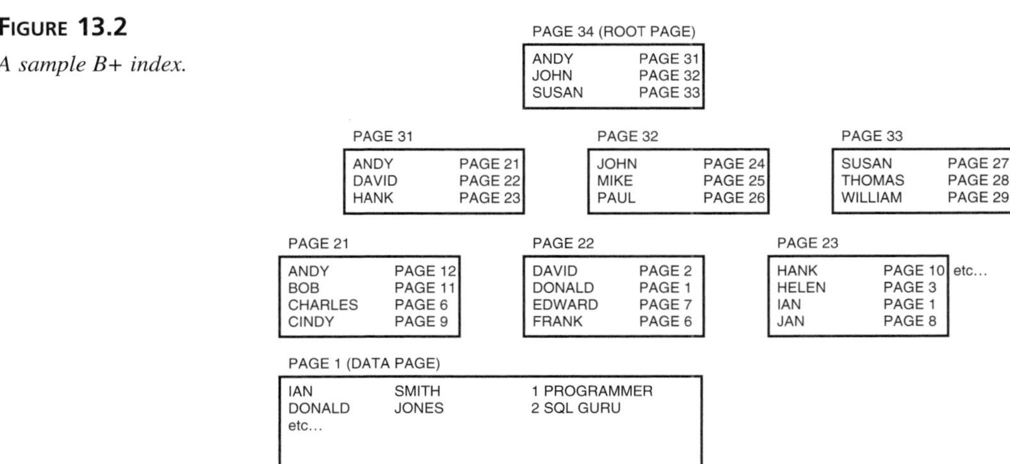

Each level of the index is a doubly linked list. Each page knows about the page before it and the page that's logically after it. On the root and intermediate levels of the index, each index value is the first value on the page of the next level below it. The leaf level of the index contains one entry for each row in the table. Notice that the index is sorted based on the column (or columns) you've chosen as your index key. This ordering doesn't change the physical sort order of the data.

When you modify data in the table, every index on that table is also modified. SQL Server guarantees consistency between the data in your tables and their indexes. This is good, in the sense that you want to have excellent data integrity. However, it also means that `INSERT`, `UPDATE`, and `DELETE` operations that might have been rather quick before now could have quite a bit more work to do and might run a little bit more slowly. Adding a new row with the `INSERT` statement normally takes two input/outputs (I/Os)—one for the data and one for the log. If you have two indexes on the table, adding a row takes at least two more I/Os, and perhaps more than that. You must balance your needs between data modifications and faster queries.

How do you use an index? Find a row of data in Figure 13.2. Pretend that the index is on first name. To find the row with a first name of Donald, you look on the root page. Because Donald is "less" than John, you follow the entry for Andy to page 6. On page 6, you find that Donald is "higher" than David but "lower" than Hank, so you go to page 22. On page 22, you find that the entry for Donald points to page 1 (which is a data page because this is the leaf level of the index). In SQL Server, you would also find the row number of the row that contains Donald as the first name, but it was left off the figure for simplicity's sake. Now you read the row from page 1 and can access any information about Donald that is stored on the page. SQL Server uses an index to find data in exactly the same way.

Index Options

Several options for indexes are available. You must specify these choices and understand them before you can create your indexes.

Clustered Indexes

New Term You have two options for physical storage of your indexes. The first type is known as clustered. A *clustered* index physically re-sorts the data. Rather than have a completely separate index structure (such as the one described earlier), the leaf level of the index is the data. Accessing data using a clustered index is almost always faster than using a nonclustered index because the additional lookup of the data page/row from the leaf level of the index isn't necessary.

Because the data is physically sorted in the order of the index key, you can have only one clustered index on a table (you wouldn't want to keep multiple copies of the data). Because only one clustered index is available, you must choose it carefully. Choosing a clustered index can be fairly complex, but some basic guidelines are included here.

One major issue that comes up with clustered indexes is free space. Creating a clustered index requires that at least 120 percent of the size of the table be available as temporary workspace. This free space must exist in the database where you are creating the index. To create the index, SQL Server copies the table, sorts the copy in the order of the index values (in ascending order), builds the index structures (the root page and any intermediate pages that are needed), and then drops the original table. When this operation is complete, the clustered index takes only about 5 percent more space than the table itself. The overhead (the nondata pages) of this type of index is relatively small but depends on the size of the values being indexed.

This overhead might not sound too bad because you need the free space only during the index creation, but it can be difficult to justify. If you have a 500MB database, but one table in the database is 100MB, and you want to create a clustered index on that table, you would need at least 120MB of unused space in the database.

Another issue of critical importance in SQL Server 2000 is that the key values (indexed columns) that you choose for your clustered index are "carried" along into the nonclustered indexes. Therefore, if you choose a wide clustered index—for example, a `Char(30)`—not only does it take longer to search the clustered index itself, but all your nonclustered indexes also have to carry the `Char(30)` value of your clustered index key on every row in the nonclustered indexes. That's a significant amount of overhead, so you should keep your clustered index keys as small as possible. You also should make sure that the clustered key you select isn't updated frequently, because all your nonclustered indexes need to be updated when the clustered index values change.

The other issue to be aware of is the order in which you create your indexes. Because the clustered index key is part of the key values for each of the nonclustered indexes, each nonclustered index needs to be rebuilt. Therefore, always create your clustered indexes first.

Figure 13.3 shows an example of a clustered index. The data is sorted in the order of the index key (the first name again), and the data on the leaf level of the index (the data page) is sorted by first name.

13

Nonclustered Indexes

New Term A *nonclustered index* is basically the same as a standard B+ tree index. Each index has a root page, one or more levels of intermediate pages, and a leaf level, which contains one row for each row in the table. Nonclustered indexes require more space overall than clustered indexes but take much less space during the creation process.

You can have up to 249 nonclustered indexes on a single table. The order in which you create them isn't significant. A nonclustered index doesn't change the order of the data, as does a clustered index. The rows in the leaf level of the index are sorted in the order of the columns chosen as part of the index. Each row contains a pointer to the page number/row number combination of the data in the table if no clustered index exists, or the value of the clustering index key if the table also has a clustered index. Refer to Figure 13.2 for an example of a nonclustered index.

FIGURE 13.3

A clustered index example.

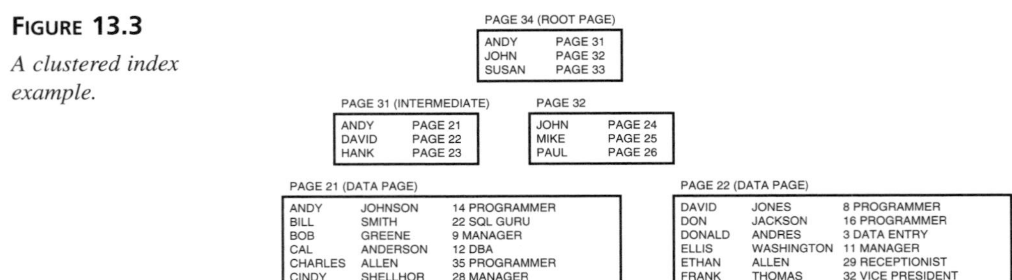

Unique/Nonunique Indexes

Uniqueness determines whether duplicate values are allowed in your index. For example, in the first name index you saw earlier, no two people would be allowed to have the same first name if the index were unique. SQL Server indexes are nonunique by default, meaning that duplicate values are allowed.

If your data supports it, making an index unique can significantly improve performance when you're using that index. When the value you are searching for is found, no more searches are necessary (if you know only one entry exists, when you find it, you can stop looking for more).

Clustered indexes are particularly good candidates for unique indexes because SQL Server internally always forces clustered indexes to be unique. If you don't create a unique clustered index, SQL Server generates a hidden additional key value to force uniqueness of the index. So, why make SQL Server generate this key if you have a good candidate key that's also unique?

Single-Column/Multicolumn Indexes

NEW TERM Many indexes have only one column; however, you can easily create a multicolumn index. Multicolumn indexes can be quite useful because you can reduce the number of indexes used by SQL Server and get faster performance. If you specify both columns together frequently during queries, the columns are an excellent candidate for a *composite index* (just another name for an index with multiple columns). Composite indexes can be clustered or nonclustered, contain anywhere from 2 to 16 columns, and be up to 900 bytes wide.

The trade-off here is that if you make an index too wide, it is no longer useful because it might take less time to scan the table rather than use the index. Indexing, unfortunately, involves many trade-offs and rarely presents obvious choices for multiple applications.

Ascending/Descending Indexes

In all previous versions of SQL Server, indexes were always assumed to be ascending (a very natural way to think of indexes). So, if you were to sort the alphabet, A would come first, and Z would come last. However, sometimes you want a list sorted in descending order (that is, sorted from Z to A in that order). SQL Server 2000 fully supports having descending indexes.

Figure 13.4 shows a nonclustered index on first name (the same index as Figure 13.2), but the index is now stored in descending order. You find rows in exactly the same fashion, simply navigating through the index starting at the root page. The advantage here is that if you want your query to return data in descending order, it can be returned without an additional sort.

FIGURE 13.4

A nonclustered descending index.

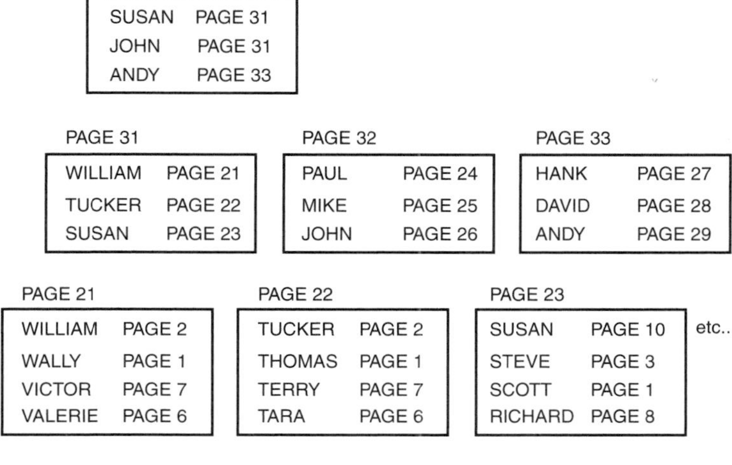

SQL Server Indexes

SQL Server implements B+ trees to build its indexes. You use the CREATE INDEX statement to create the indexes you need:

SYNTAX

```
CREATE [UNIQUE] [CLUSTERED | NONCLUSTERED] INDEX index_name
ON [owner.][table_name | view_name]
(column_name [ASC|DESC] [,...n])
[WITH
   [PAD_INDEX][[,] FILLFACTOR = x]
   [[,] IGNORE_DUP_KEY]
   [[,] DROP_EXISTING]
   [[,] STATISTICS_NORECOMPUTE]
   [[,] SORT_IN_TEMPDB]]
[ON filegroup]
```

In this syntax,

- UNIQUE specifies that no duplicates are allowed for this index. The default is nonunique; duplicate index entries are allowed.
- CLUSTERED specifies that the data itself will be physically sorted and become the leaf level of the index. Clustered index values must be unique. If you create a UNIQUE clustered index, there's no problem. However, if you create a nonunique clustered index, a 4-byte "uniqueifer" is added to each clustered index key to guarantee uniqueness.
- NONCLUSTERED specifies that a normal B+ index will be created as a completely separate object. This is the default type of index.
- *index_name* is the SQL Server unique name for this object.
- *table_name* is the name of the table that contains the columns you want to index.
- *view_name* is the name of the view containing the columns you want to index.
- *column_name* is the name of the column (or columns) to be indexed. You can create an index with up to 16 columns up to 900 bytes wide. The columns can't be of type text, image, bit, or ntext. However, new to SQL Server 2000, the column can be a computed column.
- ASC|DESC indicates whether the column is to be sorted in ascending (ASC) order (for example, A–Z) or descending (DESC) order (for example, Z–A). Ascending is the default, which is consistent with previous releases that didn't have the descending option.
- *filegroup* is the name of the filegroup on which the index should be created. If *filegroup* isn't specified, the index is created on the default filegroup.

For example, the following code lines create a table called myauthors in the pubs database and then copy all the data from the authors table. Then the code creates an index on the au_id column of the myauthors table. The resulting clustered index enforces uniqueness.

```
USE PUBS
-- CREATE THE TABLE
CREATE TABLE dbo.myauthors (
    au_id id NOT NULL ,
    au_lname varchar (40) NOT NULL ,
    au_fname varchar (20) NOT NULL ,
    phone char (12) NOT NULL ,
    address varchar (40) NULL ,
    city varchar (20) NULL ,
    state char (2) NULL ,
    zip char (5) NULL ,
    contract bit NOT NULL)
-- Copy the data from the authors table into myauthors
INSERT myauthors select * from authors
-- create the unique clustered index on the myauthors table
Create unique clustered index myauind on myauthors (au_id)
```

The following code creates a nonunique, nonclustered descending index on the au_fname column of the same table:

```
Use pubs
Create index mynamindex on myauthors (au_fname DESC)
```

Notice that this Transact-SQL command is identical functionally and might be a little more obvious:

```
Use pubs
Create nonclustered index mynameindex on myauthors (au_fname)
```

The fillfactor and pad_index Options

The fillfactor option specifies how full each page in the leaf level of an index should be. The default fill factor is 0. Because fillfactor is a configuration parameter, be sure to check that it hasn't been changed. Remember that you can check it either from SQL Server Enterprise Manager, or you can run sp_configure without any parameters. Your output should look something like this:

13

```
EXEC sp_configure
go

name                     minimum  maximum     config_value run_value
------------------------ -------- ----------- ------------ ---------
allow updates            0        1           0            0
default language         0        9999        0            0
```

```
fill factor (%)            0      100         0       0
language in cache          3      100         3       3
max async IO               1      255         32      32
max text repl size (B)     0      2147483647  65536   65536
max worker threads         10     1024        255     255
nested triggers            0      1           1       1
network packet size (B)    4096   65535       4096    4096
recovery interval (min)    0      32767       0       0
remote access              0      1           1       1
remote proc trans          0      1           0       0
show advanced options      0      1           0       0
user options               0      4095        0       0
(14 row(s) affected) ...
```

Look for the name `fill factor` in the output, and verify that the config_value and run_value columns both reflect a `fillfactor` setting of `0`.

If you don't specify `fillfactor` in your `CREATE INDEX` statement, the default value (typically `0`) is used. A value of `0` means that the leaf pages of your index are almost full but that nonleaf pages (intermediate pages and the root page) still have room for at least two more rows. If the `fillfactor` is `100`, all leaf pages are 100 percent full, with no room for additional rows. Again, the root and intermediate pages still have room for two additional rows. Any other value is the percentage of each leaf page to fill with rows. SQL Server rounds the percentage to the nearest row size, so you rarely get exactly the percentage you ask for, but the result is as close as SQL Server can get it.

If you create a clustered index with a `fillfactor` of `50`, each page would be 50 percent full. In Figure 13.5, you can see that the leaf page of the clustered index is only half full. The code might look like this:

```
CREATE INDEX aunameindex on authors (au_fname)
WITH FILLFACTOR = 50
GO
```


FIGURE 13.5

A clustered index with `fillfactor` *equal to* `50`.

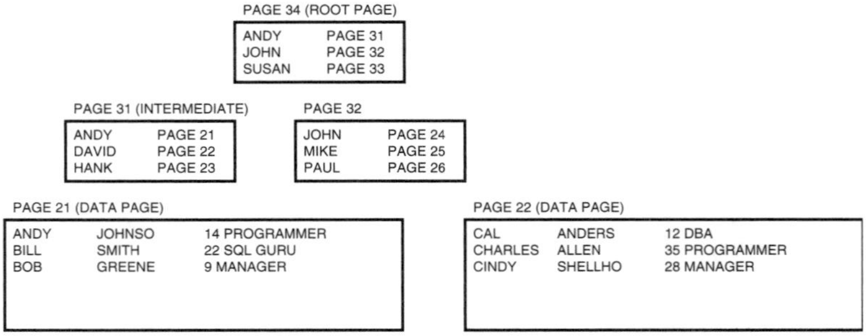

`fillfactor` isn't maintained on the index. If you create an index with a fill factor of `50` (meaning that each page is half full), over time it's likely that some pages will fill up and others will get close to empty. If you want to see your fill factor reestablished, you have to do one of the following:

- Drop and re-create the index with the fill factor specified again.
- Use the `DBCC DBREINDEX` command.
- Use the `DBCC INDEXDEFRAG` command.

Each option reinstates your fill factor. You can find the tool to help determine when you must reindex in `DBCC SHOWCONTIG`, also examined later today. However, SQL Server automatically does quite a bit of this cleanup itself.

When you use the `pad_index` option with a fill factor, the option specifies that the nonleaf pages of the index have the fill factor applied to them as well as to the leaf pages. The easiest way to understand the `pad_index` option is to look at an example.

If you create the same index as in Figure 13.5 but add the `pad_index` option, the nonleaf pages now also have the fill factor applied. Notice that if your rows don't fit perfectly, SQL Server gets as close as possible to the fill factor you've requested. For example, the following code might create an index like the one in Figure 13.6:

```
CREATE INDEX aunameindex on authors (au_fname)
WITH FILLFACTOR = 50, PAD_INDEX
GO
```

FIGURE 13.6

A clustered index with `pad_index`.

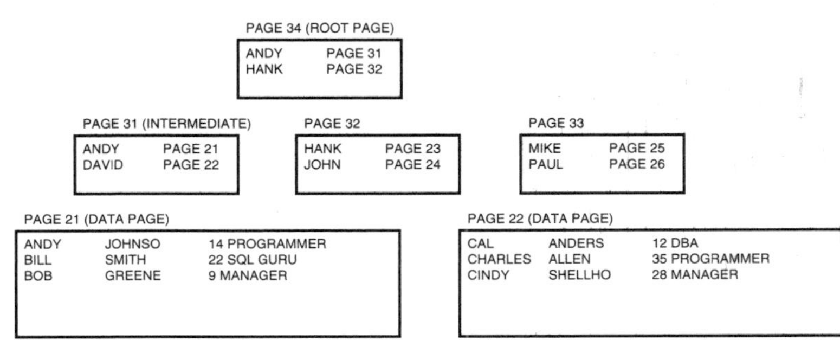

13

NEW TERM So far, you've seen how `fillfactor` and `pad_index` work, but not why you would want to use them. Often, specifying a fill factor can be quite useful. To understand why this is the case, you should know a couple of terms. The first is a *page split*. When a SQL Server page is full and another row must be put on that page, a page split occurs. A new page is assigned to the index or table, and 50 percent of the rows are moved to the new page. Then the new row is added in the appropriate location. As you might imagine, this operation can be expensive if it happens frequently. If you use a fill factor when you create your index, you can allow new rows to be added without causing page splits. Setting the appropriate fill factor will likely improve performance. However, getting the proper fill factor will mostly come from experience.

This option can be particularly useful with clustered indexes because the leaf level of the index is made up of the actual data pages. Be aware, however, that applying a fill factor such as 50 to the clustered index approximately doubles the size of the table. This approach can have a dramatic impact on space usage and should be done with some caution.

New Term Page splitting on *heaps* (tables without a clustered index) can be particularly expensive in terms of its impact because of the way nonclustered indexes are stored. Each row in the nonclustered index has a pointer to the data row's page-number/row-number combination. If a page split on the heap occurs, approximately half of the rows move. This means that half of the rows have to modify each entry for each nonclustered index. All these modifications occur while you wait for your data insert or update to occur, resulting in slower response times. Therefore, you should probably have a clustered index on most tables. As you saw earlier, the nonclustered indexes don't point to the physical location of the rows if a clustered index exists, so page splits in the clustered index don't affect the nonclustered indexes.

When you add `pad_index`, you can avoid nonleaf page splits as well. This way, you will increase space usage—but not nearly as much as you would by using the `fillfactor`.

The `DROP_EXISTING` Option

The `DROP_EXISTING` option specifies that an index should be dropped and re-created (essentially, this is a "reorganization" of the index). If you are dropping and re-creating the clustered index, you might think that nonclustered indexes would be affected. However, SQL Server 2000 is smart enough to simply drop and re-create the clustered index itself. Because the nonclustered indexes have the key value of the clustered index as their row identifier, and that value doesn't change during the `CREATE INDEX` with the `DROP_EXISTING` clause, the nonclustered indexes don't need to be changed.

This option is most useful for clustered indexes, but it can also be used on nonclustered indexes. The `DBCC DBREINDEX` option, described later today, has similar functionality, but the `DROP_EXISTING` option is probably a better long-term choice overall. However, for SQL Server 2000, Microsoft has introduced an online index reorganization utility, `DBCC INDEXDEFRAG`, which you will also examine later today.

The `STATISTICS_NORECOMPUTE` Option

SQL Server 2000 automatically recomputes statistics on indexes as needed. You can disable this feature if you want by using the STATISTICS_NORECOMPUTE option. To re-enable the automatic statistics gathering feature of SQL Server, run UPDATE STATISTICS without NORECOMPUTE. You'll learn more about UPDATE STATISTICS later today. Turning off automatic gathering of statistics for your indexes generally is a bad idea. The SQL Server 2000 optimizer is very dependent on accurate statistics to optimize your queries.

The `SORT_IN_TEMPDB` Option

SQL Server 2000 introduces the ability to use tempdb to temporarily store intermediate data structures when creating an index. This assumes that the index you are creating is larger than the amount of memory physically available to SQL Server 2000. When this is the case, SQL Server needs to spool some temporary data structures used to create the indexes out to disk. Without the SORT_IN_TEMPDB option, those structures go into the database where you're creating the index. With this option requested, these temporary structures are created in the tempdb database. If tempdb is on a separate disk, this process may result in better index creation performance but will probably require more disk space than if you create the index without using tempdb.

The `IGNORE_DUP_KEY` Option

The IGNORE_DUP_KEY option specifies that when you're running a multirow update against a table with a unique clustered index, duplicate rows from that insert are quietly discarded and the statement succeeds, but SQL Server returns a warning. The following code sample shows how this works:

```
create table t1 (col1 int not null, col2 char(5) not null)
go
create unique clustered index myind on t1 (col1) with ignore_dup_key
go
create table t2 (col1 int not null, col2 char(5) not null)
go
insert t2 values (1, 'abcde')
insert t2 values (2, 'abcde')
insert t2 values (2, 'abcde')
insert t2 values (3, 'abcde')

insert t1 select * from t2
```

13

After running this code, you get the following message:

OUTPUT

```
Server: Msg 3604, Level 16, State 1, Line 1
Duplicate key was ignored.
```

If you were to select then from table t1, you would see three rows, as expected.

Index Usage

At this point, you've examined index basics and how to create SQL Server indexes. However, you haven't seen which indexes to create or when they should be used.

When Will My Index Be Used?

You can start with the most obvious question: How do I know when an index will be used? When a query is submitted to SQL Server, the query is broken apart and analyzed. In terms of optimization for indexing, the most important part of the query is the `WHERE` clause. A statement in the `WHERE` clause of a query is the most likely way that SQL Server will know how to optimize your query to use an index. However, just because your query contains a `WHERE` clause doesn't mean that an index will be used. Consider this query, for example:

```
SELECT au_id, au_fname, au_lname
FROM pubs..authors
WHERE state = 'CA'
GO
```

If the state column has an index, but most of the authors come from California, there's no point to using an index. A table scan (reading every data page in the table) is most likely the most efficient plan to get the data. The phrase *the most efficient plan* means the most efficient in terms of minimizing the number of pages needed to be read by SQL Server. The other terms for this are *minimizing I/O* and *logical page reads*.

Given a similar query that returns only one row, it most likely makes sense to use an index. For example, if the au_id column has a clustered index, this query would almost certainly use the index:

```
SELECT au_id, au_fname, au_lname
FROM pubs..authors
WHERE au_id = '341-22-1782'
```

How Do You Verify Index Usage?

The next question is how can you verify which index will be used by your query? SQL Server 2000 includes many options to examine which indexes are used to support your queries. You can use the Transact-SQL statements `SET SHOWPLAN_ALL ON` or `SET SHOWPLAN_TEXT ON`. If you are using the SQL Server Query Analyzer to run the showplans, you can run either option. However, if you are using a command-line tool such as `isql.exe` or `osql.exe`, use the `SHOWPLAN_TEXT` statement option. To see the difference, run the script in Listing 13.1 to create a table and insert some data into the table. The script must insert some volume of data so that indexes have a chance to be used.

The SET options for showplan *must* be in a batch by themselves.

LISTING 13.1 Monitoring Indexes

```
USE PUBS
CREATE TABLE PUBS..INDEXTAB
(col1 int not null,
col2 varchar(250) not null,
col3 varchar(250) not null,
col4 varchar(250) not null,
col5 varchar(250) not null)

insert indextab values (1,'adam','col3','col4','col5')
insert indextab values (2,'bob','col3','col4','col5')
insert indextab values (3,'charles','col3','col4','col5')
insert indextab values (4,'david','col3','col4','col5')
insert indextab values (5,'edward','col3','col4','col5')
insert indextab values (6,'frank','col3','col4','col5')
insert indextab values (7,'george','col3','col4','col5')
insert indextab values (8,'hank','col3','col4','col5')
insert indextab values (9,'ida','col3','col4','col5')
insert indextab values (10,'john','col3','col4','col5')
insert indextab values (11,'kim','col3','col4','col5')
insert indextab values (12,'loni','col3','col4','col5')
insert indextab values (13,'mike','col3','col4','col5')
insert indextab values (14,'nikki','col3','col4','col5')
insert indextab values (15,'oprah','col3','col4','col5')
insert indextab values (16,'paul','col3','col4','col5')
insert indextab values (17,'quan','col3','col4','col5')
insert indextab values (18,'richard','col3','col4','col5')
insert indextab values (19,'sam','col3','col4','col5')
insert indextab values (20,'tom','col3','col4','col5')
insert indextab values (21,'uma','col3','col4','col5')
insert indextab values (22,'vera','col3','col4','col5')
insert indextab values (23,'walter','col3','col4','col5')
insert indextab values (24,'xray','col3','col4','col5')
insert indextab values (25,'yuma','col3','col4','col5')
insert indextab values (26,'zane','col3','col4','col5')
insert indextab values (27,'ann','col3','col4','col5')
insert indextab values (28,'bill','col3','col4','col5')
insert indextab values (29,'cathy','col3','col4','col5')
insert indextab values (30,'dawn','col3','col4','col5')
insert indextab values (31,'ellen','col3','col4','col5')
insert indextab values (32,'fran','col3','col4','col5')
insert indextab values (33,'grant','col3','col4','col5')
insert indextab values (34,'helen','col3','col4','col5')
insert indextab values (35,'irwin','col3','col4','col5')
```

LISTING 13.1 continued

```
insert indextab values (36,'jack','col3','col4','col5')
insert indextab values (37,'kathy','col3','col4','col5')
insert indextab values (38,'lance','col3','col4','col5')
insert indextab values (39,'molly','col3','col4','col5')
insert indextab values (40,'nancy','col3','col4','col5')
CREATE CLUSTERED INDEX CL_MYINDEX on indextab (col1)
```

> **Tip:** You will probably want to change Query Analyzer to return results in text to interpret the results of the next few statements. Reading them is very hard if you leave Query Analyzer in the default mode of returning results in a grid.

First, run with the SHOWPLAN_TEXT option:

INPUT

```
USE PUBS
GO
SET SHOWPLAN_TEXT ON
GO
select col1, col2 from indextab
where col2 = 'ann'
```

The output generated by these statements looks similar to this:

OUTPUT

```
StmtText
----------------------------------------------------------
select col1, col2 from indextab
where col2 = 'ann'

(1 row(s) affected)

StmtText
--------------------------------------------------------------------
  |--Clustered Index
    ➥Scan(OBJECT:([pubs].[dbo].[INDEXTAB].[CL_MYINDEX]),
    ➥WHERE:([INDEXTAB].[col2]=[@1]))
(1 row(s) affected)
```

As you can see from the preceding output, SQL Server chose to use a clustered index scan to run this query. Next, examine the same query using the SHOWPLAN_ALL option:

INPUT

```
USE PUBS
GO
SET SHOWPLAN_ALL ON
GO
select col1, col2 from indextab
where col2 = 'ann'
```

You get the output as shown in Figure 13.7.

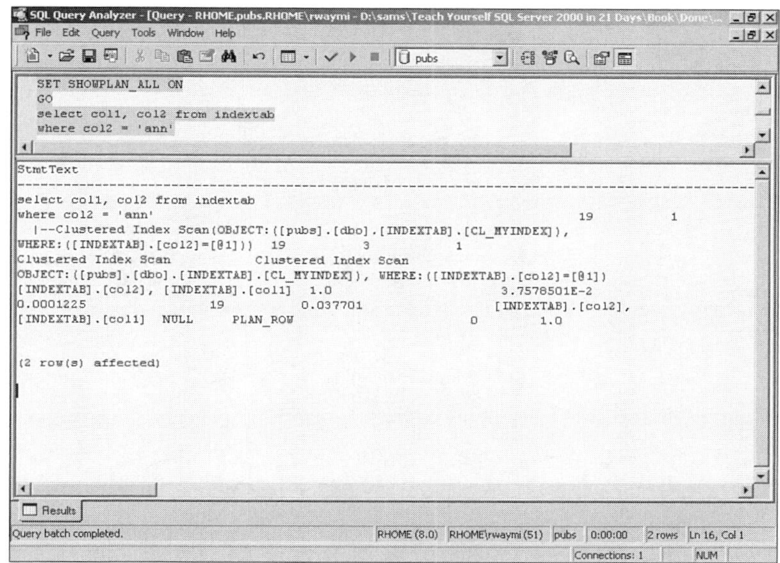

FIGURE 13.7
The SHOWPLAN_ALL *option in the SQL Server Query Analyzer.*

Notice that this is the same information that was returned with the SHOWPLAN_TEXT option, but with additional details. I recommend that you stick with using SHOWPLAN_TEXT unless you become an expert at tuning queries and understanding items such as the TotalSubtreeCost.

If you want to see which indexes are on a table, you can run the following sp_helpindex system stored procedure:

INPUT/OUTPUT

```
SET SHOWPLAN_ALL OFF (or turn off any other showplan options first)
GO
EXEC sp_helpindex indextab
GO
index_name        index_description                   index_keys
----------------- ----------------------------------- ----------
CL_MYINDEX        clustered located on PRIMARY        col1
```

Now create a second index on the table so that you can examine a plan on something other than a clustered index:

INPUT

```
CREATE INDEX NONCL_MYINDEX on indextab (col2)
GO
SET SHOWPLAN_TEXT ON
GO
select col1, col2 from indextab
where col2 = 'ann'
```

OUTPUT

```
StmtText
-------------------------------------------------------
select col1, col2 from indextab
where col2 = 'ann'

(1 row(s) affected)

StmtText
----------------------------------------------------------
  |--Index Seek(OBJECT:([pubs].[dbo].[INDEXTAB].[NONCL_MYINDEX]),
   ➥SEEK:([INDEXTAB].[col2]=[@1]) ORDERED FORWARD)

(1 row(s) affected)
```

Notice that SQL Server has now used an "index seek" on the index `noncl_myindex`. This simply means that the index is used to find all rows for `ann`.

You can also examine the plans by using the SQL Server Query Analyzer's graphical showplan options. You can actually see two plans: the estimated execution plan or the actual showplan from running the query. The difference is that the actual showplan has exact numbers, whereas the estimated plan shows you what the SQL Server query optimizer thinks will happen. You run the same query as before, except you turn on the Show Execution Plan option (either from the Query menu or by enabling the option by using the Execute Mode button). You then see something similar to Figure 13.8 when you click the Execution Plan tab at the bottom of your screen. If you move the mouse pointer over any item in the graphical window, you are presented with detailed information about that particular query step. The output here is relatively simple, but for very large plans, the graphical plan can be a blessing compared to textual showplans.

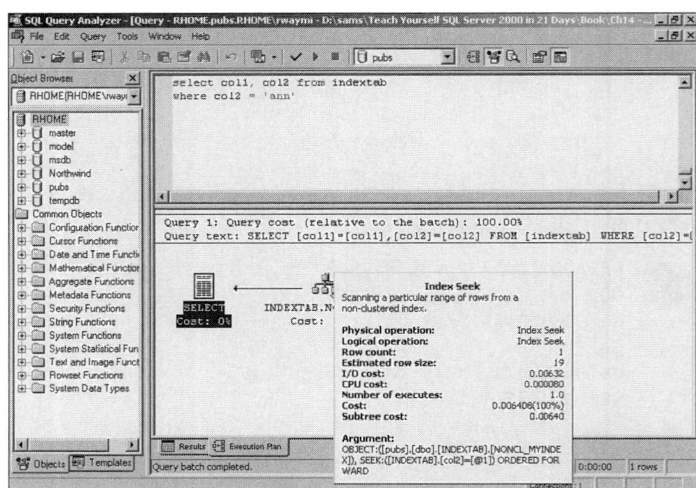

FIGURE 13.8

The graphical showplan in the SQL Server Query Analyzer.

All you've seen so far is what choice SQL Server made. The other part of the puzzle you must fill in is how SQL Server makes its decision. For the most part, the optimization is done based on how much work is required to answer your question. SQL Server wants to answer your question as quickly as it can doing the least amount of work. That usually translates into minimizing the amount of logical I/O that's done.

NEW TERM *Logical I/O* is data access by SQL Server. Each logical I/O means that SQL Server has read a single 8KB page. The total number of pages accessed is always equal to the number of logical I/Os. SQL Server differentiates between logical and physical I/O. If a query takes 50 logical I/Os and only 20 physical I/Os, it means that 30 of the 50 pages it needed were already in memory. The other 20 pages had to be retrieved physically from the disks and brought into memory so that they could be read—hence the term *physical I/O*. SQL Server tries to minimize the amount of physical I/O access. You can see the amount of I/O a query uses by using the statement `SET STATISTICS IO ON`:

INPUT

```
SET STATISTICS IO ON
GO

SELECT col1,col2
FROM indextab
where col1 < 3
GO
```

OUTPUT

```
STEP 1
col1        col2
----------- -----
1           adam
2           bob

(2 row(s) affected)

Table 'INDEXTAB'. Scan count 1, logical reads 2, physical reads 0,
read-ahead reads 0.
```


> **Note**
>
> Be sure to turn off the `NOEXEC` option before using the statistics I/O command (if you've enabled it), because you must actually run a query to get statistics I/O information. Because `SHOWPLAN` options don't actually run a query, they are also incompatible with getting `STATISTICS IO` information.

Notice that two logical reads were required to answer this query: one read to get the root page of the clustered index and one to read the leaf page of the index. Remember that because it's a clustered index, the leaf page is the data page. SQL Server normally favors using a clustered index.

In Figure 13.9, you can see how you can figure out these two logical reads. SQL Server must read the root page of the index and then the leaf level of the index to return the data. Note that this index has no intermediate pages (it's too small).

FIGURE 13.9

Your clustered index.

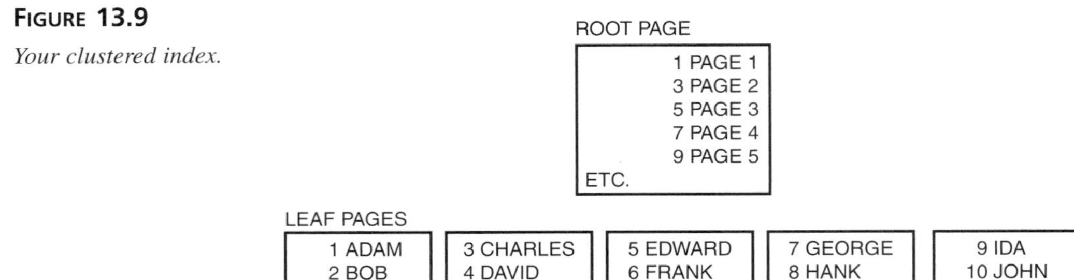

SQL Server also uses information about how much memory is available, how much central processing unit (CPU) time is required to process each query option, and how busy the system is. Therefore, you might see SQL Server choose a plan that takes more I/O than another because it actually costs less when all factors are taken together. The SQL Server optimizer is much more sophisticated than it was in versions before 7.0 and takes more of this information in to make decisions about which indexes to use. If you examine the output from the `SHOWPLAN_ALL` report, you see many of these numbers reported. How to use these numbers is beyond the scope of this book.

Now that you've seen how SQL Server tries to access your tables, what can you do about it? Also, what do you do if you've created indexes and are sure that they should be used, yet SQL Server won't use them? You can override the optimizer.

Overriding the Optimizer

To override the optimizer, you can specify optimizer hints. First, consider that most of the time the SQL Server optimizer is correct. If you're still sure that you are right and that SQL Server is wrong, and you've updated your statistics and checked the `SHOWPLAN` output, you can consider using optimizer hints. This section examines each option to provide the correct information to the SQL Server optimizer.

To select an index, specify either the index name or the index number as part of your select statement. You can find an index's number by querying the `sysindexes` system table in your database:

INPUT
```
SELECT col1, col2
FROM indextab (index = noncl_myindex)
```

Caution

SQL Server always uses the index you've selected, regardless of what the optimizer thinks is a proper choice. SQL Server never reevaluates your selection, so remember to retest your choice periodically. This is especially true when you apply service packs or upgrade SQL Server. Therefore, using optimizer hints is rarely necessary—and sometimes downright dangerous.

This query normally uses a clustered index scan, but in this case, you told it to use the nonclustered index that you created earlier.

The right approach to forcing SQL Server to use a table scan involves understanding a little bit about how indexes are numbered in the `sysindexes` table. Nonclustered indexes are numbered between 2 and 250. If a clustered index exists, it has an index number of 1. If no clustered index exists, a row with index number 0 appears in the `sysindexes` table. You can specify the index number in the optimizer hint rather than use the index name. Hence, the previous SQL statement might also look like this (assuming index number 3 is `noncl_myindex`):

INPUT
```
SELECT col1, col2
FROM indextab (INDEX = 3)
```

To force a clustered index scan, you write your query like this. You can see that SQL Server indeed does exactly as you've asked and uses a clustered index scan:

INPUT
```
SET SHOWPLAN_TEXT ON
GO
SELECT col1, col2
FROM indextab (INDEX = 0)
WHERE col1 < 3
```

OUTPUT
```
StmtText
-------------------------------------------------------------
SELECT col1, col2
FROM indextab (INDEX = 0)
WHERE col1 < 3

(1 row(s) affected)
```

```
StmtText
----------------------------------------------------------------------
  |--Clustered Index Scan(OBJECT:([pubs].[dbo].[INDEXTAB].[CL_MYINDEX]),
  ➥WHERE:([INDEXTAB].[col1]<3))

(1 row(s) affected)
```

Just to see another use of this option, drop the clustered index on the table to return the table to being a heap. Then run the same query with the optimizer hint of `INDEX=0`:

INPUT

```
set showplan_text off
go
drop index indextab.cL_MYINDEX
GO
SET SHOWPLAN_TEXT ON
GO
SELECT col1, col2
FROM indextab (INDEX = 0)
WHERE col1 < 3
```

OUTPUT

```
StmtText
------------------------------
SELECT col1, col2
FROM indextab (INDEX = 0)
WHERE col1 < 3
(1 row(s) affected)
StmtText
----------------------------------------------------
  |--Table Scan(OBJECT:([pubs].[dbo].[INDEXTAB]),
  ➥WHERE:([INDEXTAB].[col1]<3))

(1 row(s) affected)
```

Notice that a table scan was used because the table had no clustered index. Remember, a table scan and a clustered index are essentially the same type of operation. The leaf level of a clustered index is the data, so a scan of that level is the same as reading every single data page (a table scan).

Index Maintenance

Indexes must be maintained to remain efficient and useful over time. You must manually maintain these indexes (or set up automated plans to do so). Either way, you need to understand the basics of index maintenance.

Statistics

SQL Server knows statistical information about your data through a special object in the database (which I refer to as the *statistics blob*). The statistics blob contains information about how data is distributed throughout the table and also calculates the average number of duplicates for the indexed columns. When you create an index, if the table already contains data, a statistics blob is created and populated with information about the columns that you've indexed. If you create an index on a table and then add the data but haven't turned off the automatic gathering of statistics, a statistics blob is created for you. If you turn off SQL Server's capability to automatically keep updated statistics about an index, this statistics blob isn't created. If this information doesn't exist, SQL Server must guess about how your data is distributed. When your query contains a clause, such as `col1 < 3`, SQL Server consults the statistics blob to guess how many data rows will be returned. The more current your statistics blob, the better job SQL Server does selecting the proper index (or deciding to use a table scan). Therefore, don't turn off the gathering of automatic statistics.

The truly paranoid (including the authors of this book) periodically gather statistics manually as well. To update the statistics blob with current information, run the `UPDATE STATISTICS` command:

SYNTAX

```
UPDATE STATISTICS {table | view}
[index
|([index_or_column [, ...n])]
[WITH [ [FULLSCAN]
| SAMPLE number {PERCENT | ROWS}] ]
[[,] [ALL | COLUMNS | INDEX]
[[,] NORECOMPUTE] ]
```

So, the following might be an example of how to update statistics on the `authors` table:

```
UPDATE STATISTICS authors
```

As long as automatic statistics gathering is enabled, you don't need to run this command frequently. On most of our servers, we run `UPDATE STATISTICS` once a week (mostly out of habit) on each table in the database. Microsoft has shipped a handy system stored procedure to do the job for you: `sp_statistics`. To run this procedure, type **`exec sp_statistics`** in a query window. That's it; there are no parameters or anything to muck with, and it automatically gathers statistical information about each table's indexes in the database. You can specify many other options, but you don't need to examine them now.

13

Turning Off Automatic Statistics

You can turn off automatic statistics (and then, we hope, turn them back on again because they work so well) by using the system stored procedure `sp_autostats`:

```
sp_autostats 'tablename' [, 'statsflag'] [, 'indexname']
```

In this syntax,

- *tablename* is the name of the table or the view on which you want to change the autostats option.
- *statsflag* is either on or off (turning on automatic statistics or turning them off if not specified).
- *indexname* is the name of the index you want to change. If you leave this parameter off, the change affects all indexes for a given table. If you leave off both *statsflag* and *indexname*, sp_autostats returns information about the current status of automatic statistics on the indexes of the table.

So, to turn off automatic statistics on the authors table in the pubs database, you run

INPUT
```
Use pubs
Exec sp_autostats 'authors','Off'
```

Then you get

OUTPUT
```
(4 row(s) affected)
Automatic statistics maintenance turned OFF for 4 indices.
```

Column Statistics

SQL Server 2000 also can track statistics on nonindexed columns, a feature known as *keeping statistics* on columns. You use the UPDATE STATISTICS command as you did before, except specify the columns you want statistics on and use the WITH COLUMNS option. An example looks like this, which updates statistics on the city column of the authors table:

```
UPDATE STATISTICS authors (city) WITH COLUMNS
```

Why is this capability useful? The SQL Server Optimizer (the code that decides which index to use) can examine this statistical information to decide how best to read a table—much in the same way it can use indexed columns with statistics. So, if you specify a column in the WHERE clause of your select statements but don't want to index that column, it can still be used for optimization purposes with column statistics. When you examine the Index Tuning Wizard later, you'll look at column statistics again.

When Were Statistics Last Gathered?

If you somehow ended up taking over a new SQL Server (and promptly ran out and bought this book), you might need to get a handle on the current state of your SQL Server databases. You need to determine how and when statistics are updated. Fortunately, you can find out the last time statistics were gathered by using the STATS_DATE function:

SYNTAX

```
SELECT STATS_DATE(table_id, index_id)
```

This function is pretty straightforward but requires you to get the `table_id` and `index_id`. You can get them by using the `OBJECT_ID` function:

INPUT

```
Use pubs
Go
Declare @tabid int
Declare @indid int
Select @tabid = object_id ('indextab')
Select @indid = 2 /* the non-clustered index */
SELECT STATS_DATE (@tabid, @indid)
```

You get output similar to this:

OUTPUT

```
---------------------------
2000-05-19 22:12:05.920
(1 row(s) affected)
```

Note

> If you don't get the preceding results, you might still have a showplan option turned on. Open a new query window and copy the code into your new window, or run
>
> ```
> SET SHOWPLAN_TEXT OFF
> GO
> SET SHOWPLAN_ALL OFF
> GO
> ```

The DBCC UPDATEUSAGE Command

`DBCC UPDATEUSAGE` corrects information in the SQL Server `sysindexes` system table. The information in that table tells SQL Server how many pages are in the table and how many pages are used by each index, for example. That information is maintained automatically, but it's possible that the information in the system tables can become outdated. To update the information, run `DBCC UPDATEUSAGE`:

SYNTAX

```
DBCC UPDATEUSAGE ({0 | database_name} [, {'table_name' | 'viewname'}
➥[, index_id | 'indexname']])
[ WITH [COUNT_ROWS] [, NO_INFOMSGS ]]
```

In this syntax,

- `database_name` is the name of the database in which you want to work. If you specify just a database name, information in `sysindexes` is updated for all heaps and indexes in the database.

13

- *table_name* or *viewname* is the name of a table or view for which you want to have information updated in the sysindexes system table.
- *index_id* is the index number of an index for a given table for which you want to have information updated in the sysindexes system table. To find the *index_id* for an index, run the sp_helpindex system stored procedure. You can also specify the name of the index.

You probably don't need DBCC UPDATEUSAGE, but it's included here for the sake of completeness.

The DBCC SHOWCONTIG Command

Periodically, you need to reorganize your indexes. Over time, indexes don't maintain their fill factor or become fragmented and less useful. To discover whether your indexes are fragmented and need to be reorganized, use the DBCC SHOWCONTIG command:

SYNTAX

```
DBCC SHOWCONTIG [( { tablename | table_id | viewname | view_id }
            [ , indexname | index_id ] ) ]
    [ WITH { ALL_INDEXES | FAST [ , ALL_INDEXES ]
                | TABLERESULTS [ , { ALL_INDEXES } ]
                [ , { FAST | ALL_LEVELS } ] } ]
```

In this syntax,

- *table_id* or *view_id* is the ID of the table or view you want to examine for fragmentation. You can get an object's ID by using the object_id('*tablename*') function.
- *tablename* or *viewname* is the name of the table or view you want to examine. You can specify the name instead of the ID. This option is new for SQL Server 2000.
- *index_id* is the internal number for the index you want to examine. Without this value, information is gathered for the clustered index (if it exists) or for the heap.
- *indexname* is the name of the index you want to examine. Again, it is an alternative to the *index_id* and is a new option for SQL Server 2000.

You can run the following script to look at the results of DBCC SHOWCONTIG. Be sure to run this script in a new query window (or turn off SHOWPLAN and any other options you might have enabled before).

```
USE PUBS
DBCC SHOWCONTIG ('indextab')
GO
```

```
DBCC SHOWCONTIG scanning 'INDEXTAB' table...
Table: 'INDEXTAB' (741577680); index ID: 0, database ID: 5
TABLE level scan performed.
- Pages Scanned................................: 1
- Extents Scanned..............................: 1
- Extent Switches..............................: 0
- Avg. Pages per Extent........................: 1.0
- Scan Density [Best Count:Actual Count].......: 100.00% [1:1]
- Extent Scan Fragmentation ...................: 0.00%
- Avg. Bytes Free per Page.....................: 6438.0
- Avg. Page Density (full).....................: 20.46%
DBCC execution completed. If DBCC printed error messages, contact your
system administrator.
```

A cool new feature of SQL Server 2000 DBCC commands is support for the tableresults option. This support makes the DBCC command return a valid SQL Server rowset. In fact, virtually all DBCC commands allow this option, even though the official syntax doesn't always show it as valid in the SQL Server Books Online. This support allows you to do something like insert the results of a DBCC command into a table. You can do so to examine large amounts of DBCC results in a relational way. For example, run

```
USE PUBS
DBCC SHOWCONTIG ('indextab') with tableresults
GO
```

to get the answer as a single row in a virtual table (rowset).

ANALYSIS This script contains a significant amount of information, but you need to focus on just two or three key items. First, you can see from the first line, where it indicates `index ID: 0`, that this table doesn't have a clustered index. The next value to examine is the Scan Density. The higher the percentage, the better the shape your table is in. The other number to look at is the Avg. Page density (full). You want this number to be as close to your fill factor as possible.

When these numbers start to get somewhat low (there's no concrete number to use), it's probably a good time to reorganize your indexes. You could drop and then re-create them. For a clustered index, you can use the `DROP_EXISTING` option to speed up that operation. This approach puts the index back into the original shape, including reapplying your fill factor options. It also doesn't affect your nonclustered indexes because the order and overall index structures of your clustered indexes aren't affected when using the `DROP_EXISTING` option. If you drop and re-create the clustered index without this option, you reorganize the data pages as well as the index structure.

DBCC SHOWCONTIG can be run by members of the sysadmin fixed server role or either the db_owner or db_ddladmin fixed database role members.

The DBCC DBREINDEX Command

Another available option that might be a better choice is the DBCC DBREINDEX command:

SYNTAX

```
DBCC DBREINDEX (['database.owner.table_name' [, index_name
[, fillfactor ]]])
[WITH NOINFOMSGS]
```

Many of the options are the same as in the CREATE INDEX statement, so refer to that statement for a review of the sorted data and fill factor options. However, if you specify a fill factor of 0, the original fill factor specified when the index was created is used. Otherwise, it is set to the fill factor value you specify. Note, however, that if you want to specify an optional parameter, you must specify all the preceding options. For example, to specify a fill factor, you must specify an index name, even if you provide a blank name. For example, use the following to rebuild the indexes on the authors table (all of them) with the original fill factor:

INPUT

```
DBCC DBREINDEX ('authors','', 0)
```

If you specify a table, such as the following, every index on the table is dropped and re-created, as shown in the previous output:

INPUT/OUTPUT

```
DBCC DBREINDEX ('indextab')
GO
DBCC execution completed. If DBCC printed error messages,
contact your system administrator.
```

You can also specify an individual index to work with. In this example, you first create an additional nonclustered index on the authors table. Then issue the DBREINDEX command and specify the new index you just created:

INPUT

```
CREATE INDEX noncl_col2_indextab on indextab (col4)
GO
DBCC DBREINDEX ('indextab','noncl_col2_indextab')
```

Be careful when specifying a fill factor with DBCC DBREINDEX. If you don't specify a particular index but use the fill factor setting, such as

```
DBCC DBREINDEX ('indextab', '', 50)
```

it resets the fill factor on all indexes on the table (in this case, to 50). This result might or might not be what you intended.

DBCC DBREINDEX has one big advantage over dropping and re-creating indexes. As you will see on Day 14, referential integrity and American National Standards Institute (ANSI) constraints sometimes create indexes behind the scenes. DBCC DBREINDEX can safely drop and re-create the indexes created with constraints, whereas the only way to do so otherwise is to drop and re-create the constraints.

Members of the sysadmin server role, db_owner or db_ddladmin database roles, or the owner of a table can run DBCC DBREINDEX.

The DBCC INDEXDEFRAG Command

DBCC INDEXDEFRAG is a new command for SQL Server 2000. At first glance, this option may seem limited when compared to DBCC DBREINDEX, but it will probably turn into your first choice for reorganizing indexes most of the time. When you're using DBCC DBREINDEX, your table is unavailable for others to query until the reindex is complete. However, with DBCC INDEXDEFRAG, other users can still access the table. This capability is known as an *online reorg*. First, consider the syntax:

SYNTAX

```
DBCC INDEXDEFRAG
    ( { database_name | database_id | 0 }
        , { table_name | table_id | 'view_name' | view_id }
        , { index_name | index_id }
    )    [ WITH NO_INFOMSGS ]
```

Again, the options are similar enough to options examined earlier today that we don't need to enumerate the meaning of each one again here. So, what's different between this command and DBCC DBREINDEX?

DBCC INDEXDEFRAG reorganizes only the leaf levels of your indexes. So, if your goal is to have a perfectly organized index from top to bottom, this option isn't for you. However, if you want a background task to run and clean up most of your index fragmentation, or you can't afford to make a table unavailable while a DBREINDEX is run, this is the command for you.

Members of the sysadmin server role, db_owner or db_ddladmin database roles, or the owner of a table can run DBCC INDEXDEFRAG.

Indexed Views

SQL Server 2000 introduces the ability to create indexes on views. In all previous versions of Microsoft SQL Server, you could create indexes only on tables. Indexed views are easy in concept, but you might want to understand some advanced configuration issues. However, to understand the basics, you don't need to worry about all these issues quite yet.

As you've seen from your examination of indexing today, anywhere you can specify a table name in the index-related statements, you can also specify a view name. Because tables actually contain data, creating an index on them just works (and makes intuitive sense). However, what about a view, which, as you'll learn on Day 15, "Creating Views, Triggers, Stored Procedures, and Functions," is simply a stored query? The answer is that when you create an index on a view, the query results are computed and then stored. Then, any time data changes for any rows referenced by the results of the view, the view's indexes are updated.

An example is needed to explain this scenario. Imagine you have a view that combines the `titles`, `titleauthor`, and `authors` tables in the `pubs` database to present a single view of the tables. The view might look like this:

```
Create view myauthorview
With schemabinding
As
Select a.au_lname, a.au_fname, t.title, ta.royaltyper
From dbo.authors a inner join dbo.titleauthor ta on a.au_id = ta.au_id inner
join dbo.titles t on t.title_id = ta.title_id

Create unique clustered index myindexview on myauthorview(au_lname,au_fname,
title)
```

Now, if you issue the query (with showplan turned on)

```
Select * from myauthorview
```

you see the optimizer plan in Figure 13.10.

FIGURE 13.10

The graphical showplan without the clustered index being used.

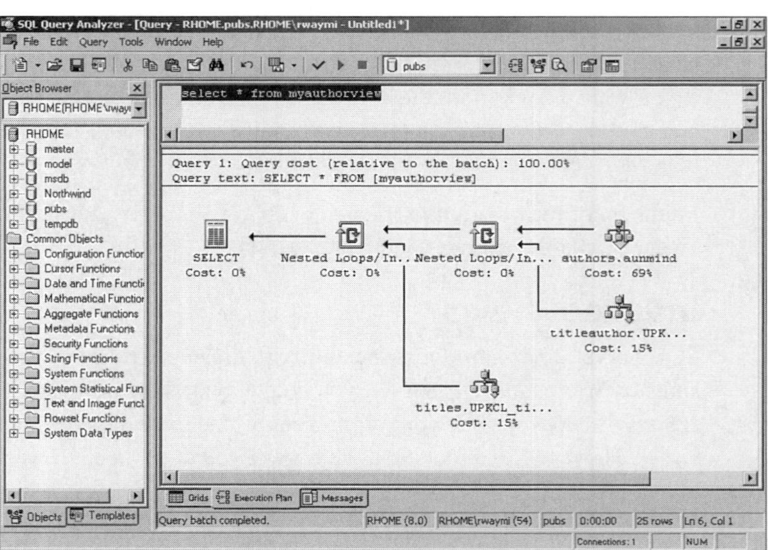

Because these tables are so small, it's hard to get the query optimizer to use the clustered index. Therefore, you can force it with a "hint" to the optimizer. Run

```
Select * from myauthorview (noexpand)
```

to get the showplan in Figure 13.11, showing that the clustered index was used.

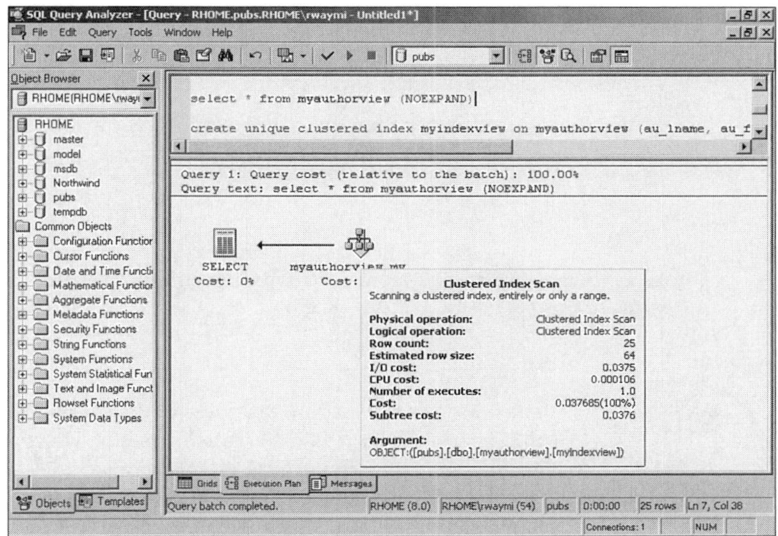

FIGURE 13.11
The graphical showplan with the clustered index being used.

For large tables with many joins, you can easily imagine that if the answer is already precalculated, your query performance will improve dramatically when you can use the indexed view. This view is particularly useful in a reporting environment where you know these kinds of queries in advance.

How is an indexed view maintained? Every time you modify a row of one of the tables referenced in the view (`authors`, `titles`, or `titleauthor`), the indexed view must also be updated. So, if you thought maintaining a regular index might be expensive, imagine the overhead of updating this index. However, if the query performance improvements for reporting are big enough, it is probably worth the trade-off.

Indexed View Restrictions

As we mentioned when we started looking at indexed views, some restrictions must be observed, including the following:

- You must first create a unique clustered index on the view before you can create nonclustered indexes.

- You must create the view by using the `SCHEMABINDING` option. You'll explore this option in detail on Day 15.
- The `ANSI_NULLS` and `QUOTED_IDENTIFIER` properties must be enabled for the database connection in which you create the view (SQL Server 2000's Query Analyzer has these options turned on by default).
- `ANSI_NULLS` must be turned on for the connection that created the tables referenced in the view.
- The view can be defined to query only tables, not other views.
- All objects used in the view must have the same owner and be in the same database as the view.
- You must include the owner name in all query references, as you saw in the sample query earlier.

Books Online actually lists more restrictions than this, but these are the most important ones.

Indexed views are used by the query optimizer only in the Enterprise Edition of SQL Server 2000. You can create indexes on views with any edition of SQL Server 2000, but only the Enterprise Edition actually uses them. You have this capability so that your Data Definition Language (DDL) doesn't fail across editions of SQL Server, even though it isn't completely used in the other editions of the product.

Managing Indexes with SQL Server Enterprise Manager

Through SQL Server Enterprise Manager, you can manage indexes by using the index properties dialog. First, you must know that there are two different index control dialogs. You can expand the database you want to work with (in the examples here, it's the `pubs` database), highlight the Tables folder, and right-click the table in the right pane that you want to work with. Then select Design Table from the pop-up menu to open (no surprise) the Design Table window. I selected `authors`, and if you do the same, you see something similar to Figure 13.12.

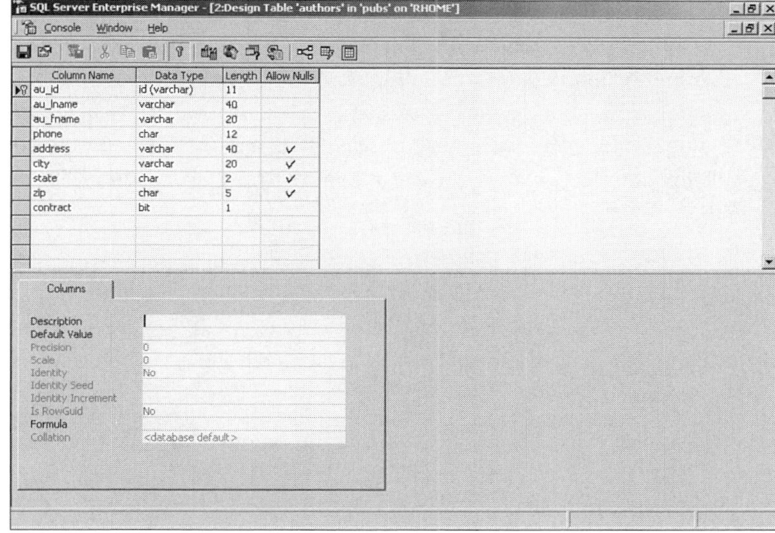

FIGURE 13.12
The Design Table window.

As you can see in Figure 13.12, if you click the second toolbar button (Table and Index Properties), you are presented with a properties dialog for the table. Notice that this dialog is different from the general properties of a table. Then click the Indexes/Keys tab (see Figure 13.13).

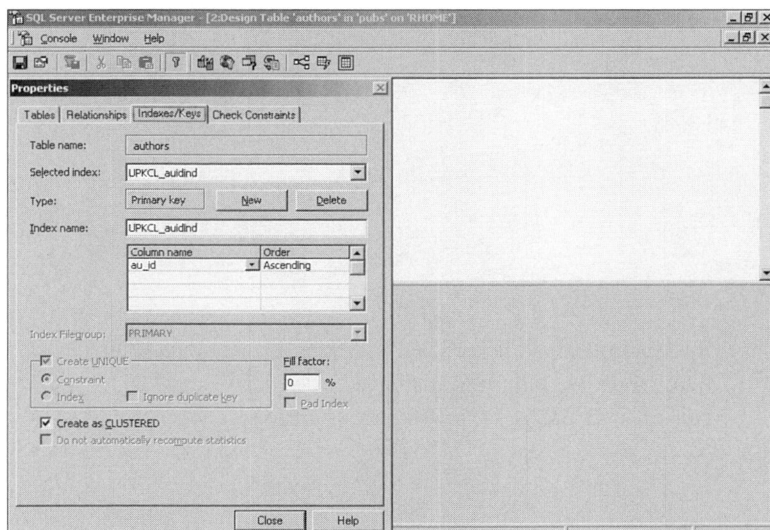

FIGURE 13.13
The Design Table window's properties.

From this dialog, you can use most of the indexing options that you've seen today. If you want to create, remove, or rename an index, you can do so here. You can choose to make an index unique and, if it's unique, decide whether it's a unique constraint or a unique index. In practice, you'll find that you usually want a unique constraint rather than a unique index. If you choose to leave it as a unique index, you can set the Ignore Duplicate Key, which you examined earlier in the section "The `IGNORE_DUP_KEY` Option."

You can also specify that the index be clustered and turn off the automatic gathering of statistics. Note that automatic statistics are turned on unless you turn them off. Fill Factor and Pad Index options are also available. The other option available here is for filegroups. If you are using filegroups (as described on Day 4, "Creating and Administering Databases and Data Files"), you can change the filegroup with which an index is associated.

However, what I consider a better index options dialog is available—it's shown in Figure 13.14. Here, you can see much more clearly which indexes are available and which columns are indexed. You get to this dialog by right-clicking a table and selecting All Tasks, Manage Indexes.

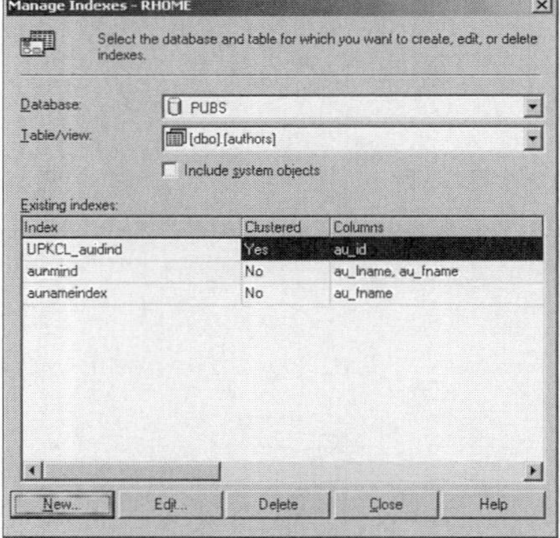

FIGURE 13.14
The Manage Indexes dialog.

The real power of this option becomes apparent when you want to create a new index. Click the New button to open the dialog in Figure 13.15. Notice that every option for SQL Server 2000 is available for you to specify graphically.

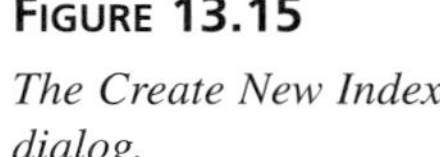

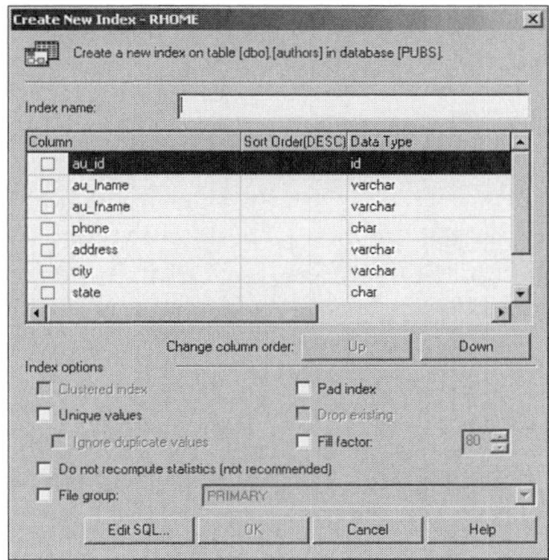

FIGURE 13.15

The Create New Index dialog.

> Why does SQL Server have two completely different manage index dialogs? The one from the table properties is from a code component that's common to many Microsoft products (such as Visual Studio). It's coded to support multiple databases, not just SQL Server 2000. However, the Manage Indexes dialog is purely for SQL Server 2000, and thus all SQL Server–specific options can be made available.

Index Selection

Now that you've seen the options available and how you build indexes, your next logical question might be, "Which columns should I index, and how should I index them?" Good candidates for indexes include

- Primary key columns (to be discussed on Day 14)
- Foreign key columns (to be discussed on Day 14)
- Columns on which you use the `ORDER BY` clause
- Columns on which you use the `GROUP BY` clause
- Columns that you specify exactly in your `WHERE` clause

In general, you should index columns that are included in your `WHERE` clause using conditions that don't include functions or calculations. In other words, the following probably indicates that a good candidate to index is the emp_id column:

```
WHERE emp_id = 5
```

However, this example probably can't use an index, so there's no point in creating one for it (for this query, anyway):

```
WHERE SUBSTRING(emp_id,1,5) = 'Annet'
```

Statements like the first WHERE clause in the preceding paragraph are known as *searchable arguments*. Searchable arguments (also called SARGs) are the types of arguments that can be used by SQL Server. In addition to exact matches, you can sometimes use approximate matches on character columns. For example,

```
WHERE emp_lname LIKE 'w%'
```

is searchable, but

```
WHERE emp_lname LIKE '%w%'
```

is not. Note that the `%` symbol specifies a wildcard. In the first example, the emp_lname column is searched for values that begin with a `w`. The second example searches the emp_lname column for values that have a `w` anywhere in them. Imagine if you tried to do a search like this yourself on the telephone book. Could you easily find the second condition? SQL Server would have the same problem as you; as long as the first letter is specified, you have somewhere to start.

One other point to consider is that not every column is a good candidate to index. You shouldn't index the following:

- Columns using the `text`, `image`, or `bit` data types
- Columns that aren't very unique (such as male or female)
- Columns that are too wide to be useful indexes

The last option depends on your application and table, but it's a good bet that a `char(200)` is an unlikely candidate for an index.

Be careful, however, because each index introduces maintenance, space usage, and performance issues. Generally, I recommend that you don't have more than three to four indexes on a table. For every rule, there are quite a few exceptions, but this is a good guideline to follow. The next step after you decide which columns to index is to figure out which type of index you need: clustered or nonclustered.

Clustered Index Choices

You get only one clustered index, so it's a good idea to choose this one first. Good candidates for clustered indexes include

- Very specific queries (where `col1 = 5`, for example)

- Queries with a range of data (for example, `WHERE col1 BETWEEN 5 AND 30` and `WHERE col1 > 20`)
- Queries on columns you order by or group by frequently

A critical concern when selecting your clustered index in SQL Server 2000 is that the key values (indexed columns) you choose for your clustered index are "carried" along into the nonclustered indexes. Therefore, if you choose a wide clustered index, such as a `Char(30)`, not only does it take longer to search the clustered index itself, but all your nonclustered indexes also have to carry the `Char(30)` value of your clustered index key on every row in the nonclustered indexes. That's a significant amount of overhead, so you should keep your clustered index keys as small as possible. You also should make sure that the clustered key you select isn't updated frequently, because all your nonclustered indexes need to be updated when the clustered index values change.

Another choice might be to index foreign key columns, which you will examine on Day 14.

Nonclustered Index Choices

After you select your clustered index, the rest of the indexes you've decided to create must be nonclustered. Good candidates include

- Specific queries (yes, they're good for both types of indexes).
- Queries that can be answered entirely by using an index (called *covering index queries*). For example, if you have an index on the au_lname and au_fname columns of the `authors` table in the `pubs` database, the following query can be answered entirely from the index without accessing the data:

  ```
  SELECT au_fname from pubs..authors where au_lname = 'White'
  ```
- Columns you order by or group by.
- Columns on which you use functions (such as `MIN`, `MAX`, or `COUNT`).

The key issue here is that you index only columns that will be used in the `WHERE` clause of your queries and that you verify that the indexes you choose will be used by SQL Server using the `SHOWPLAN` options or the graphical showplan of the SQL Server Query Analyzer.

The SQL Server Index Tuning Wizard

You will examine the Index Tuning Wizard on Day 20, "Performance Monitoring Basics and Tools." We mention it here simply so you know that it wasn't missed, if you've seen it. However, you must understand more about the SQL Server Profiler utility before you can successfully use the wizard.

Full-Text Indexing

Full-text indexes enable you to create an index on a text column, as well as any other character column. This feature is installed by default starting with SQL Server 2000 (unless you are running SQL Server on Windows 9*x*). Full-text indexing is possible because of the merging of Microsoft Index Server technology into SQL Server 2000. This feature requires that the Microsoft Search service be running (which it is by default if you installed full-text indexing during setup). It also requires a unique index on each table you want to use for full-text indexing. Only the owner of a table can create a full-text index.

You can have only one full-text index per table, and the index is physically stored outside SQL Server (in your `\mssql\FTData` directory). Unlike normal SQL Server indexes, full-text indexes aren't self-maintaining. You need to set up a periodic job to update the full-text indexes. You'll examine jobs in further detail on Day 18, "Scheduling Jobs with SQL Server Agent." The process of setting up and using full-text indexing is unlike using normal indexes, but the good news is that Microsoft has provided yet another wizard to assist you.

Highlight the table on which you want to create a full-text index in SQL Server Enterprise Manager, and select Full-Text Indexing from the Tools menu. The Full-Text Indexing Wizard starts and walks you through the process of creating your new index. The example shown here is the `pub_info` table in the `pubs` database. I made this selection to show you that you can index a column of data type text, even though this wouldn't be possible with normal SQL Server indexes. After the wizard starts, you see an introduction screen. After you read the introduction, click Next to see the dialog shown in Figure 13.16.

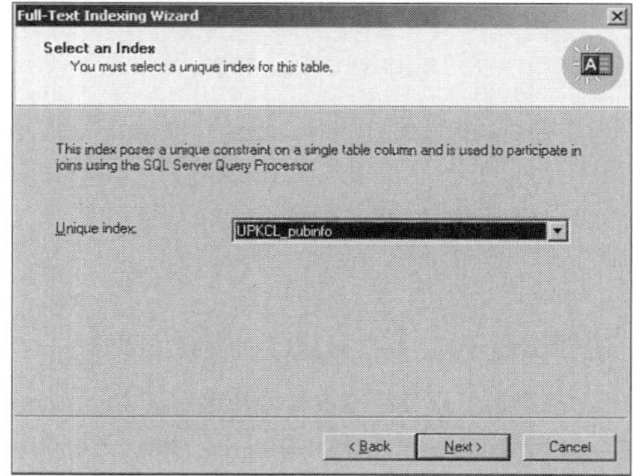

FIGURE 13.16
Selecting a unique index on your table.

As we just noted, a unique index is used for each full-text index you want to create (as a row locator). Select the unique index to use (only one is available for `pub_info`), and click Next to see the dialog shown in Figure 13.17.

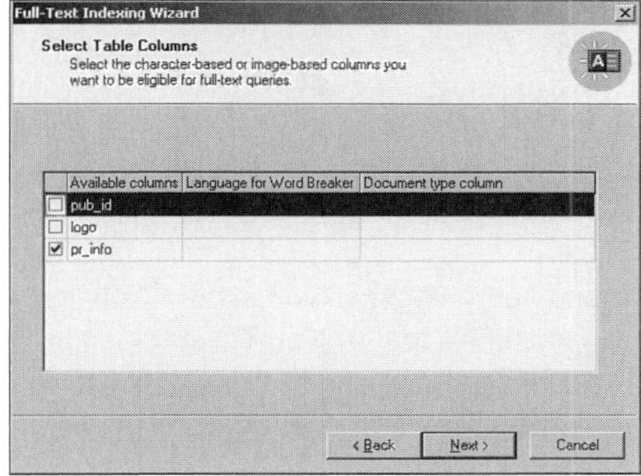

FIGURE 13.17
Selecting table columns.

As you can see, I've selected the pr_info column, which is of data type text. The other options on this dialog are new features of SQL Server 2000: You can index documents that have document filters available. Examples include Microsoft Word documents. You can even set the language of the document so that indexing filters according to the local languages. Click Next to see the dialog in Figure 13.18, in which you can select a catalog. To keep things simple, use a new one (because you probably don't have one on your system anyway), and name it `pub_info` (as shown in Figure 13.18).

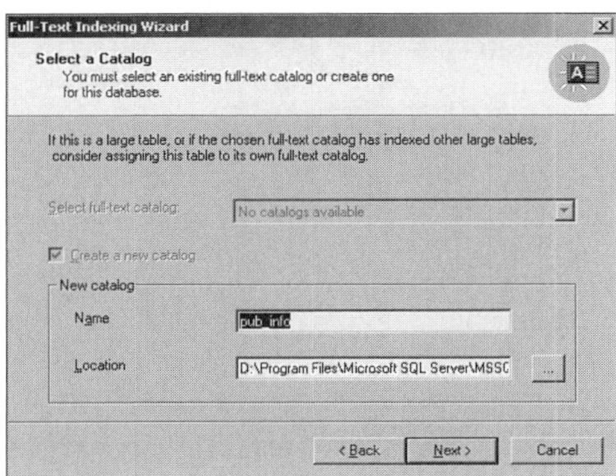

FIGURE 13.18
Selecting a catalog to store your full-text index.

Click Next, and in the resulting dialog, you have the option of setting up a schedule to populate and update your full-text index. Rather than get into scheduling, skip this dialog by clicking Next. You can still manually update the full-text index. Click Finish, and you are presented with the dialog in Figure 13.19, showing that you've succeeded in configuring your full-text index. It reports that your full-text index hasn't been populated yet.

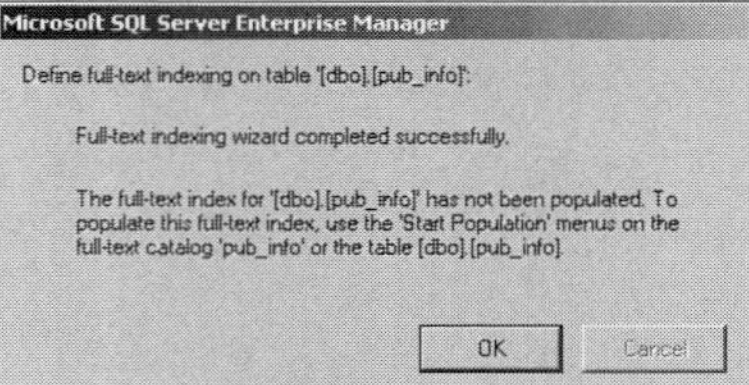

FIGURE 13.19

The finish dialog after completing the wizard.

Click OK, and then expand your `pubs` database again, if it's not already done in SQL Server Enterprise Manager. Highlight Full-Text Catalogs, right-click the catalog you just created (named `pub_info`) in the right pane of Enterprise Manager, and select Start Full Population from the pop-up menu (see Figure 13.20).

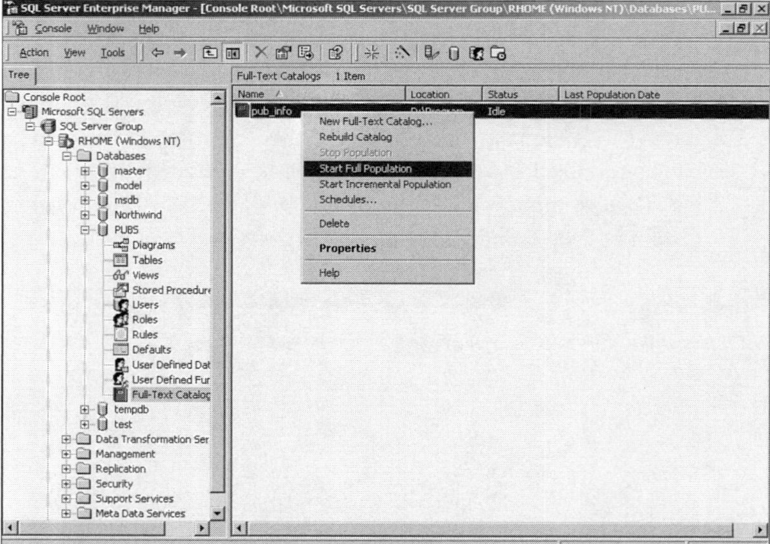

FIGURE 13.20

Initializing the population of your Full-Text Catalog.

That's it! You've populated the index and can now query against it. At this point, querying gets a bit harder. Querying full-text indexes isn't very easy in SQL Server 2000 when compared to creating ordinary queries, because you have to learn specific syntax for full-text indexes. For example, when you run the following query in Query Analyzer, all the rows that contain the word *sample* are returned:

```
select pub_id, substring(pr_info,1,100) from pub_info
where CONTAINS (pr_info, 'sample')
```

Full-text queries can be somewhat complicated, so you should consult the SQL Server Books Online if you want to run much more sophisticated queries against full-text indexes.

Summary

Indexes aren't required but are extremely useful to speed up your queries. They are essentially the "go fast" option in SQL Server—particularly with indexed views. Various options are available during the creation of your indexes, and several maintenance issues must be addressed. Your indexes can help you resolve queries faster and provide better overall performance as long as you maintain them properly.

Remember that you probably don't need to override the optimizer, but that option is available to you in the form of optimizer hints. This option requires an understanding of the query, the data being queried, and the available indexes to make a good choice for optimization. If you aren't comfortable with your knowledge of all these elements, let SQL Server pick the indexes for you. It's right almost every single time if you've performed index maintenance properly.

You can manage indexes entirely in Transact-SQL, or you can use SQL Server Enterprise Manager. In the long run, it's good to know how to perform any operation either way, but you'll most likely use the Enterprise Manager dialogs. Using it is a lot easier than trying to remember the exact syntax of the Transact-SQL commands.

Q&A

Q What are some of the differences between clustered and nonclustered indexes?

A The number of indexes available (1 for clustered, 249 for nonclustered) and the contents of the leaf level of the index (data for the clustered index, rows pointing to the data for the nonclustered index).

Q How does SQL Server determine when to use an index?

A It analyzes the `WHERE` clause in your query as well as the statistics from the statistics blob and the information stored in the `sysindexes` system table.

Q When would I specify a fill factor setting on an index?

A When you want to leave free space in your indexes to allow for growth of the data and to reduce page splits.

Q How do I override SQL Server's choice of indexes?

A By using optimizer hints such as `SELECT ... FROM indextab (index = 1)`.

Workshop

This section provides quiz questions to help you solidify your understanding of the concepts presented today. In addition to the quiz questions, exercises are provided to let you practice what you've learned today. Try to understand the quiz and exercise answers before continuing onto tomorrow's lesson. Answers are provided in Appendix A, "Answers to Quiz Questions."

Quiz

1. How do you force SQL Server to choose a table scan?
2. How much free space do you need to create a clustered index?
3. What option do you turn on to verify the index selection of SQL Server?

Exercises

1. Write a query to select data from the `sales` table in the `pubs` database, where `title_id = 'BU1032'`, and show SQL Server's index choice and how much I/O it will take.
2. Override the choice in exercise 1, and use the clustered index.
3. Create a new table, along with a unique clustered index and two nonclustered indexes—each with a different fill factor. Then use `DBCC DBREINDEX` to reorganize the indexes, and reset the fill factor to 50.
4. Do the same thing from exercise 3, but make the `DBCC DBREINDEX` and fill factor changes from within SQL Enterprise Manager.

WEEK 2

DAY 14

Ensuring Data Integrity

Yesterday you examined indexes and all the options available in SQL Server relating to indexes. Indexes can be a huge win for performance, but too many indexes can actually hurt performance. Selecting the proper indexing structure, including choosing which index to use as your clustered index, is critical to enhancing database performance. Creating indexes on views can really enhance reporting queries that join many tables together frequently.

Today's lesson focuses on data integrity. You look at two kinds of mechanisms to enforce data integrity: procedural and declarative. Declarative integrity in SQL Server, combined with the `IDENTITY` property, is often referred to in the Microsoft documentation as *declarative referential integrity* (DRI). However, it encompasses more than what the name implies.

How to Enforce Data Integrity

When you examine data integrity, you're trying to ensure that the data in your database is correct from a literal standpoint (without errors) and from a business standpoint. As you just learned, you can enforce integrity either procedurally or by using declarative integrity.

New Term *Procedural integrity* means that you can use programmatic structures and separate objects to enforce data integrity. Frequently, you do so at the application program level. However, this means that if any data modifications occur outside that program, your integrity rules aren't enforced. Therefore, it makes sense to put much of this integrity enforcement at the database level. You can perform that database integrity enforcement using objects such as triggers and stored procedures, which you'll learn about on Day 15, "Creating Views, Triggers, Stored Procedures, and Functions." The rest of today's lesson covers defaults and rules as enforcement mechanisms, as well as user-defined data types in a bit more detail.

New Term The other approach is *declarative integrity*; in other words, the mechanisms to enforce integrity are declared as part of the definition of the objects (tables) in your database. They become an integral part of these objects. You will spend most of your time examining these objects, because they provide critical functionality that would otherwise require significant amounts of programming to enforce.

Types of Integrity

Many components are used to enforce integrity in SQL Server 2000. Some of these components are more obvious than others. You can use these three types of integrity: domain, referential, and entity.

Domain Integrity

New Term Data types help determine what values are valid for a particular column. This is known as *domain integrity*. The *domain* is simply the set of valid values for a particular column. Nullability is another option to determine which values are valid in the domain—in this case, whether the unknown value (null) is valid. You can put further restrictions on a column's domain with user-defined data types, rules, and defaults if you want to use "traditional" SQL Server integrity objects. Otherwise, you can use American National Standards Institute (ANSI) constraints (default and check constraints) to enforce your domain integrity. Note that data types and nullability are always used, and the other components are optional.

Referential Integrity

New Term *Referential integrity* refers to the maintenance of relationships between data rows in multiple tables. You enforce referential integrity with DRI, as you learned earlier. You can, however, enforce integrity with triggers and programmatically control this functionality, but doing so takes quite a bit of work.

SQL Server 2000 has two kinds of cascading actions for foreign keys: cascading deletes (new for SQL Server 2000) and "no action" enforcement. The latter means that if you try to delete a customer, and referential integrity with "no action" is in place, you cannot delete that customer if invoices are still outstanding for him. With delete cascade referential integrity in place, when you delete the customer, all invoices are also removed from your database. To accomplish delete cascade integrity in all previous versions of SQL Server, you had to program it yourself (by using triggers, stored procedures, or standard Transact-SQL statements). This significant capability of SQL Server 2000 should prevent a significant amount of programming on the part of a database developer.

Entity Integrity

NEW TERM The last type of integrity you should be concerned with is *entity integrity*. This means that you can uniquely identify every row in a table. You can do so by using a unique index (as mentioned yesterday) or declarative integrity (primary-key or unique constraints), which you'll learn today.

Traditional Methods of Integrity

Traditional (meaning backward-compatible) methods of ensuring integrity include user-defined data types, defaults, and rules. Now let's examine how these database items can help enforce database integrity.

Note Although you can use user-defined data types, defaults, and rules as integrity enforcement mechanisms, I discourage you from using them and recommend that you use ANSI integrity constraints whenever possible. ANSI integrity constraints are generally more flexible. Another benefit to ANSI constraints is that the SQL Server Query Optimizer, the component that helps select the physical execution plan of your queries, understands ANSI constraints and can use them to help make better decisions about access plans.

User-Defined Data Types

User-defined data types enable you to help ensure domain integrity. Normally, when you create a table, you define each column with a system-supplied data type as well as information regarding whether the column allows nulls. You can also specify your own data types in SQL Server. Remember that you must define user-defined data types in terms of system-supplied data types. SQL Server doesn't allow you to create structures as new data types, for example.

You use these user-defined data types when you want to translate logical data types from your data model into physical data types in SQL Server. For example, if you model the use of postal codes in your data model on several tables, a user-defined data type might be appropriate. If you make the decision to define the model as a `char(10)`, you can create a data type called something like `postal_code_datatype`. The data type is a `char(10)`. To create this data type, you run this system stored procedure:

INPUT
```
EXEC sp_addtype postal_code_datatype, 'char(10)'
```

The `sp_addtype` system stored procedure uses this syntax:

SYNTAX

`sp_addtype` *`typename`*`,` *`phystype`*`[,` *`nulltype`*`][,` *`owner`*`]`

In this syntax,

- *`typename`* is the name of your user-defined data type. You use it in place of the system data type in your `CREATE TABLE` statements.
- *`phystype`* is the system data type that you want to use when you reference this user-defined data type. Quotation marks are optional in some cases, but it's safer to use them.
- *`nulltype`* is optional. Specifying it (in quotation marks) determines the nullability of a column if you don't specify it in a `CREATE TABLE` statement. If you don't specify this parameter, the data type defaults to the system default for nullability (which is `NULL` in SQL Server 2000 unless you change it).

Caution

For safety, don't rely on this functionality. Always specify nullability on your columns during your `CREATE TABLE` (and other Transact SQL) statements.

- *`owner`* is also optional. Specifying it (in quotation marks) determines the owner of the user-defined data type. By default, the creator is the owner of the data type.

Types are stored in the `systypes` system table in each database.

For example, to create a `state_code_type` data type of `char(2)` that doesn't allow nulls by default, you can run

INPUT
```
EXEC sp_addtype state_code_type, 'char(2)', 'not null'
```

To use it, you run

INPUT
```
Create Table mytable2
(col1 state_code_type)
```

col1 doesn't allow nulls because you've specified in the data type that you don't want to allow nulls. It behaves this way regardless of whether the database is set to allow nulls by default.

When you are finished with a user-defined data type (either because you never used it or because you've dropped all tables that use the data type), you can drop it by using the sp_droptype system stored procedure:

SYNTAX

```
sp_droptype typename
```

In this syntax, *typename* is the name of the user-defined data type you want to drop.

If a user-defined data type is still used anywhere, you get an error if you try to drop it. You must first drop all tables that use the data type before you can eliminate it.

As you might expect, SQL Server Enterprise Manager provides an interface to support user-defined data types. To use it, expand the database you want to work with (remember, data types are database specific), highlight User Defined Data Types, and view the data types you've created in this database. They appear on the right side of the SQL Server Enterprise Manager console. To create a new user-defined data type, right-click the User Defined Data Types icon in the left pane, and select New User Defined Data Type. You also can select New User Defined Data Type from the Action menu when you have the User Defined Data Type folder highlighted, or click the New button of the Enterprise Manager toolbar (it looks like a yellow star). Either way, you see the User-Defined Data Type Properties dialog (see Figure 14.1).

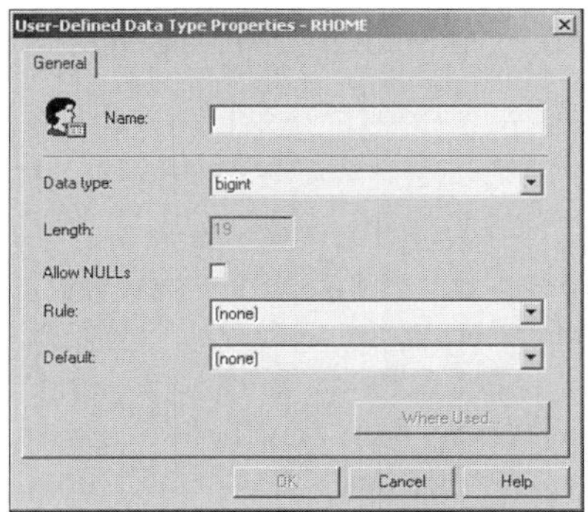

FIGURE 14.1
The User-Defined Data Type Properties dialog.

To add a new user-defined data type, type the name you want it to have, select a system data type, fill in the length if necessary (this option is dimmed if not needed), and then select Allow NULLs if you want the data type to allow nulls by default. You will learn more about the defaults and rules when you explore those objects later today. Click OK to add the user-defined data type.

To drop a user-defined data type, right-click the data type (or data types) on the right pane of SQL Server Enterprise Manager, then select Delete from the pop-up menu. In the Drop Objects dialog, click Drop All to drop the user-defined data types. You can't drop a user-defined data type that's in use. To find out where your data type is being used (if at all), highlight it and click Show Dependencies to view the list of objects that use your user-defined data type. You then see a list of the tables and columns with which the data type is used.

If you want to see this dependency list without dropping the user-defined data type (see Figure 14.2), double-click the user-defined data type (or right-click and select Properties), and then click Where Used. Optionally, right-click the user-defined data type, and select All Tasks, Display Dependencies.

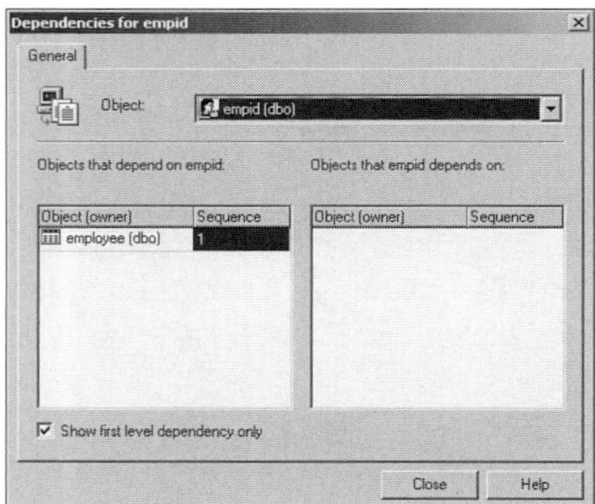

FIGURE 14.2
Viewing the list of dependencies without dropping the data type.

Defaults

Defaults specify a value to add to a column when you don't want to insert a value directly into that column. The two kinds of defaults in SQL Server are ANSI constraint defaults and standalone objects called defaults. In this section, you'll examine the latter; ANSI defaults are examined later today. You must have permission to run the `CREATE DEFAULT` statement (or be a member of either the sysadmin, db_owner, or db_ddladmin fixed database roles) .

I recommend that you use ANSI default constraints rather than defaults created with the `CREATE DEFAULT` statements. ANSI constraints provide the same basic functionality while providing consistency with the other ANSI constraints.

As you might have guessed by now, you create defaults by using the CREATE DEFAULT statement:

SYNTAX

```
CREATE DEFAULT default_name
AS constant_expression
```

In this syntax,

- *default_name* must be unique in the database (because defaults are separate objects) and must follow the rules for SQL Server identifiers.
- *constant_expression* is a constant that is appropriate for the data type of any columns you want to use for this data type. For example, if you are referencing a char(2) data type, your constant should be either x or xx, where x is any valid character. If you're referencing an integer, your constant should be an integer. If you're referencing binary data, it must start with a 0x character set (such as 0x13 for a binary value of 13). Money data types must begin with a dollar sign ($). Unicode data types begin with the letter N. You can also use system functions such as getdate() as long as they return the appropriate data for the data type.

Defaults are recorded in the sysobjects system table in each database. The text of the CREATE DEFAULT statement is stored in the syscomments table. As with other objects in SQL Server 2000, the definition of the object is stored in Unicode format.

As you learned on Day 11, "Modifying Data," you can use defaults during an insert either by using the DEFAULT keyword or simply not referencing the column in the column list.

You must address a couple of concerns when using defaults:

- The default must comply with any rules or ANSI check constraints you assign to the same columns or user-defined data types. If you have a rule on a column (such as a phone number column) that formatted the column as (xxx)xxx-xxxx, your default cannot be Unknown. It has to be something like (000)000-0000. You will examine the rules shortly.
- The default must not be incompatible with the data type of the column or user-defined data type it's assigned to. You can't have a default of Unknown for a char(2) column. Likewise, a default of Unknown doesn't work for a numeric column. (Here, Unknown is the literal string, not the null value.)

The implication so far has been that defaults apply to columns or user-defined data types. When you create a default, it's a standalone object in the database; it's not tied to any particular object. To actually use defaults, you must bind them to a column or user-defined data type. To bind a default, use the sp_bindefault system stored procedure:

```
p_bindefault defname, objname[, futureonly]
```

In this syntax,

- *`defname`* is the name of the default you've already created.
- *`objname`* is the name of the object to which you want to bind your default and must be in quotation marks. You can bind to either a column or a user-defined data type. SQL Server knows you are binding to a column if your quoted text is in the format *`tablename.columnname`*. If no period (`.`) appears in the quoted text, you can assume that it's a user-defined data type name. You can't bind a default to a system-supplied data type.
- `futureonly` applies only to user-defined data types. If this parameter is specified, the default doesn't apply anywhere that the user-defined data type has already been used. Each time you use the user-defined data type in the future, the default will be bound. I recommend that you not use this option because it's a little confusing. Sometimes the default applies and sometimes it doesn't, depending on when the `sp_bindefault` system stored procedure was run. It must be in quotation marks.

When the binding is complete, any user-defined data type or column to which the default is bound has the default applied during an insert, as appropriate.

To unbind the default, you run the `sp_unbindefault` system stored procedure:

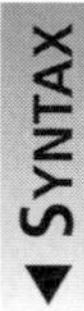

```
sp_unbindefault objname[, futureonly]
```

In this syntax,

- *`objname`* is the same as for `sp_bindefault`.
- `futureonly`, like with `sp_bindefault`, applies only to user-defined data types. It unbinds the default from the user-defined data type, but the default still applies everywhere it was used before. Future uses of the user-defined data type won't have the default applied. For the same reasons as before, I recommend that you not use this option. You can't drop the default until you explicitly unbind it from the columns it was used on before you ran `sp_unbindefault` with the `futureonly` option.

After you unbind a default from a data type or default, it's no longer used during an insert. You can't drop a default until it has been unbound from all data types and columns.

To drop a default, use the `DROP DEFAULT` command:

SYNTAX

```
DROP DEFAULT default_name[, default_name...]
```

This statement is pretty straightforward. You can drop as many defaults as you want in a single statement. If you are the owner of the default, you inherently have the right to drop the default; otherwise, you must be a member of the db_owner or db_ddladmin fixed database roles or the sysadmin fixed server role.

You can use the following sample code to create a table and user-defined data type and then apply some defaults:

INPUT

```
Use pubs
Go
EXEC sp_addtype my_uddt_type, 'money'
Go
CREATE DEFAULT intdefault as 0
Go
CREATE DEFAULT char5default as 'Hello'
Go
CREATE DEFAULT moneydefault as $10.00
Go
CREATE TABLE mytab
(intcol int not null,
 char5col char(5) not null,
 uddtcol my_uddt_type not null)
Go
```

Now bind the defaults to the data type and to the columns:

INPUT

```
EXEC sp_bindefault moneydefault, 'my_uddt_type'
EXEC sp_bindefault intdefault, 'mytab.intcol'
EXEC sp_bindefault char5default, 'mytab.char5col'
Go
```

Now insert a default row, and then select it:

INPUT

```
INSERT mytab DEFAULT VALUES
Go
SELECT * FROM mytab
Go
```

You then see this return set, showing that the defaults were indeed used:

OUTPUT

```
(1 row(s) affected)

intcol      char5col uddtcol
----------- -------- ---------------------
0           Hello    10.0000

(1 row(s) affected)
```

Look at this result through the SQL Server Enterprise Manager. In Enterprise Manager, expand the Databases folder and then the `pubs` database. Highlight Defaults in the left pane to view defaults (if you don't see the defaults you just created, click the Refresh button on the toolbar). Right-click the Defaults icon, and select New Default to open the Default Properties dialog (see Figure 14.3). You can also access this dialog by selecting New Default from the Action menu.

FIGURE 14.3

The Default Properties dialog.

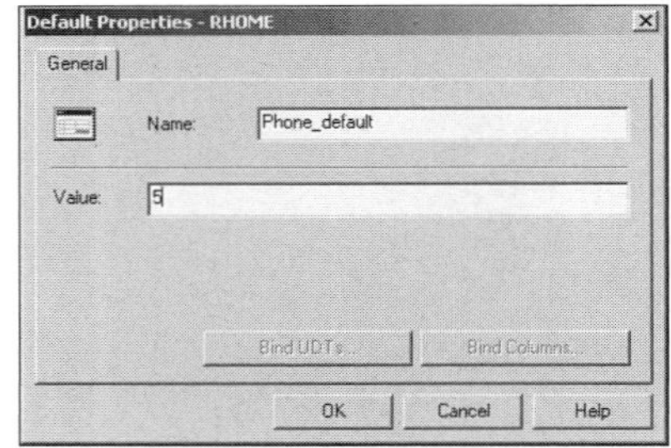

Type the name of the default you want to create. In the Value text box, type the character string, numeric value, money value, or binary value you want the default to have. After you start typing in this window, the OK button becomes available. Click OK to add your default to the database.

After you create a default, you can view it in the right pane of SQL Server Enterprise Manager. Right-click a default, and select Properties (or double-click it) to change, view, or modify bindings for a default. Click the Bind Columns button if you want to bind the default to one or more columns in your database, as shown in Figure 14.4.

FIGURE 14.4

Binding a column with Enterprise Manager.

Select the table you want to get a column from for the binding in the Table list box; then highlight the column or columns you want to bind to, and click the Add button to move them to the Bound Columns box. When you click Apply or OK, the binding is attempted. You receive an error message if the binding fails for some reason. To unbind a column, find the appropriate table, highlight the column in the Bound Columns box, and then click Remove.

To modify user-defined data types, click the Bind UDTs button to open the Bind Default to User-Defined Data Types dialog (see Figure 14.5). It contains a list of all existing user-defined data types. Simply check the box in the Bind column to bind the default to the user-defined data type.

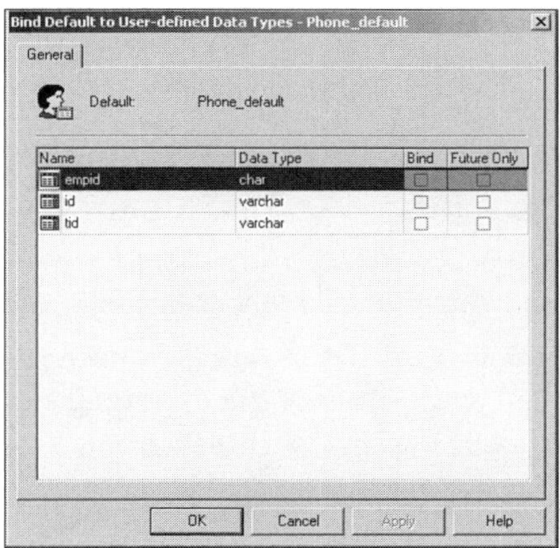

FIGURE 14.5
Binding a user-defined data type with Enterprise Manager.

To drop the default, right-click it and select Delete. Just as with user-defined data types, you can examine the dependencies the default has, and you must unbind the default from all user-defined data types and columns before you can drop the default object.

Rules

Rules further enforce domain integrity by providing more sophisticated checking of valid values. Rules are used to ensure that values

- Match a pattern (much like a *like* clause)
- Match a list of values (much like an *in* clause)
- Fall within a range of values (much like a *between* clause)

Rules, like defaults, are standalone objects that require special permission to create. You must be a member of the db_owner or sysadmin roles to create a rule. Rules are stored in the same system tables as your defaults: `sysobjects` and `syscomments`. They are checked for violations when inserts and updates are performed (whenever the column that a rule affects is referenced).

> I don't mean to sound like a broken record, but you are better off implementing ANSI constraints rather than using rules for most every instance of implementing this type of integrity. However, in special cases, such as when you want the same integrity check on 100 tables, it might be nice to create the rule once and then simply reference it 100 times. However, I still recommend ANSI constraints because the SQL Server Query Optimizer can use constraints during query optimization. This means that using constraints instead of rules could actually speed up your queries.

You create rules by using the `CREATE RULE` statement:

```
CREATE RULE rulename
AS condition_expression
```

In this syntax,

- *`rulename`* is a valid and unique name in the database in which it's created.
- *`condition_expression`* is in the form *`@variable_name`* `WHERE` *`clause`*. The `WHERE` *`clause`* can be any valid `WHERE` clause, including arithmetic operators, `BETWEEN`, `IN`, `LIKE`, `AND`, `OR`, `NOT`, and other operators. However, a rule can't refer to variable values or to other columns in the database. To do so, you must use a check constraint or a trigger.

For example, to create a rule for a part number column, when the column must start with a `p` or a `t`, you can have a rule such as

```
CREATE RULE myrule AS @myvar like 'p%' OR @myvar like 't%'
```

> The `@myvar` is arbitrarily named. You could call it `@fredandethel` if you want. Most people create the variable name to be similar to the name of the columns or data type it's used with.

Rules, like defaults, must be bound to a data type or column. You bind them by using the `sp_bindrule` system stored procedure:

SYNTAX

```
sp_bindrule rulename, objname[, futureonly]
```

In this syntax,

- *rulename* is the rule you want to bind to.
- *objname* is, as before, either a *tablename.columnname* combination or a user-defined data type.
- futureonly has the same meaning as it does for sp_bindefault.

When the rules are bound, they're used just like defaults. When you perform an insert, the inserted data is checked against the rule to ensure that it's valid. If it's not, you get a message similar to the following:

```
Server: Msg 513, Level 16, State 1, Line 1
A column insert or update conflicts with a rule imposed by a
previous CREATE RULE statement. The statement was terminated.
The conflict occurred in database 'pubs', table 'testtab', column 'c1'.
The statement has been terminated.
```

If you want to unbind the rule, you use the sp_unbindrule system stored procedure:

SYNTAX

```
sp_unbindrule objname[, futureonly]
```

In this syntax, *objname* is the name of the user-defined data type or the *tablename.columnname* combination, and futureonly means the same as for sp_unbindefault.

To drop a rule, you run the DROP RULE statement:

```
DROP RULE rulename[, rulename...]
```

When you use the DROP RULE statement, you simply specify the rule names you want to drop. As with the DROP DEFAULT statement, you can drop as many rules as you want with a single command. The rules must not be bound to any columns or user-defined data types.

You can use the same table I used earlier to examine how rules work, as well as how they work in conjunction with defaults. The following code creates several rules, which are explained in a little bit. Note that this depends on the script for the previously mentioned defaults having been run.

INPUT

```
CREATE RULE char5rule AS @col LIKE 'h%'
Go
CREATE RULE intrule AS @intval < 100
Go
CREATE RULE moneyrule AS @moneyval BETWEEN $5.00 AND $10.00
Go
Exec sp_bindrule 'char5rule', 'mytab.char5col'
```

```
Exec sp_bindrule 'intrule', 'mytab.intcol'
Exec sp_bindrule 'moneyrule', 'my_uddt_type'
Go
```

Now insert a valid column (based on these rules):

INPUT

```
INSERT mytab VALUES (90,'Howdy',$6.00)
Go
```

Test that your defaults comply with the rules:

INPUT

```
INSERT mytab DEFAULT VALUES
Go
```

In each case, you get `(1 row(s) affected)`.

Now insert an invalid set of values (based on the rules):

INPUT

```
INSERT mytab VALUES (101,'Ralph',$20.00)
Go
```

SQL Server doesn't allow you to enter the invalid data. Now you can see how the combination of Rules and Defaults together greatly increases the way you can control the domain of valid values for a column.

Of course, you can use SQL Server Enterprise Manager to perform all these operations. To access the Rule Properties dialog (see Figure 14.6), right-click the Rules icon in your database and select New Rule. As before, you can also access this dialog by selecting New Rule from the Action menu. This dialog works exactly like the Default Properties dialog you looked at earlier.

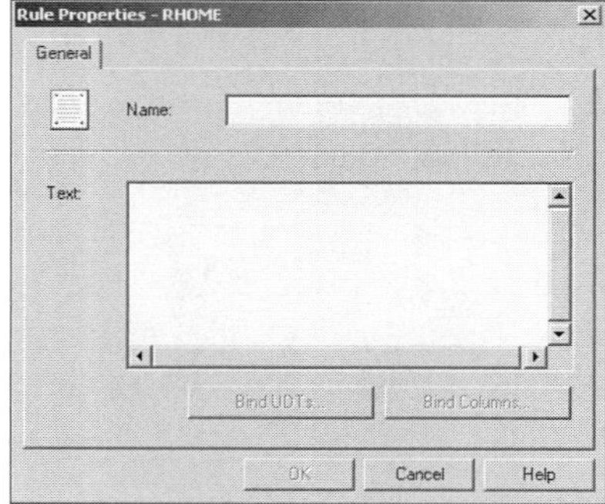

FIGURE 14.6
The Rule Properties dialog.

Ensuring Data Accuracy with ANSI Constraints and Declarative Integrity Mechanisms

You can use ANSI constraints and declarative integrity to ensure the accuracy of your data. They include the use of the `IDENTITY` property and the following constraints: default, check, primary key, foreign key, and unique.

The `IDENTITY` Property

The `IDENTITY` property enables you to use system-generated values in your tables. It is similar to the auto-number data type in Microsoft Access and Microsoft FoxPro databases. You are allowed a single column in each table with the `IDENTITY` property.

Typically, identity columns generate system-assigned keys. To enforce entity integrity, you must uniquely identify every row in a table. If no natural column or set of columns does this for you, you might want to create an identity column.

You can use the `IDENTITY` property only if the column to which it's being assigned is an integer or is compatible with an integer. Therefore, you can use the following data types:

```
tinyint      bigint
smallint     numeric
integer      decimal
```

You can use `numeric` and `decimal` only if they have a scale of 0 (such as `numeric (12,0)`). The column must also not allow nulls. You might want to use these data types that scale a bit more, because the `IDENTITY` property doesn't reuse values by default and doesn't wrap around. After it is "filled up," no more inserts are allowed.

Each time you perform an insert into a table with the `IDENTITY` property enabled for a column, the next available value is automatically inserted into that column:

SYNTAX

```
IDENTITY [(seed, increment)]
```

In this syntax,

- *`seed`* is the value identifying the starting value for the identity column. It's used for the first row inserted into the table.
- *`increment`* is the value that identifies the amount of change (expressed as an integer) that will occur between each value. This value can be positive or negative.

If you don't specify a seed or increment, they each default to 1. Hence, the first row would have a value of 1, the next, 2, and so on.

You use the `IDENTITY` property during a `CREATE TABLE` or an `ALTER TABLE` statement, as discussed on Day 9, "Data Types and Creating Tables." For example, the following results in a value of `1` for col1 when the first row is added, then `101`, then `201`, and so on:

```
CREATE TABLE mytable5
(col1 int not null IDENTITY(1,100),
 col2 char(5) not null)
```

Because identity columns don't wrap, you can see that you might run out. Because you can't change data types in SQL Server after you create a table, be sure to select a data type large enough to handle any conceivable values you might have for this column.

If you use `IDENTITY` without the optional parameters, it is set to `(1,1)`.

You can refer to the column using the keyword `IDENTITYCOL` instead of the proper column name. Because only one column in each table can have the `IDENTITY` property set, SQL Server can always figure out which column you're referring to. In the preceding example, you could run `SELECT IDENTITYCOL FROM mytable5`, and SQL Server would return only the data for col1.

To get information about an identity column on a table, you can run the `sp_help` system stored procedure, specifying the table name as a parameter. You can also use the system functions `IDENT_SEED` or `IDENT_INCR`:

SYNTAX

```
IDENT_SEED('tablename')
IDENT_INCR('tablename')
```

For these syntax lines,

- `IDENT_SEED` returns the *`seed`* parameter used during the `CREATE` or `ALTER TABLE` statement.
- `IDENT_INCR` returns the *`increment`* parameter used during the `CREATE` or `ALTER TABLE` statement.

From a programming perspective, an important question comes up right away. How would you know what value was last inserted? In comes the global value `@@IDENTITY`. Every time you insert a value into a table that has an identity column, the `@@IDENTITY` value is updated.

Try the following code to see how this change works. You'll work with `myidenttab` table which you will create now.

```
CREATE TABLE myidenttab
(col1 int not null IDENTITY(1,100),
```

```
 col2 char(5) not null)
Go
INSERT myidenttab (col2) VALUES ('howdy')
    SELECT @@identity
```

At this point, the value of `@@identity` should be `1`.

INPUT

```
INSERT myidenttab(col2) VALUES ('Movie')
SELECT @@identity
```

Now `@@identity` should be `101`.

Running the `truncate table` statement resets the identity value back to the initial seed. Ordinary deletes—even deletes of every row in the table—don't have this effect, however. Try it here:

INPUT

```
DELETE myidenttab
Go
INSERT myidenttab (col2) VALUES ('Zebra')
SELECT @@identity
```

Now `@@identity` should be `201`, even though it's the only row in the table.

INPUT

```
TRUNCATE TABLE myidenttab
Go
INSERT myidenttab (col2) VALUES ('howdy')
SELECT @@identity
```

Now `@@identity` should be back to `1` again.

A new feature of SQL Server 2000 is the function `SCOPE_IDENTITY()`, which returns `@@IDENTITY`, but with a twist. `@@IDENTITY` returns the last `IDENTITY` value updated within the database. `SCOPE_IDENTITY()`returns the last `IDENTITY` value from the current `SCOPE`. An example is the best way to show how `SCOPE_IDENTITY()`varies from `@@IDENTITY`. Suppose that you have a trigger (you'll examine triggers in detail tomorrow), and that trigger runs code that modifies another table with an identity column. When you select the value of `@@IDENTITY`, you get back the `IDENTITY` value of the table modified by the trigger, not your original table, because that's the last identity value modified. However, `SCOPE_IDENTITY()` returns the value of the last identity row you inserted directly into the original table. Not clear yet? Look at the following to make sense of it all:

INPUT/OUTPUT

```
Create table triggertab (col1 int not null identity(1,1), col2
➥char(5) null)
Create table othertab (cola int not null identity(100,1))
GO
Create trigger mytrigger on triggertab for insert as
Insert othertab DEFAULT VALUES
insert triggertab (col2) values ('howdy')
GO
INSERT othertab DEFAULT VALUES
```

```
INSERT triggertab (col2) VALUES ('doody')
select @@identity
select scope_identity()

(1 row(s) affected)

----------------------------------------
(1 row(s) affected)

----------------------------------------
2
(1 row(s) affected)
```

Notice that the result from `@@IDENTITY` is 100 because the trigger on `triggertab` modified table `othertab`'s `IDENTITY` value, so this is indeed the last identity column to be updated. That's probably not the result you were expecting, so SQL Server 2000 has added `SCOPE_IDENTITY()` so that you can check the last `IDENTITY` value you inserted on the `triggertab` table. In all previous releases of SQL Server, the data value inserted into `triggertab` would have been lost.

Identity values are kept as a pool in memory. There's no guarantee that every value will be used because some transactions might be canceled, and sometimes server crashes occur. If you want to guarantee that your identity columns are unique, you must have a unique index on that column. Some people want to reuse identity values. By default, however, you can't manually insert into identity columns. You can use the `identity_insert` option, however, to override that default for a single table from within a single session:

SYNTAX

```
SET identity_insert [database.[owner.]]tablename ON|OFF
```

The preceding turns on the capability to insert directly into a table's identity column. You must be the table owner or a member of the sysadmin, db_owner, or db_ddladmin role to turn on this option.

To use this capability on `myidenttab`, run the following Transact-SQL code. You must run it all from within the same SQL Server Query Analyzer because of the session-specific `SET` statement:

INPUT

```
SET identity_insert myidenttab ON
Go
INSERT myidenttab (col1, col2) VALUES (2,'jolly')
Go
SET identity_insert myidenttab OFF
Go
SELECT * FROM myidenttab
```

This example inserts the row you've requested into the table. You must specify the column list, even if you are specifying a value for every column in the table.

Although the UNIQUEIDENTIFER data type is not strictly a constraint or DRI option, it is another option you might consider in place of an identity (particularly for primary keys). If you define a column with the UNIQUEIDENTIFIER data type—and set a default of the NEWID() function, which automatically generates a new, globally unique value each time a row is added—you have a powerful mechanism to ensure uniqueness of your key values. Unlike the IDENTITY property, UNIQUEIDENTIFIER values are unique in every table on every system. However, they are much larger than the typical identity column using the integer data type, so you should be cautious when using them too widely. Also, referring to a 16-byte binary number onscreen instead of a simple integer is much harder.

ANSI Constraints

ANSI constraints are functionally very similar to the traditional objects you looked at earlier. However, they aren't separate objects; they are part of the definition of the tables in your database. They can enforce domain integrity with default and check constraints, as with defaults and rules, or referential integrity with primary keys and foreign keys. You can also enforce entity integrity with unique constraints or primary keys.

Using constraints can be a major improvement over using defaults and rules. You don't need to keep a separate set of objects to use with your tables, nor do you need to keep track of bindings. Constraints are stored in the `sysreferences`, `syscomments`, and `sysobjects` system tables, and possibly the `sysforeignkeys` table, in each database.

Now examine the syntax of constraints as an extension to the `CREATE TABLE` and `ALTER TABLE` statements:

SYNTAX

```
CREATE TABLE [database.[owner].]table_name
({col_name column_properties [constraint]
[[,] {next_col_name | next_constraint}...])
[ON filegroup]
[TEXTIMAGE_ON filegroup]
```

You worked with this same code on Day 9, except now you need to focus on where it says *`constraint`*. Constraints are of the following form:

```
[CONSTRAINT name] Type_of_Constraint [Constraint_Options]
```

The full syntax of the *`constraint`* option is as follows (don't worry—it's broken down in great detail later today):

```
column_constraint ::= [CONSTRAINT constraint_name]
{[ NULL | NOT NULL ]| [ { PRIMARY KEY | UNIQUE }
[CLUSTERED | NONCLUSTERED]
```

```
[WITH [FILLFACTOR = fillfactor] ]
[ON {filegroup | DEFAULT} ]]
]
| [ [FOREIGN KEY] REFERENCES ref_table [(ref_column) ]
  [ON UPDATE { CASCADE | NO ACTION }]
  [ON DELETE { CASCADE | NO ACTION }]
 [NOT FOR REPLICATION]]
| CHECK [NOT FOR REPLICATION] (logical_expression) }

table_constraint ::= [CONSTRAINT constraint_name]
{[ { PRIMARY KEY | UNIQUE } [ CLUSTERED | NONCLUSTERED]
{ ( column[ASC | DESC][,...n] ) }
[ WITH [FILLFACTOR = fillfactor] ]
[ON {filegroup | DEFAULT} ]]
| FOREIGN KEY [(column[,...n])] REFERENCES ref_table [(ref_column[,...n])]
  [ON UPDATE { CASCADE | NO ACTION }]
  [ON DELETE { CASCADE | NO ACTION }]
 [NOT FOR REPLICATION] | CHECK [NOT FOR REPLICATION] (search_conditions)
}

ALTER TABLE table
{ [ALTER COLUMN column_name
{[ new_data_type [ (precision[, scale] ) ]
[COLLATE collation_name] [ NULL | NOT NULL ]
| [ {ADD | DROP} ROWGUIDCOL ] }]
| ADD { [ column_definition ]
| column_name AS computed_column_expression [,...n]
| [ WITH CHECK | WITH NOCHECK] ADD [ <table_constraint> ] }[,...n]
|  DROP { [CONSTRAINT] constraint_name | COLUMN column }[,...n]
| {CHECK | NOCHECK} CONSTRAINT {ALL | constraint_name[,...n]}
| {ENABLE | DISABLE} TRIGGER {ALL | trigger_name[,...n]} } }
```

Note that the preceding is a simplified syntax.

Constraints come in two forms: column level and table level. Column-level constraints are applied at the column level of the create table, and table-level constraints are added as if they were additional columns. Examples are the easiest way to differentiate between them.

Column level:

```
CREATE TABLE mytablea
(col1 int not null CONSTRAINT DF_a_col1 DEFAULT (0))
```

Table level:

```
CREATE TABLE mytableb
(col1 int not null)

ALTER TABLE mytableb ADD
CONSTRAINT DF_b_col1 DEFAULT (0) FOR col1
```

The FOR col1 option specifies to which column the default applies. The column is implied during a column-level constraint.

Default Constraints

Default constraints are very much like SQL Server defaults. However, default constraints apply only to columns—never to user-defined data types. You can't apply default constraints to columns that are also identity columns. You also can't use default constraints with columns defined with the timestamp data type. The difference here is that the default is "part" of the column, as opposed to having to be bound to the column. These constraints are enforced during inserts only—just as SQL Server default objects are.

SYNTAX

Column level:

```
[CONSTRAINT constraint_name] DEFAULT {constant_expression}
```

Table level:

```
[CONSTRAINT constraint_name] DEFAULT {constant_expression} FOR col_name
```

The CONSTRAINT *constraint_name* part of the syntax is optional. This part identifies that you are adding a constraint explicitly (always a good idea from a documentation perspective), as well as giving the constraint a name. If you don't name a constraint, it ends up with a name like this:

```
DF__mytab__col1__117F9D94
```

Therefore, naming constraints is a good idea, because you'll see in a bit that you might want to run some operations that require you to name the constraints you're working with.

The keyword DEFAULT is next, and then either a constant appropriate for the data type, NULL, or a *niladic function*. Niladic functions include the following:

- CURRENT_TIMESTAMP gets the current date and time; it is equivalent to SELECT getdate().
- SYSTEM_USER gets the current login name; it is equivalent to SELECT suser_sname().
- CURRENT_USER, USER, USER_NAME, and SESSION_USER all get the current database username; they are equivalent to SELECT user_name().

Functionally speaking, no difference exists here between table-level and column-level default constraints other than the fact that default constraints must be specified as column level during a CREATE TABLE, and table or column-level constraints during an ALTER TABLE.

14

These examples show default constraints:

INPUT

```
CREATE TABLE defaulttab1
( intcol int NOT NULL CONSTRAINT df_intcol DEFAULT 0,
  char5col char(5) NOT NULL DEFAULT 'Hello',
  anumber numeric(10,0) NOT NULL
)
Go
```

Note that the first constraint is named, but the second one isn't; therefore, it gets a system-assigned name.

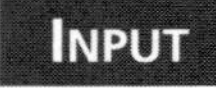

```
ALTER TABLE defaulttab1
ADD moneycol money NULL CONSTRAINT df_moneycol DEFAULT $2.00,
CONSTRAINT df_anumber DEFAULT 100 FOR anumber
Go
```

Run **`exec sp_help defaulttab1`** to verify that the constraints are properly on the table, and you see something like this in the constraint section of the report:

OUTPUT

```
constraint_type              constraint_name        ... constraint_keys
--------------------------------------------------------------------
DEFAULT on column char5col DF__defaultta__char5__702996C1 ('Hello')
DEFAULT on column anumber  df_anumber                        (100)
DEFAULT on column intcol   df_intcol                           (0)
DEFAULT on column moneycol df_moneycol                    (2.0000)

No foreign keys reference this table.
No views with schemabinding reference this table.
```

Notice the system-assigned name for the default constraint you didn't name.

Check Constraints

Check constraints function very much like rules. They provide a mechanism to enforce domain integrity for your columns. You can have as many check constraints, unlike other ANSI constraints, as you want on a single column. They have many of the same restrictions as default constraints, such as with columns' `timestamp` data type or the `IDENTITY` property. They are checked during inserts and updates, just as rules are.

However, check constraints can do something that rules can't. Check constraints can refer to other columns of the same table as part of their enforcement of conditions. You can refer to columns this way only with table-level constraints, however.

SYNTAX

Column level:

```
[CONSTRAINT constraint_name]
CHECK [NOT FOR REPLICATION] (expression)
```

Table level:

```
[CONSTRAINT constraint_name]
CHECK [NOT FOR REPLICATION] (expression)
```

In this syntax,

- `CONSTRAINT` *`constraint_name`* is optional, just as with default constraints.
- `CHECK` specifies that you are creating a check constraint. The expression can be any expression, just as with rules. However, now you can also reference other columns within the same table.
- CHECK constraints must evaluate to a Boolean value.
- `NOT FOR REPLICATION` prevents the check constraint from being enforced when the replication process inserts or updates the table.

As you learned previously, only table-level constraints can have references to multiple columns.

Examples are probably the best way to see how check constraints work:

INPUT

```
CREATE TABLE checktable
(col1 int not null CONSTRAINT ck_col1
     CHECK (col1 between 1 and 100),
 col2 char(5) null,
 zip_code char(5) null,
 col4 int not null,
 CONSTRAINT ck_col4 CHECK (col4 > col1),
 CONSTRAINT ck_zip_code CHECK
(zip_code like '[0-9][0-9][0-9][0-9][0-9]')
)

ALTER TABLE checktable
ADD CONSTRAINT ck_col2 CHECK (col2 like 'H%')
Go
```

Note that the rules are now enforced. For example,

```
INSERT checktable VALUES (1,'Howdy','99901',2)
```

works, but

```
INSERT checktable VALUES (2,'Howdy','8834A',3)
```

fails with the message

```
Server: Msg 547, Level 16, State 1, Line 1
INSERT statement conflicted with COLUMN CHECK constraint
'ck_zip_code'. The conflict occurred in database 'pubs',
table 'checktable', column 'zip_code'.
The statement has been terminated.
```

Primary-Key Constraints

Primary-key constraints combine referential integrity and entity integrity. Every column used for a primary key must be defined with the `NOT NULL` attribute, and only one primary-key constraint can exist on a single table. The primary-key constraint might be referenced by foreign-key constraints. Some processes, such as replication or open database connectivity (ODBC) applications, might require declared ANSI primary keys.

Primary-key constraints are an implied creation of a unique index. By default, a unique clustered index is created.

SYNTAX

Column level:

```
[CONSTRAINT constraint_name] [  PRIMARY KEY [ CLUSTERED | NONCLUSTERED]
[ WITH [FILLFACTOR = fillfactor] ][ON {filegroup | DEFAULT} ]
```

Table level:

```
[CONSTRAINT constraint_name] [  PRIMARY KEY [ CLUSTERED | NONCLUSTERED]
{ ( col_name[ASC | DESC][,...n] ) } [ WITH [FILLFACTOR = fillfactor] ]
[ON {filegroup | DEFAULT} ]
```

In this syntax, `PRIMARY KEY` creates the primary key (unique) index. Any index options are valid here, including changing the index to nonclustered, applying fill factors, and so on. By default, this option creates a clustered index.

No functional difference exists here, per se, between column-level and table-level constraints.

You can create a primary key on a single column or on up to 16 columns, as long as the total width of the columns doesn't exceed 900 bytes.

This example creates a unique clustered index on col1 of table `pktable`:

```
CREATE TABLE pktable
(col1 int not null CONSTRAINT pk_col1 PRIMARY KEY,
 col2 char(5) null
)
```

This next example creates a unique nonclustered index on col1 of table `pktable2`:

```
CREATE TABLE pktable2
(col1 int not null CONSTRAINT pk2_col1
     PRIMARY KEY nonclustered (col1),
 col2 char(5) null
)
```

This last example creates a unique clustered index on `(col1, col2)` of table `pktable3`:

```
CREATE TABLE pktable3
(col1 int not null,
```

```
 col2 char(2) not null,
 col3 int null,
 CONSTRAINT pk3_col1col2 PRIMARY KEY (col1, col2)
)
```

In all instances, you can view the index but can't manipulate it directly. If you attempt to drop the index, for example, on the last table, you get an error such as this:

```
Server: Msg 3723, Level 16, State 4, Line 1
An explicit DROP INDEX is not allowed on index 'pktable3.pk3_col1col2'.
It is being used for PRIMARY KEY constraint enforcement.
```

Unique Constraints

Unique constraints enable you to create unique indexes, just as primary keys can, but with a bit more flexibility. You typically create unique constraints if you have more than one column or set of columns that can be valid primary keys. Using such constraints serves two purposes: It documents the potential key choices and allows foreign keys on other tables to reference the unique constraints (in addition to being allowed to reference primary-key constraints).

Unique constraints can also be created on columns that allow nulls. You can also have more than one unique constraint on a table.

SYNTAX

Column level:

```
[CONSTRAINT constraint_name] [  UNIQUE [ CLUSTERED | NONCLUSTERED]
[ WITH [FILLFACTOR = fillfactor] ] [ON {filegroup | DEFAULT} ]
```

Table level:

```
[CONSTRAINT constraint_name] [  PRIMARY KEY [ CLUSTERED | NONCLUSTERED]
{ ( column[ASC | DESC][,...n] ) } [ WITH [FILLFACTOR = fillfactor] ]
[ON {filegroup | DEFAULT} ]
```

Just as before, the name of the constraint is optional. Also, just as with primary-key constraints, at the column level you don't have to list any columns. It assumes just the column you create the constraint on otherwise.

As an example, the following creates a primary key as well as a unique constraint. Both are unique indexes on table `myuniquetable`.

```
CREATE TABLE myuniquetable
(col1 int not null CONSTRAINT pk_myuniquetable PRIMARY KEY,
 col2 char(20) NOT NULL CONSTRAINT u_myuniquetable UNIQUE
)
```

Foreign-Key Constraints

Foreign-key constraints protect referential integrity between tables. You create a foreign key on a table, which references another table's primary-key or unique constraint. This constraint does one of three things:

- Restricts data modifications against the table with the primary key as long as the table with the foreign keys contains related rows
- Deletes all related rows in the table with the foreign keys
- Updates the primary-key value in all the related rows in the table with the foreign keys

It also prevents data from being added (or updated) on the table with the foreign-key constraint that wouldn't contain valid data from the referenced tables.

Creating a foreign key doesn't create an index on the table; however, it's likely that this is a good candidate for an index. Therefore, you typically need to follow your creation of tables with foreign keys with `CREATE INDEX` statements. You can refer to tables in the same database only when creating foreign-key constraints. You must have the appropriate permission (SELECT or REFERENCES) on the table you refer to, and any single table can have a maximum of 253 foreign keys pointing to it. You can't extend this limit.

SYNTAX

Column level:

```
[CONSTRAINT constraint_name] [FOREIGN KEY] REFERENCES ref_table
    [ ( ref_column ) ]
   [ ON UPDATE { CASCADE | NO ACTION } ]
   [ ON DELETE { CASCADE | NO ACTION } ]
 [NOT FOR REPLICATION]
```

Table level:

```
[CONSTRAINT constraint_name]  FOREIGN KEY [(column[,...n])]
    REFERENCES ref_table [(ref_column[,...n])]
   [ ON UPDATE { CASCADE | NO ACTION } ]
   [ ON DELETE { CASCADE | NO ACTION } ]
    [NOT FOR REPLICATION]
```

As usual, the constraint name is optional. As with the other referential constraints, the column name doesn't have to be referenced locally if it's a single-column constraint. Also, you don't have to name the column on the other table if the columns have the same name.

If you don't specify either `ON UPDATE` or `ON DELETE`, both are set to `NO ACTION` to be compatible with previous SQL Server releases. This means any delete or update of a primary key value is prevented if any rows are referencing the primary key in the table(s) with the foreign key.

If you specify the CASCADE option, the rows from the table(s) with the foreign key are deleted or have their referenced column values updated as appropriate.

If you reference a multiple-column primary-key/unique constraint, be careful to reference it in the same order between your column list in the FOREIGN KEY and REFERENCES lists. Self-references are supported, so you could reference the table to itself (with another column).

The following code creates an employee table and an order table (which was entered by an employee). To verify that a valid employee entered the order, you can either program the functionality or declare it with foreign keys. Then, when someone tries to delete an employee, the individual is not allowed to do so as long as there are orders for that employee.

INPUT

```
CREATE TABLE emp
(emp_id int not null CONSTRAINT pk_emp PRIMARY KEY,
 emp_name char(30) not null)
Go
CREATE TABLE orders
(order_id int not null CONSTRAINT pk_order PRIMARY KEY,
 emp_id int not null CONSTRAINT fk_order
FOREIGN KEY (emp_id) REFERENCES emp (emp_id)
   ➥ON DELETE NO ACTION ON UPDATE NO ACTION
)
Go
INSERT emp VALUES (1,'Joe Smith')
INSERT emp VALUES (2,'Ann Jones')
INSERT orders VALUES (1,1)
INSERT orders VALUES (2,2)
    Go
```

This example works fine so far. Now try to insert an order for an employee who doesn't exist:

INPUT/OUTPUT

```
INSERT orders VALUES (3,3)
Go
```

```
Server: Msg 547, Level 16, State 1, Line 1
INSERT statement conflicted with COLUMN FOREIGN KEY constraint
'fk_order'.
The conflict occurred in database 'pubs',
table 'emp', column 'emp_id'.
The statement has been terminated.
```


Okay, now try to delete an employee who has an order:

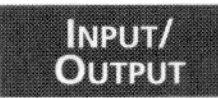

```
DELETE emp WHERE emp_id = 1
Go
```

```
Server: Msg 547, Level 16, State 1, Line 1
DELETE statement conflicted with COLUMN REFERENCE constraint
```

```
'fk_order'.
The conflict occurred in database 'pubs',
table 'orders', column 'emp_id'.
The statement has been terminated.
```

An example of the self-referencing behavior is something like this, which means that every manager must also be a valid employee:

```
CREATE TABLE emp_manager
(emp_id int not null CONSTRAINT pk_emp_mgr PRIMARY KEY,
 mgr_id int not null CONSTRAINT fk_emp_mgr FOREIGN KEY
REFERENCES emp_manager (emp_id),
  emp_name char(30) not null)
```

These two insert statements will complete successfully because they reference valid data:

```
INSERT emp_manager VALUES (1,1,'Ann Jones')
INSERT emp_manager VALUES (2,1,'Tom Smith')
```

Note, however, that if you try to reference someone who doesn't exist yet, as here,

```
INSERT emp_manager VALUES (3,4,'Bob Newett')
```

you get a similar message as before—that the foreign-key constraint was violated. This approach can be very useful in many real-world scenarios.

The code in Listing 14.1 adds to the equation an order detail table that uses the new capabilities of SQL Server 2000 to cascade any deletes and updates.

LISTING 14.1 Using Cascading Constraints

```
CREATE TABLE order_detail
(order_id int not null CONSTRAINT pk_order_detail PRIMARY KEY
➥(order_id, line_no),
 line_no int not null,
 part_no int not null,
 price money not null,
CONSTRAINT fk_order_detail FOREIGN KEY (order_id) REFERENCES orders
➥(order_id) ON DELETE CASCADE ON UPDATE CASCADE
)
-- Load some data into the table
INSERT order_detail VALUES (1,1,1,$5.00)
INSERT order_detail VALUES (1,2,2,$15.00)
INSERT order_detail VALUES (1,3,9,$2.95)
INSERT order_detail VALUES (2,1,1,$5.00)
INSERT order_detail VALUES (2,2,8,$8.00)
INSERT order_detail VALUES (2,3,4,$29.00)

-- Now delete order number 2.
```

```
DELETE orders where order_id = 2
--select * from order_detail to verify the rows for order #2 were deleted
select * from order_detail

-- Now update order #1 to be order #5 and watch it cascade to order_detail
update orders set order_id = 5 where order_id = 1
--select * from order_detail to verify the rows for order #1 were
--updated to be order #5
select * from order_detail
```

Dropping Constraints

You can drop a constraint by using the `ALTER TABLE` statement. For example, to drop the foreign-key constraint in the preceding employee/manager example, run the following:

INPUT

```
ALTER TABLE emp_manager DROP CONSTRAINT fk_emp_mgr
```

However, if you try to drop a primary-key constraint (or unique constraint) that still has foreign-key references, you cannot do so. For example, on the `emp_manager` table, if you try to drop the primary-key constraint with this code (without having dropped the foreign key),

```
ALTER TABLE emp_manager DROP CONSTRAINT pk_emp_mgr
```

you get this error message:

```
Server: Msg 3725, Level 16, State 1, Line 2
The constraint 'pk_emp_mgr' is being referenced by table 'emp_manager',
foreign key constraint 'fk_emp_mgr'.
Server: Msg 3727, Level 16, State 1, Line 2
Could not drop constraint. See previous errors.
```

Ensuring Data Accuracy with SQL Server Enterprise Manager

All this functionality could be accomplished with SQL Server Enterprise Manager. To access it, highlight the Tables icon inside your database, right-click a table in the right pane, and select Design Table. The Design Table window then opens (see Figure 14.7).

To set the primary key for a table, highlight the column or columns you want to set as the primary key, and then click the yellow key on the toolbar to set the primary key. After you set the key and save it by clicking the floppy disk in the menu, your primary-key constraint is created. Notice that the key icon is added to each column in your table that participates in the primary key.

FIGURE 14.7

The Design Table window.

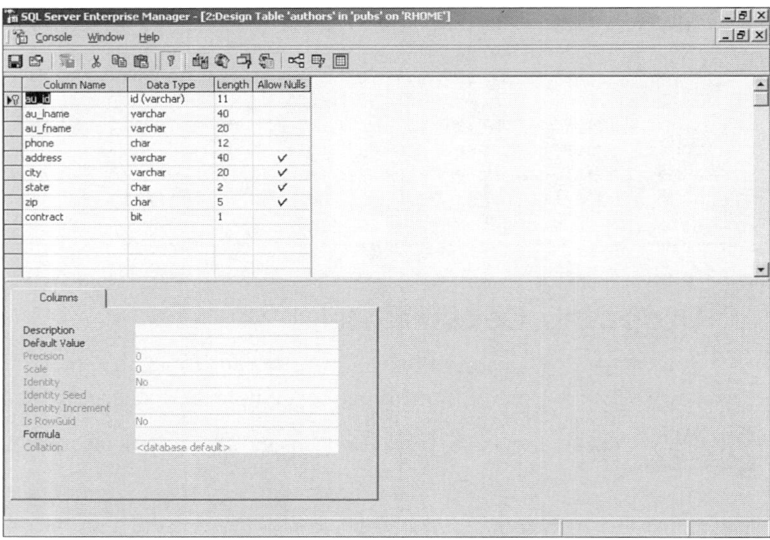

To create a unique constraint for a table, click the table and Index Properties toolbar button (second button from the left), or right-click anywhere in the table and select Properties. Click the Indexes/Keys tab, and fill in the appropriate information. You were presented with this same dialog yesterday. Remember to use the Constraint option after you select your columns and check the Create UNIQUE check box.

To illustrate this dialog and to facilitate an examination of check constraints and foreign-key constraints, as well as primary-key and unique constraints, create a table named `ConstraintTab` in the `pubs` database. After you create the table, add the following columns in design view:

Column Name	*Data Type*	*Length*	*Allow Nulls*
pkcol	`int`		
fkcol	`int`		Check
checkcol	`char`	10	
defaultcol	`int`		
altpkcol	`int`		

Highlight the pkcol column, and click the yellow key to add a primary-key constraint. Also, make pkcol an identity by right-clicking the table, selecting Properties, and then selecting pkcol for the Table Identity Column: selection (accept the default seed and increment values). Highlight the defaultcol row, and set the Default Value to 0. When completed, the table should look like Figure 14.8.

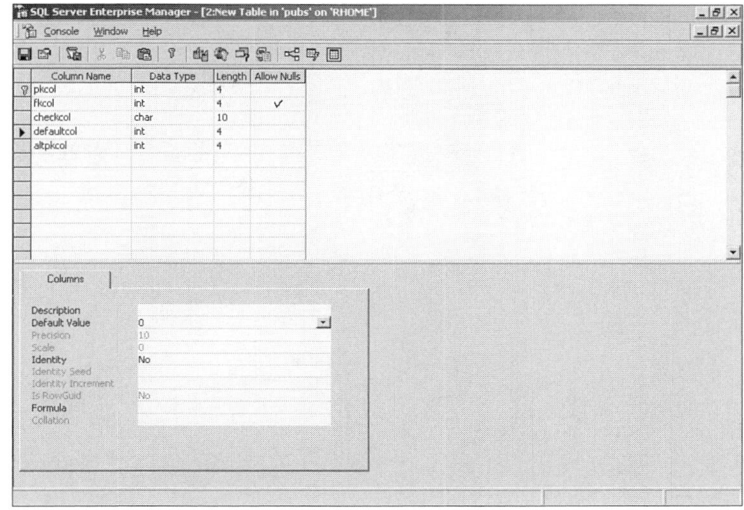

FIGURE 14.8
The Design Table window for the `ConstraintTab` *table.*

At this point, you've created a table with a default constraint on the defaultcol column and a primary key on the pkcol column. Now create one more table, called `reltab` (for relationship table), with a single column, pkcol of data type `int` not null, and make it a primary key.

Back in Enterprise Manager, right-click the Diagrams folder, and select New Database Diagram. In the Create Database Diagram Wizard, click Next, and then select the `ConstraintTab` and `reltab` tables (see Figure 14.9) .

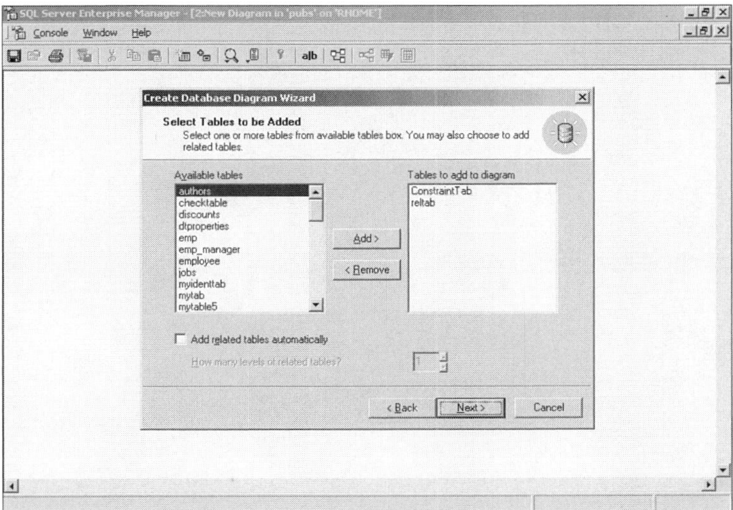

FIGURE 14.9
The Create Database Diagram Wizard dialog.

Click Next and then Finish. SQL Server Enterprise Manager notifies you that the tables you requested have been added to the database diagram. Click OK to see your new database diagram (see Figure 14.10).

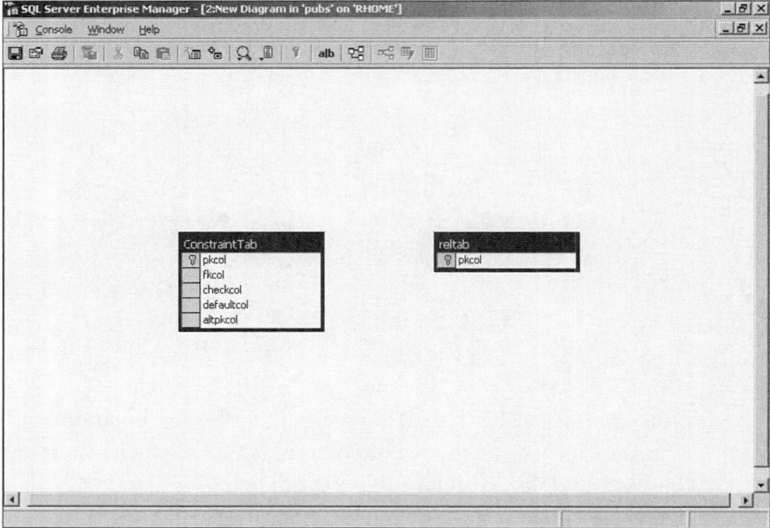

FIGURE 14.10 *The initial database diagram.*

Click the fkcol column in the `ConstraintTab` table, and hold down your mouse button. Drag your mouse to the `reltab` table and release it. The dialog in Figure 14.11 appears, showing you the primary-key to foreign-key relationship you are creating. Accept the defaults and click OK.

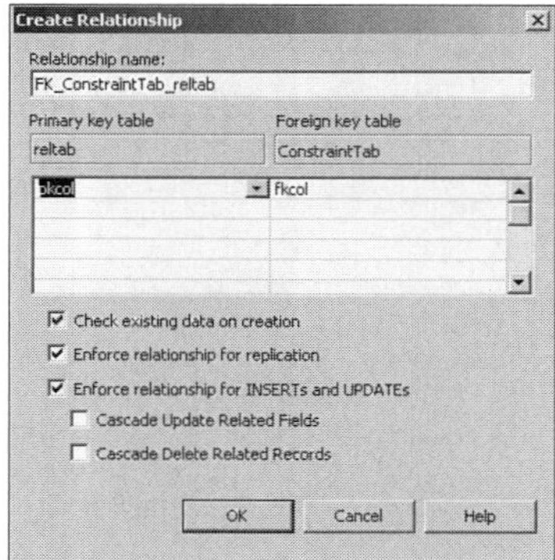

FIGURE 14.11 *Your newly created relationship.*

Notice how the diagram has changed; your relationship is reflected by a line between the tables (see Figure 14.12). You can right-click the line to change the relationship properties or move the tables around any way you like to view these relationships.

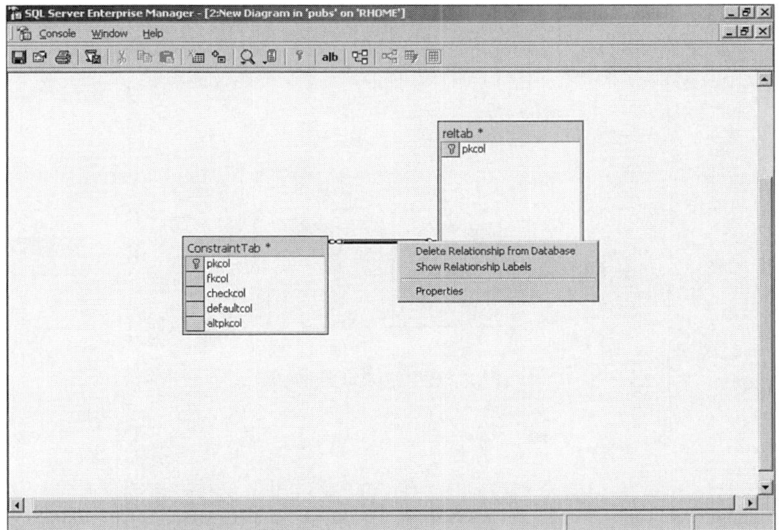

FIGURE 14.12

Your database diagram showing your newly created relationship.

Save the diagram, and accept the default name (which should be DIAGRAM1 if it's the first one you've created). SQL Server Enterprise Manager then shows you the list of tables you've changed and asks whether you want to save them. Click Yes to save your referential integrity changes.

Go back into Enterprise Manager and select the `ConstraintTab` table and enter design view (remember, right-click the table and select Design Table). Right-click the fkcol column, and select Properties. On the Relationships tab, view the relationship you created to your `reltab` table (see Figure 14.13) .

Now click the Check Constraints tab, and then click the New button to create a new check constraint. Complete the dialog as shown in Figure 14.14 to add a check constraint.

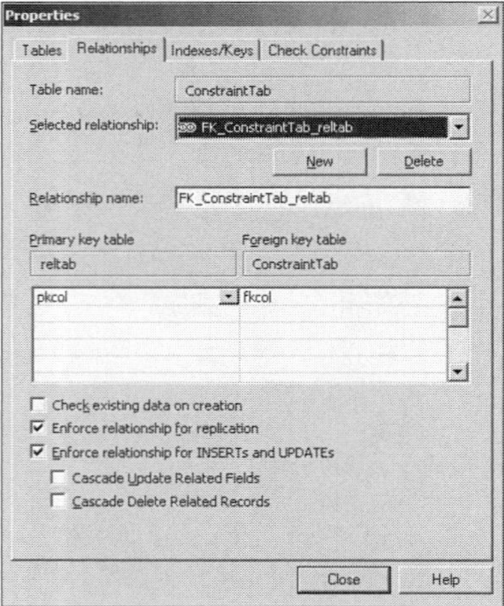

FIGURE 14.13

The completed foreign-key constraint dialog.

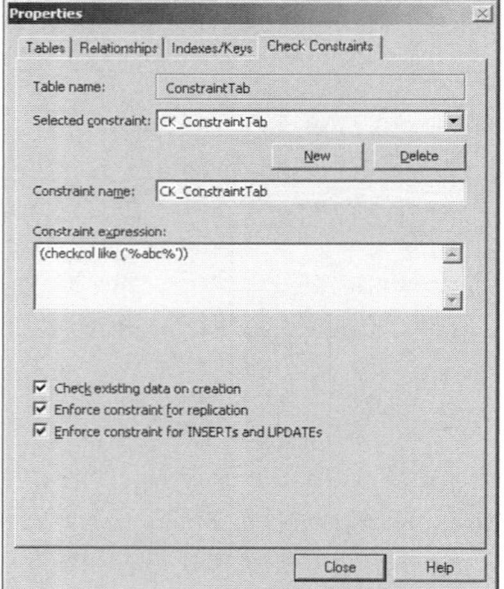

FIGURE 14.14

The completed Check Constraints dialog.

Finally, add a unique constraint as described earlier by selecting a new index on the Indexes/Keys tab of the Table and Index Properties dialogs and completing the dialog as shown in Figure 14.15. When it's complete, save the table and exit the Design Table window.

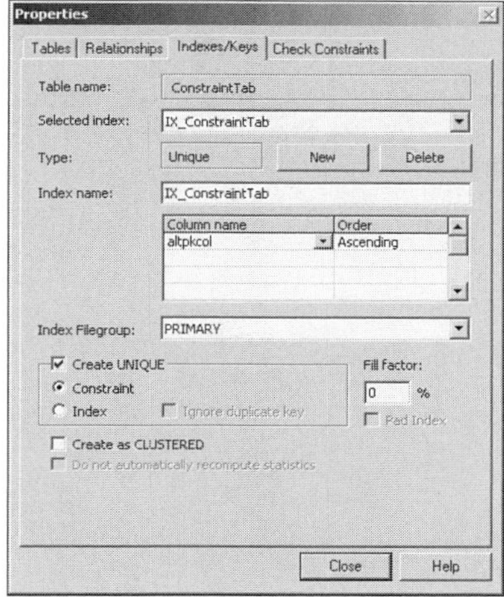

FIGURE 14.15
The completed unique constraint dialog.

Now run the `sp_help` system stored procedure on the table from the SQL Server Query Analyzer, and view the constraints:

INPUT

```
EXEC sp_help constrainttab
```

Notice that you've created one of each kind of constraint on this table as well as used the `IDENTITY` property. All the functionality relating to constraints and the `IDENTITY` property are fully exposed within SQL Server Enterprise Manager.

Deferring Constraints

You can defer foreign-key and check constraints when they are created. Primary-key, unique, and default constraints can't be deferred (because they create indexes in the case of primary-key and unique constraints, and defaults are never checked for previous data). When you alter a table, add one of these constraints, and specify the `NOCHECK` option, existing data isn't validated. If you alter a table and add a check constraint, existing data is verified for validity as in this example:

INPUT

```
CREATE TABLE mytesttable
(col1 char(5) not null
)
Go
INSERT mytesttable VALUES ('Howdy')
INSERT mytesttable VALUES ('Grant')
```

14

Now try to create a constraint that would fail for some of the data:

INPUT

```
ALTER TABLE mytesttable
ADD CONSTRAINT ck_mytest CHECK (col1 like 'h%')
```

And it fails:

```
Server: Msg 547, Level 16, State 1
ALTER TABLE statement conflicted with COLUMN CHECK constraint
 'ck_mytest'. _The conflict occurred in database 'pubs', table
 'mytesttable', column 'col1'.
```

However, if you create the same constraint by using the NOCHECK option, it now works:

```
ALTER TABLE mytesttable
WITH NOCHECK
ADD CONSTRAINT ck_mytest CHECK (col1 like 'h%')
```

The same is true of foreign-key constraints. Be careful using this option because you are identifying that you might have invalid data in your database.

Disabling Constraints

You can also disable constraints temporarily so that you can add invalid data that violates your check constraints or data that would violate your foreign-key constraints. To do so, run the `ALTER TABLE` command with the `WITH NOCHECK CONSTRAINT` *`constraintname`* or `WITH NOCHECK ALL` option to disable all check and foreign-key constraints.

Continuing the preceding example, the following disables all constraint checking:

```
ALTER TABLE mytesttable
NOCHECK CONSTRAINT ALL
```

You can then add invalid data to violate the check constraint. You can reenable the constraint by running

```
ALTER TABLE mytesttable
CHECK CONSTRAINT ALL
```

Summary

You can choose to enforce data integrity in several ways. "Traditional" integrity enforcement options in SQL Server revolve around rules, defaults, and user-defined data types. You can also enforce data integrity and referential integrity using ANSI constraints. The choice is entirely up to your individual application needs. ANSI constraints and declarative referential integrity are typically preferred because they tend to perform better and are integrated into the definitions of objects. With SQL Server 2000, delete cascade and update cascade referential integrity are now available, and you no longer need to program triggers or other program logic for this functionality.

Today you also learned about the `IDENTITY` property, which can help you create automatic key values when no natural primary key is available for a table. Automatic key values are extremely useful in most database designs.

Q&A

Q What options can I use to enforce entity integrity?

A Unique indexes, primary-key, unique constraints, rules, defaults and user-defined types.

Q What does the identity property do to a column?

A It generates an automatic value for an integer column.

Q Can a rule refer to another column in a table?

A No. Only table-level check constraints can refer to another column.

Workshop

This section provides quiz questions to help you solidify your understanding of the concepts presented today. In addition to the quiz questions, exercises are provided to let you practice what you've learned today. Try to understand the quiz and exercise answers before continuing on to tomorrow's lesson. Answers are provided in Appendix A, "Answers to Quiz Questions."

Quiz

1. Is the following a valid default definition?

```
Create default mydefault as 'UNKNOWN'
```

2. Can you drop a rule while it's still bound to a column, even if the table doesn't have any data?
3. Is a numeric data type allowed for identity columns?
4. Can a foreign key refer to a table in a different database?
5. Can a unique constraint be deferred or disabled?
6. Can you drop the indexes created by some constraints?

Exercises

1. Create three tables, each with compatible data types. Create primary-key/foreign-key relationships between them using the database diagram features of SQL Server Enterprise Manager.
2. Create several tables using the `IDENTITY` property. Try different seed and increment values, and add data to see whether they perform as you expect. Also, run the `truncate table` statement to see your identity options "reset" back to the initial seed value.

WEEK 2

In Review

Now it's time to take a quick refresher on the information you covered during this second week.

On Day 8, you looked at restoring your databases and transaction logs. You also learned the importance of having an emergency plan in place. We can't stress enough that you must verify your backup and recovery process on a timely basis.

On Day 9, you learned how to work with the different data types available in SQL Server 2000 to create your own table definitions.

On Day 10, you developed a strong foundation for programming with the `SELECT` statement. You learned how to implement the use of arithmetic and mathematical operators, how to use data conversion in your `SELECT` statements, and how to choose ranges and sort your selected data. You then extended your Transact-SQL (T-SQL) development by learning how to do some database programming, which included the use of aggregates such as `AVG`, `COUNT`, and the `GROUP BY` statements. You also learned how to take advantage of joins. You finished by correlating data using subqueries.

On Day 11, you learned how to insert, update, and delete data from your databases. With this knowledge, you can make modifications to data that already exists or add and remove data.

On Day 12, you learned the fundamentals of programming, including the creation and use of batch processing and transaction management. You learned the use of the `BEGIN TRAN`, `COMMIT TRAN`, and `ROLLBACK TRAN` statements. You also learned about the different locking mechanisms in SQL

8
9
10
11
12
13
14

Server and how to implement control-of-flow statements such as `BEGIN` and `END`, `CASE`, `DECLARE`, `IF` and `ELSE` statements, and `WHILE` loops.

Day 13 showed you how to speed up your queries through the use of proper indexing. You learned about the clustered and nonclustered indexes. You also learned about factors that can affect index performance, such as the fill factor. You finished the day with a quick look at the full-text indexing feature of SQL Server 2000.

All these backups, modifications, and data selections are virtually useless if your database lacks integrity. To be sure of your data, on Day 14 you learned about the different types of data integrity, including entity, domain, and referential. You also learned the difference between procedural and declarative integrity and examined the `IDENTITY` value, defaults, rules, and constraints.

WEEK 3

At a Glance

During this third week, you will learn more about programming in SQL Server. Your lessons in Transact-SQL (T-SQL) will cover views, user-defined functions, stored procedures, and triggers. You also learn how to streamline your administrative tasks with automation. You learn how to distribute your data over the enterprise using replication. You will examine data migrating into and out of SQL Server by using various tools and utilities. You then take some time for performance tuning and optimization of SQL Server and finish with a look at using SQL Server with the new XML capabilities.

Day 15 walks you through the use of views, user-defined functions, stored procedures, and triggers. They can be implemented for both speed, ease of use, and database accuracy.

Day 16 examines the types of replication available with SQL Server 2000 and introduces you to the terminology used for replication. Day 17 continues Day 16's replication discussion by showing you how to implement the various types of replication.

Day 18 can be useful to you as a database administrator. You learn how to automate many mundane tasks involved with running and maintaining a database. You can even have email sent to you when your automated tasks fail or succeed. These tasks are all accomplished through the SQL Server Agent.

Day 19 examines migrating data from other systems into SQL Server, as well as migrating data out of SQL Server. You are introduced to Data Transformation Services (DTS), as well as some Transact-SQL commands and command-line utilities for migrating data.

Optimizing your database for best performance and throughput is always a must. You begin to learn how to fine-tune your database on Day 20.

The hottest thing about databases today is XML, and Day 21 introduces you to using your SQL Server with XML.

As always, do all the exercises presented to you at the end of each lesson. They not only build on what you've learned, but they also give you a chance to test your understanding of the material presented.

WEEK 3

DAY 15

Creating Views, Triggers, Stored Procedures, and Functions

Yesterday you learned how to enforce data integrity by using both procedural constraints and declarative constraints. Declarative integrity in SQL Server is often combined with the `IDENTITY` property and is referred to as *declarative referential integrity* (DRI). Essentially, you were trying to ensure that the data in your database was correct (without errors) and followed the rules of your business.

Today you learn about views, stored procedures, triggers, and user-defined functions. With these database components, you can hide much of the Transact-SQL complexities from the users of your databases. The first section discusses the creation and manipulation of views. Views enable you to specify exactly how users will see data. You can think of them as stored queries. The second section covers stored procedures, which are precompiled SQL statements. Because stored procedures are precompiled, they run much more quickly than do ad-hoc queries.

Next is a section on triggers. Triggers can be very complex, and they have several rules about how and when they should be created. Triggers enable you to ensure data integrity, domain integrity, and referential integrity within your database. You also look at two categories of triggers—`AFTER` and `INSTEAD OF`—as well as three trigger styles: `INSERT`, `UPDATE`, and `DELETE`.

The final section describes a new feature of SQL Server 2000—user-defined functions (UDF). UDFs are similar to stored procedures, but unlike stored procedures, they can be used as part of your Data Manipulation Language (DML) commands. The DML includes statements such as `INSERT`, `UPDATE`, and `DELETE`.

Creating and Manipulating Views

Views enable you to partition information horizontally or vertically from one or more tables in a database. In other words, with a view you can let users see only selected fields and selected rows. Figure 15.1 shows a view that lets users see only the authors' last name and first name fields (vertical partition) and only authors with a last name that begins with the letter *M* (horizontal partition).

FIGURE 15.1

A view created from a horizontally and vertically partitioned table.

au_name	au_fname	city	state	zip
Caloney	Sarah	Fresno	CA	90225
Deitrich	Johanna	Plano	TX	76503
Dominic	Anthony	Bend	OR	97922
Ferrous	Eric	Towns	ME	2566
MacFeather	Stearns	Bowie	UT	82331
McDonald	Stephanie	London	MO	55823
Oreland	Lars	Reno	NV	89509
Spinola	Michael	Moreno	NM	73220

au_name	au_fname
MacFeather	Stearns
McDonald	Stephanie

The code used to create this view might look something like this:

```
CREATE VIEW dbo.vwAuthors AS
SELECT au_lname, au_fname FROM authors
WHERE au_lname LIKE 'M%'
```

Views can also be created to show derived information. For example, you can create a view that shows the author's last name, first name, and book title, and then a calculated or derived field showing the number of books sold multiplied by the royalty fee per book.

Views also have the following advantages:

- You control what users can see. This capability is useful for both security and ease of use. Users don't have to look at extra information that they don't require.
- You can simplify the user interface by creating views of often-used queries. With this capability, users can run views with simple statements rather than supply parameters every time the query is run.
- Views allow you to set up security. Users can control only what you let them see. This might be a subset of rows or columns, statistical information, or a subset of information from another view.
- Because a view is a database object, you can assign user permissions on the view. This approach is much more efficient than placing the same permissions on individual columns in a table.
- Views can now have indexes created on them, making them an incredibly efficient method of gaining access to frequently requested data.
- Data can be exported from a view by using the BCP utility.

Views are very powerful and useful objects in your database design. You can give users access to certain columns and rows within your table, but a view is much easier to maintain than user permissions on individual columns and is therefore the preferred method of partitioning information. This is a performance consideration as well. When you place permissions on columns in a table, every time that table is referenced for any reason, the permissions must be checked on each referenced column.

Creating Views

You can create views by using the SQL Server Query Analyzer utility or the SQL Server Enterprise Manager. This section gives some examples using the SQL Server Query Analyzer utility.

The syntax for the `VIEW` statement is as follows:

SYNTAX

```
CREATE VIEW [owner.]view_name [(column_name[, column_name...])]
[WITH attributes
AS select_statement
[WITH CHECK OPTION]
attributes: {ENCRYPTION | SCHEMABINDING | VIEW_METADATA }
```

A simple `CREATE VIEW` statement looks like this:

```
CREATE VIEW vwAllAuthors
AS SELECT * FROM authors
```

You can use this view in a variety of different ways, as shown in the following examples:

```
SELECT * FROM vwAllAuthors

SELECT au_fname, au_lname
FROM vwAllAuthors

SELECT au_lname
FROM vwAllAuthors
WHERE au_lname like 'M%'
```

You can specify several options in the `CREATE VIEW` statement: `WITH CHECK OPTION`, `WITH ENCRYPTION`, `WITH SCHEMABINDING`, and `WITH VIEW_METADATA`.

By default, data modifications made through a view aren't checked to determine whether the rows affected will be within the view's definition. In other words, inserts and updates can be made to the base table even if the view doesn't use them. For example, a view might horizontally partition a table and give you only records that have an author's last name beginning with the letter *F*. Without using `WITH CHECK OPTION`, you could potentially add a new record with a last name of Meredith. `WITH CHECK OPTION` forces all data modification statements applied through the view to use the criteria set within the `SELECT` statement that defines the view. The `WITH ENCRYPTION` option encrypts the `CREATE VIEW` statement in the `syscomments` system table. After a view definition is encrypted, it can't be seen by anyone. The only way to decrypt a view is to drop the view and then re-create it.

These sample views are created with the `WITH CHECK OPTION` and `WITH ENCRYPTION` options enabled:

```
CREATE VIEW vwMyCheck
AS select * from authors
WITH CHECK OPTION

CREATE VIEW vwMyEncrypt
WITH ENCRYPTION
AS select * from authors
```

When you create views, you should always test the `SELECT` statement before you make it into a view. This way, you can avoid unexpected results. For example, you can create a view that returns all the rows in your table. The table might have only 500 rows when you create your view. Two years from now, that same table might return 10,000 rows of data. Is this still a good `SELECT` statement?

Tip

> When you create a view, you are creating a database object. Try to avoid creating broken ownership chains by having only one developer create all the objects in your database. This person is usually the dbo or a developer with an alias as the dbo. The dbo can then assign permissions to use the view to individual database users and database groups.

The `WITH SCHEMABINDING` option forces you to use two-part names (*`owner.object`*) to refer to the base tables, views, or UDFs referenced in your view's `SELECT` statement. When this is done, the schema of those base objects can't be changed or dropped unless the view is dropped or altered. For example, if you create a view based on the au_lname and au_fname columns of table `authors` and use the `WITH SCHEMABINDING` option, you can't drop the `authors` table. You would first have to drop the view and then the `authors` table.

The `VIEW_METADATA` option specifies that SQL Server 2000 will return information about the view (metadata) rather than the result set of the view's `SELECT` statement when you request browse-mode metadata from a client. Currently, the DBLIB APIs and the OLE-DB libraries support this feature.

Be aware of these rules and restrictions when you create views:

- `CREATE VIEW` statements shouldn't be combined with other SQL statements in a batch.
- When you're creating a view, any database objects referenced by the view are verified at the time the view is created.
- When you are running a view, you must have SELECT permission on the objects referenced in the view definition unless the objects don't have an owner specified. This means that you could potentially create a view that you couldn't run. Permissions on views are checked each time the view is run, not when it's created.
- You can't include the `ORDER BY`, `COMPUTE`, or `COMPUTE BY` clauses in your `SELECT` statement within a view.
- If you drop objects referenced within a view (unless you specified the `WITH SCHEMABINDING` option), the view still remains. You will receive an error message the next time you attempt to use that view. For example, if you create a view by joining information from two base tables and then drop one of the base tables, the view remains but doesn't run. To avoid this problem, use the `sp_depends` system stored procedure to see what dependent objects the table has before it's dropped.
- Temporary tables can't be referenced in a view. This also means that you can't use a `SELECT INTO` clause in a view.

- If your view uses a `SELECT *` statement and the base table referenced in the `SELECT` statement has new columns added, the new columns don't show up in the view. The `*` is resolved at it's time of creation into a fixed list of columns. You must alter the view to include the newly added columns.
- If you create a child view based on a parent view, be aware of what the parent view is doing. You could run into problems if the parent view is large and complex.
- Data in a view isn't stored separately. This means that if you modify data in a view, you are modifying the data in the base tables.
- You can't reference more than 1,024 columns in a view.
- You must specify names for all derived columns in your view.

Gathering Information on Views

To get the text used in the `CREATE VIEW` statement, you can use the SQL Server Enterprise Manager or run the `sp_helptext` system stored procedure and pass the view name as a parameter:

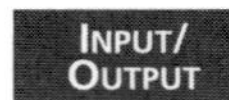

```
sp_helptext vwCheck

CREATE VIEW vwCheck AS
SELECT * FROM authors WITH CHECK OPTION
```

If a view was created with the `ENCRYPTION` option set, you can't use `sp_helptext` (or the SQL Server Enterprise Manager) to view the text used to create the view. The view must be dropped and re-created without the `ENCRYPTION` option before it can be read.

You can use the `sp_depends` system stored procedure to get a report of the tables and views on which a view depends, as well as objects that depend on your view. You can run `sp_depends` on tables, views, stored procedures, and triggers.

If you run `sp_depends` on the previous view, you get the following (Note: all of the examples shown are using the Result in Text option. If you are showing results in grid, then you may have to click the various tabs to find the right grid with your data.):

```
EXEC sp_depends vwCheck
In the current database, the specified object references the following:

Name          Type        Updated     Selected    Column
-------------------------------------------------------------
Dbo.authors   user table  no          yes         au_id
```

```
Dbo.authors   user table   no          yes         au_lname
Dbo.authors   user table   no          yes         au_fname
Dbo.authors   user table   no          yes         phone
Dbo.authors   user table   no          yes         address
Dbo.authors   user table   no          yes         city
Dbo.authors   user table   no          yes         state
Dbo.authors   user table   no          yes         zip
Dbo.authors   user table   no          yes         contract
(9 row(s) affected)
```

You can also query the following system tables to gather information about a view:

- `syscolumns` returns columns defined within a view.
- `syscomments` returns text of the `CREATE VIEW` statement.
- `sysdepends` returns view dependencies.
- `sysobjects` returns the view name.

Types of Views

Each different type of view depends on the type of `SELECT` statement used to create it. Now let's take a closer look at projections, joins, aggregates, computed columns, and views based on other views.

Projection Views

The simplest type of view is called a *projection*. A projection is simply a subset of columns in a table:

```
CREATE VIEW vwMyView
AS SELECT au_lname, au_fname
FROM authors
```

To work with the newly created view, use the following statement:

```
SELECT * FROM vwMyView
```

```
au_fname                 au_lname
-------------------     -------------
Bennet                   Abraham
Blotchet-Halls           Reginald
Carson                   Cheryl
DeFrance                 Michel
del Castillo             Innes
Dull                     Ann
Green                    Marjorie
[...]                    [...]
White                    Johnson
Yokomoto                 Akiko

(23 row(s) affected)
```

Join Views

New Term *Joins* link rows from two or more tables by comparing values in the specified columns. For example, you might like to give the users a list of authors from the `authors` table and the titles of the books they've written from the `titles` table. These two tables have a many-to-many relationship in the pubs database and therefore use the `titleauthor` table to create two one-to-many (denoted as 1-N) relationships, as shown in Figure 15.2.

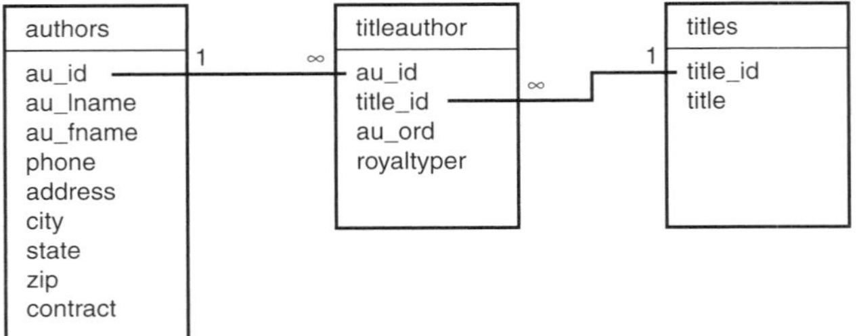

Figure 15.2
The `authors` *and* `titles` *tables are linked by the* `titleauthor` *table.*

You could type a join to gather data from the `authors`, `titles`, and `titleauthor` tables, but creating a view as follows is much more efficient:

Input

```
CREATE VIEW vwAuthorsTitles
AS SELECT authors.au_lname, authors.au_fname, titles.title
FROM authors INNER JOIN titleauthor
ON authors.au_id = titleauthor.au_id
INNER JOIN titles
ON titles.title_id = titleauthor.title_id
```

Then run the following to list the last name, first name, and title of any books that all authors with a last name beginning with the letter *M* have written:

Input/Output

```
SELECT * FROM vwAuthorsTitles
WHERE au_lname like 'M%'

au_lname      au_fname      Title
-----------   ----------    -------------------------
MacFeather    Stearns       Cooking with Computers:...
MacFeather    Stearns       Computer Phobic AND Non-Phobic...

(2 row(s)  affected)
```

Other Types of Views

You can also create views by using aggregate functions, computed columns, and views based on other views. Aggregates use aggregate functions such as `AVG`, `COUNT`, and `SUM`. You can use computed columns to create summary data for your users. You can use a view from a view to further refine the original view. For example, your original view might give you information on all products with their corresponding prices and the quantity sold. You can create a new view from this view that computes the quantity by the number of units sold for a particular item number.

The following is a computed column view:

```
CREATE VIEW vwBookTotals AS
SELECT title, (price * ytd_sales) 'Total'
FROM titles
```

You can now use this view to return all the books in the `titles` table with a column called `Total`, which lists the price multiplied by the year-to-date sales figures:

```
Select * from vwBookTotals

title                                           Total
-------------------------------------------     -----------
The Busy Executive's Database Guide             81,859.05
Cooking with Computers:  Surreptitious Balance... 46,318.20
You can combat computer Stress!                 55,978.78
Straight Talk About Computers                   81,859.05
Silicon Valley Gastronomic Treats               40,619.68
The Gourmet Microwave                           66,515.54
The Psychology of Computer Cooking              (null)
[...]                                           [...]
Fifty Years in Buckingham Palace Kitchens       180,397.20
Sushi, Anyone?                                   61,384.05

(18 row(s) affected)
```

Modifying Data in Views

You can modify data in a view. Remember that when you modify data in a view, you are modifying data in the underlying tables themselves. Several rules apply when you're modifying data through a nonindexed view and/or a nonpartitioned view:

- Modifications can't affect more than one underlying table. If your view joins data from one or more tables, you can modify data in only one of the base tables.
- You can modify data only in a base table, so aggregates, computed columns, and columns with built-in functions can't be altered.
- If you use the `WITH CHECK` option when you create or alter your views, all data to be inserted or modified through the view must conform to the restrictions in the `SELECT` statement used to create the view. For example, if your `SELECT` statement has a `WHERE au_lname LIKE 'M%'` clause, you can add or modify rows that conform to that `WHERE` clause only.
- `NOT NULL` columns defined in the base table, but not part of the view, must also have default values assigned to them for you to be able to insert a new row through the view.

- If the view contains a `UNION`, it's known as a *partitioned view* and can be used for inserts and updates though under very strict conditions. For more information, see *Creating and Maintaining Databases* in the SQL Server 2000 Books Online.

Altering Views

With SQL Server 2000, you can alter a view by using the `ALTER VIEW` statement. Its syntax is the same as that used for `CREATE VIEW`, except that you replace `CREATE` with `ALTER`. Thus, the syntax for the `ALTER VIEW` statement is as follows:

SYNTAX

```
ALTER VIEW [owner.]view_name [(column_name[, column_name...])]
[WITH { ENCRYPTION | SCHEMABINDING | VIEW_METADATA }]
AS select_statement
[WITH CHECK OPTION]
```

The advantage of using `ALTER VIEW` is that all permissions already assigned to the view are retained. If you were to drop and then re-create the view, this wouldn't be true. Note, however, that if your view accesses new objects that have an owner specified, those who have permission on your newly altered view must also have the appropriate permissions on those newly referenced objects.

Removing Views

You can remove views from your database by selecting the view in SQL Server Enterprise Manager and then right-clicking and choosing Delete. Alternatively, you can use a `DROP` statement. The `DROP` statement uses the following syntax:

SYNTAX

```
DROP VIEW [owner.]view_name[,[owner.]view_name...]
```

To drop a view called `vwMyCheck`, which is owned by the dbo, use this code:

```
DROP VIEW dbo.vwMyCheck
```

```
The command(s) completed successfully.
```

Working with Stored Procedures

NEW TERM *Stored procedures* are precompiled Transact-SQL (T-SQL) statements stored in a SQL Server database. Because stored procedures are precompiled, they usually provide the best performance of any type of query. Many system stored procedures defined with an `sp_` gather information from system tables and are especially useful for administration. You can create your own user-defined stored procedures as well.

What makes stored procedures so great? What's so special about these SQL Server objects that they get their own section in this lesson? Stored procedures are fast-running sets of T-SQL commands stored in a SQL Server database. When you run a stored procedure for the first time, all the following steps are run. The stored procedure's query plan is then placed into memory. Subsequent calls to the same stored procedure result in only step 5 being run.

1. The procedure is parsed into its component pieces.
2. The components that reference other objects in the database (tables, views, and so on) are checked for their existence. This process is also known as *resolving*.
3. The name of the procedure is stored in the `sysobjects` table, and the code to create the stored procedure is saved in `syscomments`.
4. Compilation continues, during which a blueprint for how to run the query is created. This blueprint is often called a *normalized plan* or a *query tree*.
5. When the stored procedure is first executed, the query tree is read and fully optimized into a procedure plan and then run. This saves you the time of reparsing, resolving, and compiling a query tree every time you run the stored procedure.

In SQL Server version 6.5 and earlier, stored procedures were a way to partially precompile an execution plan. At the time the stored procedure was created, a partially compiled execution plan was stored in a system table. Executing a stored procedure was more efficient than executing an SQL statement because SQL Server did not have to compile an execution plan completely, it only had to finish optimizing the stored plan for the procedure. Also, the fully compiled execution plan for the stored procedure was retained in the SQL Server procedure cache, meaning that subsequent executions of the stored procedure could use the precompiled execution plan.

Another benefit of using a stored procedure is that after it's executed, the procedure plan is stored in memory. This means that the next time you use that stored procedure in the same session, it will be read directly from the memory cache and run. You can get a performance boost over running a standard SQL query again and again.

Stored procedures have additional benefits:

- You can use stored procedures to encapsulate business rules. After they're encapsulated, multiple applications can use these rules, thus giving you a consistent data interface. This is also advantageous in that, if functionality must change, you can change it in only one place rather than once for each application.
- Performance is boosted for all stored procedures, but even more so for stored procedures that are run more than once as the query plan is saved in the procedure cache.
- With stored procedures, you can pass in arguments and get data returned, too.
- Stored procedures can be set up to run automatically when SQL Server starts up.
- Stored procedures can be used to extract or modify data (not at the same time).
- Stored procedures can have permissions assigned to them.
- Stored procedures are explicitly invoked. Unlike triggers, stored procedures must be called by your application, script, batch, or task.

In a nutshell, stored procedures are powerful database components. System stored procedures are useful for database administration and maintenance. User-defined stored procedures are useful for whatever you have designed them for. They have advantages over views and queries in that they are precompiled, and after their first execution, their execution plan is stored in the procedure cache that resides in random access memory (RAM). Another benefit of stored procedures is that you can assign permission to a user to run a stored procedure, even if that user doesn't have permissions on the underlying tables.

To look at interesting stored procedure code, run the `sp_helptext` system stored procedure on the stored procedures in the `master` database (for example, **`sp_helptext sp_helpdevice`**).

Creating Stored Procedures

You use the `CREATE PROCEDURE` statement to create stored procedures. Stored procedures are created in the current database unless you're creating temporary stored procedures which are created in `tempdb`. To create a stored procedure, you must have the create procedure statement permission.

The following are rules for creating a stored procedure:

- The name must follow the rules for identifiers.
- Referenced objects must exist when your stored procedure runs. This feature, known as *delayed name resolution*, enables you to reference objects that don't exist at compile time. You can have your stored procedure create temporary objects and then reference them later in the same stored procedure.
- You can't create and then drop or re-create objects with the same name in a single stored procedure.
- You can have up to 1,024 parameters.
- You can reference temporary tables within your stored procedure. Local temporary tables disappear when your procedure ends.
- Stored procedures can't have the following T-SQL create statements in them: `CREATE DEFAULT`, `CREATE PROCEDURE`, `CREATE RULE`, `CREATE TRIGGER`, and `CREATE VIEW`.
- You can nest procedures within procedures (up to 32 levels deep).
- Stored procedures can be up to 128MB in size.
- As with views, if you use a `*` in the stored procedure `SELECT` statement and the underlying table has new columns added to it, the new columns don't show up when the procedure is run. You must use the `ALTER` statement and recompile the stored procedure.

Test the SQL statements before creating your stored procedure. This way, you can avoid unexpected results.

The CREATE PROCEDURE syntax is as follows:

SYNTAX

```
CREATE PROC[EDURE] procedure_name {;number}
[{@parameter data_type} [VARYING] [= default] [OUTPUT]][,...n]
[WITH {RECOMPILE | ENCRYPTION | RECOMPILE, ENCRYPTION}]
[FOR REPLICATION]
AS sql_statement [...n]
```

After you look at some sample CREATE PROCEDURE statements, you'll learn about the *;number*, *parameter*, RECOMPILE, and ENCRYPTION components.

```
CREATE PROCEDURE pAuthors
AS SELECT au_fname, au_lname
FROM authors
ORDER BY au_lname DESC
```

```
The command(s) completed successfully.
```

To use this procedure, you can execute it from the Query Analyzer window:

```
EXEC pAuthors

au_fname                    au_lname
-------------------         -------------
Yokomoto                    Akiko
White                       Johnson
Stringer                    Dirk
[...]                       [...]
Carson                      Cheryl
Blotchet-Halls              Reginald
Bennet                      Abraham

(23 row(s) affected)
```

The results are a two-column table with the last and first names shown in descending order.

Gathering Information on Stored Procedures

To get the text used in a CREATE PROCEDURE statement, use the SQL Enterprise Manager or run the sp_helptext stored procedure and pass the view name as a parameter:

```
sp_helptext pAuthors

text
CREATE PROCEDURE pAuthors AS SELECT au_fname, au_lname
FROM authors ORDER BY au_lname DESC
```

Like a view, if a stored procedure was created with the ENCRYPTION option set, you can't use sp_helptext (or the Enterprise Manager) to view the text used to create the stored procedure. The procedure must be dropped and re-created without the ENCRYPTION specified before it can be read.

You can also use the sp_depends stored procedure to get a report of the objects on which a stored procedure depends. To apply sp_depends to the preceding procedure, do the following:

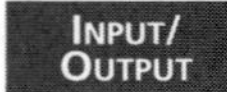

```
sp_depends pAuthors

In the current database, the specified object references the
following:

Name           Type        Updated   Selected   Column
-------------- ----------  --------  ---------  ----------
Dbo.authors    user table  no         yes       au_lname
Dbo.authors    user table  no         yes       au_fname
```

Creating a Group of Procedures

The first option you will look at is the *;number* option. By specifying a semicolon and a number, you can create a group of stored procedures. Groups of stored procedures are often created for use in the same application. Maintenance is then easier because all procedures used by a particular application reference the same group. The following is an example of creating a group of procedures:

```
CREATE PROC group_sp;1
AS SELECT * FROM authors
GO
CREATE PROC group_sp;2
AS SELECT au_lname FROM authors
GO
CREATE PROC group_sp;3
AS SELECT DISTINCT city FROM authors
GO
```

This batch of statements creates a single procedure called group_sp with three different procedures as part of it. To refer to individual procedures, execute them with their

`;number` as part of the name. For example, to get a listing of all the cities that authors live in, use the following:

INPUT/OUTPUT

```
EXEC group_sp;3

City
Ann Arbor
Berkeley
Corvallis
Covelo
Gary
Lawrence
[...]
Vacaville
Walnut Creek
(16 row(s) affected)
```

When you drop grouped procedures, you need to drop only the procedure name. Any procedure that is part of that group is also dropped:

```
DROP PROCEDURE dbo.group_sp
```

Note

You can't drop an individual procedure from a group of procedures. You must drop the entire group and then re-create it to make such a change.

Using Parameters with Stored Procedures

Parameters enable you to create stored procedures that behave a little differently every time they are called. For example, you can write a stored procedure that averages a series of test scores passed into it. You don't know what the scores are going to be when you create the procedure, but every time the procedure is run, you get a new average. The syntax for the parameter portion of the `CREATE PROCEDURE` deserves a closer look:

SYNTAX

```
@parameter data_type [= default|NULL] [VARYING] [OUTPUT]
```

`@parameter` specifies the name of the parameter within the procedure. You can declare up to 1,024 parameters within a single stored procedure. The parameter data type can be any system-defined or user-defined data type, except for image. `default` specifies a default value for the parameter. `VARYING` applies to the cursor (recordset) returned and is beyond the scope of this book. `OUTPUT` determines this as a return parameter.

The OUTPUT option allows you to pass information out of the stored procedure to the calling procedure. I'll illustrate this point with some sample code. This stored procedure accepts five parameters, averages them, and then outputs the average:

INPUT

```
CREATE PROCEDURE scores
@score1 smallint,
@score2 smallint,
@score3 smallint,
@score4 smallint,
@score5 smallint,
@myAvg smallint OUTPUT
AS SELECT @myAvg =
    ➥(@score1 + @score2 + @score3 + @score4 + @score5) / 5
```

Every parameter in a stored procedure must have a value for the procedure to run. If a parameter has a default value assigned to it, users don't have to supply a value for that parameter unless they want it to be something other than the default. Also, if you have a procedure that accepts four parameters that all have defaults assigned to them, you can call the procedure and pass values for only the first two parameters. You can't call the procedure and pass a value for the first and third parameters and leave the second parameter blank if you are passing parameters in order. It's possible to pass parameters in SQL Server *by reference*, meaning that you supply the parameter as *name = parameter*. This way, you can pass parameters in any order.

To extract the myAvg value from this procedure, you must first declare a variable and then run the procedure. Note that this example passes the parameters by position:

INPUT/OUTPUT

```
DECLARE @AvgScore smallint
EXEC scores 10, 9, 8, 8, 10, @AvgScore OUTPUT
SELECT 'The Average Score is:  ', @AvgScore
GO

----------------------    ---------
The average score is:     9
(1 row(s) affected)
```

ANALYSIS Let's review this example. You first create the procedure scores with myAvg declared as an OUTPUT variable. You then declare a temporary variable called AvgScore and pass the average score into your stored procedure call with the OUTPUT parameter. This places the value of myAvg from the stored procedure into the AvgScore variable outside the procedure. You then use a SELECT statement to print the value of AvgScore. Notice that when you pass your values into the stored procedure, you pass them in order *by position*. You can also pass by reference, which allows you to pass your variables in any order. For example, the following code passes the values out of order, yet you get the same result as before:

INPUT

```
DECLARE @AvgScore smallint
EXEC scores
@score1 = 10, @score3 = 9,
@score2 = 8, @score4 = 8,
@score5 = 10, @myAvg = @AvgScore OUTPUT
SELECT 'The average score is:  ', @AvgScore
GO
```

Note

> If you start by passing by reference, you must pass by reference for the entire procedure call. You can't switch between pass by position and pass by reference in the middle of a stored procedure call.

Another way to pass information back to the calling procedure is to use the `RETURN` keyword. It passes a variable directly to the calling procedure without using the `OUTPUT` statements needed in both the stored procedure definition and the call to the procedure. Now take a look at the code to use the `RETURN` keyword:

INPUT

```
CREATE PROC MyReturn
@t1 smallint, @t2 smallint, @retval smallint
AS SELECT @retval = @t1 + @t2
RETURN @retval
```

After you create this procedure, enter the following to run it:

INPUT/OUTPUT

```
DECLARE @myReturnValue smallint
EXEC @myReturnValue = MyReturn 9, 9, 0
SELECT 'The return value is:  ', @myReturnValue

------------------------     --------
The return value is:         18
(1 row(s) affected)
```

Using the `WITH RECOMPILE` Option

You can add the `WITH RECOMPILE` option in the `CREATE PROCEDURE` or `EXEC PROCEDURE` statement. Its location affects how the stored procedure is processed and run.

Using `WITH RECOMPILE` in a `CREATE PROCEDURE` Statement

When you use `WITH RECOMPILE` in the `CREATE PROCEDURE` statement, the execution plan isn't saved in the procedure cache. The entire procedure is recompiled every time it's run. This is similar to the way a standard query is handled. Recompiling can be useful in stored procedures with parameters that make the normal execution plan run poorly. By recompiling every time, the procedure can be optimized for the new parameters. This example shows a stored procedure with the WITH RECOMPILE option:

```
CREATE PROCEDURE MyRecompileProc
WITH RECOMPILE
AS SELECT * FROM authors
ORDER BY au_lname
```

Using WITH RECOMPILE in an EXEC PROCEDURE Statement

You can also use the WITH RECOMPILE option in the EXEC PROCEDURE statement. It compiles the stored procedure for that single execution and then stores the new plan in the procedure cache for subsequent EXEC PROCEDURE commands. This next example uses WITH RECOMPILE in an EXEC PROCEDURE statement:

```
EXEC pAuthors
WITH RECOMPILE
```

```
au_fname                   au_lname
-------------------        -------------
Yokomoto                   Akiko
White                      Johnson
Stringer                   Dirk
[...]                      [...]
Carson                     Cheryl
Blotchet-Halls             Reginald
Bennet                     Abraham

(23 row(s) affected)
```

The results are a two-column table with the last and first names shown in descending order. The procedure is also recompiled, and the new plan is stored in the procedure cache.

Forcing All Stored Procedures to Be Recompiled

You can force all stored procedures and triggers that reference a particular table to be recompiled at their next runtime by executing the sp_recompile stored procedure:

```
EXEC sp_recompile authors
```

Making Your Stored Procedures Run Automatically at SQL Startup

You can have stored procedures "autoexecute" at the startup of SQL Server. The execution of these stored procedures begins after the last database is recovered at startup time.

Tip

> You can have as many autoexec stored procedures as you like, but each separate stored procedure uses up a user connection. You can have one stored procedure call other stored procedures and thus use only one user connection to the server.

To create these autoexec stored procedures, use the `sp_procoption` stored procedure. See the Books Online or *Microsoft SQL Server 2000 Unleashed* for more information.

Using the `WITH ENCRYPTION` Option

The `WITH ENCRYPTION` option encrypts the SQL statements used to create the procedure and stores the encrypted text in the `syscomments` table. This example uses the `WITH ENCRYPTION` option:

```
CREATE PROC encrypted_proc
WITH ENCRYPTION
AS SELECT * FROM authors
```

Of course, this code does the same thing as when you use the `WITH ENCRYPTION` option with the `CREATE VIEW` statement. You can't use `sp_helptext` or the SQL Enterprise Manager to view the text of the stored procedure.

Using Remote Stored Procedures

You can implement and run stored procedures, called remote stored procedures, on other SQL Servers. Enabling the use of remote stored procedures requires the following:

- The remote server must allow remote access, which is the default when SQL Server is installed. Unless you reconfigured your server without this option, you don't need to worry about turning it on.
- Both servers must have each other registered in their `sysservers` tables.
- Both servers must have your login ID in the `syslogins` table.

After you set up this access, you execute the stored procedures in a similar fashion as you do locally. The difference is that you must preface the stored procedure like this:

SYNTAX

```
EXEC servername.dbname.owner.storedprocedure
```

For example, if you want to run the system stored procedure `sp_addlogin` on the Accounting server, run the following code to add the Muriel login ID to the server:

```
EXEC Accounting.master.dbo.sp_addlogin Muriel
```

Working with Triggers

NEW TERM A *trigger* is a special type of stored procedure that's automatically invoked when you try to modify data that it's designed to protect. Triggers help secure your data's integrity by preventing unauthorized or inconsistent changes from being made. Suppose that you have `customers` and `orders` tables. You can create a trigger that ensures that when you create a new order, it will have a valid customer ID with which to be attached. Likewise, you can create the trigger so that if you try to delete a customer from the `customers` table, the trigger will check to see whether you have any orders still attached to that customer and, if so, halt the delete process. Of course, you could also implement this functionality by using declarative referential integrity.

You can also use triggers to enforce more complex business rules than you can with constraints. For example, an `INSERT` trigger can fire when a new record is added to your `orders` table. The trigger can check the customer's payment history and determine an appropriate payment term.

Triggers don't have parameters and can't be explicitly invoked. This means that you must attempt a data modification to fire off a trigger.

You can nest triggers up to 32 levels. Nested triggers work like this: A trigger on your `orders` table can add an entry to your accounts receivable table that in turn fires a trigger to check to see whether the customer has any overdue accounts receivable and then notifies you. One trigger makes an update to another table, which in turn fires its own trigger.

By default, all triggers (`INSERT`, `UPDATE`, `DELETE`) fire after data modification is performed. They are known as `AFTER` triggers and were the only type available in prior versions of SQL Server. SQL Server 2000 introduces the `INSTEAD OF` trigger, which fires instead of the intended data modification.

From a performance standpoint, triggers have a relatively low amount of overhead. Most of the time involved in running a trigger is used up by referencing other tables. The referencing can be fast if the other tables are in memory or a bit slower if they must be read from disk.

Triggers are always considered a part of the transaction. If the trigger or any other part of the transaction fails, it's rolled back.

In the past, triggers were the only means of enforcing referential integrity. Starting with SQL Server 7, you can use DRI, which makes most triggers unnecessary.

In SQL Server 2000, Microsoft introduced CASCADING UPDATE and CASCADING DELETE which makes many triggers which formerly performed these actions redundant.

Understanding the inserted and deleted Tables

Triggers use the special inserted and deleted tables, both of which contain the same structure as the base table or the "trigger table" where the trigger has been created. The inserted and deleted tables reside in RAM because they are logical tables. If you add a new record to the base table, the record is recorded in the base table itself, as well as in the inserted table. Having the values available in the inserted table enables you to access the information without having to create variables to hold the information. When you delete a record, the deleted record is stored in the deleted table. An update is like a combination of both an insert and a delete, with the old value of the updated data being stored in the deleted table and the new value of the updated data being stored in the inserted and base table. If you update a record, the original is stored in the deleted table, and the modified record is stored in the base table, as well as in the inserted table.

Creating Triggers with the CREATE TRIGGER Statement

You create triggers by using the CREATE TRIGGER statement:

SYNTAX

```
CREATE TRIGGER [owner.]trigger_name
ON [owner.]table_name | view_name
[FOR..AFTER | INSTEAD OF] {INSERT | UPDATE | DELETE}
[WITH ENCRYPTION]
AS sql_statements
```

A table can have as many triggers as you want to create on any of the three trigger actions defined: INSERT, UPDATE, or DELETE. You also can create default triggers to fire after the data modification is completed, or you can create triggers to fire instead of the data modification.

Each action can be stored in a single trigger or multiple triggers. If the action is stored in different triggers, each trigger name must be unique. For example, you can create a trigger called trInsUpdAuthors on the authors table with a trigger designed for INSERT and UPDATE actions. You can then create an additional trigger called trDelAuthors with the DELETE action defined.

If you want to modify the trInsUpdAuthors trigger, you must drop the whole trigger and then re-create it or use the ALTER TRIGGER statement.

If you modify a trigger by using the ALTER TRIGGER statement, the old trigger is completely replaced with the new trigger. If you drop a table with triggers on it, the triggers are automatically dropped as well.

Other rules apply to creating triggers as well:

- Triggers can't be created on temporary tables. They can, however, reference views and temporary tables.
- Triggers can't return result sets. Therefore, be careful when you include SELECT statements. Using the IF EXISTS clause as part of a SELECT statement in trigger code is a common practice.
- Triggers should be used to maintain data integrity, maintain referential integrity, and encapsulate business rules.
- Triggers can be encrypted in the syscomments table if you specify the WITH ENCRYPTION option.
- TRUNCATE TABLE commands do not activate triggers.
- WRITETEXT statements don't activate triggers. You use WRITETEXT to modify text or image data, and it's a nonlogged transaction.
- The following SQL statements can't be used in a trigger: all CREATE statements, all DROP statements, ALTER TABLE and ALTER DATABASE, TRUNCATE TABLE, GRANT and REVOKE, RECONFIGURE, LOAD DATABASE or TRANSACTION, UPDATE STATISTICS, SELECT INTO, and all DISK statements.
- Rollback transaction statements inside triggers can cause unexpected behavior in your calling programs.

Triggering Inserts and Updates

Now look at a sample trigger for both inserts and updates to a table. The default trigger style is FOR..AFTER (you don't need to include the AFTER keyword).

INPUT/OUTPUT

```
USE pubs
GO
CREATE TRIGGER trAddAuthor
ON authors
FOR INSERT, UPDATE
AS raiserror ('%d rows have been modified', 0, 1, @@rowcount)
RETURN
```

```
The command(s) completed successfully.
```

This trigger fires every time you try to add or update a record in the authors table. The trigger sends you a message about how many rows have been modified. Try inserting a new author and see what happens:

```
USE pubs
GO
INSERT authors
(au_id, au_lname, au_fname, phone,
 address, city, state, zip, contract)
```

```
VALUES
('555-66-7777', 'Leap', 'Frog',
'800 444-5656', '123 Sesame Street',
'West EastBrooke', 'CA', '90221', 0)
1 rows have been modified
(1 row(s) affected)
```

You've successfully added your Leap Frog record to the `authors` table. The message `1 rows have been modified` tells you that your trigger did indeed fire.

Triggering Deletes

When you use the `DELETE` action, realize that this trigger won't fire if a `TRUNCATE TABLE` statement has been executed. `TRUNCATE TABLE` deletes all rows from the table.

To test the `DELETE` action, first add another record to your table that's similar to the first record you created. You can change the primary-key field only for your Leap Frog record as follows:

INPUT/OUTPUT

```
INSERT authors
(au_id, au_lname, au_fname, phone, address, city, state, zip, contract)
VALUES
('444-55-6666', 'Leap', 'Frog', '800 444-5656',
'123 Sesame Street', 'West EastBrooke', 'CA',
'90221', 0)

1 rows have been modified
(1 row(s) affected)
```

Now you've successfully added a second Leap Frog record to the `authors` table. Notice that the `au_id` field changed to `444-55-6666`.

Now create a `DELETE` action trigger that tells how many rows will be deleted when you run this trigger:

INPUT/OUTPUT

```
CREATE TRIGGER trDelAuthors
ON authors
FOR DELETE AS raiserror
('%d rows are going to be deleted from this table!',
0, 1, @@rowcount)
```

```
The command(s) completed successfully.
```

Now delete all records with a first name of Leap:

INPUT/OUTPUT

```
DELETE FROM authors
WHERE au_lname = 'Leap'

2 rows are going to be deleted from this table!
(2 row(s) affected)
```

Enforcing Data Integrity with Triggers

You can use triggers to enforce data integrity within your database. In the past, referential integrity was enforced only with triggers. With later versions of SQL Server, you can use referential integrity constraints. Triggers are still useful, however, to encapsulate business rules and force cascading changes in your database. A cascading change can be created with a trigger. Suppose that a particular bookstore is no longer in business. You can create a cascading trigger that removes the store from the `stores` table and removes all sales associated with that stor_id from the `sales` table. You can create a `DELETE` action cascading trigger. (Keep in mind that SQL Server 2000 introduced cascading triggers as part of the DRI. This example is here for backwards compatibility and to ensure that the concept is understood.)

First, create a couple of dummy tables to work with:

INPUT/OUTPUT

```
sp_dboption pubs, 'Select Into', TRUE
go
SELECT * INTO tblStores from pubs..stores
SELECT * INTO tblSales from pubs..sales

 (6 row(s) affected)
(21 row(s) affected)
```

Now run a `SELECT` statement to see what you have:

```
SELECT sa.stor_id, st.stor_name
FROM tblStores st INNER JOIN tblSales sa
ON st.stor_id = sa.stor_id

stor_id          stor_name
----------       ------------------------------------
6380             Eric the Read Books
6380             Eric the Read Books
7066             Barnum's
7066             Barnum's
7067             News & Brews
7067             News & Brews
7067             News & Brews
[...]            [...]
7131             Doc-U-Mat: Quality Laundry and Books
8042             Bookbeat

(21 row(s) affected)
```

You will be deleting the four `7067` stor_ids. Next, create the trigger on `tblSales` that tells you how many sales will be deleted when the associated store from `tblStores` is deleted:

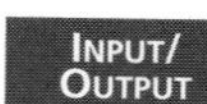

```
CREATE TRIGGER trDelSales
ON tblSales
FOR DELETE AS
```

```
raiserror('%d rows are going to be deleted from the sales table!'
➥, 0, 1, @@rowcount)
```

```
The command(s) completed successfully.
```

Now create the `DELETE` trigger on `tblStores`:

```
CREATE TRIGGER trDelStore
ON tblStores
FOR DELETE AS
DELETE tblSales FROM deleted where deleted.stor_id =
➥tblSales.stor_id
```

```
The command(s) completed successfully.
```

Finally, delete stor_id `7067`, which is the News & Brews store:

INPUT/OUTPUT

```
DELETE FROM tblStores
WHERE tblStores.stor_id = '7067'
```

```
4 rows are going to be deleted from the sales table!
(1 row(s) affected)
```

The `DELETE` trigger fires and deletes all associated records in `tblSales`. The trigger also delivers the message that four rows are being deleted. If you rerun the previous `SELECT` statement, you will see that News & Brews is gone and that you no longer have 21 rows of data, but 17.

Encapsulating Business Rules

Encapsulating business rules are normally made with constraints, defaults, data types, and rules, but you can also use triggers. Triggers are especially useful when you must reference other tables, because this action isn't allowed in constraints, defaults, data types, and rules. To continue with the earlier examples, you can modify your trigger `trDelSales` on the `tblSales` table to run the business rule. Don't allow any store to be deleted if sales are greater than or equal to 20.

You might need to drop this trigger before you can re-create it:

INPUT/OUTPUT

```
DROP TRIGGER trDelSales
GO
CREATE TRIGGER trDelSales
ON tblSales
FOR DELETE AS
IF (SELECT COUNT(*) FROM deleted
WHERE deleted.qty >= 20) > 0
BEGIN
PRINT 'You cannot delete any of these stores.'
PRINT 'Some stores have more than 20 sales!'
PRINT 'Rolling back your transaction!'
ROLLBACK TRANSACTION
END
```

```
The command(s) completed successfully.
```

Now test this new trigger:

```
DELETE FROM tblSales
WHERE stor_id = '7066'

You cannot delete any of these stores.
Some stores have more than 20 sales!
Rolling back your transaction!
```

At least one store with a stor_id of `7066` has more than 20 sales. To verify, run this `SELECT` statement:

```
SELECT stor_id, qty FROM tblSales
stor_id         qty
----------      -------
6380            5
6380            3
7066            50
7066            75
7067            10
[...]           [...]
8042            10
8042            25
8042            30

(21 row(s) affected)
```

Now run the `DELETE` statement again using stor_id `6380`. As you can see from the previous code, this statement should delete those stores because neither entry has a qty field of more than 20:

```
DELETE FROM tblSales
WHERE stor_id = '6380'

(2 rows(s) affected)
```

Rerun the `SELECT` statement, and you will see that both stores with an ID of `6380` are gone, and you have 15 rows of data left rather than 17.

Enforcing Referential Integrity

You also can use triggers to enforce referential integrity. This is their primary purpose in a database. They are especially useful in cascading updates and deletes. Triggers are tested last when data modifications occur. Constraints are checked first on the trigger table. If a constraint is violated, the trigger will never fire.

The following trigger enforces referential integrity. It ensures that before a sale is added to the `sales` table, a valid store ID exists in the `stores` table.

```
CREATE TRIGGER trInsUpdSales
ON tblSales
FOR INSERT, UPDATE AS
IF (SELECT COUNT(*) FROM tblStores, inserted
WHERE tblStores.stor_id = inserted.stor_id) = 0
BEGIN
PRINT 'The stor_id you have entered does not exist'
PRINT 'in the stores table!'
ROLLBACK TRANSACTION
END
```

This trigger works on any single `UPDATE` or `INSERT` to `tblSales`. It makes sure that you have a valid stor_id in `tblStore`. If you run `SELECT INTO`, though, this trigger might not fire properly. When you have multiple rows to deal with, you should check to make sure that the rowcount of inserted stor_ids equals the amount of sales you added. You code this trigger to handle multiple rows like this (again, you might have to drop this trigger before re-creating it here):

```
DROP TRIGGER trInsUpdSales
GO
CREATE TRIGGER trInsUpdSales
ON tblSales
FOR INSERT, UPDATE AS
DECLARE @rc int
SELECT @rc = @@rowcount
IF (SELECT COUNT(*) FROM tblStores, inserted
WHERE tblStores.stor_id = inserted.stor_id) = 0
BEGIN
PRINT 'The stor_id you have entered does not exist'
PRINT 'in the stores table!'
ROLLBACK TRANSACTION
END
IF (SELECT COUNT(*) FROM tblSales, inserted
WHERE tblSales.stor_id = inserted.stor_id) <> @rc
BEGIN
PRINT 'Not all sales have a valid stor_id '
PRINT 'in the stores table!'
ROLLBACK TRANSACTION
END
```

Using `INSTEAD OF` Triggers

When you use an `INSTEAD OF` trigger, the original code that made a modification to the table isn't run; instead, the trigger code is run. For example, you could create a trigger on the `authors` table to notify users that authors can't be deleted. You could do the same with a regular FOR..AFTER trigger, however, that would require that the data actually be modified first and then rolled back from within the trigger code. If you use an INSTEAD OF trigger, the update is never performed. It is the more efficient trigger of the two just described. Now check out this sample code for the INSTEAD OF trigger:

```
USE pubs
GO
CREATE TRIGGER trIO_DelAuthors
ON authors INSTEAD OF DELETE AS
PRINT 'You cannot delete authors from the authors table.'
```

To test this trigger, try deleting an author with the last name White:

```
USE pubs
GO
DELETE authors WHERE au_lname = 'White'

You cannot delete authors from the authors table.

(1 row(s) affected)
```

Gathering Information on Triggers

As with the other components you've looked at today, you can run the sp_helptext system stored procedure to look at the text of a trigger statement. Of course, encrypted triggers have no syscomments entries that you can look at. You shouldn't encrypt any objects unless you absolutely have to. When you upgrade your database, encrypted objects must be dropped and re-created. Unencrypted objects are automatically upgraded to the newer version.

Working with User-Defined Functions

A powerful new feature of SQL Server 2000 is the user-defined function (UDF). You can create a UDF to return either a scalar value (a single value) or a table. The RETURNS clause in the UDF determines whether it's a scalar or a table function. Getting used to UDFs takes a little practice, but I predict that they'll be one of the most often used additions to SQL Server 2000.

You can use two types of table functions:

- If you return a table from a single SELECT statement, this is referred to as an *inline* table value function. Creating a table this way means that all the column names and data types are determined by the SELECT statement.
- If you specify new column names and different data types as part of your function definition, this is called a *multistatement* table value function.

When working with multistatement functions, you can include all the following statements. Keep in mind that if the statement isn't in this list, it can't be used.

- Assignment statements
- Control-of-flow statements
- Cursor operations local to the function
- Declare statements for variables and cursors local to the function
- `INSERT`, `UPDATE`, and `DELETE` statements local to the function
- `SET/SELECT` statements used to assign values to local function variables

SQL Server 2000 nondeterministic functions aren't allowed inside a function because these functions may return different values even though they are given the same input parameters. This list includes functions such as `@@CONNECTIONS`, `GETDATE`, and `RAND`.

Scalar Functions

The most straightforward functions to create and work with are the scalar functions. The basic syntax is as follows:

SYNTAX

```
CREATE FUNCTION [owner_name.]function_name
([{@parameter_name scalar_parameter_data_type [ = default]} [...,n]])
RETURNS scalar_returnd_data_type
[WITH ENCRYPTION | SCHEMABINDING]
[AS]
BEGIN
RETURN [(] select_statement [)]
END
```

In this syntax,

- *`owner_name`* specifies the object owner.
- *`function_name`* specifies the name of the UDF. Keep in mind that it must follow the rules for SQL Server identifiers.
- *`@parameter_name`* identifies any parameters that need to be passed to the function. You can have as many as 1,024 parameters. This is similar to the way you used parameters earlier today in the stored procedures section.
- *`scalar_parameter_data_type`* is the data type of this function's return value. Nonscalar data types (nonsingle value data types) aren't supported, including tables and cursors. `rowversion` and `timestamp` can't be returned either. You could use a `uniqueidentifier` and a `binary(8)` in place of them.

Now let's put this information together and create a UDF. The sample UDF in Listing 15.1 returns the last day of the month when you pass in a date. The basic logic here is to break down the date into its component parts. Add one month to the date, go to the first day of that next month, and then subtract one day. The result is the last day of this month.

LISTING 15.1 Creating a User-Defined Function to Find the Last Day of the Month

```
CREATE FUNCTION dbo.fnLastDayOfMonth (@mydate datetime)
RETURNS datetime
AS
BEGIN
-- Declare variables to hold the various date components
  DECLARE @yy int
  DECLARE @mm int
  DECLARE @dd int
  DECLARE @tempdate datetime
  DECLARE @foo varchar(10)

-- Store the date components
  SET @yy = DATEPART(yy, @mydate)
  SET @mm = DATEPART(mm, @mydate)
  SET @dd = DATEPART(dd, @mydate)

-- If the month is December, then set the month to January
-- and the year to year + 1,  otherwise increment month by 1
  IF @mm = 12
    BEGIN
      SET @mm = 1
      SET @yy = @yy + 1
    END
  ELSE
    BEGIN
      SET @mm = @mm + 1
    END

--Set the day of the temporary string to the date with the day
--set to the first day of the following month.  Then convert the
--temporary string to a real date.  Then subtract one day from
--the date and return that value.
  SELECT @foo = CONVERT(varchar(2), @mm) + '/01/' + CONVERT(varchar(4), @yy)
  SET @tempdate = CONVERT(datetime, @foo)
  SET @tempdate = DATEADD(dd, -1, @tempdate)

  RETURN @tempdate
END
```

To test your new function, run the following statements:

INPUT

```
SELECT dbo.fnLastDayOfMonth('12/12/99')
SELECT dbo.fnLastDayOfMonth('02/02/99')
SELECT dbo.fnLastDayOfMonth('02/02/2000')
```

15

Your results should look similar to the following:

OUTPUT

```
1999-12-31  00:00:00.000

(1 row(s) affected)

1999-02-28  00:00:00:000

(1 row(s) affected)

2000-02-29  00:00:00:000

(1 row(s) affected)
```

Inline Table-Valued Functions

Of the two table functions, the inline table-valued function is more straightforward:

SYNTAX

```
CREATE FUNCTION [owner_name.]function_name
([{@parameter_name scalar_parameter_data_type [ = default]} [...,n]])
RETURNS TABLE
[WITH ENCRYPTION | SCHEMABINDING]
[AS]
RETURN [(] select_statement [)]
```

It uses the same parameters as the scalar function with one exception—the *select_statement*. It is a single standard `SELECT` statement. Keep in mind that all columns must be named, including your computed columns.

The example in Listing 15.2 returns a table with royalties to date calculated by author.

LISTING 15.2 Creating a User-Defined Function to Display the Royalties Paid by Author

```
CREATE FUNCTION dbo.fnRoyaltiesByAuthor()
RETURNS TABLE AS
    RETURN (SELECT a.au_fname, a.au_lname, t.title,
    'RoyToDate' = (t.ytd_sales * t.price * t.royalty / 100)
    FROM authors a, titles t, titleauthor ta
    WHERE a.au_id = ta.au_id AND t.title_id = ta.title_id)

SELECT * from dbo.fnRoyaltiesByAuthor()
SELECT au_fname, RoyToDate FROM dbo.fnRoyaltiesByAuthor()
```

Multistatement Table-Valued Functions

You use the multistatement table-valued functions to return a table:

SYNTAX

```
CREATE FUNCTION [owner_name.]function_name
([{@parameter_name scalar_parameter_data_type [ = default]} [...,n]])
RETURNS @return_variable TABLE table_type_definition
[WITH ENCRYPTION | SCHEMABINDING]
[AS]
BEGIN
    function_body
    RETURN [(] select_statement [)]
END
```

The table that's returned, however, may not necessarily be created by a single `SELECT` statement (hence the *multistatement* name). For example, you may want to do some processing on data and create a temporary table. Then you can do some additional processing based on that temporary table and return a new table with your results.

The following example expands on the last example. In the preceding example, the `RoyaltyByAuthor` function returned the royalties to date based on books sold. The problem with this function is that many books have more than one author. If books with multiple authors split their royalties, you are giving back incorrect results.

To fix this problem, you need to figure out the royalties by title, divide those royalties by the number of authors on each title, and then return a table with the author's name, the title, and the newly modified royalties. Assume that the royalties are divided evenly among multiple authors.

Although you use multiple statements and a temporary table in this example, you could accomplish the same thing by writing a complex correlated subquery:

```
CREATE FUNCTION dbo.fnRoyaltySplitByAuthor()
RETURNS @RoyByAuthor TABLE
  (au_lname varchar(40) NOT NULL,
   au_fname varchar(20) NULL,
   title varchar(80) NOT NULL,
   RoyToDate float)
AS
BEGIN
--Create a temp table to store my author count per title
    DECLARE @temptbl TABLE (title_id varchar(6) NOT NULL,
    num_authors tinyint NOT NULL)
    INSERT @temptbl
      SELECT title_id, COUNT(au_id) FROM titleauthor
      GROUP BY title_id

--Load my return table with a join between my temp table and all
--other appropriate tables.

    INSERT @RoyByAuthor
        SELECT a.au_fname, a.au_lname, t.title,
```

```
    'RoyToDate' = ((t.ytd_sales * t.price * t.royalty / 100)
         / tt.num_authors)
    FROM authors a, titles t, titleauthor ta, @temptbl tt
    WHERE a.au_id = ta.au_id AND t.title_id = ta.title_id
        AND t.title_id = tt.title_id
    RETURN
END

SELECT * FROM dbo. fnRoyaltySplitByAuthor()
```

Summary

Today you learned about four powerful database objects: views, stored procedures, triggers, and user-defined functions. Views enable you to give users access to certain columns and rows within your table(s). System stored procedures are useful for database administration and maintenance. User-defined stored procedures are useful for whatever you have designed them for, such as encapsulating complex business logic. Stored procedures have the advantage of being precompiled and therefore run much more quickly than views do. Triggers are a special type of stored procedure that are executed automatically when data is modified in the trigger table. Triggers help secure the integrity of your data by preventing unauthorized or inconsistent changes from being made. User-defined functions are a powerful new feature of SQL Server 2000 that gives you, as a database developer, incredible flexibility when writing SQL scripts.

Q&A

Q Which are faster: triggers, views, or stored procedures?

A Stored procedures and triggers are faster than views. As precompiled SQL statements, they both run at the same speed and generally have the same amount of overhead. SQL Server's order of operations runs stored procedures and views before it executes triggers. So, for efficiency, if you can catch problems with a stored procedure, you won't get down to the trigger level just to have to roll back everything that has been done already.

Q How can I get a list of all stored procedures in my server?

A You can retrieve a list of stored procedures names, database by database, by running this query:

```
SELECT name
FROM sysobjects
WHERE type = 'P'
```

Q How can I get a list of all triggers on my server?

A You can look at triggers database by database if you run the following query, which returns each table with its associated triggers:

```
SELECT name,
'INSERT' = object_name(instrig),
'UPDATE' = object_name(updtrig),
'DELETE' = object_name(deltrig)
FROM sysobjects
WHERE type = 'U'
AND (instrig <> 0 OR updtrig <> 0 OR deltrig <> 0)
```

The second example returns the trigger information on a single table:

```
EXEC sp_helptrigger authors
```

Q How can I get a list of all the different objects in my database?

A Run the following `SELECT` statement to retrieve object information from the `sysobjects` database system table:

```
SELECT * FROM sysobjects
```

Q How can I gather information about the T-SQL used to create a trigger, stored procedure, view, or UDF?

A The most straightforward method is to use the `sp_helptext` stored procedure. The following are a few examples:

```
EXEC sp_helptext fnRoyaltySplitByAuthor
EXEC sp_helptext titleview
```

Workshop

This section provides quiz questions to help you solidify your understanding of the concepts presented today. In addition to the quiz questions, exercises are provided to let you practice what you've learned today. Try to understand the quiz and exercise answers before continuing on to tomorrow's lesson. Answers are provided in Appendix A, "Answers to Quiz Questions."

Quiz

1. What do triggers enforce?
2. You can have _____ number of triggers per table.
3. *True or false*: Views can focus on only the data needed, provide security, and allow modifications to base tables, and they are faster than stored procedures.
4. *True or false*: You can update multiple base tables with a view.

5. *True or false*: You can use a stored procedure that returns information from base tables on which you don't have permission.
6. *True or false*: You can use a view that returns information from base tables on which you don't have permission.
7. *True or false*: Declared referential integrity (DRI), constraints, data types, defaults, and rules have eliminated the need for triggers.
8. When you drop a table, which of the following database objects are also dropped: views, stored procedures, or triggers?
9. *True or false*: You can drop a table that has a view created on it with the `SCHEMABINDING` option enabled.
10. *True or false*: User-defined functions can return scalar values as well as tables and can be used as part of the `SELECT` statement or in the `FROM` clause of a query.

Exercises

1. Create a view that shows which authors have written which books.
2. Create a trigger that prevents you from adding a new book title without having a valid publisher.
3. Create a stored procedure that shows which books are selling in which stores. (*Hint:* You need to join three tables to do so.)
4. Create a UDF that averages the price of all books sold to date.

WEEK 3

DAY 16

Understanding Replication Design Methodologies

Yesterday you learned how to create views, triggers, stored procedures and functions. These objects allow you to create very robust and powerful database applications.

Today you learn about SQL Server replication: what defines replication, why you might want to use replication, and what you might publish. You also look at the different methods of data distribution and determine what best suits your needs. Replication uses a publisher/subscriber metaphor complete with articles and publications. You learn about the different agents SQL Server uses to move your data from one location to another. You then look at the different replication scenarios and examine the advantages of each. You finish this day by looking at replicating data in heterogeneous environments.

Okay, that sounds like a lot—and you're right, it is. You might also be asking yourself, "What about actually implementing a replication scenario?" Well, as to the first part, you must have a good foundation in what replication is, what it can accomplish, and what its uses are. As to the actual implementing, you'll learn about that tomorrow. So, now is a great time to get to work on replication.

What Is Replication?

Replication creates an environment that allows multiple copies of the same information to be distributed to multiple databases throughout your enterprise. Replication has the following benefits:

- Data is closer to the user.
- It removes the impact of read-intensive OLAP (Online Analytical Processing) environments from the transaction-intensive OLTP (Online Transaction Processing) environments.
- It reduces conflicts between multiple sites trying to work with the same data.
- Database sites can operate autonomously with the replicated data. They can define their own rules, procedures, and views on their copy of the data.

The two basic types of replication are replication and distributed transactions. Both replication types allow you to keep the different copies of your data current. You can even use both strategies at the same time in your environment.

NEW TERM *Replication* duplicates and distributes copies of your data to the different locations in your environment. You can make these updates intermittently, so you can keep those replicated sites more autonomous. The databases at each site don't have to be connected to the server publishing the data all the time. Replication can involve just moving transactions or moving an entire snapshot of the data.

Distributed Data Factors

You must consider many different factors when you're trying to decide on a particular method for distributing your data, including the following:

- *Site autonomy* depends on the answers to the following questions: How much independence from the publishing database must your subscribing sites have? For how long is a version of the data at a subscription site good? How often do you need to connect to the publishing site and update your copy of the data?

- *Transactional consistency* refers to the transactions themselves. Do all the stored transactions need to be applied at the same time or not at all? If a delay occurs in applying the transactions, but they are all processed in order, is this acceptable? Are the transactions being applied in a manner that doesn't conflict with the consistency of your data?
- *Latency* refers to the time the copies of the data are applied. Does your data need to be 100 percent in sync 100 percent of the time, or is it acceptable to have data updated periodically? If you can have some latency, how big a lag is acceptable?

Before you get into the various distribution methodologies, keep these questions in mind when you're trying to decide where and what to publish:

- What am I going to publish? Do the subscribers receive all the data or just subsets of my data? Should my data be partitioned by region values or ZIP codes? Should I allow subscribers of my data to send me updates? If I allow updates, how should they be implemented?
- Who can have access to my data? Are these users online or offline? Are they across the country and connected with expensive phone lines?
- How often should I synchronize my data with the subscribers? How often are changes sent to them?
- What does the network look like? Is it fast? Should I do more data partitioning to minimize replication-bound traffic? Is the network reliable? Are all network nodes available at all times?

Now look at the different distribution methodologies that put these factors into practice.

Distribution Methodologies

With latency, transactional consistency, and site autonomy in mind, you can use several different methods to implement replication in SQL Server. In the following sections, you'll take a closer look at distribution methodologies and determine which methodology is most applicable in a given scenario.

Three basic types of replication can be combined to various degrees to create seven different methodologies. The replication types are transactional replication, snapshot replication, and merge replication. When you add in latency, transactional consistency, and site autonomy, you get the following methods of data distribution:

- Merge replication
- Snapshot replication

- Transactional replication
- Updateable subscriptions
- Snapshot replication with updating subscribers
- Transactional replication with updating subscribers
- Distributed transactions

Merge Replication

Merge replication has the highest amount of site autonomy and can afford the most latency. However, it has the lowest amount of transactional consistency.

Merge replication allows each site to make changes to its local copy of the replicated data. At some point, the changes from the site are sent to the publishing database, where they are merged with changes from other sites. Sooner or later, all sites receive the updates from all the other sites. This is known as *data convergence*. The changes from all the sites converge, and sooner or later all sites have the same information, as illustrated in Figures 16.1 and 16.2.

FIGURE 16.1
Modified records converge at the publishing server.

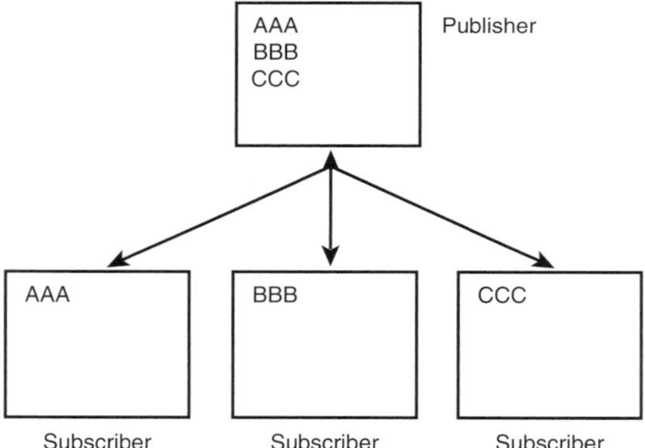

Transactional consistency is thrown out the window here because different sites might be updating data at different times. A particular site doesn't wait for its updates to be sent to every other site before continuing its work. In other words, every site is guaranteed to converge to the same result sets but not necessarily at the same time.

Merge replication sometimes can generate conflicts. For example, Site A makes some changes to record 27. Site B also makes changes to record 27. They both send their versions of data back to the publishing server. The publishing server now sees that both of them made changes to record 27. Which version of record 27 is correct? The version that was modified first? The version that was modified last? What about other dependencies? For example, if changes in record 27 are based on data found in record 26, and record 26 is different on both machines, which one is correct? Determining the right answer can be complex. You'll take a closer look at this issue later today.

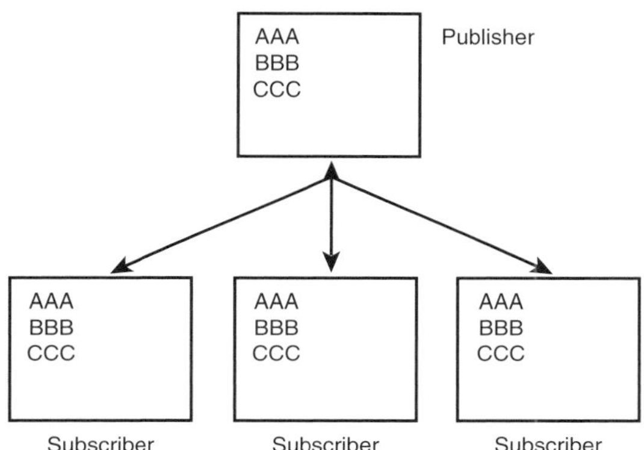

FIGURE 16.2
Converged records are sent back to all subscribers.

Who should use merge replication? Good question. Because of the potential conflicts that can occur, merge replication is better suited to environments in which the chances of these conflicts are minimized. For example, sites that tend to make changes to their records only (indicated by a location ID in each record), but need the information from all the other locations, are good candidates for merge replication.

For example, you might create a database that tracks the criminal history of individuals. A large state like Alaska, where every little town might like to have a copy of this criminal history but can't afford to be in contact with the central database at all times, might be an excellent location to implement merge replication. Each town would be autonomous, and latency could be very high. The local police or sheriff could add new criminal information to the database and then send it back to headquarters to be merged with data from many other towns. Conflicts might still occur if a criminal is moving from town to town and causing problems, but these conflicts can be detected and the appropriate records can be updated—ahem, converged—and sent back to all the little towns.

Snapshot Replication

In snapshot replication, an entire copy of the items to be replicated is copied from the publishing server to the subscribing database (see Figure 16.3). This type of replication is the easiest to set up and maintain. Snapshot replication has a high level of site autonomy. It also guarantees transactional consistency because all transactions are applied at the publication server only. The site autonomy can be very useful for locations that need read-only versions of the data and don't mind a higher amount of latency. When you are using snapshot replication, the subscription database should consider the replicated data as read-only because any changes made to the data won't be sent back to the publication database. Also, all changes that might have been made to the data will be wiped out when the next snapshot is downloaded.

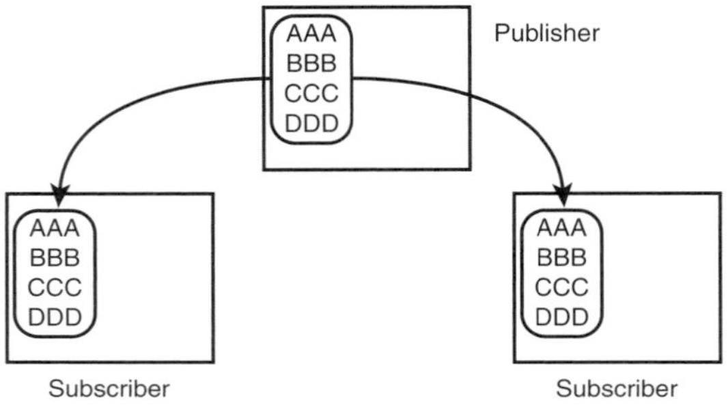

FIGURE 16.3

Snapshots of the entire data set are sent to each subscriber. Changes to the data can take place only at the publishing server.

OLAP servers are excellent candidates for snapshot replication. The ad hoc queries that Management Information Systems (MIS) administrators apply to data are generally read-only, and data that is several hours or even several days old doesn't affect their queries. For example, a company MIS department might want to do some research on the demographics of items sold two months ago. Information from last week, or even today, won't make any difference in its queries. Furthermore, the department isn't planning to make changes to the data; it just needs the data warehouse. The site autonomy allows the MIS department to implement additional indexes on the data without affecting the OLTP publication database.

Transactional Replication

In transactional replication, the transactions are sent from the publisher to the subscribers. This type of replication is one way. The only way a subscriber can make changes to data is directly to the publishing database. The changes are then replicated back to the subscriber at the next synchronization (see Figure 16.4).

This type of replication allows for a medium amount of autonomy. The subscriber should treat the replicated data as read-only. This point is important because changes made on the replicated data might not allow the future replicated transactions to be performed. Suppose that you change the country field from USA to Korea in the `suppliers` table at the subscriber. If you then run a transaction on the publisher that updates all the suppliers from the USA, your new Korea record wouldn't get the update that all the other subscribers received. This causes consistency problems in your database and should be avoided. A medium amount of latency is generally involved in this type of replication as well. The subscriber doesn't have to be in touch with the publisher at all times, but regular synchronizations are useful, and the amount of data being moved is relatively small. Remember that snapshot replication must move all the published data from the publisher to the subscriber (whether or not it has been modified). In transactional replication, only committed transactions are sent to the subscribers. This type of replication was used primarily in SQL Server 6.5, in which you didn't have the option of using any type of merge replication.

Transactional replication is most useful in scenarios in which the subscribers can treat their data as read-only, but they need changes to the data with a minimal amount of latency. An excellent example of transactional replication is found in an order-processing/distribution system. In this type of scenario, you might have several different publishing sites taking orders for goods. These orders are then replicated to a central distribution warehouse where pick tickets are created and the orders are filled and shipped. The warehouse, which can treat the data as read-only, needs new information in a timely manner.

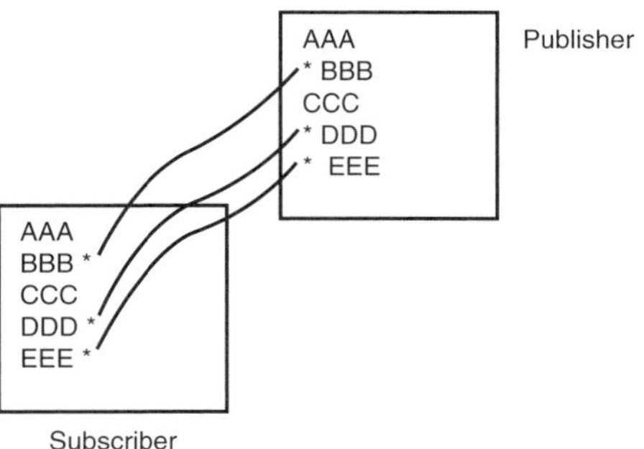

FIGURE 16.4

In transactional replication, changes can be made only at the publisher. The changes (transactions) are then applied at each subscriber.

Updateable Subscriptions

Although replicated data is generally treated as read-only, SQL Server 7.0 provided options to allow subscribers to update data at the publisher. These options increased your subscriber's ability to work with its data autonomously. Updating subscribers in SQL Server 7.0 used the two-phase commit (2PC) protocol to maintain transactional integrity and data consistency. The limiting factor in this approach is that a persistent network connection must exist between publisher and subscriber. SQL Server 2000 addresses this limitation with a new update option called *queued updating*.

Three options are now available for updateable subscriptions, whether or not you're configuring snapshot or transactional replication:

- Immediate updating
- Queued updating
- Immediate updating with queued updating as a failover

Immediate Updating

Immediate updating subscribers use 2PC to make simultaneous changes to the publisher and subscriber as they did in SQL Server 7.0. This option requires the publisher and subscribers to be available and connected. When a change is committed, the update is then propagated to additional subscribers through snapshot or transactional replication.

Queued Updating

New in SQL Server 2000, queued updating takes advantage of the store-and-forward mechanism used in message queuing technologies. In this case, modifications are sent to a queue where they can be applied when a network connection is available. The asynchronous application of updates to the publisher can lead to conflicts if another subscriber had applied its updates. To handle this situation, you need to create a conflict-resolution policy for the queue reader agent on your publication.

Conflict resolution for queued updating is handled differently than for merge replication. Merge replication handles conflicts at the row level based on a policy you configure for the publication. Queued updating, however, resolves conflicts at the transaction level to guarantee atomicity of transactions. The conflict resolver can make three choices when a conflict is detected:

- Publisher wins and the subscription is reinitialized
- Publisher wins
- Subscriber wins

Configuring the option to reinitialize the subscriber ensures the highest degree of transactional consistency, whereas configuring the subscriber wins option results in the lowest degree. The default is the middle-of-the-road publisher wins option.

With respect to the queue itself, by default, it's implemented as a table (`MSReplication_queue`) in the subscription database. It is referred to as a SQL Server 2000 queue. The advantage of this type of queue is that it works with all SQL Server platforms, including the desktop edition for Windows 98. Using a SQL Server 2000 queue, the queue reader agent runs on the subscriber, which reads and empties the queue when a network connection with the publisher is re-established.

If your distributor and subscribers are running on the Windows 2000 operating system, you can configure your subscribers to use the queuing mechanism provided by Microsoft Message Queue 2.0 (MSMQ). With this configuration, updates are packaged as messages and sent to the distributor using 2PC. When subscribers are offline, their changes are cached in the local queue until they can be delivered to the distributor. Although this approach is more complex to implement, the advantage is extended message routing capabilities, centralized queue administration, and enhanced monitoring that can't be achieved using SQL Server 2000 queues.

Immediate Updating with Queued Updating as a Failover

The final option, immediate updating with queued updating as a failover, is a best-of-breed approach in which immediate updating using 2PC is the method you're counting on to propagate changes to the publisher and other subscribers. If you lose network connectivity, you can enable queued delivery so that you don't necessarily lose your intended updates. When you're ready to revert to immediate updating, you can restore the network connection and begin immediate updates after the queues are cleared. This option is very useful when you need to pull a publisher offline for maintenance.

Snapshot Replication with Updating Subscribers

Snapshot replication with updating subscribers is an interesting animal. It combines snapshot replication, as previously described, with one of the updateable subscriber options.

With this methodology, you have a certain amount of autonomy because the subscription database doesn't have to be in contact with the publishing database at all times. The subscriber is working with the publisher only when a snapshot is being downloaded or the subscriber is using one of the updating options to update a transaction at the publishing database. Figure 16.5 shows an example of snapshot replication using the immediate updating subscriber option.

In this case, a high degree of transactional consistency is maintained because transactions must be applied at both the subscription database and the publication database. That other subscribers might have made changes to the publication database since your subscriber last downloaded a snapshot is irrelevant. The consistency is maintained by the transaction failing on the publication server if the data being modified at both the publisher and subscriber is different. This method works even with the latency-involved snapshot replication.

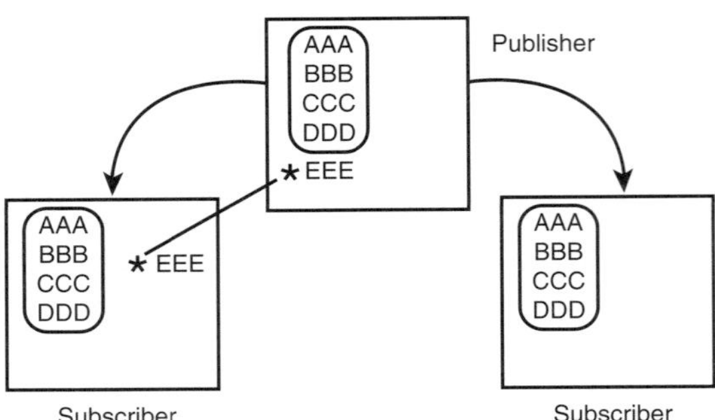

FIGURE 16.5

Snapshots are sent to each subscriber regularly. For a subscriber to make a local change to replicated data, the same change must be successfully applied at the publisher; otherwise, no change is allowed.

Regardless of update methodology, the subscription server can immediately begin working with the changed data, because it either knows that it has successfully updated the publication server (immediate update); or the publication server will converge the information (queued update), and in time all servers involved in the replication will receive the changes.

This methodology is useful in scenarios in which few but occasional modifications take place at the subscription servers. The longer the latency, the more likely that your 2PC will fail. It may fail because there's a better chance that the data at the publisher has been changed but hasn't yet been replicated to the subscriber, in which case queued updating may prove to be a better methodology.

Transactional Replication with Updating Subscribers

With transactional replication with updating subscribers, you lose even more autonomy at the subscription sites but minimize latency. With this methodology, you use the transactional replication described earlier in the "Transactional Replication" section.

When a subscription database is updated, the update is made to both subscriber and publisher using a 2PC. This means that the change is written to both the subscriber and the publisher at the same time. As a result, you have guaranteed transactional consistency. The change is then converged with other updating subscribers and sent back out to all the subscription databases. As you learned in the section on options for updateable subscriptions, queued updating resolves conflicts at a transactional level.

Transactional replication with updating subscribers has less latency than using snapshot replication with updating subscribers because the transactions being replicated are much smaller (and quicker to move) than synchronizing an entire snapshot of your data.

Useful scenarios for this type of replication include low-volume reservation systems. In this type of system, a subscriber can look through a schedule of availability and then attempt to make a reservation. After the reservation is scheduled, it can be replicated within a few minutes (or however long you determine) to all the other subscription databases. All their schedules are updated. You might be thinking to yourself, "Yeah, that looks good, but what if I try to make a reservation that someone else already has booked, but that booking hasn't been replicated to this subscriber yet?" In this case, it would be better to use immediate updates, because this type of replication uses 2PC, and you would know whether your reservation was successfully committed, it was available, and you didn't overwrite anyone else's reservations.

Distributed Transactions

Distributed transactions available in SQL Server 6.5 and SQL Server 7.0 are still available in SQL Server 2000. Distributed transactions, or 2PC, have almost no autonomy, no latency, and guaranteed transactional consistency.

As you learned earlier, changes are either all replicated simultaneously or not at all. This type of replication takes advantage of the MSDTC (Microsoft Distributed Transaction Coordinator), which implements the 2PC protocol and applies transactions at all sites simultaneously.

Because every subscriber must be in contact with the publisher and each other at all times, this leaves little autonomy and no latency. This type of replication is useful in scenarios in which everyone must have real-time versions of the data.

High-volume reservation systems can take advantage of this type of replication. For example, an airline reservation system would find this type of replication very useful. Subscribers are offsite and reduce some of the workload on the publication server. The guaranteed transactional consistency is displayed when a person in New York tries to get seat 2A on flight 2400 and another person in Idaho tries to get the same seat on the same flight. Only one of them can book the seat, and the one who doesn't get the booking will know immediately.

The Publisher/Subscriber Metaphor

You have probably figured this out already. SQL Server replication uses a publisher/subscriber metaphor. Just like a real publisher, several different pieces play a role in this metaphor:

- The *publisher* is the owner of the source database information. The publisher makes data available for replication and sends changes to the published data to the distributor.

- The *subscriber* database receives copies of the data (snapshot replication) or transactions held in the distribution database.
- The *distributor* receives all changes made to published data. It then stores the data and forwards it to subscribers at the appropriate time. A single distribution server can support multiple publishers and multiple subscribers at the same time.

One or more publishers and subscribers and a distributor are involved. A SQL Server in your enterprise can play any or all of these roles simultaneously. The way in which you implement these roles gives you the different replication models, which you will learn about a little later.

To continue the publisher/subscriber metaphor, a publishing database creates articles. Articles are then bundled together to create a publication.

Articles

NEW TERM An *article* is a single table or subset of data in a table. Articles are bundled together into publications. To publish a subset of data in an article, you must use some type of filtering to partition data in your table. You can use vertical partitions, horizontal partitions, or both (see Figure 16.6). A vertical partition selects only certain columns from the table, whereas a horizontal partition selects only certain rows from the table. In addition to using SQL statements to create your articles, you can also use stored procedures.

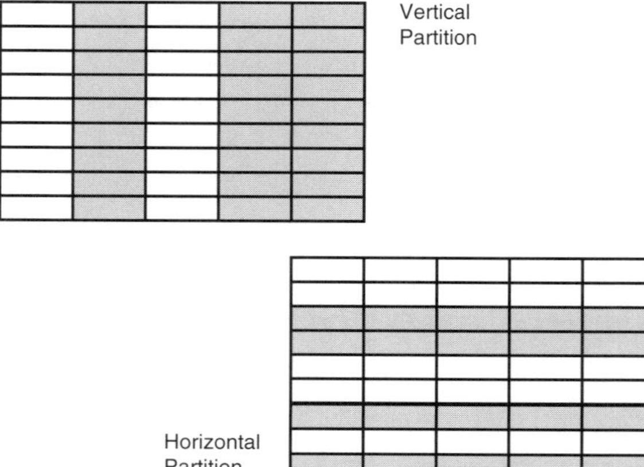

FIGURE 16.6
Data partitioning.

Each partitioned table becomes a single article that can then be subscribed to. You might find it more useful to actually change the physical implementation of your tables. For example, you might have a `sales_info` table that services three different regions. If you physically redesign your database, you can implement three separate `sales_info` tables (one for each region). As an enhancement to merge replication, dynamically filtering data subscriber by subscriber is even possible. Dynamic filters are row filters implemented as either SQL Server functions or user-defined functions. If you want to filter data based on the data in other tables, you can also implement a join filter.

SQL Server 2000 also allows you to publish database objects such as stored procedures, views, indexed views, and user-defined functions. In fact, you can even replicate schema objects such as indexes (clustered and nonclustered), key constraints, user triggers, and collations.

Data Definition Considerations

Keep in mind a few rules when you're creating your articles:

- IDENTITY columns are replicated, but the property isn't. When an initial synchronization occurs, the values in the IDENTITY column are copied as integer values.
- Timestamp data types (different from date/time data types) indicate the sequence of SQL Server activity on a row of data. They provide a history or lineage of changes made to that row. These values are replicated as binary data types.
- `Uniqueidentifier` creates GUIDs (globally unique identifiers). These 128-bit IDs are used with merge replication. They make it possible for each row to be uniquely identified even if you are converging rows from two separate tables. You can use the `NEWID` function to generate a GUID. The data type is replicated, but the function isn't.
- User-defined data types can be replicated only if they also exist in the subscription database.

Working with the `IDENTITY` Property

You must deal with some special considerations when working with the `IDENTITY` property. Remember that autonumber-type columns are changed to binary numbers (which don't automatically generate values) on the subscribers. This change occurs so that subscriber and publisher information matches. If you want to partition your tables at the subscription site, you should add a new IDENTITY column. If you decide to add this column, you have to use seed values and `CHECK` constraints to avoid any conflicts with incoming transactions. You can also use the `uniqueidentifier` data type with the `NEWID` function to guarantee unique keys.

When you get into scenarios in which you have multiple publishers and subscribers of the same information, you might want to allow subscribers to change data from their local region only but still view data from other regions. You do so by using the `NOT FOR REPLICATION` statement when you initially create an `IDENTITY` property, `CHECK` constraint, or trigger.

You can use NOT FOR REPLICATION when you add data at the subscriber. The CHECK constraint or trigger can fire and make sure that that particular subscriber owns the data you are modifying at the subscriber. In this fashion, you can maintain referential integrity because a subscriber can add a local record with a valid IDENTITY column value. This IDENTITY column value is then replicated as a binary number, as discussed earlier.

Publications

Publications are made up of one or more articles and are the basis for a subscription. When you create a subscription, you are subscribing to an entire publication. When you've subscribed to a publication, you can then "read" individual articles. You can maintain referential integrity with publications because all articles in a single publication are synchronized at the same time. You can create as many publications per database as you like.

When you work with publications and subscriptions, you can set up either push or pull subscriptions. The real difference between these two methods of data transfer is the place where the administration of the subscription is taking place.

You can publish to non-SQL servers and even implement replication on articles that have a different sort order and data type; however, doing so isn't recommended.

You should be aware of some other publishing restrictions:

- Tables must have a primary key to ensure integrity. (The exception occurs when you are using snapshot replication.)
- You can't replicate master, model, MSDB, tempdb, or any distribution databases.
- Publications might not span multiple databases. Each publication can contain articles from one database only.
- IMAGE, TEXT, and NTEXT data have limited support. Transactional and merge replication can't detect changes in these values because they are stored separately from the tables and not logged (by default) when they're changed. The best type of replication to work with these data types is snapshot replication. You can schedule snapshots of your tables (including these fields) to occur regularly. This process is often referred to as a *scheduled table refresh*.

Push Subscriptions

When you set up a subscription at the same time you create your publications, you are essentially setting up for a push subscription. This type of subscription helps centralize subscription administration because the subscription is defined at the publisher along with the subscribers' synchronization schedule. All administration of the subscription is handled from the publisher. The data is "pushed" to the subscriber when the publisher decides to send it.

> You can set up multiple subscribers at the same time when you're working with push subscriptions.

Push subscriptions are most useful when your subscribers need updates sent to them as soon as they occur. Push subscriptions also allow for a higher level of security as the publisher deems who is allowed to subscribe and when. Push subscriptions do take some additional overhead at the distribution database because it manages the replication.

Pull Subscriptions

A pull subscription is set up from each individual subscriber. The subscribers initiate the transfer of information on a timely basis. This subscription type is useful for applications that can allow for a lower level of security. The publisher can allow certain subscribers to pull information, or the publisher can allow anonymous subscriptions. Pull subscriptions are also useful in situations in which a large number of subscribers might be involved. Internet-based solutions are good candidates for pull subscriptions.

Anonymous Subscriptions

Another type of pull subscription, anonymous or non-trusted subscriptions, don't maintain detailed information about the subscription, or subscriber information isn't maintained at the publisher. The subscribers themselves are left to keep track of their subscriptions and the details of what the data was when a subscription was last synchronized. For anonymous subscriptions, the subscriber doesn't need to be explicitly named at the publisher. All rules for pull subscriptions still apply. This type of subscription is appropriate when you don't want the overhead of maintaining subscriber information at the publisher and distributor. Applications with a large number of subscribers and Internet subscribers are best suited to this subscription option.

How Does Replication Work?

Replication might seem very complex on the surface, but when you break it down into its component parts, it's not too bad. Essentially, replication is handled by five different agents. Each agent has its own specialized job to do. When you put all the following agents together, you get replication:

- A *distribution agent* moves information from the distribution database to the subscribers.
- A *log reader agent* monitors the transaction log of all published databases that are using it for replication. When it finds transactions that are part of a publication, it copies them to the distribution database where they can then be applied to the subscribers by the distribution agent.
- A *merge agent* merges modifications from multiple sites.
- A *snapshot agent* moves a snapshot of the data before replication can begin. This data transfer is required. If a snapshot of the data doesn't exist at the subscriber, you can't apply transactions to the subscriber. It's also used for the various types of snapshot replication.
- A *queue reader agent* reads messages from the SQL Server queue on each subscriber and applies the transactions to the publication. When you're using MSMQ 2.0, the queue reader agent reads the messages stored in the central queue created at the distributor.

Now take a closer look at how each agent differs in its task when faced with the different replication methodologies covered earlier. Keep in mind that a replication methodology is applied at the individual publication level and that each subscriber can take advantage of different methodologies that have been applied to different publications.

How Does Merge Replication Work?

In merge replication, the merge agent can live on the distribution server or on each subscription server. In a push scenario, the merge agent lives on the distribution server. In pull scenarios, the agent lives on each subscriber. Figure 16.7 outlines the replication process presented in the following steps:

1. The snapshot agent (which lives on the distribution server) takes an initial snapshot of the data and moves it to the subscribers. Remember that the subscribers must first be synchronized with the publishers for replication to begin (with the exception of snapshot replication).
2. A distribution working folder is created on the distribution server to handle merges.
3. Replication begins.
4. The merge agent takes modifications from the publishers and applies them to the subscribers.
5. The merge agent takes modifications from the subscribers and applies them to the publishers.
6. The merge agent receives any update conflicts and takes the appropriate action.

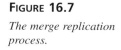

FIGURE 16.7
The merge replication process.

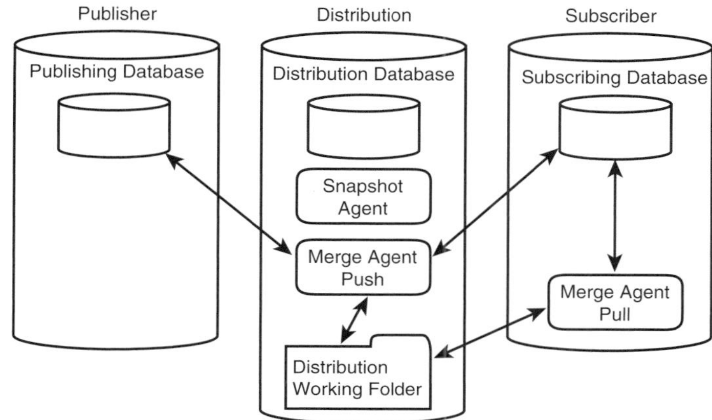

> **Note**
>
> Merge replication is best used when there are few chances for changes to be made to the same records by different locations.
>
> Horizontally segmented tables are useful with merge replication. You can have separate publications created and subscribed to based on a region code or some other discriminatory mechanism.

For merge replication to work properly, some changes are made to the table schema as well as the distribution database. These changes are made to allow SQL Server to perform conflict resolution. Keep the following schema changes in mind when you decide to use merge replication:

- System tables are added to the distribution working folder. They track changes for use during synchronization as well as for conflict resolution.
- SQL Server creates triggers on the publishing and subscription servers involved in merge replication. These triggers are fired when a data modification occurs in one of the tables involved in replication. Information about the change is stored in the system tables added to the distribution working folder. These saved changes allow you to track changes to each row or column of modified information.
- SQL Server creates a new `uniqueidentifier` column for each row in tables being replicated. A GUID or ROWGUID is then added to uniquely identify that row. In this fashion, when a record is updated at different sources, the different updates can be differentiated.

Remember that you can't vertically partition information when you are using merge replication.

When you allow updates to the same data to occur at multiple locations, you will run into conflicts. To resolve these conflicts, SQL Server does the following.

NEW TERM The system tables stored in the distribution working folder track every change to a row. Each row's changes are listed, and each entry has a ROWGUID. This history of modifications to a record is called the record's *lineage*, a history of changes made to a row involved in merge replication. Changes are identified by a ROWGUID attached to the row and stored in the distribution working folder on the distribution server.

By using the lineage, the merge agent can evaluate the current and arriving values and automatically resolve conflicts based on assigned priorities. You can customize these priorities, which are stored as triggers, to create your own conflict-resolution process. You'll learn more about this process tomorrow.

Remember that SQL Server 2000 allows you to define multiple triggers on a single table. Your conflict resolution scheme can be very complex.

I suggest you pick a record to be the current record and then save both records in a separate table for a manual review. In this fashion, you can test the quality of your conflict-resolution process.

After you pick a record, the synchronization process continues and the whole cycle repeats itself.

Merge Replication and SQL Server CE

You can set SQL Server 2000 Windows CE Edition up as an anonymous subscriber in merge replication. This is an ideal solution for PDA devices. Merge replication allows you to update data at both the PDA (subscriber) as well as at the Publisher.

When the PDA is connected with the network again, the replication can take place and data from other subscribers and the publisher will be merged and sent back to the PDA running SQL Server 2000 for Windows CE.

The SQL Server 2000 Windows CE Edition uses SQL Server CE replication object. When you create a publication, ensure that you have specified that Servers running SQL Server CE are a type of subscriber. This will create the anonymous subscriptions for the publication automatically.

When the subscription is created, the initial snapshot is sent to the PDA through the SQL Server CE Replication Object. Synchronizations are handled by the SQL Server CE Replication object.

Snapshot Replication Internals

Remember that snapshot replication copies the entire article or publication wholesale from the publisher to the subscriber. This includes snapshot replication with updating subscribers. The updates are done at both subscriber and publisher, but when a synchronization occurs, the incoming replicated article completely overwrites the subscriber's data.

In snapshot replication, no merge agent is involved; however, the distribution agent is used. If you are using a pull subscription, the distribution agent is found on the subscription server. If you are using a push subscription, the distribution agent is located on the distribution server. Using a push or pull subscription in this scenario depends on many factors, not the least of which is how busy your distribution server is and how you want to manage subscriptions. Do you want to manage subscriptions centrally (push subscription), or do you want to manage subscriptions at each subscriber (pull subscriptions)?

Figure 16.8 outlines the snapshot replication process presented in the following steps:

1. The snapshot agent reads the published article and creates the table schema and data in the distribution working folder.
2. The distribution agent reads these schema and rebuilds the tables on the subscriber.
3. The distribution agent moves the data into the newly created tables on the subscriber.
4. Indexes (if used) are re-created on the newly synchronized subscription database.

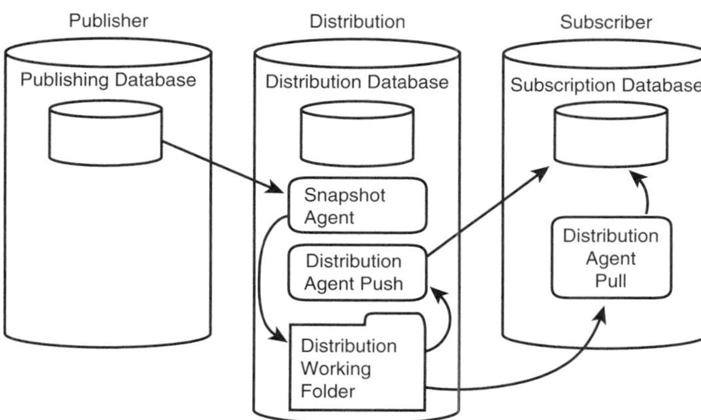

FIGURE 16.8
Snapshot replication process.

Snapshot replication occurs on demand. This means that the data snapshot isn't stored in the distribution database, as occurs with the store-and-forward algorithm used in transaction-based replication. Only status information about a snapshot is stored in the distribution database. The snapshot agent and the distribution agent do all the work at the time the synchronization is initiated.

Transaction Replication Internals

Remember that transaction-based replication copies just the transactions that occurred in the published databases to the distribution database. The updates are then applied to the subscription database generally as they occur, which reduces latency. The subscription database should be thought of as read-only, because this type of replication is one-way. Changes to the data can be made only at the publisher.

Although you should think of the subscription database as read-only, don't set the read-only database option to true. If you do, you can't apply replicated transactions to it.

Transaction-based replication doesn't use a merge agent anymore, but it does use a log reader agent. Keep in mind that the snapshot agent is still around as well. You must have a basis for applying your transactions, which the snapshot agent accomplishes for you. As in snapshot replication, the distribution agent is used. If you're using a pull subscription, the distribution agent is found on the subscription server. If you're using a push subscription, the distribution agent is located on the distribution server.

Figure 16.9 outlines the transaction replication process presented in the following steps:

1. The snapshot agent reads the published article and creates the table schema and data in the distribution working folder in the same manner as shown in Figure 16.8.
2. The distribution agent reads these schema and builds the tables on the subscriber.
3. The distribution agent moves the data into the newly created tables on the subscriber.
4. Indexes (if used) are re-created on the newly synchronized subscription database.
5. Normal transactional replication can begin.
6. The log reader agent watches the transaction logs of the publishing databases. When it finds a transaction, the agent moves it to the distribution database, where the transaction will be stored until the next synchronization process begins.

7. When the synchronization process is called (either by a push from the distributor or a pull from a subscriber), the transaction is read by the distribution agent and then applied to the subscription database.

FIGURE 16.9
Transaction replication process.

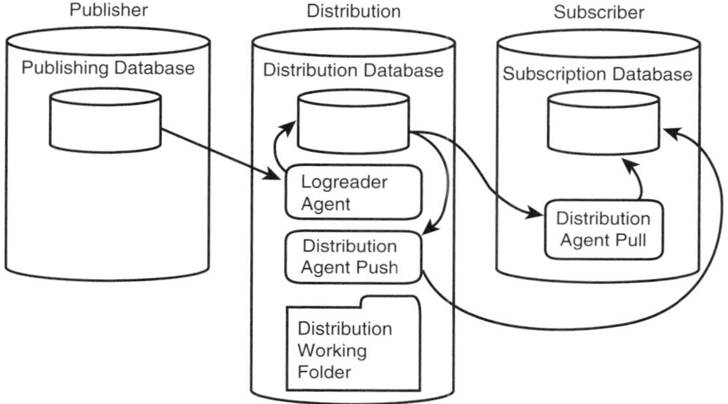

Note

Transaction replication is commonly used when you want minimal latency and can consider your subscription database as read-only. This type of scenario is useful when you want to remove the impact of OLAP services from your OLTP servers.

Queued Updating Internals

When a publication is enabled for queued updating, the data modifications made at a subscriber are held in a queue until they can be applied to the publisher. Figure 16.10 outlines the queued updating process presented in the following steps:

1. Triggers on the subscribing tables capture updates made at the subscriber. These triggers, created as part of the subscription process, store the updates in a queue, the default being a SQL Server 2000 queue.
2. For SQL Server 2000 queues, the updates are stored in a table called `MSReplication_queue`, which is also created during the subscription process. For MSMQ 2.0 queues, the updates are stored in a central queue at the distributor. When the subscriber is disconnected from the network, the updates are stored locally and automatically forwarded to the queue at the distributor after a network connection is restored.
3. The queue reader agent applies queued transactions to the appropriate publication. For SQL Server 2000 queues, the updates are read directly from the queue at the subscriber. With MSMQ 2.0, the transactions are read from the central queue stored on the distributor.

4. Any conflicts detected while applying the queued transactions are resolved according to the conflict policy set when the publication is created. Conflicting transactions can then be rolled back at the subscriber that sent them using the standard transactional distribution process.
5. The changes made at the publisher are propagated to all the other subscribers according to the configured schedules of the distribution agent.

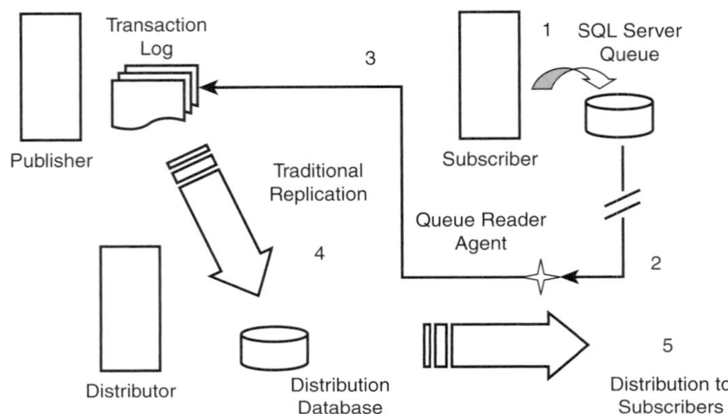

FIGURE 16.10
Queued update process.

Replication Scenarios

You can implement replication in various scenarios. Each scenario benefits a given business situation.

Central Publisher

In the central publisher scenario (see Figure 16.11), you can reduce the impact of OLAP services from the OLTP environment. In this scenario, the publishing server is also the distribution server. Keep in mind that the more subscribers you have, the larger the impact will be on the distribution server. This impact can be reduced somewhat by using a pull subscription in which the distribution agent resides on each subscriber. Although the distribution database lives on the publication server, it can support multiple publication servers and multiple subscription servers.

Central Publisher with a Remote Distributor

In the central publisher with a remote distributor scenario, you can further reduce the impact of the distribution database on your high-volume OLTP environment by moving it to its own server (see Figure 16.12). As before, a single distribution server can support multiple publishers and multiple subscribers. This scenario is preferred when you have situations with multiple publishers and subscribers.

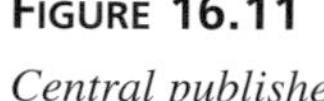

FIGURE 16.11

Central publisher replication scenario.

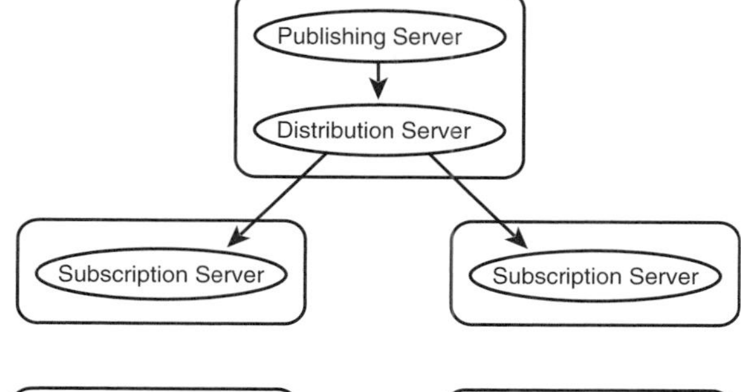

FIGURE 16.12

Central publisher with a remote distributor scenario.

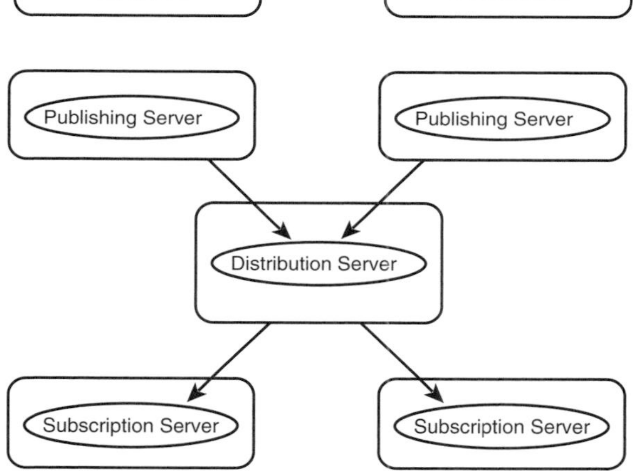

Republisher

In the republisher scenario, your subscription server is also a publishing server. This scenario can be very beneficial when you have a slow and expensive link (regular telephone lines) between the main publisher and a group of subscribers (see Figure 16.13). In this scenario, the subscriber also acts as a publisher for a series of subscription databases. In this manner, you can minimize the cost of your slow link by updating a single subscriber and then republishing the newly synchronized information to the rest of the subscription servers.

In Figure 16.13, your main publishing database is located in New York City. You can now synchronize on a schedule that minimizes your phone line costs to the main subscriber in Hamburg. Hamburg can then redistribute that data more locally to the Berlin and Munich locations.

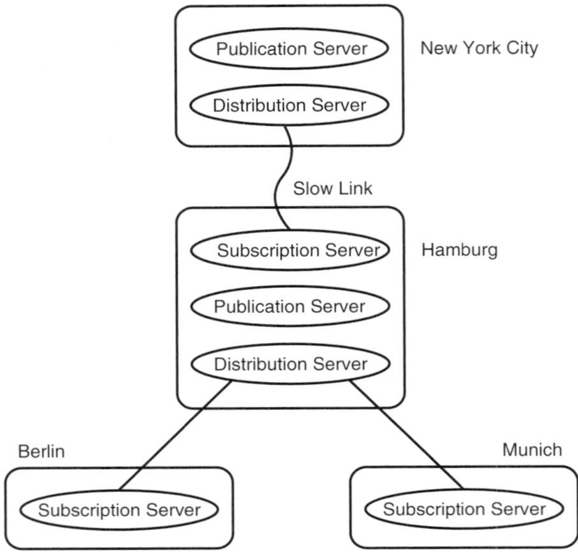

FIGURE 16.13
Republisher scenario.

Central Subscriber

In the central subscriber scenario, your subscription server is centrally located and one or more publishing servers sends it updates. This scenario is useful for rollup reporting situations or central processing. For example, Figure 16.14 shows a central publisher scenario in which branch offices in Seattle, Los Angeles, and Detroit (the publishers) send orders to the Denver location. From the Denver location, these orders are then processed and the product is shipped.

To differentiate between orders coming from various locations, you should make some schema changes to your data as outlined here:

- Add a separate RegionCode column to your orders table.
- Make the new RegionCode column part of the primary key.

By creating a RegionCode column and making it part of your primary key, you can avoid conflicts. For example, what would happen if Los Angeles had an order number 2000 and Detroit also had an order number 2000? When they are both applied at the subscriber, a conflict will occur. By adding the region code, you now have a primary key that might look like 2 2000 for Los Angeles and 3 2000 for Detroit, as shown in Figure 16.15.

FIGURE 16.14

Central subscriber scenario.

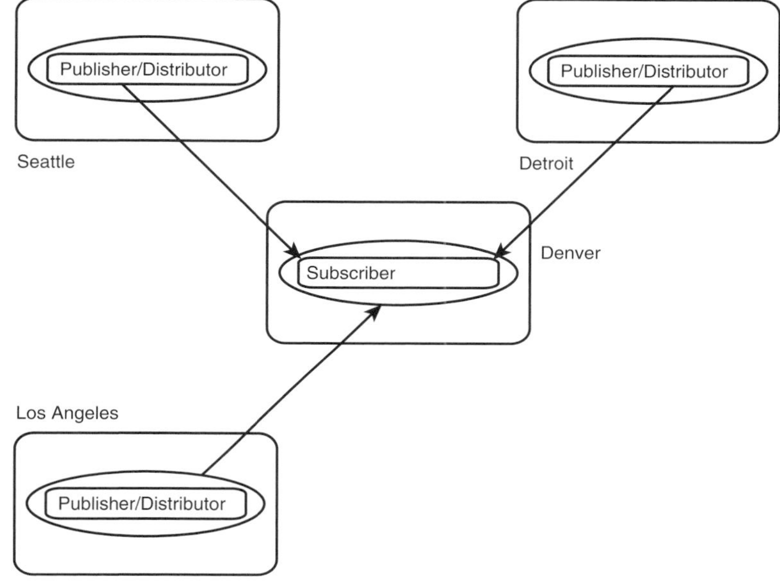

FIGURE 16.15

Use some type of region code to differentiate rows of data coming from separate locations in the central subscriber scenario.

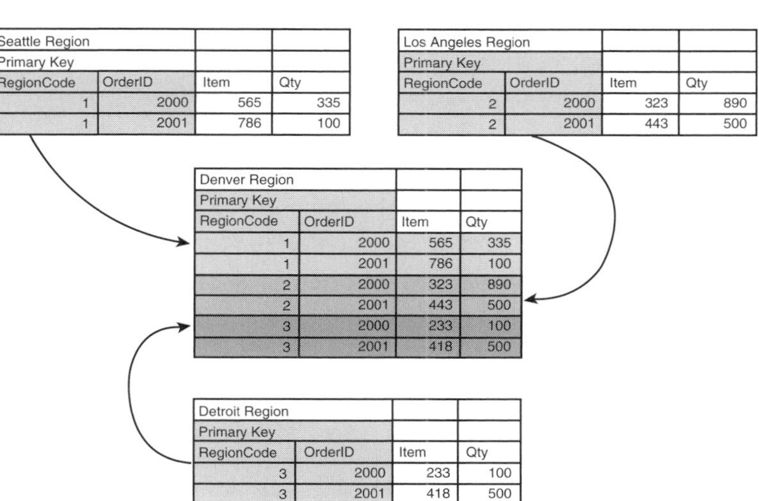

Seattle Region			
Primary Key			
RegionCode	OrderID	Item	Qty
1	2000	565	335
1	2001	786	100

Los Angeles Region			
Primary Key			
RegionCode	OrderID	Item	Qty
2	2000	323	890
2	2001	443	500

Denver Region			
Primary Key			
RegionCode	OrderID	Item	Qty
1	2000	565	335
1	2001	786	100
2	2000	323	890
2	2001	443	500
3	2000	233	100
3	2001	418	500

Detroit Region			
Primary Key			
RegionCode	OrderID	Item	Qty
3	2000	233	100
3	2001	418	500

The central subscriber scenario lends itself well to a transaction-based replication. Each location that orders an item will have the item order replicated to the central location where it will be processed and shipped.

Multiple Publishers and Subscribers

Multiple publishers and subscribers are useful for reservation-type systems or any other system in which information about other regions must be available at each region. I like to look at an example of 800 call centers. When you dial an 800 number to order a particular product or to check on the status of an order, your call might be routed to any of the geographically dispersed call centers around the country. Figure 16.16 shows call centers in Bend, Boulder, and Atlanta. Each call center must have information that could have been gathered at another call center to support customers who want to check on the status of orders.

FIGURE 16.16
Multiple publishers and subscribers scenario.

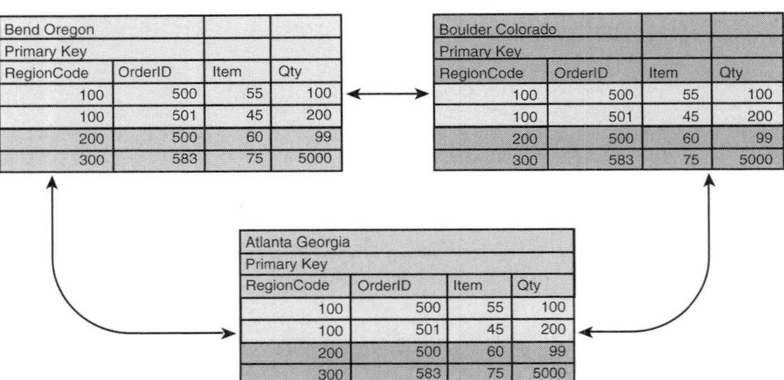

In a reservation-type system, you can implement this form of replication as well. I suggest that you use distributed transactions to do this so that all locations have the same data at the same time. (You don't want to double-book an airline reservation or hotel room, do you?)

As shown in Figure 16.16, each location is both a publisher and a subscriber of information. Each shop subscribes to the other shops' published articles. Each shop should publish only the articles it owns. In other words, use a RegionCode field to differentiate data owned by one or more shops. In this way, you avoid the conflicts discussed in the central subscriber section. For this scenario to work properly, each shop should update data only from its own location. If you use an updating subscriber type of scenario here, be sure to make your updates to all sites simultaneously to avoid conflicts.

Transforming Published Data

For snapshot and transactional replication, SQL Server 2000 allows you to leverage the power of Data Transformation Services (DTS) to tailor your publications subscriber by subscriber. This is another option you can specify when creating a publication. When the option to allow transformations is set, you can build a replication DTS package, using wizards or the DTS Designer, to which subscribers can attach and incorporate as part of their replication data flow. This functionality is limited, however, to SQL Server 2000 and OLE DB subscribers.

Publishing SQL Server 2000 Databases to the Internet

To enable publishing of your SQL Server database to the Internet, you must take care of some additional configuration changes. Day 21, "Using XML with SQL Server 2000," covers this in more depth. For our purposes here, however, keep the following in mind when you're working with push and pull subscriptions:

- TCP/IP must be enabled and installed on the computers running the distribution agent and the merge agent and any computers connected to those running these agents.
- Your publishing and distribution servers should have a direct network connection other than through the Internet. This is not only for security but also to handle potential problems with latency.
- Your publishing and distribution servers should be on the same side of the firewall (preferably the secure side of the firewall).

Publishing Through a VPN

The most secure method for publishing data over the Internet, Virtual Private Networking (VPN) technology, allows remote users to connect to a corporate network while maintaining secure communications. A VPN connects one network to another using the Internet as a wide area network (WAN) link between the sites. Two commonly used tunneling protocols for the purpose are Point-To-Point Tunneling Protocol (PPTP), available with Windows NT 4.0, and Layer Two Tunneling Protocol (L2TP), included with Windows 2000. After a VPN is configured, replication can be configured as though the publisher and subscriber were on the same LAN.

Publishing Through Microsoft Proxy Server

Internet replication in SQL Server 2000 can be configured to take advantage of the security provided by Microsoft Proxy Server. In this approach, Internet pull subscriptions are configured to connect to the proxy server instead of directly to your SQL Server. The proxy server can be configured to prevent unauthorized access to your internal network resources.

Publishing Through File Transfer Protocol (FTP)

If you're going to allow pull subscriptions from the Internet, you must make the following additional configuration changes to your servers:

- Internet Information Server (IIS) must be installed on the same server as your distribution server.
- The merge and distribution agents must be configured with the correct FTP address. This address can be configured through the distribution agent utility or from a command prompt on the distribution server.
- The FTP paths and ports under the publication's properties need to be configured with an FTP site used for the snapshot folder location. Or you can set the FTP home directory to be the snapshot folder (by default, `\Microsoft SQL Server\MSSQL\Repldata\FTP`) and configure this home directory as an FTP site.
- The snapshot folder must be available to your subscription servers.

Best Practices

To help ensure the best performance, keep the following points in mind when you're determining the type of replication to use and the scenario you want to implement:

- Ensure network speed and availability.
- Immediately updating subscribers can be useful when sufficient network bandwidth is available.
- Publish partitioned data. You don't need to always send all the information all the time. Give the subscribers what they need, and reduce network and distribution overhead.
- Pull subscriptions can take much of the workload off the distribution server. Remember that you will lose your centralized management of replication but gain some performance.
- Use a remote distributor in your scenarios to move the bulk of the workload involved in replication from your OLTP database. This tool is also useful if you have a slow and expensive link between your distribution and subscription servers.
- Minimize updating conflicts by minimizing the chance for them to occur when you're using merge replication or updating subscribers.
- In merge replication or updating subscribers, be sure to include a region code as part of your primary key.

Replicating Issues in a Heterogeneous Environment

Because SQL Server 2000 supports replication in a heterogeneous environment, you can use a SQL Server publisher to send publications subscribers through open database connectivity (ODBC) drivers and object linking and embedding database (OLE DB) providers. In certain instances, you can even use SQL Server as a subscriber to a non-SQL Server publisher.

Replication is supported on Windows 9*x*/NT platforms. Replication to other platforms is supported through the use of the appropriate ODBC drivers or OLE DB providers and communications software. SQL Server 2000 supports replication to Microsoft Access, Oracle, and any other database that complies with the SQL Server ODBC subscriber requirements. SQL Server ships with drivers for Oracle, Access, and IBM's Distributed Relational Database Architecture (DRDA) data protocol.

The ODBC subscriber driver must

- Support ODBC Level 1 conformance
- Support T-SQL DDL (data definition language)
- Run in 32-bit mode
- Be thread-safe
- Allow updates

Publishing Data to Non-SQL Server 2000 Databases

Keep these points in mind when you're attempting to replicate to non-SQL Server 2000 ODBC subscribers:

- SQL Server 2000 doesn't support pull subscriptions. You must use push subscriptions from a SQL Server 2000 publisher.
- Batched statements aren't supported to ODBC subscribers.
- Data types are mapped to the closest data type available on the subscription database. For example, Microsoft Access has no concept of a text field. Access would receive a replicated text field as an Access memo data type.
- The ODBC DSN (data source name) must conform to SQL Server's naming rules for identifiers.
- When you use snapshots, the data to be transferred uses the Bulk Copy Program (BCP) character format. You'll learn about the BCP utility in detail on Day 19, "Migrating Data Between Database Servers."

Publishing Non-SQL Server 2000 Data to SQL Server 2000

Third-party databases can become publishers in the SQL Server 2000 environment. To accomplish this feat, you must write a program that takes advantage of the SQL-DMO (SQL Database Management Objects). After you create your programs to do so, you can support all the various replication features found in SQL Server 2000.

The SQL-DMO exposes the following Component Object Model (COM) objects for use in replication:

- Objects for replication administration
- Objects for replication monitoring
- Objects to take advantage of the distribution agent to forward transactions to subscription servers
- Objects to work with the distribution database for storing replicated transactions
- SQL Server performance counters, several of which are grouped into the SQL Server performance objects and displayed in the SQL Server Performance Monitor
- Objects to expose your publisher to the SQL Server Enterprise Manager for graphical administration

Summary

Today you learned about the replication methodologies in SQL Server 2000. You covered information about what defines replication. You also learned about the three prime factors in determining what type of replication to use: autonomy for subscribers, transactional consistency, and latency.

You then learned the distribution methodologies. They include merge replication, in which both subscribers and publishers can update data. You then looked at snapshot replication, which is the easiest type of replication to install and maintain because the entire publication is transferred all at once. Remember that with snapshot replication, data at the subscriber is considered read-only.

You then learned about transactional replication, which is the most popular form of replication. Again, subscription information is considered read-only. Next, you looked at options for updating subscribers. Carried over from SQL Server 7.0, immediate updating subscribers use 2PC to guarantee changes are made simultaneously at the publisher and subscriber. Queued updating uses the store-and-forward mechanisms of message queuing to handle asynchronous transactions. Both immediate and queued updating can be used with snapshot and transactional updating subscribers. Finally, you looked at distributed transactions, which work through the 2PC protocol and take advantage of the Microsoft Distributed Transaction Coordinator, which is part of the Microsoft Transaction Server. With distributed transactions, all sites are updated at the same time, or none of them are.

Five types of replication agents work in SQL Server. Each agent has its own set of tasks and responsibilities. The merge agent is responsible for handling conflict resolution and converging your records. The snapshot agent moves snapshots of your data from a publisher to a subscriber. The distribution agent moves transactions from the distribution database to the subscribers. The log reader agent handles transactional replication and monitors the transaction logs of replicated databases. When it finds transactions, it moves them to the distribution database where the distribution agent takes over. The queue reader agent moves transactions stored at the subscriber to the distributor when a network connection is re-established. You also covered several different replication scenarios. SQL Server 2000 supports replication in heterogeneous environments, including support for Access, Oracle, and any ODBC- or OLE DB–compliant database that also supports the SQL Server ODBC subscriber conformance issues.

All in all, it was a long day. Congratulations on finishing it. Tomorrow you will implement several different types of replication in SQL Server.

Q&A

Q Which is most important: transactional consistency, latency, or autonomy?

A Generally speaking, transactional consistency is of utmost importance. Latency and site autonomy are really up to you, but having the correct data should be the most important issue. Keep in mind that only merge replication has a chance to lose transactional consistency. All other types of replication support full transactional consistency.

Q Which type of replication do you see the most often?

A Currently, transactional replication is most common because SQL Server 6.5 supported only transactional replication and distributed transactions. Transactional replication with updating subscribers will probably become the most popular form of replication because it supports transactional consistency, a reasonable level of site autonomy, and a low level of latency. It really is the best of all worlds.

Q Should I use merge replication or queued updating?

A This question is tough to answer without stepping on anyone's toes. Merge replication handles conflicts at the row level, whereas queued updating handles conflicts at the transaction level. One company successfully using queued updating is Damascus Software within its point-of-sale module. In this case, cash registers update a local SQL Server 2000 server with sale information, which in turn periodically connects with a central SQL Server 2000 server to synchronize sale and inventory information. For these purposes, queued updating makes more sense than merge replication. In situations like the one described today to explain merge replication, queued updating wouldn't be as appropriate. Basically, the answer depends on whether a row or a transaction is more important to your application.

Q How hard is it to modify the conflict-resolution triggers?

A Modifying them isn't too difficult. They are just triggers with code in them. When you feel good enough about programming in SQL Server, these triggers should be a snap. You can implement your triggers to move both the chosen version of a record as well as the unchosen version of the conflicting record to a separate table and evaluate how well your trigger code is working. Also, keep in mind that because you're coding it, you can make the conflict-resolution process as picky as you want it to be. The old magic 8 ball can help you decide which version of a conflicting record to update and which one to toss out.

Q How does this ROWGUID thing work? What is it?

A A ROWGUID is a 128-bit unique identifier. It's alleged to be a globally unique number. SQL Server uses an algorithm that generates these numbers based on many factors. ROWGUIDs are commonly added to tables marked for merge replication. Using these ROWGUIDs, you can track the history or lineage of changes made to a particular record.

Q Can the distribution server support all types of replication at the same time?

A Yes. In fact, you can set up publications and subscriptions on the same servers that use different types of replication on a per-publication basis.

Workshop

This section provides quiz questions to help you solidify your understanding of the concepts presented today. In addition to the quiz questions, exercises are provided to let you practice what you've learned today. Try to understand the quiz and exercise answers before continuing on to tomorrow's lesson. Answers are provided in Appendix A, "Answers to Quiz Questions."

Quiz

1. Which agent reads the transaction log of published databases and then moves the data to the distribution database?
2. What does the distribution agent do?

3. What replication scenario is best suited to doing rollup reporting?
4. Where does the merge agent reside in a push subscription with merge replication?

Exercise

1. In this exercise, determine the best replication scenario to use given the following facts:

   - You have four sites in the United States that handle order processing. You have a central warehouse located in Wichita, Kansas, that must have pick tickets made up so that merchandise can be shipped.
   - You have three sites located in Great Britain that handle MIS duties and other types of administration. The British sites must have copies of all records of shipped items and the orders placed for them.
   - The British locations don't want to have a dedicated line to the United States because it's deemed far too expensive.

DAY 17

Implementing Replication Methodologies

Yesterday's lesson was long, with many issues that those of you who are new to SQL Server might have found confusing. Take a few minutes here to review what you covered.

You learned about SQL Server 2000's replication methodologies. You also learned about the three prime factors in determining the type of replication to use: autonomy for the subscribers, transactional consistency, and latency. You then covered the distribution methodologies, including merge replication, where both subscribers and publishers can update data. You then looked at snapshot replication, the easiest type of replication to install and maintain because the entire publication is transferred all at once. Remember that with snapshot replication, data at the subscriber level is considered read-only.

You then looked at transactional replication, where subscription information is considered read-only. You then looked at the SQL Server 2000 options for updating subscribers. You looked at immediate updating subscribers, which take advantage of the 2PC protocol to make updates at both the subscriber and publisher levels simultaneously. You also looked at the new option of queued updating, which sends transactions to a message queue when servers are offline. Finally, you looked at distributed transactions. Distributed transactions work through the 2PC protocol and take advantage of the Microsoft Distributed Transaction Coordinator, which is part of the Microsoft Transaction Server. With distributed transactions, all sites are updated at the same time, or none of them are.

You then covered the five replication agents that work in SQL Server. The merge agent is responsible for handling conflict resolution and converging your records. The snapshot agent moves snapshots of your data from a publisher to a subscriber. The distribution agent moves transactions from the distribution database to the subscribers. The Log reader agent, used in transactional replication, monitors the transaction logs of replicated databases. When it finds transactions, it moves them to the distribution database, where the distribution agent takes over. The queue reader agent moves queued transactions from their respective message queues to be applied at the publisher.

You next covered the different replication scenarios, which included the central publisher, central publisher with a remote distributor, republisher, central subscriber, and multiple publishers and subscribers. You finished with some information regarding replication in a heterogeneous environment. This type of replication includes support for Access, Oracle, and any database that's compliant with ODBC (open database connectivity) or OLE DB (object linking and embedding database) but also supports the SQL Server ODBC subscriber-conformance level.

Today you learn about the security issues involved with replication. You then learn how to set up publishing, distribution, and subscribing databases. Then you will focus on how to create a publication and learn about publication restrictions. You learn how to do the initial synchronization of your data and begin the replication process. You also look at how to implement both push and pull subscriptions and some considerations of each.

Replication management is covered next. You cover the issues involved with monitoring replication, creating replication scripts (used to make backups of your replication scenarios), Windows NT/2000's performance monitor as it applies to replication, distribution database backup issues, and replication agent histories. You finish up with a short section on troubleshooting the replication process.

If you're like me, you spend a lot of time reading through technical information (such as this book) and would prefer to do it in a comfortable chair away from your computer. This lesson has many figures so that you can read it while you are away from a computer and still get a good feel for what you would see and what's going on.

Today's lesson is laid out with many step-by-step walkthroughs and their associated screen captures. I hope that you find the additional visual information useful.

Understanding Security Issues

To begin the replication process, you must first meet some basic replication requirements:

- Each server involved in the replication process must be registered in Enterprise Manager.
- For Windows NT, if you are working with SQL Servers from different domains, trust relationships between the domains must be established. Windows 2000 implements the domain model differently, and two-way transitive trusts are the default (if you are using Active Directory, trusts are only implemented between domains if they belong to the same forest).
- Replication uses the same security context of the SQLServerAgent service under Windows NT/2000. This account must have administrative privileges and should be a member of the local administrators group.
- The account must have the logon as a service advanced user right.

I strongly suggest that you create a single Windows 2000 account that all SQL Server agents will share. This way, you can avoid any potential connectivity issues. If you decide to use alternative accounts, these accounts must be able to access the distribution server's working folder. You have to add these accounts to the distribution server's Windows NT Administrators local group. You can also use SQL Server login accounts when you are using non-Windows NT computers.

Local system accounts *don't* have network access and therefore can't participate in replication.

Setting Up Your Servers

In this section, you will prepare your servers using the Configure Publishing and Distribution Wizard in the SQL Enterprise Manager.

You must first install the distribution server before you can install any dependent publishing servers. You must have sysadmin rights to create the distributor. After you install the distribution service, you can view both local and remote distribution server properties. The distribution database is installed automatically when you set up your distributor. You can create additional distribution databases on a local or remote distributor.

You must ensure the accessibility of the distribution working folder as well. By default, the distribution working folder is located in `\\`*`computer_name`*`\C$\Program Files\Microsoft SQL Server\MSSQL\Repldata`. This folder is installed by default on Windows 2000.

Finally, make sure that the distribution server has enough memory. By default, you must have at least 32MB on the server and 16MB allocated to SQL Server for the server to participate in replication as a distributor. If you're supporting many publishers or many subscribers, you might want to add memory.

You can uninstall a distribution server by using the Uninstall Publishing and Distribution Wizard in the Enterprise Manager. Keep in mind the following when you remove a distribution server:

- All publishers that use the distributor are disabled.
- All publications residing on those servers are deleted.
- All subscriptions to those publications are deleted.
- All distribution databases on the distribution server that is being uninstalled are deleted.

The next sections begin the process of installing and configuring your server for replication. You can use the same server for publishing, distribution, and subscribing. If you have multiple servers and want to try this process, the steps are the same. As you go through each section, you will receive additional information as necessary. This format is very similar to that of Day 2, "Installing Microsoft SQL Server 2000."

Installing Replication

You must perform three distinct steps to install and enable replication:

1. Install a distribution server.

2. Create publications.
3. Subscribe to these publications.

You will learn more about each of these steps as you do them.

Installing the Distribution Server

A distribution server requires additional disk space to store snapshots and the distribution database. The various replication agents running on that server also need additional processor time. When you install your distributor, keep these points in mind:

- Make sure that you have enough disk space for the distribution working folder and the distribution database.
- The distribution database must be able to store all transactions between publishers and subscribers if you're using transactional replication.
- You must manage the distribution database's log file carefully for transactional replication because each transaction published to it and each subscription applied is logged.

Note

> Snapshot and merge replication store data in the distribution working folder. The distribution database tracks only the status of your replication jobs in these replication methodologies. Remember that for transactional replication, all transactions are stored in the distribution database.

If you are a bit apprehensive about the size of your distribution database, you might think about the following in terms of the size requirements for your distributor:

- The number of articles to be published.
- The size of the articles being published.
- Whether any text or image data types are in the articles. If so, you must use either a scheduled table refresh or snapshot replication because these items aren't replicated during transactional replication.
- How much latency between synchronizations can significantly increase the space requirements. Transactional information at the distribution is retained until it's applied to the subscriber, which might be offline.
- If you're using transactional replication, the number of `INSERT` and `UPDATE` statements. Remember that these statements contain actual data changes. If you insert 500 rows into a server, 500 rows of data need to be on the distribution server.

- If you're using transactional replication, how many transactions in a given time period will stack up. For example, how many transactions per half hour do you expect to be replicating?

Now with those issues out of the way, follow these steps to install a distribution server:

1. Connect to your SQL Server through the SQL Enterprise Manager.
2. Highlight your server and select Replication and then Configure Publishing, Subscribers, and Distribution from the Tools menu.
3. A welcome screen appears (see Figure 17.1). Click Next to continue.

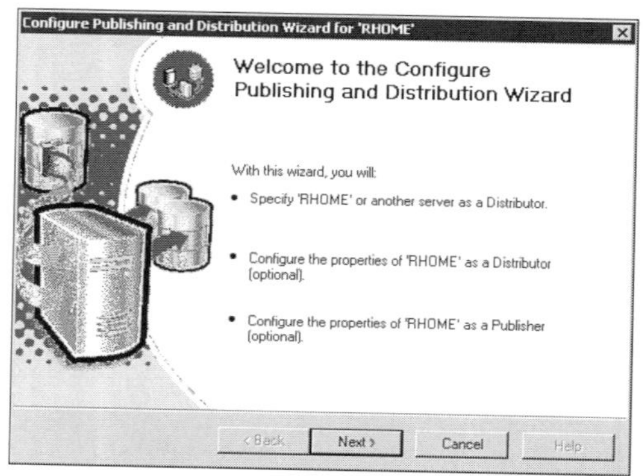

FIGURE 17.1

Configure Publishing and Distribution Wizard welcome screen.

4. Choose a server to use as your distribution server (see Figure 17.2). By default, the computer you are connected to is selected as the distributor. You can choose a different distribution server by selecting Use the Following Server and then selecting another registered server in your enterprise. Click Next to continue.

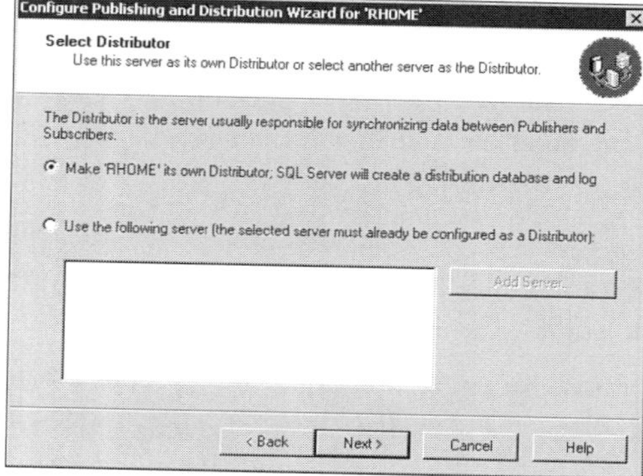

FIGURE 17.2

Choose a distributor dialog.

5. You are asked to specify the Snapshot folder. Take the default and click Next. If you receive a notification from SQL Server that the snapshot folder you chose is accessible only by logins with admin privileges on the local server, click OK to continue.
6. Choose whether to use a default configuration or to customize your settings. For this example, choose Yes, Let Me Set the Distribution…. In Figure 17.3, the default settings specify that RHOME (my computer name) is used as the distributor. RHOME can subscribe to RHOME and publish to RHOME. The distribution database also is stored in the `\MSSQL\Data` folder. Any other SQL Servers registered in Enterprise Manager also show up in this list. For example, if you have a SQL Server registered as Leap, you can publish and subscribe with the Leap computer. When you are ready, click Next to continue.

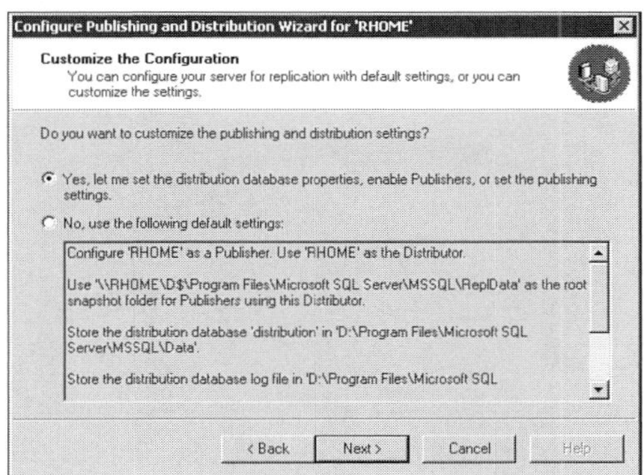

FIGURE 17.3
The Customize the Configuration dialog.

7. From the Provide Distribution Database Information dialog (see Figure 17.4), specify the name of the distribution database, the folder in which to store the database file, and the folder used to store the distribution log. These files must reside on the distribution server (in this example, RHOME). Click Next to continue.

Configure Publishing and Distribution Wizard for 'RHOME'

Provide Distribution Database Information

Select the name and location of the distribution database and log files.

The distribution database stores changes to transactional publications until Subscribers can be updated. It also stores historical information for snapshot and merge publications.

Distribution database name: distribution

Folder for the distribution database file: D:\Program Files\Microsoft SQL Server\MSSQL\Data

Folder for the distribution database log file: D:\Program Files\Microsoft SQL Server\MSSQL\Data

The paths must refer to disks that are local to 'RHOME' and begin with a local drive letter and colon (for example, C:). Mapped drive letters and network paths are invalid.

< Back | Next > | Cancel | Help

FIGURE 17.4
The Provide Distribution Database Information dialog.

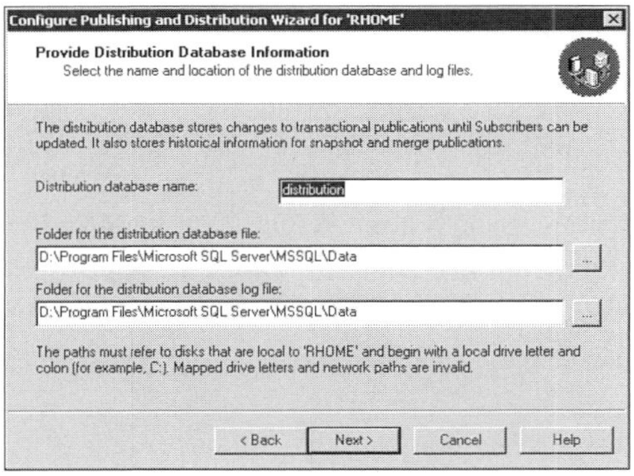

8. In the Enable Publishers dialog, you can give permissions for other publishers to use this distributor. Just select the registered server you want to give access to, and then click the … button to set the security options. If you don't see your server listed, click the New button to add one. Be sure to place a check mark next to the name of your computer, and click Next to continue.
9. In the Enable Publication Databases dialog (see Figure 17.5), specify whether to use transactional replication (including snapshot) or merge replication on your databases. Either click the check boxes next to the databases or click the command buttons on the right to affect all selected databases. In this example, select the Trans check box for the pubs database, and then click Next.

FIGURE 17.5

The Enable Publication Databases dialog.

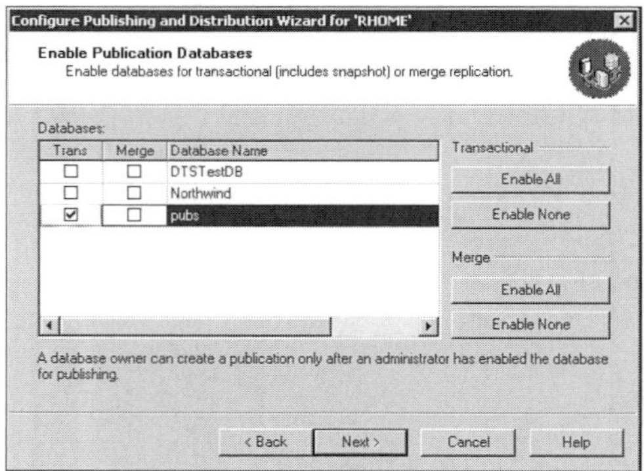

Keep these rules in mind when you're enabling a publication database:

- You must be a member of the sysadmin fixed server role.
- After you enable a database for publishing, members of the db_owner fixed database role can create publications.

10. In the Enable Subscribers dialog (see Figure 17.6), all registered servers are available for subscribing. You can also register additional servers by clicking the New button. To enable a server, click the check box next to the server you want to have as a subscriber.
11. You might have noticed the buttons with the … next to your servers. You use this button to bring up the login information used in replication as well as the default

replication schedules you want to implement. Click the … next to your computer name. You should see something similar to Figure 17.7.

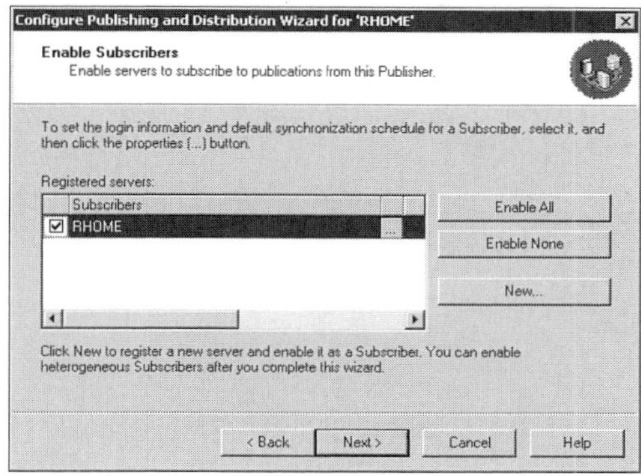

FIGURE 17.6

The Enable Subscribers dialog.

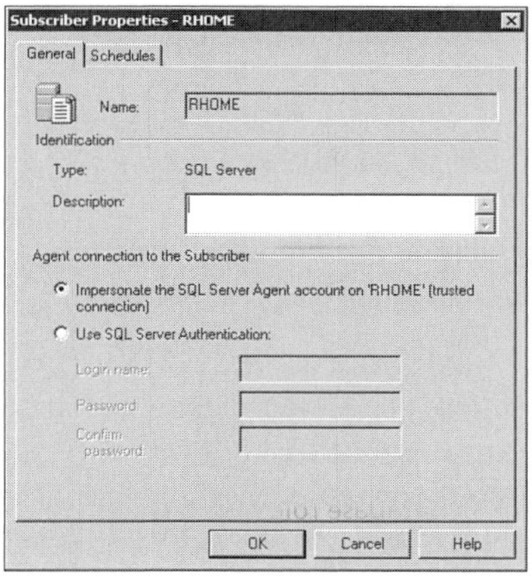

FIGURE 17.7

The General tab of the Subscriber Properties dialog.

12. In this dialog, you can specify that you want to connect to the subscriber by impersonating the SQL Server Agent account on the subscriber's computer, or you can use the SQL Server Authentication. If you use SQL Server Authentication, you must specify a login name and a password.

13. On the Schedules tab (see Figure 17.8), you can specify whether the distribution agent and the merge agent will run continuously or at scheduled intervals. The default is to run the distribution agent continuously. If you click the Change button, you see options to schedule replication times. You will look at these options later. Be sure that the default Continuously option is selected, and click OK to close the properties dialog. You then return to the Enable Subscribers dialog (refer to Figure 17.6). Click Next to continue.

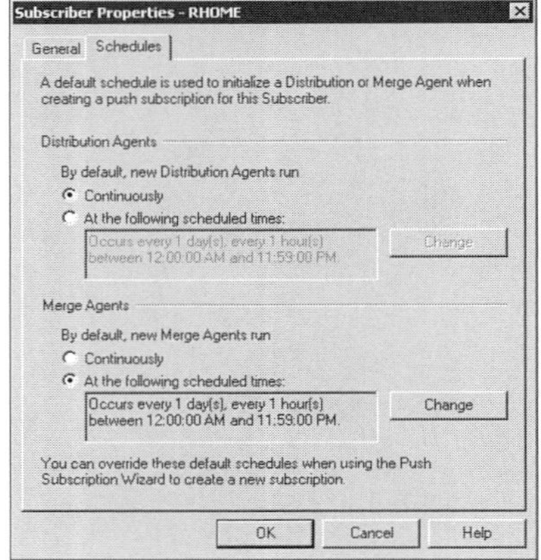

FIGURE 17.8

The Schedules tab of the Subscriber Properties dialog.

14. The Completing the Configure Publishing and Distribution Wizard dialog appears. This screen provides a summary of what you are doing. Click Finish to complete this portion of the replication process.

After clicking Finish in the last step, you see a progress dialog detailing which portion of your selections are being implemented (see Figure 17.9). A final dialog then appears, telling you that the Enterprise Manager has successfully enabled your computer as a distribution server. If you see a replication monitor installation screen, click Close.

Notice that Replication Monitor now appears in the console tree on the left side of Enterprise Manager. This item isn't available until replication is configured on a particular server.

Congratulations, you have successfully installed a distribution server! Let's quickly review what you just did:

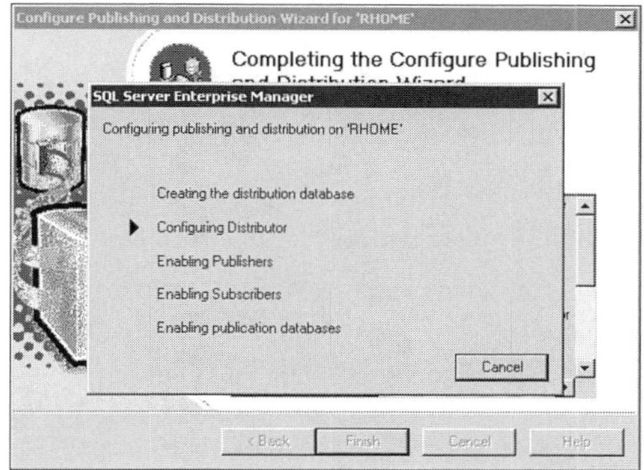

FIGURE 17.9
Completing the Configure Publishing and Distribution Wizard.

- You installed the distribution database on your server.
- You determined which servers can use this server (your distribution server) as a remote distribution server.
- You configured which servers can publish data.
- You enabled subscribers.
- You verified the distribution schedule for your subscribers using push replication with transactional replication methodology.
- You ensured that your publisher has enough memory and hard disk space. You might need additional hard disk space if your distribution server is unavailable.

Creating a Publication

In this section, you will create a publication, determine the replication type, determine snapshot requirements, specify whether anonymous or updating subscribers or pull subscriptions will be allowed, and define partitions on your data.

You can create publications in several different ways: You can use the wizards, the console tree in Enterprise Manager, or menu options.

The Create Publication Wizard creates publications and specifies the following options:

- Whether one or more articles are available
- Whether to schedule the snapshot agent

- Whether to maintain a snapshot at the distribution server
- The tables you want to publish
- The stored procedures you want to publish
- Publications that share agents
- Whether to allow anonymous updates from subscribers
- Whether to allow updates from subscribers
- Whether to allow pull subscriptions

In this example, you will create a publication that uses the `authors` table from the `pubs` database. You will install and use transactional replication to replicate this table to a new table called `rplAuthors`. You will then make changes to the original table and verify that the data was successfully replicated to the `rplAuthors` table. Follow these steps:

1. Connect to your server in the Enterprise Manager. Highlight your server, and select Replication, Create and Manage Publications from the Tools menu. The Create and Manage Publications dialog opens (see Figure 17.10). Click the Create Publication button, and then click Next on the Welcome screen. You should see a dialog similar to Figure 17.11, with the Northwind, `pubs`, and any other databases that you might have created.

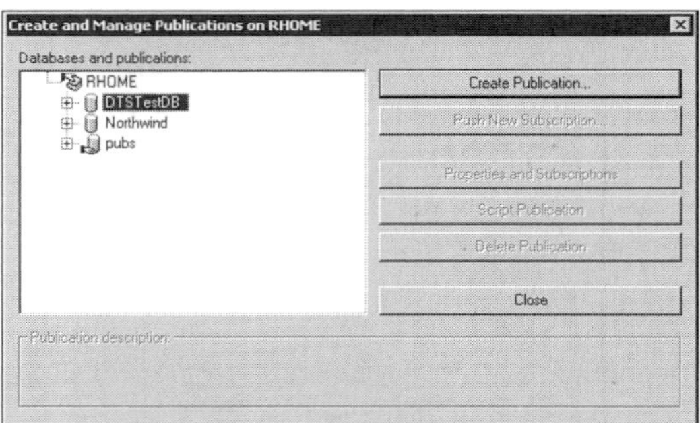

FIGURE 17.10
The Create and Manage Publications dialog.

2. Select the `pubs` database and click Next.
3. You need to specify the type of publication to use (see Figure 17.12): Snapshot, Transactional, or Merge. Select Transactional Publication, and then click Next.
4. Specify what type of subscriber to support (see Figure 17.13). Your choices include SQL Server 2000, SQL Server 7.0, or products other than Microsoft SQL Server. Leave the default of Servers Running SQL Server 2000, and click Next.

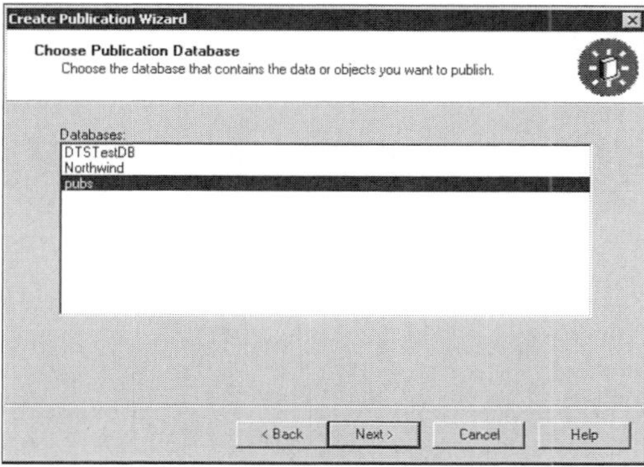

FIGURE 17.11
The Create Publication Wizard.

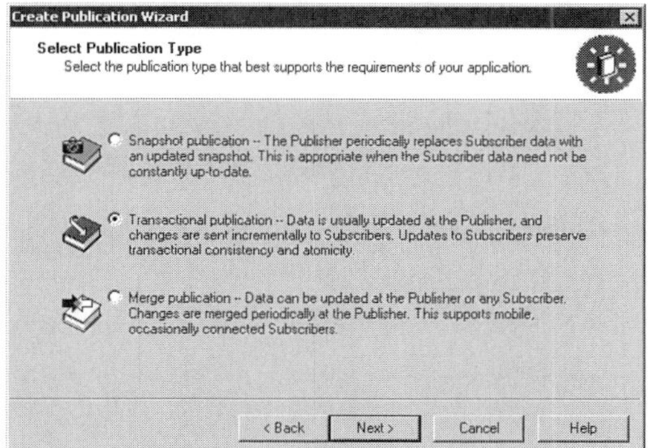

FIGURE 17.12
Choose a publication type.

> If you are running the Personal Edition of SQL Server, you can't select a transactional publication because the Personal Edition is allowed only to subscribe to publications, not to publish publications.

5. Specify articles, as shown in Figure 17.14. On the right side of the dialog, you can list both published and unpublished articles or just published articles. You can also publish views and stored procedures by clicking the corresponding check boxes on the left side of the dialog. For this example, click the check box for dbo.authors. Click Next to continue.
6. Specify the publication name, and give it a description (see Figure 17.15). I changed the publication name to pubs_authors. Click Next to continue.

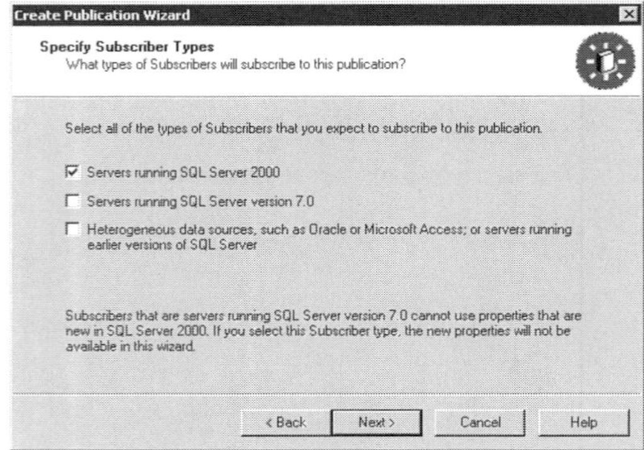

FIGURE 17.13

Specify a subscriber type.

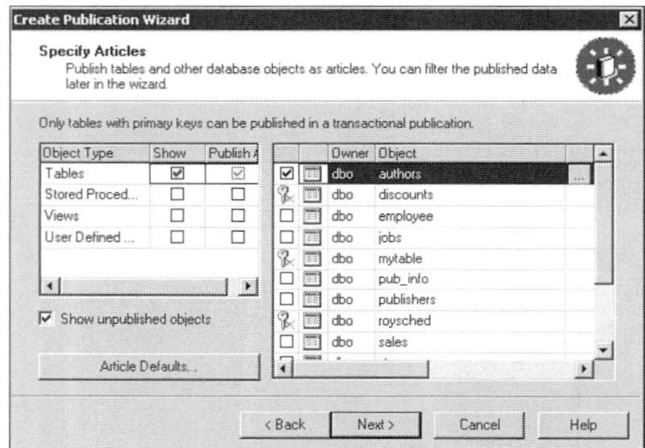

FIGURE 17.14

Specifying articles.

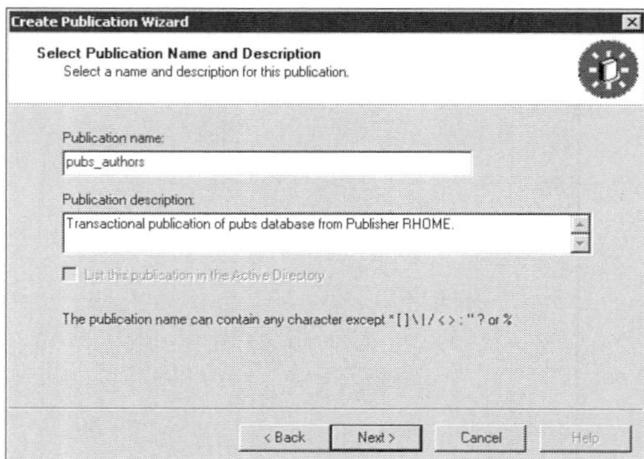

FIGURE 17.15

Choosing a publication name and description.

7. The Customize the Properties of the Publication dialog appears (see Figure 17.16). From here, you can specify filters (partitions) for your data, or create the publication without filters and with the properties specified in the box. I chose Yes. Click Next to continue.

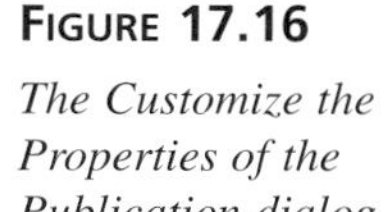
FIGURE 17.16
The Customize the Properties of the Publication dialog.

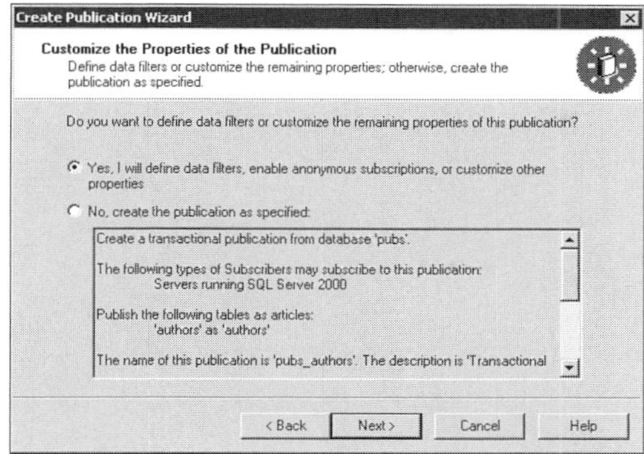

8. You are asked how you want to filter data. As you might recall from yesterday, you filter or partition when you use `SELECT` statements to gather only certain columns (vertical partition) or only certain rows (horizontal partition). Leave the check boxes unchecked, and click Next to continue.
9. In the next dialog, you can specify whether to allow anonymous subscribers. Choose No and click Next to continue. Anonymous subscriptions are used in special pull subscription situations. Normally, the information about each subscriber is stored at the publisher, and subscriber performance information is stored at the distributor. You can avoid this performance overhead by specifying an anonymous subscription. Each subscriber keeps performance information in its local subscriber database. Anonymous subscriptions are useful when your publication has a large number of subscribers or the subscribers are coming in over the Internet.
10. The Set Snapshot Agent Schedule dialog appears with the default schedule listed (see Figure 17.17). If you click the Change button, you see a scheduling dialog that you have worked with in other lessons. Click OK to return to the Set Snapshot Agent Schedule dialog; then click Next to continue.
11. The completion dialog for this wizard appears. Click Finish to see a list of tasks that SQL Server is completing and then a successfully completed dialog.
12. After the publication is created, you have an opportunity to set the publication's properties (see Figure 17.18). Click the Publication Properties button to continue.
13. Click the tab marked Publication Access List (see Figure 17.19). On this dialog tab, you can modify the list of users who have access to your publication. You can customize this list or choose to use the list the publisher has already created for you. Click OK and then click Close to return the Enterprise Manager.

FIGURE 17.17

Set Snapshot Agent Schedule dialog.

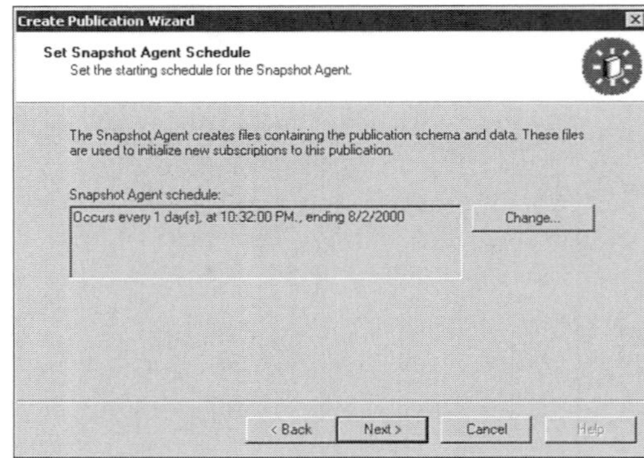

FIGURE 17.18

Configure the publication's properties.

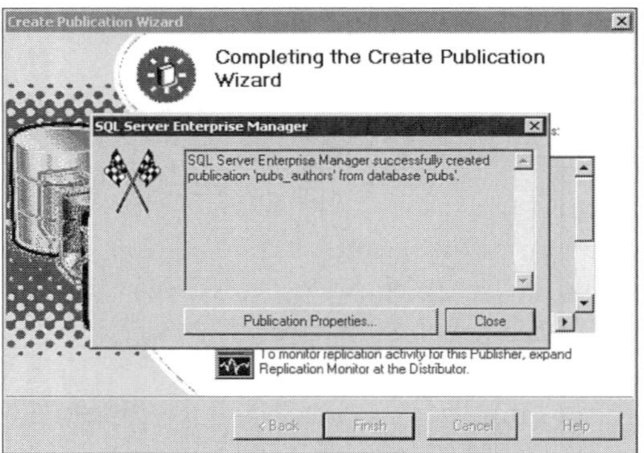

Back in the Enterprise Manager, notice that your new pubs_authors publication is listed under the Replication\Publications folder. From the Enterprise Manager, you can create a new push subscription, create additional publications, look at the properties of the distributor and the subscriptions, or delete publications. You will look at some of the items later today.

Creating a Subscription

Now you will create a subscription to gather the information you just published. When you configure subscribing, you can make the following specifications:

- Select the publishers to which you want to subscribe.
- Specify the destination database that will receive the replicated data.
- Verify that you have a valid account to access the distributor.

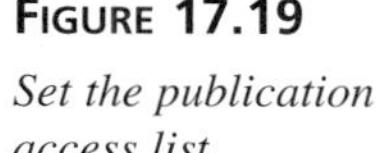

FIGURE 17.19
Set the publication access list.

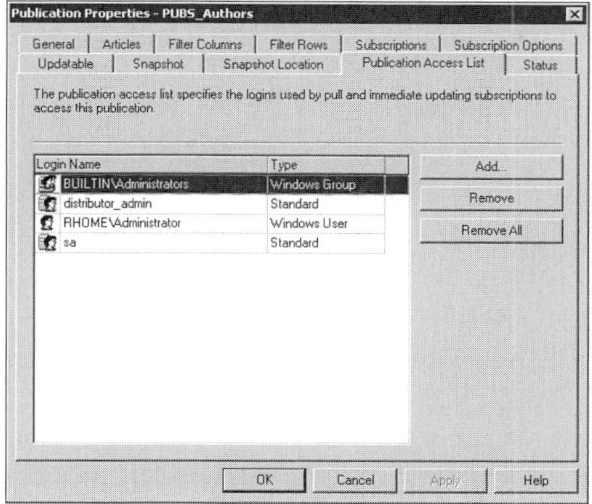

- Specify a description of your subscriber.
- Set a default schedule.
- Specify the security mode.

Follow these steps to enable your subscriber and complete the replication process:

1. You are creating a pull subscription in this example, so connect to your server in Enterprise Manager. Highlight your server, and choose Replication, Pull Subscriptions to *computername* from the Tools menu. You should see a Pull Subscription dialog similar to Figure 17.20.
2. Click the Pull New Subscription button to continue. The standard welcome dialog appears. Click Next to continue.
3. A dialog asks where to look for publications. Leave the default of Look at Publications from Registered Servers, and click Next.
4. The Choose Publication dialog appears. You should see your server here. Click the plus symbol (+) to expand the server and view the available publications (see Figure 17.21). Click the pubs_authors:pubs publication, and then click Next to continue.
5. You might see a Synchronization Agent login dialog. If you do, fill in the appropriate credentials, and click Next to continue. If you don't see this dialog, you see the Choose Destination Database dialog (see Figure 17.22). Because you're working on a single server, you will create a new database. Click the New button. Give the new database the name `rplPubs`. Click OK in the Database Properties dialog to

select the defaults for the rest of the create database process. Back in the Choose Destination Database dialog, click `rplPubs`, and then click Next to continue.

6. You must specify how to do your initial synchronization (see Figure 17.23). Be sure the Yes option is selected, and then click Next to continue.
7. You are asked about the Snapshot Delivery. Select the default and click Next.
8. In the next dialog, you control how frequently the distribution agent updates the subscription you are creating (see Figure 17.24). You can specify that it run continuously, run on a specific schedule, or have no schedule, in which you will perform a manual synchronization. Select Continuously and click Next to continue.
9. The Start Required Services dialog appears (see Figure 17.25). If the service isn't started, clicking the check box next to the service starts it automatically after the subscription is created. Be sure the check box next to the SQL Server Agent on your computer is selected. Click Next to continue.

FIGURE 17.20

The Pull Subscription dialog.

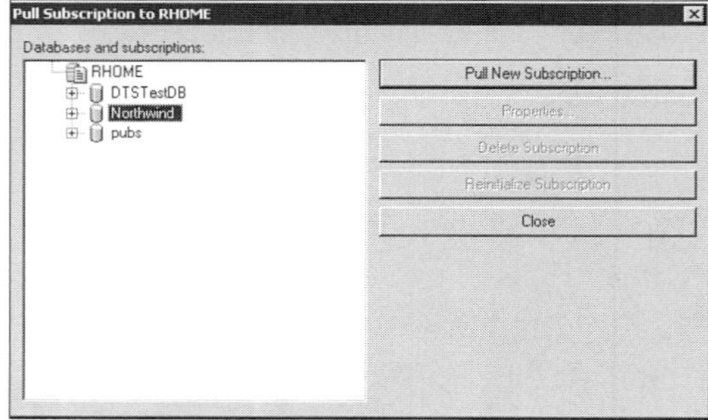

FIGURE 17.21

The Choose Publication dialog.

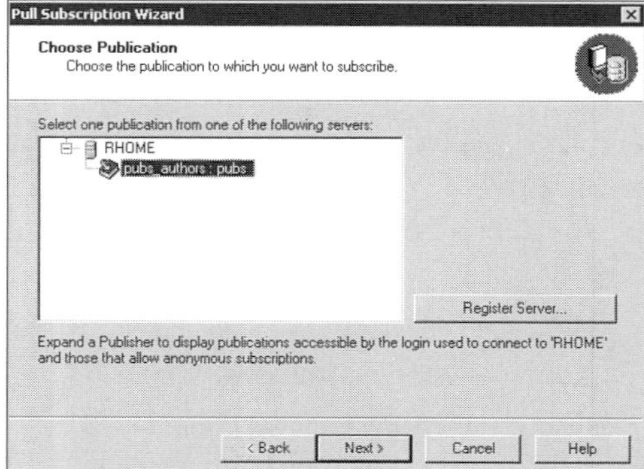

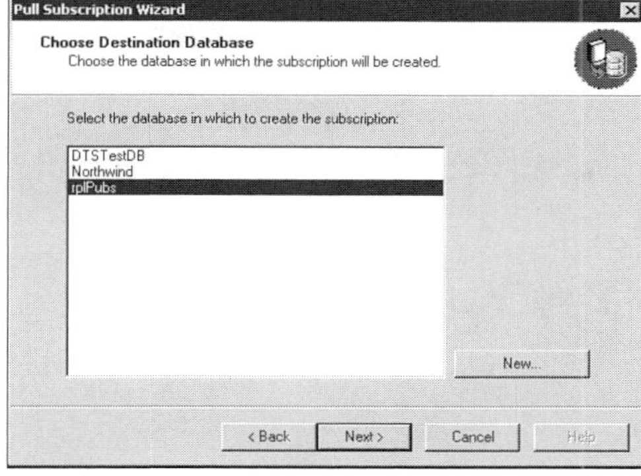

FIGURE 17.22
Choose a destination database.

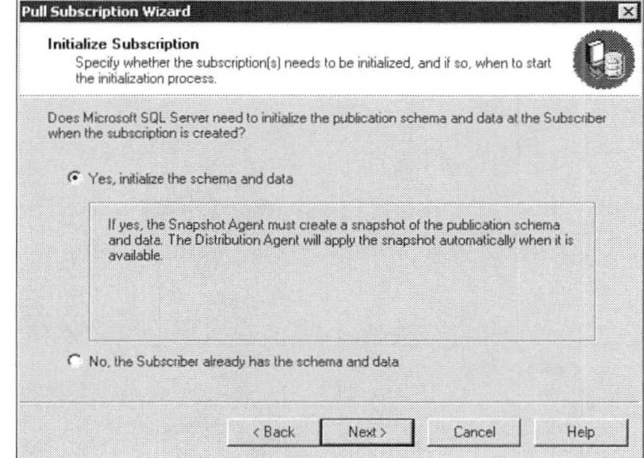

FIGURE 17.23
The Initialize Subscription dialog.

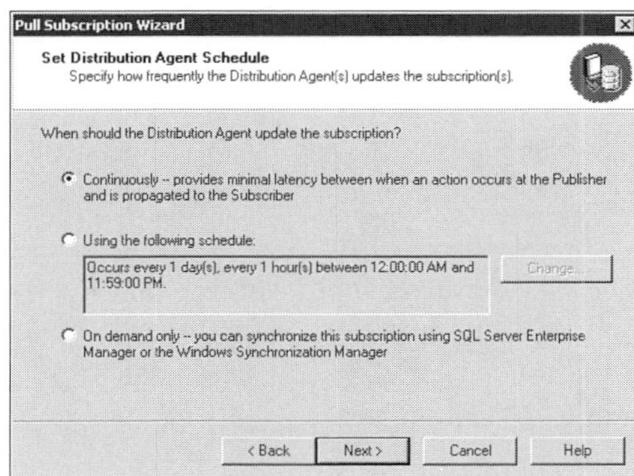

FIGURE 17.24
Set the distribution agent schedule.

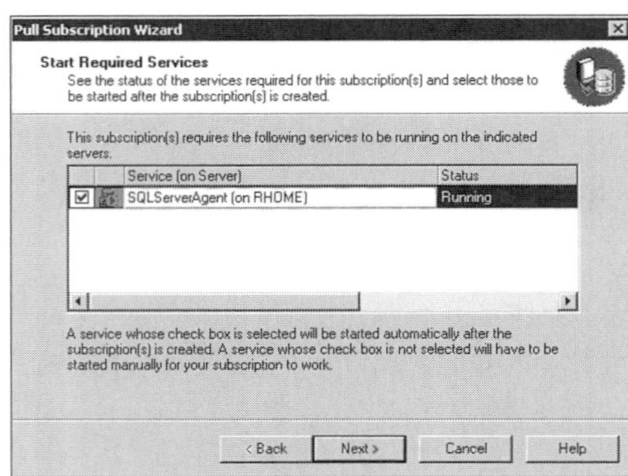

FIGURE 17.25

The Start Required Services dialog.

10. You should see the completion dialog. Click Finish to finish the installation. You see a progress dialog and then a final successful completion dialog. Click OK to dismiss the dialog and finish.
11. The Pull Subscription dialog should now appear. If you drill down, you will see that the pubs:pubs_authors subscription has changed (see Figure 17.26). Now you can check the subscription properties by clicking the Properties button.

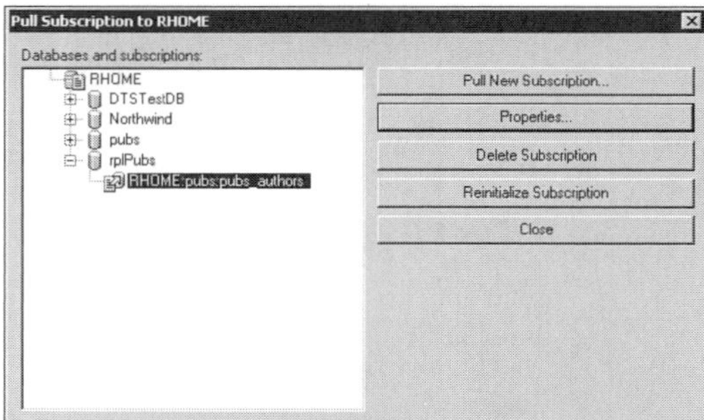

FIGURE 17.26

The Pull Subscription dialog.

12. The Pull Subscription Properties dialog appears (see Figure 17.27). The General tab details the publisher, publisher database, description, and whether anonymous or updateable subscriptions are allowed. On the Security tab, you can modify the SQL Server Agent login credentials.
13. Click OK to close the Pull Subscription Properties dialog. Finally, click Close to close the Pull Subscription dialog. You should now be back at the Enterprise Manager.

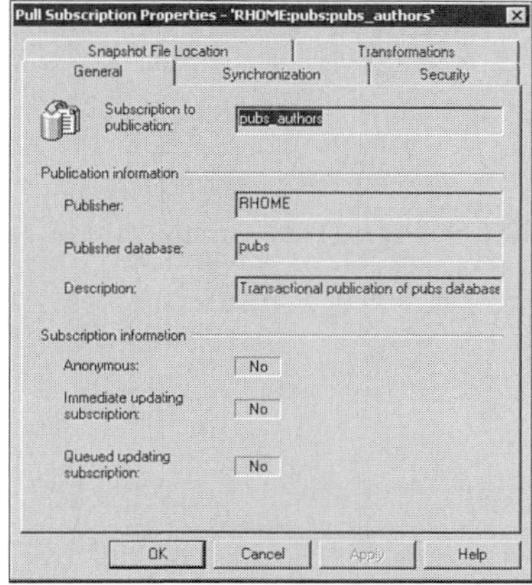

FIGURE 17.27

The Pull Subscription Properties dialog.

Manual Synchronization

The snapshot agent runs when you specify it should. After this occurs, the replication process begins. You can force a synchronization to occur. Follow these steps to have the initial synchronization run by starting the snapshot agent:

1. In the Enterprise Manager, expand the Replication Monitor, Publishers, and then your server; then click the pubs_authors:pubs item (see Figure 17.28). Depending on your current configuration, the first time you access the Replication Monitor you might be asked whether you want it to refresh itself automatically. If you choose Yes, you can set the refresh schedule.

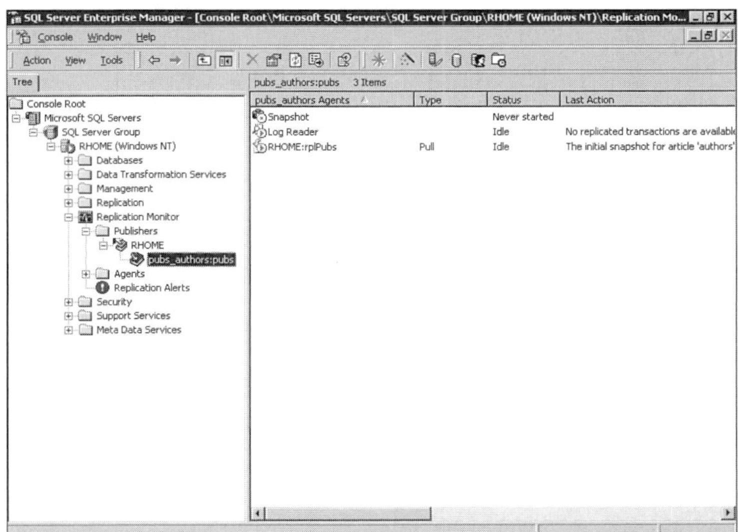

FIGURE 17.28

The Snapshot Agent in the details pane.

2. Right-click the snapshot item in the details pane, and choose Start Agent. The snapshot agent shows a status of running for a few seconds, and then the status changes to Succeeded. The snapshot agent's icon changes to a stop sign after it finishes moving the snapshot.

If you press the "F5" key, you can see the progress of the tasks that the Snapshot agent is running.

3. If you right-click the snapshot agent after it succeeds, you can see the agent history. Take a moment now to review the agent history.

Verifying the Initial Synchronization

You can verify that the snapshot agent has performed its duties appropriately and that the database schema and data were copied by using queries to view data in the new table. To view the data, run the following query in the Query Analyzer:

INPUT

```
USE rplPubs
GO
SELECT * FROM authors
GO
```

If you get data back, you know that the initial synchronization worked correctly.

Testing the Replication

Now you can test to see whether the replication will actually work. To do so, you will run several queries against the `pubs` and `rplpubs` databases.

The first query determines how many rows are in the `authors` table:

INPUT/OUTPUT

```
SELECT COUNT(*) FROM pubs..authors
GO
- - - -
23

(1 row(s) affected)
```

Check this outcome against the count in your other table by modifying your query slightly and then rerunning it:

INPUT/OUTPUT

```
SELECT COUNT(*) FROM rplPubs..authors
GO
- - -
23

(1 rows(s) affected)
```

Now add a row to your table by running the following query:

INPUT/ OUTPUT

```
USE pubs
GO
INSERT INTO authors VALUES
('555-55-5555', 'Johnson', 'Susan', '555 555-5555',
'123 Anystreet', 'Fresno', 'CA', '90000', '1')
GO
- - -
(1 row(s) affected)
```

Rerun the `SELECT COUNT` query on both databases, and verify that you now have 24 rows in your `pubs..authors` table as well as your `rplPubs..authors` table.

To double-check that the data was brought over, run the following query:

INPUT

```
SELECT * FROM rplPubs..authors
WHERE au_lname = 'Johnson'
GO
```


You should get your row of data back. Now delete this record from the publisher, and verify that a deleted record will be replicated as well. Run the following query to delete the Susan Johnson record from the `pubs..authors` table:

INPUT/ OUTPUT

```
DELETE FROM pubs..authors
WHERE au_lname = 'Johnson'
GO
(1 row(s) affected)
```

You can run your `SELECT COUNT` queries again to verify that both the publisher (`pubs`) and the subscription (`rplPubs`) databases now have 23 rows. Close the query windows when you're finished.

Replication Considerations

You need to remember several different points when you work with replication in SQL Server. They include some publishing restrictions and considerations when using updating subscribers. There are some performance considerations to keep in mind as well. In the following sections, you will examine these topics more closely.

Publishing Issues

When you're using merge replication, you must ensure that every row of data that will be involved in the replication process has a unique identifier. You can do so by using the `uniqueidentifier` constraint and the `ROWGUIDCOL` property. When SQL Server finds a column with this constraint and property associated with it, it automatically uses that column as the row identifier for the replicated table. If that column isn't found, SQL Server automatically creates it when you use the Merge Replication Wizard.

Also keep in mind the following restrictions:

- The system databases—`master`, `model`, `tempdb`, MSDB, and distribution—can't be replicated.
- Each table or portion of a table involved in replication must have a primary key to ensure entity integrity. The only exception is snapshot replication, in which the entire contents are copied as a single unit.
- Publications can't span multiple databases. When you create a publication, all the data must come from a single database.

Keep these restrictions in mind when you are replicating with data used in non-logged operations, including text, ntext, and image data types. The following summary describes the three main types of replication methodologies and how they are affected by these data types:

- With merge replication, changes aren't detected and data isn't replicated.
- Transactional replication uses the Logreader to detect changes. Because these are non-logged operations, the Logreader doesn't detect them nor replicate the data.
- Because snapshot replication copies the entire contents of the article, these non-logged values are replicated.

> If you plan to use text, ntext, or image data types in your replication scenarios, you should either use snapshot replication or have the snapshot agent run regularly to transfer these values to the subscribers.

Subscriber Issues

When you use the Immediate Updating subscriber option when creating a publication, you specify that the subscriber make updates to both the local copy of data and the publisher's copy of the data. After that change is put into effect, data is replicated to other subscribers at the next scheduled synchronization. (You can't do this with merge replication.)

In SQL Server 7.0, you could use a timestamp column in your article to avoid potential conflicts. However, in SQL Server 2000, timestamp data is no longer used for conflict detection. For merge replication and queued updating subscribers, a timestamp column is replicated, but its literal values aren't. Client applications can use timestamps at the subscriber for functions such as locking. In this fashion, you can always tell which record was modified first such that an application can take an appropriate action.

Performance Issues

Consider these suggestions for optimizing the performance of your replication methodologies:

- Use pull subscriptions to offload work on your distributors. Although this option isn't as convenient for administration, it can have a major impact on the distribution server's performance.
- Use a remote distributor, which can support multiple publishers and multiple subscribers. By moving the distribution task to a different SQL Server, you can reduce the impact of distribution on your OLTP (Online Transaction Processing) servers.
- Replicate only the data you need. By taking advantage of partitioning (filtering) your data, you can replicate a minimum amount of information and thus reduce the overall impact of replication on your SQL Servers and network.
- Keep in mind that most types of replication increase network traffic. Make sure that you've configured your network with the appropriate amount of bandwidth. For SQL Servers involved in heavy replication use, you might want to place involved computers on a separate physical subnet.
- Use primary keys on all your tables involved in replication to ensure relational and entity integrity.
- Use the same domain user account (SQL Server Agent) for all your SQL servers involved in replication. Because all servers can be part of the domain or involved in a trust relationship with the domain, they can all take advantage of the same SQL Server Agent account. This takes much of the administrative headache out of maintaining SQL Server security.

Maintaining Replication

In the following sections, you'll learn more about maintaining and monitoring replication. By using the Replication Monitor, you can administer your publishers, subscribers, and publications. You can look at agent profiles and modify their properties. You can also work with replication histories and set replication alerts.

As part of replication maintenance, you need to monitor the size of your distribution database as well as track the cleanup jobs to ensure that they run at the appropriate times. You should also prepare for the possible failure of your replication servers. By maintaining good backups of your distribution database, you can ensure that recovery and resynchronization will flow smoothly.

You can administer many replication servers through the Enterprise Manager. You can create replication scripts to ease the task of replication configuration for multiple subscribers.

Using the Replication Monitor

The Replication Monitor is available only on the SQL Server acting as the distributor. It's used to view status information about publishers, subscribers, and publications. You can also view scheduled replication agents and their historical data, such as information about inserts, updates, and transactions. The Replication Monitor also allows you to view and modify the agents' profiles and properties.

To gather information about the replication agents, follow these steps:

1. Open Enterprise Manager on the SQL Server designated as the distribution server (for the installation here, it's the same server as the publisher).
2. Connect to your server, drill down through the Replication Monitor to Agents, and select Snapshot Agents in the console tree (see Figure 17.29).

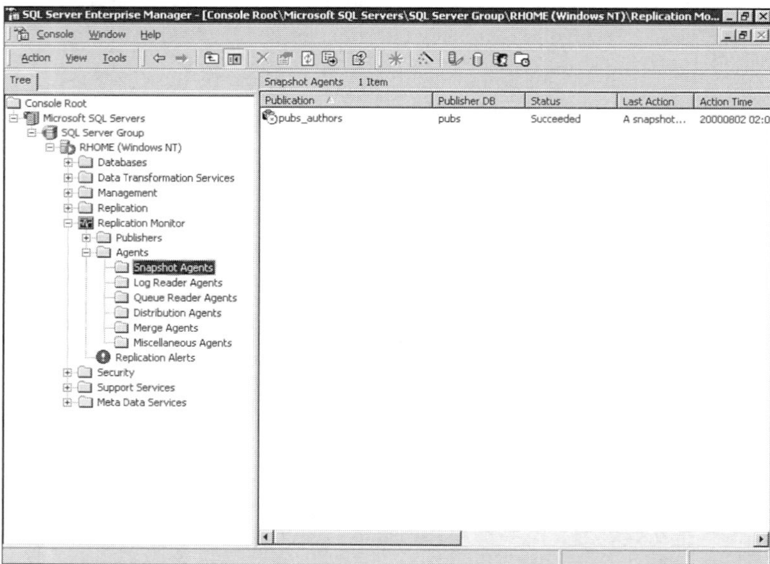

FIGURE 17.29
The Agents folder of the Replication Monitor.

3. Right-click the pubs_authors item in the details pane, and then choose Agent History to open the Snapshot Agent History file. The list can be filtered to show the following sessions:

- Sessions with errors
- All sessions
- Sessions in the last 24 hours
- Sessions in the last two days
- Sessions in the last seven days
- The last 100 sessions

4. If you view the last 100 sessions, you should see a list of attempts, but no new subscription is available. If you scroll to the bottom of the list, you see at least one item that states `A snapshot of 1 article(s) was generated`. That was the initial synchronization taking effect, as shown in Figure 17.30.

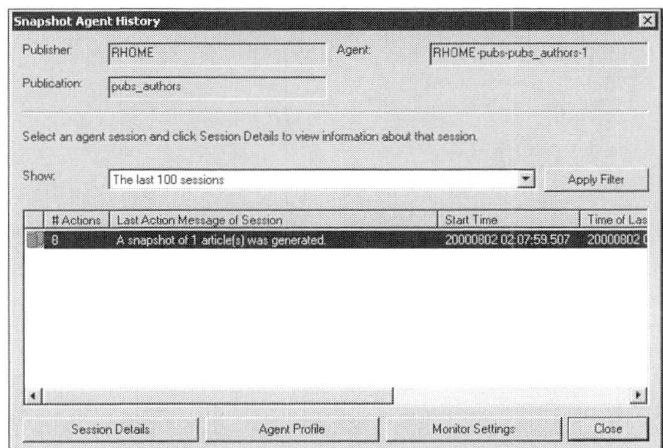

FIGURE 17.30

The Snapshot Agent History dialog.

5. Select that item in the list, and then click the Session Details button to see additional information as to what exactly took place during the snapshot process (see Figure 17.31).

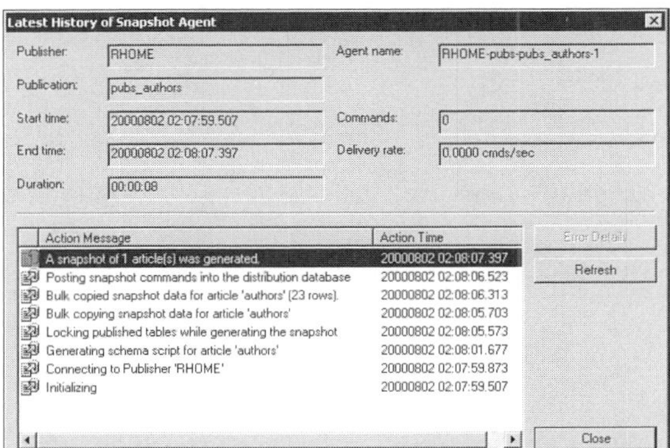

FIGURE 17.31

Session details.

6. Click Close to close the Session Details dialog. Click Close again to close the Snapshot Agent History dialog.
7. In the console tree and details pane, right-click your pubs_authors agent again, and this time choose Agent Properties. The job properties dialog for this particular agent appears (see Figure 17.32).

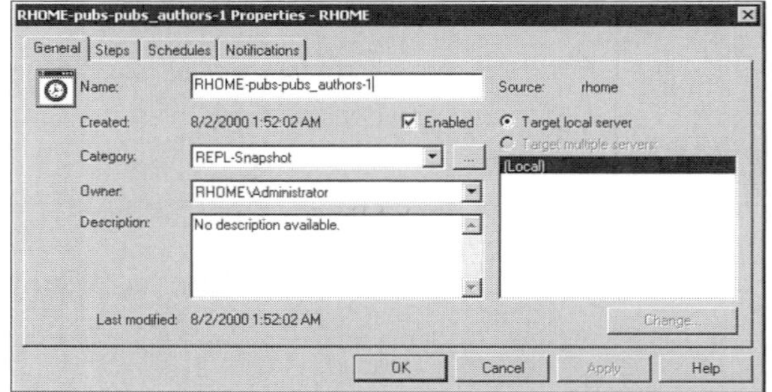

FIGURE 17.32

Job properties General tab, showing general information about this replication agent.

8. Click the Steps tab to see the steps involved with running this particular job. As shown in Figure 17.33, the snapshot agent's job has three steps: log the startup message, run the replication agent, and detect non-logged shutdown. You also see whether each job succeeded (green check mark) or failed (red ×). You can move these steps around, delete steps, or add steps.

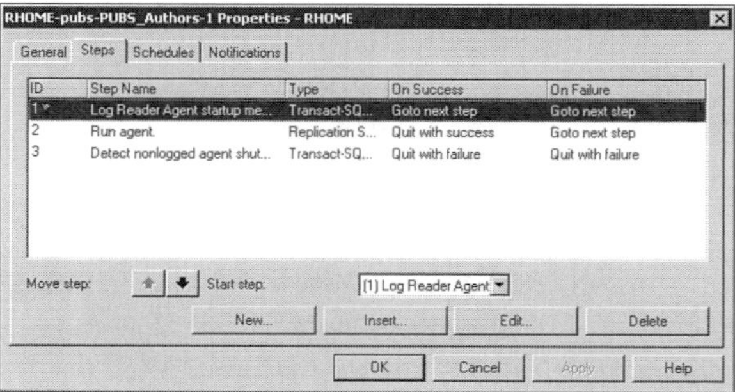

FIGURE 17.33

The Job properties Steps tab.

9. Click the Schedules tab to see the scheduling information for your replication agents (see Figure 17.34). You can edit and delete jobs here. You can also create a new job or alert here.

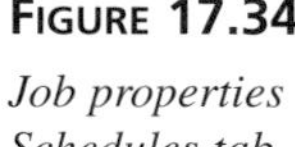

FIGURE 17.34

Job properties Schedules tab.

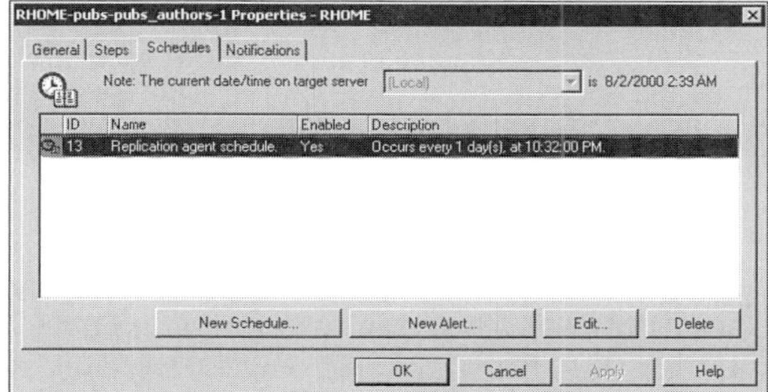

10. Click the Notifications tab (see Figure 17.35), on which you can specify email and page operators, as well as a net send operator to notify on success or failure of this operation. You can also have it write to the Windows 2000 application log. (Please select this option as shown in the figure.) The final check box enables you to automatically delete the job after it is completed. Click OK to close the job properties dialog.

FIGURE 17.35

Job properties Notifications tab.

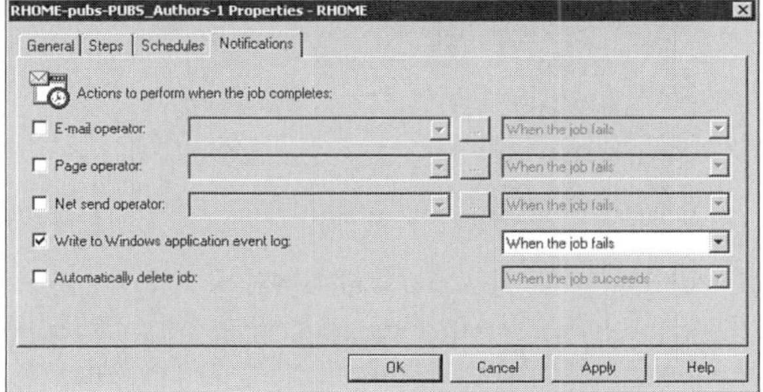

Distribution Server Management

Now it's time to look at some replication maintenance issues. You should develop a plan for managing the size of your distribution database as well as develop distribution database backup strategies.

You should monitor the size of the distribution database to ensure that enough space is available for all your replication jobs. You can do so by determining the retention period for your replication history and replication transactions. Also, track your cleanup jobs, which occur whenever items in your replication history or replication transactions are removed. You can configure these options through the Distributor Properties dialog.

At least one cleanup occurs on each distribution server for each subscriber. If you have a distribution server with 10 subscribers, that distribution server will have at least 10 cleanup jobs.

Follow these steps to work with distributor properties:

1. Right-click Replication Monitor in your console tree, and choose Distributor Properties. You should see something similar to Figure 17.36.

FIGURE 17.36
Publisher and Distributor Properties dialog.

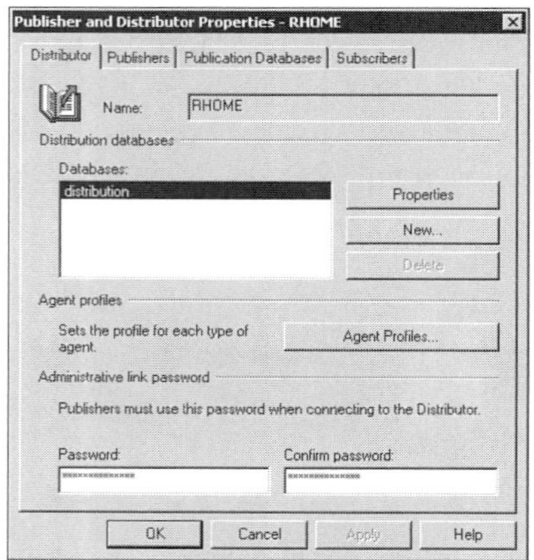

2. From this dialog, you can look at all kinds of information. After you install replication, you can monitor and manage all aspects of your replication scenario here. Click the distribution database and then click Properties. You should now see a dialog similar to Figure 17.37. You can specify that you want to store transaction records for at least some minimum length of time, but not more than some maximum length of time. The defaults are 0 and 72, respectively. You can also specify a minimum length of time to store your replication performance history. After you're done, click OK to return to the Publisher and Distributor Properties dialog.

The Publisher and Distributor Properties dialog is available after you install your distribution database. On the Publishers tab, you can specify the available publishers. The Publication Databases tab allows you to modify databases available for publication. The Subscribers tab allows you to add and edit subscribers.

You can look in Management\SQL Server Agent\Jobs in the console tree to check on your replication cleanup jobs. (Be sure to close the Publisher and Distributor Properties Dialog first.) These cleanup jobs process on a normal schedule (see Figure 17.38).

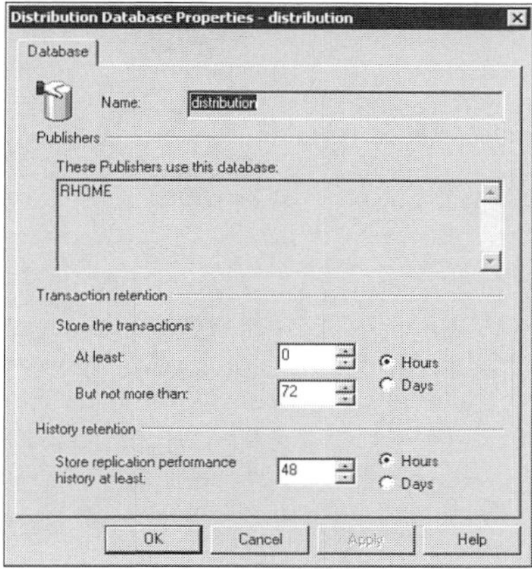

FIGURE 17.37

Distribution Database Properties dialog.

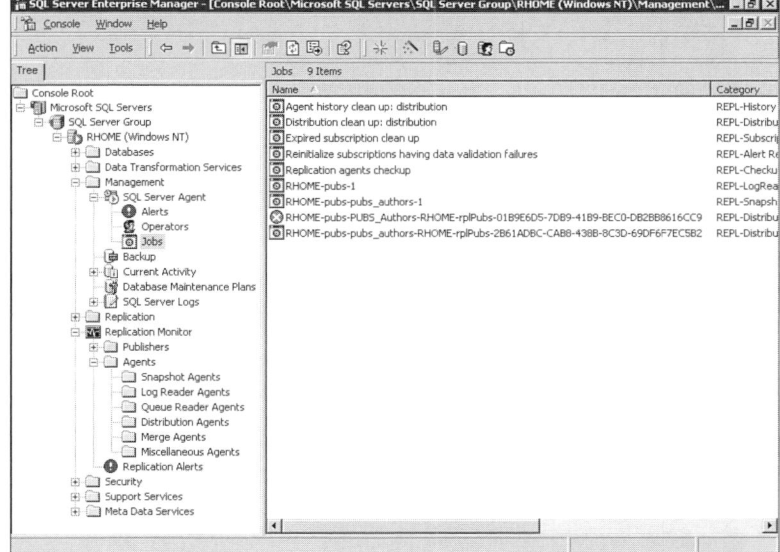

FIGURE 17.38

Replication cleanup tasks.

As you can imagine, with all the additions and deletions from these databases, as well as the regular logged transactions involved with replication, the distribution database and its transaction log can grow very quickly.

Even if you don't actually make a backup of your distribution database, you should at least truncate the transaction log regularly. If you keep backups of the distribution database and the database fails for some reason, you won't have to go through the whole process of re-creating the distribution server, the publishers, and the subscribers. You can simply restore the database and resynchronize your data.

Here's an excellent reason to make backups of your distribution database: *If the distribution database runs out of space, any transactions waiting to be published can't be removed from the transaction log on the publisher.*

At first, that doesn't sound so bad, but think it through for a second. If the items can't be removed from the publisher's transaction log, the publisher can't do standard transaction log dumps, which in turn means that sooner or later your publishing databases' transaction log will fill to capacity and you will no longer be able to make modifications at the publisher. So, make backups of your distribution database, or at least use the `BACKUP TRANSACTION` with `TRUNCATE_ONLY` statements to clear the logs.

Replication Scripts

Replication scripts contain the Transact-SQL statements necessary to create and configure a particular replication scenario. They have the following benefits:

- You can use a script to configure many servers identically. Doing so saves you the trouble of continually using the wizards.
- You can use the scripts to track different versions of your replication environment. As you make changes to your environment, you can create additional scripts.
- You can quickly and easily customize an existing replication environment.
- You can use the scripts as part of your recovery process. You can use the scripts to essentially reinstall any or all aspects of your replication environment.

When you create a script for multiple servers, you have to make slight modifications. Mainly, you must change the computer name referred to in the script. Although making these changes might be time consuming, it's far quicker than walking through the wizards several times.

Follow these steps to create a replication script:

1. Highlight your server in the console tree, and choose Replication, Generate SQL Scripts from the Tools menu. The dialog shown in Figure 17.39 appears.

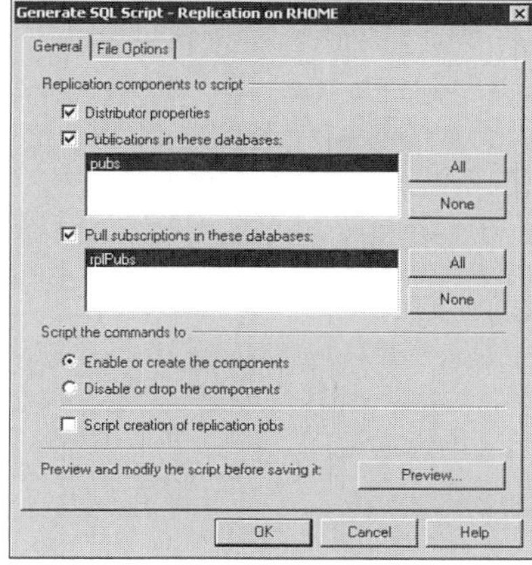

FIGURE 17.39
Generate SQL Script dialog's General tab.

2. On the General tab, select which replication components you want scripted. You can select the distributor properties and as many publications as you want. You can also specify whether to have the script enable or create the selected components, or disable or drop the selected component. Click the Preview button to see the generated script (see Figure 17.40). From here, you can specify a filename and storage location for your script. Click Close to close the dialog.

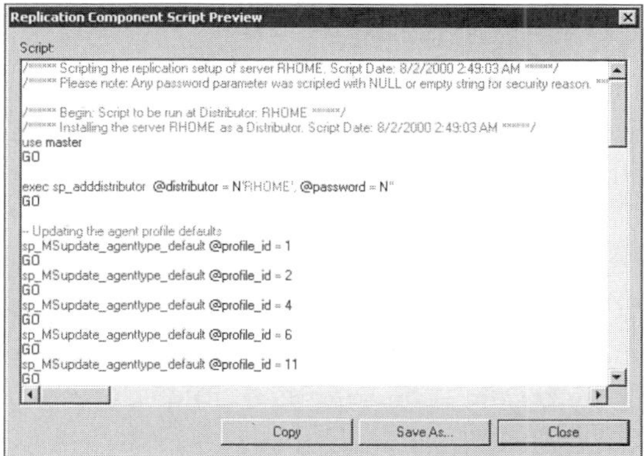

FIGURE 17.40
Replication Component Script Preview dialog.

3. Click the File Options tab in the Generate SQL Script dialog. On this tab, you can specify in what format the script will be saved (see Figure 17.41). By default, the script is saved in Unicode and appended to an existing file (if you are saving it to an existing file).

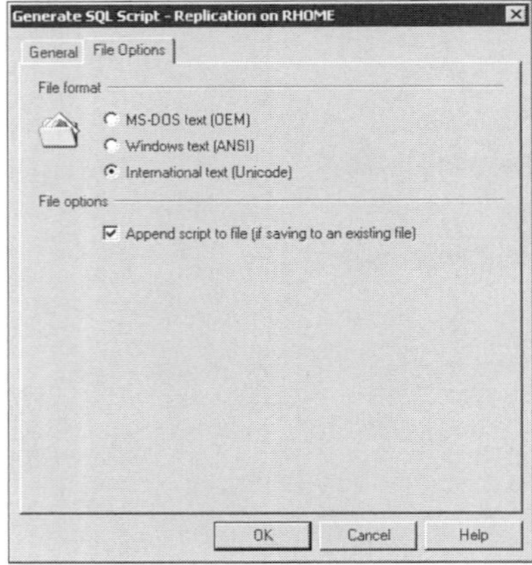

FIGURE 17.41

Generate SQL Script dialog's File Options tab.

4. Click OK. You are asked to specify a file location and filename for your new script file. The default location, `\MSSQL\Install`, is excellent because this folder contains many other scripts used during the installation of your SQL Server. Enter the default filename `replication.sql`, and click Save.

To execute a replication script, use the Query Analyzer. Open the script file there, and execute it as you would any other saved script.

Performance Monitor and Replication

SQL Server is tightly integrated with Windows NT/2000. One component of this integration is through the Windows NT/2000 performance monitor. SQL Server creates counters, several of which are combined into a performance object. For example, one Windows NT/2000 performance object is Processor. This object has many counters—for example, %Processor Time, %User Time, and Interrupts/sec.

Replication in SQL Server also exposes some performance objects and counters you can use to track the performance of the various aspects of replication. Table 17.1 lists some of the replication-related counters and their associated values.

TABLE 17.1 SQL Server Performance Objects

Counters	*Explanation*
	Replication Agents
Running	Number of replication agents now running, including Distribution, Logreader, Merge, Queue Reader, and Snapshot

TABLE 17.1 continued

Counters	*Explanation*
	Replication Distributors
Dist:Delivered Cmds/sec	Logreader commands delivered per second in the last batch
Dist:Delivered Trans/sec	Logreader transactions delivered per second in the last batch
Delivered Latency	Logreader latency in milliseconds
	Replication Logreader
Logreader:Delivered Cmds/sec	The number of commands per second delivered to the distributor
Logreader:Delivered Trans/sec	The number of transactions per second delivered to the distributor
Logreader:Delivery Latency	The current amount of time, in milliseconds, elapsed from when transactions are applied at the publisher to when they are delivered to the distributor
	Replication Merge
Conflicts/sec	Number of merge replication conflicts per second
Downloaded	Number of download changes per second that Changes/sec are merged from the publisher to the subscriber
Uploaded	The number of rows per second merged from Changes/sec the subscriber to the publisher
	Replication Snapshot
Snapshot:Delivered Cmds/sec	The number of commands per second delivered to the distributor
Snapshot:Delivered Trans/sec	The number of transactions per second delivered to the distributor

17

Using Stored Procedures

All right, you knew it was coming. You saw how to do all the implementation through the Enterprise Manager. Of course, you can use stored procedures to build the same implementation of your replication scenarios. Probably the easiest way to do so is to create everything you need in the Enterprise Manager and then generate your replication scripts. On the upside, creating your own replication scenario exclusively through scripts is beyond the scope of this book. However, you can use some useful stored procedures to gather additional information about the replication process in place of a given server. The following is a short list of the stored procedures used to manage SQL Server 2000 replication. A double asterisk (**) marks stored procedures you will most likely use to gather information about your replication scenario.

```
sp_browsereplcmds
sp_check_for_sync_trigger
sp_help_agent_default
sp_help_agent_parameter
sp_help_agent_profile
sp_help_publication_access
sp_helparticle
sp_helparticlecolumns
sp_helpdistpublisher
sp_helpdistributiondb
sp_helpdistributor**
sp_helpmergearticle
sp_helpmergearticleconflicts
sp_helpmergeconflictrows
sp_helpmergedeleteconflictrows
sp_helpmergefilter
sp_helpmergepublication
sp_helpmergepullsubscription
sp_helpmergesubscription
sp_helppublication**
sp_helppublication_snapshot
sp_helppullsubscription
sp_helpremotelogin
sp_helpreplfailovermode
sp_helpreplicationdb
sp_helpreplicationdboption
sp_helpreplicationoption
sp_helpsubscriber**
sp_helpsubscriberinfo**
sp_helpsubscription**
sp_helpsubscription_properties
sp_link_publication
sp_linkedservers
sp_mergedummyupdate
sp_mergesubscription_cleanup
sp_publication_validation
sp_refreshsubscriptions
sp_reinitmergepullsubscription
sp_reinintmergesubscription
sp_reinitpullsubscription
sp_reinitsubscription
sp_removedbreplication
sp_replcmds**
sp_replcounters**
sp_repldone**
sp_replflush
sp_replication_agent_checkup
sp_replicationdboption
sp_replicationoption
sp_repltrans**
sp_resynch_targetserver
sp_revoke_publication_access
sp_subscription_cleanup
```

You can use others, but this list is long enough as it is.

Administration Considerations

Managing replication can be a fairly administration-intensive task, but it doesn't have to be. The following suggestions can help keep the replication management tasks more streamlined:

- Create and monitor replication alerts. With appropriate alerts set, you can proactively administer your replication enterprise. You can see potential problems coming and take corrective action before they have a chance to get out of hand.
- Ensure that replication jobs and agents are running properly. You can find this information by periodically checking the replication histories and error logs to verify whether replication is occurring as scheduled.
- Ensure that disk space is available. The distribution database needs space to store transactional information as well as track the replication process itself. Be sure to back up the distribution database or at least monitor the distribution database's transaction log closely.

- Create a recovery and resynchronization plan. Create and store replication scripts. They are useful for recovery and version control (though you will need to manage the versioning of scripts yourself) as well as for duplicating multiple identical servers. Test the recovery and resynchronization plan occasionally, and time how long it takes.
- Security is probably the largest troubleshooting problem you will encounter in SQL Server replication. If possible, have all servers involved in replication use the same SQL Server Agent account. In this manner, you avoid many potential security issues.
- Network connectivity is another troublesome issue. Ensure that you have enough bandwidth on your network to support your replication tasks.
- Remove the impact of the distribution database on your OLTP server by using some type of remote distribution.
- When you build your replication scenarios, try to implement snapshot replication first. This form of replication is the simplest to implement and maintain. When you are satisfied that no connectivity and security issues exist, change the replication type to whatever you want.

Troubleshooting

Troubleshooting replication takes some technical know-how and a lot of practice. This section will help make you technically adept at troubleshooting replication and certainly give you some excellent suggestions for tracking down the source of the errors plaguing your system.

When you are dealing with replication, problems can occur in only a few places:

- Security
- Logreader agent
- Distribution agent

Take a closer look at how errors here affect the system.

Initial Snapshot Jobs Aren't Applied at the Subscriber

Remember that before replication can begin, an initial snapshot of your data must be applied to the subscriber. When it's not applied, the most likely cause of the problem is with the snapshot agent itself. Check the snapshot agent histories and see what's happening. Has the snapshot even been scheduled? If it has been scheduled, was the attempt made to take a snapshot of your data? Do your snapshot agent and your subscriber have appropriate levels of access?

If the snapshot agent isn't getting any data and therefore not trying to apply a snapshot to the subscriber, there might be a problem with the security between the snapshot agent and the publishing database.

If the snapshot agent is doing absolutely nothing, verify that it has been enabled and that the distribution server is online and available.

No Subscribers Are Receiving Replicated Information

If none of your subscribers are receiving replicated information, it's unlikely that the distribution agent is at fault, because no subscriber is getting data. It's more likely that the Logreader agent can no longer (or will no longer) read data from the published databases' transaction logs. To verify whether the Logreader agent or the distribution agent is failing, check the agent histories. Verify that jobs are being passed from one to the other.

If these tasks don't appear to be running, try changing their schedule a little bit to see what happens.

One Subscriber of Many Isn't Receiving Replicated Data

If only one (or several of many) isn't getting replicated information, you know that the Logreader agent is working properly (otherwise, how would the other subscribers be getting their information?). You should check for the following problems:

- The distribution agent for the failing server is working properly. (Check the agent histories.)
- The subscribing database is unavailable. The database might have been marked for read-only, DBO-use only, and so on.
- The subscription server is unavailable. Has the server been shut down? Do you have network connectivity?
- The SQL Server Agent's security credentials have been modified.
- The distribution agent is waiting to perform a manual synchronization of your data.

Replication Recovery Issues

The manner in which SQL Server replication is designed allows it to recover itself in most instances. Keep in mind the following considerations regarding your publishing server, distribution server, and subscribing servers.

Publishing Server Recovery

The Logreader agent uses pointers in every published database to keep track of the place it left off reading transactions. Having these pointers makes recovery a relatively simple process if the publishing server is offline for some reason. When the publishing database is back online or again available, the Logreader agent will begin where it left off.

If, for some reason, the publishing databases are rebuilt and reloaded with data, the pointers will be off. You should resynchronize your publishers and subscribers to continue the process of replication.

Distribution Server Recovery

Distribution servers generally keep track of the place they left off sending jobs (transactions) to the subscribers. When your distribution is offline and then comes back online, it will continue processing where it left off. Normally, all will be well. If the distribution experiences an extended period of downtime, you might need to restore your distribution server. You should have a coordinated backup scheme to guarantee that the distribution server is backed up with the publishing servers. In this way, the Logreader agent is in sync with the publishing database, and automatic recovery will take place.

If they are out of sync and the Logreader agent's pointers are off (you have conflicting restored databases between the publisher and distributor), you have to resynchronize your publishers and subscribers. If this approach doesn't work, unsubscribe and resubscribe to the databases.

Subscription Server Recovery

If a subscription server goes down, simply bring it back online. Replicated transactions are stored on the distribution server and are applied when the subscriber is back online. If you use snapshot replication, the entire snapshot is sent down at the scheduled time. If you use merge replication, the merged records are converged back down to you at the synchronization. This is all true if your subscriber is down for only a short while.

If your subscriber is offline for an extended period of time, transactions that are to be applied to the subscriber might have aged out of the distribution database. If you know a subscriber will be down for an extended period of time and don't want to hassle with resynchronization (you might have an extremely large database and don't want to snapshot it across the network again), you can edit the cleanup jobs associated with that snapshot agent. You can also modify the retention period for transactions associated with that subscriber, as discussed earlier today. As always, we are backup freaks. You should back up your Subscription database on a regular basis and especially if you know it is going to be down for an extended period of time.

Summary

You began today's lesson by studying how security is handled with respect to replication. You learned that replication uses the SQL Server Agent to interact with different servers (publishers, distributors, and subscribers). You then looked at the requirements necessary for your server to be involved in replication.

From there, you went through an extensive step-by-step process to install and configure your distribution server. After installing the distribution server, you could then create publications. You walked through another step-by-step process to create a publication. After you created the publication, you used the same machine to build a subscriber. You ran the snapshot agent for the initial synchronization process and tested replication.

The next major section you examined was on replication considerations, which included information about issues concerning the publishing servers, subscription servers, distribution servers, and other replication issues.

You then looked at the process of maintaining your replication scenarios. You looked at the replication monitor item in the console tree of the Enterprise Manager. You then took a closer look at the replication agents (snapshot, distribution, Logreader, and merge agents) and at their histories and scheduled tasks.

You next looked into the management of your distribution server. This section included information about managing the size of your transaction log as well as the replication history files. You also learned about replication scripts. Recall that replication scripts can be extremely useful as part of the recovery process, for use in creating multiple identical subscribers, and for replication scenario histories.

Counters and objects exposed by SQL Server to the Windows NT/2000 performance monitor were discussed next. You saw many items that you can use to track the efficiency of your replication scenario. You then looked at the stored procedures associated with replication. When you have some spare time, take a closer look at the stored procedures highlighted for you.

You finished today's lesson with a look at some administrative considerations. You learned how you "should" set up your SQL Server replication scenarios. You then looked at some methods for tracking down and alleviating errors in the replication process. Remember that very little can go wrong with replication. When something does, it's most likely a security issue, the Logreader agent, or the distribution agent. In most cases, the replication scenario will fix itself. In a few cases, resynchronization is all that's necessary. In very few extreme cases, you will have to unsubscribe and resubscribe.

Q&A

Q Which type of replication is most common?

A Transactional replication. It guarantees transactional consistency and has a low to moderate amount of overhead.

Q Do you expect merge replication to become one of the most used types of replication?

A It's possible with the number of remote users out there that this will be the case. Try to minimize the impact of merge replication by using region codes in your tables. In this manner, the same piece of data is less likely to be altered at two locations at the same time.

Q Should I use scripts to create and install replication?

A That depends. For the initial replication, publication, and subscription, use the Enterprise Manager and then, through the Replication Monitor, generate replication scripts. In this way, you use the easy interface to create what you need and then have the interface create scripts for you that are excellent for use in a recovery scheme.

Q How important is replication recovery?

A The answer really depends on your business needs. Keep in mind that replication is pretty much self-sustaining. If a publisher goes down for a while, automatic recovery works. If a distribution server goes down for a short period of time, it simply picks up where it left off and catches up. If a subscriber goes down for a short period of time, it is caught up when it comes back online. The only real problem you have to worry about with recovery is that transactions don't age out of the replication agents before they have a chance to be applied. The other point is to ensure that you are regularly managing the size of the distribution database's transaction log.

Workshop

This section provides quiz questions to help you solidify your understanding of the concepts presented today. In addition to the quiz questions, an exercise is provided to let you practice what you've learned today. Try to understand the quiz and exercise answers before continuing on to tomorrow's lesson. Answers are provided in Appendix A, "Answers to Quiz Questions."

Quiz

This lesson was much more of a walkthrough than an exercise in study. No quiz is provided for this lesson. Please take the time to try the exercise, however.

Exercise

Modify the publication and subscriptions you did today to reflect merge replication rather than transactional replication.

WEEK 3

DAY 18

Scheduling Jobs with SQL Server Agent

Yesterday you examined advanced replication features, including how to use merge replication and update subscribers to transactional replication. These features can be extremely beneficial to extend your replication architecture. They are particularly useful for laptop users who might be disconnected periodically or users at remote sites who must give immediate updates to a central publisher.

Today you examine SQL Server's automation features, including the SQL Server Agent service, which provides many advanced features for SQL Server 2000. This feature set includes the capability to run scheduled jobs, monitor SQL Server events, and set alerts that can launch a job or notify you via email, pager, or a `net send` command. Also, replication is built entirely around SQL Server Agent scheduled jobs.

Why Automate SQL Server?

You might be wondering why you should automate SQL Server in the first place. As an administrator who's done my share of 2 a.m. support calls, I can tell you that it's not much fun to get up at that time of night, so anything you can do to enable a database to help you avoid those calls is worthwhile. If SQL Server is configured properly, you can set up the server so that when problems happen, the most common errors can be intercepted and resolved without a call to wake you up. You can also automate routine database maintenance, such as data loading, integrity checking, and backups.

The SQL Server Agent service enables you to automate fully this maintenance using scheduled jobs. You can schedule job types, including database maintenance jobs, a full-text job, a Web assistant job, or various replication jobs. You also can use a generic job type to support running Transact-SQL commands, Windows 2000 command files, or Active Script (VBScript or JavaScript). Replication tasks are an advanced option and are examined fully in *Microsoft SQL Server 2000 Unleashed* from Sams Publishing.

You can create jobs that don't necessarily run on a regular schedule but are preconfigured to run when you need them. They include any type of job mentioned here. You can also create jobs that run only when you explicitly request them to run rather than schedule them.

You can also configure alerts that can respond appropriately when a particular event occurs or a specific error message is generated. The response could be to generate an email, to page an operator, or to launch a job to correct a problem. The capability to use alerts is central to making SQL Server easier to administer and avoiding those 2 a.m. phone calls!

You can run everything yourself, and you don't need to use the SQL Server Agent service. However, even in an environment in which only one SQL Server is being used, you will find that several tasks are easier to manage if you let the system perform them for you. If you take advantage of this built-in functionality, you can focus on designing your databases properly and on dealing only with true exceptions to normal processing.

Which Scheduling Tool Should You Use?

After you decide to take advantage of automating SQL Server, your next question might be whether the proper tool to use is the SQL Server Agent service. SQL Server Agent is much more than a simple scheduling engine; it allows you to set up responses to error conditions and emails or even pages you. However, if your background is in Windows 2000, and you've scheduled other jobs (such as Windows backups) with the Windows schedule service, you might consider using that scheduling engine to support SQL Server.

The Windows 2000 Schedule Service

Because the Windows schedule service is a pure scheduling engine, you might be inclined to consider using it with the AT command. AT schedules commands and programs to run on a computer at a specified time and date. The Windows schedule service must be running to use the AT command.

If you ask for help on the AT command by typing

INPUT
```
C:> AT /?
```

at the Windows command prompt, you get the following help:

OUTPUT
```
AT [\\computername] [ [id] [/DELETE] | /DELETE [/YES]]
AT [\\computername] time [/INTERACTIVE]
   [ /EVERY:date[,...] | /NEXT:date[,...]] "command"

\\computername     Specifies a remote computer. Commands are
                   scheduled on the local computer if this
                   parameter is omitted.
id                 Is an identification number assigned to a
                   scheduled command.
/delete            Cancels a scheduled command. If id is
                   omitted, all the scheduled commands on the
                   computer are canceled.
/yes               Used with cancel all jobs command when no
                   further confirmation is desired.
time               Specifies the time when command is to run.
/interactive       Allows the job to interact with the desktop
                   of the user who is logged on at the time the
                   job runs.
/every:date[,...]  Runs the command on each specified day(s) of
                   the week or month. If date is omitted, the
                   current day of the month is assumed.
/next:date[,...]   Runs the specified command on the next
                   occurrence of the day (for example, next
                   Thursday). If date is omitted, the current
                   day of the month is assumed
"command"          Is the Windows 2000 command, or batch program
                   to be run.
```

18

For example, to schedule an automated backup, you could type

INPUT
```
C:> AT \\MYSERVER 12:00 /EVERY:M,T,W,TH,F d:\Program Files
➥\mssql\backup.cmd
```

to set up a call to the backup.cmd program in the SQL Server 2000 installation directory, which could contain calls to isql.exe or osql.exe to perform backups. This command would run every weekday at midnight.

This option certainly helps to allow you to schedule your backups. It's also a good option if you're already familiar with using the AT command and scheduling tasks this way. You can also purchase the Windows 2000 Resource Kit and use a graphical version of the AT command. Both versions rely on the Windows schedule service to perform the scheduled tasks.

The SQL Server Agent Service

The SQL Server Agent service allows you to set up simple jobs or more complex multi-step jobs. You can graphically set up email integration so that you don't need to write your own calls to the mail subsystem on your computer. The jobs can call Windows command files as the AT command does, take advantage of direct use of T-SQL commands, or even use Active Script language options. The interface is also much more intuitive than figuring out the AT commands and writing batch files.

The SQL Server Agent service is made up of a set of components that work together to automate your SQL Server:

- The *scheduling engine* performs the equivalent of the Windows schedule service. It starts scheduled jobs at the appropriate intervals based on the date and time of the Windows clock on the SQL Server computer.
- The *alert engine* monitors messages written to the Windows 2000 Event Log, receives events from the SQL Server Event engine, and performs an action (such as launching a job or sending an email or pager notification). It can also monitor SQL Server performance counters that would normally be read by the Windows 2000 Performance Monitor utility.
- The *event engine* monitors the Windows 2000 application event log and captures messages posted by SQL Server. It then passes those messages to the alert engine.
- The *job engine* runs jobs either on a predetermined schedule or when dynamically requested. It records whether a task runs successfully or fails, and it can also send email or write a message to the Windows 2000 event log on success or failure. A job consists of one or more job steps, as you will see later today.

These engines work together to automate administrative control of your SQL Server environment. When an event occurs that's written to the Windows 2000 application event log, the event engine captures the message and passes it to the alert manager. The alert manager determines whether the alert is one it has been configured to watch for; if so, it might launch a job or send an email or page. The job might also then cause a message to be written to the Windows 2000 event log, and the cycle starts again.

SQL Server Agent Configuration

When you first install SQL Server, you select a service account to run the SQL Server services, including the SQL Server Agent service. It is just one configuration option you might set to control the Agent service.

To begin configuring your Agent service, start up SQL Server Enterprise Manager (if it's not already running). Then connect to your server, and expand the Management folder. Right-click the SQL Server Agent service, and select Start if the service isn't running.

After you start the service and the icon shows the green play button, right-click the icon or the text, and select Properties to open the dialog shown in Figure 18.1.

FIGURE 18.1
The SQL Server Agent Properties dialog.

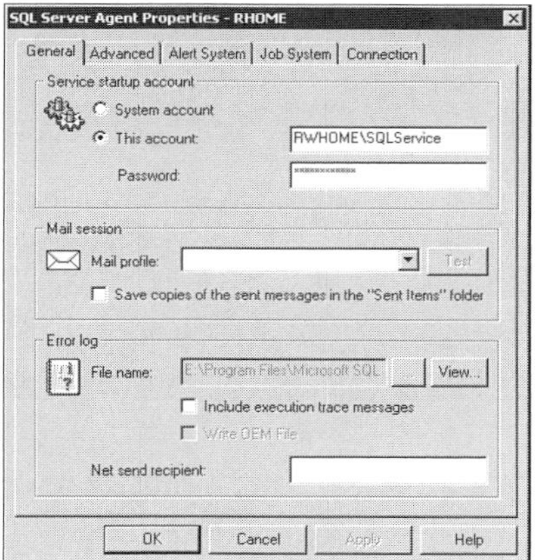

The General Tab The first option on the General tab of this dialog configures which Windows account runs the SQL Server Agent service (on Windows 9*x* platforms, this option isn't available). I have the service running under a domain user's context (shown as `RWHOME\SQLService` in the dialog) as my account on my Windows 2000 server. If you don't use a user account (meaning that you don't use the System Account option), you can't take advantage of SQL Server's email integration features. You also can't run any jobs that would otherwise run on multiple servers or need to access remote servers for resources (such as backing up to a remote file server).

Configuring the Mail Session Option for the SQL Server Agent The next option after the service account is the Mail Session configuration option. Here, you select the email profile you've set up. Setting up SQL Server Agent Mail to work properly requires several steps, so you will look at how to do so shortly. For now, leave the Agent Mail Profile blank.

Configuring the Error Log for the SQL Server Agent The last option on the General tab is to configure the error log for the SQL Server Agent. This error log is completely separate from the SQL Server error log (the log for the SQL Server service). This error log is primarily used for difficulties with jobs. Figure 18.2 shows the error log for the SQL Server Agent on my system. You can view your log by right-clicking the SQL Server Agent icon and selecting Display Error Log. Several filtering options are available—for example, you can view only errors, warnings, or information types—or you can simply view the entire error log, as Figure 18.2 shows.

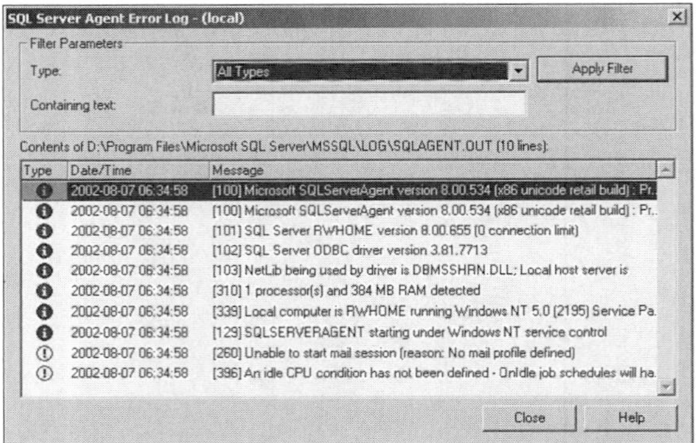

Figure 18.2
The SQL Server Agent error log.

Back on the General tab for the SQL Server Agent, the following configuration options are available for the error log:

- Include Execution Trace Messages includes all details of events for the SQL Server Agent service. You usually turn on this option when you're troubleshooting problems with the SQL Server Agent.
- The SQL Server Agent error log is written in Unicode format by default, which makes the log file usable anywhere in the world but doubles its size. If you want the log to be written in non-Unicode text, select the Write OEM File option.
- Net Send Recipient specifies the Windows 2000 account name of an operator who should be notified when a pop-up error occurs. The user is notified via a `net send` command in Windows 2000, and a message box appears on any computer into which the user is logged.

The Advanced Tab After you complete your general configuration changes, click the Advanced tab (see Figure 18.3). Here, you can configure options to restart your SQL Server services in the event of a failure, to forward events to another SQL Server, and to set the CPU Idle configuration for your server.

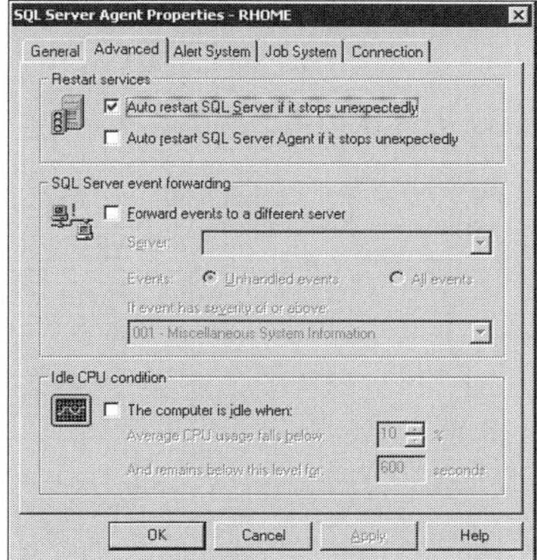

FIGURE 18.3

The Advanced configuration of the SQL Server Agent.

Restart Services You can set the option to automatically restart either the SQL Server service or the SQL Server Agent in the event of an unexpected shutdown. As you see in the Restart Services section, the option is already set for the SQL Server service by default. Simply check or uncheck the box next to the option to turn this feature on or off. It's just one more way to automate your SQL Server environment to require less manual intervention. If your SQL server crashes for some reason, you can avoid a call in the middle of the night to simply restart the services.

SQL Server Event Forwarding In the SQL Server Event Forwarding section of the Advanced tab, you can specify another SQL server to send your events to if you don't want to configure event handling on the local SQL server. The idea behind this option is that you can choose to forward events from your server to a central SQL server system. The central SQL server can be configured with alerts for multiple servers and can then be centrally controlled. Configuring the server this way can offload a considerable amount of work to the central server; however, it also potentially slows down the response to events on your server because the events need to be forwarded to the central server.

Configuring an event-forwarding server also increases network traffic to the central server as more messages are sent to that server. Therefore, you don't want to specify an event-forwarding server that's already busy handling a production database.

By setting the If Event Has Severity of or Above option, you can configure for only errors with a severity level of the level you specify (or higher) to be forwarded to the event forwarding server. Only unhandled events are forwarded; this means that if you configure an alert locally to respond to an event, it is not forwarded. The following table explains the severity levels:

Severity 0–10	Considered informational in nature.
Severity 11–16	Indicates that a user can fix the errors.
Severity 17	Indicates insufficient resources, such as running out of locks.
Severity 18	Indicates that an internal error has occurred in SQL Server. The error is nonfatal, and your connection to the server isn't interrupted.
Severity 19	Indicates that an internal non-configurable resource has been exceeded.
Severity 20	Indicates that a fatal error has occurred with your connection.
Severity 21	Indicates that a fatal error has occurred in your connection, which affects all connections to a database.
Severity 22	Indicates that the table or index you're using has become corrupted.
Severity 23	Indicates that the database you're using has been corrupted by a hardware or software problem.
Severity 24	Indicates that some kind of hardware-level error has occurred.
Severity 25	Indicates that an internal system error has occurred.

As you can see, errors with a severity level higher than 18 are really nasty errors. These errors often result in a call to Microsoft SQL Server product support.

Idle CPU Condition One option for SQL Server Agent jobs is that they run when the Central Processing Unit (CPU) is considered to be idle. When you check the box for The Computer Is Idle When, you can edit the CPU percentage and the amount of time for that percentage to remain in effect. The default is that the CPU must be less than 10 percent busy for at least 10 minutes (600 seconds) before the server is considered to be idle. If you want to change the default values, simply enter different ones here.

Again, think carefully before changing these defaults, because you typically invoke processor or disk-intensive tasks only during idle conditions and don't want other users on the system when these jobs are run.

The Connection Tab You will examine the Alert System and Job System tabs later today when you examine each of those systems. For now, click the Connection tab to complete the initial configuration of your SQL Server Agent (see Figure 18.4).

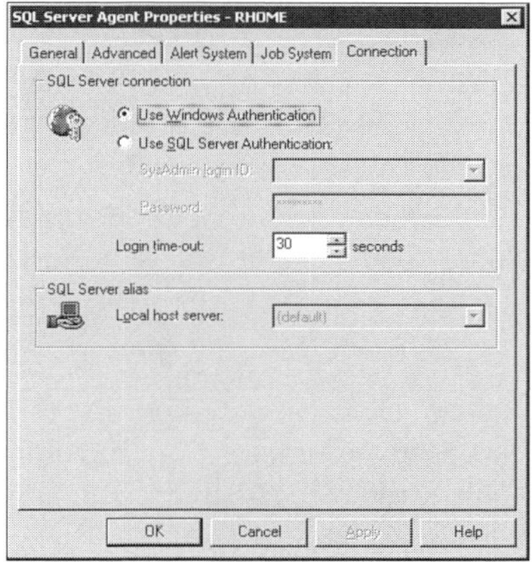

FIGURE 18.4

The connection configuration of the SQL Server Agent.

You can use a SQL Server Authentication mode account for the SQL Server Agent service. The default on a Windows 2000 computer is to make a Windows authenticated connection to your SQL Server. If you want to use SQL Server authentication or are on the Windows 9*x* platform, simply select Use SQL Server Authentication, and supply the appropriate credentials. The account used in either case should be a member of the sysadmin fixed server role.

Login Time-Out specifies how long the SQL Server Agent will wait after it requests a connection to SQL Server before it assumes that the SQL Server service isn't running. The default is 30 seconds.

The other option on the Connection tab is to use an alias to connect to your SQL Server. If you configured a server alias using the SQL Server Client Network Utility as examined on Day 3 (for example, forcing Transmission Control Protocol/Internet Protocol [TCP/IP] sockets to a non-default socket number), you specify that alias here. This advanced configuration option shouldn't be changed in most environments.

SQLMail Integration

As you've seen, you must complete several configuration tasks before using the SQL Server Agent. Although you can use the default options, it's useful to look them over and verify the settings before you begin.

One feature you just learned about was the option to integrate email with SQL Server. This option, which has historically been called SQLMail, enables you to configure a mail profile and then have the SQL Server services use this profile to send (and receive) email. Receiving reports indicating whether your jobs have completed successfully can be really useful. You also can have SQL Server page you if something serious goes wrong that you need to know about, though this will require the purchase of additional software to achieve this functionality.

You can actually set up two different SQL Mail configurations in SQL Server 2000:

- The SQL Server service can use extended stored procedures to send and receive email. This mail configuration is the SQLMail option you see in the Support Services folder of SQL Server Enterprise Manager.
- The SQL Server Agent's implementation of email integration is used for the most exciting options of SQLMail—the capability for SQL Server itself to automatically notify you under the conditions examined earlier. This option is often referred to in the Microsoft Literature as "SQL Server Agent Mail."

If your SQL Server and SQL Server Agent services are using the same Windows 2000 account configuration for their respective services, you can configure and use a single mail profile for both services. This recommended configuration is assumed for this book.

If your SQL Server services are using the Local System account, change them to use a user account now. You just saw how to change the SQL Server Agent Service, and you examined how to change the service account for the SQL Server service on Day 2, "Installing Microsoft SQL Server 2000." If you haven't set up the Windows 2000 account yet, refer to Day 2 to see how to set up and properly configure an account to run the SQL Server services.

The mail profile you create MUST be under the user name of the SQL Server and SQL Server Agent service account(s). Therefore the rest of the mail configuration steps here *must* be completed while logged in to Windows with the service account (SQLService in this book). Your mail configuration will not work otherwise.

Configuring a Microsoft Outlook Messaging Profile

When you have your SQL Server services running under your specified service account, you will need to log in to your Windows 2000 computer that is running SQL Server using the service account credentials. If you accepted the setup configuration from Day 2, you log in as SQLService with a password of `password` (in the real world you should use a much more difficult/less hackable password; this is simply for the purposes of learning the product in the book). The SQL Server services need you to specify the name of the mail profile they should use. Any mail profile you select will come from the profile of the user configured for the services. Therefore, you must log in using that account.

Right-click the inbox on your desktop or on the Microsoft Outlook icon. This book references Outlook XP, the most recent mail client available from Microsoft as of the writing of this book. Select Properties to open the dialog shown in Figure 18.5.

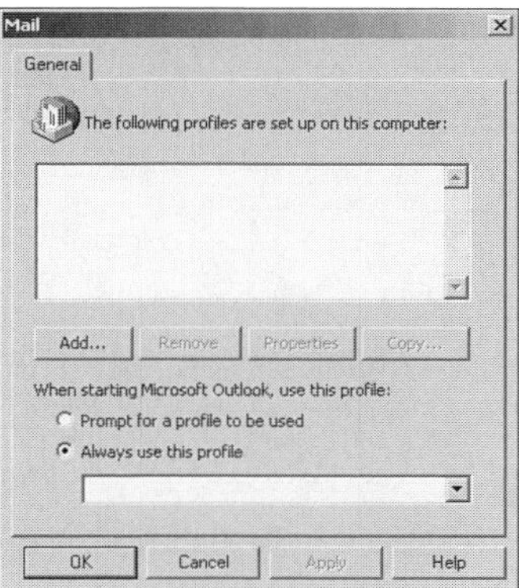

FIGURE 18.5
The default Mail properties dialog.

Now click Add to create a new mail profile. When prompted for a new mail profile, type **`SQLMail`** (as shown in Figure 18.6). The name of this mail profile is what SQL Server will use when talking to the mail services of the server.

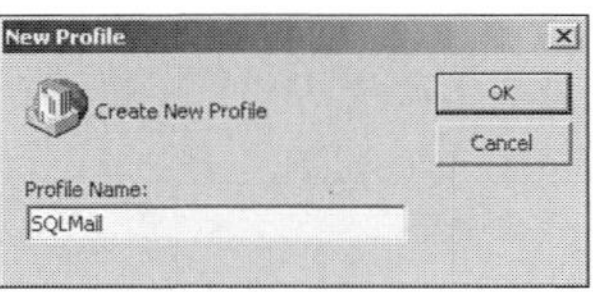

FIGURE 18.6
The name of the Mail profile to configure and use.

When you click OK, you will be presented with Email Accounts dialog (Figure 18.7). This is the starting page for configuring your email.

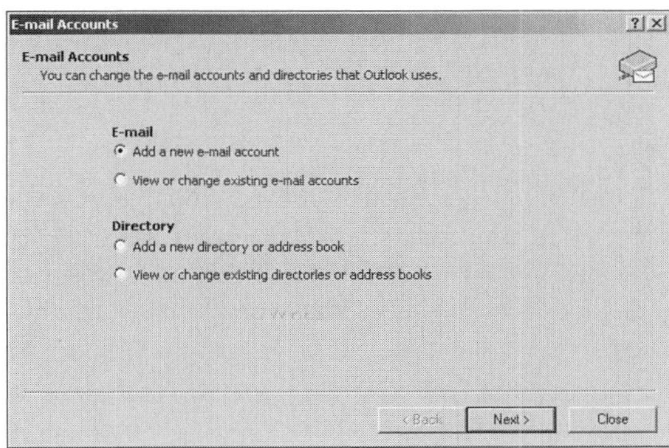

FIGURE 18.7
Email Configuration Start Page.

Click Next, and Outlook will ask what kind of email server you wish to connect to (Figure 18.8).

FIGURE 18.8
Select your email server type.

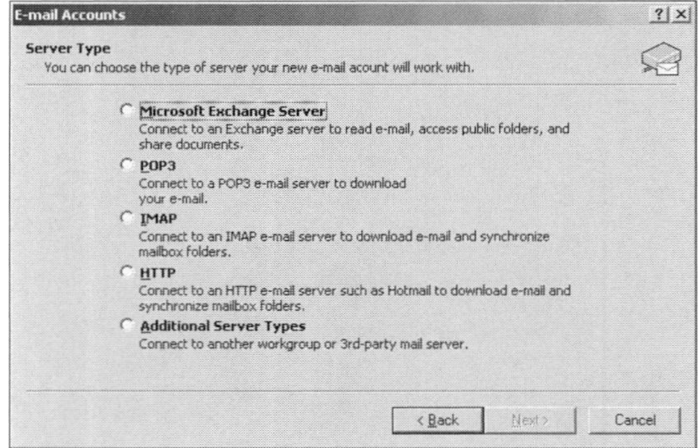

Microsoft Exchange Server

If you select Microsoft Exchange Server, the dialog in Figure 18.9 appears. Simply type the name of the Microsoft Exchange Server computer, and specify either your full name or your email alias.

FIGURE 18.9
Microsoft Exchange Server configuration.

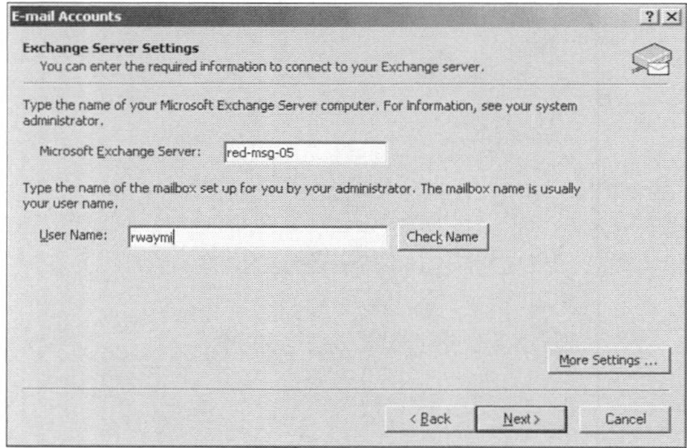

Click the Check Name button to confirm you entered everything correctly (your user name and mail server will become underlined). Then, click Next and you're done! The dialog in Figure 18.10 shows that you've successfully configured your Microsoft Exchange Server.

Internet Mail

Not everyone uses Microsoft Exchange Server yet as a mail server. Another popular option is to use an Internet mail provider. If you check the POP3 E-mail option (from Figure 18.8) and click Next, the dialog in Figure 18.11 appears. Note that for today POP3 is assumed to be the most likely Internet mail client type.

As you can see, I've entered my name and email address in the dialog. I've chosen to use my personal email account for SQL Server. Next, enter the name of your Simple Mail

Transfer Protocol (SMTP) email server for outgoing mail, the Post Office Protocol 3 (POP3) server for incoming mail, and your login information. You should obtain this information from your Internet service provider (ISP).

FIGURE 18.10
The configuration is complete dialog.

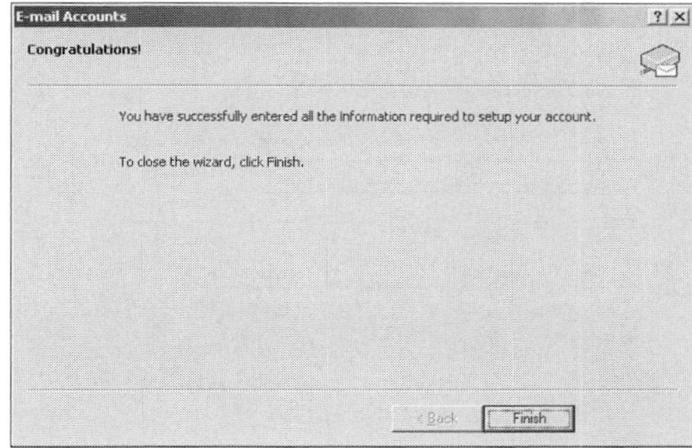

FIGURE 18.11
Configure your POP3 email account.

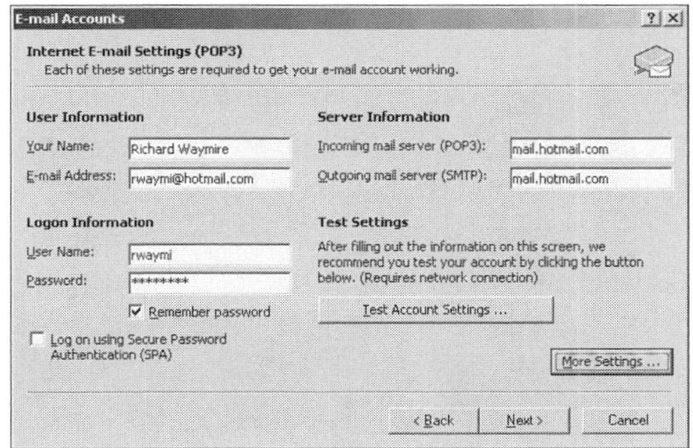

If you are on a local area network (LAN), you're probably ready to click next. If you're working on a home computer, and you want SQL Server to automatically dial your ISP when it's time to send any mail (and you don't have a DSL or cable-modem connection), click the "More Settings" button, then click on the Connection tab (see Figure 18.12) Connect Using My Phone Line option. If you want SQL Server to connect only when you have manually dialed up to the Internet, leave the option set to the default (Connect using my Local Area Network (LAN). If you aren't dialed into the Internet, SQL Server logs an error when attempting to connect to your mail server. Click OK after you select the option you want to use.

Click Next and you're once again presented with something like Figure 18.10; you're done configuring your POP3 mail account.

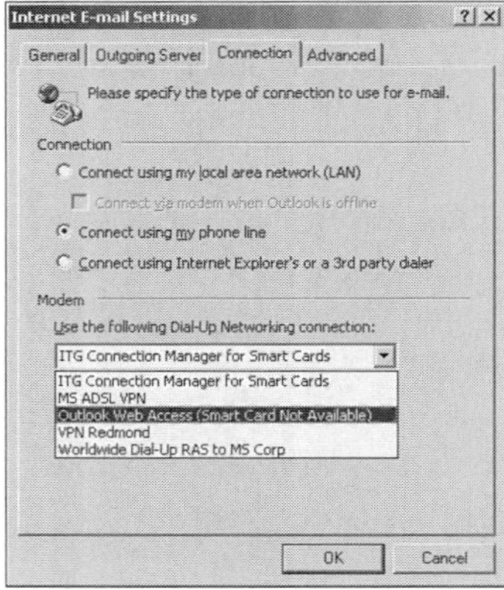

FIGURE 18.12
Entering your email server information

HTTP Mail

As you can see from the email address I provide in this book, I use the popular Hotmail email service. A new option added into Office XP is to use a web-based email service as part of your mail profile. You use the same options as above to get to the email type selection (Figure 18.8), but this time select HTTP. Click Next, the dialog in Figure 18.13 appears. I've entered my Hotmail account information and Outlook figured out the correct web address for me since it knows all about Hotmail. Once again, complete your personal information, your email address, and your password. Click Next to complete the wizard and your email profile is configured.

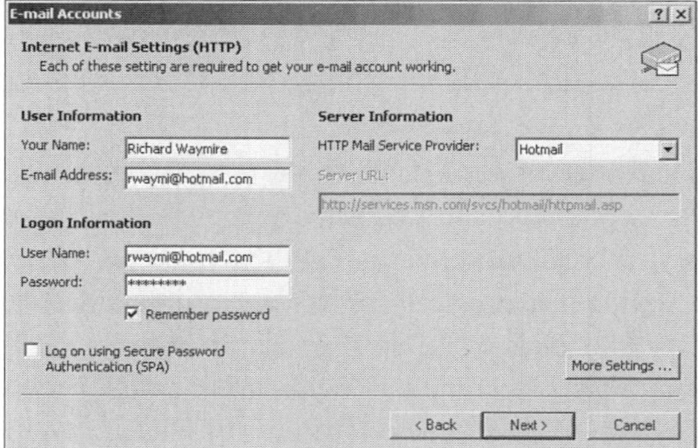

FIGURE 18.13
Configure your HTTP email account.

Configuring SQLMail for SQL Server

It doesn't matter which of the three options examined above you use, but do select one of them at this time. For the rest of the day I'm going to use my Hotmail account via HTTP mail. Now that you've successfully configured a mail profile, it's time to configure SQL

Mail for SQL Server. First, configure SQL Mail to support the use of the mail-related extended stored procedures. Switch back to SQL Server Enterprise Manager, expand the Support Services folder for your server, and right-click SQL Mail. Select Properties, and complete the SQL Mail Configuration dialog (see Figure 18.14).

FIGURE 18.14

The completed SQL Mail Configuration dialog.

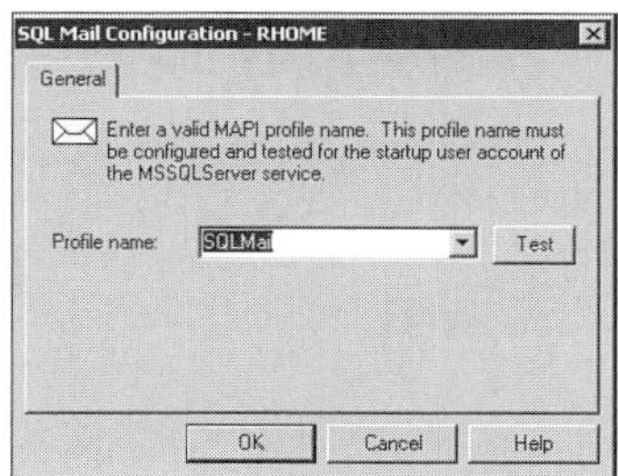

Enter the SQL Mail profile name as shown in Figure 18.14. You can test that everything works correctly by clicking the Test button. If something goes wrong, troubleshooting SQLMail can become rather involved. Look at Microsoft Knowledge base article q321183, (located in English at the time of this writing at `http://support.microsoft.com/default.aspx?scid=kb;en-us;q321183`), for helpful steps in troubleshooting email configuration issues.

After you complete the SQL Mail configuration dialog and successfully test your profile, click OK.

Configuring SQL Mail to Use with SQL Server Agent

To configure the same profile for the SQL Server Agent, right-click the agent (in the Management folder), and select Properties. Under Mail Session, select SQL Mail from the drop-down list, and click the Test button to confirm that everything works here as well. If you get any kind of error, verify that your SQL Server Agent service is using the same account as your SQL Server service. When you click OK, you are prompted to restart the agent so that the changes you've made will take effect. Select Yes, and the agent stops and restarts. Now SQL Mail is fully functional. You should note here that SQLMail and SQL Server Agent email are different and do have minor behavioral differences which I'll not get into in this book as they're not relevant for most administrators of SQL Server.

Sending Email from SQL Server

To send email from SQL Server via a T-SQL query, use the extended stored procedure `xp_sendmail`:

SYNTAX

```
xp_sendmail {[@recipients =] 'recipient[; recipientn]'}
    [, [@message =] 'message']
    [, [@query =] 'query']
    [, [@attachments =] attachments]
    [, [@copy_recipients =] 'recipient[; ...recipientn]'
    [, [@blind_copy_recipients =] 'recipient[; ...recipientn]'
    [, [@subject =] 'subject']
    [, [@type =] 'type']
    [, [@attach_results =] {'true' | 'false' | 'NULL'}]
    [, [@no_output =] {'true' | 'false'}]
    [, [@no_header =] {'true' | 'false'}]
    [, [@width =] width]
    [, [@separator] = separator]
    [, [@echo_error =] {'true' | 'false'}]
    [, [@set_user =] 'user']
    [, [@dbuse =] 'dbname']
```

This syntax has several options, but you will focus on only the most important ones here. The following are the most common parameters:

- `@recipients = recipient` specifies the name of the email recipient. If you want to specify multiple recipients, put semicolons (;) between their names.
- `@subject = subject` specifies the subject of the message.
- `@message = message` specifies the text that will be in the body of the message that's sent.
- `@query = query` specifies a query to be run. The results are then sent to the user specified in the `@recipients` parameter.
- `@attachments = attachments` specifies the pathname and filename of an attachment to be sent with the message.

As with any stored procedure, you can pass parameters by either name or position. For example, the following sends you an email with a subject of "test mail":

```
Use Master

GO

xp_sendmail @recipients = 'your email', @subject = 'test mail'
```

You can also send the message without specifying the parameters (by specifying them in order):

```
Use Master
go
xp_sendmail 'your email', 'This is a message from SQL Server'
```

SQL Server can also receive email. You can send a query to SQL Server and run the `sp_processmail` stored procedure to process incoming messages. If the mail message is formatted properly, the message body is interpreted as a query, the query is run, and the results are sent back to the user as a text file attachment.

SYNTAX

```
sp_processmail [[@subject =] 'subject'][, [@filetype =] 'filetype']
    [, [@separator =] 'separator'][, [@set_user =] 'user']
    [, [@dbuse =] 'dbname']
```

The following are the most common parameters:

- `@subject = subject` specifies that SQL Server should process only email messages with the subject line you specify.
- `@filetype = filetype` specifies the extension of the attachment to be returned as part of the query. The default is to return a `.txt` file.
- `@separator = separator` specifies the separator in the query output. The default is a tab.
- `@set_user = user` specifies the security context of the query. The default user is Guest.
- `@dbuse = dbname` specifies in which database the queries should be run. The default is the `master` database.

18

If you were to send a message to SQL Server's mailbox, with a message body of

```
Select au_fname, au_lname from pubs..authors
```

and then log on to SQL Server as a member of the sysadmin fixed server role and run the query

```
EXEC sp_processmail
```

your message would be processed, the query would be run, and an email message would be returned to you with the results of the query as a text file attachment.

Scheduling Jobs

As you learned earlier today, *jobs* are the SQL Server objects that you configure to run tasks you need to complete. You usually create a job if you want one or more sets of commands to be run repeatedly.

Setting up a job requires four steps: You create the job, create your job steps, set the schedule for the job, and then set notification options for the job. Now switch to SQL Server Enterprise Manager and expand the Management folder; then expand the SQL Server Agent. You see folders labeled Alerts, Operators, and Jobs. Highlight the Jobs folder, and in the right pane, you can see any jobs that have already been created.

Creating a New Job

To create a new job, right-click the Jobs icon and select New Job. The New Job Properties dialog appears (see Figure 18.15).

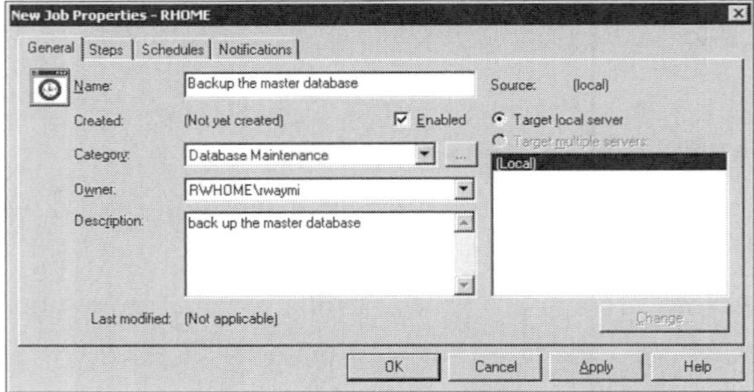

FIGURE 18.15
The New Job Properties dialog.

First, give the job a name. Because it's likely that you will want to have a job to create a backup for the `master` database anyway, name the job **`Backup the master database`**. Select the category Database Maintenance, because this is what you are doing here.

For the job owner, the default is that the user you are logged in as becomes the owner. Anyone can create a job in SQL Server 2000. However, members of the sysadmin role can create jobs that are owned by other users. Leave this job owner at the default value.

In the Description text box, enter a description for your job.

You'll examine the target server options shortly, but for now leave the option at the default of Target Local Server.

Setting Up Job Steps

Click the Steps tab to prepare to create steps for the job (see Figure 18.16). Each step is a separate command or set of commands to run.

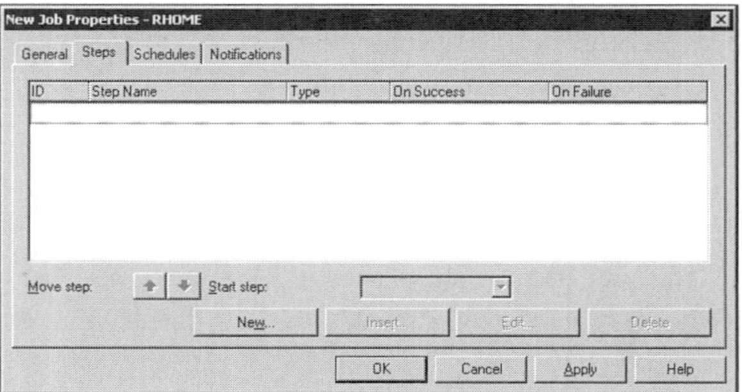

FIGURE 18.16
The Job Steps dialog.

Click the New button to build the first job step. You then are presented with the New Job Step dialog (see Figure 18.17).

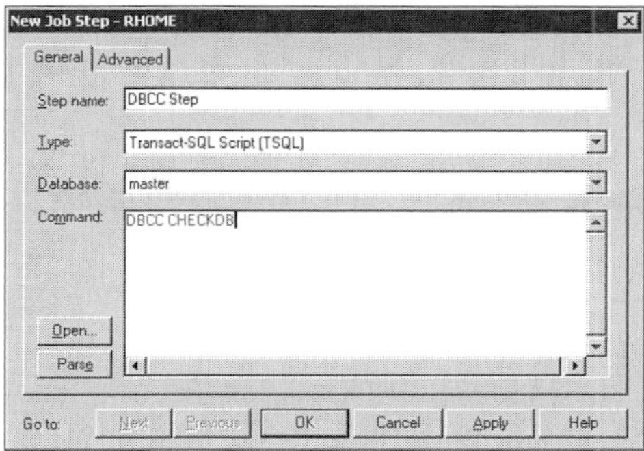

FIGURE 18.17

The New Job Step dialog.

For this job, first run `DBCC CHECKDB` on your `master` database. Then run `BACKUP DATABASE` to actually back up the `master` database. However, back up the `master` database only if the DBCC checks don't report any errors.

As you can see in Figure 18.17, I've already completed the dialog for the DBCC step. Click the Parse button to verify that you've entered your T-SQL commands properly.

Next, click the Advanced tab (see Figure 18.18). Here you can choose options that control the flow of execution, specify what to do in case of failure of this job step, and specify whether to keep the results of your T-SQL commands as an output file.

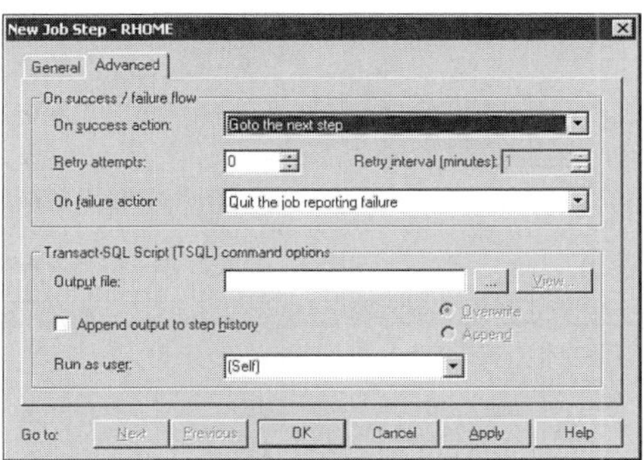

FIGURE 18.18

The Advanced tab of the New Job Step dialog.

If you want to keep the results of this job step in the history of the job as a whole rather than in a separate file, select Append Output to Step History. Accept all the other defaults, and click OK to finish this job step.

Now add another step to run the backup command. As a reminder, a valid command might be

```
BACKUP DATABASE master TO master_backup WITH INIT
```

Set the On Success Action option as Quit the Job Reporting Success. Figure 18.19 shows the completed New Job Step dialog.

FIGURE 18.19

The configured New Job Step dialog.

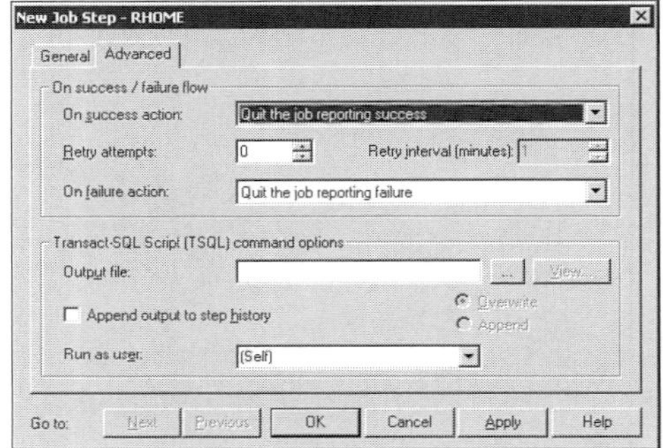

You should explore the dialogs for other job types as well. Specifically, look at the Active Script and Operating System Command (CMDExec) job types. They tend to be the three types of jobs you run most often. Notice how the dialogs change depending on the type of job you select.

Job Scheduling

Now you must define the schedule for this job. To do so, click the Schedules tab (see Figure 18.20) and then click the New Schedule button to set up the schedule (see Figure 18.21).

FIGURE 18.20

The Job Schedules dialog.

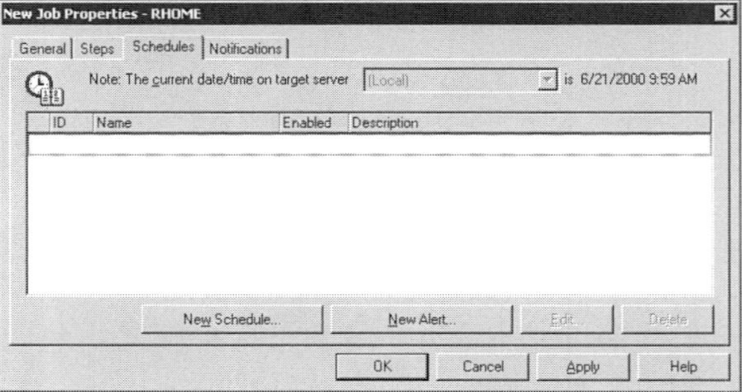

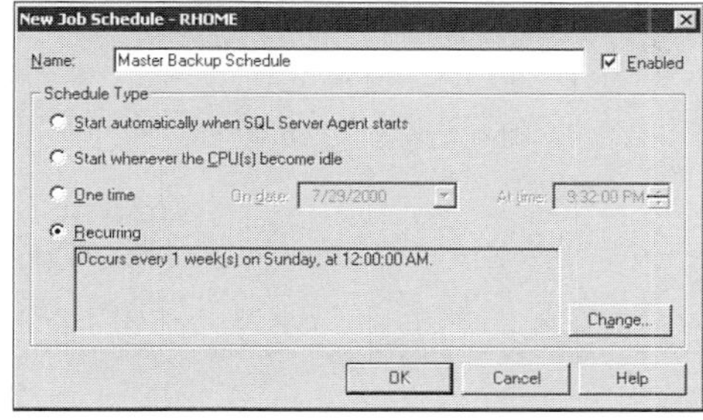

FIGURE 18.21

The New Job Schedule dialog.

The options here are mostly self-explanatory. You can have this job automatically start when the SQL Server Agent service starts, you can have the job run when the CPU is idle (as you defined earlier today), or you can schedule the job for a one-time run. Another option would be to not configure anything in this dialog, which would make the job run only when you explicitly request it to run.

The final option (which is also the default) is to set a fixed schedule for the job. Notice that the default is to run the job once a week—on Sunday at midnight. Click the Change button to change to a different schedule. You then see the dialog shown in Figure 18.22.

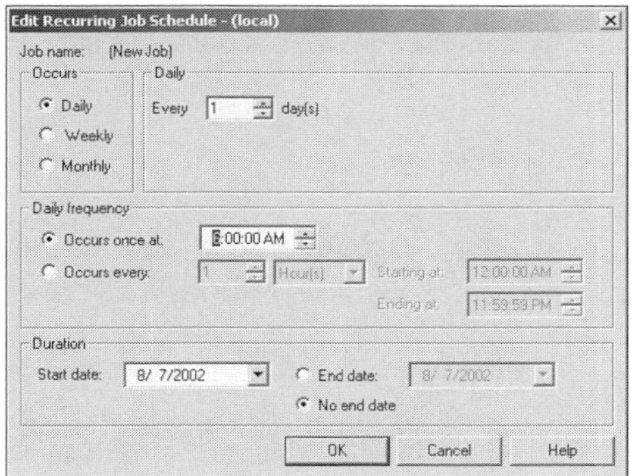

FIGURE 18.22

The Edit Recurring Job Schedule dialog.

The Occurs section specifies whether the job occurs daily, weekly, or monthly:

- When you specify Daily, the Daily section appears next to the Occurs section. This option enables you to specify that the job occurs every *x* days (every day, every second day, and so on).
- The Weekly option, when selected, displays the Weekly section. This section displays the option to run every *x* weeks (with the default being one). You can also specify which day of the week the job will run, and you can check as many days as you want. You can, for example, specify that a job occurs weekly, every one week, on Monday through Friday.

- Selecting the Monthly option allows you to run a job on a specific day of the month (or every *x* number of months) or on the first, second, third, fourth, or last day, weekend day, or weekday of every x number of months. As you can see, this option is quite flexible.

The Daily Frequency section specifies at what time of day the job will run. You can also set up the Occurs Every option to run a scheduled job every *x* number of hours or minutes. You can specify a start time and end time for the job to run.

The Duration section specifies a Start Date (defaulting to the current date) and an End Date (or the No End Date option). If you want to have a scheduled job that runs only for a specific duration and then stops running, you can set the End Date. When that date is reached, the job won't run again.

For this job, set Occurs to Daily, and run the job at 6 a.m. Click OK to return to the New Job Schedule dialog. Then name the schedule (I chose Daily at 6 a.m.). Finally, click OK and return to the Schedules tab, which should now look like Figure 18.23.

FIGURE 18.23

The completed Schedules tab.

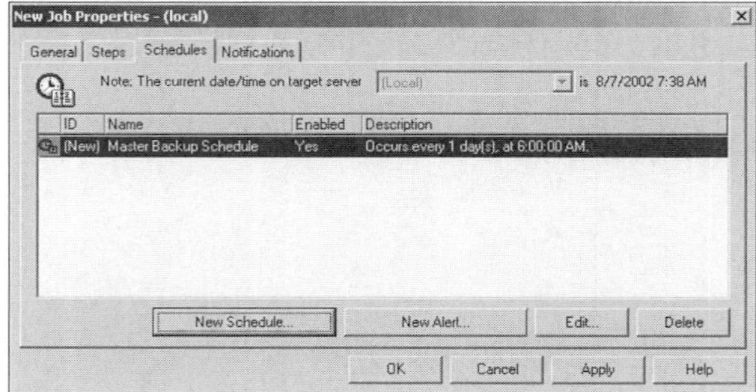

Job Notifications

On the Notifications tab (see Figure 18.24), you can set options to have an email sent, have an operator paged, use the Windows 2000 Net Send function to send a message (only on Windows NT/2000/XP), and write to the Windows 2000 event log. For each option, you can specify whether the notification will happen when the job fails, when it succeeds, or whenever it completes (always).

You can also request that the job be deleted if the job succeeds or fails. Configure the dialog as shown in Figure 18.24. You will set email options for this job a bit later—after you add an email operator. Click OK, and you've successfully created your first job!

FIGURE 18.24

The completed Notifications tab.

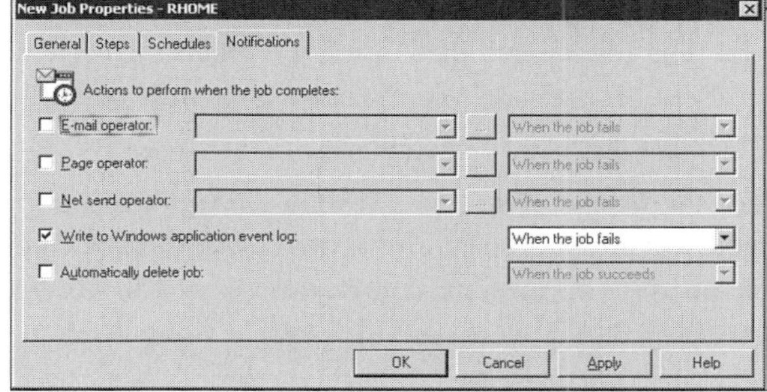

Setting Job System Options

Some job options are universal across all jobs. To set some job system options, right-click your SQL Server Agent (within the Management folder in Enterprise Manager), and select Properties. Then click the Job System tab (see Figure 18.25).

FIGURE 18.25

The Job System configuration tab.

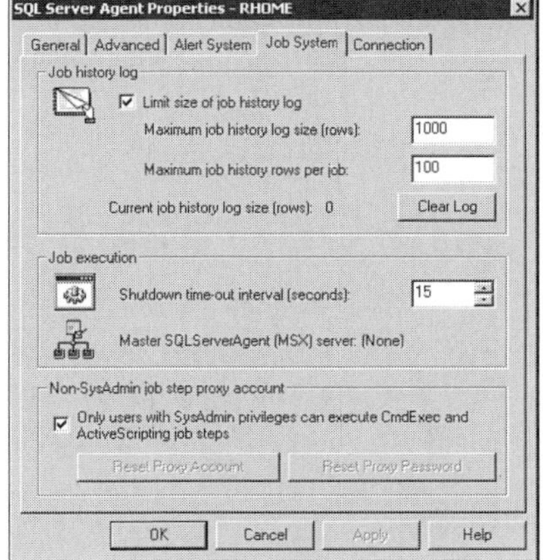

You can choose to limit the size of the history kept for all scheduled jobs on your SQL Server installation. Your two options are to limit the maximum job history log size (1,000 rows by default) or limit the maximum job history rows per job (100 rows by default).

If you disable this option, the history of your tasks will be kept forever. This task history is kept in the `sysjobhistory` table of the MSDB database. Therefore, if you change these parameters or turn off the maximum size options, you will most likely need to increase the size of the MSDB database. The job definitions are kept in the `sysjobs`, `sysjobschedules`, `sysjobsteps`, and `sysjobservers` system tables in the MSDB database.

18

The Job Execution section allows you to configure how long the SQL Server Agent will wait for any running jobs to complete after you request that the service stop. The default is 15 seconds. The other option in this section is specific to Multiserver operations, which are beyond the scope of this book.

Finally, notice that the last option, to allow only users who are members of the sysadmin fixed server role the right to run jobs of type ActiveScript or CmdExec, is checked. You should leave it checked because these job types allow you full access to the server (or even the network) as though you were the account used to run SQL Server. This restriction prevents anyone who isn't a SQL Server administrator from having that kind of access.

Click OK to set your Job System options.

Multiserver Jobs

You might have noticed several options throughout the last few pages that reference multiserver jobs. This advanced feature generally isn't used unless you have at least three SQL Server machines on your network. If you want to understand multiserver jobs, refer to the SQL Server Books Online or, better yet, *Microsoft SQL Server 2000 Unleashed* from Sams Publishing.

Setting Up Alerts and Operators

Alerts allow you to specify events that SQL Server should watch for. When these events occur, you can have the alert send you an email, a page, issue a `net send` command on Windows 2000/XP systems, or launch a job if needed. Some alerts are preconfigured when you install SQL Server, and others you might want to add.

Configuring Operators

To configure an operator, right-click the Operators option under the SQL Server Agent. Then select New Operator to open the New Operator Properties dialog (see Figure 18.26).

Name the operator (I've added my own name, see figure 18.27), and then click the … button next to the E-mail name to add an email address for your operator. The same options apply for the Pager e-mail name because it's based on SQL Server's email capabilities. When you click the … button next to the email name space, you see your personal address book. If it doesn't contain any entries (because it's new, for example), click the New button to add a new operator. Select Internet Mail Address, and complete all the options you want. At a minimum, you must provide a name and email address.

FIGURE 18.26

The New Operator Properties dialog.

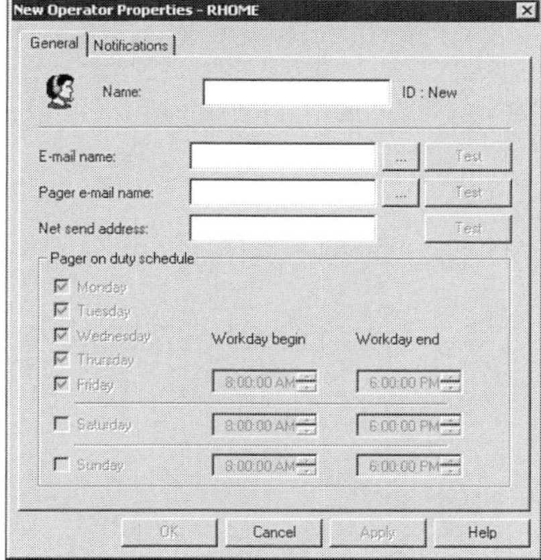

Click Add to add the email address back to your operator to the New Operator Properties dialog (as well as the personal address book of SQL Server). Click OK in the dialog (see Figure 18.27), and you've successfully created an operator. If you created a pager entry, you can also set the schedule for the operator to be paged. You don't need to click the Notifications tab yet, because this will examine the alerts assigned to this operator, which you'll look at next. However, now is a good time to configure alerts.

FIGURE 18.27

Adding a new email address for a user.

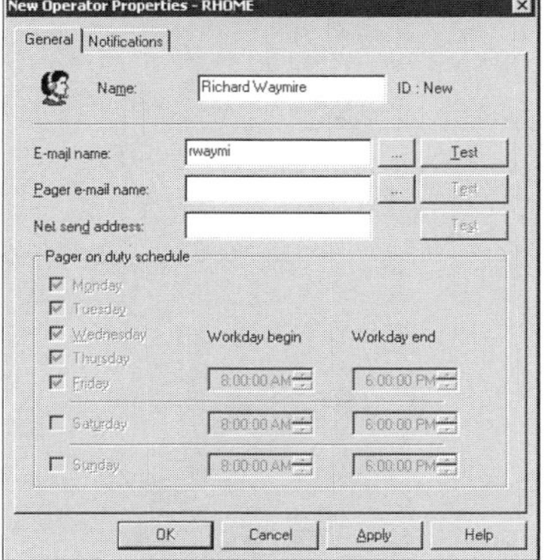

Creating Alerts

Highlight the Alerts option under the SQL Server Agent. Notice that several alerts are preconfigured on your server. These alerts are preconfigured to cover the most severe errors that can occur in SQL Server (see Figure 18.28).

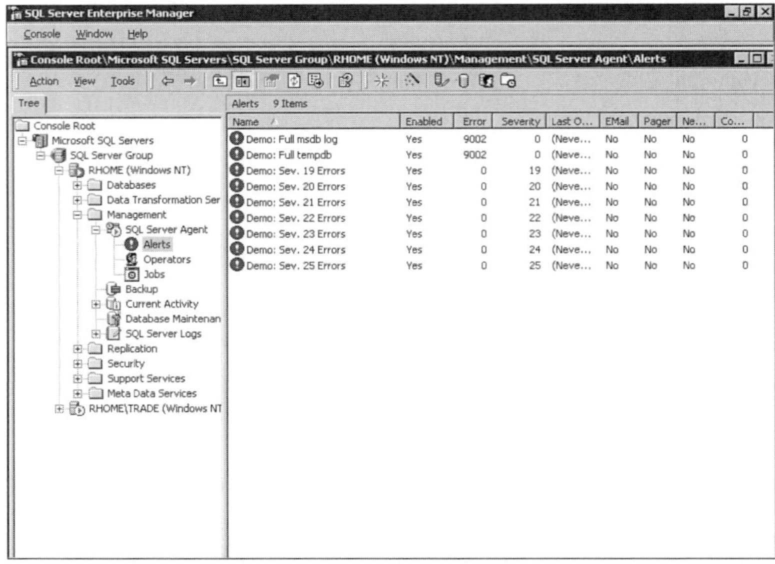

FIGURE 18.28
SQL Server 2000's preconfigured alerts.

To create a new alert, right-click the Alerts option under the SQL Server Agent, and select New Alert. The New Alert Properties dialog then opens (see Figure 18.29).

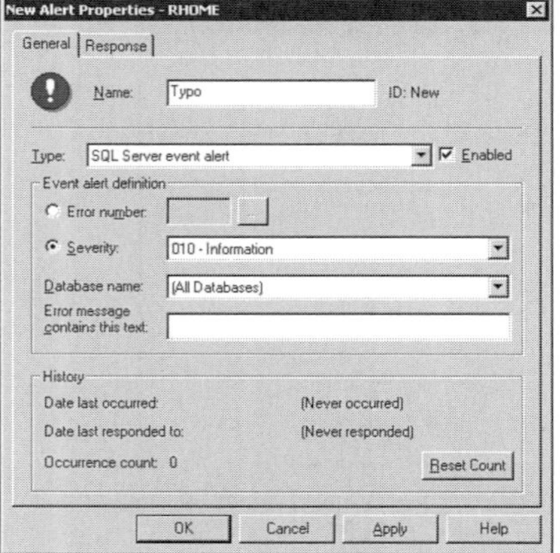

FIGURE 18.29
The New Alert Properties dialog.

In Figure 18.29, I've begun creating an alert named Typo. Click the … button next to the Error Number option to search for an error message that this alert should watch for. To make one that's easy to reproduce, configure error 208 (Object not found in a query).

Type **208** in the Error Number text box (within the Manage SQL Server Messages dialog), and click Find. You then see a dialog with the error displayed. Click Edit to view the Edit SQL Server Message dialog (see Figure 18.30). Here, you need to change a default option for this error message.

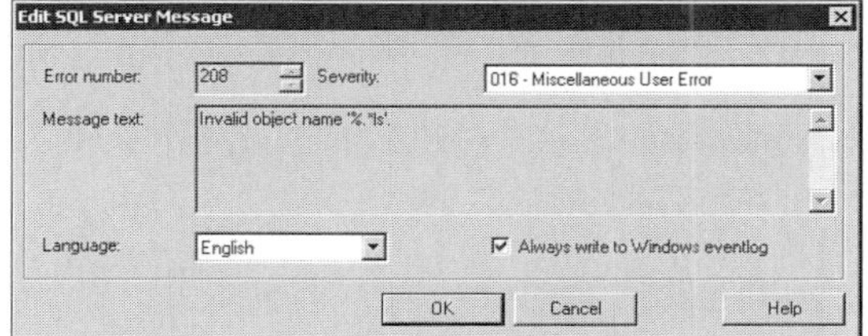

FIGURE 18.30

The Edit SQL Server Message dialog.

The SQL Server Agent can see messages only if they are posted to the Windows 2000 event log (or are configured to do so at a minimum on the Windows 9*x* platform). Click the Always Write to Windows NT Eventlog check box, as shown in Figure 18.30. Click OK twice to complete the selection of this error. Change the database name to `pubs` so that you aren't overwhelmed with this error if others are using your SQL Server. The fully configured alert should look like Figure 18.31.

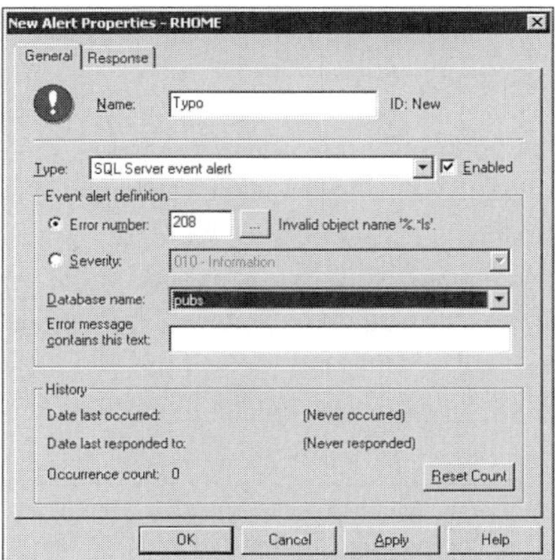

FIGURE 18.31

The fully configured alert.

Click the Response tab (see Figure 18.32). Configure the options as shown—that Richard Waymire (or you on your server) will be notified when this alert occurs. Notice that you can also configure the alert to launch a job by checking the Execute Job check box and then selecting a job in the drop-down list. You can even launch the New Job Properties dialog from here. Here, I have configured the alert to back up my `master` database when this error occurs. Click OK after you configure the response options.

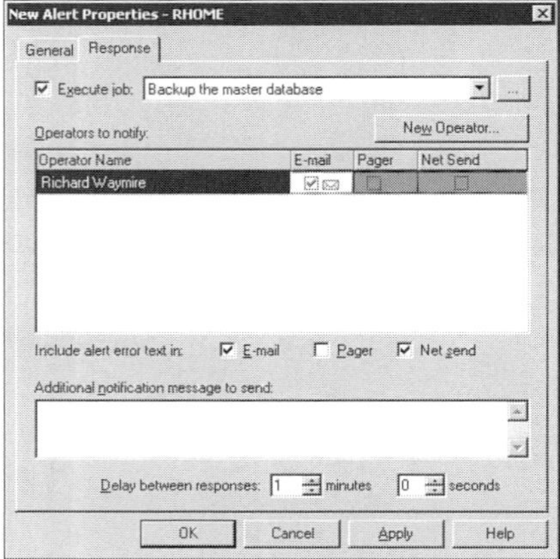

FIGURE 18.32
The Response tab options for an alert.

Testing Your Alert

Now is a great time to test this alert. Start the SQL Server Query Analyzer, switch to the pubs database, and run the following query:

```
Select * from nonexistenttable
```

You should get back

```
Server: Msg 208, Level 16, State 1
Invalid object name 'nonexistenttable'.
```

This output signals your alert and causes an email to be sent as well as your master database backup job to be launched. Switch to the Alerts entries for your server, and you should see that the Typo alert has a last-occurred value as well as a count of 1 (to show that the error has happened one time). You can also verify that you now have an email from SQL Server. Highlight your Jobs folder, and you can see that your job has run as well. If you don't see these changes reflected, right-click the Jobs or Alerts options in the left pane, and select Refresh (or use the shortcut key F5).

Alerts are kept in the sysalerts system table in the MSDB database.

Setting Alert System Options

Now go back to the SQL Server Agent, right-click, and select Properties. Click the Alert System tab (see Figure 18.33).

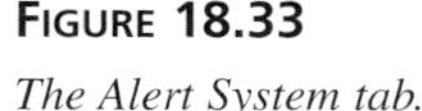

FIGURE 18.33

The Alert System tab.

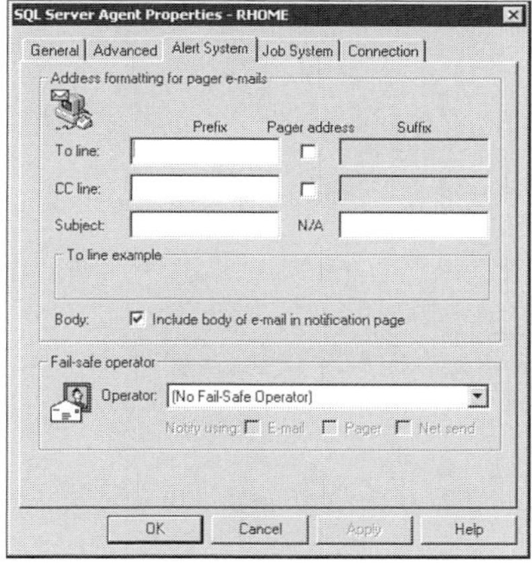

Most of these options are necessary only for pagers, such as adding a special prefix or suffix for pager emails. The documentation for your paging software describes what must be entered here. You can also choose to have the body of your email in the notification page sent to the operator (if the operator has a text pager, that is).

The Fail-Safe Operator section specifies the fail-safe operator to use, as well as whether to use email, a pager, or the Net Send option for that operator. If something should go wrong with an alert and none of the operators who should be paged are paged for some reason, you can designate an operator to receive a message about the notification failure. To do so, select an operator from the Operator drop-down list. You can also create an operator here by selecting the New Fail-Safe Operator option, which opens the New Operator dialog. To not specify a fail-safe operator (the default), select (No Fail-Safe Operator).

Taking Advantage of Performance Monitor Integration

The Windows 2000 Performance Monitor utility has been fully integrated with SQL Server through alerts in the SQL Server Agent. To take advantage of this integration, go back to the New Alert Properties dialog (right-click Alerts under the SQL Server Agent, and select New Alert). Notice the alert Type drop-down list on the General tab. If you click this drop-down list, you can select the SQL Server performance condition alert, which enables you to pick then any SQL Server performance counter and configure an alert—just as you did with SQL Server error messages. Figure 18.34 shows a performance counter alert for the transaction log of the `pubs` database. When the transaction log is 80 percent full (or greater), this alert is triggered.

FIGURE 18.34

An alert using a Performance Monitor counter.

Using the Database Maintenance Plan Wizard

The Database Maintenance Plan Wizard creates a job (or multiple jobs) to automatically check the integrity of your database, reorganize your indexes, clean up unused space in your database, and create database and transaction log backups. You examined the program that actually runs behind the scenes, `sqlmaint.exe`, on Day 3, "Working with SQL Server 2000 Management Tools and Utilities." Using this wizard on your databases is a good idea unless you want a highly customized maintenance plan for your databases.

To start the wizard, select a server in the SQL Server Enterprise Manager, and then choose Wizards from the Tools menu. Expand the Management entry, and select the Database Maintenance Plan Wizard. Click OK to launch the wizard, and you are presented with the wizard's Welcome dialog. Click Next to see the dialog in Figure 18.35, which asks you to select one or more databases to perform regular maintenance on.

Select just the `pubs` database for now to keep things simple. Click Next to move to the dialog in Figure 18.36. Here, specify whether you want indexes reorganized, statistics updated, and unused space removed from your database. Which options you select depend on your database environment. This dialog has the option to reorganize your indexes selected, which automatically re-creates statistics for you. For `pubs`, you don't need to clean up unused space, but you could set the appropriate entries for your database.

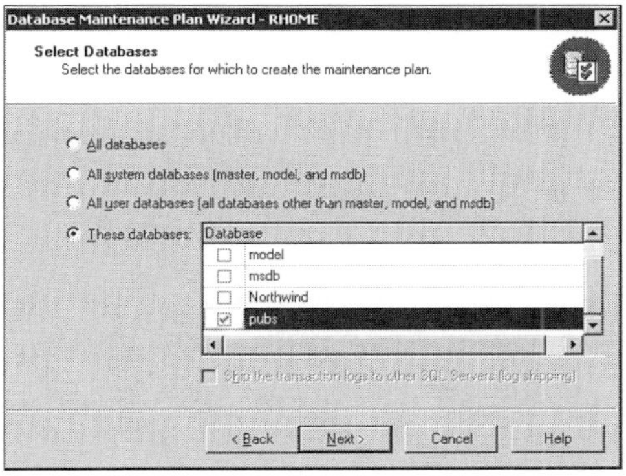

FIGURE 18.35

Select one or more databases for the Database Maintenance Plan Wizard.

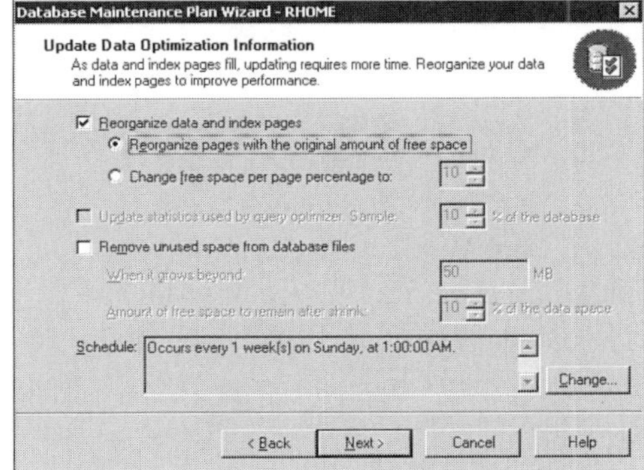

FIGURE 18.36

The wizard's Update Data Optimization Information dialog.

Establish the schedule of the data optimizations by clicking the Change button next to the schedule, as you did earlier today. Click Next after you complete the data optimizations and scheduling options, and you move to the Database Integrity Check dialog (see Figure 18.37).

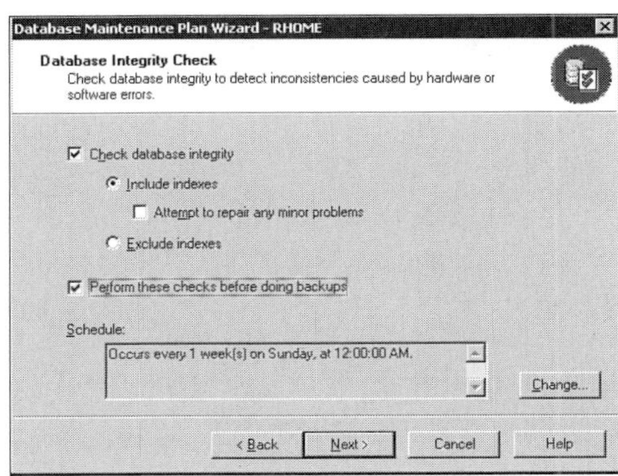

FIGURE 18.37

Data integrity optimizations with the Database Maintenance Plan Wizard.

Don't set the option Attempt to Repair Any Minor Problems. As tempting as this option sounds, it puts your database in single-user mode so that it can run DBCC with `REPAIR` turned on. This seriously affects your database's availability.

Specifying most options here is probably best, allowing full integrity checks to be run and directing that your backups be run only if no database corruption is found. Again, set the schedule for these integrity checks, and click Next. You then move to the dialog in Figure 18.38, where you configure the backup options. They should be very familiar to you now, so select the options you want and set the schedule. Then click Next.

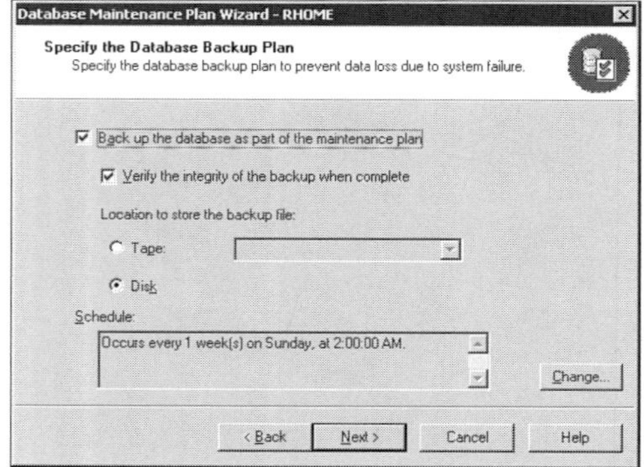

FIGURE 18.38
Specifying your database backup plan.

Indicate where you want your backups to be stored. If you're backing up to disk, specify a disk drive other than the one on which your data is stored. I recommend that you make a subdirectory for each database (locating your backups is easier that way) and that you have the backups automatically deleted as they get old. These options are set in Figure 18.39.

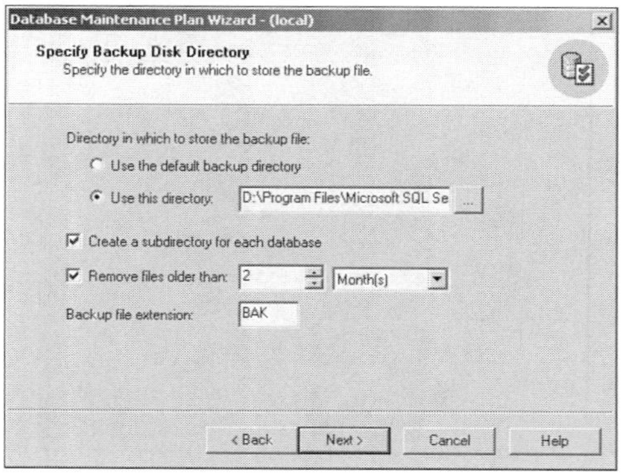

FIGURE 18.39
Database backup options in the Database Maintenance Plan Wizard.

Click Next to see the transaction log backup options (see Figure 18.40). Again, select the appropriate options for your log backups, and click Next. You see a dialog similar to the one you saw earlier in Figure 18.39 —except now it's for your transaction logs. Complete the appropriate entries, and click Next.

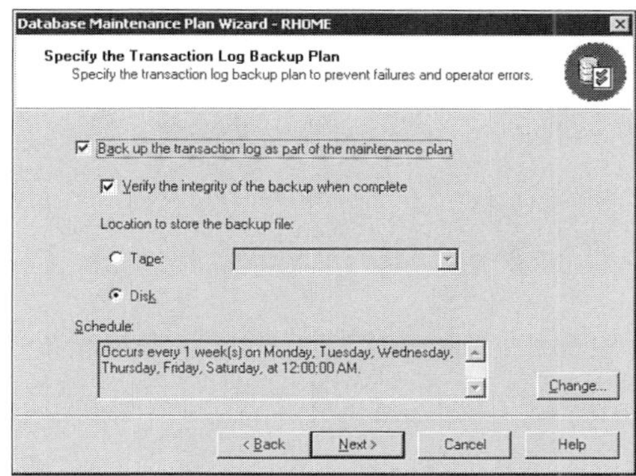

FIGURE 18.40

Transaction log backups in the Database Maintenance Plan Wizard.

The dialog in Figure 18.41 then appears, giving you the opportunity to set the location and options for your transaction log backups. Accept the defaults and click Next.

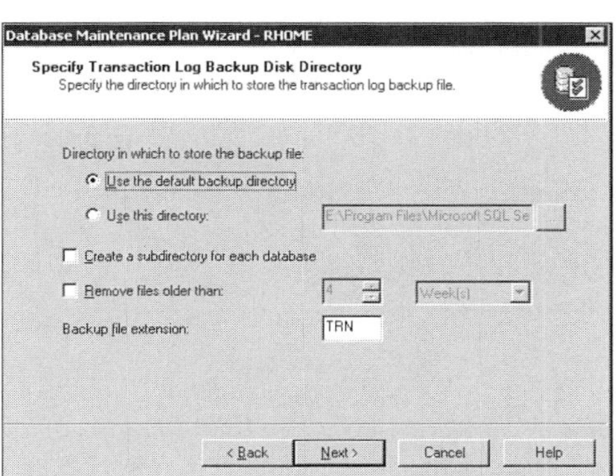

FIGURE 18.41

Specifying the Transaction Log Backup Disk Directory in the Database Maintenance Plan Wizard.

You then have the option of having reports generated about the success or failure of your maintenance plans. As you would expect, you can also configure an email recipient for the maintenance plan (see Figure 18.42).

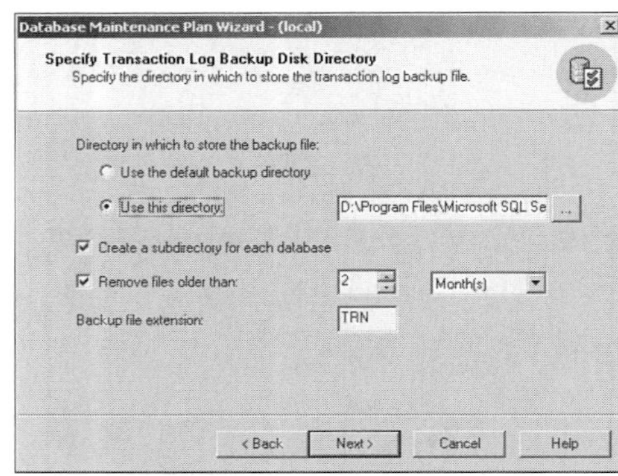

FIGURE 18.42
Specifying reporting options for the Database Maintenance Plan Wizard.

Finally, you have the option to keep historical information about your maintenance plans in the system tables of the MSDB database, and you can limit the number of rows of history kept (see Figure 18.43).

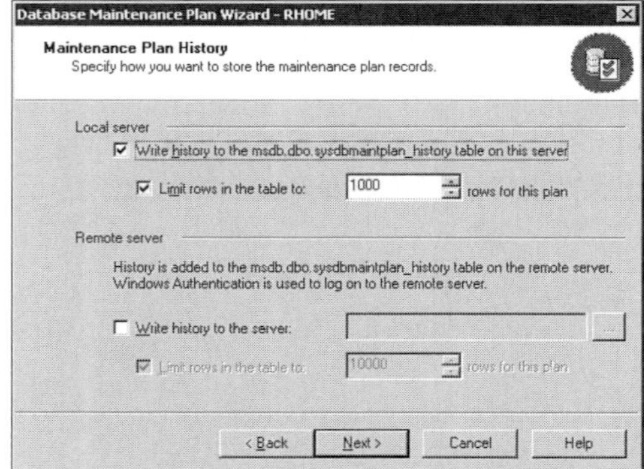

FIGURE 18.43
Capturing historical reporting information for the Database Maintenance Plan Wizard.

Click Next to see a summary of the options you've chosen and a request to name the plan. After you complete this option, several scheduled jobs are configured on your behalf. You can observe them in the Jobs window as described earlier today. After you do this, 90 percent of your database maintenance needs are taken care of for you.

Summary

The SQL Server Agent service isn't required when you're using SQL Server, but it can dramatically increase the functionality of your server. You can set up sophisticated jobs to automate functions such as backups and database integrity checks. You can set up alerts to react when events occur on your SQL Server databases, and you can even use the Windows 2000 performance counters for alerts. You've also seen the power of integrating email and paging features within SQL Server to notify an administrator (or set of administrators) when an alert occurs or when a job is executed.

By taking advantage of SQL Server integration with these features and with a little bit of planning, you can dramatically improve the reliability and responsiveness of your server to problems. Planning ahead for the more common errors that can occur (and setting up tasks to respond to these errors) can dramatically reduce your server's unavailable times and make your users much happier with the job you're doing.

Q&A

Q Which service is responsible for managing scheduled tasks?

A The SQL Server Agent service.

Q Which system table contains the alerts I define on my SQL Server system?

A The `sysalerts` system table in the MSDB database.

Q Which severity level indicates a severe problem with SQL Server itself?

A Severity 17 or higher.

Q What must I do to take advantage of the Performance Monitor integration in SQL Server 2000?

A Set up an alert with the type set to SQL Server performance condition.

Workshop

This section provides quiz questions to help you solidify your understanding of the concepts presented today. In addition to the quiz questions, exercises are provided to let you practice what you've learned today. Try to understand the quiz and exercise answers before continuing on to tomorrow's lesson. Answers are provided in Appendix A, "Answers to Quiz Questions."

Quiz

1. What is the Windows NT/2000 alternative to the SQL Server Agent service to schedule tasks?
2. What profile is SQL Server referring to when it requests a mail profile name?
3. Which command would you use to receive a query via email and send the reply back to a user as a text file attachment?

4. How many scheduled tasks would you create if you wanted your transaction log to be backed up every three hours daily? The first backup should be `with init` (at 5 a.m.), and the rest of the log backups should be `with noinit`.
5. Which tool or wizard would you use to perform regular backups, database reorganizations, and integrity checks?

Exercises

1. If you didn't do so during the chapter, integrate email with SQL Server on your system.
2. Configure a Performance Monitor alert, and then cause the alert condition to fire. Verify that it works as expected.
3. Create a scheduled job to run a Windows 2000 command file. Experiment with the success and failure options of the job steps.
4. Configure the Database Maintenance Plan Wizard for each database on your system.

WEEK 3

DAY 19

Migrating Data Between Database Servers

Yesterday you learned how to automate much of your SQL Server administration duties by using the SQL Server Agent. Today you learn how to move and modify data from one data source to another.

SQL Server 2000 has three principal methods for moving data:

- A backup-and-restore methodology moves all data and other objects, such as tables, from one location to another. This approach doesn't make changes to your data.
- The Bulk Copy Program (BCP) transfers just data from one location to another. Although this utility doesn't make changes to your data, you can use it to gather certain columns and rows from one data source and transfer them to another.
- A bulk insert quickly moves data from a file to your database.

SQL Server 2000 also has a method for both moving and transforming data—the Data Transformation Services (DTS) Manager. This utility, at first glance, is similar to the old Transfer Manager Interface found in SQL Server 6.*x*. You can use DTS to move data, schema, or both. DTS also includes the capability to transform (modify) your data. You can use DTS to change the format of your data from one data type to another, restructure and map your data to different tables, make your data consistent, and validate your data. You can include data logic to summarize, decode, convert, and decompose data.

In the past, much of this logic had to be handled through another utility or programming language such as Delphi or Visual Basic. SQL Server 2000 includes this programmability with DTS through data transformation packages. Because these packages are complete modular units, you can incorporate them into your job scheduler for automated information transfer and modification.

Now it's time to get to work. You'll first review using the backup-and-restore technique to move data from one location to another. You'll then look more closely at the BCP program and then learn about the advantages of using a bulk insert. You will finish today's lesson with a discussion of DTS.

Moving Data with a Backup and Restore

You can use backup and restore to move your databases between servers, but it's probably not the optimal solution. When you back up the database, you also back up all the system tables, including the `sysusers` system table in the database. Backing up this table can cause problems when you recover the database on another server. If the new server doesn't have all the same logins, security mappings might be compromised.

> Using backup and restore to move data from one SQL Server to another isn't recommended for day-to-day movement of your data. You might run into database security issues if users from the originating server don't exist in the destination server. We recommend instead using SQL Server Replication, Transaction Log Shipping, or DTS.
>
> The backup-and-restore technique is recommended in situations in which you are creating a "backup" or "standby" server.

Microsoft now ships SQL Server 2000 with a system stored procedure called `sp_change_users_login`. This stored procedure fixes the biggest problem with using the backup-and-restore technique: the invalid security mappings (SQL Server 2000 validated logins only). After you complete the restore, verify that the logins are appropriately matched to users, and then run this system stored procedure:

SYNTAX

```
sp_change_users_login {Auto_fix | Report | Update_One}
[, 'UserNamePattern'[, 'LoginName']]
```

The `Auto_fix | Report | Update_One` code indicates which action should be taken. Now look at what each part does:

- `Auto_fix` tries to map usernames to login names. However, it assumes things that might not be true. Be wary of using this option.
- `Report` (the default) lists all the broken named links. If you don't specify a parameter, a report is generated to the screen, unless you specify a filename.
- `Update_One` fixes only one specific broken link, as specified by the next set of parameters.
- The `UserNamePattern` is a *like* comparison operator (such as `%` for all users, if you specify `Auto_fix`). The default is `NULL` for `Report` (report on all users). For `Update_One`, it reports on the username you specify here.
- The `LoginName` parameter is the name of a login from the `sysxlogins` table in the `master` database. If you are using `Update_One`, specify the mapping you want corrected. Otherwise, it should be `NULL`.

For example, after a recovery, you have a login of Ted on the new server. Ted has a particular SID or GUID (SIDs are used for Windows 2000-authenticated users; GUIDs are used for SQL Server-authenticated users). When you query the `sysusers` table in the newly recovered database, you might find that a different GUID has been applied for Ted (SIDs are created and maintained by Windows 2000 and don't change). To return Ted's original GUID, you can run the following:

```
sp_change_users_login Update_One, 'Ted', 'Ted'
```

This example changes the GUID field in the `sysusers` table in your recovered database to match the GUID for Ted in the `sysxlogins` table in the `master` database on this server.

19

Using BCP to Load Data

Now that you have seen the potential issues involved with transferring data using the backup-and-restore technique, it's time to look at using the Bulk Copy Program. You can use BCP to load data either into SQL Server from a file or from SQL Server to a file. You can use this utility when you must move data from SQL Server 2000 to a previous version of SQL Server or to another database such as Oracle. You can also import data from another program, another database, or a legacy system.

This utility transfers only to or from a flat file, and it transfers only data. To transfer a database schema, you must use backup and restore or use DTS.

You can append data to an existing table, just as you can with any other program you write that inserts data into a table. However, BCP usually runs faster than a program you can write to perform this kind of data load.

You can also export the data to a file. A new file is created if the file didn't previously exist; otherwise, the file's contents are replaced with the newly downloaded data.

The following common naming conventions for files are generally followed with the BCP program:

`.bcp`	Native-mode data files
`.txt`	ASCII text files
`.csv`	Comma-separated files
`.fmt`	Format files
`.err`	Data-error files

BCP Permissions

To copy data from SQL Server to a file, you must have SELECT permissions on the table or view from which you get data, as well as on the system catalog. Everyone can view the system tables by default if they have a database username, so this shouldn't be much of a concern. You also need operating system permissions to create or modify the file to which you want to write. Of course, file permissions are applicable only in the Windows NT/2000/XP environments, because Windows 9*x* doesn't implement file system permissions. In a Windows NT/2000/XP environment, this typically means the Change or Full Control permissions on the directory, as well as file permissions if you are creating a new file. File allocation table (FAT) and FAT32 partitions aren't secured, so no special permissions are necessary at the file or directory level.

To import data into SQL Server from a file, you need READ permissions on the file (if on an NTFS partition). You also need INSERT permissions on the table you want to load in SQL Server.

Using the BCP Program

Look at the BCP program's syntax:

SYNTAX

```
bcp [[databasename.]owner.]tablename | view_name | "Query"}
{in | out | queryout | format } datafile
[/m maxerrors]
[/f formatfile]
[/e errfile]
[/F firstrow]
[/L lastrow]
[/b batchsize]
[/n] [/c] [/w] [/N]
[/V (60|65|70)] [-6] [/q]
[/C code_page]
[/t field_term]
[/r row_term]
[/i inputfile]
[/o output_file]
[/a packet_size]
[/S server_name\Instance_Name]
/U login_id
[/P password]
[/T] [/v] [/R] [/k] [/E]
[/h "hint [, n]"]
```

Here are the required parameters (those not in square brackets or those contained within braces { and }):

- `tablename` is the name of the table you want to export from or import to. It can be a global temporary table, a view, or a query. The *`databasename`* defaults to the default database of the user running the BCP command. The *`owner`* defaults to the database username of the logged-in user. You might want to specify all the parameters here, such as `pubs.dbo.authors` for the `authors` table owned by user dbo (database owner) in the `pubs` database.
- `in | out | queryout | format` specifies whether data is being loaded into SQL Server or out of SQL Server into a file, or returned as a query.
- *`datafile`* is the name of the file you want to load data from or put data into when running your BCP program. You must specify the full path and filename of the file you want to use. (Be careful with the filenames. If you have spaces in your filenames, you should encapsulate the entire filename and path in double quotes.) As with any Windows 2000 program, it defaults to the local directory from which you run the BCP program if you don't specify a path.

19

Note

Although the data file is required, you might not get an error message if you run BCP without a filename. You can use this to your advantage, however. If you want to create a format file (discussed shortly) but don't actually want to export data, you can leave off the *`datafile`* parameter and just create the format file. Follow the previous naming standards when creating or referencing this file.

- `/U` is followed by the login name you want to be validated with.

The following are the optional parameters:

- `/P` is followed by the password for the login name you provide with the `/U` parameter. If you don't specify a password, you are prompted for one. Needless to say, you should provide a password when running batch BCP programs.
- `/S` is followed by the server name you want to connect to. If you don't specify a server name, BCP attempts to connect to the local copy of SQL Server. If you do specify a server name, BCP connects to your server over the network. From a performance perspective, it's best to load a data file onto the server without the `/S` parameter.
- `/m` *`maxerrors`* indicates the maximum number of errors you can get when importing data into SQL Server (such as poorly formatted rows) before the bulk copy is canceled. This option is particularly useful for testing large data imports. If you type something wrong or have some other problem, you can cause the load to stop quickly rather than run for a long time and then find that the load failed. The default value if you don't provide this parameter is 10 errors.
- `/f` *`formatfile`* specifies the path and filename of the file used to determine how you format a file when extracting data from SQL Server or used to describe how SQL Server should interpret your file when loading data. If you don't provide this parameter on output, BCP prompts you for formatting information. When it's finished, it saves the file as `bcp.fmt` by default.
- `/e` *`errfile`* specifies the path and filename of the file that BCP copies rows to when the rows fail during data loads into SQL Server. With this information, you can examine each row that failed to load properly, correct problems, and then use the error file as your source file and run another BCP. If you don't specify an error file, none is created, and problem rows aren't specifically identified. The naming conventions mentioned earlier suggest an extension of `.err` for this file.
- `/F` *`firstrow`* is a parameter that, if specified, can start you at a relative row number within your file during a data load. If you don't specify this parameter, your load starts with row 1.
- `/L` *`lastrow`* specifies the last row to copy from your file during a data load. The default is to load all rows until the end of the file.
- `/b` *`batchsize`* specifies the number of rows being inserted that will be treated as a batch. In this context, SQL Server treats each batch as a separate transaction. (You'll learn more about this option shortly.) If you don't specify this parameter, the entire load is treated as a single batch.

- `/n` specifies that the data will be exported (or imported) using the native format for SQL Server data types. You should use this option only when moving data from one copy of SQL Server to another and only when moving data on the same platform (Intel, Alpha, and so on).
- `/c` specifies that data imports/exports use character data types instead of SQL Server internal data types. It creates (or uses) a tab-delimited format between each column and a carriage return/line feed to indicate the end of a line.
- `/w` specifies that the data will be transferred using a Unicode format.
- `/N` specifies that the transfer will use Unicode characters for character data and native format for non-character data.
- `/V (60|65|70)` specifies that you are transferring data from a SQL Server 6.0, 6.5, or 7.0 database. When copying from one SQL Server 2000 server to another, this parameter isn't required. This parameter also isn't required to transfer data in character mode, as we don't have to do any type of data type matching.
- `/6` specifies that the transfer uses SQL Server 6.*x* data types. This parameter is provided for backward compatibility.
- `/q` specifies that quoted identifiers are being used. When this is the case, you must be sure that all references to quoted identifiers have double quotation marks around them.
- `/C` *`code_page`* allows you to specify a code page for the data file. This code page applies only to extended characters in the character set.
- `/E` specifies that BCP should load identity columns with values from your data file rather than use the `identity` property of the identity column on your table. For more information about the `identity` property, refer to Day 14, "Ensuring Data Integrity." Otherwise, identity values are assigned as normal.
- `/t` *`field_term`* specifies the default field terminator.
- `/r` *`row_term`* specifies the value that BCP should use to determine when one row ends and another begins.
- `/i` *`inputfile`* allows you to save time. If you don't want to type all these parameters each time you run BCP, you can add them to an input file and then run BCP with that file. When you specify the input file, you must use the full path and filename.
- `/o` *`outputfile`* indicates the name of the file that will receive messages and so on from BCP. You can capture output from running the program and then analyze the output later. This capability is particularly useful when you're running in batch mode.

19

- `/a packet_size` indicates the packet size that will be used on the network. The default value is 4,096 bytes (4KB) except on MS-DOS workstations, where it's 512 bytes. You can configure this option on the server as well.
- `/T` specifies that BCP will connect to SQL Server using a trusted connection.
- `/v` reports the current DB-Library version number.
- `/R` specifies that the date and time data, as well as currency data, aren't ignored but are transferred using the regional settings found on the client computer.
- `/k` specifies that empty columns retain their `NULL` values rather than have a default applied to them.
- `/h "hint"` allows you to specify hints like sort orders on columns and check constraints. See the SQL Server Books Online for additional information on these hints.

Native Mode versus Character Mode

As you just learned, you can transfer data in two ways: native mode and character mode. Character mode specifies that data will be transferred into human-readable format. For example, numbers from an integer column will be human readable. The number 12,500 is readable just the way it is. In native mode, the data is kept in its internal format. The number 12,500 is stored in four bytes: 0x000030D4 (in hex).

Character mode is my preferred format because it's much more flexible. You can use native mode only when transferring data among SQL servers and preferably among servers on the same platform using the same character set. Character mode allows the data to be transferred from or to just about any program. Also, if an error occurs in the file, character mode files are much easier to fix.

If you specify `/c`, you aren't prompted for additional information when running BCP. It is assumed that your data is formatted as plain ASCII text. If you specify `/n`, you also aren't prompted for additional information. Otherwise, you are required to provide information about how you want your file to be formatted.

BCP was run to export a table with a single char(5) column in Figure 19.1.

If you add the `/c` parameter, notice that BCP no longer prompts you to format the output rows and build a format file (see Figure 19.2).

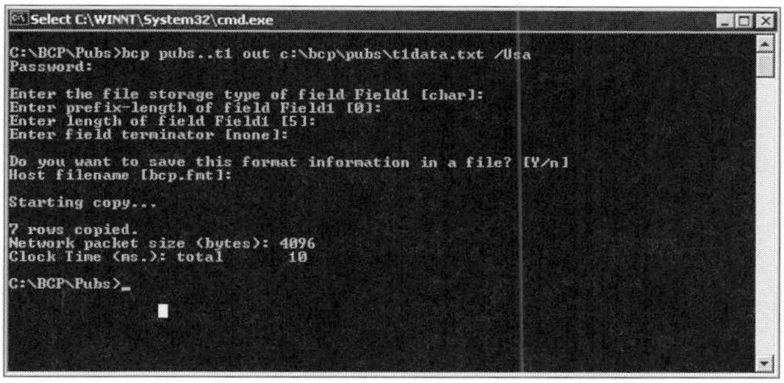

FIGURE 19.1
A basic BCP export.

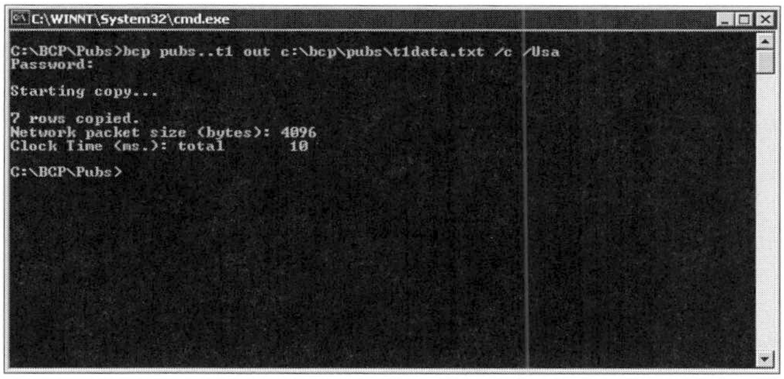

FIGURE 19.2
Exporting data with BCP.

Format Files

Format files specify the layout of data in your files or document the layout for import. When you export data with BCP, you can build a format file if you choose not to use the `/n` or `/c` parameter. For import, you can build a format file yourself.

For example, you can examine each option you are presented with when you specify that you want to create a format file during a BCP export. You receive an additional request for a field length for character data, as represented in the following code. Otherwise, the requested information is consistent between data types.

```
Enter the file storage type of field COL1 [char]:
Enter prefix-length of field COL1 [0]:
Enter length of field COL1 [5]:
Enter field terminator [none]:
```

The file storage type refers to how the data is stored in the file. For character data or a character-only data type, use the data type char. Otherwise, accept the default value from SQL Server. You can use any valid SQL Server data type.

The prefix length determines how much space is reserved to indicate how long this particular field is. For many types, this length can be 0 bytes. For char or varchar data, it can be 1 byte long. For text or image data types, the default length is 4 bytes.

The field length specifies how long the data fields will be when exported. You should probably accept the default values requested by SQL Server.

The last option is the field terminator. Just about any single character is a valid field terminator; however, it's best to specify a character that won't appear in your data. You can specify any value, including these special characters:

- `\t` for a tab
- `\n` for a new line
- `\r` for a carriage return
- `\\` for a backslash
- `\0` for a "null terminator" (no visible terminator)

You can use these terminators for both field terminators (the previous `/t` option) or row terminators (`/r`).

The example produces a format file like this:

```
8.0
1
1       SQLCHAR       0       5       ""       1       COL1
```

The `8.0` on line 1 refers to the version with which this format file is associated. The next line references the number of columns in this format file. Then you see one line showing each column of data represented in the file.

The first number on this line is the relative column number in the data file. The second entry on the line is the data type. BCP format files don't contain SQL Server data types; they contain special data types specific to these BCP files. Valid BCP format file data types include the following:

BCP Data Type	*Used for SQL Server Data Types*
SQLBINARY	binary, image, timestamp, varbinary
SQLBIT	bit
SQLCHAR	char, sysname, text, varchar
SQLDATETIME	datetime
SQLDECIMAL	decimal
SQLFLT8	float

SQLMONEY	money
SQLNUMERIC	numeric
SQLFLT4	real
SQLDATETIM4	smalldatetime
SQLMONEY4	smallmoney
SQLTINYINT	tinyint

The next field is the length of the prefix as described previously. Then the actual data length is listed. The next entry is the field terminator. Then the order of the column in the table data definition language (DDL) is necessary (also called the server column number), finally ending with the column name in the server.

Batch Sizes

When you load data into SQL Server with BCP, by default all data is copied in a single batch and a single transaction. This means that the entire load either completely succeeds or completely fails. Even if you are loading a million rows of data, the entire set of data is still copied in a single transaction. All this data can easily fill a database's transaction logs. Therefore, it's probably appropriate to issue a "commit" periodically and begin a new batch to improve concurrency and allow you to truncate the logon checkpoint, for example. For more information on transactions, see Day 12, "Using Transact-SQL Extensions."

Fast BCP

BCP can operate in two modes: regular BCP and fast BCP. BCP at its lowest level is fundamentally running inserts. This means that each row is processed as an insert operation. It is written to the transaction log, the data is modified, and then any indexes are added. This method isn't the fastest way to add data to SQL Server.

If you drop all indexes on a table and set the Select Into/Bulk Copy option to true for a database, a fast BCP is executed. In this mode, inserts aren't written to the transaction log. Because there are no indexes to be maintained and no transaction logging occurs, this operation runs very quickly. Data types and defaults are still enforced, even during a fast data load. However, rules, constraints, and triggers aren't enforced.

To get a fast data transfer to occur, follow these steps:

1. (Back up your database.) Drop all indexes on the affected tables. (You should script the indexes first so that you can quickly recreate them.)
2. Set the Select Into/Bulk Copy option.
3. Load your data with BCP.

4. Verify integrity that would otherwise be checked by rules, constraints, and triggers (for example, run queries).
5. Re-create your indexes.
6. Turn off the Select Into/Bulk Copy option.
7. Back up your database.

Now perform a couple of BCPs to see how you might use them in the real world. If you want to follow along, you need to copy the data presented here into files on your system. You will work with this table in both examples:

```
USE pubs
GO
CREATE TABLE mytable
(cust_id integer not null,
    cust_name char(30) null,
    city char(20) null ,
    state char(2) not null DEFAULT 'WA',
    zip  char(10) null)
```

This table represents customer data you will get from another system. The only required fields are cust_id and state. Additional data, such as the city, cust_name, and zip fields, are optional (and hence, allow nulls). If a value isn't supplied for state, it defaults to Washington ("WA").

In the first example, load a table from a data file that doesn't have as many columns of data as the table. Your comma-delimited data file should look like this:

```
cust_id,city,state,zip_code
```

For example, two sample rows might look like the following:

```
1,Seattle,WA,98102
2,Bellevue,WA,98004
```

To load this file properly, you need to create a format file. In this case, use this format file (which you should copy if you want to run this example):

```
8.0
5
1     SQLINT     0    9     ","       1     cust_id
2     SQLCHAR    0    0     ""        0     cust_name
3     SQLCHAR    0    20    ","       3     city
4     SQLCHAR    0    2     ","       4     state
5     SQLCHAR    0    10    "\r\n"    5     zip
```

Notice that you must change the server column number for cust_name to 0. This value tells BCP that the data isn't being passed in this file. You also must reset the field length of this column to 0 and specify no row terminator.

Now, when loading with BCP and with fewer columns in the data file than in the table, you see something similar to Figure 19.3.

FIGURE 19.3
Loading with BCP.

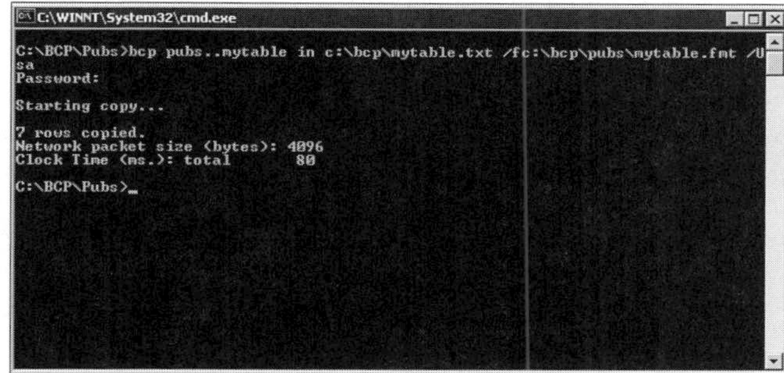

Now perform the second example. This time your file has more data than you want to load. Your file should be in the following format, where the address is 30 characters long:

```
cust_id,cust_name,cust_addr,city,state,zip_code
```

Again, examine the two rows of sample data:

```
1,Joe Smith,1200 First Ave,Seattle,WA,98102
2,Marilyn Jones,123 116 Ave NE,Bellevue,WA,98004
```

This time a format file reflects the column that exists in the data file but doesn't exist in SQL Server:

```
8.0
6
1     SQLINT     0    9     ","        1    cust_id
2     SQLCHAR    0    30    ","        2    cust_name
3     SQLCHAR    0    0     ","        0    cust_addr
4     SQLCHAR    0    20    ","        3    city
5     SQLCHAR    0    2     ","        4    state
6     SQLCHAR    0    10    "\r\n"     5    zip
```

In this example, you add a field for cust_addr but indicate that it doesn't exist in the table by specifying its server column number as 0 and its data length as 0. Notice that you still need the field terminator so that BCP knows how much to skip over in your file.

As you can see, BCP is quite flexible, but working with format files can require some time to get right.

The real beauty of bulk copy and format files is that the bulk copy is a command-line utility that you can add to your batch scripts for automated processing.

Working with the BULK INSERT Command

With the `BULK INSERT` command, you can read a data file as though it were an OLE DB recordset. This way, SQL Server can move the entire recordset into the table in one step, or in several steps, if you are using a predetermined batch size. The syntax of the `BULK INSERT` command is as follows:

SYNTAX

```
BULK INSERT [['database_name'.]['owner'].]{'table_name'
FROM data_file}[WITH
([ BATCHSIZE [= batch_size]]
[[,] CHECK_CONSTRAINTS]
[[,] CODEPAGE [= 'ACP' | 'OEM' | 'RAW' | 'code_page']]
[[,] DATAFILETYPE [= {'char' | 'native' | 'widechar' | 'widenative'}]]
[[,] FIELDTERMINATOR [= 'field_terminator']]
[[,] FIRSTROW [= first_row]]
[[,] FIRE_TRIGGERS]
[[,] FORMATFILE [= 'format_file_path']]
[[,] KEEPIDENTITY]
[[,] KEEPNULLS]
[[,] KILOBYTES_PER_BATCH [= kilobytes_per_batch]]
[[,] LASTROW [= last_row]]
[[,] MAXERRORS [= max_errors]]
[[,] ORDER ({column [ASC | DESC]}[,...n])]
[[,] ROWS_PER_BATCH [= rows_per_batch]]
[[,] ROWTERMINATOR [= 'row_terminator']]
[[,] TABLOCK]))
```

In this syntax,

- *`'database_name'`* is the name of the database in which the table you want to bulk-insert data into is located.
- *`data_file`* is the full path and filename you want to import.
- `CHECK_CONSTRAINTS` specifies that table constraints are checked during the bulk insert operation.
- `CODEPAGE` specifies the code page found in the data file. This option is necessary only when the data is of a character data type and uses extended characters.
- `DATAFILETYPE` specifies what format the data in the file is stored as.
- `FIELDTERMINATOR` specifies what character to use as a field terminator. The default is a tab (`\t`).
- `FIRSTROW` specifies with which row you want to start the bulk insert process. The default is the first row in the data file (that is, `FIRSTROW = 1`).
- `FIRE_TRIGGERS` specifies that `INSERT` and `INSTEAD OF` triggers defined on the destination tables will fire for each row that is inserted by the bulk copy. By default, BCP does not fire triggers.

- `FORMATFILE` specifies a full path and filename of a format file to be used with the bulk insert. It works similarly to the format file created for the BCP command.
- `KEEPIDENTITY` specifies that bulk-inserted `IDENTITY` values keep their values rather than have new values assigned as part of the insert process.
- `KEEPNULLS` specifies that `NULL` values retain their values when bulk-inserted.
- `KILOBYTES_PER_BATCH` specifies the number of bytes to transfer at a time. There's no default value because the `BULK INSERT` command seeks to move the entire data set in one chunk.
- `LASTROW` specifies the last row of data to move. By default, it is the last row in the data file.
- `MAXERRORS` specifies the maximum number of errors allowed before SQL Server terminates the `BULK INSERT` process. The default is `10`.
- `ORDER` allows you to specify the sort order within the data file. If the data file is sorted and has a different sort order from the data in your table, specifying this option can greatly enhance performance.
- `ROWS_PER_BATCH` specifies how many rows to move in each batch. You can use this option when `BATCHSIZE` isn't specified.
- `ROWTERMINATOR` specifies the end of a row of data. The default is the newline (`\n`) character.
- `TABLOCK` specifies that a table lock will be used for the duration of this bulk insert. This lock can have performance benefits for the bulk insert operation.

For additional information on using `BULK INSERT`, refer to the Microsoft SQL Server Books Online or *Microsoft SQL Server 2000 Unleashed* by Sams Publishing.

Working with Data Transformation Services

Data in your organization might be stored in a large variety of formats and locations. With DTS, you can import and export data between multiple heterogeneous data sources and data destinations. All this takes place through the use of OLE DB providers. You can transfer data and schema; and if you are working with two Microsoft SQL Server 2000 computers, you can also transfer database objects such as indexes, data types, constraints, and tables by using the Object Transfer within the DTS component.

DTS exposes several different interfaces that allow you to do the following:

- Schedule DTS packages to transfer and transform data automatically
- Create custom DTS packages that can be integrated into third-party products through the Component Object Model (COM) interface

- Transfer data to and from the following:

  Microsoft Access

  Microsoft Excel

  SQL Server

- Open database connectivity–compliant databases such as Oracle, DB2, and Informix
- Open ASCII text files (both flat files and delimited files)

A data transformation can be one of any operations applied to your data before it's stored in the destination. Operations can include the calculation of new values, the concatenation of values, breaking of values like a name field into a first name and last name field, as well any type of data cleaning you want to enforce.

DTS can be broken down into three major sections:

Packages	A package encompasses all the steps and tasks needed to perform an import, export, or transformation.
Import and Export wizards	Use these wizards to interactively create a DTS package. These wizards are also available from the command line as `dtswiz` and `dtsrun`. Using them from the command line allows you not only to script them but also to bypass many of the dialogs the wizards show.
DTS Designer	This desktop environment comes complete with toolboxes and palettes, which experienced administrators can use to visually create complex tasks and packages. The DTS Designer is beyond the scope of this book. See *Microsoft SQL Server 2000 Unleashed*, published by Sams Publishing, or the SQL Server Books Online for additional information.

Understanding Data Transformation Packages

As you learned earlier, a DTS package is a set of one or more tasks executed in a coordinated sequence. These packages can be created automatically through the Import and Export wizards, manually through the use of a scripting language, or visually through the DTS Designer. After you create a DTS package, it's completely self-contained and can be run from the Enterprise Manager, the Task Scheduler, or the `dtsrun` command-line utility.

When you create a DTS package, you can store it in various formats, each with its own distinct advantages.

SQL Server's MSDB Database

You can store your DTS packages in the MSDB database. When they are stored here, other SQL Server 2000 servers can connect to the packages and use them. Less storage overhead is involved in storing them here than in using the Microsoft Repository. Having less overhead can help minimize the amount of space and time required to access and use the package.

Meta Data Services

When you store a package in the Repository, you can make it available to other SQL Server 2000 computers. The Repository has the advantage of making metadata available to other applications. The other major advantage of the Repository is its capability to track the lineage or history of transformations that the data has gone through. This information includes data sources, destinations, and changes applied to the data.

COM-Based Structured Storage

COM supplies a storage architecture made up of data objects and data streams. Data objects are analogous to directories in a file system, whereas stream objects are analogous to the files. One major advantage of the COM-based storage model is that stream objects can easily be distributed through network file servers or email. Any COM-compliant program or programming language can then access the COM objects.

Note Because DTS is a COM-based set of components and servers, you can use any COM-compliant programming language such as Visual Basic, PerlScript, or JScript to define your own customized transformations, packages, scripting objects, and data pump interfaces.

Note You can also store your packages as Visual Basic .bas modules.

Package Security

All packages can have two types of security applied to them: the DTS owner and password and the DTS operator password. A DTS package stored in COM-based structured storage can also be encrypted. When a package is encrypted, all its components are encrypted except for the CreationDate, Description, ID, Name, and VersionID information.

A user or application with the DTS Owner password has complete access to all package components. When a package is saved without an owner password, it's not encrypted. When you save a package with an owner password, it's encrypted by default.

A user or application with the DTS Operator password can execute the package but can't access any package components directly.

Package Components

A DTS package is made up of several components that interact to form the package and the workflows: task objects, step objects, connection objects, and the data pump. Take a closer look at each of these individual components. You will then see how these components interact within the package architecture.

Task Objects

Packages are made up of one or more tasks. Each task defines a process or action that should be taken. Tasks are used to do the following work:

- Run a SQL command or batch
- Move data from one OLE DB data source to an OLE DB data destination
- Launch external programs, command executions, or batch files
- Gather results from another DTS package
- Execute another DTS package
- Execute a COM-compliant script (Visual Basic, JScript, PerlScript, and so on)

Although a task can be associated with more than one step, that task can have only one instance of itself running at any one time. This means that if step 2 and step 4 are both associated with Task A, and step 2 is now running, step 4 can't begin until Task A in step 2 has completed.

Step Objects

Step objects coordinate the flow of tasks that make up your DTS package. Tasks that don't have an associated step object are never executed. Step objects are used to create your workflow.

Steps can be executed in several different ways. For example, you can design a step to fire only when the prior step finishes, only when the prior step finishes successfully, or only when the prior step fails. This type of relationship is based on precedence constraints. This means that the latter step has a precedence constraint on the prior step. After all the precedence constraints for a step are satisfied, the step can execute.

Suppose that you have a two-step package you want to run. Step 1 is a `CREATE TABLE` statement. Step 2 is a `CREATE INDEX` statement. Step 2 fires only after step 1 finishes successfully.

Because task objects are separate from step objects, you can associate one or more steps to a particular task object.

New Term Step objects can also be executed conditionally based on different runtime conditions. You can also execute multiple steps simultaneously to improve your performance. This is known as running steps *in parallel*. To do so, create steps that don't have any precedence constraints assigned to them.

To assign precedence constraints, you can use the following values from prior steps, or you can use return codes generated by a scripting language:

- **On success**—Step 2 waits until step 1 finishes successfully before beginning.
- **On failure**—This code allows an alternative branch of steps to run when an error is encountered.
- **Unconditional**—Step 2 doesn't begin until step 1 finishes, regardless of success or failure.

Using the scripting languages allows you to implement `IF...THEN...ELSE`–style logic to your workflows.

DTS Connection Objects

DTS packages that connect to data sources have connection objects. The two types of connection objects are as follows:

- *Data source* connections specify the data source and destination servers, location, and format of the data and necessary passwords.
- *Data file* connections specify the source and destination files, including the location and format of the data.

A connection is made when a task object that needs it is invoked in a step. Otherwise, the connection is dormant.

DTS Data Pump

The data pump is an OLE DB service provider that handles the importing, exporting, and Data Transformation Services. It loads as an in-process COM server in the SQL Server 2000 process space. The data pump is used with two or more connection objects. Because the data pump is COM based, you can extend its functionality by using any COM-compliant programming language. Through these extensions, you can create your own complex procedural logic programs that you can implement and reuse. Figure 19.4 represents the flow of information through the data pump component.

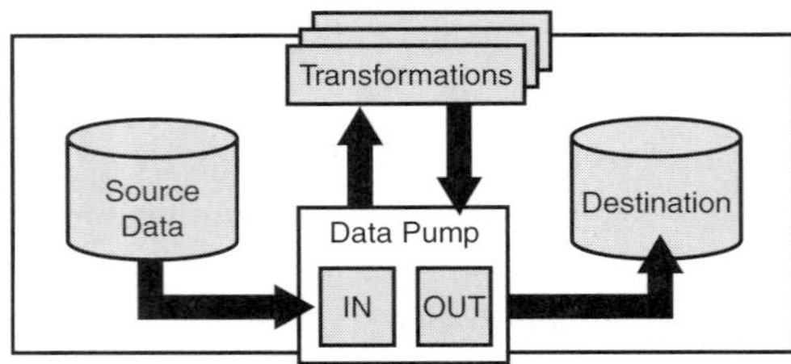

FIGURE 19.4
The DTS architecture.

DTS Object Transfer

The DTS Object Transfer is the upgrade to SQL Server 6.*x*'s Transfer Manager Interface (TMI). With the DTS Object Transfer, you can move data, schema, and objects from SQL Server to other SQL Server data sources. You do so by using the Import and Export Wizards, which you'll learn about later today.

DTS Object Transfer uses the SQL-DMO rather than the OLE DB functionality to make connections to data sources and data destinations.

Exporting Data with the DTS Import and Export Wizards

Through the use of the wizards, you can interactively create DTS packages for importing, exporting, and transforming your data. DTS is smart enough to check the destination objects for their existence. If the objects already exist, you can have the wizard include a step to drop and re-create the objects.

As a DTS user, you can do all the following:

- Copy a table
- Copy the results of a query
- Create a query with the Query Builder inside the wizard
- Specify connection settings for data sources and destinations
- Transform data, including column headings, data type, size, scale, precision, and nullability
- Run a COM-compliant script
- Save packages in the Repository, in the MSDB, or to a COM-structured storage location
- Schedule a completed package for execution

Using the DTS Export Wizard

Follow these steps to export data:

1. Open the SQL Enterprise Manager, and connect to your server.
2. From the Tools menu, select Wizards.
3. In the Select Wizard dialog, expand the Data Transformation Services node, and then select the DTS Export Wizard (see Figure 19.5). Click OK to continue.

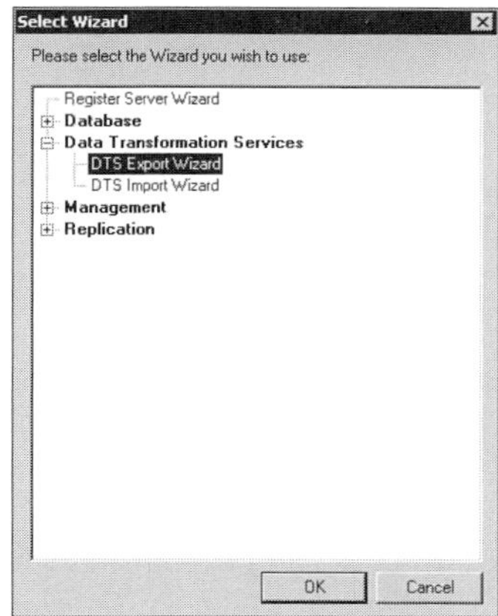

FIGURE 19.5
Select the DTS Export Wizard.

4. In the DTS Export Wizard dialog, click Next to continue.
5. From the Choose a Data Source dialog (see Figure 19.6), you can select an export server, login authentication credentials, and the export database. Select the `pubs` database from your local SQL Server as the export database.

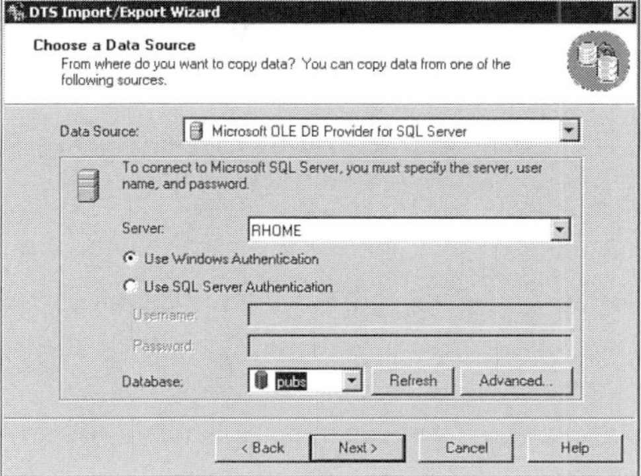

FIGURE 19.6
Choose a data source.

6. Click the Advanced button to see the advanced properties you can attach to this package. Return to the Choose a Data Source dialog, and click Next to continue.
7. In the Choose a Data Destination dialog, you can set the same types of properties as shown in the Choose a Data Source dialog. You are going to create a new database in your local server to export your data to. From the database combination box, select <new>. The Create Database dialog appears (see Figure 19.7).

FIGURE 19.7
Create a database.

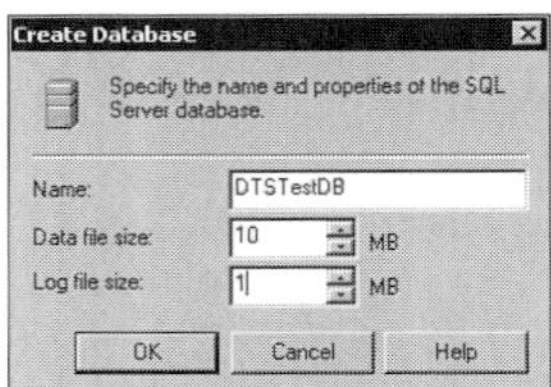

8. Fill in the Create Database information as shown in Figure 19.7. The database name is `DTSTestDB`, the file size is 10MB, and the log size should be left at 1MB. When you're finished, click OK. The Choose a Destination dialog appears, ensuring that DTSTestDB is selected (see Figure 19.8). Click Next to continue.

FIGURE 19.8
Choose a destination.

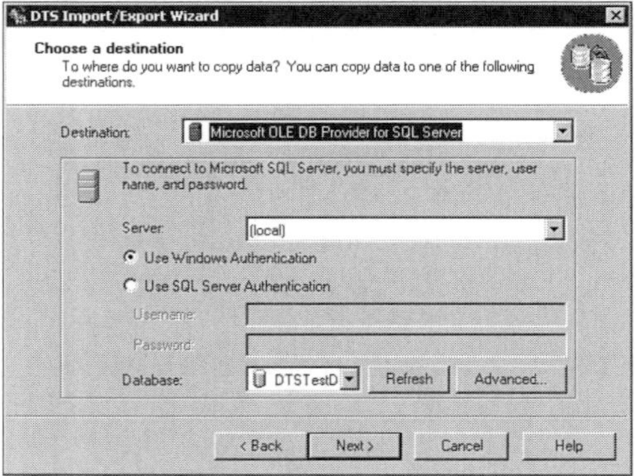

9. From the Specify Table Copy or Query dialog (see Figure 19.9), you can choose to gather tables, run a query, or transfer database objects. Click Next to continue.
10. From the Select Source Tables and Views dialog (see Figure 19.10), select the `authors`, `titles`, and `titleauthor` tables. Leave the destination tables to their defaults. You might have noticed that each table has a Transform (…) button. If you click this button, you are given some advanced transformation options, as shown in Figures 19.11 and 19.12.

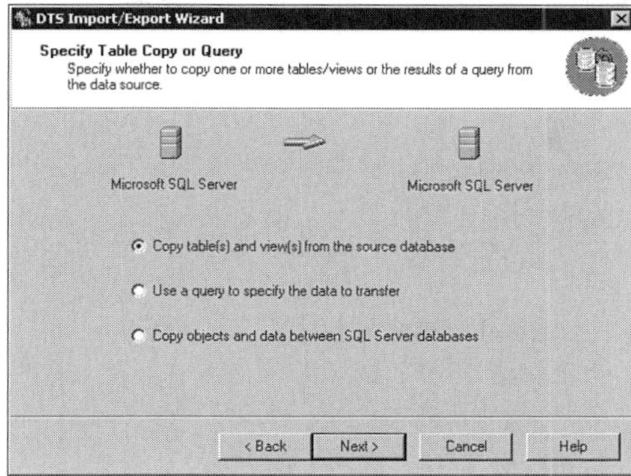

FIGURE 19.9

Specify a table copy or query.

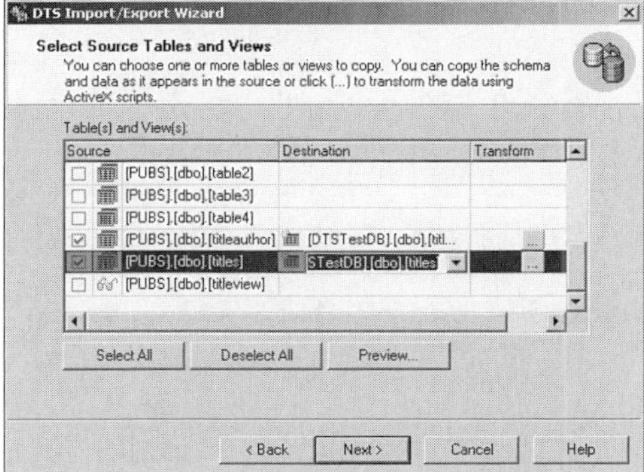

FIGURE 19.10

Select source tables and views.

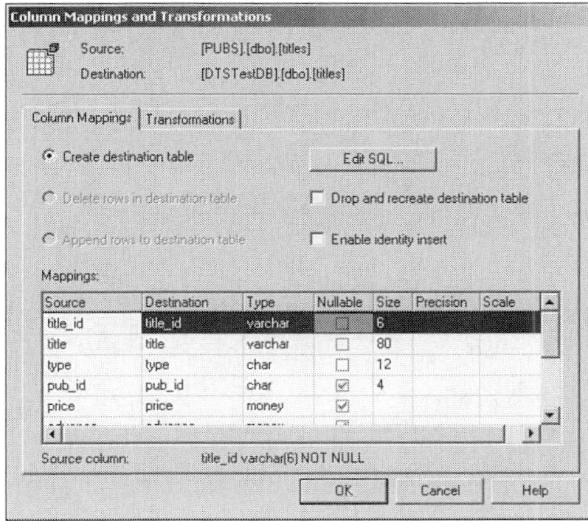

FIGURE 19.11

The Column Mappings tab.

19

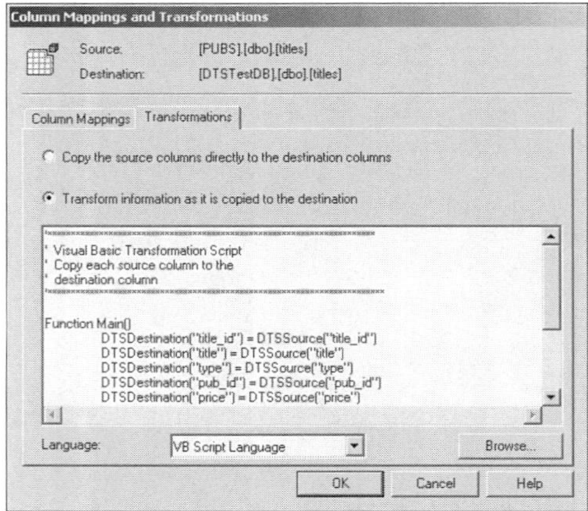

FIGURE 19.12

The Transformations scripting tab.

11. Click OK to close the Advanced window, then click Next on the Select Source Tables and Views dialog to continue. The Save, Schedule, and Replicate Package dialog appears (see Figure 19.13). From this dialog, specify that you want to run the package immediately and save the package in SQL Server.

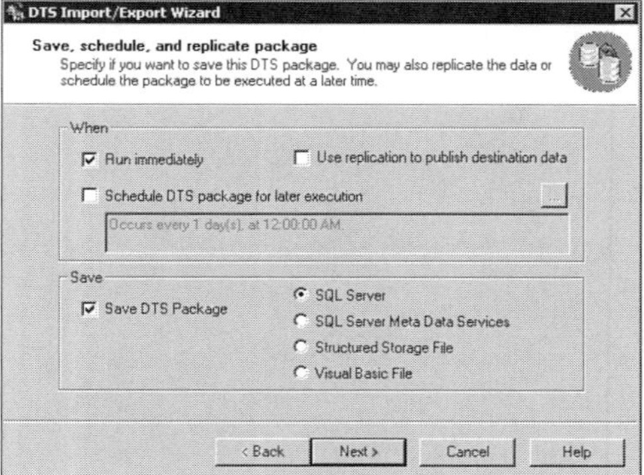

FIGURE 19.13

Save, schedule, and replicate the package.

12. The Save DTS Package dialog appears. You should select a package name like TestExport. You should also specify the storage location, as shown in Figure 19.14.
13. When the Finish dialog appears, click Finish to complete the package creation and save. Because you scheduled the package to run immediately, you see the transfer take place and a summary grid, which shows the completed process (see Figure 19.15).

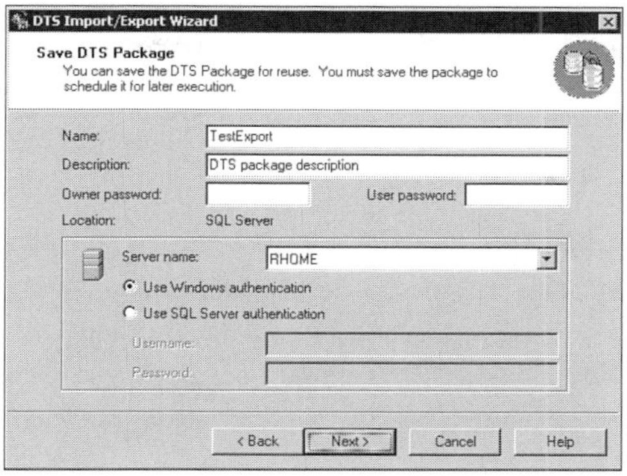

FIGURE 19.14
Save a DTS package.

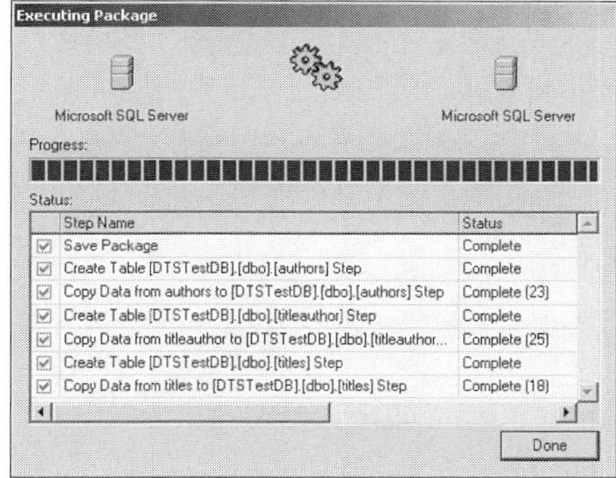

FIGURE 19.15
Transferring data.

14. Click OK to the message box (which reports the overall status of the package execution), and then click Done when you're finished. Look at your new database and the tables that were transferred.

19

Transferring Database Objects

You can use the DTS Object Transfer within the DTS screens to transfer database objects such as stored procedures and views from one SQL Server 2000 computer to another. This type of transfer can be done across different platforms and different sort orders.

To work with the Object Transfer, follow steps 1 through 9 from the "Using the DTS Export Wizard" section. In step 9, specify the Copy Objects and Databases Between SQL Server 2000 Databases option, as shown in Figure 19.9. You then can specify that you want to transfer all objects, or if you deselect that option, you can pick and choose individual objects to transfer, including tables, views, stored procedures, user-defined data types, and others.

Summary

Today you learned several different methods for moving data from one location to another. SQL Server 2000 has three principal methods for moving data and one for both moving and transforming data.

You can use a backup-and-restore methodology to move all data and table schema from one location to another. This approach doesn't make changes to your data. You can use the Bulk Copy Program (BCP) to transfer just data from one location to another. Although this utility doesn't make changes to your data, you can use it to gather only certain columns and rows from one data source and transfer them to another.

The final element is the new Data Transformation Services (DTS) Manager in SQL Server 2000. This utility is similar to the old Transfer Manager Interface found in SQL Server 6.*x*. You can use DTS to move data, schema, or both. DTS also includes the capability to transform (modify) your data. You can use DTS to change the format of your data from one data type to another, restructure and map your data to different locations, make your data consistent, and validate it. You can include data logic to summarize, decode, convert, and decompose data.

Q&A

Q Should I use DTS or replication to move data around?

A Normally, when you want to make data available to other SQL servers, you should use replication, because it runs regularly and includes functionality to guarantee consistency.

Q The DTS looks interesting, but will I really use it?

A In our consulting practices, we have found that a large part of our job is data cleaning. Many companies have large mainframe databases that dump flat ASCII text files regularly. These ASCII files must be imported into SQL Server. The DTS program allows you not only to import the data but also to make the necessary data type changes, split columns (like Name into First Name and Last Name), and perform many other transformations.

Q You talked briefly about the DTS Designer. Is it really difficult to work with?

A The answer really depends on you. Administrators familiar with a visual interface for programming like Visual Basic or Delphi will find the DTS Designer fairly easy to use. For a beginner, it can be a daunting task because so much functionality is exposed through the designer. I suggest that you save your packages from the wizards and then look at them in the Designer. This approach helps ease you into its use.

Workshop

This section provides quiz questions to help you solidify your understanding of the concepts presented today. In addition to the quiz questions, exercises are provided to let you practice what you've learned today. Try to understand the quiz and exercise answers before continuing on to tomorrow's lesson. Answers are provided in Appendix A, "Answers to Quiz Questions."

Quiz

1. What permissions are required for you to use the BCP program?
2. What database objects does BCP enforce and ignore when you're transferring data into a table?
3. What's required to do a fast BCP?
4. When using DTS, what can you do to your data?
5. You want to upgrade a database from an Intel Pentium II 400MHz server running Windows 2000 to a DEC Alpha running Windows NT 4.0. You also are changing your sort order. How can this be accomplished?

Exercises

1. Use the DTS Import Wizard to do the following:
    - Create a new database called `DTSNWind`.
    - Transfer all objects, but no data, from the Northwind database.
2. Use the Export Wizard to move all data from the Northwind database to your newly created `DTSNWind` database.

WEEK 3

DAY 20

Performance Monitoring Basics and Tools

Yesterday you examined the Data Transformation Services (DTS), BCP, and `BULK INSERT`. You learned how to move data from one SQL Server to another and load data into SQL Server from operating system files such as text files or comma-delimited files (CSV)—for example, those that might come from an Excel spreadsheet.

Today you examine how to configure and monitor SQL Server 2000. This lesson includes configuring your hardware, Windows 2000 (you can't do much with Windows 9*x*), and SQL Server itself. In terms of monitoring SQL Server, various tools are available to monitor how SQL Server is performing. These tools include the Windows performance monitor, the SQL Server Profiler, and the Index Tuning Wizard.

One point must be clear from the start. The best thing you can do to make your database perform is to implement a properly normalized physical database design. If you implement your database design poorly (or don't design your database), nothing you can do with hardware or software will ever make your database perform well.

Hardware Selection and Tuning

First, consider the proper selection of hardware. People often ask what the most important component of a SQL Server system is. A well-functioning machine requires components that work well together. However, if you had to pick one component, it would have to be memory. SQL Server rarely has too much random access memory (RAM). Nevertheless, you should examine each component in detail.

Memory

SQL Server requires RAM to hold all data and index pages, as well as log records, in memory. It also holds compiled queries and stored procedures. SQL Server addresses one major area of concern about memory by automatically using all available memory on your computer. You can tune this memory usage, and you will examine how to do so later today.

Asking how much RAM your computer should have is a separate question. A good starting point on Windows 2000 or Windows XP systems being deployed with SQL Server is probably 256MB of RAM. If you can afford more, RAM is a good place to invest your money. For small implementations of SQL Server (and *small* is a hard term to describe), 128MB of RAM might be enough; but given today's inexpensive memory, you should start with the largest amount of RAM possible. On Windows 9*x* computers, the same recommendation applies. Although SQL Server can run with 32MB of RAM on your computer, this amount might not be enough to get the best performance possible out of SQL Server. SQL Server 2000 can take advantage of 2GB of RAM on Windows NT 4.0 and 3GB of RAM on Windows NT 4.0 Server Enterprise Edition. With AWE (Addressing Windowing Extensions) support, SQL Server can support 8GB of RAM on Windows 2000 Advanced Server and 64GB of RAM on Windows 2000 Datacenter Server. For more details on AWE, see your Windows 2000 documentation.

Processor

As with any system, having plenty of central processing unit (CPU) power never hurts. Although SQL Server isn't necessarily the most CPU-intensive program, it certainly can use the CPU, depending on the workload being run. SQL Server and Windows 2000 can both take advantage of multiple processors. SQL Server 2000 Standard Edition can take advantage of up to four processors. SQL Server 2000 Enterprise Edition can support 32 processors. SQL Server is programmed to run a workload spread out over multiple CPUs and to provide thread parallelization (running SQL Server simultaneously on multiple CPUs, including parallelization within a single query). Most parallel features only function in parallel in SQL Server Enterprise Edition.

Network

Although the network is often overlooked, it is critical to the success of your deployment of SQL Server. First, consider what kind of network card you should use in your server. You should use a 32 or 64-bit bus mastering network card. Not only does it have the best throughput in terms of raw amounts of data, but it also tends to have the least impact on the CPU. Also, consider the type of network card. Most networks are still 10MB Ethernet, although local networks with servers are often 100MB networks. You can also use other fast networking technologies, including GigaNet CLan, Compaq ServerNet, ATM (Asynchronous Transfer Mode), and FDDI (Fiber Distributed Data Interface). Remember that all your database activity has to be sent through the network. If you have a 10MB Ethernet network card, you can expect throughput of about 1.2MB per second (MBps). If you want more than that amount of data to be sent out of SQL Server, you need to add a second or even a third network card, or use a faster technology.

Note

> Be sure to put each network card on a separate physical network. If you place multiple network cards on a single network, you get duplicate name errors, and some or all network cards could be disabled because your SQL Server machine announces its presence on the network one network card at a time. When the second network card announces its server name, the first card announces that it already has this name. Because Network Basic Input/Output System (NetBIOS) has a flat name space, all names must be unique on the network. Therefore, the secondary network cards return errors about name problems and do not function properly. Again, simply place each network card on its own subnet to avoid this problem. If you are using DNS only with the Active Directory, this consideration probably isn't as big a concern, but most environments will use both NetBIOS and DNS for some time.

Disks

Disks are a critical component of any server because the data is located there. If you want access to your data, you typically must access it from your hard disk. The speed with which the data is written back to the disks is also important. You also must consider bandwidth. Then there's…okay, I'll stop. You first must examine what kinds of disks you should use. More small disks are better than fewer large disks. Small computer system interface (SCSI) disks tend to perform better than integrated development environment (IDE) disks, but they cost a little bit more. However, they're worth the money. It's also worthwhile to use multiple SCSI cards in your computer, with disks distributed among them. Make sure that all components of the SCSI system are the same speed (all fast/wide, for example). Mismatches can cause devices to default to the slowest possible speed.

Another question that comes up frequently is the recommended layout of disks. System files and transaction log files should be duplexed. This means that they are mirrored, preferably on different SCSI controllers. The data files have two different options, either of which will work. The most expensive option is to have disk stripes and then mirror the stripes. You can configure mirrored stripes by using hardware striping, and then use Windows 2000 mirroring of the stripes. This way, any disk in the system can be lost without causing any performance loss. Many newer hardware systems now natively support this type of disk protection (known as RAID 1+0, or RAID 10). You can also set up the disks using RAID 5 (redundant array of inexpensive disks), the less expensive option. However, your performance isn't as good using this option, and if you lose one of the disks, you see a significant loss of performance. Figures 20.1 and 20.2 show recommended intermediate and advanced configurations.

FIGURE 20.1

A high-fault–tolerant /moderate-performing server configuration.

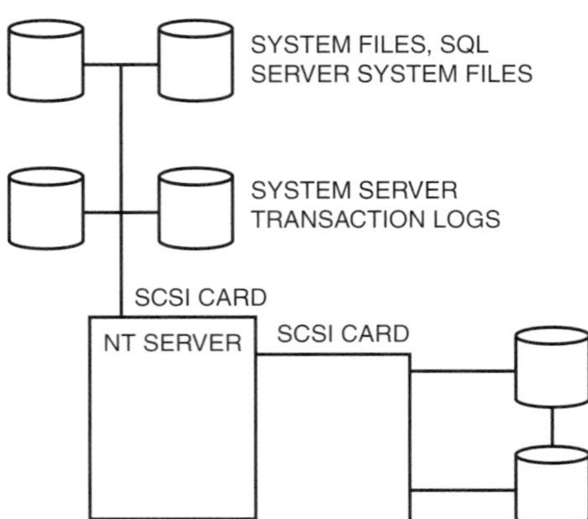

You must consider a lot of information about disks. Most well-known server vendors do an excellent job of putting together packages with all this in mind. We've worked with servers from Compaq, HP, Data General, and IBM and had good luck with them. Most are superbly engineered, and the support staffs from the vendor companies understand how to tune and configure SQL Server and recommend systems that support Windows 2000 and SQL Server well.

FIGURE 20.2

A high-fault–tolerant/high-performing server configuration.

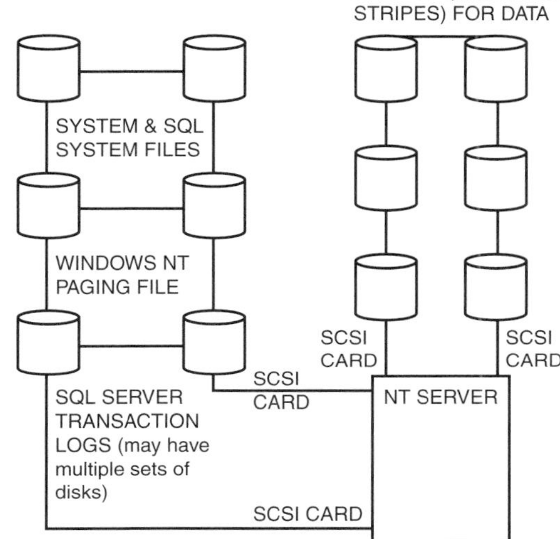

Windows 2000 Configuration Parameters

Most Windows 2000 configuration options that must be set are chosen by default by the setup program. The most important configuration option is to Maximize Throughput for Network Applications as the configuration value of the File and Printer Sharing for Microsoft Networks (your Server service). To find it, go to Control Panel, Network and Dial-up Connections, your network card (probably called Local Area Connection), select Properties, and then select the properties of File and Printer Sharing for Microsoft Networks (see Figure 20.3). The SQL Server setup program sets this value correctly, and you shouldn't change it.

FIGURE 20.3

The File and Printer Sharing for Microsoft Networks Properties dialog.

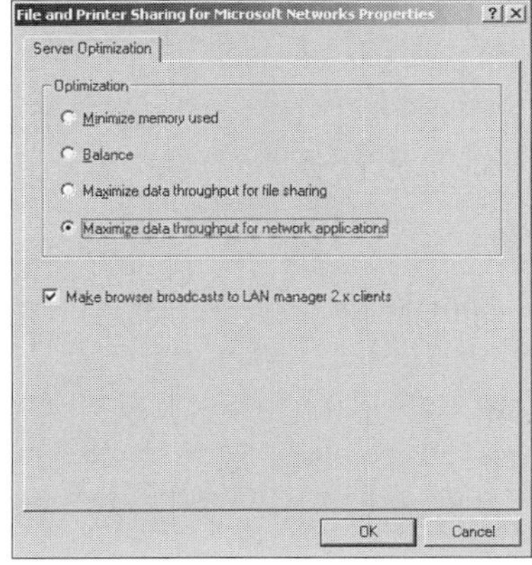

20

As you learned on Day 2, "Installing Microsoft SQL Server 2000," SQL Server should be installed on a member server (or standalone server—they're basically the same thing). SQL Server can function on a domain controller, but this implementation isn't recommended. Domain controllers have additional demands on their memory that can conflict with SQL Server's memory needs.

This brings up the topic of additional services running on the SQL Server machine. Being a domain controller is mostly a function of another service running on the server. Other services such as Dynamic Host Configuration Protocol (DHCP) Server, Windows Internet Naming Service (WINS) server, Domain Name Service (DNS) server, or other Microsoft server applications will most likely interfere with SQL Server's performance. You shouldn't run these services on the same machine as your database.

Another consideration is the Windows 2000 paging file. You should place the paging file on a disk not being used by SQL Server. Otherwise, usage of the page file might interfere with SQL Server.

The earlier section on "Disks" mentions using RAID to protect data. Using a hardware implementation of mirroring or RAID 5, rather than Windows 2000 Server's RAID capabilities, is a good idea. Most hardware implementations will outperform Windows 2000 server's built-in RAID capabilities.

Windows 2000 Performance Monitor Counters

This book doesn't attempt to provide a thorough discussion of Windows 2000 performance monitoring or performance counters. The Windows 2000 Resource Kit provides a good discussion of Windows 2000 performance monitoring. However, a few counters are very important for SQL Server and deserve mention.

The objects and counters described here can be monitored with the Windows 2000 performance monitor tool (the Performance MMC snap-in). Now let's look at each of the four types of resources you already learned about today.

Memory

One consideration for a machine dedicated to SQL Server is memory. In general, you should keep page faults to a minimum. Page faults occur when data is needed in memory but isn't found and must be fetched from disk. You can monitor this counter by using the MEMORY object, Page Faults/Sec counter. Although the value won't be 0, it shouldn't be a high value (that is, whatever isn't normal for your server). In general, you want this value to be as close to 0 as possible.

Another memory counter to consider is the MEMORY object, Available Bytes counter. This value shouldn't fall below 4MB. If it does, Windows 2000 attempts to reclaim memory from applications (including SQL Server) to free up some memory. If this value falls below 4MB frequently, you might have assigned too much memory to SQL Server. However, SQL Server automatically prevents paging unless you turn off automatic memory tuning.

Processor

The counter most commonly monitored is the PROCESSOR object, % Processor Time counter. It tells you how busy the CPU is overall. Each CPU in the system has an instance number, starting at 0, or you can monitor all CPUs with the _Total counter.

Network

For network monitoring, you can use either the performance monitor tool or a network monitoring tool, such as Microsoft Network Monitor. Too many network objects and counters are available to mention them all here. You can monitor objects based on each separate network protocol, such as NetBEUI, Transmission Control Protocol (TCP), User Datagram Protocol (UDP), Internet Protocol (IP), and so on. You'll learn about some SQL Server–specific counters later today.

Disk

You can monitor disk usage only after you turn on the Windows 2000 disk counters. You enable them by using the command `diskperf -y` from a Windows 2000 command prompt and then restart the server. Otherwise, all disk counters reflect a value of 0.

You might choose to monitor the PhysicalDisk object. The difference between this and the LogicalDisk object is that the PhysicalDisk counter monitors physical hard drives, whereas the LogicalDisk counter tells you about drive letters. Hence, if you have two logical disks on a single physical drive, you can use the PhysicalDisk counter to show how much activity is happening on the physical disk, as well as break it down logically, disk by logical disk.

If you see too much activity going to a single disk, you might want to use filegroups to move data to other physical disks on your computer.

Configuring SQL Server

Configuring SQL Server 2000 is relatively straightforward. Several options are still available to tune, but the good news is that you almost never need to change these options. However, it's still useful to at least see what is available and know when you might need to change them.

This section deals with tuning only for Windows 2000–based SQL servers. For the Personal version of SQL Server on Windows 9*x*, you would be wasting your time to put too much effort into tuning SQL Server for most implementations. The automatic tuning options take care of the most important configuration options for you.

To begin examining these configuration options, turn on the Show Advanced Options configuration option to see all the configuration parameters available to you. Do so by using the `sp_configure` system stored procedure:

INPUT
```
EXEC sp_configure 'Show Advanced Options',1
GO
RECONFIGURE with Override
GO
EXEC sp_configure
```

You then see something like the following results:

OUTPUT
```
name                           minimum  maximum    config_value run_value
------------------------------ -------- ---------- ------------ ---------
affinity mask                  0        2147483647 0            0
allow updates                  0        1          0            0
awe enabled                    0        1          0            0
c2 audit mode                  0        1          0            0
cost threshold for parallelism 0        32767      5            5
cursor threshold               -1       2147483647 -1           -1
default full-text language     0        2147483647 1033         1033
default language               0        9999       0            0
fill factor (%)                0        100        0            0
index create memory (KB)       704      2147483647 0            0
lightweight pooling            0        1          0            0
locks                          5000     2147483647 0            0
max degree of parallelism      0        32         0            0
max server memory (MB)         4        2147483647 2147483647   2147483647
max text repl size (B)         0        2147483647 65536        65536
max worker threads             10       32767      255          255
media retention                0        365        0            0
min memory per query (KB)      512      2147483647 1024         1024
min server memory (MB)         0        2147483647 0            0
nested triggers                0        1          1            1
network packet size (B)        512      65536      4096         4096
open objects                   0        2147483647 0            0
priority boost                 0        1          0            0
query governor cost limit      0        2147483647 0            0
query wait (s)                 -1       2147483647 -1           -1
recovery interval (min)        0        32767      0            0
remote access                  0        1          1            1
```

```
remote login timeout (s)      0      2147483647 20        20
remote proc trans             0      1          0         0
remote query timeout (s)      0      2147483647 0         0
scan for startup procs        0      1          0         0
set working set size          0      1          0         0
show advanced options         0      1          1         1
two digit year cutoff         1753   9999       2049      2049
user connections              0      32767      0         0
user options                  0      16383      0         0
```

Despite its huge increase in functionality, SQL Server 2000, like SQL Server 7.0, has fewer options than previous releases. As we stated before, you never need to tune the vast majority of these options. Most of them are set to 0 in the `config_value` and `run_value` options, meaning that SQL Server automatically tunes the option for you. Unless you have a compelling reason to change these automatic settings, you shouldn't do so. Notice that the `run_value` is currently applied; the config value would be different if you requested a change but hadn't restarted SQL Server or run the `RECONFIGURE` command.

From a performance and tuning perspective, you might want to change a few configuration parameters. Again, we can't say it too often: The odds are good that for all but the largest SQL Server implementations, you don't need to change these parameters. However, if you are managing an eight-processor or greater SQL Server, you might need to consider these configuration options. To make the analysis of these options easier, today's lesson groups them into four categories: processor options, memory configuration options, input/output (I/O) options, and query/index options.

Processor Options

The first set of options to examine relates to SQL Server's use of the processors on your computer. You can configure the relative priority of the SQL Server process, which CPUs on your computer SQL Server will use, and the total number of operating system threads SQL Server can use on your computer. You can also set the maximum number of CPUs that can be used during parallel query operations. Each option is listed in a logical order to consider when making changes to your SQL Server configuration. In other words, it's probably better to consider changing the priority boost option (examined first) before considering changing the cost threshold for the parallelism option (examined last).

Priority Boost

The priority boost option determines whether the SQL Server threads on your computer run at normal priority (priority level 8 on Windows 2000) or high priority (priority level 13 on Windows 2000). When this option is set to the value 0, you run at normal priority; when it's set to the value 1, you run at high priority. These settings are for a single-processor computer. On a multiprocessor computer, normal SQL Server priority at the operating system level is 15 and high priority is 24. When you change this option, you need to restart the SQL Server service for the change to take effect.

Monitor your computer carefully after setting this option, because you could hurt any other process running on your SQL Server computer. However, on a dedicated SQL Server machine, you'll see improved performance by setting this option.

Affinity Mask

The affinity mask option is a bitmap representing which CPUs will be used for SQL Server on a multi-CPU system. So, to set processors 0, 1, and 3, you must set the bitmap pattern to 00001011 (because you set them from right to left, with position 1 equal to CPU 0, position 2 set to CPU 1, and so on). To make this simple, you enter the base 10 (normal number) equivalent to this, which is 11—(8×1) + (4×0) + (2×1) + (1×1), starting from the first set bit. By default, SQL Server takes advantage of all your system's processors; you change this option only when you want some processors to be reserved for Windows 2000 or another process running on your server. Letting SQL Server use all available processors most of the time is a good idea.

Parallel Query Options

SQL Server 2000 has two parallel query options. Parallelism really takes two forms in SQL Server. The first form is SQL Server's capability to run some parts of a query in parallel and then recombine the processing to produce a single result. This kind of parallelism happens all the time in SQL Server.

The second kind of parallel query—and the one you configure—is SQL Server's capability to dedicate processors to a single query in parallel. This kind of parallel query is available only on multiprocessor systems and typically runs only when you have more processors than users.

For example, on Saturday night at 9 p.m., no users are on the system, and you start a job to run a huge report. If you have a four-processor system, SQL Server can choose to use all four processors to complete this report much more quickly than it would be able to otherwise. However, after the parallel query starts, it runs until completing, using all the configured CPUs. If another user connects and tries to run another query, the new user's query performance suffers because of this parallel query. For this reason, you should configure parallelism carefully if you have multiple processors.

Max Degree of Parallelism The max degree of parallelism option specifies the number of threads available to use for parallel queries (between 1 and 32). A value of `0` indicates that all configured processors (from the affinity mask configuration) can be used, with one thread per processor. A value of 1 effectively turns off the parallel query. Any other value specifies the maximum number of CPUs used for a parallel query. Again, parallel queries are considered only when your SQL Server is relatively free of other activity.

On single-processor computers, this option is ignored. Changes to this configuration parameter take effect immediately, without restarting SQL Server.

Cost Threshold for Parallelism The cost threshold for parallelism option specifies the number of seconds a query will take if executed without parallel query before a parallel execution plan is considered. The default value is 5 seconds, and the option can be set up to 32,767. In other words, if a query will take at least 5 seconds to run without parallel query, SQL Server will examine the option to use the parallel query facilities.

This option applies only to multiprocessor computers when the SQL Server affinity mask and max degrees of parallelism options are set to allow parallel queries to occur. Changes to this parameter take effect immediately, without restarting SQL Server.

SQL Server Enterprise Manager

Each configuration "group" has a property page in the configuration of your server as part of the SQL Server Enterprise Manager utility. To access the processor properties of your server, right-click your server, select Properties, and click the Processor tab (see Figure 20.4). The options in this dialog are self-explanatory now that you've examined them in detail.

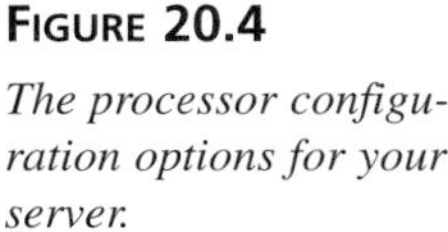

FIGURE 20.4

The processor configuration options for your server.

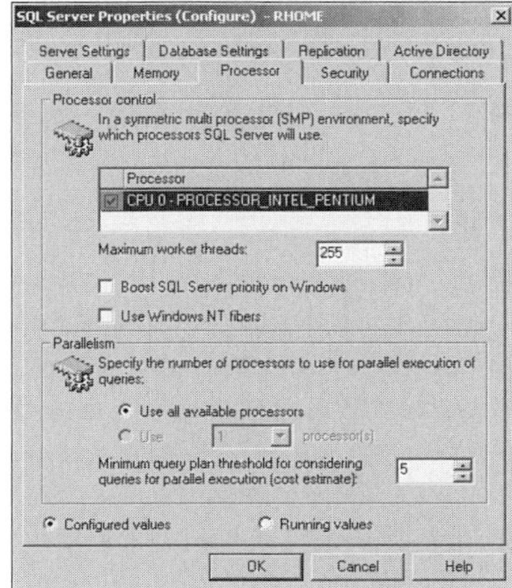

Memory Configuration Options

You will examine two memory configuration options: min server memory and max server memory. By default, SQL Server sets min server memory to 0 and max server memory to 2,147,483,647MB (a really, really big number). This configuration means SQL Server uses automatic memory management. As SQL Server needs more memory, it takes more memory. However, to prevent paging, SQL Server's default keeps it from expanding so much that the total memory load on the server takes more than the amount of physical RAM—5MB. So, on my 128MB system, SQL Server never commits more RAM than 123MB (including Windows 2000 and any other running processes). However, you can set these options manually as well.

You would normally leave these settings unchanged; SQL Server 2000 does an excellent job of dynamically allocating and deallocating memory as needed. However, if you're running another memory-intensive program, such as Microsoft Exchange Server, on the same computer, you might want to restrict how much RAM is assigned to SQL Server. Having a dedicated SQL Server machine is always a good idea.

Min Server Memory

If you set the min server memory, you are telling SQL Server to never use less than *n* megabytes of memory. For example, if you configure min server memory to 50 (megabytes), when you start SQL Server, it always requests 50MB of memory to start.

If you also set the max server memory to 50MB, you're setting a "fixed" amount of memory that SQL Server will always use.

Max Server Memory

Setting the max server memory restricts the maximum amount of memory SQL Server can ever use. Again, the value is set in megabytes.

Min Memory Per Query

The min memory per query option specifies the minimum amount of memory allocated for each user on your SQL Server for each query each server runs. The default value is 1,024KB, or 1MB. For most SQL Server computers, this default is enough memory. However, if you are using SQL Server 2000 as a decision-support or data-warehousing database, you might want to increase this value. You can increase performance of queries doing large sorts or joins by allocating more memory before the queries actually need the memory (rather than finding the memory at runtime).

SQL Server Enterprise Manager

If you again select the properties of your server and click the Memory tab, you see the dialog shown in Figure 20.5. You can leave the server set to allocate memory dynamically, set a fixed memory size, or tune the minimum and maximum memory allocations. You can also set the minimum memory allocation per query.

FIGURE 20.5

The memory configuration options for your server.

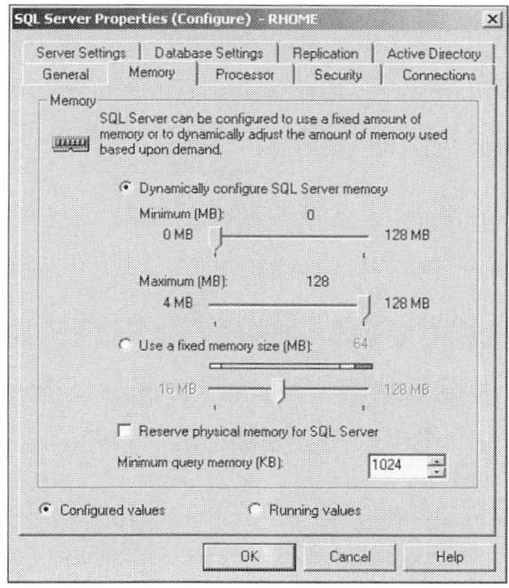

Tip

> The option Reserve Physical Memory for SQL Server sets the Set Working Set Size configuration parameter. Setting this option never seems to make any improvement in SQL Server (perhaps even hurts), so it's not examined further here.

I/O Options

There are no I/O configuration parameters to tune on SQL Server 2000. In SQL Server 7.0 and previous releases, you tuned the max async I/O parameter, but it was eliminated in SQL Server 2000. Now SQL Server always starts the needed threads to issue I/O to the operating system. So, the best thing you can do for your SQL Server disk and I/O performance is to spread your data across multiple disks and multiple controllers, as you learned earlier today.

Query/Index Options

Two options are available to tune or limit the running of queries or to tune indexes. They include the fill factor, which you already examined on Day 13, "Indexing for Performance." The other option is the built-in query governor cost limit.

The default value for the query governor cost limit is 0, meaning all queries are allowed to run. However, when you set this option to a nonzero number, you are telling SQL Server that any query predicted to run for longer than *n* number of seconds will be prevented from executing. Be careful when setting this option because you can easily prevent users from running queries that they need to run to perform their jobs. On the other hand, you can prevent those runaway one-hour queries from running as well. This option doesn't have a SQL Server Enterprise Manager interface.

Monitoring SQL Server Performance

Several utilities, as well as Transact-SQL commands, are available to help you monitor SQL Server performance. Among them are the performance monitor counters (which you saw briefly yesterday when examining alerts), SQL Server Enterprise Manager's Current Activity windows, the SQL Server profiler, and some key system stored procedures. You'll examine each in the following sections.

SQL Server Performance Monitor Counters

The first stop on your monitoring tour will be with the Windows 2000 performance monitor again. This time, however, you will examine the performance monitor counters that SQL Server exposes. As with the configuration options, today's lesson doesn't attempt to examine each counter (there are more than 100), just the big ones you should know about.

Memory

Consider the SQLServer:Buffer Manager object, Buffer Cache Hit Ratio counter to determine how efficiently memory is being used on your server. This value reflects how frequently data was found in memory when SQL Server went to find it. This value should be higher than 90 percent and preferably as close to 100 percent as possible. If you haven't done so, start the performance monitor (located in the Administrative Tools program group), and click the plus sign (+) on the toolbar. Scroll down to the SQLServer:Buffer Manager object (or MSSQL$Instancename:Buffer Manager for a named instance), and you will see a dialog resembling Figure 20.6. Here, you can see the Buffer Cache Hit Ratio counter we are discussing. You can find other counters and objects by selecting the appropriate drop-down menu items.

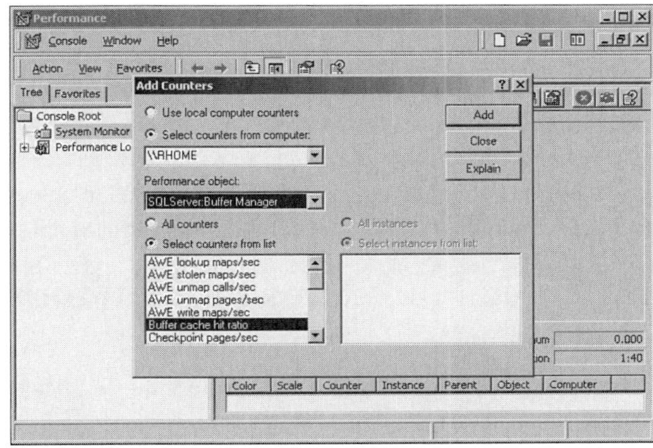

FIGURE 20.6

The performance monitor view for the SQL Server counters.

You might also want to monitor the SQLServer:Buffer Manager object, Database Pages counter to view how much memory is being used to hold your data and indexes. This information is returned as pages, so you multiply the result by eight to return the approximate number of kilobytes of memory being used.

Processor

If you want to monitor how much of the CPU SQL Server is using, you can monitor the `PROCESS` object, % Processor Time counter, with an instance of `SQLSERVR`. If you're running multiple instances of SQL Server, you can see them all here (and, unfortunately, they look basically identical). You can monitor how much processor time the SQL Server Agent service is using by monitoring the instance of SQLAgent.

Network

SQL Server doesn't provide a way to monitor your network activity. Each network protocol can report its own statistics.

If you're using Transmission Control Protocol/Internet Protocol (TCP/IP), you must install the Simple Network Management Protocol (SNMP) service for the TCP/IP-related performance counters to appear on Windows NT 4.0.

Disk

You need to monitor a significant number of I/O counters for the SQLServer object. For example, in the SQLServer:Buffer Manager object, the Page Reads/sec counter monitors read activity (from disk), and the Page Writes/sec counter monitors how much write activity is occurring on the server. Another counter you might want to monitor is in the SQLServer:Databases object, Log Flushes/sec. This counter indicates how many log records are written to disk each second and gives you an idea of how much work is being done. Related to this counter is the SQLServer:Databases object, Transactions/Sec, which indicates how many active transactions are in a database at any given time. Notice that these last two options are database specific, so you need to select one or more databases from your Instance window to monitor the activity in that database.

System Stored Procedures for Monitoring Performance

You can use a few system stored procedures to monitor your SQL Server's performance. The most important two are `sp_who` and `sp_monitor`.

SYNTAX

```
sp_who [[@login_name =] 'login']
```

In this syntax, *`login`* is the name of a login you want to monitor. If you don't specify the login, information is returned for all logins. If you specify the keyword `ACTIVE` instead of a *`login`*, only information on users who are now running queries is returned. System connections are always returned, even when you specify `ACTIVE`.

The output from `sp_who` tells you who's connected, what computers the users are using, what databases they are using, and what command states they are in. For example, when I run

```
EXEC sp_who
```

I get

```
spid ecid status     loginame          hostname blk dbname  cmd
----------------------------------------------------------------------------
1    0    background sa                         0   NULL    LAZY WRITER
2    0    sleeping   sa                         0   NULL    LOG WRITER
3    0    background sa                         0   master  SIGNAL HANDLER
4    0    background sa                         0   NULL    LOCK MONITOR
5    0    background sa                         0   master  TASK MANAGER
6    0    sleeping   sa                         0   NULL    CHECKPOINT SLEEP
7    0    background sa                         0   master  TASK MANAGER
8    0    background sa                         0   master  TASK MANAGER
9    0    background sa                         0   master  TASK MANAGER
10   0    background sa                         0   master  TASK MANAGER
51   0    runnable   RHOME\rwaymi      RHOME    0   master  SELECT
52   0    sleeping   RHOME\rwaymi      RHOME    0   master  AWAITING COMMAND
53   0    sleeping   RHOME\rwaymi      RHOME    0   master  AWAITING COMMAND
54   0    sleeping   RHOME\SQLService RHOME    0   msdb    AWAITING COMMAND
55   0    sleeping   RHOME\SQLService RHOME    0   msdb    AWAITING COMMAND

(15 row(s) affected)
```

The other system stored procedure is `sp_monitor`, which returns the amount of system activity that has occurred since the system stored procedure was last run:

SYNTAX

```
EXEC sp_monitor
```

This system stored procedure has no parameters.

For example, on my system I ran `sp_monitor`, performed some activity, and then ran `sp_monitor` again. Here are the results:

```
last_run                     current_run                  seconds
---------------------------- ---------------------------- ---------
2000-04-18 01:53:23.693      2000-06-10 18:39:41.270      4639578

cpu_busy                  io_busy                   idle
------------------------- ------------------------- ----------------
25(22)-0%                 0(0)-0%                   69532(69467)-1%

packets_received         packets_sent             packet_errors
------------------------ ------------------------ ------------
2390(1687)               2383(1941)               0(0)

total_read          total_write         total_errors        connections
------------------- ------------------- ------------------- -----------
2021(1902)          579(-3410)          0(0)                38(27)
```

As you can see, this system stored procedure reports quite a bit of useful information, including how busy the CPU was, how busy your disks were, how much network activity occurred, and how much disk activity occurred. Although this information is useful, it does require that you run the command before and after an activity you want to measure.

The Current Activity Window of SQL Server Enterprise Manager

An easier way to view SQL Server performance information is through the Current Activity window of SQL Server Enterprise Manager. To access this window, expand the Management folder for your SQL Server, and then expand the Current Activity option. Then highlight the Process Info item in the left pane. You are presented with the window in Figure 20.7. (If you see icons instead of this window, select Detail from the View menu.)

In this window, you can see each connection in SQL Server. When you highlight a particular process and then right-click it, you can kill that process (if you are a member of the sysadmin or processadmin fixed server roles). You can also send the user a message (via Windows, not to the user's query tool), or select properties from the pop-up menu to see the last command the user has run (see Figure 20.8). You can also examine the details of locking by selecting either Locks/Process ID or Locks/Object in the left pane to view locks by those groupings.

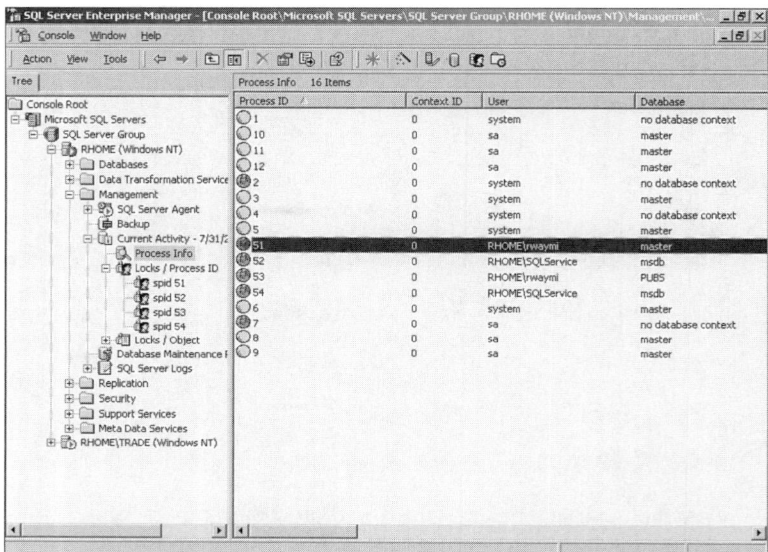

FIGURE 20.7

The Current Activity window.

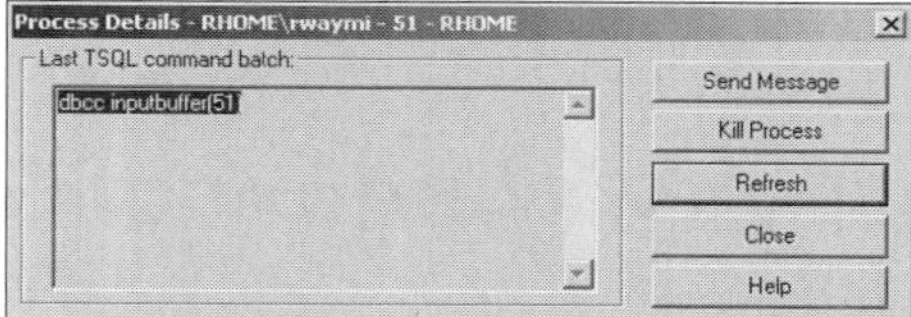

FIGURE 20.8

You can highlight an item and kill the process or send a message via the Process Details dialog.

Using the SQL Server Profiler

With the SQL Server Profiler utility, you can monitor all activity on your SQL Server. You can capture and record an amazing array of events when using the SQL Server Profiler. The most useful part of using this utility, however, is the simple ability to capture the Transact-SQL commands that are run on your server. You can use this information as an audit trail or simply as a way to see what kind of work is being performed on your computer. You can also use a captured trace as input to the SQL Server Index Tuning Wizard. This wizard helps you select the proper indexes for a given set of queries. It's handy when you can simply run a trace for a typical business day and then hand the trace over to the Index Tuning Wizard. It runs for a while and then spits out the optimal set of indexes for you to use.

Setting Up and Starting a Trace

The first step in using the SQL Server Profiler is to set up a trace. Start the Profiler from your SQL Server 2000 program group, and you see the window in Figure 20.9.

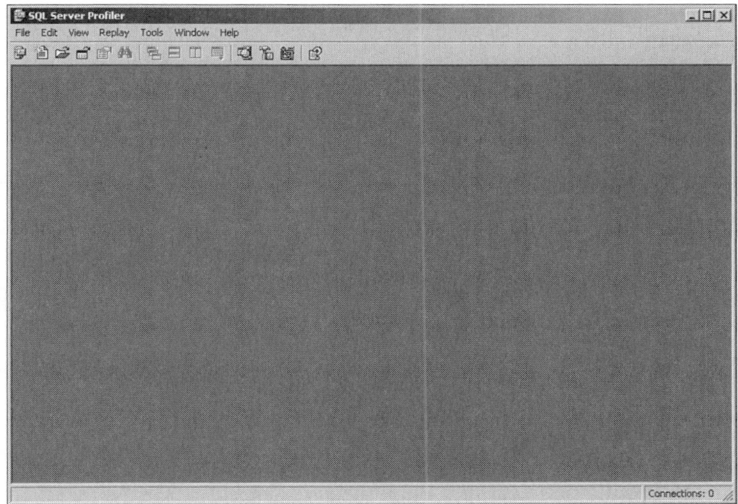

FIGURE 20.9

You can use the SQL Server Profiler to set up a trace.

To begin a preconfigured trace, select New and then Trace from the File menu. You are prompted to log in to an instance of SQL Server. After you're connected, the Trace Properties dialog appears (see Figure 20.10). SQL Server 2000 ships with several preconfigured traces in the form of Trace Templates. By default, SQL Server Profiler loads the template SQLServerProfilerStandard.

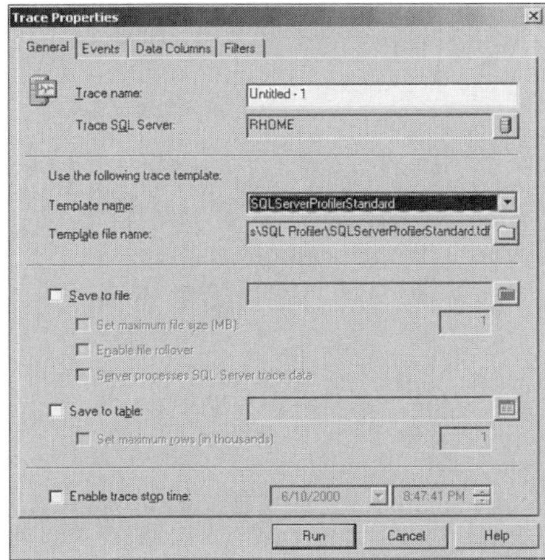

FIGURE 20.10

The SQL Server Profiler Trace Properties dialog.

Each template defines a standard set of events (sets of information you want to know about) and data columns (the individual bits of information about each event). Accept the defaults for this trace, and click the Run button to start recording a trace. Start the SQL Server Query Analyzer (notice the icon on the toolbar for the Query Analyzer), and run the following query:

INPUT

```
Use pubs
Select * from authors
```

Now return to the Profiler and look at the T-SQL statements (and other information) that were captured. Although the queries you ran (the `USE` command followed by the `SELECT` command) were captured, several other commands were also captured. These commands are run every time the SQL Server Query Analyzer starts. They configure the environment before you begin to run queries. All commands that are run, even when you don't know they're being run, are captured here.

> **Note**
>
> SQL Server Profiler doesn't show any passwords sent in as passwords from system stored procedures.

To stop the trace, simply click the stop button inside the query window. The trace stops, and no more information is captured.

Now customize a trace to your requirements. Close the trace you were looking at, and click the New Trace button on the toolbar (the first one on the left). You are presented with the dialog in Figure 20.11 and can start entering the properties of your trace. You first must name the trace (I used My Trace, but you should probably use something more descriptive if you intend to keep your trace).

FIGURE 20.11

The SQL Server Profiler trace.

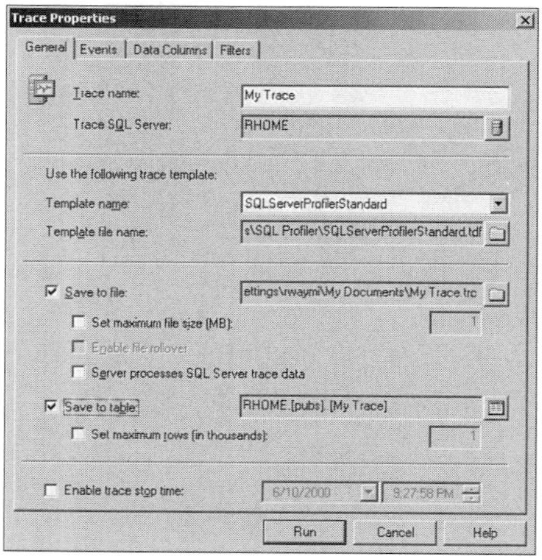

You can also save your traces to a file or to a SQL Server table rather than simply have it displayed in the user interface. If you select the Save to File option, you are prompted for a location. The default location is in your My Documents folder, with a filename of `tracename.trc`. So, for the trace I named My Trace, the filename would be `My Trace.trc`. You can also save your trace to a SQL Server table. If you check the Save to Table option, you are prompted for the server name, database name, owner name, and table name. Select a database on your SQL Server, and accept the default table name of [My Trace]. Notice that the table has the same name as your trace, so it's a good idea to create your trace name with a valid SQL Server identifier. Figure 20.11 reflects all these selections.

If you click the Events tab (see Figure 20.12), you can select the information you want to capture in your trace. The default is to capture when users connect, when they disconnect, and which users are connected when the trace starts. You also see any Remote Procedure Call (RPC) events or SQL Batch events when they are complete. SQL Batch events are the calls into SQL Server that aren't RPC events.

FIGURE 20.12

The Events tab of a new trace.

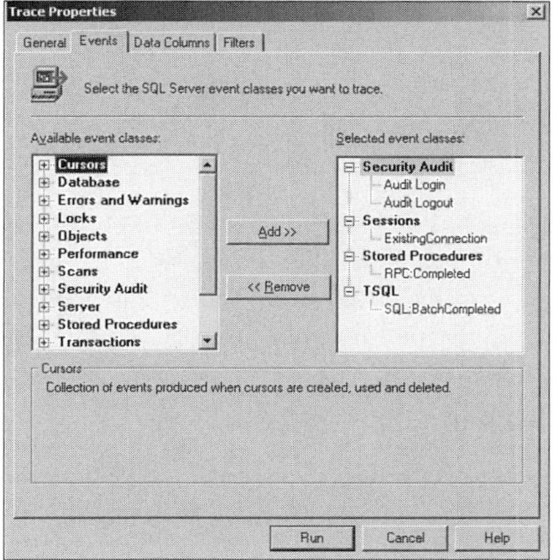

Notice that on the left side of the trace dialog is a significant number of additional events you can capture. Exploring these events takes time, but when you master them, you will discover that you can do just about anything with the Profiler.

Click the Data Columns tab to see which items show up on your trace report (see Figure 20.13). By default, you capture items such as which user was running a query, what application he was using, what SQL Server Login name he was using, various performance information, and, of course, the text of the command he ran. You also can group items of similar types. For example, if you want to group events by SQL Server username, you can highlight the SQL User Name item and then click the Up button until SQL User Name appears under the Groups item. Your report then groups its trace by SQL User Name rather than listing events sequentially. You can use grouping to make your reports more readable onscreen.

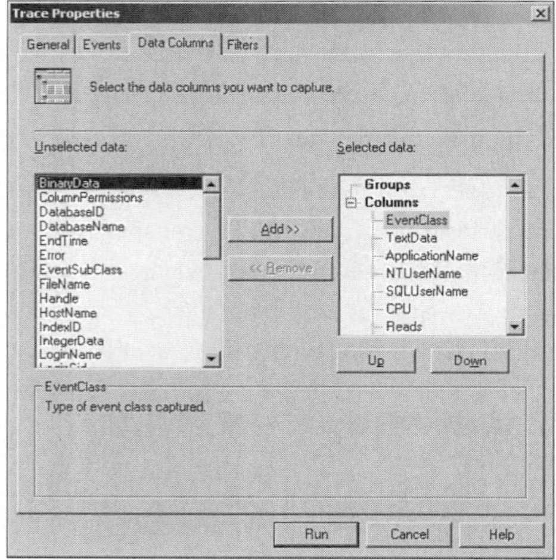

FIGURE 20.13
The Data Columns tab of a new trace.

And last, but not least, you can filter your trace so that you gather only the information you really want. Notice in Figure 20.14 that the Profiler excludes its T-SQL commands by default. To see that the Profiler utility is calling an extended stored procedure when it starts, remove this restriction by highlighting (underneath Not Like) the words `SQL Server Profiler%` and then pressing Delete. Deleting them removes the restriction so that you see the work the Profiler itself performs.

For each restriction you want to place on your trace, highlight the option in the Trace Event Criteria window; then type the item you want to include or exclude in the appropriate text box. For each event criterion, the appropriate text box appears.

Click Run, and your trace starts automatically. Notice in Figure 20.15 that the SQL Server profiler is calling the stored procedure `sp_trace_create`. Using the graphical interface is much easier than figuring out which stored procedures to call, but if you want, you can set up calls to this procedure (and all the others you need) yourself.

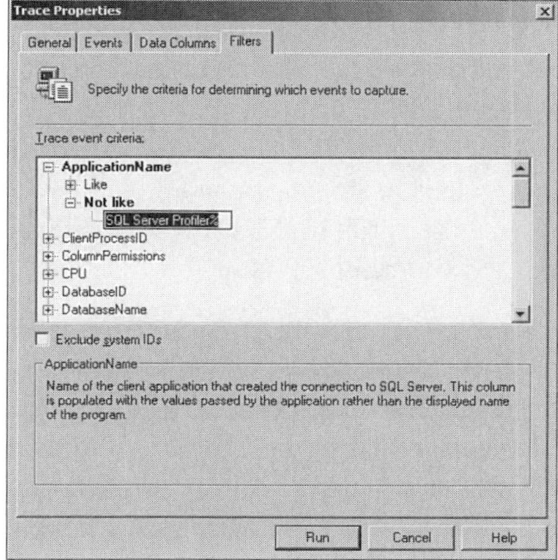

FIGURE 20.14
The Filters tab of a new trace.

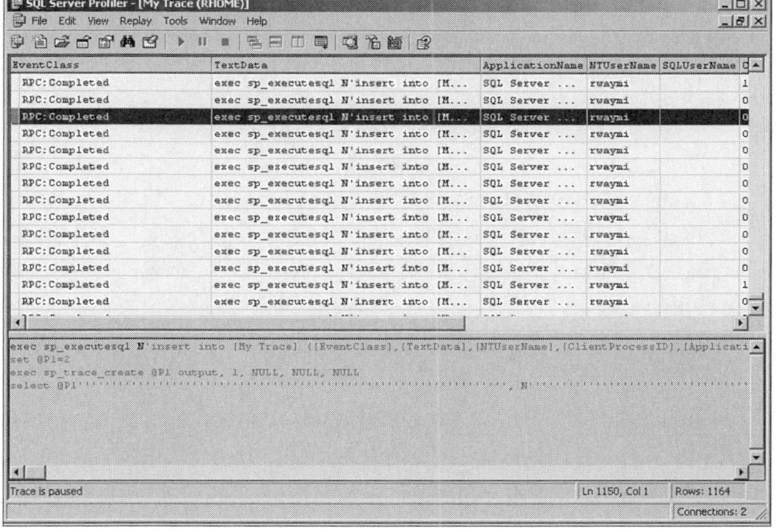

FIGURE 20.15
A captured trace.

Again, this trace simply captures all T-SQL statements and RPC events that occur on your SQL Server. If you leave it running, it will continue to do so. However, stop the trace now, and verify that the trace file has been created by clicking File, Open, Trace File. You should see `My Trace.trc`. When you open this trace, you should see that, indeed, all the commands you were viewing were captured and recorded in the trace file.

20

Setting Up an Audit Trail

As you can see, you've already set up the beginnings of an audit trail. All you must do is select all Security Audit events, add all data columns, and then leave the trace running all the time on your server. SQL Server 2000 can even roll over the file when it reaches a certain size so that you never need to shut down auditing to back up each audit trace. When the previous audit trace file is full to the size you configured, a new file is opened, the previous file is closed, and you can back it up.

You might also consider setting a Profiler trace to start automatically when SQL Server starts. You can do so in two ways: You can wrap all the calls to configure a trace within a stored procedure and then mark that stored procedure as startup. This method is actually quite simple: Configure the trace and then run it. Then, from the File menu, select Script Trace, and SQL Server Profiler builds all the calls to create the trace. Now all you have to do is wrap a stored procedure around these calls and mark that stored procedure to autostart with SQL Server.

You can also set C2 Audit Mode by using `sp_configure`. After you restart SQL Server, a full audit trace will always run. More information about C2 Audit Mode is available in the SQL Server Books Online.

Using a Trace to Monitor Performance

The easiest way to use the Profiler to find your performance problems is to select a different trace template; `SQLServerProfilerTuning` should do nicely to start. Then click the Filters tab to restrict items to look for. For example, you might filter only the database you're interested in and restrict the results to queries that run more than some amount of time (such as 1 second). Notice that the value is in milliseconds, so 1,000 is actually only a 1-second query. Figure 20.16 shows a filter that restricts the profiler results to queries that run for at least 1 second in the `pubs` database.

That's it! Now run the trace, and watch queries pile up in your environment that qualify based on the filters you set. Don't forget to set the file location to which the trace should be recorded.

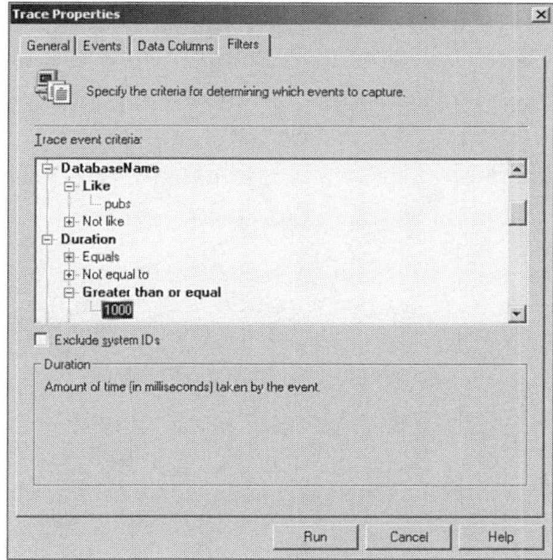

FIGURE 20.16
Filtering for performance issues.

The Index Tuning Wizard

The preceding discussion of traces leads rather nicely into a description of the Index Tuning Wizard. This wizard reviews a saved trace file and then recommends changes to your indexes on the server to enhance the performance of the queries captured during the trace. Here's how to use the wizard:

1. Select Index Tuning Wizard from the Tools menu in the SQL Server Profiler. Read the introductory screen, and then click Next to see the Select Server and Database dialog (see Figure 20.17) after you log in to SQL Server.

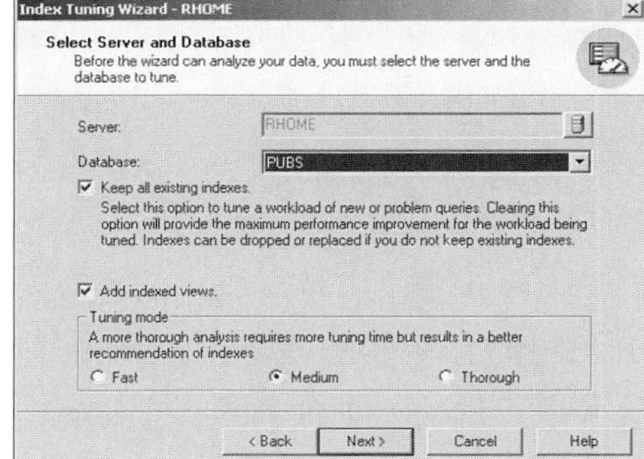

FIGURE 20.17
Select your server and database for the Index Tuning Wizard.

2. Select a different server if you've changed your mind in the last five seconds. Then select a database. The Index Tuning Wizard recommends indexes for only one database at a time. The default is not to remove any indexes you already have and to perform a less thorough analysis. Selecting the option to perform a thorough analysis is a good idea because you would hate to have the wizard recommend indexes that aren't as good as they could have been.
3. Click Next. You're asked to identify the workload to be analyzed (see Figure 20.18). If you already have a trace captured, you can either select the trace file or point the Index Tuning Wizard at a table containing your trace data.

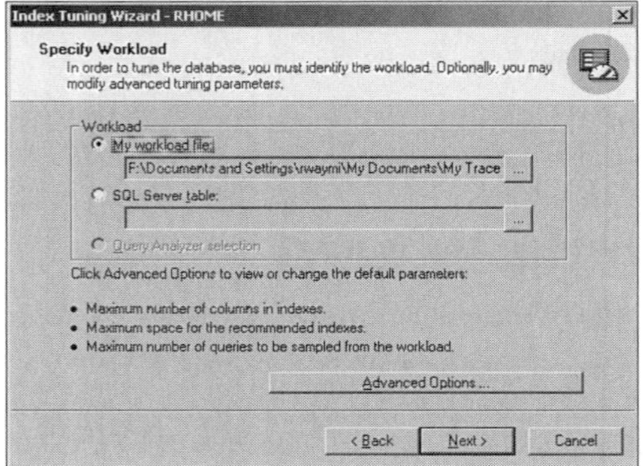

FIGURE 20.18
Specify Workload dialog for the Index Tuning Wizard.

4. Select an existing trace file (such as `My Trace.trc`, as shown in Figure 20.18), or select the SQL Server table with your saved trace information. Click the Advanced Options button to view the dialog shown in Figure 20.19.

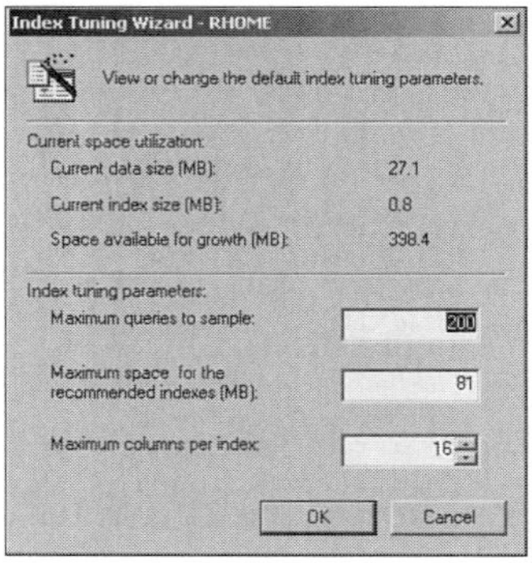

FIGURE 20.19
Advanced configuration options for the Index Tuning Wizard.

5. Click OK to accept any changes you make, and then click Next to view the Select Tables to Tune dialog (see Figure 20.20). By default, the wizard doesn't attempt to optimize any tables, so select all tables in your database. Then click Next.

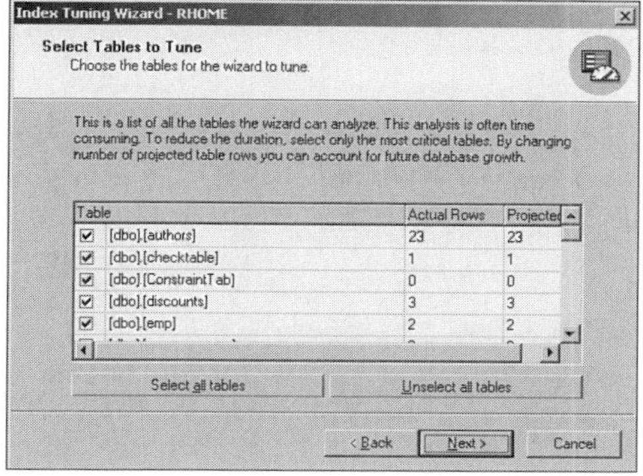

FIGURE 20.20

The Select Tables to Tune dialog of the Index Tuning Wizard.

The Index Tuning Wizard then analyzes the workload you've given to it. This process might take awhile, depending on the size of your trace file. When it's completed, the recommended indexes are shown in the Index Recommendations dialog (see Figure 20.21).

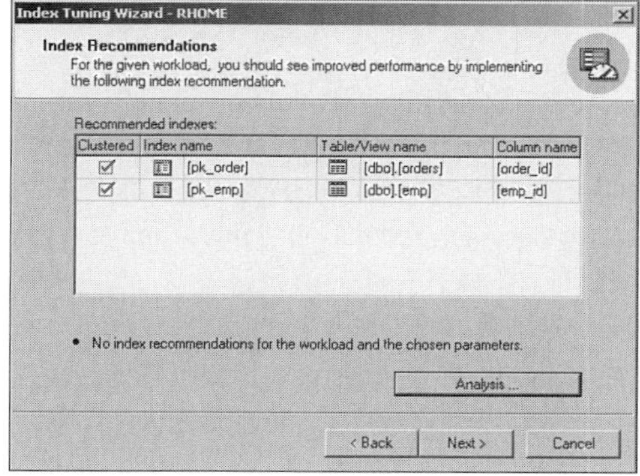

FIGURE 20.21

Index Recommendations dialog of the Index Tuning Wizard.

6. Because the trace My Trace contained only two simple queries, the Index Tuning Wizard didn't recommend any changes. You can see the recommendation by clicking the Analysis button and viewing the Original Configuration report; notice that it's identical to the Recommended Configuration report.
7. Click Next again, and if any changes were recommended, you can select to run the wizard's recommended changes on a given SQL Server Agent Job Schedule, or save the changes as a T-SQL script and review or run them at your leisure (see Figure 20.22).

FIGURE 20.22
The Schedule Index Update Job dialog.

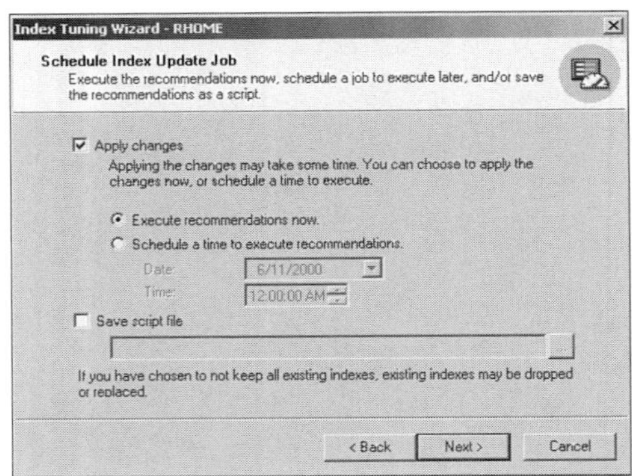

8. Because the wizard didn't recommend any changes in this case, you won't see the dialog in Figure 20.22; you'll just see the finished dialog. If you do get this dialog, it means some changes are recommended. Choose to apply them immediately, click Next, and then click Finish.

That's it! The SQL Server team has turned a horribly complex job (selecting which indexes are needed on a server) into a few clicks of a wizard.

As you might have guessed, information about the Index Tuning Wizard and the SQL Server Profiler could fill books themselves. So, for additional information about them, refer to *Microsoft SQL Server 2000 Unleashed* from Sams Publishing, which has much more detailed performance tuning information—including information about these utilities and wizards.

Summary

Today you learned how to configure Windows 2000 and SQL Server for optimal performance. You also examined how to monitor SQL Server with the Windows 2000 performance monitor, as well as several built-in SQL Server tools. They include the SQL Server Profiler, the Index Tuning Wizard, and the Current Activity window of the SQL Server Enterprise Manager. Over time you will learn these tools in great detail, and they will become your closest friends when performance problems arise on your SQL Server.

Q&A

Q If I want a quick snapshot of activity on SQL Server, where should I look?

A In the Current Activity window of SQL Server Enterprise Manager.

Q What kind of network card should I install in my server?

A A 32- or 64-bit bus mastering network card.

Q What kind of RAID array is best to use with my transaction logs?

A A mirrored, or even duplexed, set of disks is best.

Q Which tool should I use to select the proper indexes for my databases?

A The Index Tuning Wizard.

Workshop

This section provides quiz questions to help you solidify your understanding of the concepts presented today. In addition to the quiz questions, exercises are provided to let you practice what you've learned today. Try to understand the quiz and exercise answers before continuing on to tomorrow's lesson. Answers are provided in Appendix A, "Answers to Quiz Questions."

Quiz

1. In terms of overall performance impact, what component of the system deserves the most attention for performance tuning?
2. Why should the transaction logs be kept on different disks than the Windows 2000 paging file?
3. If you manually configured SQL Server's memory and are concerned that you overallocated memory for SQL Server, what Windows 2000 counter would you monitor?
4. What parameter would you change in SQL Server to adjust the processors used by SQL Server?
5. Which SQL Server performance counter would you watch to determine how much work was being done by SQL Server?

Exercises

Performance tuning usually involves monitoring a system with many users. Because you might or might not have such a system available to you, you can do your best to simulate a multiple-user system.

1. Start the SQL Server Profiler and begin a trace. Be sure to save the trace information to a trace file. Then start up several SQL Server Query Analyzer sessions, and run stored procedures and queries from each connection to SQL Server.

2. Start up SQL Enterprise Manager and monitor the activity with the current activity window. Observe what information can be seen, and try each of the options, such as the `Kill` command. Observe the behavior of the client programs (the Query Analyzer, in this case).
3. After you capture a bunch of queries with a trace, stop the trace. Then run the Index Tuning Wizard to see what kinds of changes the Wizard can recommend for you. Script out the changes, and see what the Wizard can do for you.

WEEK 3

DAY 21

Using XML with SQL Server 2000

Yesterday you examined the tools available to monitor the basic health and performance of both Windows and SQL Server. You looked at the SQL Server profiler to trace queries and to perform security audits. You also examined the Windows Performance Management console, including relevant performance counters for both Windows and SQL Server. As you can see, the Windows 2000 and SQL Server 2000 combined platform provides various ways to view information so that you can properly optimize your server.

Today's lesson focuses on an exciting new technology in SQL Server 2000—XML. Previously we had commented that XML was on track to be a technology fundamental to business processes. Since publishing the first edition, we've found this to be true in our consulting practices, especially now that Microsoft's .Net platform has been formally released. XML allows you to trade data in a self-describing way. This capability should go a long way toward facilitating easier electronic commerce, including business to business (B2B) and business to consumer (B2C) markets. The SQL Server 2000 engine has a significant amount of support for XML built right in.

What Is XML?

NEW TERM XML stands for *Extensible Markup Language*. You are probably already familiar with a markup language but don't necessarily know it. HTML, which stands for Hypertext Markup Language, is used to display the Web pages you view on the Internet. HTML is built on a well-defined set of tags (such as `<P>` and `</P>`). A big part of the power of HTML is that it's easy to support and universally available, but that is also its biggest limitation.

Many folks have tried a number of tricks to extend HTML, such as Microsoft's Dynamic HTML (DHTML). However, exchanging data is something that these other markup languages haven't been able to do well. XML is an attempt to do several things. The goals of XML are as follows:

> **Note:** References here are taken from the W3C specification of XML. You can read the complete XML specification at `http://www.w3.org/TR/REC-xml`.

- XML will be usable over the Internet.
- XML will support a wide variety of applications.
- XML will be compatible with SGML.
- It will be easy to write programs that process XML documents.
- The number of optional features in XML is to be kept to the absolute minimum—ideally, zero.
- XML documents should be human-legible and reasonably clear.
- The XML design should be prepared quickly.
- The design of XML will be formal and concise.
- XML documents will be easy to create.
- Terseness in XML markup is of minimal importance.

As you can see, it's an ambitious project. Our focus on XML will be to use its data interchange capabilities. You can use XML to support data interchange, because you can define your own tags.

Suppose that you have a customer name, address, and phone number. You could define them in SQL Server as a table as follows:

```
Create table customer
(customer_id int not null,
lastname nvarchar(50) not null,
firstname nvarchar(50) not null,
```

```
address nvarchar(500) not null,
City nvarchar(50) not null,
State nvarchar(30) not null,
Postal_code nvarchar(10) null)
```

You could create the same thing in XML, and it might look like this:

```
<?xml version="1.0" encoding="ISO-8859-1" ?>
<Customer>
<Customer_Id></Customer_Id>
<lastname></lastname>
<firstname></firstname>
<address></address>
<city></city>
<state></state>
<postal_code></postal_code>
</Customer>
```

NEW TERM The first difference that should jump out at you is that the XML document doesn't tell you the data type of each column of data. That information is built into the schema definition of SQL Server, but not necessarily into XML. You can get these definitions in something called a *Document Type Definition* (DTD) . DTDs hold the schema information that define what's in your XML document. DTDs are limited somewhat and do have a lot of overhead associated with them. More and more people are moving toward XML schemas instead. XML schemas accomplish the same purpose as DTDs, but they are written in XML; they are easier to understand and extensible.

NEW TERM Style sheets are also referenced. A *style sheet* is the formatting and display information you use to format your XML documents. The Extensible StyleSheet Language (XSL) is the formatting language you use with XML documents.

However, after you agree to these definitions, data interchange becomes very possible. If you put data into a document in the XML format, you can trade the data with any other system that supports XML. It doesn't matter whether you keep your data in a SQL Server database, an Excel spreadsheet, or an ordinary text file. The point is it no longer matters that you store your data in the same way, only that you transmit the data between systems using this common format.

You can learn more about XML by reading *Sams Teach Yourself XML in 21 Days*. What we've covered here should be enough to get you through the rest of the day.

SQL Server 2000 exposes XML in various ways. You can access SQL Server through Internet Information Server (IIS). You can submit queries directly as URLs (your traditional `http://www.microsoft.com/sql`–type string), you can process SQL Server result sets into preformatted documents, and you can select data directly from SQL Server via the `SELECT` statement. You can even open XML-formatted documents via Transact-SQL (T-SQL). With the latest (as of this revision August 2002), SQLXML libraries (freely downloadable from Microsoft's download site) XML has been extended in SQL Server to include an XML BULK LOAD processes.

Installing SQLXML 3.0 Service Pack 1

SQLXML is a set of technologies to enhance the basic XML functionality of SQL Server 2000. As of the writing of this book, the latest update is SQLXML 3.0 Service Pack 1. This service pack includes both security enhancements as well as bug fixes and some new technology. The new functionality includes:

- .NET framework support through SQLXML Managed Classes and the DiffGram format.
- Updategrams—which allow you to modify data in SQL Server 2000 from existing XML documents.
- XML Schema Definition Language (XSD)—XSD allows you to create schema annotations in an XML view of relational information.
- Web Services (SOAP) support—which allows you to send SOAP requests to an IIS server in order to execute stored procedures and user-defined functions.
- FOR XML support on the client side.
- XML BULK LOAD—allows you to bulk load XML documents into SQL Server.

SQLXML can be straight-forward (as documented throughout the rest of this day's reading) but there are many things that are significant features in their own right (such as Updategrams, XSD, SOAP, etc.) that require significant research on their own. If you'd like to dig into the meat of them, the help file is downloaded and installed when you install SQLXML 3.0 SP1, additionally you can look for a book such as *Teach Yourself XML in 24 Hours* from SAMS publishing.

As with any service pack or other upgrade, you should always read the documentation associated with the service pack and do some testing before putting your upgrades into a production environment.

SQLXML 3.0 (sp1) has some caveats that you should be aware of:

- Not completely backwards compatible
- Older DLL files from SQLXML 2.0 and 1.0 installs are not removed. You can run these side by side. If you are running them side by side, it is important to understand how the PROGIDs are handled. You should use dependent or explicit

PROGIDs in your applications. By explicitly referencing the version of SQLXML you wish to work with, you will not have version problems.

- Registry keys are modified in each version of the release. (See the documentation that comes with the service packs for complete details.)
- SQLXML 3.0 must use MSXML 4.0 (sp1) or later. Of course, installing MSXML 4.0 has the same issues that we are covering here for SQLXML 3.0. This includes PROGIDs and registry keys.
- You must have the SQL Server 2000 client installed prior to installing the SQLXML 3.0 service pack.
- To take advantage of the Web Service (SOAP) functionality, you must have the SOAP Toolkit 2.0 SP2 installed. To use the SQLXML Managed Classes, you must have the .NET framework installed.

Accessing SQL Server via Internet Information Server

The first way you can access SQL Server using XML is through Microsoft's Web server, IIS. You can expose a database with a special extension that the SQL Server team has written for IIS. This way, you can run queries against SQL Server via XML, and of course, display the results directly on a Web site. Better yet, the data returned via XML is preformatted using your XML schema and is self-describing to someone who understands the same XML schema.

The first step in allowing access via IIS is installing the Virtual Directory for SQL Server.

Virtual Directories and SQL Server

When you want to set up SQL Server to support direct access from the Internet, you need to go through a few configuration steps. First, set up IIS and establish a virtual directory. Assuming that you performed a default installation of Windows 2000, you have IIS already installed and running on your computer. If not, in Control Panel, open Add/Remove Programs, select Windows Components, and add in IIS.

After IIS is available, proceed to setting up the virtual directory.

Setting Up IIS and the Virtual Directory

Choose Start, Programs, Microsoft SQL Server, Configure SQL XML Support in IIS to start the IIS Virtual Directory Management for SQL Server utility (see Figure 21.1).

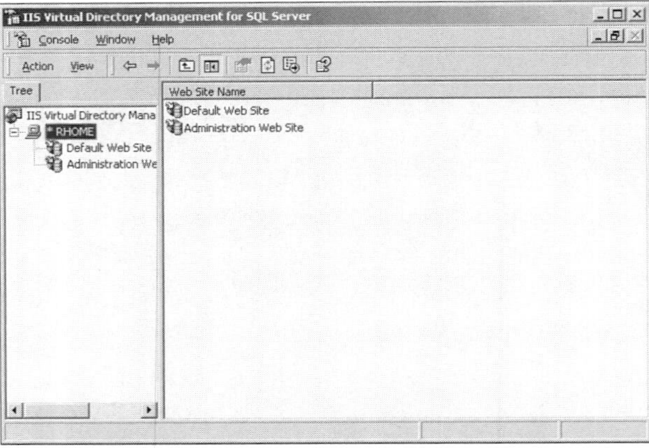

FIGURE 21.1
The IIS Virtual Directory Management for SQL Server console.

Expand your server name, select Default Web Site, select New, and then Virtual Directory from the Action menu to bring up the New Virtual Directory Properties dialog. Now you can create a virtual root. For the purposes of this book, create a virtual directory to reflect the `pubs` database. So, select the virtual directory name `pubs`. You should also create a directory under your `inetpub\wwwroot` directory. As you can see in Figure 21.2, I created the `pubs` directory under my IIS root directory.

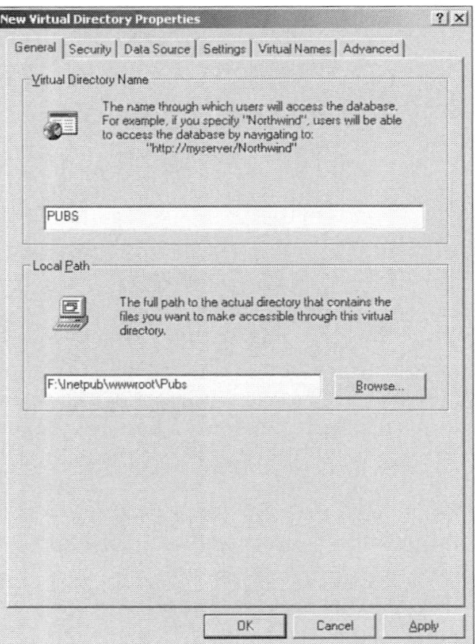

FIGURE 21.2
The General properties of your new virtual root.

Now click the Security tab, and configure the security for your virtual root. You have several important choices on this tab, so select carefully (see Figure 21.3).

FIGURE 21.3

The Security properties of your new virtual root.

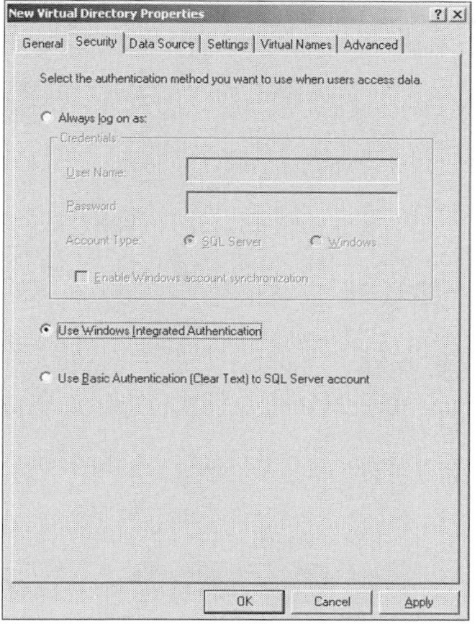

The default selection is Always Log on As. If you've set up your SQL Server in mixed security mode, you can configure your standard security credentials in this dialog. As we've stated repeatedly in this book, you shouldn't use standard security if you can help it. You can use Windows Integrated security in a couple of different ways. You can set the Account Type to Windows, and by default the IIS service account (`IUSR_COMPUTERNAME`) is used. You also can override this setting and use any arbitrary account.

The disadvantage of these methods is that you won't know who anyone is when they get to SQL Server—everyone will log in as the user you configure here, and everyone will have the same security rights. You'll want to think this one through before you choose to set an account here.

A better alternative might be to select the option Use Windows Integrated Authentication. With this option set, SQL Server may receive the credentials of the end user. I say *may* because, if SQL Server is on a different computer than IIS, normally a user's Windows NT/2000 security credentials aren't passed along to the next computer. However, if Windows 2000 and Kerberos security delegation are set up properly, the end user's security credentials are passed along to SQL Server. You can learn more about Kerberos and delegation in the SQL Server Books Online.

Kerberos is the new security protocol introduced with Windows 2000. It's much more secure than previous implementations, and a bit more complex. However, it introduces the capability to perform delegation as mentioned earlier.

Finally, you can set the option Use Basic Authentication (Clear Text) to SQL Server Account. As you might have guessed, in terms of security, it may not be your best choice. The end user is prompted for his security credentials (a standard security SQL Server login), and those credentials are passed on to SQL Server. They, by default, flow over your network without any kind of encryption (at least between the user and IIS).

For now, set the Use Windows Integrated Authentication option, and then click the Data Source tab (see Figure 21.4).

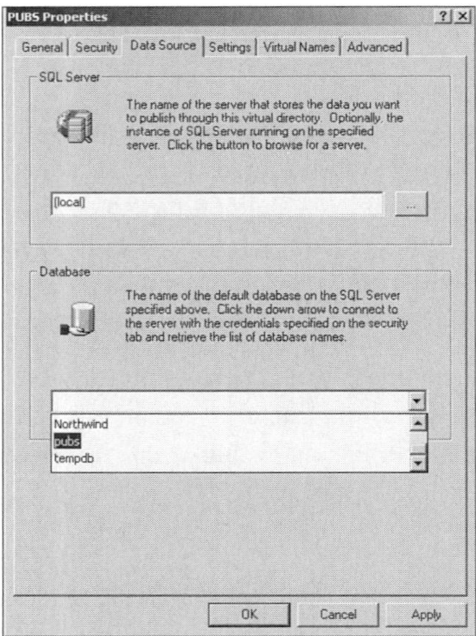

FIGURE 21.4

Select a data source.

Here, you select which SQL Server you want to connect to; *(local)* means the default instance of a local copy of SQL Server. You can type the name of your SQL Server or browse for a list of SQL Servers available on the network. Then click the drop-down list of databases, as shown in Figure 21.4, to select which database you want to use. Select `pubs` to follow along in this example.

Next, select the Settings tab (see Figure 21.5). Again, you make several critical choices here.

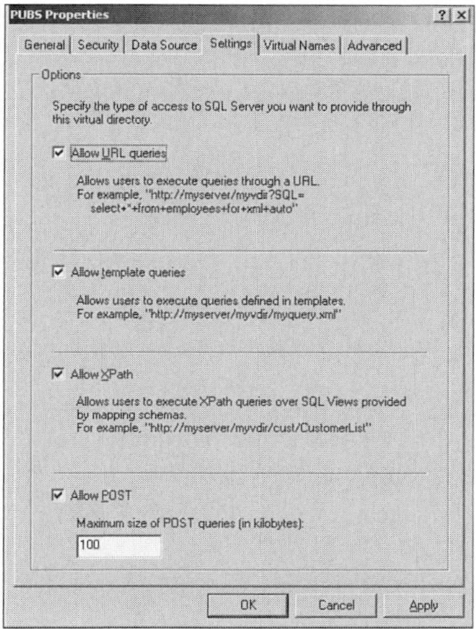

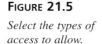

FIGURE 21.5
Select the types of access to allow.

By default, the option to allow template queries is the only one set. Relatively speaking, this option is the safest to have on. As you can see in Figure 21.5, I have enabled all these options so that you can see how each one works. Let's examine them:

- *Allow URL Queries* allows users to specify the Transact-SQL statements they want to run directly in the URL (uniform resource locator). You type this line into Internet Explorer to specify an Internet address. This option can be a little scary to enable in the sense that absolutely no restrictions are placed on the type of T-SQL that can be submitted. Queries are entered in the form

  ```
  http://rhome/pubs?SQL=select+*+from+authors+for+XML+AUTO
  ```

  where you substitute your server name for `rhome`. Note that the `?SQL=` is case sensitive.

> *Any* kind of T-SQL statement is valid for these URL queries. When you get it all working, give it a try. Run **`CREATE DATABASE randomtest`** and guess what? If you have the rights to SQL Server, you can create the database. You might want to take a second look at those options on the Security tab.

- *Allow Template Queries* is, relatively speaking, the safest option to select because users can run only queries you have preconfigured in template files. A sample call would be in the form `http://rhome/pubs/myquery.xml`.

- *Allow XPath* allows you to use the XPath query language to submit queries that use SQL Server views. Schema mapping occurs between the XML queries and the SQL Server database. You can learn more about XPath in *Sams Teach Yourself XML in 21 Days*.
- *Allow POST* allows you to create an HTML form and then have the customer fill out the form. Finally, the form's fields are used to fill in parameters to complete a T-SQL query. You can limit the size of `POST` queries so that excessively large queries aren't submitted to SQL Server.

Turn on each option so that you can try them out in a few minutes.

On the Virtual Names tab (see Figure 21.6), you can optionally set remappings so that you can have more complicated directory structures within IIS and not have to burden customers with knowing the detailed paths. You can also use a virtual name as an alias so that you can move files around as necessary without customers having to learn new URLs.

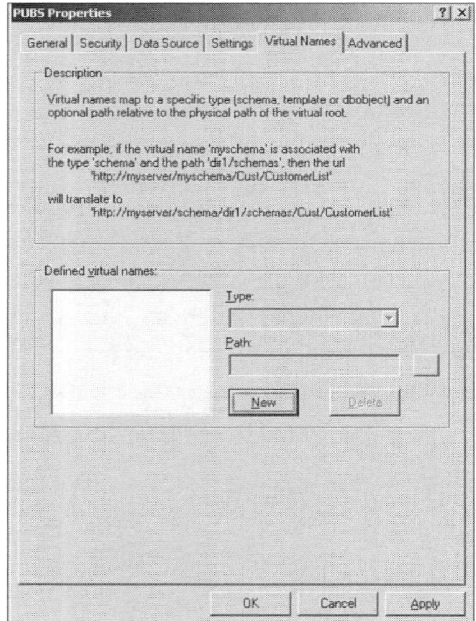

FIGURE 21.6

The Virtual Names tab.

Finally, on the Advanced tab (see Figure 21.7), you can set advanced options for your virtual directory. Don't change any of these options now. Refer to the SQL Server Books Online as you become more sophisticated using these capabilities to determine whether you even want to change these settings (I'll give you a hint—you probably won't ever need to do so).

Click OK to finish creating your virtual directory. Congratulations! You've created your SQL Server Virtual Directory in IIS to allow XML access to SQL Server.

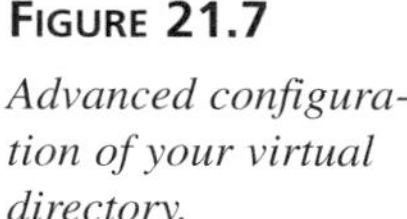

FIGURE 21.7

Advanced configuration of your virtual directory.

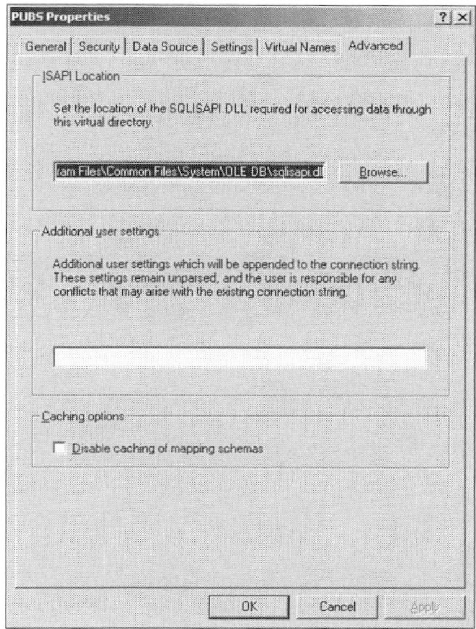

Using SQL Server Through URLs

Now for the fun part: After you set up this Web site, you can use SQL Server directly from the Internet. You can run SQL statements as part of the URL you type into your Web browser, or you can predefine queries via template files. First, you may have to use some special characters to get around the limitations of using the URL interface.

Special Character Mappings

Be aware that some characters on the Internet are special, and you don't have a proper URL unless you reference them via their special representation:

Value	*Meaning*
`%20`	A space (" ")
`%23`	Bookmarks (`#`)
`%25`	Special characters (`%`)
`%26`	Separator within a URL (`&`)
`%2F`	Directory separator (`/`)
`%3F`	Separates the query from the URL (`?`)

Executing Queries

To execute a query, simply start the URL with your server name, then the virtual root you created earlier today, and then the query (a `?sql=` and then the query). Finally, it should end with `&root=ROOT` (yes, it's case sensitive). For example, type the following into your Web browser, substituting your server name as appropriate:

INPUT

```
http://rhome/pubs?sql=Select+au_id,+au_lname,+au_fname+from+
➥authors&root=ROOT
```

Unfortunately, you get the error shown in Figure 21.8.

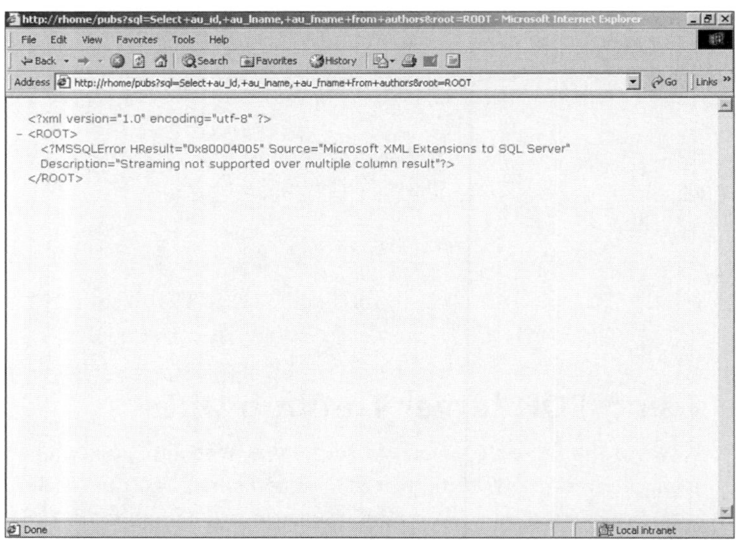

FIGURE 21.8
XML error when the `FOR XML` *clause isn't specified.*

This error resulted from the Web browser expecting to get XML back, not a real SQL Server result set. So, you have to tell SQL Server to return XML. You'll examine how to do that a bit later today, but for now simply add `for xml raw` to the query as follows to get the results shown in Figure 21.9.

INPUT

```
http://rhome/pubs?sql=Select+au_id,+au_lname,+au_fname+
➥from+authors+for+xml+raw&root=ROOT
```

Basically, you can now submit any query you want in the `pubs` database. Try another one to see how powerful this capability can be:

INPUT

```
http://rhome/pubs?sql=create+database+SQLXML&root=ROOT
```

This time, you get back

OUTPUT

```
<?xml version="1.0" encoding="utf-8" ?>
<ROOT />
```

But now look at Figure 21.10 (and your own Enterprise Manager). Because the virtual directory you created is using your Windows 2000 security credentials to log in to SQL

Server, it can do whatever you can do. So, if you are a sysadmin role member (as I am on my system), you can do anything. As you can see in Figure 21.10, a database named SQLXML was created by the preceding URL query. If you can create a database, imagine what else you could do.

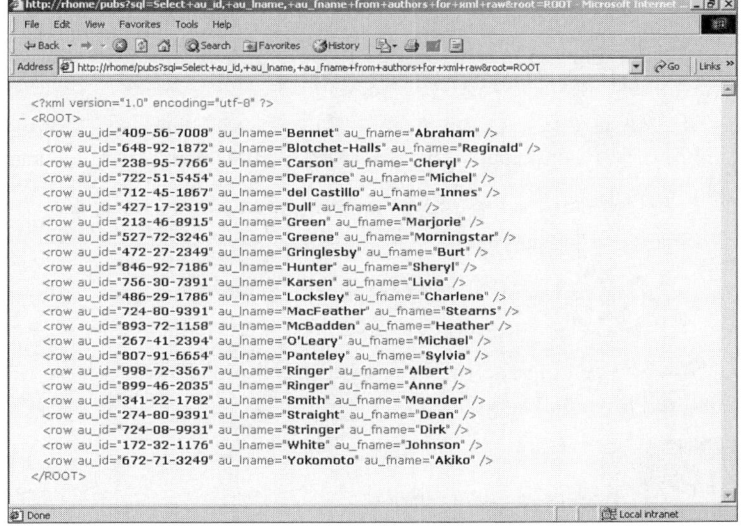

FIGURE 21.9

Your first query returning XML to the Internet.

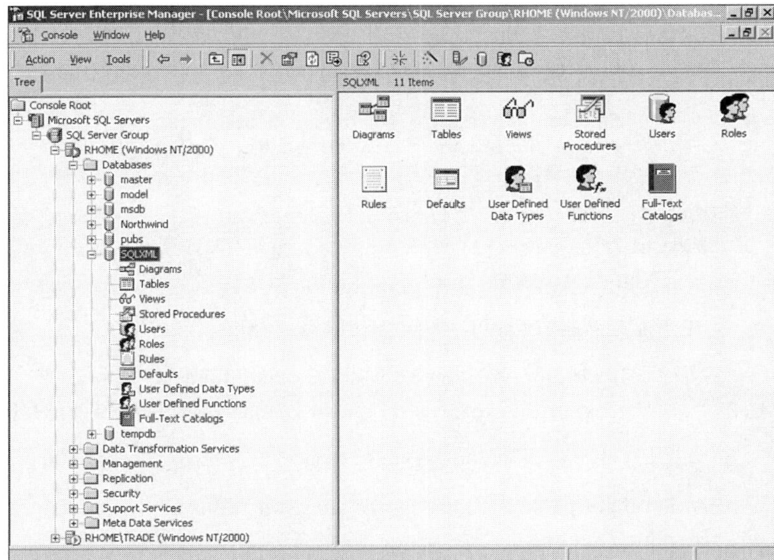

FIGURE 21.10

Enterprise Manager showing the newly created database.

> Not nervous yet? Try a few more commands, such as
>
> `http://rhome/pubs?sql=drop+database+SQLXML&root=ROOT`
>
> and you might be. So, what should you do about it? Make sure only authorized personnel using the correct security accounts have access through this interface.

Executing Stored Procedures

As long as you can submit T-SQL queries, you can also submit calls to stored procedures. You can actually call stored procedures using two mechanisms:

- You can use the traditional execute command, such as

  `Exec sp_helpdb`

- You can use the ODBC call syntax, such as

  `{call+sp_helpdb}`

Now try creating and then calling a stored procedure. Run the following to create two stored procedures to call:

INPUT

```
Use Pubs
GO
Create proc testxml1
As
Select au_lname, au_fname from authors for xml auto
Return
Go
Create proc testxml2 (@lastname nvarchar(255))
As
Select au_lname, au_fname from authors
where au_lname = @lastname for xml auto
Return
GO
```

First, call the `testxml1` stored procedure. This stored procedure doesn't take any parameters. You then see the results in Figure 21.11.

```
http://rhome/pubs?sql=exec+testxml1&root=ROOT
```

Now call stored procedure `testxml2`, which takes a parameter of `lastname`. Select one from the list in Figure 21.11 (I chose Johnson White). So, the URL now looks like

```
http://rhome/pubs?sql=exec+testxml2+'White'&root=ROOT
```

and you get back just the row for Johnson White. You can also reference the parameter by name, such as

```
http://rhome/pubs?sql=exec+testxml2+@lastname=+'White'&root=ROOT
```

FIGURE 21.11

Results of a stored procedure (no parameters).

```
http://rhome/pubs?sql=exec+testxml1&root=ROOT - Microsoft Internet Explorer
Address http://rhome/pubs?sql=exec+testxml1&root=ROOT

<?xml version="1.0" encoding="utf-8" ?>
- <ROOT>
    <authors au_lname="Bennet" au_fname="Abraham" />
    <authors au_lname="Blotchet-Halls" au_fname="Reginald" />
    <authors au_lname="Carson" au_fname="Cheryl" />
    <authors au_lname="DeFrance" au_fname="Michel" />
    <authors au_lname="del Castillo" au_fname="Innes" />
    <authors au_lname="Dull" au_fname="Ann" />
    <authors au_lname="Green" au_fname="Marjorie" />
    <authors au_lname="Greene" au_fname="Morningstar" />
    <authors au_lname="Gringlesby" au_fname="Burt" />
    <authors au_lname="Hunter" au_fname="Sheryl" />
    <authors au_lname="Karsen" au_fname="Livia" />
    <authors au_lname="Locksley" au_fname="Charlene" />
    <authors au_lname="MacFeather" au_fname="Stearns" />
    <authors au_lname="McBadden" au_fname="Heather" />
    <authors au_lname="O'Leary" au_fname="Michael" />
    <authors au_lname="Panteley" au_fname="Sylvia" />
    <authors au_lname="Ringer" au_fname="Albert" />
    <authors au_lname="Ringer" au_fname="Anne" />
    <authors au_lname="Smith" au_fname="Meander" />
    <authors au_lname="Straight" au_fname="Dean" />
    <authors au_lname="Stringer" au_fname="Dirk" />
    <authors au_lname="White" au_fname="Johnson" />
    <authors au_lname="Yokomoto" au_fname="Akiko" />
  </ROOT>
```

In either case, they return exactly the same result, as shown in Figure 21.12.

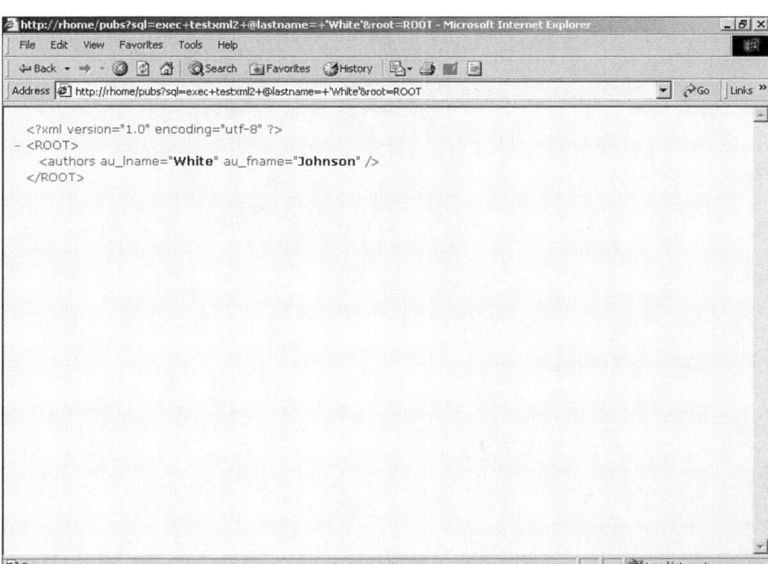

FIGURE 21.12

Calling a stored procedure with a parameter.

As you can see, submitting queries via a URL is really quite simple and powerful—so powerful, in fact, that you might want to restrict the type of T-SQL that can be sent. In this case, template files can fit in nicely.

21

Using Template Files

Template files allow you to restrict what users can run as far as T-SQL statements go. You can restrict users to running only the SQL statements you code in the template file, or you can restrict them to calling a SQL statement and specifying parameters (including calls to stored procedures).

The easiest way to see how these restrictions work is to simply create a few templates. Start by creating a template directory under your pubs virtual directory using Windows Explorer. In my case, I created the folder f:\inetpub\wwwroot\pubs\template. Next, create a simple template file, and store it in the folder. Here is your first template file:

```
<ROOT xmlns:sql="urn:schemas-microsoft-com:xml-sql">
  <sql:query>
    SELECT au_lname, au_fname
    FROM   Authors
    FOR XML AUTO
  </sql:query>
</ROOT>
```

Now you must enable the template virtual directory in the IIS Virtual Directory Management tool. Right-click your pubs virtual directory, select Properties, and then select the Virtual Names tab. Click New to see the dialog shown in Figure 21.13. Complete it with the same values, noting that you should use the template directory you just created under your pubs virtual directory.

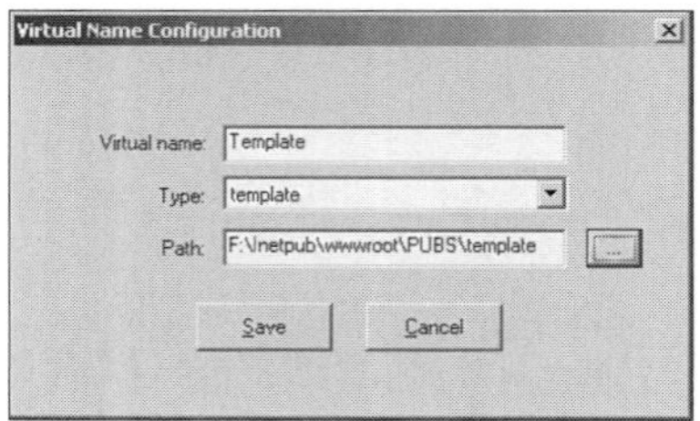

FIGURE 21.13
Creating a new virtual configuration.

Click Save and then OK, and your changes are saved. Now start Internet Explorer to view your Web site (in my case, http://rhome/pubs/template/authors.xml). The site is shown in Figure 21.14.

What about passing parameters? The following example shows another template file, this one containing a call to the stored procedure you created earlier, testxml2. You must pass this stored procedure a parameter. The following XML file (which I called sp.xml) accepts the parameter you pass or defaults to a value of White for the last name:

```
<ROOT xmlns:sql='urn:schemas-microsoft-com:xml-sql'>
  <sql:header>
```

```
    <sql:param name='LastName'>White</sql:param>
  </sql:header>
  <sql:query >
     exec testxml2 @LastName
  </sql:query>
</ROOT>
```

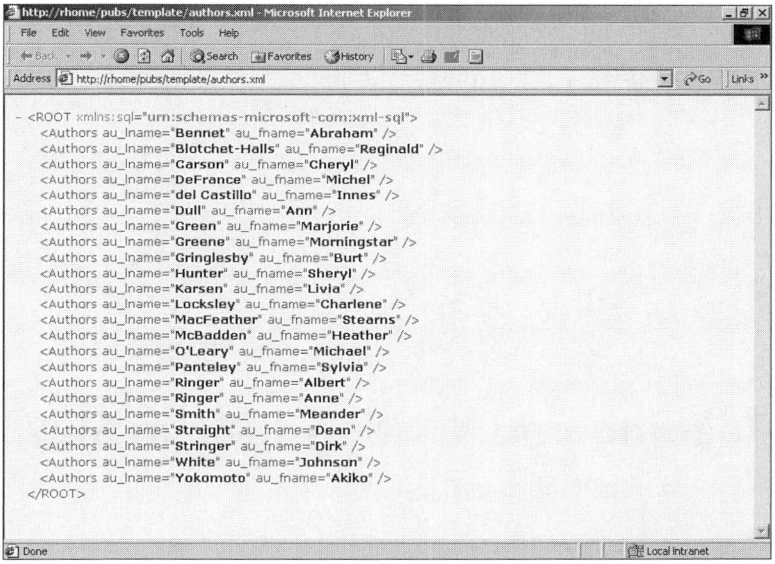

FIGURE 21.14

Results from your XML template file.

```
http://rhome/pubs/template/authors.xml - Microsoft Internet Explorer
File Edit View Favorites Tools Help
Address http://rhome/pubs/template/authors.xml

- <ROOT xmlns:sql="urn:schemas-microsoft-com:xml-sql">
    <Authors au_lname="Bennet" au_fname="Abraham" />
    <Authors au_lname="Blotchet-Halls" au_fname="Reginald" />
    <Authors au_lname="Carson" au_fname="Cheryl" />
    <Authors au_lname="DeFrance" au_fname="Michel" />
    <Authors au_lname="del Castillo" au_fname="Innes" />
    <Authors au_lname="Dull" au_fname="Ann" />
    <Authors au_lname="Green" au_fname="Marjorie" />
    <Authors au_lname="Greene" au_fname="Morningstar" />
    <Authors au_lname="Gringlesby" au_fname="Burt" />
    <Authors au_lname="Hunter" au_fname="Sheryl" />
    <Authors au_lname="Karsen" au_fname="Livia" />
    <Authors au_lname="Locksley" au_fname="Charlene" />
    <Authors au_lname="MacFeather" au_fname="Stearns" />
    <Authors au_lname="McBadden" au_fname="Heather" />
    <Authors au_lname="O'Leary" au_fname="Michael" />
    <Authors au_lname="Panteley" au_fname="Sylvia" />
    <Authors au_lname="Ringer" au_fname="Albert" />
    <Authors au_lname="Ringer" au_fname="Anne" />
    <Authors au_lname="Smith" au_fname="Meander" />
    <Authors au_lname="Straight" au_fname="Dean" />
    <Authors au_lname="Stringer" au_fname="Dirk" />
    <Authors au_lname="White" au_fname="Johnson" />
    <Authors au_lname="Yokomoto" au_fname="Akiko" />
  </ROOT>

Done                                   Local intranet
```

You can call this new XML template file (`sp.xml`) two ways. You can run `http://rhome/pubs/template/sp.xml`, and you get the results for the default value (White). However, you can also pass the parameter as part of the URL. Try running `http://rhome/pubs/template/sp.xml?LastName=Bennet`, and you get the results for the author with the last name Bennet (see Figure 21.15).

As you can see from these examples, calling template files is very easy (and requires a lot less typing). It's also inherently more secure because you can specify the T-SQL statements that will be allowed ahead of time.

Both `XPATH` and `POST`, the other two types of access described in the option settings for your `pubs` virtual directory, are beyond the scope of this book. More detailed information is available in the SQL Server Books Online should you want to learn more about these options.

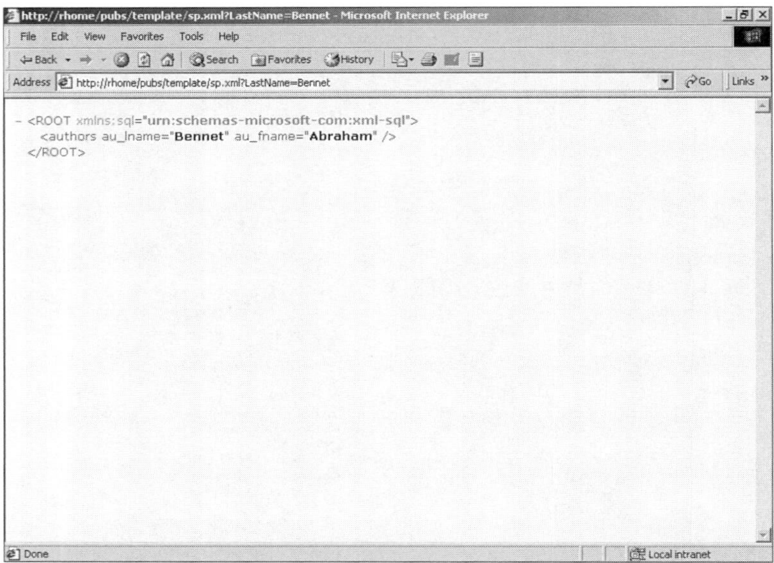

FIGURE 21.15

Results from your XML template file with parameters.

Reading and Writing XML in SQL Server

Now that you know how to get data from SQL Server via your Web browser using XML, you can examine going from the other direction. The SQL Server database engine has been enhanced to support XML directly from T-SQL. You used these capabilities earlier today with nearly every query. Whenever you add a `FOR XML` clause to your `SELECT` statements, you tell the SQL Server engine to return your results formatted for XML. You've also been specifying exactly how you want to format those results. Let's explore these options now.

Valid SELECT Statements

Unfortunately, some restrictions are placed on the types of `SELECT` statements you can specify a `FOR XML` clause on:

- You can't specify `FOR XML` within a T-SQL subselect (a `SELECT` within a `SELECT`).
- The `SELECT` statement must be returning a real result set, and options that don't return "normal" relational rowsets aren't supported, such as the `COMPUTE BY` clause.
- Aggregations such as `GROUP BY` aren't supported when you use `FOR XML AUTO`.
- You can't specify `FOR XML` within a `CREATE VIEW` statement.
- You can't specify `FOR XML` in the select part of an `INSERT SELECT` statement.
- Your select statement can't `CONVERT` or `CAST` a column into image or text data types.

- Some valid SQL Server column names are invalid for XML and are translated as the results are returned. You can find details on valid names in the Books Online, but if you're sticking with normal alphabetic letters, you'll be fine.

Basically, these restrictions all boil down to two rules:

- The data must be leaving SQL Server.
- It must be a proper relational result set.

Using the `FOR XML` Clause

For most valid T-SQL statements, you can append the clause `FOR XML`. The syntax looks like this:

SYNTAX

```
FOR XML mode, [XMLDATA][,ELEMENTS][,BINARY Base64]
```

Three tree modes are available with `FOR XML`: `RAW`, `AUTO`, and `EXPLICIT`.

`FOR XML RAW`

The `FOR XML RAW` option turns each row of your result into an XML document with the identifier of *row*. Each column is specified with an attribute name of the T-SQL column name. All the rows are returned as a single set of data to the client. Figure 21.16 shows what Query Analyzer looks like running this command:

```
Select au_lname from authors FOR XML RAW
```

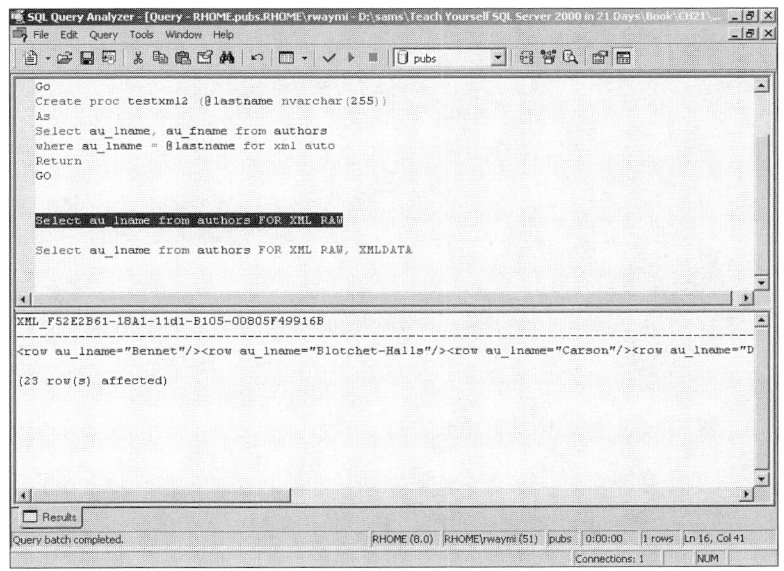

FIGURE 21.16
Results from your `SELECT...FOR XML RAW` statement.

21

Now, run the same command but add the XMLDATA option, which returns information describing the schema (think of it as the create table information), along with the data:

```
Select au_lname from authors FOR XML RAW, XMLDATA
```

You then see the results of your query, as shown in Figure 21.17.

FIGURE 21.17
Results from your SELECT...FOR XML RAW, XMLDATA *statement.*

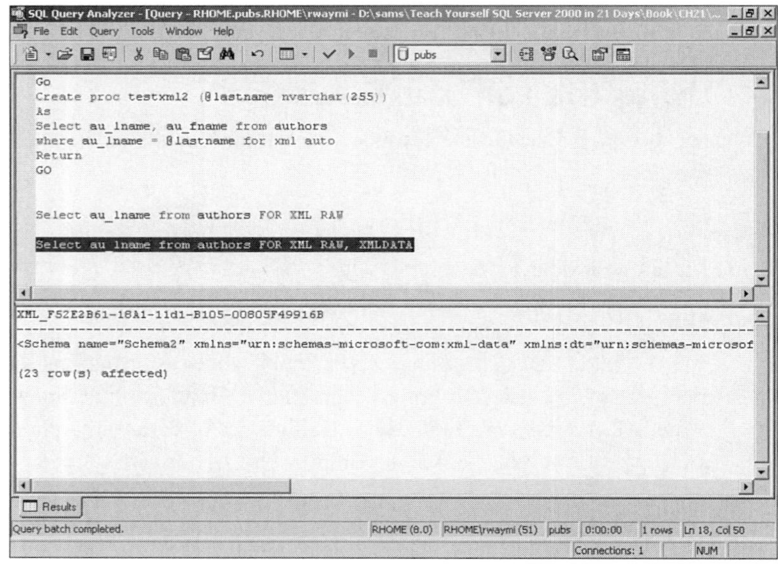

> When you specified FOR XML RAW, XMLDATA, the results were probably truncated. From the Tools menu, choose Options, Results in Query Analyzer, and change the Maximum Characters Per Column setting to something like 1000 to see all the data returned by this command.

Using the XMLDATA Option

As you saw with FOR XML RAW, when you specify the XMLDATA option, you get back a great deal of information in addition to your results. This option returns schema information beyond what's normally returned in XML. Microsoft recommends that you don't specify this option, because it slows down your server, and most XML data coming back is simply text strings anyway.

FOR XML AUTO

The AUTO option is similar to RAW but returns more information about the returned data. It also returns each table from your query in a nested format to the XML results. The easiest way to understand this option is to view results from running queries with this option set. Let's run the same query as before as a start (the results are shown in Figure 21.18):

```
Select au_lname from authors FOR XML AUTO
```

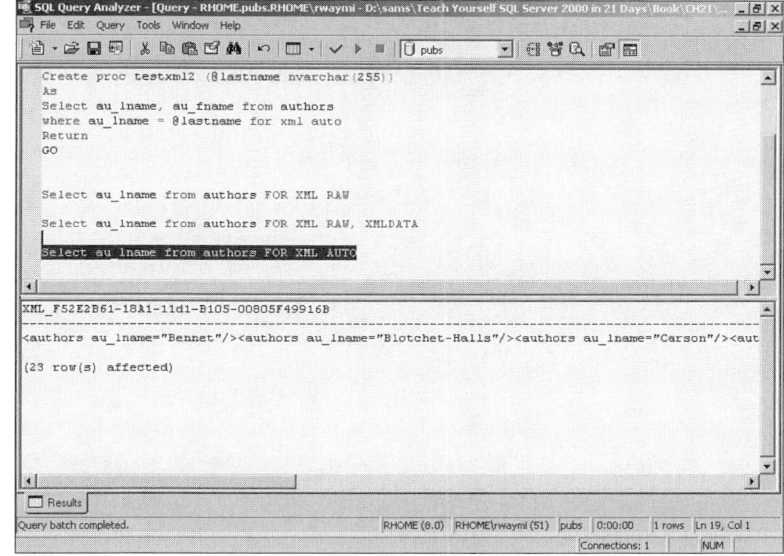

FIGURE 21.18
Results from your `SELECT...FOR XML AUTO` *statement.*

However, running a multiple-table select statement really shows the difference. So, run the following query:

INPUT
```
Select au_lname, title, royaltyper
From authors inner join titleauthor on authors.au_id = titleau-
thor.au_id
Inner join titles on titleauthor.title_id = titles.title_id
FOR XML AUTO
```

You see the results as shown in Figure 21.19.

Notice that the results are all qualified with which table they came from, are all nested, and include the column name that they represent, as well as the data. Because Query Analyzer doesn't format these results too well, look at what a little creative use of Notepad did to the results in Figure 21.20. Now you can clearly see the hierarchy of the results and what `FOR XML AUTO` has done for you.

With the `FOR XML AUTO` option, you can specify the additional option `ELEMENTS`:

INPUT
```
Select au_lname, title, royaltyper
From authors inner join titleauthor on authors.au_id = titleau-
thor.au_id
Inner join titles on titleauthor.title_id = titles.title_id
FOR XML AUTO, ELEMENTS
```

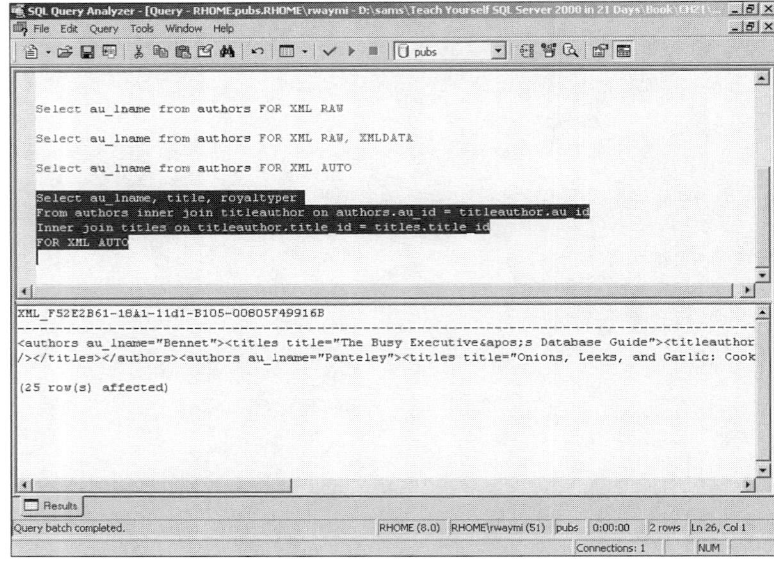

FIGURE 21.19

Multiple table join results for the `FOR XML AUTO` statement.

FIGURE 21.20

The same results viewed and formatted in Notepad.

Untitled - Notepad

File Edit Format Help

```
<authors au_lname="Bennet">
        <titles title="The Busy Executive&apos;s Database Guide">
                <titleauthor royaltyper="60"/>
        </titles>
</authors>
<authors au_lname="Blotchet-Halls">
        <titles title="Fifty Years in Buckingham Palace Kitchens">
                <titleauthor royaltyper="100"/>
        </titles>
</authors><authors au_lname="Panteley">
        <titles title="Onions, Leeks, and Garlic: Cooking Secrets of the Mediterranean">
                <titleauthor royaltyper="100"/>
        </titles>
</authors>
...
```

When you specify this option, each column title is broken out separately as an XML element. Review Figure 21.21 to see what this minor change in your query has done to your results.

`FOR XML EXPLICIT`

Finally, you can specify the option `FOR XML EXPLICIT`, which allows you to specify exactly how the XML will be formatted from your query results. In the previous edition our coverage of this topic was a bit light. However as we've gained experience implementing this technology, we've come to instances where it's more cumbersome to return an XML stream with `FOR XML AUTO` than it is to explicitly define what you want. Also, by our own admission, Books Online's coverage of this topic leaves a little to be desired. Without further ado, let us investigate how to use this option.

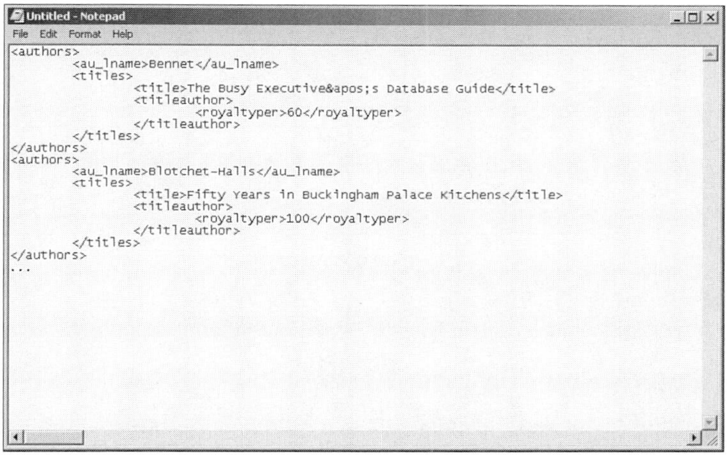

FIGURE 21.21
Same query with the `ELEMENTS` *option specified.*

```
Untitled - Notepad
File  Edit  Format  Help
<authors>
        <au_lname>Bennet</au_lname>
        <titles>
                <title>The Busy Executive&apos;s Database Guide</title>
                <titleauthor>
                        <royaltyper>60</royaltyper>
                </titleauthor>
        </titles>
</authors>
<authors>
        <au_lname>Blotchet-Halls</au_lname>
        <titles>
                <title>Fifty Years in Buckingham Palace Kitchens</title>
                <titleauthor>
                        <royaltyper>100</royaltyper>
                </titleauthor>
        </titles>
</authors>
...
```

The Universal Table

NEW TERM The key to understanding explicit XML formatting is understanding the structure of what's called the *Universal Table*. The Universal Table is a structure used by SQL Server to determine how it should render a result set within an XML stream. This table always contains the two columns "Tag" and "Parent", which are defined with integer data–types. The remaining columns are named with a format that contains meta–data used by the SQL Server process that converts the result set to XML.

```
<element name>!<tag number>[!<attribute name>][!<directive(s)>]
```

The first part of the name defines the XML element this particular column is associated with. The second part contains the "Tag" number, which relates to this element's position within the XML hierarchy. Next we have an optional part of the name that is used to associate the column with a particular attribute. Finally, another attribute exists, which can be used to give the conversion process additional instructions as to the purpose of the column. We'll examine these options after we give an example of what we've just covered.

If you recall our first example using `FOR XML AUTO`, we asked SQL Server to return a list of author last names from the Pubs database. The following is the first few elements returned from that query:

```
Select au_lname from authors FOR XML AUTO

<authors au_lname="Bennet"/>
<authors au_lname="Blotchet-Halls"/>
<authors au_lname="Carson"/>
```

The Universal Table behind this result set would look something like this:

```
Create table universal
(tag int not null,
parent int null,
[authors!1!au_lname] varchar(40) null)
```

We've used a `CREATE TABLE` statement here for illustrative purposes only. When using `FOR XML EXPLICIT` you do not have to create this table yourself.

In this example notice that *authors* is the name of our element. Also, this is our first element indicated by tag ID *1,* and this element contains an attribute called *au_lname*.

The Role of Tag and Parent

One of the most frequently asked questions in SQL Server newsgroups is how to retrieve data in a hierarchical format? This question gives rise to what we call the storage–presentation paradox. The term *relational* in relational databases stems from the mathematical term *relation*. A relation is a correspondence between two or more sets. For example, mathematically the function given by $f(x) = 2x - 1$ is a relation between the set of real numbers and the set of real numbers. Geometrically, we'd describe this relation as a line. In relational databases, we describe relations using primary and foreign key relationships. The greatest strength of this model is its inherent ability to avoid storing redundant data. On the other hand, for the presentation layers of the applications that consume our data, it's more convenient to display and use data in a hierarchical fashion.

The *Tag* and *Parent* columns of the Universal Table are used to communicate the nesting of our XML hierarchies. In the second example of using `FOR XML AUTO`, we had SQL Server render author last names, titles they've written, and the royalty they're being paid for the title.

```
Select au_lname, title, royaltyper
From authors inner join titleauthor on authors.au_id = titleauthor.au_id
Inner join titles on titleauthor.title_id = titles.title_id
FOR XML AUTO, ELEMENTS
```

In this case we have two elements, *titles* and *titleauthor,* that appear in the results as children of *authors*. Our Universal Table in this example would look like this:

```
Create table universal
(tag int not null,
parent int null,
[authors!1!au_lname] varchar(40) null,
[titles!2!title] varchar(80) null,
[titleauthor!3!royaltyper] int null)
```

Notice that each of our elements are uniquely identified by their corresponding tag number. This is important because element names need not be unique in an XML hierarchy, only their position within the schema needs to be unique. The parent number is used to identify an element which an element should be nested under.

Writing `FOR XML EXPLICIT` Queries

If you've ever tried to understand the documentation on `FOR XML EXPLICIT`, this may very well be the moment you've been dreading in our discussion. For our first example, we'd like to show you how to achieve the author last name, title, and royalty XML we retrieved previously, but this time using `FOR XML EXPLICIT`. Although this may look confusing, we'll analyze each part of the query in terms of the Universal Table to demystify the syntax.

```
Select 1 as [Tag], null as [Parent], au_lname as [authors!1!au_lname],
null as [titles!2!title], null as [titleauthor!3!royaltyper]
From authors
Union
Select 2, 1, au_lname, title, null
From authors inner join titleauthor on authors.au_id = titleauthor.au_id
Inner join titles on titleauthor.title_id = titles.title_id
Union
Select 3, 1, au_lname ,title, royaltyper
From authors inner join titleauthor on authors.au_id = titleauthor.au_id
Inner join titles on titleauthor.title_id = titles.title_id
Order by [authors!1!au_lname], [titles!2!title], [titleauthor!3!royal-
typer]
For xml explicit
```

At this point it's time to reflect on the advice given on the cover of *The Hitchhiker's Guide To The Galaxy*: DON'T PANIC! This is much simpler than it may appear. The first thing to point out is that we have three distinct elements, which requires us to compose our result set from three separate queries. Next, if you examine the first `SELECT` statement, you'll see that each of the columns are aliased as the column names from the Universal Table we defined for this query.

Note

When result sets are combined with a `UNION` statement the column names from the first `SELECT` become the column names for the final result.

You may also have noticed the use of NULL in the first two queries. In the first query, parent, title, and royalty have been assigned the value NULL rather than values from a particular column in a table. When rendering XML, explicitly NULL is used to indicate that there's no data for a particular column that may need to be rendered. In the case of the parent column though, NULL is used to indicate that the tag had no parent, that is to say it's a root node in the XML. The final part to point out is the ORDER BY clause. When you create a query for explicit XML, you are responsible for specifying the sort order of the resulting XML.

If we look at the result of this query without the FOR XML EXPLICIT clause, the hierarchy we're rendering becomes more apparent. The following is a sample of just that.

OUTPUT

```
Tag        Parent  [authors!1!au_lname]    [titles!2!title]
➥[titleauthor!2!royaltyper]
1  NULL     Bennet  NULL     NULL
2  1        Bennet  The Busy Executive's Database Guide     NULL
3  1        Bennet  The Busy Executive's Database Guide     60
1  NULL     Blotchet-Halls  NULL     NULL
2  1        Blotchet-Halls  Fifty Years in Buckingham Palace Kitchens       NULL
3  1        Blotchet-Halls  Fifty Years in Buckingham Palace Kitchens       100
```

You might also have noticed that we repeated certain columns in our queries, which appear redundant in our Universal Table. This is also necessary for the conversion process to be able to associate, in our case, authors with titles and royalties being paid to that author for a particular title.

If you're thinking to yourself that FOR XML AUTO is infinitely simpler, we share your sentiments. In fact we wouldn't recommend writing such a trivial query with explicit formatting. Bear with us however as we're about to show you the power of explicit formatting.

Advantages of Explicit Formatting

Suppose the consumer of this XML stream needs the associated royalty as an attribute of the *titles* element, rather than within its own *titleauthor* element. It turns out you cannot do this with FOR XML AUTO in a convenient fashion; however, it's a snap with explicit formatting. The new query would look like so.

```
Select 1 as [Tag], NULL as [Parent], au_lname AS [authors!1!au_lname],
null as [titles!2!title], null as [titles!2!royaltyper]
From authors
Union
Select 2, 1, au_lname ,title, royaltyper
From authors inner join titleauthor on authors.au_id = titleauthor.au_id
Inner join titles on titleauthor.title_id = titles.title_id
```

```
Order by [authors!1!au_lname], [titles!2!title]
For xml explicit
```

Hopefully, you're curiosity has been piqued by this example, because it gets even better! You may have noticed that each author is a distinct element in our XML, but a title can be written by more than one author. To better represent this observation, we could rewrite our query as such.

```
Select 1 as [Tag], NULL as [Parent], title AS [titles!1!title],
null as [authors!2!au_lname], null as [authors!2!royaltyper]
From titles
Union
Select 2, 1, title, au_lname ,royaltyper
From authors inner join titleauthor on authors.au_id = titleauthor.au_id
Inner join titles on titleauthor.title_id = titles.title_id
Order by [titles!1!title], [authors!2!au_lname]
For xml explicit
```

A sample from our resulting XML would look like this.

```
<titles title="But Is It User Friendly?">
    <authors au_lname="Carson" royaltyper="100"/>
</titles>
<titles title="Computer Phobic AND Non-Phobic Individuals: Behavior
Variations">
    <authors au_lname="Karsen" royaltyper="75"/>
    <authors au_lname="MacFeather" royaltyper="25"/>
</titles>
```

Looks great for that accounting application!

Taking It to the Next Level

Working with unions can get cumbersome to say the least, and there are difficulties in their use, mostly stemming from limitations of ordering. So now that we've made you suffer though the difficult part, we'll show you a much simpler, more flexible, and quite frankly, more elegant way to use this technique.

Our previous discussion on the structure of the Universal Table was not only to help clarify element–attribute naming conventions and organization, it also was meant to give you a bit of background on what we're going to cover here. In our consulting practices, it's quite common to receive requests for XML schemas that contain complicated nesting, particularly when rendering a stream to an ASP page where you want to eliminate unnecessary trips to the database. In this case, it's useful the stage your data and select it once using a *table variable*.

21

NEW TERM A *table variable* is similar to a *temporary table* in previous versions of SQL Server. The primary difference being that table variables exist in memory, while temporary tables exist on disk within tempdb. There are several other limits on their use, such as an inability to create an index on them that are of no consequence for our purposes. You can find more information on this in Books Online.

> **Caution** Although temporary tables can be used just as easily as table variables, you're better off not using them, especially if your SQL Server connections are being pooled from IIS. Temporary tables are local to a connection, but in an effort to more efficiently allocate resources, they may wind up actually being shared if two connection instances are created with the same connection string. In this case it's possible for these connections to corrupt each other's data, which leads to some interesting result sets and even more interesting debugging!

Declaring a table variable is just like declaring any other local variable, except its data–type is `TABLE` and you include your column definitions. The following is an example of how you might declare a table variable for the example we've been working with.

```
Declare @tblXML table
([tag] int not null,
[parent] null,
[au_lname] varchar(40) null,
[title] varchar(60) null,
[royaltyper] int null)
```

> **Tip** When creating a table variable to serve as a stage for your explicit XML queries, it's useful to specify your non–tag columns to allow null.

Before proceeding with our final example, we need to discuss the optional directive parameters we deferred in our discussion of the Universal Table. For our purposes, the only two we're concerned with are *element* and *hide*.

- **element** is used when we want to indicate that a particular column should not be rendered as an attribute, but instead be displayed on its own as an element within our XML.
- **hide** is used when we do not want a particular attribute to be displayed within our XML. The most common use of this directive is for ordering our results by an attribute that does not need to be part of the XML, but is required for an `ORDER BY` clause in our `SELECT`.

There are several additional directives that only apply when using the `XMLDATA` option. Information on their use can be found in Books Online.

Rather than continue with our ongoing example, we'll demonstrate how to use table variables and `FOR XML EXPLCIT` in a more practical light. Suppose we've been tasked to create a stored procedure that will render our list of authors, titles, publishers and royalties to our new web application. It's been decided that we want to minimize our trips to the database to present the data and we also want to capitalize on the latest XML features within Internet Explorer. The developers of the presentation layer have decided that the best way for them to receive our data is using the following XML schema.

```
<TitleList>
    <Authors>
        <Author ID="" Name="" />
    </Authors>
    <Publishers>
        <Publisher ID="" Name="" City="" State="" Country="" />
    </Publishers>
    <Titles>
        <Title Name="" Type="" Price="" PudID="" PubDate="" >
            <Author ID="" RoyaltyPercentage="" />
        </Title>
    </Titles>
</TitleList>
```

Ask a wise man how to eat an elephant and he'll reply, "One bite at a time." The good news is in our experience it doesn't get much more complicated than this. In the technique that follows, we're going to take the wise man's advice and break this problem into a series of tasks that are much simpler. The first step in our approach is to determine what the Universal Table would look like. Take a moment to think about this and then compare your result with ours below.

```
DECLARE   @tblXml TABLE (
[Tag] INT NOT NULL,
[Parent] INT NULL,
[TitleList!1!element] INT NULL,
[Authors!2!element] INT NULL,
[Author!3!ID] VARCHAR(12) NULL,
[Author!3!Name] VARCHAR(62) NULL,
[Publishers!4!element] INT NULL,
[Publisher!5!ID] CHAR(4) NULL,
[Publisher!5!Name] VARCHAR(40) NULL,
[Publisher!5!City] VARCHAR(20) NULL,
[Publisher!5!State] CHAR(2) NULL,
[Publisher!5!Country] VARCHAR(30) NULL,
[Titles!6!element] INT NULL,
[Title!7!ID!hide] VARCHAR(6) NULL,
[Title!7!Name] VARCHAR(80) NULL,
[Title!7!Type] VARCHAR(12) NULL,
[Title!7!Price] MONEY NULL,
[Title!7!PubID] CHAR(4) NULL,
[Title!7!PubDate] DATETIME NULL,
```

```
[Author!8!ID] VARCHAR(12) NULL,
[Author!8!RoyaltyPercentage] INT NULL)
```

If you didn't get the hidden attribute, that's perfectly alright. The ID attribute of our Title element is used within our process to ensure the correct ordering and associations are maintained between titles and authors in our hierarchy. The code listing that follows is a stored procedure that populates the schema for this example. See if you can notice why we chose to use a hidden attribute.

```
CREATE PROCEDURE dbo.GetTitleListWithExplicitXml
AS
SET NOCOUNT ON

DECLARE   @tblXml TABLE (
[Tag] INT NOT NULL,
[Parent] INT NULL,
[TitleList!1!element] INT NULL,
[Authors!2!element] INT NULL,
[Author!3!ID] VARCHAR(12) NULL,
[Author!3!Name] VARCHAR(62) NULL,
[Publishers!4!element] INT NULL,
[Publisher!5!ID] CHAR(4) NULL,
[Publisher!5!Name] VARCHAR(40) NULL,
[Publisher!5!City] VARCHAR(20) NULL,
[Publisher!5!State] CHAR(2) NULL,
[Publisher!5!Country] VARCHAR(30) NULL,
[Titles!6!element] INT NULL,
[Title!7!ID!hide] VARCHAR(6) NULL,
[Title!7!Name] VARCHAR(80) NULL,
[Title!7!Type] VARCHAR(12) NULL,
[Title!7!Price] MONEY NULL,
[Title!7!PubID] CHAR(4) NULL,
[Title!7!PubDate] DATETIME NULL,
[Author!8!ID] VARCHAR(12) NULL,
[Author!8!RoyaltyPercentage] INT NULL)

-- INSERT THE <TitleList> NODE
INSERT @tblXml ([Tag]) VALUES (1)

-- INSERT THE <Authors> NODE
INSERT @tblXml ([Tag], [Parent]) VALUES (2, 1)

-- INSERT THE <Author> NODES
INSERT @tblXml ([Tag], [Parent], [Author!3!ID], [Author!3!Name])
SELECT    3, 2, au_id, au_lname + ', ' + au_fname AS 'Name'
FROM dbo.authors
ORDER BY 'Name'

-- INSERT THE <Publishers> NODE
INSERT @tblXml ([Tag], [Parent]) VALUES (4, 1)
```

```
-- INSERT THE <Publisher> NODES
INSERT @tblXml ([Tag], [Parent], [Publisher!5!ID], [Publisher!5!Name],
    [Publisher!5!City], [Publisher!5!State], [Publisher!5!Country])
SELECT    5, 4, pub_id, pub_name, city, state, country
FROM dbo.publishers
ORDER BY pub_name

-- INSERT THE <Titles> NODE
INSERT @tblXml ([Tag], [Parent]) VALUES (6, 1)

-- GET OUR LIST OF TITLES
DECLARE @Titles TABLE (
k INT IDENTITY(1,1) NOT NULL,
title_id VARCHAR(6),
title VARCHAR(80),
type VARCHAR(12),
price MONEY,
pub_id CHAR(4),
pubdate DATETIME)

INSERT @Titles (title_id, title , type, price, pub_id, pubdate)
SELECT    title_id, title , RTRIM(type), price, pub_id, pubdate
FROM dbo.titles
ORDER BY title

-- ITERATE OUR LIST OF TITLES TO RETRIEVE THE AUTHORS
DECLARE @i INT, @c INT, @title_id VARCHAR(6), @title VARCHAR(80), @type
VARCHAR(12),
    @price MONEY, @pub_id CHAR(4), @pubdate DATETIME

SET @i = 1
SELECT @c = COUNT(*) FROM @Titles

WHILE @i <= @c
BEGIN
    SELECT @title_id = title_id, @title = title, @type = type,
        @price = price, @pub_id = pub_id, @pubdate = pubdate
    FROM @Titles WHERE k = @i

    -- INSERT OUR <Title> NODE
    INSERT @tblXml ([Tag], [Parent], [Title!7!ID!hide], [Title!7!Name],
[Title!7!Type],
        [Title!7!Price], [Title!7!PubID], [Title!7!PubDate])
    VALUES (7, 6, @title_id, @title, @type, @price, @pub_id, @pubdate)

    -- INSERT THE <Author> NODES
    INSERT @tblXml ([Tag], [Parent], [Title!7!ID!hide], [Author!8!ID],
        [Author!8!RoyaltyPercentage])
    SELECT 8, 7, ta.title_id, a.au_id, ta.royaltyper
    FROM dbo.titleauthor ta INNER JOIN dbo.authors a ON ta.au_id =
a.au_id
    WHERE ta.title_id = @title_id
```

```
    ORDER BY a.au_lname

    SET @i = @i + 1
END

-- FINALLY RENDER OUR STREAM
SELECT * FROM @tblXml
FOR XML EXPLICIT

RETURN 0
GO
```

The first thing we've done in the procedure is declare a table variable that looks like the Universal Table we need to render this XML stream. Once we've done this, we simply load our elements in the order that they appear in the schema. One primary advantage of this technique is that it allows us to sort each element group individually. Once we get to the titles themselves, we've used a new technique you may not be familiar with. Because our titles contain nested elements which relate to them, we need some means of working with a title at a time. In fact you may have seen a similar technique using TRANSACT-SQL `CURSORS`.

Essentially, what we've done here is declare another table variable to hold all the data we needed for a title. We created this table with an `IDENTITY` column you learned about previously. We're using the fact that the rows are now sequentially numbered so that we can iterate the table with a while loop. Starting with the number 1, we can stop after we exceed the count of rows in the table. We could also have used a TRANSACT-SQL `CURSOR` for this, but for this example, the approach we've used here is much more appropriate.

Did you notice why we used the hidden attribute? As mentioned previously, we're using title_id to specify which title the nested Author elements are linked to. We could've used our existing title column, but this would've required us to join the titles table to our query. This final step in our procedure is to select the results from our *@tblXml* variable for explicit formatting.

Of course there's other ways to achieve these results, but this is a technique we've used professionally. Another advantage we'd like to point out is, when using a staging table, you're not subject to the limitation of not being able to use `GROUP BY` as with `FOR XML AUTO`.

New Features in SQLXML 3.0

Some of the new features in SQLXML 3.0 (over the functionality included in the box with SQL Server 2000 originally) include client-side XML formatting. Here is how it compares to server-side formatting.

- GROUP BY and other aggregate functions are supported on the client side.
- Multiple rowset queries are not supported on the client side.
- Client side formatting of VARIANT types converts the variants to Unicode strings.
- There are others that are more in-depth than we have time for here. Take a look at the documentation which is installed with the service pack for more information.

XML BULK LOAD Overview

The XML Bulk Load program is actually a COM object that loads structured XML data into SQL Server 2000. It can quickly move large amounts of XML data into SQL Server 2000.

When you execute an XML Bulk Load, you need to specify a couple of parameters. These include the XML Schema Definition or XML-Data Reduced schema which specifies the data mappings and the XML document file or stream.

The XML Bulk Load operation can load data in either a transactional or non-transactional state. The same rules for doing a fast bulk copy apply here. (Tables to be loaded are empty and do not have indexes.)

The SQLXML 3.0 documentation has some wonderful examples of doing an XML BULK LOAD. They include the XML, XSD/XDR, and some VB Script to instantiate the COM object and move the data into SQL Server.

Summary

As you've seen today, Microsoft has provided excellent support for XML either through Internet Information Server or directly in Transact-SQL. Both options have their place. You can allow users to write queries as part of their URL strings, or you can provide the safer option of allowing users to query your database by using XML template files.

Several more advanced features of XML support are available in SQL Server 2000, and the XML team is planning to continue releasing additional features. You might want to periodically check `http://www.microsoft.com/sql` for updates to SQL Server 2000's XML capabilities.

Q&A

Q Which tool should I use to establish XML query capabilities to SQL Server 2000?

A The IIS virtual directory management utility.

Q What does the `FOR XML` clause do for me?

A It automatically generates XML tags appropriate for your data.

Q Can I automatically submit queries via a URL to SQL Server?

A No. You must first enable support for these types of queries in the Virtual Directory Management utility.

Q How can obtain aggregations such as those I get with `COMPUTE` and `COMPUTE BY` using `FOR XML`?

A Both `COMPUTE` and `COMPUTE BY` return non-standard rowsets, so unfortunately you cannot use these clauses within your `SELECT` statements to load your staging variable. However, you can use our `WHILE` loop technique and another local variable to select the aggregation you desire and insert that value into the stage.

Workshop

This section provides quiz questions to help you solidify your understanding of the concepts presented today. In addition to the quiz questions, exercises are provided to let you practice what you've learned today. Answers are provided in Appendix A, "Answers to Quiz Questions."

Quiz

1. Is this a valid URL query?

   ```
   http://rhome/pubs?SQL=select city from authors for XML AUTO&root=ROOT
   ```

2. What kinds of statements are allowed through URL queries?
3. What does the `FOR XML RAW` option do differently from `FOR XML AUTO`?

Exercises

1. Write some XML template files to call stored procedures and queries, specifying parameters. This is likely to be the way you'll allow XML access to SQL Server.
2. Add a new virtual directory to the virtual directory management utility, and point to a system database, such as `master`. Try queries against the `INFORMATION_SCHEMA` views, and then imagine how you could use them to maintain reports about your database schema on a Web site.
3. Rewrite our GetTileListWithExplicitXml stored procedure as a user–defined function.

WEEK 3

In Review

Now it's time to look at what you covered this last week.

On Day 15, you looked at views, user-defined functions, and stored procedures and how to create and execute them. You also learned about creating triggers to enforce referential integrity as well as business rules. They included triggers on `INSERT`, `UPDATE`, and `DELETE`.

On Day 16, you learned the terminology used with replication and the types of replication available, including replication with SQL Server CE. Day 17 continued Day 16's discussion by showing you how to implement replication.

On Day 18, you learned how to automate many of the day-to-day tasks involved with maintaining a SQL Server. You learned how to implement tasks, alerts, and events and then how to connect these components to your email system for notification purposes.

On Day 19, you learned how to use the BCP program to import and export data between SQL Server and other storage locations. You also learned about the Data Transfer Services Wizard for moving data and database schema between any compatible components.

Day 20 focused on fine-tuning your SQL Server. We could write an entire 21-day book on performance tuning and optimization. This lesson, however, introduced you to enough of the major tuning functions to get your SQL Server to about a 90 percent efficiency. The other 10 percent is difficult to implement and varies for each environment and server. Implementing it requires many hours of studying the operation of the server and the use of its components. This lesson described hardware, Windows 2000, and SQL Server parameters that you can set and how to monitor SQL Server performance.

Day 21 examined SQL Server 2000's capabilities with XML. You saw how to expose SQL Server on the Internet via Internet Information Server, as well as how to retrieve data in XML format so that it can be easily interchanged on the Web.

Bonus Days

At a Glance

In these last two bonus days, you will look at some of the "extra" features that come with SQL Server 2000. These features, which are included with the product for free, provide significant functionality that you should at least be aware exists (you already paid for it).

Day 22 introduces you to SQL Server Analysis Services (formerly OLAP) and gives you some background information on data warehousing. You will also launch and start the Analysis Services Tutorial.

Day 23 introduces the English Query product and gives you an overview of its capabilities.

Bonus Days

Day 22

An Overview of Analysis Services

Today's bonus lesson focuses on an overview of Microsoft's Analysis Services. Analysis Services, formerly known as OLAP Services in SQL Server 7.0, enables you to support *data warehousing*. This lesson also introduces data mining and the Microsoft Meta Data Services components (known as the Microsoft Repository in SQL Server 7.0).

Today you also install Analysis Services and start the tutorial for Analysis Services, including data mining.

Understanding Data Warehousing

New Term *Data warehousing* is the art of putting data together in such a way that you can analyze and extract information from what's traditionally been viewed as strictly operational data. *Operational data* is the data your production systems use to run your business.

Not that long ago the data gathered in operational systems was used for day-to-day needs, archived as required by business or legal restrictions, and then discarded. Then smart companies started asking questions—why are we discarding this data? Sales and marketing departments have been forecasting future business for a long time. They've rarely had enough data to make the correct decisions, however. In the end, when your production systems are formatted and correctly transformed, they contain mountains of useful information for business purposes such as forecasting.

When I was younger, I worked at a cosmetics company. The business already had reports about sales, but it wasn't readily available. We had to wait for the reports to come out, generate huge printouts, and then wade through those printouts to find information. This was hardly a model for rapid business decision-making.

Then we decided to build a data warehouse. We took data from various production systems, gathered the required amount of historical data, and built a data warehouse. The data warehouse consisted of sales, down to the individual product level, of every item in every store the product was available in throughout the world. The data was aggregated into interesting business categories and correlated by time.

We could then use the data warehouse to ask questions such as: How do sales compare for this shade of lipstick in region X as compared to region Y? Does it sell better in stores of brand X or brand Y? Can we correlate sales to other factors, such as display types, or similar products being sold in the same display case? How were sales this week by product by category compared to the same week last year? Perhaps most importantly, we could ask all these questions online. We didn't have to wait for someone to write a report—we could do it ourselves and have an answer in no time at all.

That's the excitement of data warehousing—the ability to glean information you couldn't have found before or had to wait for while someone wrote a program for you. Not only that, but you can begin to ask questions no one has asked before. The data warehouse database is flexible enough to allow you to think of new questions and get them answered in short order.

Data warehouses are typically time based and made up of several components: fact tables, dimensions, and levels of aggregation. They usually pull together data from many different systems, based on different data formats, and unify them into something useful. Data warehouses can be quite large. The system I worked on had about 1GB of base information but grew to about 40GB when aggregating and building the data warehouse was completed. Of course, building a data warehouse is never complete because new data is constantly being generated by your business or organization.

By today's standards, 40GB is a fairly small data warehouse. Some vendors are publishing that they have terabyte-sized data warehouses. It's rumored that some companies have much larger data warehouses, but sometimes the very existence of these systems is considered company proprietary information because the business value of a data warehouse can be tremendous—generating a huge competitive advantage.

Fact Tables

New Term Most data warehousing database designs are centered around *fact tables*. A fact table is the central source of information you build your data warehouse with. The easiest way to explain a fact table is to give you an example.

Pretend that you were that cosmetics manufacturer. Your fact table would likely contain information such as the product you sold, who precisely you sold it to, how much you charged, how much it cost to manufacture this product, how much it was sold for at retail, and the date and time you shipped it. You could then use this fact table to answer questions, such as how much product you sold this month and how much money you made by shipping today.

Dimensions

New Term A single fact table in isolation still isn't terribly useful. What's useful is to join that fact table with dimensional support tables. A *dimension* is simply a breakdown of something familiar, such as time. Your time dimension might include century, decade, year, month, week, day, and hour. You might have a product category dimension, which groups information about each kind of product you can sell and how you logically group them. You might also keep geographic information, such as continent, country, region, state, county, and city.

You can then take each dimension and join it to the fact table, so you could find the answer to questions such as, "Tell me by state, by product category, by week, what were sales of product X this year compared to last? Also, compare that to sales in other regions."

Aggregation

New Term Of course, having one large fact table with several dimension tables can indeed answer your data warehousing questions. However, getting answers may take awhile if you ship tens or hundreds of millions of individual products. So, you'll probably *aggregate* data—that is, pre-calculate the answers to questions you think will be asked or pre-calculate data by dimension up to a certain level.

For example, you may anticipate frequently getting asked about product sales by week. So, to save time when people run queries, you could calculate sales by week by product, or by product category. Then, when someone asks a question that your aggregation has already figured out, you can return the results much more quickly and have happy customers.

As you might imagine, the hard part about aggregation is knowing when to stop and how to know that you have the right set of aggregations. The best way to do so is to capture the types of questions folks are asking and review your aggregation designs. You can also use some predictive modeling tools, such as those included with SQL Server 2000 Analysis Services.

Understanding Data Marts

NEW TERM Data marts are becoming increasingly popular. A *data mart* is simply a mini data warehouse. Imagine that you have indeed built the world's best data warehouse for your company. How many users will be using the data simultaneously? How much data will be in that data warehouse? It may be just too much information in one place for some customers. So, what do you do about this problem?

The answer: Build a data mart. A data mart is simply a section of your data warehouse customized for a particular community of customers of the data. For example, in the cosmetics company example, perhaps the sales representative for a large national chain is interested only in data for her particular customer but doesn't want the rest of the data warehousing dimension. You could create a data mart to address this customer's needs and slice out just the required data from the data warehouse. Given the affordability of tools such as SQL Server 2000, the process of building and maintaining data marts is becoming easier all the time.

Building a Data Warehouse

You must perform a few steps to build your data warehouse. Of course, each step probably involves a tool provided with SQL Server 2000. Your first step is to design the data warehouse and identify where you'll get the data. This step typically requires a team effort and may take quite a bit of time.

Step 1: Create a Holding Area for the Data

After you figure out where to get data, you need to create a temporary holding area. It may be a totally separate installation of SQL Server, but will more than likely be an isolated database. It's *very* likely that the data won't be ready for you to simply load into your data warehouse. So, putting it here for safekeeping is a good idea until you're ready to transform the data to the correct formats and filter out just the information you need.

Step 2: Get Data from a Legacy or OLTP System

The second step usually involves getting the cooperation of a number of other administrators and developers in your company. You need to find the authoritative source of data for each piece of information you want to retain in your data warehouse. Then you need to arrange for regular information feeds from those systems to your holding area. SQL Server replication, as well as heterogeneous distributed queries, can be used here to connect to these systems and get the data.

Step 3: Transform the Data, If Necessary

When you have the information, you'll likely need to massage the data somewhat before it is useful. It's likely that not all data will be in the exact format you need, and it's also likely you'll need to combine or separate columns to get them into the format you need for your data warehouse.

A classic example is a name column. If you normalize your database, you may have last name, first name, middle initial, title, and suffix. However, suppose that your data warehouse needs only a simple name field. You can transform the data by combining the individual columns that make up a name into a single field for your data warehouse.

Data Transformation Services (DTS) is often used in this step to transform your data to the proper format. DTS can perform complicated look-ups, perform conversions, and combine or tear apart information as needed. Because DTS uses OLE DB to connect to a data source, this step and Step 2 can often be combined.

Step 4: Load the Transformed Data into Your Warehouse

After you have the data in the proper format, load it into your data warehouse. Here, you can take advantage of DTS again, or use SQL Server's `BULK INSERT` and `BCP` utilities to load your data. Each process is built with the expectation that you're simply adding on to the existing data warehouse.

Step 5: Build and Update OLAP Cubes in Analysis Services

After you have your basic fact tables, you can perform aggregation and prepare to answer all these interesting business questions. You should probably do so by using

OLAP cubes and Microsoft Analysis Services. When you do so, you get the answers to questions very, very quickly, even when querying very large sets of information joining one or more fact tables with many dimension tables.

Understanding the Components of Analysis Services

Analysis Services is part of the foundation for data warehousing available with SQL Server 2000. As you've just seen, you need more than the basic components of SQL Server 2000 to build a data warehouse. You also need help from the components provided by Analysis Services. Analysis Services in the context of today's lesson is made up of three components: OLAP, data mining, and Meta Data Services.

OLAP

OLAP stands for OnLine Analytical Processing, or the ability to learn something meaningful from your data without having to use an offline batch system. SQL Server 2000 has full support for OLAP and data warehousing with the availability of Analysis Services.

SQL Server 2000's OLAP features allow you to view data in more than relational tables. You can combine data in new and interesting ways and view it "multidimensionally." You can choose to store data within traditional SQL Server tables (known as ROLAP, for Relational OLAP), in a Microsoft proprietary format known as MOLAP (for Multidimensional OLAP), or HOLAP (Hybrid OLAP, with some data stored in SQL Server and some in MOLAP cubes).

NEW TERM A *cube* is simply a set of data stored in such a way as to allow quick and easy analysis of data. Data stored in cubes is analyzed based on dimensions. A dimension is typically something very intuitive, such as time or region. For example, you could have sales by year, quarter, month, week, day, and even hour or minute. You could also have sales broken up by region, for example, country, state, county, and city, and perhaps even postal code within city.

Now, put your sales data into a cube with the time and region dimensions, and you can start asking questions such as, "Were sales higher in the southern United States for ice cream during the month of June?" That's interesting, but then you could drill down further into your data and ask detailed questions, correlating additional information, such as the weather in each region at the time.

As you can imagine, adding more dimensions can allow you to ask very hard questions and get nearly instant answers. You can store data at nearly any level of detail (depending on how much disk space you have) and be able to resolve questions as large as sales for the last five years to sales for every department of every store in every region for every product. All of this in a single OLAP cube, and, perhaps most importantly, with extremely fast response times because the answers are already there in the cube.

OLAP Services has its own query language, MDX (MultiDimensional Expressions). If you use a HOLAP or MOLAP cube rather than Transact-SQL to manipulate data, you use the MDX language. MDX is fully supported from both OLE DB and ADO.

Data Mining

Analysis Services includes data-mining capabilities. Data mining allows you to use existing OLAP cubes to search for relationships that may be interesting in your data. For example, if you conducted a survey and asked several questions, you could create an OLAP cube of the survey results and then answer questions about the data, such as, "If someone answered yes to question 2, how likely is it that that person will answer yes to question 5?"

Sounds boring, but imagine if that meant that if the person comes to a store to buy diapers and he's a male under 35, he'll probably buy some beer as well. You, as an enterprising retailer, could then move the beer between the diapers and the checkout counter as a less-than-subtle hint. And, assuming that your data was correct, beer sales will probably increase.

Another example: You've been sending out mailings to your customer list. Each piece of mail costs money, so you would much rather send mail to just customers likely to take advantage of your services. With data mining, you can analyze whom you've sent mail to previously and whether that got a response. You can also factor in socioeconomic data about your customers to determine who's most likely to respond to your mailing. This way, you can reduce the amount of mail you send and possibly increase the responses from the customers to whom you do send mail.

Both examples show how collecting data and then performing analysis (mining your data) can lead to increased profits and the ability to provide better customer service. Providing this kind of data to the company can contribute directly to the financial bottom line (and justify that pay increase you've been waiting for).

As with OLAP, data mining has API interfaces as well, such as Decision Support Objects (DSO), an object model for OLAP, and data mining.

Meta Data Services

Meta Data Services is an object-oriented system to store metadata, or information about data. It does so via a Meta Data engine that comes with SQL Server 2000, the tools for viewing metadata, as well as an SDK (Software Development Kit) for writing applications to use Meta Data Services.

Metadata can significantly enhance the value of a data warehouse. It can answer questions about your data, such as

- Where did this row of data come from originally?
- When was it last modified, and by whom?
- Was it transformed by DTS from the original system?
- If so, what did the DTS package look like?

Of course, these are just questions you could ask based on SQL Server 2000's built-in features. By using the SDK, you can build your applications to support storing and using metadata.

Meta Data Services abstracts information into an object-oriented model. After you define the models, information fits very naturally (if you think object-oriented information fits naturally). The basic models are based on an industry standard model known as the Open Information Model, defined by a group known as the Meta Data Coalition. The Meta Data Coalition is a group of software vendors (of which Microsoft is a member) that have joined to provide standards and infrastructure to support metadata.

Installing Analysis Services

Installing Analysis Services is very straightforward. Insert the SQL Server CD-ROM, select SQL Server 2000 Components, and then select Install Analysis Services (see Figure 22.1).

After you click this option, you see the Welcome to SQL Server 2000 Analysis Services Setup, as shown in Figure 22.2.

Click Next and review the license agreement (see Figure 22.3). Click Yes after you read it.

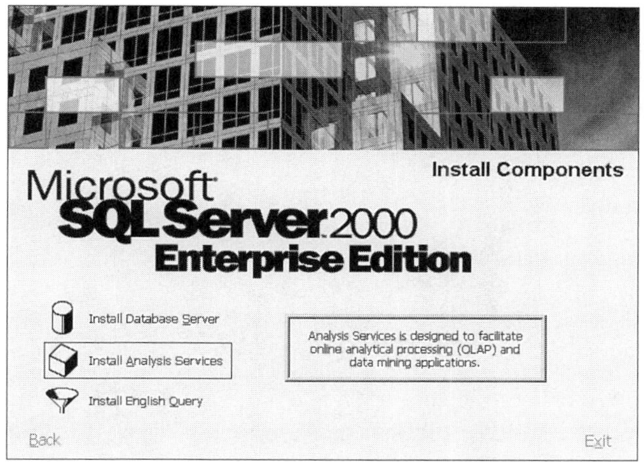

FIGURE 22.1
Selecting to install Analysis Services.

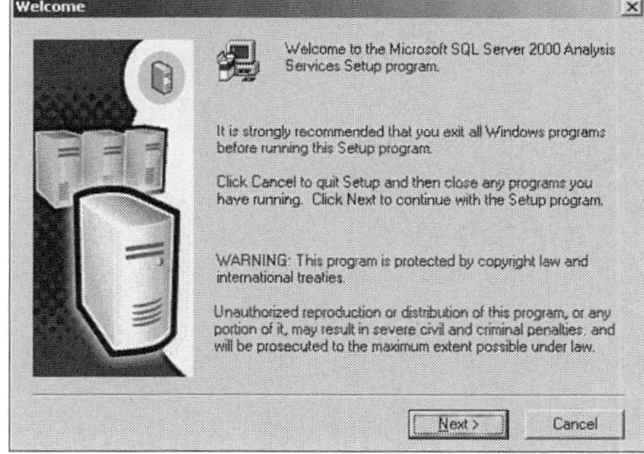

FIGURE 22.2
Welcome to SQL Server 2000 Analysis Services Setup.

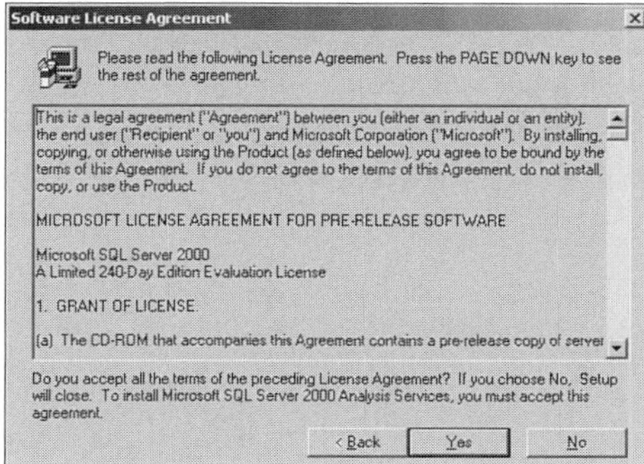

FIGURE 22.3
Review and agree to the license agreement.

You then see the Select Components dialog (see Figure 22.4). By default, Analysis Services installs every component, so don't change anything on this dialog (unless you want to change the default installation location).

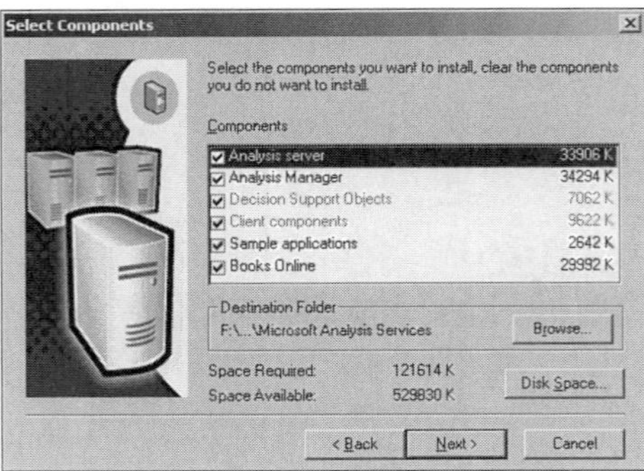

FIGURE 22.4

Selecting Analysis Services components.

Click Next to move to the dialog shown in Figure 22.5. Here, you select the default location to store your OLAP cubes as they are created, as well as the location for the sample cubes that ship with Analysis Services. Change the location if necessary, and then click Next.

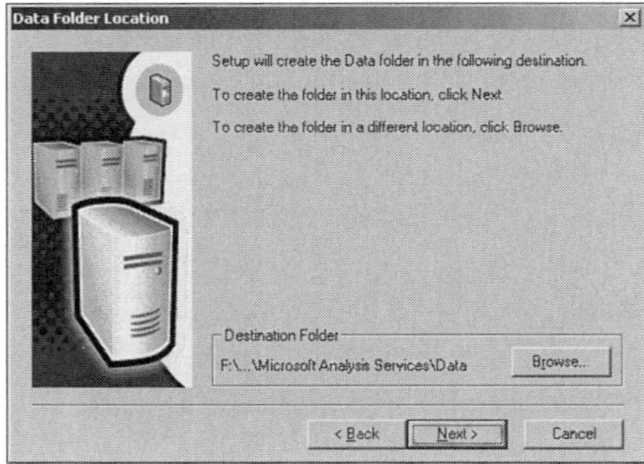

FIGURE 22.5

Selecting the Data Folder Location.

Finally, setup asks you which program group on your Start menu you want the tools installed to. By default, the Analysis Services program group goes in the Microsoft SQL Server program group. Accept the default, click Next, and then setup installs Analysis Services.

As you can see, installation of Analysis Services is quite straightforward. Now, start the sample applications and explore the product a little.

Accessing the Sample Application for Analysis Services

From the Start menu, choose Programs, Microsoft SQL Server, Analysis Services, Analysis Manager to start the equivalent of SQL Server Enterprise Manager for Analysis

Services. Expand the Analysis Services folder; then click the plus sign for your computer name. You then see a window like Figure 22.6, showing that Analysis Services is running on your computer and that a single OLAP cube, FoodMart 2000, is installed.

FIGURE 22.6

The Analysis Manager.

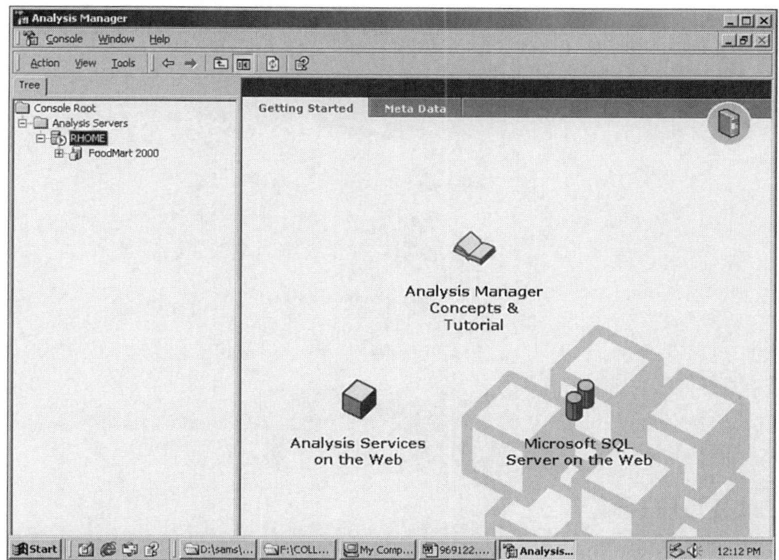

Your best bet at this point is to try the sample application. By far the easiest way to proceed is to select the Analysis Manager Concepts & Tutorial link in the right pane of Analysis Manager. When you select this link, you go to the tutorial shown in Figure 22.7.

Rather than walk through the tutorial in this book, the best thing for you to do is simply give it a try. Click Quick Start, and then follow each step as presented. Going through the tutorial takes a few hours, so it's probably best for you to tackle one piece at a time. Estimated time to complete each section is shown in Figure 22.7.

As you can also see, a data mining tutorial has also been integrated. You should probably get a good understanding of OLAP cubes and Analysis Services in general before attempting to dive into data mining.

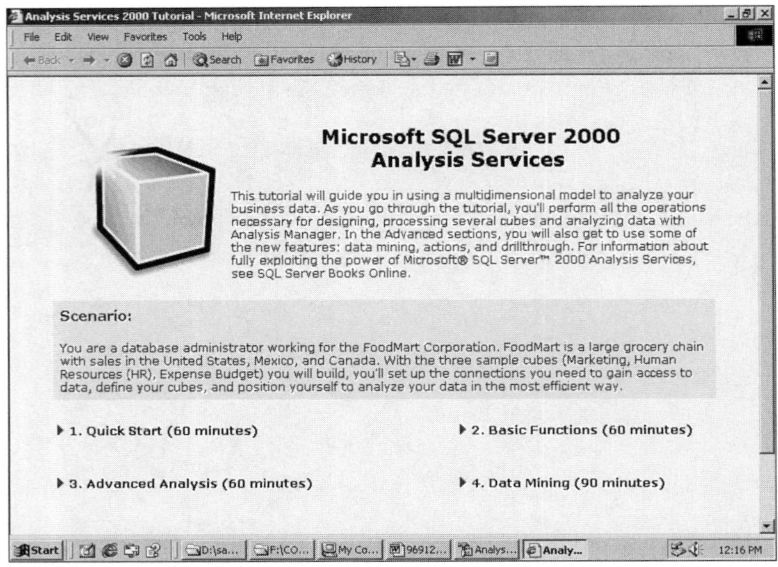

FIGURE 22.7

Analysis Services 2000 Tutorial.

Summary

Analysis Services, including OLAP server, data mining, and Microsoft Meta Data Services, provides a powerful set of features to support data warehouses. You can aggregate your data into cubes of information with Analysis Services, drill into your cubes with data mining to identify new and interesting information about your data, and use Meta Data Services to track information about your data.

These products together, along with DTS, are a huge set of features and generally require someone to be trained completely separately from the typical SQL Server database administrator.

Q&A

Q What's a dimension table?

A A table that identifies how to break down data by some kind of measurement, such as time or geographic region.

Q What's a fact table?

A A table that rolls up (aggregates) your data—for instance, retail sales data.

Q What's a star schema?

A A set of tables with one central fact table and many dimension tables.

Q Why would I want to use SQL Server's Data Mining capabilities?

A To learn previously undiscovered relationships that expand understanding (and maybe make additional money).

BONUS DAYS

DAY 23

An Overview of English Query

Today you will learn about Microsoft English Query, a natural language-processing tool that abstracts the complexity of SQL by allowing users to ask questions in plain English.

When developing database applications, you can generally plan for canned reports your users will require from functional specifications. However, these types of reports can go only so far when it comes to true analysis, especially when "why" questions arise. Yesterday you were introduced to a powerful tool for answering "why." Although SQL and MDX may seem pretty straightforward to you, these query languages will probably seem mystical to your users. To conduct truly ad hoc analysis, you need to be familiar with using one of these query languages.

You're probably thinking to yourself, "As if I don't have enough to do with maintenance and performance monitoring, now I have to write queries, too!" In the past, the answer would have been yes. However, English Query comes to the rescue by translating plain English into Transact-SQL. The best part, though, is that you don't have to be a programmer to set up these queries. The graphical development environment allows you to import a database schema and begin configuring the semantics. From there, you can build a project and your users can ask questions without your intervention.

English Query Components

English Query applications are built on three components, two of which Microsoft supplies:

- An *English Query model* is the combination of database objects and language objects that tie them together to form an English Query application. For example, if you have tables that store data about customers and products, you could configure your model with those entities. From there, you could create relationships between the entities, such as *customers buy products*.
- The *English Query Model Editor* (see Figure 23.1) is the graphical development environment used to create your English Query models. This development environment includes a diagramming tool that enables you to drag and drop entities to create relationships. English Query itself knows only about the English language, so it's up to you to tell English Query about the specifics of your database.

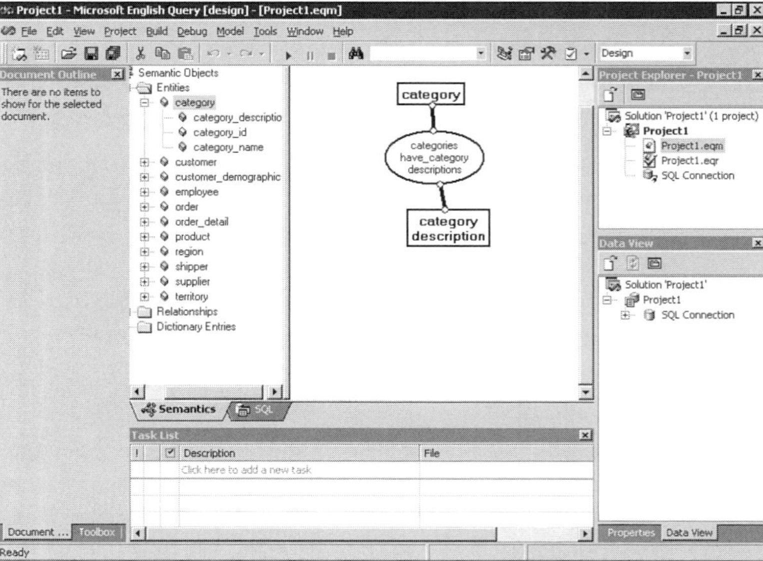

FIGURE 23.1
The English Query Model Editor.

- The *English Query runtime engine* is the component that actually makes the magic happen. The runtime engine is a COM server that parses English into query statements, which can be executed against a data store.

How English Query Works

Because the runtime engine is COM compliant, English Query applications can be called from any COM platform, such as Visual C++, Visual Basic, Visual Basic for Applications (VBA), and even Active Server Pages. An English Query application follows the flow illustrated in Figure 23.2 and in the following steps.

1. A user submits a question in English to the application.
2. The application submits the question to the English Query runtime engine.
3. The runtime engine parses the query and sends a query statement back to the calling application.
4. The application establishes a connection to the data source and passes it the query statement.
5. The data source executes the statement and sends the application a result set.
6. The result is presented to the user.

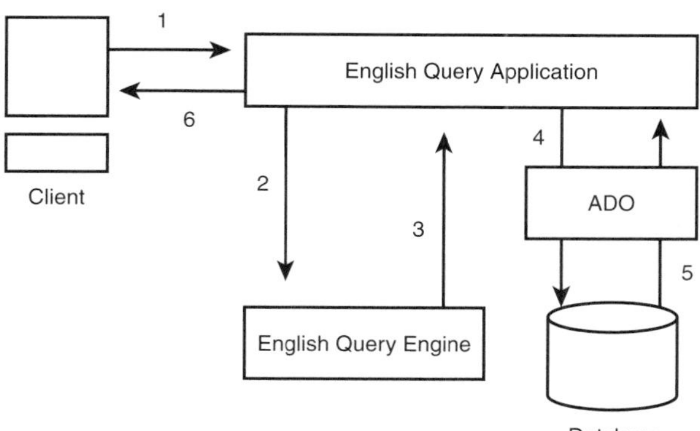

FIGURE 23.2

The flow of an English Query application.

A user never works with the runtime engine directly. Instead, your application sends a question to the runtime engine on your user's behalf. Similarly, the runtime engine never communicates directly with the data store. This modularity lends itself to scalability and platform independence. You can use the same English Query runtime to create statements that will execute across SQL Server 6.5 SP3, SQL Server 7.0, and SQL Server 2000.

Normalization Requirements

It's time for some relational database theory. On Day 9, "Data Types and Creating Tables," you learned about creating tables. If you recall, when I defined a table, I stated that it represents an entity in the database and that a row represents a single occurrence of an entity. This definition is actually for a normalized table. Normalization, if you'll recall, is the process of eliminating redundant data from your database. There are varying degrees of normalization—from first normal form, which is basically a spreadsheet, to fifth normal form, where things like area codes would exist in their own tables. Most databases aren't normalized to this extreme.

In general, you try to normalize a database to third normal form, which means that every non-key column must relate to the key column(s). Consider the Northwind database. The `orders` table has columns for customerid and employeeid instead of names. These columns are used because the names are related to their respective key values within their tables.

I've brought up normalization because English Query applications work best with a normalized database. Unfortunately, you may not have the luxury of designing the database schema for which you are building your English Query application. Fortunately, you have the option of specifying views that can be used in place of tables that may be ambiguous to the runtime engine. The following rules are recommended by Microsoft to achieve the best performance and reliability:

- The instances of an entity and the rows of the table should have a one-to-one relationship.
- A field should have the same meaning in each row of the table.
- Each table should represent at most one entity.
- Multiple instances of an entity shouldn't be represented by multiple rows in a table.
- Multiple instances of an entity shouldn't be represented as multiple columns.
- Multiple instances of an entity shouldn't be represented as multiple tables.
- Joins should be based only on primary and foreign-key equality.

If your database doesn't meet these rules, again you can use views to overcome the runtime engine's challenges with your schema.

Creating an English Query Application

In this section, you'll create an English Query application based on the Northwind sample database:

1. Open the English Query development environment in Visual Studio. When you start the development environment, a dialog prompts you to create new projects or modify existing projects. Double-click the English Query Projects folder, and select the SQL Project Wizard. Name your project **NorthwindEQ** (as I've done in Figure 23.3), and click Open.

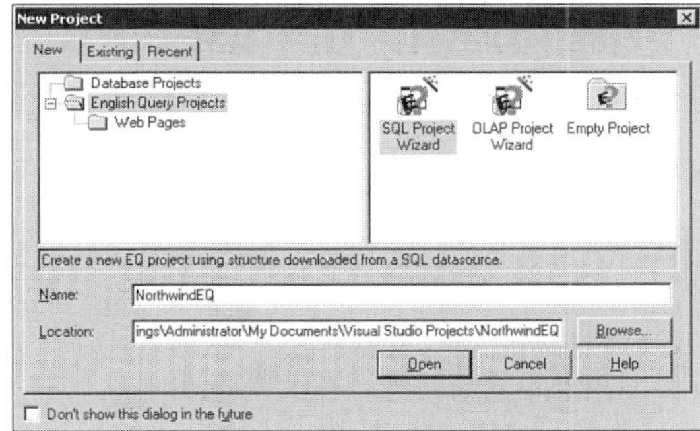

FIGURE 23.3

The New Project dialog.

2. A dialog prompts you to set your data source properties (see Figure 23.4). Select Microsoft OLE DB Provider for SQL Server, and click Next.

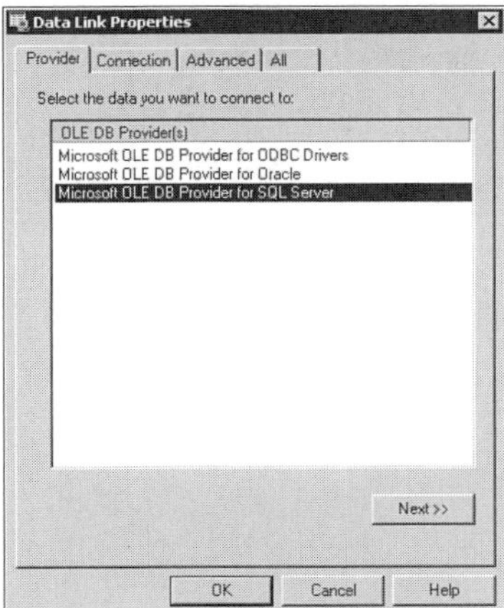

FIGURE 23.4

The Data Link Properties dialog.

3. You need to provide information as to which server you will be connecting. In my example, I am connecting to SQL Server on the same computer I'm running the development environment. In the next dialog, you can connect by using either Integrated or SQL Server security. I will connect using SQL Server security as the sa user. Next, choose the Northwind database from the drop-down menu (see Figure 23.5). Finally, click Test Connection; if you get a message saying that the connection succeeded, everything worked. Click OK to continue.

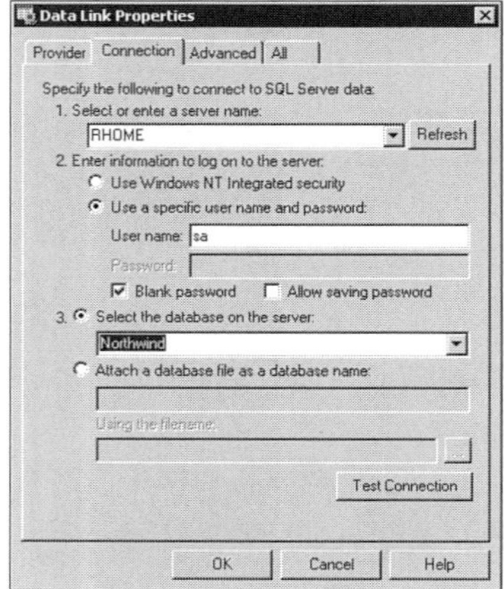

FIGURE 23.5

Configuring the database connection.

4. Select which database objects to make available to the project. Click the >> button to select all available objects, as in Figure 23.6. Click OK to continue.

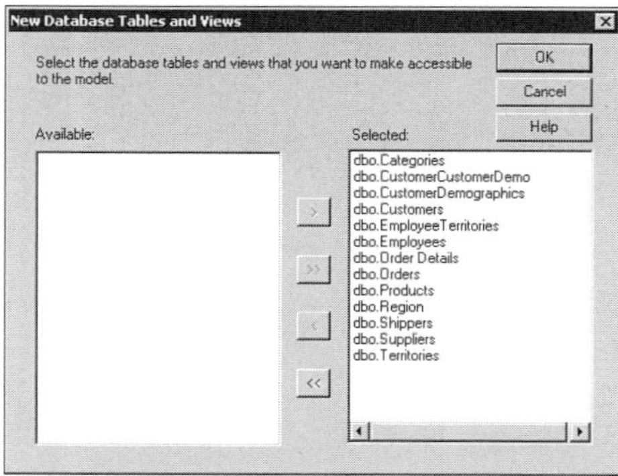

FIGURE 23.6

The New Database Tables and Views dialog.

5. The wizard displays all the possible entities (see Figure 23.7) based on the tables and views you previously imported. You can choose to remove an entity by deselecting its corresponding check box. For this example, don't clear any check boxes.

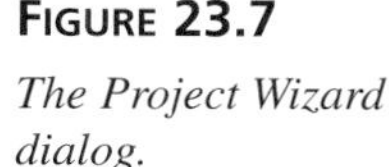

FIGURE 23.7

The Project Wizard dialog.

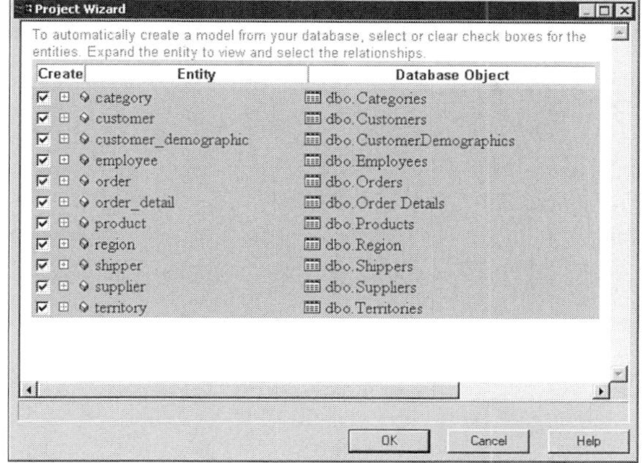

6. Click the plus sign next to `product`. Notice that it already contains several relationships (see Figure 23.8). In the previous version of English Query, you would have had to configure all these relationships yourself. Now click the plus sign next to `customer`. Notice how some of the relationships have yet to be defined. To add or remove a relationship, check or clear the desired check box. Don't change anything (leave them all selected), and click OK to continue.

FIGURE 23.8

Exploring the wizard's relationships.

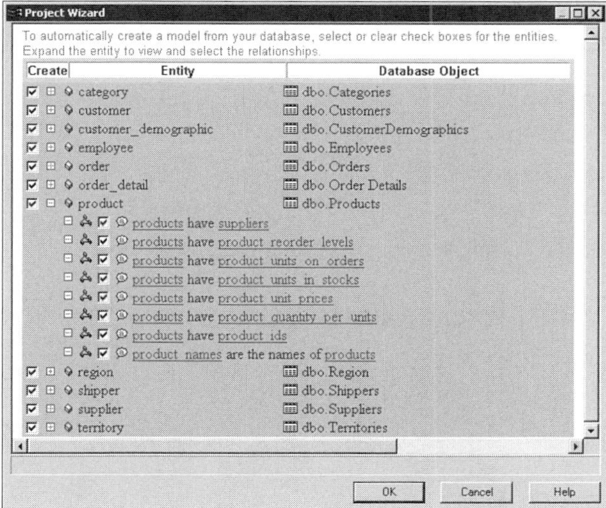

The wizard finishes the application's framework (see Figure 23.9), and you are ready to refine your semantics (language translations).

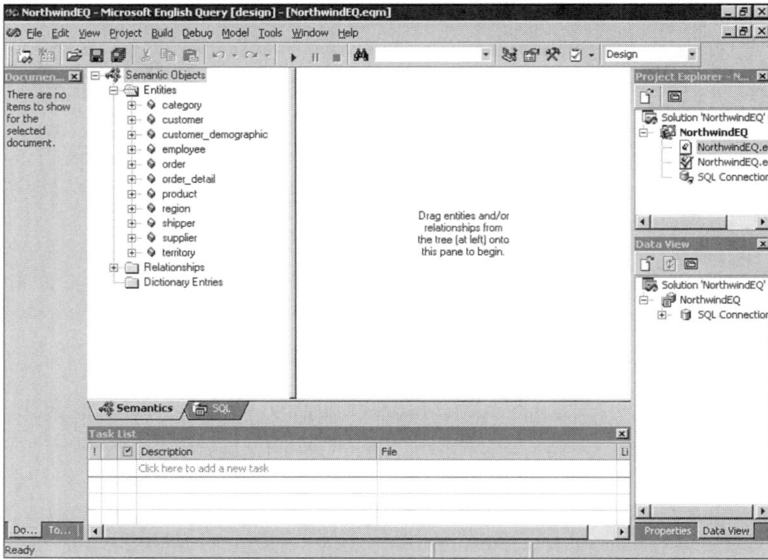

FIGURE 23.9

Framework after the wizard finishes.

Adding Synonyms to Your Entities

The first thing you'll want to do is add synonyms for your entities. Right now, the attributes of your entity are known by their column names from the respective table. Follow these steps:

1. Expand the `supplier` entity and double-click supplier_`home_page`. Click the ... next to supplier_`home_page`. Notice that `home_page is also a valid alias`.
2. Click the text box again and type **`website`**. You should see a list of words to describe the `home_page` attribute (see Figure 23.10).
3. Click OK to return to the development environment.

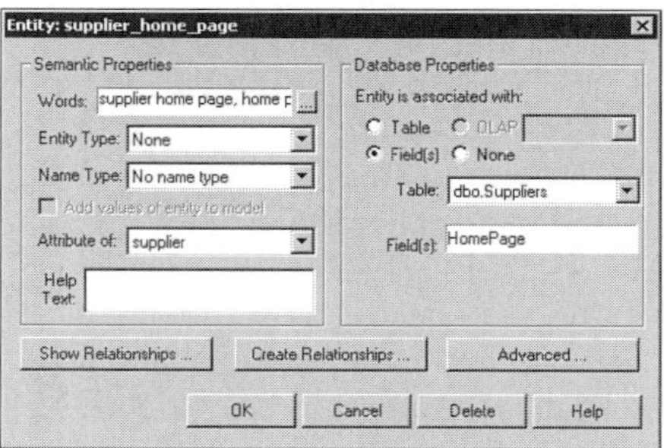

FIGURE 23.10

Adding a synonym.

Adding Relationships to Your Model

Follow these steps to add a relationship to the model between the `supplier` entity and the entity's supplier_`contact_title` attribute:

1. Double-click the supplier_`contact_title` attribute under the `supplier` entity, and select the Add Values of Entity to Model check box (see Figure 23.11). Click OK to continue.

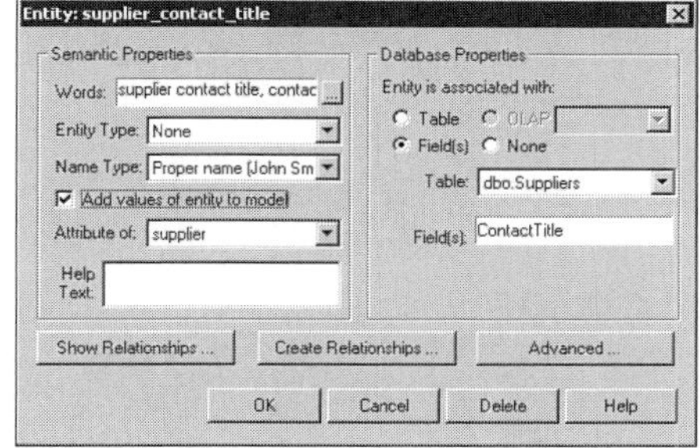

FIGURE 23.11

Adding an entity to the model.

2. Drag the supplier_`contact_title` attribute to the canvas pane to the right. Then drag the `supplier` entity to the canvas, and drop it on the supplier_`contact_title` attribute to open the New Relationship dialog (see Figure 23.12).

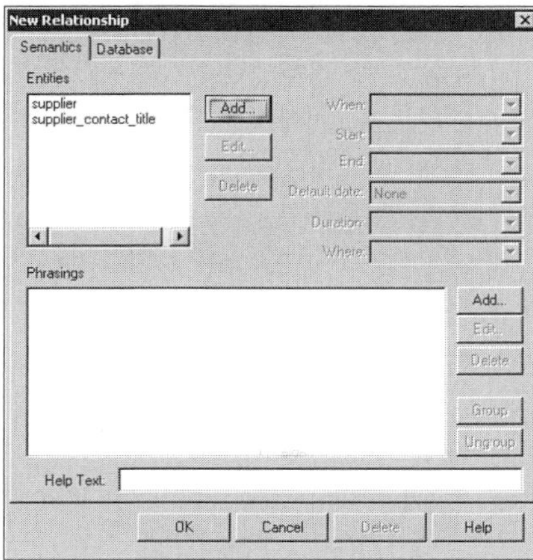

FIGURE 23.12

The New Relationship dialog.

3. Click the Add button next to the Phrasings list box to launch the Select Phrasing dialog.

4. Because `supplier_contact_title` is an adjective you'll be using to describe `supplier`, select Adjective Phrasing from the list (see Figure 23.13), and click OK to continue.

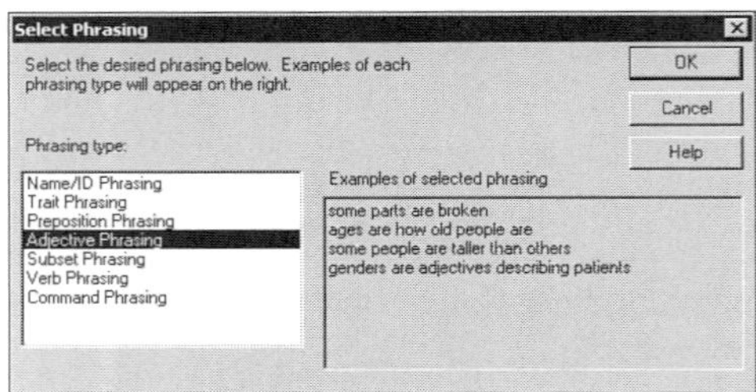

FIGURE 23.13
The Select Phrasing dialog.

5. You see the Adjective Phrasing dialog. From the Subject drop-down list, select `suppliers`. For Adjective Type, select Entity Contains Adjectives. Finally, in the Entity That Contains Adjectives drop-down list, choose `supplier_contact_titles`. Your dialog should look like Figure 23.14. Click OK to continue.

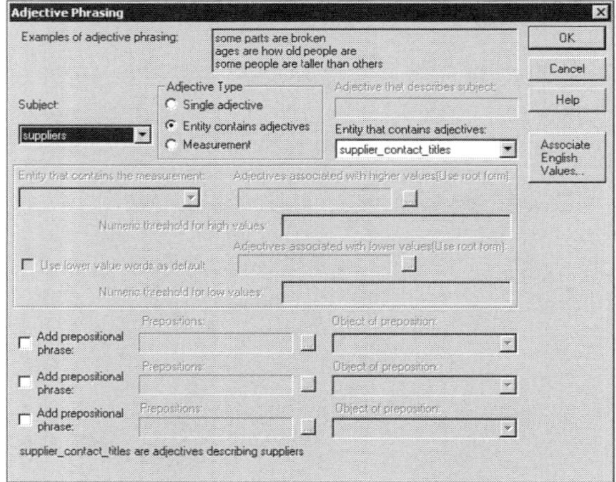

FIGURE 23.14
The Adjective Phrasing dialog.

6. Click OK (as many times as necessary) to return to the development environment, which should look similar to Figure 23.15 (re-arranged for visibility in the figure).

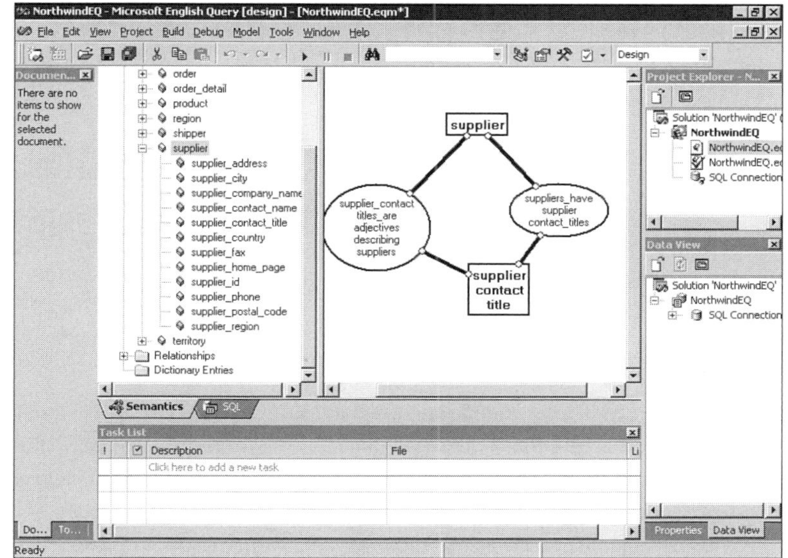

FIGURE 23.15

The English Query development environment with the query mapped.

Testing an English Query Application

Before deploying your English Query application, you should test the results it will produce. A convenient way to test your application is provided within the development environment. From the Debug menu, choose Start. Your application is then compiled, and an instance of the testing tool starts. In the query text box, type **`List all the customers`** and press Enter. You then see an analysis that shows the query syntax. You can also display the results of the query by clicking the View Results button. The question "What is the supplier of New Orleans Cajun Delights?" produced the results shown in Figure 23.16.

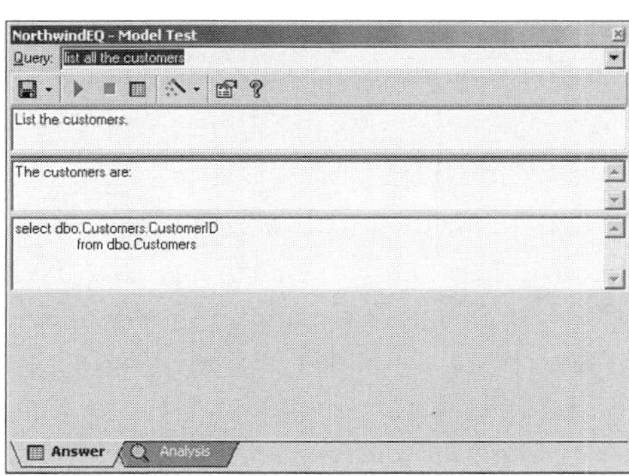

FIGURE 23.16

The Model Test dialog.

Building an English Query Application

After you complete your testing and are satisfied that English Query can answer the questions your users will ask, it's time to build the application. From the Build menu in the development environment, choose Build. This option compiles your model into an English Query application file, which in the example would be `NorthwindED.eqd`. When you have an application file, you can then use English Query to query your databases through any COM-compliant language, such as Visual Basic, Visual C++, and Active Server Pages.

Summary

If you stop to consider it, the English language is one of the most complicated on the planet. The English Query development team and the natural language researchers at Microsoft have come up with a very impressive product. Today you learned about their product, English Query. The lesson started with an overview of how English Query can make your life simpler by allowing users to conduct their own ad-hoc analysis. Then you learned about the core components of the system, followed by a tour through the flow of an English Query application.

Next, you delved into the technical portion with a discussion of database normalization. In this section, you reviewed several rules to improve the success of the applications you build. In the event that your database schema deviates from these rules, all hope isn't lost. You can implement views to achieve the desired results and use these views to represent entities within your English Query model.

From there, you went through the process of building a rudimentary English Query application for the Northwind database. First, you used the new SQL Project Wizard to establish the framework, which included importing your database schema and establishing basic entities and relationships. Next, you configured synonyms for your entities. The default name for an entity's attributes are the column names from the table. Although it wasn't specifically mentioned, you need to ensure that you configure synonyms that correspond to the terminology your users may use to formulate their questions. Then you learned how to create new relationships for your model.

After you created the model, you learned how to test it within the development environment. If you asked questions other than the ones in the book, you may have been prompted that English Query didn't have enough information about your database to answer. This is exactly the response you want to avoid sending back to your users. When you encounter this message in the test environment, it means that you have more work to do in defining synonyms and relationships.

When you are satisfied that your application is producing the proper results within the test environment, it's time for you to build the application. The build phase creates the `.eqd` file that contains the information about your model. From your client application, you reference this file so that the runtime engine knows where to get its information.

From a user's perspective, it's very annoying for English Query to reply with a request to rephrase the question. Because your users will undoubtedly come from various demographical backgrounds, designing a model to accommodate a wide range of syntactic nuances would be very difficult. To make it easier for everyone, you might want to consider listing several samples of how to format questions to be asked of English Query.

Q&A

Q Is English Query widely used in real-world applications?

A Unfortunately, not as much as it could and should be. If you worked with the domain editor in SQL Server 7.0, you may have found it clunky and tedious. This is unfortunate because it's such a powerful product. Also, when the first version of English Query was released, I think many potential users may have thought it too good to be true. With the innovation in the development environment and support for Analysis Services, English Query will be used more frequently.

Q Why doesn't English Query include a spelling checker?

A It would be possible but not very practical. To be honest, the programming challenge for this type of functionality is very overwhelming—not to say that a spelling checker won't appear in a future version. However, consider the nature of the data you're potentially querying. Storing abbreviations and symbols in tables is quite common. Similarly, it's also likely you will have tables containing names. The spelling checker that ships with Office 2000 is perhaps one of the most sophisticated on the market, yet it can't overcome these challenges.

APPENDICES

A

B

C

APPENDIX A

Answers to Quiz Questions

Day 1

Quiz Answers

1. The table.
2. Tables, columns, data types, stored procedures, triggers, rules, keys, constraints, defaults, and indexes.
3. Usually the SQL Server administrator.

Exercise Answer

Following is one way to look at creating objects and organizing them into tables and columns. Day 9, "Data Types and Creating Tables," covers more details on different data types.

Normalizing Your Database Design

Normalizing the database consists of taking related objects and grouping them into tables. For example, look at the used-car dealership database as though it were a spreadsheet. The columns would be Vehicle Identification Number (VIN), Make, Model, Color, Mileage, Photograph, Air Conditioning, Size of Engine, Transmission, Four-Wheel Drive, Power Locks, Other Features, Cost, List Price, Asking Price, Date Bought, Date Sold, Deposit, Deposit Date, Customer Name, Customer Address, Customer Phone, Salesperson Name, Salesperson Address, Salesperson Commission, and Salesperson ID.

You have 25 columns to save for each car. Putting them in a spreadsheet would work for a small shop, but for large shops, a spreadsheet would quickly become too cumbersome. You need a unique identifier to link these tables. Vehicles have a natural unique ID in their VIN. You can assign customers and salespeople unique numbers or use existing identifiers (such as Social Security or last name plus address). In this case, an assigned ID for the salespeople and the customer's Social Security number will work as identifiers.

You can see that information about vehicles, salespeople, cost and sales, and customers are related data. These variables can go into several tables, as appropriate:

- **Vehicle**—VIN, Make, Model, Color, Mileage, Photograph, Air Conditioning, Size of Engine, Transmission, Four-Wheel Drive, Power Locks, Other Features
- **Salespeople**—Salesperson Name, Salesperson Address, Salesperson Commission, Salesperson ID
- **Sales Data**—VIN, Cost, List Price, Asking Price, Date Bought, Date Sold, Deposit, Deposit Date, Customer ID, Salesperson ID
- **Customer**—Customer Name, Customer Address, Customer Phone, Customer ID, Comments

Finalizing the Database Design

To finalize the design, choose column names, the data type, and the length of each column (when appropriate). Also, split names into first and last because you might want to alphabetize them later.

A database's detailed design is often referred to as the *data dictionary,* because it defines the variables and tables in the database. A breakdown of your data dictionary follows.

Vehicle This table will contain vehicle information and have the following variables:

- *VIN* (primary key) is the vehicle identification number. This character field has a variable length of 30 characters (for nonstandard cars and so on).

- *Make* is the make of the car. Valid responses are something like Ford, Nissan, and so on. This character field has a variable length of 30 characters.
- *Model* is the model of the car. Valid responses are something like Ranger, Altima, and so on. This character field has a variable length of 30 characters.
- *Color* is the car's color. This character field has a variable length of 20 characters.
- *Mileage* is, no surprise, the car's mileage. This numeric field is seven characters long (maximum of 9,999,999—it won't track mileage to the tenth of a mile).
- *Photo* is a photograph of the car, taken in 640×480×256 Joint Picture Experts Group (JPEG) format, so it can be easily published on the Internet. This is an image field.
- *AC* indicates whether the car has an air conditioner. Valid responses are Y or N. This character field is set to a length of one.
- *Size_of_Eng* indicates how many cylinders the engine has. Valid responses are 3, 4, 6, 8, 10, and 12. This is a `tinyint` (tiny integer, ranges from 0 to 255) field.
- *Trans* is the type of transmission, with valid responses being "standard" or "automatic." This variable character field has a maximum length of nine.
- *FWD* indicates whether the vehicle is four-wheel drive. Valid responses are Y or N. This character field is set to a length of one.
- *PL* indicates whether the vehicle has power locks. Valid responses are Y or N. This character field is set to a length of one.
- *Comment* holds comments about the vehicle and is a text variable.

tblSalespeople This table will contain information about the salespeople:

- *Sales_ID* (primary key) lists the ID of each salesperson. All salespeople will be assigned an ID to help track sales and so on. This field is a `smallint` (small integer, ranges from –32,768 to 32,767).
- *Fname* is the salesperson's first name. This variable character field has a maximum of 30 characters.
- *Lname* is the salesperson's last name. This variable character field has a maximum of 30 characters.
- *Addr* is the salesperson's address. This variable character field has a maximum of 30 characters.
- *City* is the salesperson's city. This variable character field has a maximum of 30 characters.

- *State* is the salesperson's state. This character field has two characters.
- *Zip* is the salesperson's ZIP code. This character field has nine characters.
- *Commission* is the salesperson's base percentage for his commission. You can later use this information to calculate commissions based on profits on cars sold. This is a `tinyint` variable.

tblSales This table will track information about the purchase and sale of the vehicle:

- *Invoice* (primary key) is the invoice number of the original purchase of the vehicle. This `varchar` field has a maximum length of 20.
- *VIN* (foreign key) is the same as the field found in the vehicle table and is used to create a key to that table.
- *CustID* (foreign key) also exists in the customer table and is a key to that table.
- *SalesID* (foreign key) also exists in the sales table and is a key to that table.
- *Cost* is the actual vehicle cost. This `smallmoney` field can handle up to $214,000.
- *List* is the list (blue book) price for the car. This is a `smallmoney` field.
- *Ask* is the asking price. This price might change because of a sale, advertisement, or incentive. This is a `smallmoney` field.
- *DateIn* is the date that the dealer purchased the vehicle. This is a `smalldatetime` field (keeps track of dates down to one-minute intervals).
- *DateOut* is the date the vehicle was sold to a customer. This is a `smalldatetime` field.
- *Deposit* is the amount of a deposit (if any) that the customer has put down on a vehicle. This is a `smallmoney` field.
- *Deposit Date* is the date the deposit was made. This is a `smalldatetime` field.

tblCustomer This table will keep track of the customers.

- *CustID* (primary key) holds the customer's Social Security number, which will also double as the customer's ID number. It is a nine-digit character field.
- *Fname* is the customer's first name. This variable character field has a maximum of 30 characters.
- *Lname* is the customer's last name. This variable character field has a maximum of 30 characters.

- *Addr* is the customer's address. This variable character field has a maximum of 30 characters.
- *City* is the customer's city. This variable character field has a maximum of 30 characters.
- *State* is the customer's state. This character field has two characters.
- *Zip* is the customer's ZIP code. This character field has nine characters.
- *Phone* is the customer's phone number. It is a 10-digit character field.
- *Comments* is a text field where comments about the customer can be added.

Figure A.1 shows how your tables and their relationships might look.

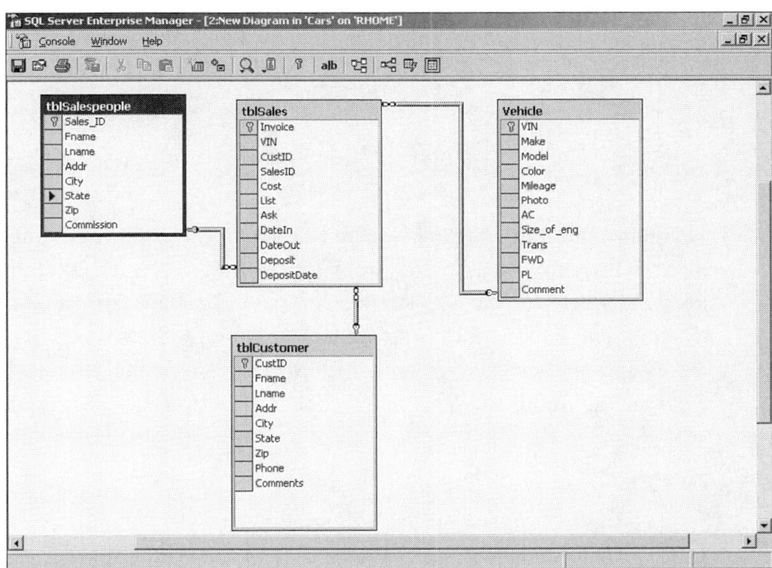

FIGURE A.1
Relationships between tables.

SQL Server ships with two default databases that you can use to learn how to program SQL Server 2000. If you've used SQL Server in the past, you will recognize the `pubs` database, an assortment of tables that track books, publishers, authors, stores, and sales. Figure A.2 provides a sample view of the tables in the `pubs` database and their relationships.

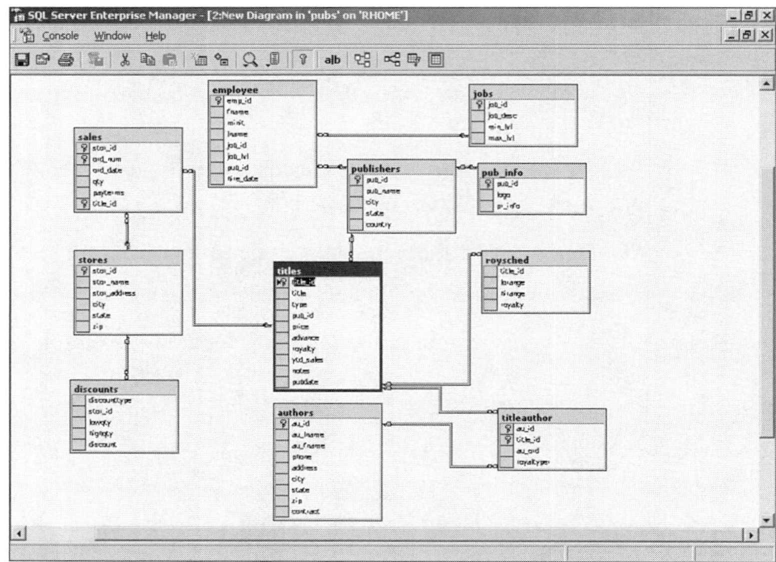

FIGURE A.2
The pubs *database.*

If you are familiar with the Northwinds database from Microsoft Access, you will also have an easy time making the transition into SQL Server 2000, because a SQL Server version of the Northwinds Traders company database is included. Northwinds Traders is a fictitious company that buys and sells exotic foods from all over the world. The various tables and queries used to work with the data are in SQL Server 2000. Figure A.3 shows a sample layout of the Northwinds database and its associated tables and fields.

Day 2

Quiz Answers

1. The binary sort order would return data in ASCII order.
2. Only Unicode data columns in SQL Server 2000.
3. The MDAC (Microsoft Data Access Components).
4. You should set up a special account that's a member of the administrator's group on the local computer.
5. Use the SQL Service Manager or SQL Server Enterprise Manager, or run several Windows 2000 utilities. You can also run `NET START MSSQLServer`.
6. NTFS—it has better security and reliability.
7. Select Full-Text Indexing under Server Components during a custom setup.

FIGURE A.3
The Northwinds database.

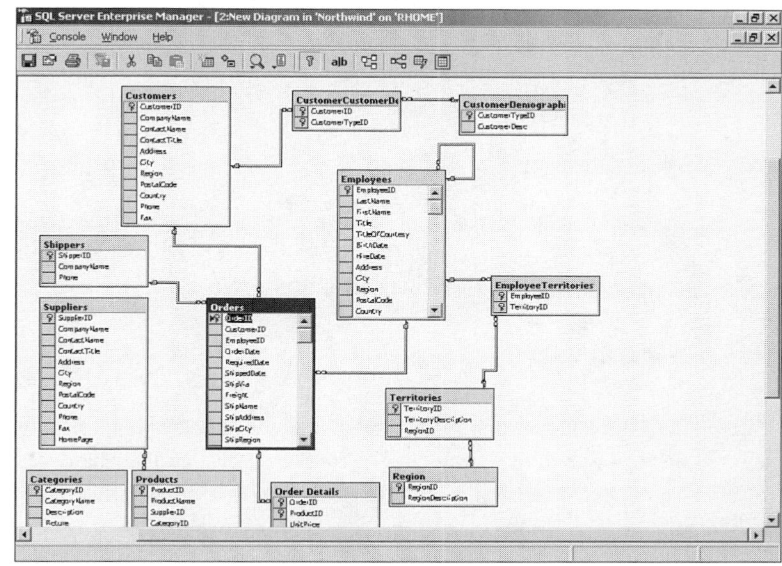

Day 3

Quiz Answers

1. Configure the registration information to not keep your login information by default, and require a separate login at every connection.
2. In the Client Network utility.
3. In the Server Network utility.
4. Performance Management console, SQL Server Profiler, and SQL Server Query Analyzer.
5. `SQLDiag.exe`.

Day 4

Quiz Answers

1.
```
CREATE DATABASE Accounting
ON
(NAME = Accounting_Data,
```

```
FILENAME = 'D:\Program Files\Microsoft SQL Server\mssql
            ➥\data\Accounting_Data.mdf',
SIZE = 20,
FILEGROWTH = 2,
MAXSIZE = 40)
LOG ON
(NAME = Accounting_Log,
FILENAME = 'D:\Program Files\Microsoft SQL Server\mssql
            ➥\data\Accounting_Log.ldf',
SIZE=5,
FILEGROWTH = 1,
MAXSIZE=10)
```

2. This code adds a new data file called `TestData2` with a filename of `TestData2.ndf` in the default directory. The initial size is 10MB. The default autogrowth of 10 percent is being used, and the file has no maximum size.
3. Make sure that you are in the `master` database when you run this query:

```
DROP DATABASE Von, Ron, Don, Christina
```

Exercise Answers

1.

```
CREATE DATABASE Frog
     ON
     (NAME = FrogData1,
      FILENAME = 'D:\program files\Microsoft SQL Server
                ➥\mssql\data\FrogData1.mdf',
      SIZE = 3,
      FILEGROWTH = 2,
      MAXSIZE = 20),
     (NAME = FrogData2,
      FILENAME = 'D:\program files\Microsoft SQL Server
                ➥\mssql\data\FrogData2.ndf',
      SIZE = 3,
      FILEGROWTH = 2,
      MAXSIZE = 20)
     LOG ON
     (NAME = FrogLog1,
      FILENAME = 'D:\program files\Microsoft SQL Server
                ➥\mssql\data\FrogLog1.ldf',
     MAXSIZE = 5),
```

```
(NAME = FrogLog2,
 FILENAME = 'D:\program files\Microsoft SQL Server
            ➥\mssql\data\FrogLog2.ldf',
MAXSIZE = 5)
GO
```

2. ```
   ALTER DATABASE Frog
         ADD FILE
         (NAME = FrogData3,
          FILENAME = 'D:\program files\Microsoft SQL Server
                     ➥\mssql\data\FrogData3.ndf')
         GO
   ```
3. ```
   DBCC SHRINKDATABASE (Frog, 80)
         GO
   ```
4. ```
   USE Frog
         GO
         DBCC SHRINKFILE (FrogLog2,EMPTYFILE)
         GO
   ```
5. ```
   ALTER DATABASE Frog
         REMOVE FILE FrogLog2
         GO
   ```
6. ```
   USE Master
         GO
         EXEC sp_dboption Frog, 'Single User', True
         GO
         EXEC sp_renamedb 'Frog', 'TreeFrog'
         GO
         EXEC sp_dboption TreeFrog, 'Single User', False
         GO
   ```
7. ```
   USE MASTER
         GO
         DROP DATABASE TreeFrog
         GO
   ```

A

Day 5

Quiz Answers

1. By deleting the BUILTIN\Administrators group in Enterprise Manager or by running the `sp_revokelogin` system stored procedure. This approach would revoke

their rights to log in to SQL Server at all, however. You could also run the sp_dropsrvrolemember system stored procedure to remove these administrators from membership in the sysadmin fixed server role.

2. You can add someone to the dbo user in the database, but a better solution is to add the individual to the database as a user and make her username a member of the db_owner fixed database role.
3. When the individual user needs specific permissions that are different from other members' permissions of every single group he is a member of. This scenario should be rare.

Exercise Answers

1. You can use sp_addlogin and sp_adduser or the SQL Server Enterprise Manager. The code would look like this:

```
Exec sp_addlogin 'george'
Exec sp_addlogin 'Henry'
Exec sp_addlogin 'Ida'
Exec sp_addlogin 'John'
Use pubs
Exec Sp_adduser 'George'
Exec sp_adduser 'Henry'
Exec sp_adduser 'Ida'
Exec sp_adduser 'John'
```

2. Remove John from the database user, and then run sp_changedbowner to make John the dbo:

```
Use pubs
Exec sp_changedbowner 'John','TRUE'
-- Oops -- received an error
exec sp_dropuser 'John'
exec sp_changedbowner 'John','TRUE'
```

Day 6

Quiz Answers

1. GRANT SELECT ON MyTable TO MARY.
2. Paul needs permission to SELECT on Joe.JoeView and SELECT on Mary.MaryTable.
3. Joe can't SELECT from MYTABLE. DENY overrides all other permissions.
4. Joe can SELECT from MYTABLE.
5. Have all objects created by or with the owner of dbo.

6. `GRANT SELECT ON MYTABLE TO PUBLIC.`
7. All statement permissions except `CREATE DATABASE`.

Exercise Answers

1. Many answers are possible, but this script would work as well:

```
use pubs
exec sp_addapprole 'testrole','password'
grant select on authors to testrole
deny select on titleauthor to testrole
--now log in and run:

exec sp_setapprole 'testrole','password'
select * from titleauthor
-- and the select from titleauthor will fail because the
-- permissions of the approle have taken effect.
```

2. Again, answers vary.

Day 7

Quiz Answers

1. RAID 1 performs better (in general) than RAID 5 for writes; hence, it's a better option for holding transaction logs.
2. Yes. Network locations are available for backup devices.
3. If the Truncate Log On Checkpoint database option is set or Select Into/Bulk Copy has been set and a full database backup hasn't been made, you can't make a transaction log backup.
4. In an offsite storage vault, if one is available.
5. No, a checkpoint is merely a copy of the data pages from memory to disk. It doesn't affect your transaction log backups.

Exercise Answers

1. To create the backup devices, use SQL Server Enterprise Manager or run the following:

```
exec sp_addumpdevice 'disk', 'master_backup',
➥ 'd:\program files\microsoft sql server\mssql\backup\master_backup.dat'
exec sp_addumpdevice 'disk', 'msdb_backup',
➥'d:\program files\microsoft sql server\mssql\backup\msdb_backup.dat'
exec sp_addumpdevice 'disk', 'model_backup',
➥'d:\program files\microsoft sql server\mssql\backup\model_backup.dat'
```

```
exec sp_addumpdevice 'disk', 'pubs_backup',
➥'d:\program files\microsoft sql server\mssql\backup\pubs_backup.dat'
exec sp_addumpdevice 'disk', 'northwind_backup',
➥'d:\program files\microsoft sql server\mssql\backup\northwind_backup.dat'
```

To back up the databases, use SQL Server Enterprise Manager or run the following:

```
BACKUP DATABASE MASTER TO master_backup WITH INIT
BACKUP DATABASE MSDB TO msdb_backup WITH INIT
BACKUP DATABASE MODEL TO model_backup WITH INIT
BACKUP DATABASE PUBS TO pubs_backup WITH INIT
BACKUP DATABASE NORTHWIND TO northwind_backup WITH INIT
```

To view the database options, use SQL Server Enterprise Manager or run the following:

```
exec sp_helpdb
```

2. `NOINIT` is included just to prevent you from erasing your previous full database backups on the same backup devices. You could just as easily have created new backup devices.

```
BACKUP DATABASE PUBS TO pubs_backup WITH NOINIT, DIFFERENTIAL
BACKUP DATABASE NORTHWIND TO northwind_backup WITH NOINIT,
➥DIFFERENTIAL
```

3.
```
exec sp_addumpdevice 'disk', 'pubs_log_backup',
➥'d:\program files\microsoft sql server\
➥mssql\backup\pubs_log_backup.dat'
use pubs
go
--turn off the truncate log on checkpoint option
exec sp_dboption 'pubs', 'trunc. Log on chkpt.', FALSE
go
--You must perform a full backup after turning off truncate log
--on checkpoint
BACKUP DATABASE PUBS TO pubs_backup WITH INIT
--Finally, back up the log.
BACKUP LOG PUBS TO pubs_log_backup WITH INIT
```

Day 8

Quiz Answers

1. All system databases other than `master`, as well as `pubs` and Northwind, are reinitialized. You need to recover or reattach all user databases.
2. A list of the files for each backup you examine on a backup file or tape.
3. Yes, you can restore a parallel striped backup by using fewer tape drives than you used to make the backup.
4. The recovery interval option. It's set to automatic by default, and you probably shouldn't change it.
5. Restore the last full database backup, and then apply the transaction logs, specifying the `STOPAT` parameter to recover to a particular point in time.

A

Day 9

Quiz Answers

1. When maximum speed is needed and storage space isn't.
2. When storage space is the most important concern but speed isn't.
3. Store the data in a file outside the database, and store the filename in your table. You can also store your text and images in a separate table. You might also be able to break down a text data type into several smaller `char` fields.
4. Always specify `NULL` or `NOT NULL`. Use `ROWGUID` for global unique values, the `IDENTITY` property for autoincrementing values, and Unicode for international databases.
5. a. For a five-digit ZIP code, use `char(5)`. If it can hold 10 digits, as in 40317-2291, use `varchar(10)`.

   b. `smalldatetime`.

   c. To store just the year value, `tinyint`; otherwise, use a `smalldatatime`.

   d. VIN (assuming up to 20 chars) `char(20)`.

   e. `char(10)`.

   f. `varchar(50)`.

   g. `smalldatetime`.

   h. `numeric(,6)`. If you said `money`, remember that those data types support a scale of 4 only.

6. The maximum size is 10 + 15 + 15 + 255 + 3 (3 bytes of overhead for the varchar column) = 298 bytes per row.
7. Yes. Note that the fname field will be changed to a varchar field, and the text and image columns will have a 16-byte pointer to the data pages where their data is stored. The maximum row size should be 582 bytes plus any associated overhead involved with the variable length fields.

Exercise Answers

1.
```
sp_addtype zip_code, 'char(5)', 'NOT NULL'
sp_addtype phone_number, 'char(14)'
sp_addtype store_id, 'int', 'NOT NULL'
sp_addtype fax, 'char(14)'
sp_addtype email, 'varchar(50)'
```
2.
```
CREATE TABLE stores(
id store_id,
name varchar(30),
addr1 varchar(50),
addr2 varchar(50),
city varchar(30),
state char(2) NOT NULL,
zip zip_code,
owner varchar(30),
contact varchar(30),
fax fax,
email email
)
```
3.
```
CREATE TABLE sales (
id store_id,
sales_date datetime,
tot_sales money,
tot_returns money,
deposit money
)
```

Day 10

Quiz Answers

1. a. This query returns all columns from the `authors` table, when the author's last name begins with the letter *M*.

   b. This query returns all rows from the `employee` table and the emp_id, fname, and lname columns. The column headings have been aliased as EmployeeID, LastName, and FirstName.

   c. This query rounds the dollar amount with a single digit to the right of the decimal point as 7725.5.

   d. This query returns a column aliased as Name and the emp_id column aliased as EmployeeID from the employee table. The Name column is in the form of the last name, a comma (`,`), and the first initial of the first name.

2. Yes, in most cases, a subquery can be implemented as a join and vice versa.
3. False. `ROLLUP` and `CUBE` are designed to give you summary information.
4. Yes, to create this table, make sure you prefix the table name with the `##` symbol.

Exercise Answers

1. ```
   SELECT title_id, title, price
   FROM titles
   WHERE (pub_id = '0877'
   OR title LIKE '%computer%')
   And price is not NULL
   (Returns 14 rows)
   ```
2. ```
   SELECT * FROM titles
   WHERE price IS NOT NULL
   (Returns 16 rows)
   ```
3. ```
   SELECT title, price
   FROM titles
   ORDER BY price DESC
   (Returns 18 rows)
   ```
4. ```
   SELECT AVG(ytd_sales) FROM titles
   ```
5. ```
   SELECT title_id, count(title_id)
   FROM titleauthor
   GROUP BY title_id
   HAVING count(title_id) > 1
   ```
   ```

6. ```
   SELECT stor_id, qty
   FROM sales
   ORDER BY stor_id
   COMPUTE SUM(qty) BY stor_id
   ```
7. **ANSI Syntax**

   ```
   SELECT authors.au_fname, authors.au_lname, titles.title
   FROM authors
   INNER JOIN titleauthor ON authors.au_id = titleauthor.au_id
   INNER JOIN titles ON titleauthor.title_id = titles.title_id
   ORDER BY authors.au_lname
   ```

   SQL Server Syntax

   ```
   SELECT authors.au_fname, authors.au_lname, titles.title
   FROM authors, titles, titleauthor
   WHERE authors.au_id = titleauthor.au_id
   AND  titleauthor.title_id = titles.title_id
   ORDER BY authors.au_lname
   ```
8. ```
   SELECT * FROM authors
   WHERE authors.state IN
   (SELECT state from stores)
   ```
9. ```
   SELECT *
   INTO #tmpEmployees
   FROM employee
   GO
   SELECT * FROM #tmpEmployees
   GO
   ```

Day 11

Quiz Answers

1. A `DELETE` without a `WHERE` removes every row from a table. It's more efficient to use `TRUNCATE TABLE` if you really want to remove all rows.
2. False. Identity values are never supplied. They are calculated by the SQL Server. For any column that has a default value or allows nulls, you don't need to supply a value, but you can supply one if you want.
3. Joins in a `DELETE` or `UPDATE` statement allow you to access values in another table to determine which rows to modify. The second table is used only as a lookup table and isn't affected. The data modification operations can change only one table at a time.
   ```

Exercise Answers

1.
```
select title_id, title, pub_id, price
into #cook_books
from tmpTitles
where type = 'mod_cook'
```
2.
```
insert into #cook_books
    select title_id, title, pub_id, price
    from tmpTitles
    where type = 'trad_cook'
```
3.
```
update #cook_books
set price = price * 1.2
```
4.
```
update #cook_books
set price = price * 0.9
where pub_id =
     (select pub_id from publishers
      where pub_name = 'Binnet & Hardley' )
```
5.
```
delete #cook_books
where price < $10
```
6.
```
delete #cook_books
where title_id in
     (select title_id from tmpTitles
      where ytd_sales > 10000)
```

Day 12

Quiz Answers

1. CREATE DATABASE, CREATE TABLE, CREATE INDEX
2.
```
BEGIN TRAN
    UPDATE authors SET au_lname = 'Johnson' WHERE au_lname = 'Smith'
    INSERT publishers VALUES ('9991','SAMS','Indianapolis','IN','USA')
    SELECT * FROM publishers (HOLDLOCK)
COMMIT TRAN
```
   The UPDATE statement takes two exclusive row locks on the authors table as well as two intent-exclusive page locks (the deleted and the inserted rows). The INSERT statement takes an exclusive row lock on a data page on the publishers table (page 99 in the following table). Finally, the SELECT statement takes several

key-range locks on the `publisher` table (because of the `HOLDLOCK` option). Here are the results of `sp_lock`:

```
spid  dbid  ObjId     IndId  Type Resource       Mode  Status
----- ----- --------- ------ ---- -------------- ----- ------
8     2     0         0      DB                  S     GRANT
8     5     0         0      DB                  S     GRANT
8     2     0         0      EXT  1:80           X     GRANT
8     5     117575457 1      PAG  1:87           IX    GRANT
8     5     117575457 2      PAG  1:122          IX    GRANT
8     5     197575742 1      PAG  1:99           IX    GRANT
8     5     117575457 0      TAB                 IX    GRANT
8     5     197575742 1      KEY  (ffffffffffff) IS-S  GRANT
8     5     117575457 2      KEY  (d59632855aa8) X     GRANT
8     5     197575742 0      TAB                 IX    GRANT
8     5     117575457 2      KEY  (39747cc5fc43) X     GRANT
8     5     117575457 1      KEY  (02c094e89f8a) X     GRANT
8     5     197575742 1      KEY  (030431363232) IS-S  GRANT
8     5     197575742 1      KEY  (030130373336) IS-S  GRANT
8     5     197575742 1      KEY  (040131373536) IS-S  GRANT
8     5     197575742 1      KEY  (090a31333839) IS-S  GRANT
8     5     197575742 1      KEY  (070f30383737) IS-S  GRANT
8     5     197575742 1      KEY  (000039393939) IS-S  GRANT
8     5     197575742 1      KEY  (000139393938) IS-S  GRANT
8     5     197575742 1      KEY  (0c0b39393532) IS-S  GRANT
8     5     197575742 1      KEY  (090839393031) IS-S  GRANT
8     5     197575742 1      KEY  (000839393931) X     GRANT

(22 row(s) affected)
```

3. By setting the `REMOTE_PROC_TRANSACTIONS` configuration item. You can set it by using the stored procedure `sp_configure` or the configuration screen in SQL Server Enterprise Manager. You first have to set up either remote servers or linked servers for each server you want to connect with.
4. With either the `ROLLBACK TRAN` or `ROLLBACK WORK` statement.
5. Yes. The `ROLLBACK TRAN` inside the trigger would cancel the transaction as well as the batch. The `SELECT * FROM AUTHORS` is in the second batch and would therefore run. Note that the `COMMIT TRAN` would fail, however.

```
Server: Msg 3902, Level 16, State 1
The COMMIT TRANSACTION request has no corresponding BEGIN TRANSACTION.
```

Exercise Answer

```
BEGIN TRAN
INSERT publishers VALUES ('9993','WAYCOOL PUBLISHERS',
 'Indianapolis', 'IN', 'USA')
INSERT authors VALUES ('111-11-1111','Jackson','Ann','425 999-9000',
'PO Box 1193','Snoqualmie','WA', '98065', 1)
```

```
INSERT authors VALUES ('111-22-1111','Greene','Bob','425 999-9000',
'1204 Sycamore Lane','Boulder City','NV', '89005', 1)
INSERT TITLES VALUES ('BU1403','How to Surf the Net in 3 Easy Steps',
 'business', '9993', $19.95, $3000.00, NULL, NULL, NULL,'8/1/1998')
INSERT TITLEAUTHOR VALUES ('111-11-1111','BU1403', 1, 50)
INSERT TITLEAUTHOR VALUES ('111-22-1111','BU1403', 1, 50)
COMMIT TRAN
```

This script adds a new publisher, the two authors, and the new book title. It then adds the authors as having written the book (50/50 cut). Your answer might differ, but it should include the same set of tables within a single transaction.

Day 13

A

Quiz Answers

1. By specifying an optimizer hint with an index number of 0.
2. At least 120 percent of the size of the table with which you're creating the index.
3. Set `SHOWPLAN_TEXT` to on or the graphical showplan of the SQL Server Query Analyzer.

Exercise Answers

1.
```
set showplan_text on
go
Select * from pubs..sales where title_id = 'BU1032'
Go
Set showplan_text off
Go
Set statistics io on
Go
Select * from pubs..sales where title_id = 'BU1032'
Go
```
   (Remember that you can't run a query and see the showplan in a single step.)
2.
```
Select * from pubs..sales (index=1) where title_id = 'BU1032'
Go
```
3. Answers will vary; however, here is one potential answer:
```
Create table myindextab2
(col1 int not null,
 col2 char(5) not null,
 col3 varchar(50) null)
go
```

```
create unique clustered index myclindex on myindextab2 (col1)
➥with fillfactor = 100
go
create index mynonclindex1 on myindextab2 (col1,col2)
➥with fillfactor = 25
go
create index mynonclindex2 on myindextab2 (col3)
➥with fillfactor = 75
go
dbcc dbreindex ('myindextab2',' ',50)
go
```

4. Graphical answer: If you can do step 3, you can figure out step 4.

Day 14

Quiz Answers

1. Yes.
2. No, it must be referenced elsewhere.
3. Yes, as long as the scale is 0.
4. No, foreign keys can refer only to tables in the same database.
5. No, it creates a unique index that can't be disabled.
6. Not directly. You must manage them by controlling the constraints.

Day 15

Quiz Answers

1. Data integrity, referential integrity, and business rules.
2. As many as you want. You can have different triggers for `INSERT`, `UPDATE`, and `DELETE` statements.
3. False. Views aren't faster than stored procedures. All the other criteria are true of views, however.
4. False. You can update only a single base table with a view.
5. True. This is one benefit to creating a stored procedure.
6. False. You must have permission on the base tables to run a view. It's interesting, however, that you can create a view on base tables that you don't have access to.
7. False. Although these things have made most triggers unnecessary, triggers still have many valid uses—for example, cascading updates and deletes.

8. Only triggers are dropped.
9. False. The whole point of the SCHEMABINDING option is to keep this from happening.
10. True. This is exactly how they are supposed to be used.

Exercise Answers

1. ```
   CREATE VIEW myView AS select au_lname, au_fname, t.title from
   authors inner join titleauthor ta on authors.au_id =
   ➥ta.au_id inner join titles t on ta.title_id = t.title_id
   ```
2. ```
   Create trigger mytrigger on titles for insert as
   if(select count(*) from inserted I inner join publishers p on
   ➥i.pub_id = p.pub_id) <> 1 raiserror(50001, 10, 1)
   ```
3. ```
   CREATE PROC myproc AS
   SELECT s.stor_name, t.title FROM
   stores s, titles t, sales sa
   WHERE t.title_id = sa.title_id
   AND s.stor_id = sa.stor_id
   ORDER BY s.stor_name
   ```
4. Here's one possible solution:
   ```
   CREATE FUNCTION dbo.fnAvgPriceBooksSold(@MyDate datetime)
   RETURNS money
   AS
   BEGIN
     DECLARE @RetVal money
     SET @RetVal = (SELECT CONVERT(money, AVG(s.qty * t.price))
     FROM sales s, titles t
     WHERE s.title_id = t.title_id
     AND s.ord_date <= @MyDate)
     RETURN @RetVal
   END
   ```
   You can use the following two queries to test your results:
   ```
   SELECT dbo.fnAvgPriceBooksSold('10/10/94')
   SELECT dbo.fnAvgPriceBooksSold('10/10/93')
   ```

Day 16

Quiz Answers

1. The log reader agent.
   ```

2. The distribution agent moves replicated transactions from the distribution database to the subscribers.
3. The central subscriber scenario.
4. The merge agent resides on the distribution server when you're using push replication. When you use pull subscriptions, the merge agent is on each subscriber.

Exercise Answer

You could implement several solutions, but given the facts in this scenario, I suggest a hybrid type of installation. One approach is to implement a central subscriber scenario at the warehouse in Wichita. The other four sites throughout the United States would publish data to the central location. The Wichita data could then be used in a publishing subscriber scenario with one of the British sites. The data coming into the Wichita database could be sent over the slow and expensive phone lines to a single database in the British Isles. That British database could then republish the data to the other administrative sites located in Great Britain.

Day 17

No quiz or exercise answers.

Day 18

Quiz Answers

1. The `AT` command and the Windows 2000 Schedule service.
2. The name of the mail profile of the Windows 2000 user account being used to run the SQL Server or SQL Server Agent service.
3. `Exec sp_processmail`.
4. Two scheduled tasks (one for the `with init` command and one without that runs every three hours).
5. The Database Maintenance Plan Wizard.

Day 19

Quiz Answers

1. You must have SELECT permissions in the source database on both the data and the system tables. You must be the dbo in the destination database.
2. BCP always enforces defaults and data types. It also always ignores rules, constraints, and triggers.
3. You must have the Select Into/Bulk Copy database option enabled and drop all indexes on the table.
4. You can transfer your data directly, transform it into other data types, summarize it, concatenate it, break it into component columns, and perform many other transformations.
5. You can't use a backup-and-restore methodology here because the sort order and processor architecture changed. I suggest that you install SQL Server 2000 on the new Alpha machine and then use the DTS Object Transfer Manager to move all objects, users, and permissions from the Intel machine to the Alpha machine.

Day 20

Quiz Answers

1. The physical implementation of the logical database design. No amount of hardware or software tuning will make up for a poor design.
2. So that the log's disk activity can have the highest priority and speed up SQL Server's overall throughput.
3. You would monitor the `MEMORY` object, Pages/Sec counter to look for a high level of swapping from memory to the paging file.
4. The affinity mask configuration with the `sp_configure` system stored procedure.
5. The SQLServer:Databases object, Log Flushes/sec counter would give you the best approximation of how many changes were being made on your SQL Server. CPU usage from the `PROCESS` object, % Processor Time counter, with an instance of `SQLSERVR` could also be used to measure activity. In fact, there is no one best counter. Monitoring isn't as easy as using a single counter.

Day 21

Quiz Answers

1. No, spaces aren't allowed in a URL. The correct URL would be `http://rhome/pubs?SQL=select+city+from+authors+for+XML+AUTO&root=ROOT`.
2. Any kind, so you must set security carefully.
3. It provides fewer detailed XML tags by default.

APPENDIX B

Installing MSDE 2000

In today's lesson you will learn how to install MSDE (The Microsoft Database Engine), and you will examine the components of the database server that are included with MSDE.

You will also examine the setup configuration you need to perform and discuss how to apply a service pack to MSDE.

What Is MSDE 2000?

MSDE is a set of technologies based on the SQL Server Database Engine. It is 100% compatible with the SQL Server product suite. This means that you can use MSDE to develop your SQL Server-based applications and be assured that they will work if you choose to install and use any type of SQL Server 2000 product.

MSDE is primarily targeted at application developers as a replacement database engine for Microsoft's JET database technologies. When you buy selected products from Microsoft, a copy of MSDE 2000 is now included (such as Visual Studio.NET, Microsoft Office XP Professional, and now with the Microsoft

ASP.NET Web Matrix Project at `http://www.asp.net`). When you develop applications with one of these products, you can re-distribute MSDE along with your application.

MSDE has a built-in resource governor that limits optimal performance to five concurrent workloads (roughly equivalent to five concurrent queries). As you run more simultaneous queries against MSDE, response times and overall query performance will degrade.

The following other restrictions apply to MSDE 2000 as well:

- Databases have a maximum size of 2GB (not including the transaction log).
- You can't use MSDE as a publisher for Transactional Replication.
- SQLMail is unavailable
- MSDE will only use up to two processors on a multi-processor computer.

If your application is going to exceed these limits, you will need to use either the standard or Enterprise Edition of SQL Server 2000.

MSDE Licensing

When I look at the Microsoft Support newsgroup for MSDE, I find that there are far more licensing than technical questions about MSDE. The biggest questions are around re-distribution of MSDE with developer's applications. There's good news and bad news here. The good news is that usually you can get an answer from the documentation provided with the product you purchased (i.e. Visual Studio.NET or Office XP), or in the redist.txt file in the MSDE directory of your product CD. The bad news is that the redistribution rights do vary from product to product, so examine these documents carefully. Your best bet is to read the redist.txt file, as well as your EULA (End-User License Agreement). Additionally, you can visit the SQL Server Web site (at `http://www.microsoft.com/SQL/howtobuy/msde.asp` at the time this was written) for this information as well:

> Customers using the Processor licensing model enjoy unlimited connections to the server running the licensed SQL Server. Customers using the Server/CAL (versus Per-Processor) licensing model must have a CAL dedicated to any device using MSDE, either in stand-alone form or as part of one of the products mentioned above.
>
> Redistribution rights and guidelines for MSDE are defined in the end-user license agreement (EULA) of each product that includes MSDE. For more information about MSDE, visit the `MSDE Product Overview` page.

There are additional restrictions on licensing that aren't always obvious. Basically, if you use MSDE to connect to a SQL Server (i.e. replication, distributed queries, etc.), you need to have either a CAL (Client Access License) for the machine that's running MSDE or you need to have the SQL Server running in per-processor mode.

Additionally, the administrative tools that come with the evaluation CD can only be used during the 120-day period against MSDE. You must have purchased a SQL Server CAL for the machine running MSDE in order to use the graphical administrative tools against MSDE (in other words, the tools are not free).

Neither of us are lawyers, and in no way is this section meant to give you legal advice. If you have legal questions about your license agreement or re-distribution rights, you should consult either a Microsoft licensing specialist or your attorney. You can visit `http://www.microsoft.com/licensing` for more info, and if you're in the United States, you can call 1-800-426-9400 Monday through Friday, 6:00 AM to 6:00 PM (Pacific Time) to speak directly to a licensing specialist.

MSDE Components

MSDE comes with several components, including

- The core database engine
- The SQL Server Agent service
- The osql.exe utility
- The SQL-DMO programming model
- The DTS run-time engine
- Microsoft Data Access Components (MDAC)

Each of these components is described on Day 2 or Day 3 as appropriate (except for the core database engine, which is most of the book).

Installing MSDE 2000

There are several steps involved in the installation of MSDE. Just like SQL Server 2000, MSDE 2000 has pre-requisite software that must be present for MSDE 2000 to function properly. There are some special considerations for running setup as MSDE is targeted more at a developer audience than a regular SQL Server install, so some of the setup steps are a bit more difficult for the average customer at first.

Prerequisites for Installing MSDE 2000

Understanding the prerequisites is critical before you begin the installation of MSDE 2000. Hardware and software requirements must be met. Also, when you're running SQL Server on Windows NT or Windows 2000 computers, you must deal with a few additional considerations.

Hardware and Software Options

The lowest-powered CPUs supported are Pentium 166 processors. Pentium, Pentium Pro, Pentium 2, Pentium 3, and Pentium 4 computers were available at the time this lesson was written. Of course, Pentium instruction-set–compatible systems are also supported. You need at least 32MB of RAM, although you need 64MB of RAM on Windows 2000 or Windows XP.

Although a Pentium 166 is the lowest-powered configuration supported, MSDE 2000 will probably work (albeit run more slowly) on any Pentium-based computer. It can't run on a 486 or any processor that doesn't support the *full* Pentium instruction set.

MSDE requires about 44MB of disk space to install.

Supported Operating System Choices

When you have the supported hardware, you must select or consider which operating systems are supported. MSDE 2000 can run on a Windows NT computer (version 4.0 or later with service pack 5 or later), any version (Workstation, Server, Small Business Server, or Server Enterprise Edition). MSDE 2000 can also run on any version of Windows 2000 or Windows XP and on a Windows 98 or Windows ME computer. You must consider some restrictions for the Windows platforms, however.

No 32-bit version of MSDE is supported when running on a 64-bit version of Microsoft Windows.NET Server.

Windows 9*x* Restrictions

MSDE behaves differently on the Windows 9*x* platform (Windows 98, or Windows ME) because of restrictions built into the operating system:

- Named Pipes, Banyan VINES, and AppleTalk network libraries aren't supported.
- Windows Authentication Mode (also known as integrated security) isn't available.
- Server-side multi-protocol encryption isn't supported.
- Asynchronous input/output (I/O) and scatter-gather I/O aren't available.
- The MSDE components don't run as services because Windows 9*x* doesn't support services. They run as applications, just like any other program you can run.
- Performance monitor and event viewer aren't available.
- Memory tuning is optimized for minimal memory usage.

Some of these terms might not mean much now, but before your 21 days are up, you will understand all these restrictions and their implementation details. However, you won't notice most of them.

Windows NT/Windows 2000 Options

Now that you have examined some issues with the Windows 9*x* platform, it's time to examine some of the Windows NT and Windows 2000-specific features. Windows 2000 or Windows XP is definitely the recommended platform, because all product features are available.

The most important Windows NT/2000/XP options are security and the NTFS file system. Therefore, you will briefly examine each here. However, you might choose Windows NT/2000/XP for several other reasons. This book assumes that all features are available on most platforms but highlights features available only on Windows NT/2000/XP. Because it would be too confusing to reference all operating system features specific to each version, we have also chosen to use Windows 2000. Therefore, all parts of the book that reference operating system components assume Windows 2000 unless otherwise stated.

Security Options

NEW TERM Perhaps the most important option available with Windows NT/2000/XP is security. Windows NT, Windows 2000, and Windows XP are secure operating systems, allowing you to restrict who can do what to files, as well as control access rights with Windows NT/2000 security accounts. This feature, known as *Windows Authentication Mode* or *integrated security*, allows you to use Windows user and group accounts directly in SQL Server. You'll examine this feature in detail on Day 5, "Setting Up Login and User Security."

File System Options

You can use the file allocation table (FAT), FAT32 (Windows ME/2000/XP), or NTFS file systems with SQL Server 2000. I strongly recommend using the NTFS file system for security and reliability. If you install with the NTFS file system, SQL Server setup secures your installation files, including your system database files. NTFS is also much faster in terms of new database creation. With Windows 2000, you can also take advantage of the Encrypted File System (EFS) support to encrypt your database files so that no one can copy them without having the username and password of the SQL Server service account.

Creating the Setup Parameters File

This is where some of the fun of setting up MSDE 2000 starts (when compared to installing SQL Server 2000). If you want to install a default instance of MSDE 2000 on your computer, you can skip to the next section (and basically you just get to double-click setup and be happy).

However, if you have any other copy of MSDE 1.0, MSDE 2000, or any version or edition of SQL Server on your computer, you are likely to already have a default instance of SQL Server or MSDE installed. You can check by going to Control Panel -> Administrative Tools -> Services and look for a service named MSSQLServer. If you can find that service, you have a default instance of SQL Server or MSDE installed.

For the purposes of this day's lesson, we're going to install a named instance of MSDE 2000.

For a discussion of Named verses Default instances, look at the topic "Named versus Default Instances" in Day 2, Installing Microsoft SQL Server 2000.

To accomplish this selection (going with a named instance), we'll need to create an INI file so that setup can accept the INI file as a parameter.

To create this INI file, select Start -> Run -> Notepad.exe to start the Windows notepad application. Then type in:

```
[Options]
TARGETDIR="C:\Program Files\Microsoft SQL Server\Mssql$SQL2k\Binn"
DATADIR="C:\Program Files\Microsoft SQL Server\Mssql$SQL2k\Data"
INSTANCENAME=SQL2k
```

If you're short on space in the C drive of your computer, you can change the drive letter above.

Now, select File, Exit and select Yes to save your changes. When prompted to save the file, select C:\MSDE.INI, as shown in figure 1.

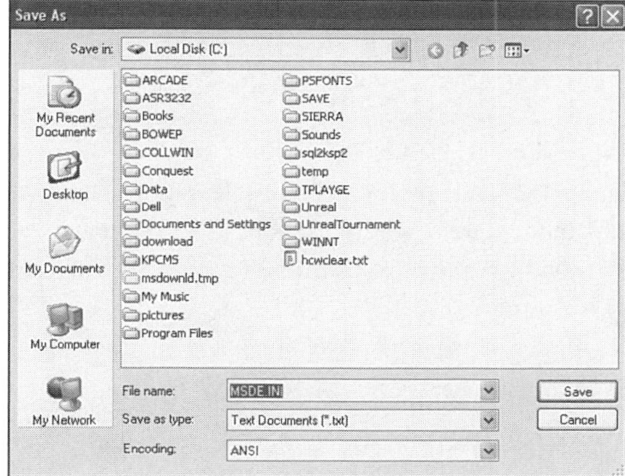

FIGURE MSDE.1

Saving the Setup INI file.

Running Setup for MSDE 2000

Now you're ready to run setup. The first step is to examine the setup parameters.

```
setup [/?]
  [[  /i package_file
   [ /settings ini_file ]
   |  [  [ CALLBACK=Dllname!CallbackFunctionName ]
           [ COLLATION="collationname" ]
           [ DATADIR="data_path" ]
           [ INSTANCENAME="instancename" ]
           [ SECURITYMODE=SQL ]
           [ TARGETDIR="executable_path"]
           [ UPGRADE=1]
           [ UPGRADEUSER=sa]
       ]
   ]
   | [ /x package_file ]
  ]
  [ /L*v [filename] ]
  [ /qn | /qb ]
```

You won't need to worry about the majority of these parameters (they're more relevant to developers re-distributing MSDE 2000, but the ones that may be used in your INI file are worth reviewing (not all of these will necessarily be in there)).

- `[ DATADIR="data_path" ]`

  This parameter indicates the folder name that your actual database files will be stored in. The path referenced in your INI file is the standard path for named instances of MSDE (substituting the instance name as appropriate).

- `[ TARGETDIR="executable_path"]`

  This parameter indicates where the program files for your installation will be located. Typically, this is the same path as your datadir with the exception that its default name is the `BINN` directory.

- `[ INSTANCENAME="instancename" ]`

  This parameter indicates the name of the instance you're installing. When you specify an instance name, you're creating a named instance install and will use this name every time to connect to or reference your MSDE 2000 installation (so keep it short and meaningful).

- `[ SECURITYMODE=SQL ]`

  This parameter is used to install MSDE 2000 in mixed security mode rather than the default mode of Windows Integrated Security only. Don't select this option unless you absolutely must run in mixed security mode (See Day 5 for more information).

- `[ /L*v [filename] ]`

  This parameter will produce a verbose setup log. If your setup fails when you re-run it, specify this parameter on the command line (i.e. `setup.exe /Settings c:\msde.ini /L*v c:\msde.log`) to see what went wrong.

- `[ /qn | /qb ]`

  `/qn` will not present any user interface, and `/qb` will only present a minimal user interface for setup. For the purposes of the book, we want as much information as possible.

Okay, now that you know what most of the options mean, go ahead and run setup. Open up a command prompt (Select Start -> Run -> Cmd (or command.exe on Windows 9*x* systems)). Now switch to your CD-ROM with the evaluation CD (drive G:\ on my computer in the screenshots), and then into the MSDE directory. Then run the following command line from setup (also see Figure MSDE.2):

```
Setup /Settings C:\MSDE.INI
```

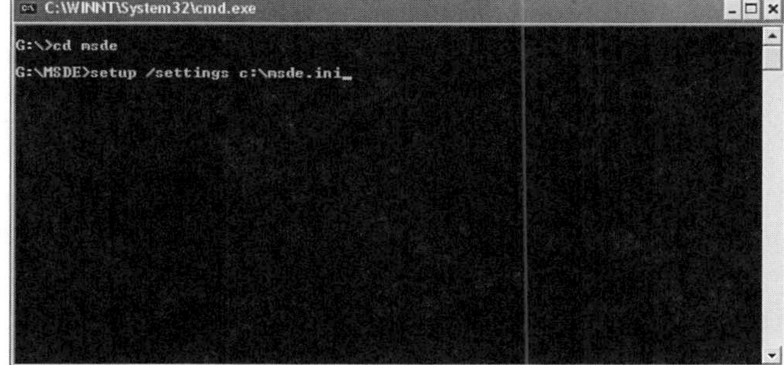

FIGURE MSDE.2
Starting MSDE 2000 Setup.

You will see setup start, as shown in Figure MSDE.3.

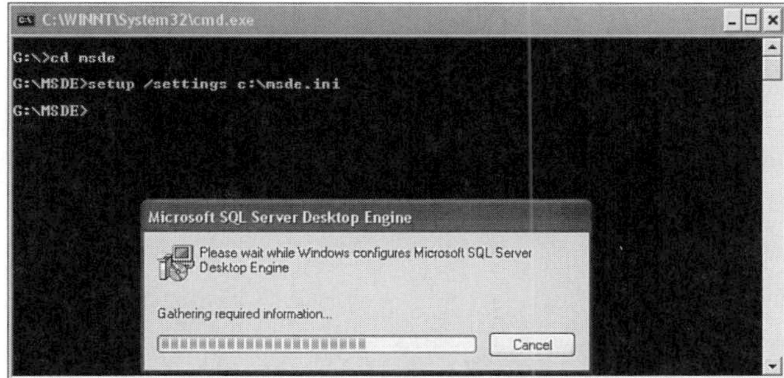

FIGURE MSDE.3
MSDE 2000 Setup Running.

Assuming you didn't make any mistakes in the INI file, you'll next see something like Figure MSDE.4 (with the time counting down to zero seconds remaining).

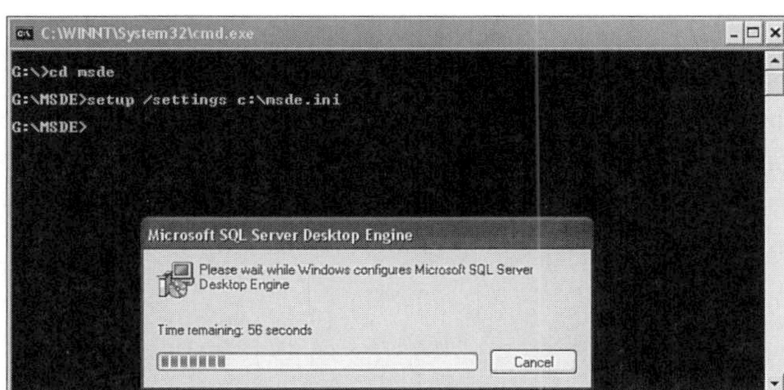

FIGURE MSDE.4
MSDE 2000 Setup Finishing.

And that's it. When setup is done, it just goes away, so don't be surprised – this is the expected behavior.

B

Installing an MSDE 2000 Service Pack

The next logical setup is to install the service pack. The bad news here is that the downloadable service pack for MSDE from `http://www.microsoft.com/sql` is only applicable to a default instance installation of MSDE 2000. Unfortunately this means you'll almost certainly need to order a CD with the service pack. We certainly hope Microsoft fixes this problem, as it's silly to have to order a CD to put the patches on in this day and age.

When you do install the service pack, make sure you get the MSDE-specific service pack, as it is different from the regular SQL Server service packs.

Summary

MSDE is a very powerful database server and is available from an increasing number of sources. If you want to build and distribute an application that just needs a local data store (or a network store that won't get more than five simultaneous users), MSDE may be right for you. The best thing about MSDE is that your customers can then upgrade directly to SQL Server with no changes in your application programs.

Q&A

Q Is MSDE 2000 Free?

A No. You only get the right to use and redistribute MSDE with either a SQL Server 2000 Client Access License (CAL) or by buying and developing with a qualifying product such as Visual Studio.NET.

Q Why would anyone buy SQL Server when MSDE is nearly free?

A SQL Server 2000 has many features, particularly in the Enterprise Edition, that are oriented toward high availability and increased performance. Additionally, SQL Server has no size limits on the database, has much more replication functionality, and includes Analysis Services and English Query.

APPENDIX C

High Availability Overview

This chapter focuses on high availability solutions with Microsoft SQL Server 2000. There are several levels of high availability. You can keep a warm standby server by using log shipping, or you can create a cluster of SQL Servers using Microsoft Cluster Server.

In this chapter, we will take a look at both of these methodologies. Let's start the day with Cluster Service. In order to understand how SQL Server clustering works, you need to have a little background in Microsoft Cluster Service.

Microsoft Cluster Service

In this section, you will learn about the following parts of the Microsoft Cluster Service:

- Cluster Terminology
- Cluster Service Architecture

- Cluster Resources
- Cluster Administration
- Failure Detection

Overview of High Availability

Microsoft developed two clustering technologies for use on their Windows 2000 family of server products. Windows 2000-based servers running Cluster service can provide failover support for back-end applications and services that require high availability and data integrity. The other type of clustering is called load balancing. In a load balancing scenario, several computers share the responsibility of running an application. Web servers can be load balanced. When incoming requests for web pages reach a server, they may be passed to another server that has less work to do. Clustering is the other method.

The Cluster service was first designed to run on the NT 4.0 platform. It has been substantially enhanced in the Windows 2000 Advanced server products. These enhancements have been carried over into Windows .Net server as well.

As designed, the Cluster service enables multiple servers and data storage components to join into a single easily managed unit known as the server cluster. This interconnectedness allows Microsoft Clustering Service (MSCS) to provide high availability, improved scalability, and improved manageability:

- High availability – By enabling services and applications in the cluster to continue to provide service during both hardware and/or software component failures. This can also be applied to scheduled downtime for maintenance as well.
- Improved scalability – MSCS supports upgradeable servers. This means that you can begin with a relatively small server (say a two processor system) and then add additional processors and memory as needed.
- Improved manageability – Managing cluster resources is simplified. Through the cluster administrator, all of the devices and resources are treated as if they were being managed on a single computer.

The other complementary clustering technology is referred to as Network Load Balancing. This type of clustering is used for the support of front-end applications. It improves their availability and speed by spreading the processing of requests across multiple servers. This type of service is most useful for applications like Internet Information Server (IIS), web-based applications, media streaming, and Microsoft Terminal Services.

Since SQL Server 2000 is a back-end application, we will focus on clustering rather than load balancing.

NEW TERM Cluster Service is the Windows 2000 Advanced Server name for Microsoft Cluster Service. Cluster Service was first introduced in Windows NT 4.0 Enterprise. In Windows 2000 Advanced Server, the Cluster Service has been integrated into the operating system making it far more stable and reliable. When running Cluster Service under Windows NT 4.0 Enterprise, the clustering technology built into Windows 2000 Advanced Server had to be virtualized. Due to this virtualization, Cluster Service under Windows NT 4.0 Enterprise was spurious at best.

Terminology

In this section, you will learn more about the terminology used to describe and work with clusters:

- Cluster Service – The Windows 2000 name for MSCS. It also refers to the collection of components on each node that perform cluster-specific activities.
- Nodes – Individual servers that are members of a cluster are referred to as nodes.
- Resource – Hardware and software components within a cluster that are managed by the Cluster Service.
- Server Clusters – 2-node or greater MSCS clusters.
- Virtual Servers – Resources may be located on any node in the cluster, however, the client does not know this. To the client, all resources appear to be on a single computer.
- Resource Groups – A logical collection of clustered resources. These are generally related objects such as applications and their associated data and peripherals. When operations are performed on the resource group, the operation is applied to all objects that comprise the group.

Cluster Resources

Resources are hardware and software components that are managed by the Cluster Service within the cluster. Resources can be online or offline.

A resource is online when it is providing its service to the cluster and is available to the client applications.

Resource Characteristics

Resources themselves can be logical or physical components that have the following characteristics:

- Can be brought online and offline
- Can be managed in a server cluster
- Can be owned by only one node at a time

Resource Components

Resources would include components like the following:

- Disk drives
- Network cards
- IP addresses
- Application databases and the application itself

Local Resources

Each cluster will have its own local resources. These are resources that are owned and managed on a particular node by the resource running on that node.

Quorum Resources

Clusters need to have common resources as well. There might be a data storage array or a private network just for the cluster. Each node in the cluster must be able to access these common resources.

The quorum resource is a physical disk in the common cluster disk array that is used to manage cluster operations. It must be present for nodes to form and join a cluster.

Server Clusters

Cluster Service is based on the shared-nothing model of clustering architecture. Servers in the shared-nothing cluster manage their own local resources and devices.

Shared resources and quorum resources (like a common disk array) and connection media are selectively owned and managed by a single server at any given time.

Using a shared-nothing model allows management of devices and applications to be more streamlined. Special cabling and applications are not required for management of your Windows 2000 and Windows NT-based resources.

Cluster Service uses standard Windows 2000 and Windows NT drivers for storage devices and media connections. When using external devices for common use on the cluster, you must use devices that support SCSI and standard PCI-based SCSI connections. You can also use SCSI over fiber channel and SCSI buses with multiple initiators.

Fiber connections are SCSI devices, simply hosted on a fiber channel bus instead of a SCSI bus. Conceptually, fiber channel technology encapsulates SCSI commands within the fiber channel and makes it possible to use the SCSI commands needed to support Cluster Service. These commands include: Reserve/Release and Bus Reset.

FIGURE XC.1
Clustering diagram.

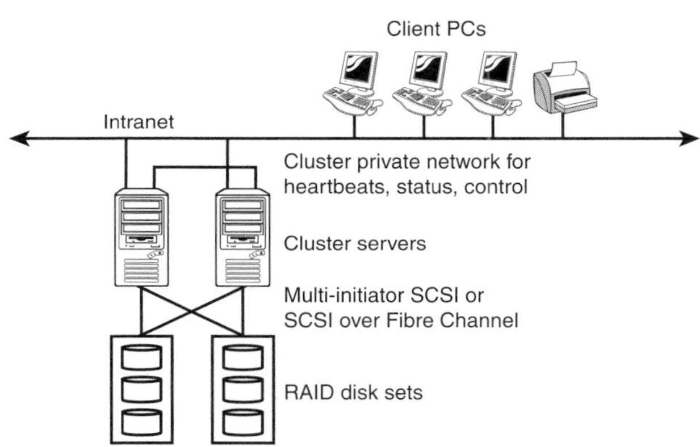

Virtual Servers

Application and services running on a server cluster can be exposed to users and workstations as a virtual server. The cluster service manages the virtual server and exposes an IP address and a network name as a resource. The cluster service itself maps the IP address and the network name to a particular node's IP address. These virtual addresses are how cluster service provides for high availability.

Application clients only need to know the IP address or the network name of the application or service that is exposed.

You can create services and applications that run on a cluster node without managing those resources through a virtual server. Although this may work, it is not a recommended solution as the applications will not automatically failover.

Since clients only need to know the IP address of the virtual resource, when a node failure occurs, the cluster server can move the entire resource to another node in the server cluster. This allows for highly available applications and services.

When a failure of this type occurs, the client will detect a failure in its session with the application and attempt to reconnect to the application as if the application were running on an individual computer. The client will successfully reconnect even though the resource has been moved to a different physical computer in the server cluster. The cluster service will simply remap the virtual IP address and network name to another node.

While virtual servers provide a highly available application or service, there are some caveats. Session state information related to a particular client is lost, unless that clustered application is specifically designed and configured to store client session data on disk for retrieval during application recovery.

Session state information is data related directly to an individual client. For example, a client may open a non-standard session with the service. When this is done, that specialized session information would be called the session state and stored with the service. As multiple clients connect to a service, each client will have its own private set of information about how it is connected and what it is doing within the application or service. This is state information.

Applications can avoid this problem if they are built to support some type of fault tolerant transaction behavior. Microsoft's DHCP service and SQL Server are examples of applications that provide this type of service. Both of the applications store transaction information in a type of database for recovery purposes. With DHCP, client IP address reservations are saved in the DHCP database. If the DHCP resource fails, the database can be moved to an available node in the cluster and restored with the same state information for all of its clients.

Resource Groups

A resource group is a logically related set of cluster resources. This is usually applications and their associated data and peripherals. You can create a resource group based around administrative needs as well. For example, you might create a resource group of IP addresses and their virtual server names.

Keep the following facts in mind when dealing with resource groups:

- Owned by only one node at a time
- Individual resources within the group must exist on the node that currently owns the group
- Different servers within the cluster cannot own different resources in the same resource group

Cluster-wide Policies

Cluster-wide policies allow you to dictate which server the resource group prefers to run on and which server the group should move to in the event of a failure.

Each resource group has these additional characteristics:

- Network name and IP address to allow clients to bind to the service
- Can be failed over and moved as atomic units from a failed node to another available node on the cluster

Dependencies and Relationships

Resources often depend on other resources in the cluster. These relationships may be as simple as having one resource loaded and running before another related resource can be started and running. For example, the SQLServerAgent service cannot run unless the MSSQLServer service is running first. Other examples may include a database application waiting on the availability of a disk or IP address.

Resource dependencies are identified with the Cluster Service. Once the various properties and dependencies are added, the Cluster Service can then control the order in which resources are brought online and taken offline.

Keep the following in mind when dealing with resource group dependencies:

- The scope of an identified dependency is only the resources found in the resource group.
- Cluster managed dependencies cannot extend beyond the resources within the group.
- Resources can be brought online and offline and moved independently.

Cluster Server Architecture

In this section, you will learn more about the modifications made to the operating system. You will learn about the components that make the cluster service work. The key components will be covered in more detail, including the Node Manager and the Failover Manager. Failover and Failback will be covered in their own sections as well.

Operating System Modifications

In general, when Microsoft developed the cluster service, they created it to work as a set of components that complement and work with the current operating system. By designing clustering in this fashion, Microsoft avoided the introduction of complex processing and operating system interdependencies.

Despite their best efforts to leave the operating system alone, there were several minor changes made to enable clustering to work. These include the following:

- Support for the dynamic deletion and creation of IP addresses and network names.
- File system modifications to allow cluster service to close open files during disk drive dismounts.
- I/O subsystem modifications to allow volume sets and disks to be shared across multiple nodes.

Cluster Service Components

Let's cover the components that make up Cluster Service and how they interact. The components are:

- Checkpoint Manager – Saves application registry keys in a cluster directory stored on the quorum resource.
- Communications Manager – Manages communications between cluster nodes.
- Configuration Database Manager – Maintains cluster configuration information.
- Event Processor – Receives event messages from cluster resources such as status changes and requests from applications to open, close, and enumerate cluster objects.
- Event Log Manager – Replicates event log entries from one node to all other nodes in the cluster.
- Failover Manager – Performs resource management and initiates appropriate actions, such as startup, restart, and failover.
- Global Update Manager – Provides a global update service used by cluster components.
- Log Manager – Writes changes to recovery logs stored on the quorum resource.
- Membership Manager – Manages cluster membership and monitors the health of other nodes in the cluster.
- Node Manager – Assigns resource group ownership to nodes based on group preference lists and node availability.
- Object Manager – Manages all the cluster service objects.
- Resource Monitors – Monitors the health of each cluster resource using callbacks to resource DLLs.

The Node Manager

The node manager runs on each node and maintains a local copy of all of the nodes that belong to the cluster. To maintain the health of the cluster, the node manager will periodically send out a message to other node managers within the cluster. This message is called a *heartbeat*. All nodes in the cluster must have the same view of the cluster and all nodes will periodically send out heartbeats to ensure synchronization.

Communication failures force the broadcast of error messages to the entire cluster. This causes all members of the cluster to verify their current view of the cluster membership. This is known as a *regroup* event.

During a regroup event, the cluster service prevents write operations to any disk devices common to all nodes in the cluster until the cluster membership has stabilized.

When a node manager on an individual node doesn't respond, the node is removed from the cluster and the active resource groups are then moved to another active node. Node selection is based on the resource group properties. The node manager will move resources to the node that they prefer. In a two-node cluster, all resource groups are moved to the surviving node. In three and four node clusters, the node manager will selectively distribute resource groups among the surviving nodes.

Note

> When cluster service or one of its component processes fail, resources attached to the node experiencing the failure are stopped under the assumption that they will be restarted on an active node in the cluster.

Failover Manager

The failover manager is responsible for stopping and starting resources, managing resource dependencies, and initiating failover of resource groups. These actions are performed when the failover manager receives notification from the Resource Monitors and the Node.

In addition to these activities, the failover manager is responsible for managing resource dependencies and deciding which node in the cluster should own which group. When the failover manager completes this arbitration process, control of the resource group is handed over to the Node manager.

When a failure occurs, the failover manager will work with the other nodes to re-arbitrate ownership of the resource group.

When a failure occurs, the failover manager can take one of several actions:

- Restart the resource.
- Take the resource offline and indicate that resource ownership should be transferred to another node (*failover)*.
- Take the resource offline and restart it on another node after failover.

The Failover Process

Failover can occur automatically because of an unplanned hardware failure, or the cluster administrator can trigger it manually. The only difference between the two is how the resources shut down. Under a manual failover, the resources shut down normally and gracefully while automatic failover may be forceful.

When an entire node fails, its resource groups are moved to one or more available servers in the cluster. When done automatically, the administrator can choose the reassignment of resources. When automatic failure occurs, the failover managers re-arbitrate resources according to the node preference lists. The node preference list is found on each node and is part of the resource group properties.

When a cluster has more than two nodes, the node preference list can specify a preferred server plus one or more prioritized alternatives. In this scenario, if a node fails, the resource groups are moved to a preferred server. If that server fails, the resources are moved to the next server in the list of alternatives. This ability to survive multiple server failures is known as a *cascading failover.*

Keep in mind that the cluster administrator can specify different preference lists and alternatives for each resource group. This allows the administrator to maintain some level of workload balance across surviving servers in the event of a failure.

When the cluster administrator sets the node preference list of all cluster groups, this is known as N+1 failover. The preference list identifies the standby cluster nodes to which resources should be moved during the first failover. The standby nodes are servers in the cluster that are mostly idle or whose own workload can be easily pre-empted in the event a failed server's workload must be moved to the standby node.

When choosing between cascading and N+1 failover, determine how you want to use the excess capacity on your other servers and the amount of excess capacity available.

With cascading failover, the assumption is that every other server in the cluster has some excess capacity to absorb a portion of any other failed server's workload.

With N+1 failover, the assumption is that the +1 standby server is mostly idle and is the primary location for excess capacity.

Once a node is brought back online, the failover manager can decide to move the resource groups back to the recovered node. This is known as a *failback*.

In order for this to occur several things must happen:

- The node must be successfully restarted or recovered.
- The resource group must have a preferred owner defined.

There is failback protection that can be defined in the failback properties. These include:

- Prevention of failbacks from occurring at peak processing times.
- Prevention of a failback to an incorrectly restarted or recovered node.
- Limitation on the number of times a failback can be attempted.

Cluster Formation and Operation

In this section, we will cover cluster formation and operation. When the cluster service is installed and running on a server, the server is available for participation in a cluster. Cluster operations will reduce single points of failure and enable high availability of clustered resources. The following section will briefly describe the node behavior during cluster creation and operation. These include

- Creating a cluster
- Forming a cluster
- Joining a cluster
- Leaving a cluster
- Failure Detection

Creating a Cluster

Creating a cluster involves three main steps. These include running the cluster installation utility on the first member of the cluster, adding common data storage devices, and running the cluster installation utility on the remaining nodes of the cluster.

Creation of First Node

The first step in creating a cluster is to run the cluster installation utility on the first server to be a member of the cluster. When you run the utility, you define the new cluster, give it a name, and create the cluster database and initial cluster membership list.

Add Common Data Storage Devices

The next step is to add the common data storage devices that will be available to all members of the cluster. This establishes the cluster with a single node with its own local data storage devices and the cluster common resources. The common resources generally include data storage devices and connection media resources.

Run Cluster Installation Utility on Additional Nodes

The final step is to run the installation utility on each additional computer that will be a member in the cluster. As each new node is added to the cluster, it will automatically receive a copy of the existing cluster database from the original member of the cluster. When a node joins or forms a cluster, the cluster service updates the node's private copy of the configuration database.

Forming a Cluster

A server can form a cluster if the following are true:

- The node is running cluster service.
- The node cannot locate other nodes in the cluster. (If the node can locate other nodes, it is already a member of a cluster and cannot form one of its own.)
- The node can acquire exclusive ownership of the quorum resource.

Quorum Resource Attributes

The quorum resource maintains data integrity and cluster unity. It must be present for node operations such as forming and joining a cluster. The quorum resource is a physical disk in the common cluster disk array and has the following attributes:

- Supports low-level commands for persisting ownership arbitration enabling a single node to gain and control the quorum resource.
- Can be accessed by any node in the cluster.
- Can be formatted with NTFS.

Low-level commands that enable persistent arbitration include the SCSI disk

Reserve and Release commands.

Resource Performs Tiebreaker

The quorum resource performs the role of tiebreaker when a cluster is formed or when the network connections between nodes fail. When a cluster is initially formed, the first node in the cluster contains the cluster configuration database. As each additional node joins the cluster, it receives and maintains its own local copy of the cluster configuration database. The quorum resource on the common cluster device stores the most current version of the configuration database in the form of recovery logs that contain node-independent cluster configuration and state data.

Quorum recovery logs are used during cluster operations to perform the following:

- Guarantee that only one set of active, communicating nodes is allowed to form a cluster.
- Enable a node to form a cluster only if it can gain control of the quorum resource.
- Allow a node to join or remain in an existing cluster only if it can communicate with the node that controls the quorum resource.

Nodes Can Be in One of Three States

When a cluster is formed, each node in the cluster may be in one of three distinct states. These states are recorded in the Event Processor and are replicated to the other nodes by the Event Log Manager. The states are

- Offline – The node is not a fully active member of the cluster. The node may or may not be running.
- Online – The node is a fully active member of the cluster. It honors cluster database updates, contributes votes to the quorum algorithm, maintains heartbeats, and owns and runs resource groups.
- Paused – The node is a fully active member of the cluster. It assumes the responsibilities of being *online,* however, it cannot accept resource groups. It will continue to support resource groups that it already owns.

Joining a Cluster

To join an existing cluster, the following must be true:

- Location of another node in the cluster must be found.
- The joining server must be authenticated for membership in the cluster.
- The joining server will then receive a replicated copy of the cluster configuration database.

Joining begins when the Cluster Service mounts the local data device. Joining a cluster begins when the NT or Win2k Service Control Manager starts the Cluster Service on the node. During the start-up process, the cluster service does the following:

- Configures and mounts the local data devices.
- Does not bring the common cluster data devices online as nodes, because the existing cluster may be using these devices.

The next step is the discovery process. When the node discovers any member of the cluster, it performs an authentication sequence. The first cluster member authenticates the newcomer and returns a status of success if the newcomer is authenticated.

An unrecognized joining node or an invalid account password may cause unsuccessful authentication. In these cases, the request to join is refused.

After successful authentication, the first node online in the cluster checks the copy of the configuration database on the joining node. If the database is out of date, it is updated and synchronized. Once the joining node receives its replicated copy of the database, the joining node can now use the database to find shared resources and bring them online as needed.

Leaving a Cluster

A node can leave a cluster under three conditions:

- When the node shuts down.
- When the cluster service is stopped.
- Eviction.

Eviction occurs when a node fails to perform cluster operations, such as failure to commit an update to the cluster configuration database.

When a node leaves a cluster, in the event of a planned shutdown, it will send a *ClusterExit* message to all other members in the cluster. The node doesn't wait for any messages back, but simply shuts down all resources and closes cluster connections.

Since the remaining nodes receive the exit message, they do not have to perform a regroup process to re-establish cluster membership. Keep in mind that this is during a planned shutdown or eviction. Under node failure conditions, the normal failover process will occur.

Failure Detection

Failure detection and prevention are key benefits provided by Cluster service. Cluster service failure detection and prevention includes bi-directional failover, application failover, parallel recovery, and automatic failback.

The cluster service is designed with two different failure detection mechanisms:

- Heartbeat—used for detecting node failures.
- Resource Monitor and resource DLLs—used for detecting resource failures.

Heartbeats

Periodically each node exchanges datagram messages with other nodes using the private cluster network. These are heartbeats. Heartbeats allow each node to check the availability of other nodes and their applications. If a server fails to respond to a heartbeat exchange, the surviving servers initiate failover processes. This includes ownership arbitration for resources and applications owned by the failed server.

Failure to respond can be caused by several events:

- Computer failure
- Network interface failure
- Network failure

When all nodes are communicating, the Configuration Database Manager sends global configuration database updates to each node. When a failure is detected, the Log Manager will save the configuration database changes to the quorum resource. Persisting state information to the quorum resource allows the surviving nodes access to the latest configuration database information for use during the regroup and recovery process.

Resource Monitor Polls Resources

The Failover Manager and the Resource Monitors work together to detect and recover from resource failures. The monitors keep track of resources by periodically polling the resources. Polling involves two steps: the brief *LooksAlive* query and a more detailed *IsAlive* query. When a failure is found, the Failover Manager is notified.

Once a resource failure is detected, the Failover Manager can perform recovery actions. This includes restarting the resource and its dependent resources or moving the entire resource group to another node. The recovery operation performed is determined by resource and resource group properties as well as node availability.

Review:

- Cluster Service
- Nodes
- Resources and Resource Groups
- Server Cluster Virtual Servers
- Clustering Architechture
- Failover and Failback

Keep in mind that during failover the resource group is treated as a failover unit to ensure that resource dependencies are correctly recovered. Once a resource recovers from a failure, the Resource monitor notifies the Failover Manager, which then performs automatic failback of the resource group. Keep in mind that failback is based on the configuration of the resource groups failback properties.

Cluster Installation and Configuration

As with any type of work you do in the database world, careful planning is essential to the success of your project. This is also true of clustering and SQL Server.

There is a very careful process you must follow in order to properly install SQL Server 2000 on a Microsoft Cluster Service Server. Installation of the cluster as well as the database and its devices are key.

There are a list of other factors to consider as well, such as potential replication issues and SQLMail issues. For the latest tips, whitepapers, and other clustering considerations, please check the Microsoft Web site at `http://www.microsoft.com/sql`.

Now let's take a closer look at log shipping.

Log Shipping in SQL Server 2000

Standby servers mirror your production server. When the production server goes down (either scheduled or unscheduled), you can have the standby server take over. The standby server may also be used as a read only version of the production server. This may be useful for offloading reporting and other information management queries from the production server.

You keep the production and standby servers synchronized by using log shipping. Log shipping is the process by which you copy the transaction log from the production server to the standby server and then load it on to the standby server.

There are a few things to keep in mind when using log shipping. Since we are moving transaction logs, you should use the full recovery model on your database.

Another key to keep in mind is security. The SQL Server Agent service must have the appropriate permissions on both the production and standby servers to do the backup and restore operations.

You can put all of this together manually, or you can let SQL Server take care of it for you.

Database Maintenance Plan Wizard

This wizard can help you set up and maintain log shipping services. If you did this process manually, you would have to remember what you did and when you did things. The wizard not only automates this work for you, but it also tracks all the operations that take place.

The wizard allows you to do the following:

- Pick standby servers which can become production servers in the event of a failure.
- Create a copy of the database on all of the standby servers. You can create a new database or use an existing database.
- Specify how often logs are shipped.
- Pick a server to monitor the status of the log shipping operations.

You should keep the following rules in mind when you are setting up log shipping:

- Only one database at a time can be configured for log shipping.
- You must be a member of sysadmins to configure log shipping.
- Automated log shipping is supported for disk backups. Tape backup is not currently supported.
- You should have good connectivity to the standby servers.
- The standby servers should be of similar quality, speed, and size as well as operating system and collation sequence.

Performing a Failover/Failback

While this process isn't automatic with log shipping, it is still fairly straightforward using the following stored procedures (included in SQL Server 2000).

Once you have set up log shipping, you can run these stored procedures:

- sp_change_primary_role—Run this on the production server to disable the log backup job and make a final log backup.
- sp_change_secondary_role—Run this on the standby server to disable the copy and restore process. This will copy the final log backup and restore it. It will then put the database online as the production server.
- sp_resolve_logins—If you have not copied the syslogins table from the master database on the production server to the standby server, then you will need to. Once the logins are copied, you must match them up with the database users in the log shipped database. You can do this manually with sp_change_users_login, or you can run this procedure and do them all at one time.
- sp_change_monitor_role—This procedure allows you to update the monitor server with the new primary and standby server information.

Here is a short list of the final steps that you may need to perform. You should rename the standby server to the old production server's name. (The production server must be taken off the network segment you are on.) You may also need to modify the IP address of the new production server to match the old server's IP address. This way, your clients will not all have to be updated. They will use the new standby server as if it were the old production server.

When you change the computer name, you will have to reboot the server. SQL Server 2000 will also need to have setup run again. The setup process will only take a few seconds as it is just updating the registry with the new server name and IP address.

When you are ready to failback, you can either have log shipping set up on the old production server and follow the same process, or you can do it manually by making a backup of the database and restoring it on the production server.

Summary

Today you learned about high availability choices in SQL Server 2000. You can go with a 24 x 7 type of availability and scalability with clustering, or you can use a more economical, but not as scalable and not 24 x 7, model of availability with log shipping.

Q&A

Q Which high availability model should I use?

A This really depends on what type of availability you need. The log shipping process is easy to develop and maintain and does not require special hardware or software. It should be considered a warm standby. You can switch to a standby server in just a few minutes. If you have the money and you need 24 x 7 uptime, then using Microsoft Clustering Services with SQL Server 2000 is a great way to go. Keep in mind that there are some issues with clustering and dealing with SQLMail and replication. The maintenance in a clustered environment is more difficult, and you must use specialized hardware and the clustering software.

Q If I do log shipping or clustering, should I still keep backups?

A Absolutely. Did I mention that we are paranoid database admins and that we always keep backups in a secure off-site location? The fun aside, you should always maintain a rigorous backup cycle and stick to it.

Workshop

This section provides a short workshop to solidify your understanding of the concepts presented today.

Exercises

For this exercise, you must install an additional instance of SQL Server. You can do this on your local machine or you can load SQL Server on another computer on your network.

1. Using the Database Maintenance Plan Wizard, configure the Northwind database for log shipping between your two instances of SQL Server.
2. Add some data to one of the tables (I like to use categories) and have the log ship process take place.
3. Verify the data on the standby server.
4. Perform the failover process using the stored procedures outlined in this chapter.
    - sp_change_primary_role
    - sp_change_secondary_role
    - sp_resolve_logins
    - sp_change_monitor_role

Index

Symbols

A

B

C

E

F

G-H

I

J-K

L

M

P

Q

R

S

T

U

X-Z

Installing the Evaluation Copy of Microsoft SQL Server 2000

The CD-ROM includes a 120-day evaluation copy of Microsoft SQL Server 2000. Follow these steps to perform the install:

1. Insert the CD-ROM into your CD-ROM drive.
2. From the Windows desktop, double-click the My Computer icon.
3. Double-click the icon representing your CD-ROM drive.
4. Double-click the `autorun.exe` icon and follow the onscreen instructions to finish the installation.

> **Note**
>
> If you have the Windows AutoPlay feature enabled, `autorun.exe` starts automatically whenever you insert the disc into your CD-ROM drive.

Licensing Agreement

By opening this package, you are agreeing to be bound by the following agreement:

You may not copy or redistribute the entire CD-ROM as a whole. Copying and redistribution of individual software programs on the CD-ROM is governed by terms set by individual copyright holders.

This software is sold as is, without warranty of any kind, either expressed or implied, including but not limited to the implied warranties of merchantability and fitness for a particular purpose. Neither the publisher nor its dealers or distributors assumes any liability for any alleged or actual damages arising from the use of this program. (Some states do not allow for the exclusion of implied warranties, so the exclusion may not apply to you.)

> **Note**
>
> This CD-ROM uses long and mixed-case filenames requiring the use of a protected-mode CD-ROM driver.

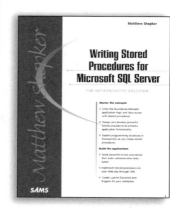

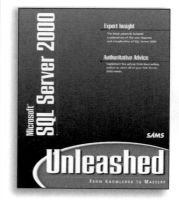

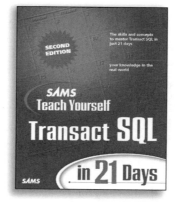